Comparative
Education Reader

REFERENCE BOOKS IN INTERNATIONAL EDUCATION
Edward R. Beauchamp, Series Editor

RUSSIAN AND SOVIET EDUCATION,
1731-1989
A Multilingual Annotated Bibliography
by William W. Brickman
and John T. Zepper

EDUCATION IN THE ARAB GULF STATES
AND THE ARAB WORLD
An Annotated Bibliographic Guide
by Nagat El-Sanabury

EDUCATION IN ENGLAND AND WALES
An Annotated Bibliography
by Franklin Parker
and Betty June Parker

UNDERSTANDING EDUCATIONAL
REFORM IN GLOBAL CONTEXT
Economy, Ideology, and the State
edited by Mark B. Ginsburg

THREE DECADES OF PEACE EDUCATION
AROUND THE WORLD
An Anthology
edited by Robin J. Burns
and Robert Aspeslagh

EDUCATION AND DISABILITY IN
CROSS-CULTURAL PERSPECTIVE
edited by Susan J. Peters

RUSSIAN EDUCATION
Tradition and Transition
by Brian Holmes, Gerald H. Read,
and Natalya Voskresenskaya

EDUCATING IMMIGRANT CHILDREN
*Schools and Language Minorities
in Twelve Nations*
by Charles L. Glenn
with Ester J. de Jong

TEACHER EDUCATION
IN INDUSTRIALIZED NATIONS
Issues in Changing Social Contexts
edited by Nobuo K. Shimahara
and Ivan Z. Holowinsky

THE UNIFICATION OF GERMAN
EDUCATION
By Val D. Rust and Diane Rust

WOMEN, EDUCATION, AND
DEVELOPMENT IN ASIA
Cross-National Perspectives
edited by Grace C. L. Mack

QUALITATIVE EDUCATIONAL RESEARCH
IN DEVELOPING COUNTRIES
Current Perspectives
edited by Michael Crossley
and Graham Vulliamy

SOCIAL JUSTICE AND THIRD WORLD
EDUCATION
edited by Timothy J. Scrase

QUALITY EDUCATION FOR ALL
Community-Oriented Approaches
edited by H. Dean Nielsen
and William K. Cummings

EDUCATION AND THE SCANDINAVIAN
WELFARE STATE IN THE YEAR 2000
Equality, Policy, and Reform
edited by Arild Tjeldvoll

POLITICS OF CLASSROOM LIFE
*Classroom Management
in International Perspective*
edited by Nobuo K. Shimahara

EDUCATION, CULTURES, AND
ECONOMICS
Dilemmas for Development
edited by Fiona E. Leach
and Angela W. Little

SCHOOLING IN SUB-SAHARAN AFRICA
*Contemporary Issues
and Future Concerns*
edited by Cynthia Szymanski Sunal

GENDER ISSUES IN INTERNATIONAL
EDUCATION
Beyond Policy and Practice
edited by Maggie Wilson
and Sheena Erskine

CHINA'S NATIONAL MINORITY
EDUCATION
Culture, Schooling, and Development
edited by Gerard A. Postiglione

Comparative Education Reader

edited by
Edward R. Beauchamp

RoutledgeFalmer
Taylor & Francis Group

NEW YORK AND LONDON

MI

Published in 2003 by
RoutledgeFalmer
29 West 35th Street
New York, New York 10001
www.routledge-ny.com

Published in Great Britain by
RoutledgeFalmer
11 New Fetter Lane
London EC4P 4EE
www.routledgefalmer.com

Library of Congress Cataloging-in-Publication Data

Comparative education reader / edited by Edward R. Beauchamp.
    p. cm.
  Includes bibliographical references and index.
    ISBN 0-415-93037-5 — ISBN 0-415-93036-7 (pbk.)
    1. Comparative education. 2. Education—Cross-cultural studies. I. Beauchamp,
  Edward R., 1933–

LB43 .C667 2002
370'.9—dc21

                                                                2002069654

3/10/03

Acknowledgments

Robert Cowen, "Comparing Futures or Comparing Pasts?" from *Comparative Education*, 36(3), (2000) 333–342. Reprinted by permission of Taylor & Francis, Inc. © 2000 by Taylor & Francis, Inc.

Rolland G. Paulston, "Mapping Comparative Education after Postmodernity," from *Comparative Education Review*, 43(4), (1999) 438–463. © 1999 by the Comparative and International Education Society. All rights reserved.

Zebun N. Ahmed, "Mapping Rural Women's Perspectives on Nonformal Education Experiences," from *Occasional Paper Series*, Department of Administrative & Policy Studies, School of Education, University of Pittsburgh (2000) 31 pages. Reprinted by permission of Zebun N. Ahmed.

Rolland Paulston, "Imagining Comparative Education: Past, Present and Future," from *Compare,* 30(3), (2000) 353–367. Reprinted by permission of Taylor & Francis, Inc. © 2000 by Taylor & Francis, Inc.

Ronald F. Price, "Comparative Education Redefined?," in Robin J. Burns and Anthony R. Welch (eds.), *Contemporary Perspectives in Comparative Education* (New York: Garland Publishing, 1992) 69–87. Reprinted by permission of Taylor & Francis, Inc. © 1992 by Taylor & Francis, Inc.

Leslie J. Limage, "Education and Muslim Identity: The Case of France," from *Comparative Education,* 36(1), (2000) 73–94. Reprinted by permission of Taylor & Francis, Inc. © 2000 by Taylor & Francis, Inc.

Frank Youngman, "The State, Adult Literacy Policy and Inequality in Botswana," from Anthony R. Welch (ed.), *Third World Education* (New York: The Falmer Press, 2000) 251–278. Reprinted by permission of Taylor & Francis, Inc. © 2000 by Taylor & Francis, Inc.

Irving Epstein, "Juvenile Delinquency and Reformatory Education in China," from Judith Liu, Heidi Ross and David Kelly (eds.), *The Ethnographic Eye: An Interpretative Study of Education in China* (New York: Falmer Press, 2000) 73–96. Reprinted by permission of Taylor & Francis, Inc. © 2000 by Taylor & Francis, Inc.

John Knodel, "The Closing of the Gender Gap in Schooling: The Case of Thailand," *Comparative Education,* 33(1), (1997) 61–86. Reprinted by permission of Taylor & Francis, Inc. © 1997 by Taylor & Francis, Inc.

Robin J. Burns and Robert Aspeslagh, "Peace Education and the Comparative Study of Education," from Robin J. Burns and Robert Aspeslagh (eds.), *Three Decades of Peace Education Around the World: An Anthology* (New York: Garland Publishing, 1996) 3–23. Reprinted by permission of Taylor & Francis, Inc. © 1996 by Taylor & Francis, Inc.

Angela Little, "Development Studies and Comparative Education: Context, Content, Comparison and Contributors," from *Comparative Education*, 36(3), (2000) 279–296. Reprinted by permission of Taylor & Francis, Inc. © 2000 by Taylor & Francis, Inc.

Kai-Ming Cheng, "Qualitative Research and Educational Policy-Making: Approaching the Reality in Developing Countries," from Michael Crossley and Graham Vulliamy (eds.), *Qualitative Educational Research in Developing Countries: Current Perspectives* (New York: Garland, 1997), 65–85. Reprinted by permission of Taylor & Francis, Inc. © 1997 by Taylor & Francis, Inc.

William K. Cummings, "The Limits of Modern Education," from H. Dean Nielsen and William K. Cummings (eds.), *Quality Education for All: Community-Oriented Approaches* (New York: Garland, 1997) 5–24. Reprinted by permission of Taylor & Francis, Inc. © 1997 by Taylor & Francis, Inc.

Rosa-María Torres, "Improving the Quality of Basic Education? The Strategies of the World Bank," from Nelly P. Stromquist and Michael L. Basile (eds.), *Politics of Educational Innovation in Developing Countries: An Analysis of Knowledge and Power* (New York: The Falmer Press, 1999) 59–91. Reprinted by permission of Taylor & Francis, Inc. © 1999 by Taylor & Francis, Inc.

Sheila Aikman, "Alternative Development and Education: Economic Interests and Cultural Practices in the Amazon," from Fiona Leach and Angela Little (eds.), *Education, Culture and Economics: Dilemmas for Development* (New York: The Falmer Press, 1999) 95–110. Reprinted by permission of Taylor & Francis, Inc. © 1999 by Taylor & Francis, Inc.

Carmen Colazo, "Public Policies on Gender and Education in Paraguay: The Project for Equal Opportunities," from Regina Cortina and Nelly P. Stromquist (eds.), *Promoting Education for Girls and Women in Latin America* (New York: Routledge-Falmer, 2000) 13–27. Reprinted by permission of Taylor & Francis, Inc. © 2000 by Taylor & Francis, Inc.

Reijo Raivola, "Comparative Perspectives on Professionalism Among American, British, German and Finnish Teachers," from Arild Tjedvoll (ed.), *Education and the Scandinavian Welfare State in the Year 2000: Equality, Policy and Reform* (New York: Garland Publishing, 1998) 133–148. Reprinted by permission of Taylor & Francis, Inc. © 1998 by Taylor & Francis, Inc.

Nobuo K. Shimahara, "Classroom Management in Japan: Building a Classroom Community," from Nobuo K. Shimahara, *Politics of Classroom Life: Classroom Management in International Perspective* (New York: Garland Publishing, 1998) 215–238. Reprinted by permission of Taylor & Francis, Inc. © 1998 by Taylor & Francis, Inc.

H. Dean Nielsen, "Reforms to Teacher Education in Indonesia: Does More Mean Better?, from *Asia-Pacific Journal of Education*, 18(2), (1998) 9–25. Reprinted by permission of *Asia-Pacific Journal of Education*. © 1998 by *Asia-Pacific Journal of Education*.

Stephen J. Duggan, "Education, Teacher Training and the Prospects for Recovery in Cambodia," from *Comparative Education* 32, (1996) 361–376. Reprinted by permission of Taylor & Francis, Inc. © 1996 by Taylor & Francis, Inc.

Contents

Part Three: Education, Development and Policy Planning

Part Four   Teachers and Teaching

Introduction

Edward R. Beauchamp

One of the West's most distinguished post-World War II scholars, the late George Z. F. Bereday of Teachers College, Columbia University, once wrote that "education is a mirror held against the face of a people. Nations may put on blustering shows of strength to conceal public weakness, erect grand facades to conceal shabby backyards, but how they take care of their children tells unerringly who they are" (Bereday, 1964). This observer agrees with Bereday's comment and suggests that a good litmus test of how much any society, including that of the United States, truly values education can be found in looking at the gap between its rhetoric about the importance of education, and the extent to which that society lives up to its own professed belief.

Although the study of comparative education over the years has utilized a multidimensional approach starting with the so-called "traveler's tales" of its early history and has developed into what many of Bereday's successors refer to as a "science" of comparative education (Noah and Eckstein, 1969), the truth is that there are virtually as many approaches as there are practitioners of the subject. Although I firmly believe that the organizational pattern chosen for this volume, and the articles used to illuminate them, are contributions that are widely esteemed within the field of comparative education, I also must admit to the undeniable fact that the vast majority of them reflect my own interests, biases, etc. This is, I believe, inevitable in any such collection.

It is also undoubtedly true that anyone teaching an introductory course in comparative education has, on more than one occasion, been sorely tempted either to write their own textbook, or compile a set of readings for their students' use that reflects their own understanding of the field. Indeed, this thought has often been on my mind over the past three decades, but as is often the case other pressures and obligations intervened to prevent it from being accomplished. Now, however, the time has come to check off this item from my personal "to do" list.

As one whose teaching style revolves around a long held, inherent aversion to traditional textbooks, the compilation of a set of diverse essays, broadly grouped under four themes was an easy choice to make. It seems likely to this writer that virtually every introductory course in comparative education deals, in one form or another, with "Ways of Thinking about

Comparative Education" or, to phrase it a bit differently, methodologies of comparative education. A second theme, especially during these days of heightened sensitivity that is highly unlikely to be omitted from an instructor's course syllabus, is the range of issues that are encompassed by "Equity and Education." Another set of issues invariably covered in introductory comparative education courses falls under the rubric of "Education, Development, and Policy Planning." Finally, when all is said and done, the core value of teaching at any level, and in any country, revolves around "Teachers and Teaching." It is a commonsense notion to remind ourselves that the key to everything good that happens in the classroom is directly related to the presence of a good, caring, and knowledgeable teacher with an ability to impart not only knowledge and skills, but also values, morality, and a sense of ethical integrity.

Although the chosen themes seem sufficiently significant and diverse to be relevant to all but the most esoteric or specialized courses, a number of other very important thematic groupings could have easily been chosen for inclusion in this book, but in that case we would have produced a multivolume series without exhausting all of the possibilities! Such a multivolume collection would also have been too unwieldy for use in a one-semester course, not to mention inflating the cost beyond the ability of students to acquire it. So, after a great deal of thought about how to reconcile the "ideal" with the "practical," it was decided to choose selections on the basis of the four sections outlined above, and to choose the very best articles that could be found to illustrate them. In using this selection mechanism, a great deal of attention was paid to the scholarly strengths, contributions, and reputations of the authors who wrote the essays. All collections are, by definition, selections that represent what the editor considers the most valuable and interesting available, but his or her judgment is always open to question. Thus, it is certain that readers will have strong disagreements with at least some of the selections, and I welcome such disagreements, for it is through this process that we all learn.

REFERENCES

Bereday, G. Z. F. (1964). *Comparative Method in Education*. New York: Holt, Rinehart and Winston, p. 5.

Noah, H. J. and Eckstein, M. A. (1969). *Toward a Science of Comparative Education*. New York: Macmillan.

Part One

Ways of Thinking About Comparative Education

Chapter 1

Comparing Futures or Comparing Pasts?

Robert Cowen

ABSTRACT   *This article, firstly and briefly, suggests that there is no single or unified "comparative education" but that there are multiple comparative educations. How may such a variety of comparative educations be distinguished? Rather more importantly and secondly, what might an "interesting" comparative education constructed in universities look like, and on what criteria would it be interesting? The specific suggestion offered here is that at least one kind of comparative education, for a decade or so, should concentrate on exploring moments of educational metamorphosis, rather than assuming that the equilibrium conditions and the dynamic linearities of development of educational systems can be predicted. Thus for the moment the correct answer to the question, how far can we learn anything of practical value from the study of foreign educational systems is: "Not a lot." The correct question is, why have we as scholars taken that question so seriously for so long?*

Introduction

It is possible to begin at the end. That is, it is possible to begin where I left off in an article which was also published in *Comparative Education* (Cowen, 1996). In that article I suggested that a good comparative education would (i) read the global; (ii) understand transitologies; (iii) comprehend "the other" and (iv) analyze pedagogies.

Kindly critics who include my own MA students have indicated that this message is not as clear as I once thought it was, and colleagues have indicated that the propositions can easily be missed amid the flurry of other ideas offered in that article. I myself see the ideas in a more complex way four years after they were first sketched.

Thus, for this millennium issue of *Comparative Education* where the theme is the contemporary condition, and the putative future condition, of comparative education I would like to re-address those themes, showing something of their individual significance. Some compression will be necessary to meet editorial guidelines. Thus, on this occasion I have chosen to compress the themes of "attributes of identity"—the last two themes—to permit space for a conclusion, which I hope remains rather open. Correctly there should be no "conclusion" if one is discussing comparative educations of the past, and potential comparative educations of the future. At best, and also at least, there is a continuing conversation.

In such a conversation it is important to avoid a messianic tone. Even to imply that I know with clarity what should be done, that I have firm "solutions" to our pressing little "problems," would not only be foolish; it would also be untrue. Equally it is important to avoid a sense of *déjà vu* as we rehearse yet again what everyone calls the state of the art, even though they never mean it. Discussions of the state of the art of comparative education normally finish up with propositions about a new and improved science. The aspiration to be a certain sort of science has haunted comparative education over a period of about 170 years, and in one decade in particular came close to destroying it.

In that sense it is also possible to begin at the beginning (Fraser, 1964). Jullien's message about a positive science permitted two things: a start date for legitimating "comparative education" as a discipline and the construction of histories of comparative education; and a considerable diversion of intellectual effort about 140 years later.

The histories of comparative education are always an interesting read, for a while. There are magnificent histories which mention persons one has never heard of, in places one has never visited, in assemblies of readings which are richly antiquarian (Fraser *et al.*, 1968). There are also documented histories that unfold the evolution of the discipline until the magical moment of teleological denouement: the field developed until it culminated in the epistemological position favored by the writer of that particular history. Thus the histories of the field are comforting. They confirm a collective identity, they give us something to gossip about, and we can always ask our students (or colleagues) to read them when they ask tiresome questions, such as what is comparative education?

However, the second consequence of Jullien was more serious. By stressing the idea of a positive science he provided a theme from which it has been almost impossible to recover. The fascinating thing about the methodological debates of the 1960s is not that they struggled to construct versions of a science of comparative education (positivist, post-relativist, Baconian or otherwise). It is that they distracted attention from the most important first step in the construction of a good comparative education: "reading the world," where this means to offer an interpretation of the political, economic, and historical worlds in which we variously live and in which education takes place. From that "reading" of the world, a substantive perspective can be constructed for the interpretation of educational processes and systems.

Thus, for example, if life in the world really is nasty, brutish and short, Machiavelli's writing on the education of princes has to be reassessed; and read by more than princes. The text becomes compulsory reading for comparative educationists. Thus, for example, despite its peculiarities, the great virtue of the work of Nicholas Hans after 1945 is that it "read the world": an interpretation of the world was the starting point and comparisons in education followed from that (Hans, 1950). Thus, for example, the sociologists and the economists of the 1960s, as symbolized by the text *Education, Economy and Society* (Halsey *et al.*, 1961), read a world of convergence, in which the technological imperative would produce economic modernity and the institutionalization of innovation, and educational convergence around the selective functions of educational systems and their relation to the world of work. Thus, for example, in the 1970s there was a break from the reading of the world by classical or neo-classical development theory, a world of the gradualist improvement of land and labor, and the transfer of capital and, for that matter, of the Protestant ethic. The fresh reading of the world was provided in the work of Arnove (1980) and Carnoy (1974) and Altbach & Kelly (1978). The world was a system, or to put the point another way, there was a world-system, which could be understood in neo-Marxist terms.

In contrast, in the 1960s a narrower world of text (about philosophies of science, and other social sciences) and an institutional world where a university was a collection of disciplinary identities justifying themselves as "sciences" was being read. That reading produced the methodologically-centered comparative education of the 1960s. I think it is moot and interesting whether the Cold War produced a paralysis in the political readings of the world by comparative educationists, other than emigrés, and a rush of foundation money and scholars into development studies.

Less moot, I think, is the idea that there was another equally serious corrosion occurring. In the methodological literature of the 1960s what was being read was a world with an implicit politics: a Weberian rationalized world in which "the expert" was all that one aspired to become and in which the social sciences would become useful technologies. We now live in a world in which social technologies are ideologically triumphant: effective schools, efficient universities, and mass distance learning techniques—all these, it seems to be widely known to policy-makers, can be managed and the expected results can be safely delivered.

Equally fortunately, this vision of education is so appalling that a range of academic perspectives is being revitalized. Among these perspectives is comparative education. So it is likely that we are at yet another turning point.

We are coming out of a world of multiple comparative educations, dealing with nationalism, with national character, with trends, with convergence, with dependency, with neo-colonialism, and with powerful specialist sub-literatures, such as comparative higher education. However, these comparative educations were not only reading different worlds—it is crucial to remember they were in different worlds. The Hans' world of nationalism was dramatically different from the political and economic structures of the world-system of Arnove.

The world continues to change. Therefore we are probably headed back into a world of multiple comparative educations, where two survivors can be predicted. Trends analyses, so reassuring for governments and international agencies, and the classical surface form of a "comparative article" (juxtaposed descriptions of at least two educational processes separated by national boundaries) which are so reassuring for editorial boards, will survive. Or will they? Probably not, and for more than trivial reasons.

The world of "comparative education," despite the massive discontinuities and contradictions in the deep structures of its discourses—the views of the world, the range of praxis embedded in each discourse, the different sociologies of knowledge of each discourse—was united at least on the surface by two sets of political and sociological assumptions. With the exception of the neo-Marxists, most of the discourses were and are incrementalist and melioristic: gradually things can and should be made better through educational action. Furthermore, and this time with the inclusion of the neo-Marxists, the discourses were and are (r)evolutionist. Social change is time-linear, sequenced, controllable and even borrowed, as are educational structures.

After all, that is what comparative education is about—learning things of practical value from the study of foreign educational systems, is it not? Therefore bits and pieces of foreign educational systems have to be borrowable, transferable, cooptable. Our professional ideology says so. The transfer business is the central political point of trends analyses (at least since the time of Pedro Rossello). The transfer business is the public legitimation of the field, the reason we can command scarce resources (and ought to be given more). Defining and analyzing "cultural borrowing" and the terms on which it is possible becomes the intellectual agenda of the field.

So an important key to at least one range of future comparative educations is whether they will indeed be informed by questions of how to borrow, questions of urgent pragmatism, questions of melioristic action. Such questions can be partially answered by juxtaposing descriptions of policies in the classic form of the comparative article, normally written by academics or, in the classic action of the international agencies, by commissioning trends reports, normally from academics.

But what if the core question of comparative education—which has been visible for so long since Jullien and apparently, on a casual reading of Sadler's question (Sadler, 1964), so powerfully relegitimated by him—changes? That is, what if we reject the question: how can we get a pragmatically useful science of educational borrowing?

What if our core question becomes something like: what are the codings of educational processes and educational sites and how may they be described and explained, comparatively, in a way that captures the intersections of the forces of history, social structures and the pedagogic identities of individuals?

In other words, and there are lots of other words and lots of other ways of approaching approximately the same problem, what if we insist for a while that much "comparative education" should be done self-consciously from inside and as part of the conversation of the intellect formerly important in the university? The process has certainly restarted (Schriewer, 1990; Rust, 1991; Crossley & Broadfoot, 1992; Welch, 1993; Bray & Thomas, 1995; Paulston, 1996; Watson, 1998). And that such a conversation is different from the conversation about action held in agencies?

What if we insist that the comparative education written by university academics should, except under extreme political circumstances, be concerned with a long-term understanding of the social world and not merely short-term action upon it? What if we insist that some of the comparative education written in universities should aspire to make truth statements (or at least temporarily "warranted assertions") of a theoretical kind? That kind of distinction is used in other social science areas, for example, in the distinctions between pure and applied economics or in the distinctions between sociology and studies of social policy or social administration. Comparative educationists working from a university base could experiment with a similar distinction for a while.

Given our contemporary anxieties, the suggestion is disturbingly unconventional but as the universities of many countries are pulled more and more tightly into measures of performance constructed by the "evaluative state," this may be the correct moment to be politically incorrect. But if we are going to be politically incorrect in distancing some of our work from policy relevance, and if we deliberately seek to strengthen an older and slightly buried tradition within comparative education, that of theorization, what could we take as a fresh starting point? In what ways might we read our own contemporary and future worlds? In the remaining part of the article I sketch ways of thinking about comparative education in the hope that later, in combination and after much substantive descriptive work, these perspectives might contribute something to the difficult art of doing comparative education.

READING THE GLOBAL

It is probably important in the year 2000 to assert immediately that "reading the global" is not synonymous with understanding globalization. Reading the global could also involve seeing civilizations as central categories of analysis, following Le Thanh Khoi (1986, 1990). Reading the global could involve placing at the center of comparative education the issue of global peace and international understanding. That is, it can be argued that unless humankind resolves issues of peace and war, partly through educative action, it really will not matter whether we all die in modest economic circumstances, or in great luxury with our knowledge economies working well and our universities efficient.

Thus, reading the global does not automatically mean reading globalization; or lamenting the death of comparative education as the nation state is no longer a powerful unit of analysis. Economic globalization and the nation state as a powerful source of cultural codes and institution building both have to be "read" in combination with, and in contradiction to, concepts and realities such as "region" or "rim." Comparative education becomes more interesting, not less, with such complexities. (Anyway, it can be doubted whether the nation state was the preferred unit of analysis even in "old" comparative education.)

More concretely, are the European Union, or the North American Free Trade Area useful arenas for the analysis of current and emerging educational patterns? For example, given the concerns for intra-European mobility illustrated by schemes such as ERASMUS/SOCRATES, what are the multiple contradictions between European economic integration and national and European cultural identities? MERCOSUL is not merely a legally defined, cross-border arena for economic activity. It is a regional institutional structure within Latin America. Indeed, for a new comparative education, Latin America itself is a promising category of analysis, a region in which the mixtures of positivism, former agricultural economies, a powerful Church, well-educated élites and "men on horseback" in the political arena produce dramatically similar educational patterns. In the Latin American region, for example, could a future comparative education identify high illiteracy rates not merely as an empirically measurable phenomenon but as a decipherable "educational code": the condensed educational expression of a political process?

Similarly, the concept of "rim," as in the expression Mediterranean Rim or Pacific Rim, raises theoretically powerful puzzles of importance to a future comparative education. Rims are arenas of possibility for international political and educational relationships. The patterns of actual inter-nation educational relations are embedded in the political insulators around and across a specific rim. France, for example, trades relatively little with Libya in either economic or educational terms. Turkey does not routinely exchange educational ideas with Greece. The Baltic Rim until recently was, in educational terms, seriously frozen. The northern Atlantic Rim has historically been one of the most open for the exchange of educational ideas, but the southern Atlantic Rim carries only a small trans-rim traffic of educational ideas and advisors. The Pacific Rim has contained examples of both one of the most powerful of insulations and one of the most powerful of conduits, in educational ideas and practices. The barriers between the People's Republic of China and the USA (and for that matter, Taiwan) may be contrasted with the political, military, economic and educational conduits between the USA and Japan (or for that matter, the Philippines).

Thus, for comparative education, both regions and rims as units of analysis contain the category of border (as in the sense of a legal boundary between nations) and the terms on which that may be collapsed, for example, for free trade or to establish common equivalences in educational qualifications for the freer movement of skilled labor. Both regions and rims as units of analysis also contain the category of border or boundary in the sense of socially structured immunity to the polluted, or a socially structured embracement of the pure.

Thus what shall not pass in a particular time or place is not merely the German army, but the ideas of Chiang Kai Shek, for consumption as school knowledge. What may perhaps be embraced (in other places) with enthusiasm—for they are both politically pure and economically useful—are "magnet schools" or Japanese modes of teaching mathematics.

However, while we can list examples of blockage and permeability to the "foreign" we have no theory of it, except in the neo-colonialist literature. Similarly, while we may be able to describe some of the educational work of the World Bank or UNESCO, or indeed participate in it, we have no theory of linearities. That is, given the tendency of those international organizations to offer universalized educational policy solutions for all contexts, we have no theory of the social permeabilities and immunologies which might permit us to understand coherently anything much more than a couple of cases of "success" or "failure."

Thus, reading the global, even if we quite sensibly stress the significance of economic "globalization" and knowledge economies, leaves room for a range of categories of analysis which also stress the political, the social and the cultural. The vision of a globalized economy which is a knowledge economy—driven by information and communications technology, mobile labor, mobile capital and mobile sites of production and the turning of certain kinds of knowledge into economic wealth—leaves unresolved a number of difficult sociological questions which could take a comparative answer.

It remains of importance, for example, whether we speak and write of a "knowledge economy" or a "knowledge society." The concept of a knowledge society, a little like the motto on the Brazilian flag (*ordem e progresso*), raises the question of whose order and whose progress. Whose knowledge society are we talking about? Questions about knowledge societies (as distinct from knowledge economies) rapidly stop being questions about adjusting education systems to new economic forms and forces, producing new skills and training systems, and asking about how to turn the rhetoric of "lifelong learning" into action.

The concept of a new kind of society whose wealth-basis has shifted to a "knowledge society," raises older questions. Even a hint of the possibilities for the emergence of a literate but economically useless "Lumpenproletariat" in knowledge societies raises in very dramatic form political questions about social justice and social cohesion, social identities and social futures. As comparativists we do not have any theories about that—though possibly we have seen an early precursor of some of the political and social problems in a range of transitologies recently.

A hint about knowledge societies is visible not only in the new social structures of the "silicon valleys" of the USA or Japan or Germany and in the science parks of Malaysia and South Korea but also in the extension of the world-system of capitalism to incorporate[sic] and to change the social structures and production systems of Central and Eastern Europe. We are seeing, there, examples of particular kinds of transitologies.

TRANSITOLOGIES

Transitologies are also part of a "reading of the global" with considerable potentials for the future shape of comparative education.

Transitologies can be taken to be the more or less simultaneous collapse and reconstruction of (a) state apparatuses; (b) social and economic stratification systems; and (c) political visions of the future; in which (d) education is given a major symbolic and reconstructionist role in these social processes of destroying the past and redefining the future. Transitologies may be distinguished from revolutions rather arbitrarily. I assert that transitologies occur in ten years or less (Cowen, 2000). Thus the Cuban "revolution" of Castro was a transitology; the Chinese "revolution," which arguably took over thirty-five years from the collapse of one dynasty to the beginnings of the construction of another, was a revolution.

There are numerous examples of transitologies available for analysis, such as Attaturk's Turkey, Thatcher's Britain, the end of the regimes such as those of Franco in Spain or the Shah in Iran, or the Meiji Restoration in Japan. Two of the two most dramatic media pictures in the last couple of decades illustrate transitological moments: in China, a tank and a transitology being stopped; the other, the collapse of the Berlin Wall, symbolically marks a whole series of transitologies.

Clearly the frequency of occurrence of transitologies has no simple or single cause, although many transitologies occur as Empires (of a variety of kinds) expand. The expansion of Western economic and political power into south and east Asia in the middle of the nineteenth century produced a flurry of transitologies in the countries we now call Cambodia, Laos, Malaysia, the Philippines, Singapore and Vietnam, as well as Japan itself. Colonialism, whether by the Japanese in Korea or the French and the British in Africa, and liberation by the USSR, produced transitologies. The collapse of empire also produces transitologies, although not axiomatically so and not in patterns which we can easily anticipate. For example, the political and educational experience of Algeria, Egypt and Libya is rather different from that of Morocco and Tunisia.

But transitologies should be part of a comparative education of the future, not merely because we do not understand them but because transitologies act for comparative education as lightning storms do on dark days. Transitologies are drama, they occur at remarkable speeds and often with stunning suddenness. They reveal to us, behind their drama and their rhetoric, the educational patterns that are ordinarily, in ordinary daylight as it were, difficult to see. Transitologies reveal new "educational codings," that is, the compression of political and economic power into educational forms.

Thus transitologies, these moments of major metamorphosis, permit comparative education to escape from incorporating into the future one of the key concepts which it took for granted in its past—the concept of equilibrium and equilibrium theorizing. Transitologies suggest a reading of the world in which equilibrium is an unusual condition, and in which educational reform itself helps to construct not sequential equilibrium conditions but more transitologies, as in contemporary Iran or in Meiji Japan, or in China after 1949.

Transitologies make the political and the sociological visible for a comparative education that is increasingly taking questions of economics and efficiency into its routine agenda of research. Sometimes this is occurring because of the interests of, say, the World Bank (1996). Sometimes this is because those more accustomed to investigating topics of, say, effective schooling decide to try their hand at a bit of comparison (Reynolds & Farrell, 1996; Scheerens & Bosker, 1997).

In contrast, transitologies are pleasantly complex mixtures of the political, economic, ideological and sociological. They are major historical events. They suggest simple questions that probably need very complex answers. What is the relation of ideologies of the future to the educational practices of the present? Answers are normally visible in transitologies, for example in the actions of Mori in Japan or Sarmiento in Argentina in the nineteenth century. What is the kind of destruction required in the educational part of a transitology—how much of the historical, social and professional past must be discredited and destroyed? Answers are normally visible in transitologies, for example in the struggles of Kemal Attaturk, a radical, or Margaret Thatcher, a radical, with different patterns of conservatism. Michael Sadler's specifications for a comparative education included a concern for "impalpable forces"; by definition, not an easy task (Sadler, 1964). Transitologies are palpable. Sadler also indicated that educational systems are partly shaped by the "spirit of battle long ago." Transitologies tell us of the spirit of battles still to come.

Thus, reading the global and reading transitologies edges us toward reading the forces of history and the interplay of the domestic and the international in the construction of educational patterns. (More precisely, what I am calling here educational codings.) Reading the global and reading transitologies are exercises in "big" comparative education in the simple sense that such a comparative education requires both an historical perspective and an emphasis on international political and economic and cultural relationships.

In such readings of the global and transitologies, and of course they must sooner or later be brought together, even some of the potential subordinate categories are large, again in a very simple sense. Concepts of rims and regions subsume geographic areas larger than most nation states and they throw up complex categories of relation, through the necessity to take seriously concepts such as border and permeability and immunology.

The challenge is a delightful one. Having been limited, as it were, to chess played in three or four dimensions (cross-national borrowing, forces and factors, the nation state as a cultural envelope, and a lot of normal puzzles taken from education policy reform) the world is now inviting us to play chess in at least eight or nine dimensions. Of these eight or nine dimensions, two others can be discussed more or less straight away. These are elements in "comparing futures" that got displaced in comparisons of the past.

THE OTHER AND PEDAGOGIES

To a surprising extent the classical comparative education literature showed a concern for both of these themes (although not in those vocabularies). Several of the "factors" of Nicholas Hans (1950) are, for example, markers of personal identity: language, race, religion. Hans' comparative education covers the possibility that certain policy choices in education in, say, Belgium or South Africa may not be possible because of particular combinations of his factors. Hans' comparative education also covers the possibility that people feel and behave in certain ways in education because of their attributes of identity—some of which are his factors written at the personal level. Thus Hans constructs a comparative education which is at the same time a sketch of possibility for a multicultural education, at least in the sense of getting a grasp on the principles of exclusion which inform educational systems.

It is not difficult to find updated accounts of exclusionary principles which are thus available for a specification of the "contemporary other." Coulby & Jones (1996), for example, find exclusionary principles in the knowledge tradition of the Enlightenment itself and in three critiques of it: the feminist critique (knowledge is male), the culturalist critique (knowledge is White and Western) and the Marxist class critique. Thus modernist knowledge is exclusionary knowledge and contains within it strong possibilities for racism and xenophobia. These tendencies are expressed in state dominated educational systems including curriculum patterns. Quite logically, the contemporary joint work of Coulby & Jones is on the theme of war and education, situations in which "the other" is not merely defined as different but is legitimately killed because they are different.

However, the huge sweep of the literature on intercultural education, positional knowledge including gender and race, and the literature on postcolonialism, means that comparative education should now take back into itself these literatures on identity. Any reading of the contemporary world in terms of the scale of diaspora and migration suggests that comparative education is now too separated from a literature about "the other" which it helped to pioneer. (It is ironic that this should have happened when many of our major scholars in comparative education were themselves émigrés.)

If, adapting the thinking of C. Wright Mills (1959), a good comparative education would combine an understanding of the intersection of the forces of history, social structures and individual biography, then it is crucial to absorb the theme of personal identities into our literature.

Again, as with the theme of "the other" it can be readily argued that the theme of personal identities and pedagogies is already in our literature. A variety of "models of man," or models of curriculum made an early effort to specify the nature of the identity of educands as this was constructed, comparatively, in a range of educational systems. Contemporaneously these models will no longer suffice (Lauwerys, 1965). They are models of identities of position—the taken-for-granted knowledge which a well-educated American, or Frenchman [sic] or Englishman [sic] would acquire in an academic high school. The models are gender and class biased and biased by cultural and political region—they refer to countries of empire and, for example, ignore Asian countries.

It is also probably true that we are nowhere near coming fully to grips with the themes of curriculum, pedagogic styles and evaluation as powerful message systems which form identities in specific educational sites, and which are even more complex when transfer to another country is discussed (Cowen, 1994). Even though schools are increasingly well looked at, we are weak in pedagogic analyses of the university and we have hardly begun on a comparative treatment of the pedagogic relations of distance education, despite the existence of mega-universities and distinct possibilities for the gradual collapse of mass instruction in schools as we have known that for over a hundred years.

Indeed, it is perhaps this last point which constitutes one of our major challenges in a comparative education of the future. We normally write of an educational system, with age-graded schools, age-linked examinations, teachers and classrooms and so on (Archer, 1979; Ringer, 1979; Green, 1990; Muller *et al.*, 1993).

However, that gives us a fascinating theoretical problem: the majority of our descriptive categories in comparative education are drawn from the vocabulary of the naming of the parts of public educational systems.

Our very descriptors will need to be changed, which makes it rather urgent to embark on a search for concepts which can handle the political and economic compressions that produce what I called earlier "educational codes." It is their relationship with reading the global, reading transitologies, reinventing and using concepts of the other and of pedagogies which may help us produce a powerful comparative education of and in the future.

CONCLUSION

For the moment we can perhaps note that education, its patterns in particular places, is not merely the result of political action. Educational forms themselves are politics compressed and educational patterns are themselves codings. Traditionally comparative educationists like Michael Sadler have tried to understand educational systems by trying to understand the political, economic and social contexts that have surrounded them. Educational sites can perhaps be read as distillations of crucial political and economic messages, including the redefinitions of the past and the visions of the future.

Educational codings are perhaps most visible in transitologies which seem to occur most frequently when there is a collapse (and rapid redefinition) of international political boundary, of political regime and of political vision. All three dramas may be more or less simultaneous, as they were in the former "East" Germany and as they are likely to be in North Korea. Another major stage for the drama of transitologies is the end of wars, for example in Japan and the multiple Germanies after 1945; and the end of empire, as in the case of Austro-Hungary.

However, any one of these dramas, collapse of international political boundary, of political regime, or of political vision, can be sufficient. Following Turkish military occupation, northern Cyprus went through a transitology. The 1979 electoral victory of Margaret Thatcher in the UK of Great Britain and Northern Ireland produced a transitology, without any suggestion in the UK of the early 1980s that there was occurring a shift in international political boundaries or a change in political regime.

In all these cases, it is being hypothesized that educational codings changed. At the moment, amid the challenges of reading the global, seeing "the other" and understanding pedagogies, we cannot even read the codings. I am not even sure if they exist, although of course I suspect they do. I am not sure that ways to read them well can be invented. But the effort should be made by comparative educationists. It seems improbable that most of our categories of educational description, which are about 150 years old and which have become our categories of analysis, will be useful much longer.

REFERENCES

Altbach, P.G. and Kelly, P.G. (Eds) (1978). *Education and Colonialism*. London: Longmans.

Archer, M.S. (1979). *The Social Origins of Educational Systems*. London: Sage Publications Ltd.

Arnove, R.F. (1980). Comparative Education and World Systems Analysis. *Comparative Education Review*, 24, pp. 48–62.

Bray, M. and Thomas, R.M. (1995). Levels of Comparison in Educational Studies: Different Insights from Different Literatures and the Value of Multilevel Analyses. *Harvard Educational Review*, 65, pp. 472–490.

Carnoy, M. (1974). *Education as Cultural Imperialism: A Critical Appraisal*. New York: David McKay.

Coulby, D. and Jones, C. (1996). Postmodernity, Education and European Identities. *Comparative Education*, 32(2) pp. 171–184.

Cowen, R. (1994). Schools and Selected Aspects of Culture from the Perspective of Comparative Education: Neither a Borrower nor a Lender Be, in: E. Thomas (ed.) *International Perspectives on Culture and Schooling: A Symposium Proceedings*. London: Institute of Education.

Cowen, R. (1996). Last Past the Post: Comparative Education, Modernity and Perhaps Post-modernity. *Comparative Education*, 32(2) pp. 151–170.

Cowen, R. (2000). Fine-tuning Educational Earthquakes, in: D. Coulby, R. Cowen and C. Jones (eds) *Education in Times of Transition: World Yearbook of Education 2000*. London: Kogan Page.

Crossley, M. and Broadfoot, P. (1992). Comparative and International Research: Scope, Problems and Potential. *British Educational Research Journal*, 18(2), pp. 99–112.

Fraser, S. (1964). *Jullien's Plan for Comparative Education 1816–1817*. Teachers College: Columbia University, Bureau of Publications.

Fraser, S.E. and Brickman, W.W. (eds) (1968). *A History of International and Comparative Education: Nineteenth Century Documents*. Glenview, IL: Scott, Forseman & Company.

Green, A. (1990). *Education and State Formation: The Rise of Educational Systems in England, France and the United States*. London: The Macmillan Press.

Halsey, A.H., Floud, J. and Anderson, C.A. (eds) (1961). *Education, Economy and Society: A Reader in the Sociology of Education*. London: Collier-Macmillan.

Hans, N. (1950). *Comparative Education*. London: Routledge & Kegan Paul.

Khoi, Le Thanh (1986). Towards a General Theory of Education. *Comparative Education Review*, 30(1), pp. 12–39.

Khoi, Le Thanh (1990). Conceptual Problems in Inter-cultural Comparisons, in J. Schriewer and B. Holmes, (eds) *Theories and Methods in Comparative Education*, 2nd ed. Frankfurt am Main: Peter Lang.

Lauwerys, J.A. (1965). General Education in a Changing World. *International Review of Education*, 11(4), pp. 385–401.

Mills, C.W. (1959). *The Sociological Imagination*. London: Oxford University Press.

Muller, D.K., Ringer, F. & Simon, B. (eds) (1993). *The Rise of the Modern Educational System: Structural Change and Social Reproduction 1870–1920*. Cambridge: Cambridge University Press.

Paulston, R.G. (ed) (1996). *Social Cartography: Mapping Ways of Seeing Social and Educational Change*. New York: Garland.

Sadler, M.E. (1964). How Far Can We Learn Anything of Practical Value from the Study of Foreign Systems of Education? *Comparative Education Review*, 7(2), pp. 307–314.

Reynolds, D. and Farrell, S. (1996). *Worlds Apart? A Review of International Surveys of Educational Achievement Including England*. London: Her Majesty's Stationery Office.

Ringer, F.K. (1979). *Education and Society in Modern Europe*. Bloomington, IN: University Press.

Rust, V.D. (1991). Postmodernism and Its Comparative Education Implications. *Comparative Education Review*, 35, pp. 610–626.

Scheerens, J. and Bosker, R. (1997). *The Foundations of Educational Effectiveness*. Oxford: Pergamon.

Schriewer, J. (1990). The Method of Comparison and the Need for Externalization: Methodological Criteria and Sociological Concepts, in: J. Schriewer and B. Holmes (eds) *Theories and Methods of Comparative Education*. Frankfurt am Main: Peter Lang.

Watson, K. (1998). Memories, Models and Mapping: the Impact of Geopolitical Changes on Comparative Studies in Education. *Compare*, 28(1), pp. 5–31.

Welch, A.R. (1993). Class, Culture and the State in Comparative Education: Problems, Perspectives and Prospects. *Comparative Education*, 29, pp. 7–27.

World Bank (1996). *World Bank, World Development Report: From Plan to Markets*. Washington, DC: World Bank.

CHAPTER 2

Mapping Comparative Education after Postmodernity

Rolland G. Paulston

To Isaiah Berlin, in Memoriam

Two extravagances: to exclude Reason, to admit only Reason.

—BLAISE PASCAL, *Penséées*

He who would do good to another must do so in Minute Particulars: General Good is the plea of the scoundrel, hypocrite and flatterer; For Art and Science cannot exist but in minutely organized Particulars.

—WILLIAM BLAKE, *Jerusalem*

This article examines the postmodern challenge to how we have come to see, represent, and practice comparative and international education. More specifically, I ask three questions: (1) Can a close reading of the relevant literature identify and type major positions or arguments in the postmodernism debate in our field? (2) How might these positions or knowledge communities be mapped as a discursive field of diverse perspectives and relations? Then, using this "heterotopia" of different ways of seeing Blake's minute particulars or mininarratives, (3) What might we reasonably conclude about the postmodern challenge of multiperspectivism and its impact on how we as comparativists choose to represent our world?

But first a few words concerning key concepts and methods used in this study. I make no distinction in using the terms postmodern, postmodernism, or postmodernity, although numerous books have been written that do so.[1] My only interest in these terms is to identify and map some sixty texts, which is all I could find on the topic. By presenting the postmodernity debate in comparative education and its related discourse as an ensemble of textual relations, I hope to avoid giving the appearance of dualism and a binary struggle of opposites. On the contrary, I view all positions in the field as interrelated and perhaps best understood as an intertextual space that allows the negotiation of meanings and values.

I thank Professor Roger Boshier and his students at the University of British Columbia who invited me to present a version of this paper as a keynote address at the Western Regional Meeting of the Comparative and International Education Society, June 1998. I also thank the three reviewers for their helpful comments.

In order to type and map, I must first enter into the texts and uncover how reality is seen (i.e., ontology), on what historical rules or codes truth claims are based (i.e., genealogy), and how the narrative framing process chosen produces a perspective, or narrative of transmission (i.e., narratology). In choosing narrative as a thematic frame, I seek to highlight specific dimensions of texts in the debate, while acknowledging that some aspects of the text are foregrounded at the expense of others.

Accordingly, my reading can only be understood in light of the possible heterogeneity of each text. Readings by others, including the authors themselves, would most likely produce different interpretations and mappings. Sharing and critiquing our interpretive and cartographic collaborations will help us to better know ourselves, others, and the world we jointly construct. The point to remember here is that my purpose is to read and interpret written and figural texts, not authors. This requires that, to the extent possible, texts be allowed to speak for themselves, to tell, with the use of quotes, their own stories.

I have always understood the postmodern condition as ironic sensibility, as a growing reflexive awareness, as an increasing consciousness of self, space, and multiplicity. Where the Enlightenment project has typically used reason and science in efforts to make the strange normal, advocates of the anti-Enlightenment,[2] and most recently the postmodernists, have sought to render the familiar strange, or uncertain. This brings to mind the earlier contrast of Apollonian harmony and rationality and Dionysian decentering and deconstruction found in classical thought. The specific theses of postmodernist advocates, that is, the present-day Dionysians, tend to focus on what they have seen as the false certainties of modernity since the 1960s. Perhaps we might take note of five postmodern theses in particular.[3] Foremost is a rejection of the Enlightenment foundations found in the grand narratives of progress, emancipation, and reason. These metanarratives are viewed as "terror," silencing the small narratives, or in Blake's terms, the minutely organized particulars of the Other.

A second thesis is the rejection of universal or hegemonic knowledge, any a priori privileging of a given regime of truth (i.e., functionalism, Marxism, postmodernism, or the like), and the need for a critical antihegemonic pluralism in social inquiry. A third thesis critiques attempts to adjudicate between competing cognitive and theoretical claims from a position of assumed or usurped privilege. Rather, postmodern texts see all knowledge claims to be problematic. The idea of universal unsituated knowledge that can set us free is seen to be a naive, if perhaps well-intentioned, self-delusion. Feminist texts, in their rejection of patriarchal truth claims, add the notion of a heterogeneous self to the postmodernist's critique. In total contrast to the Cartesian autonomous actor found in modernity texts, identity in the postmodern era is seen to be mutable and contextually variable. Bodies are also seen as a contested terrain upon which to think differently about who we are and who we might become.

A fourth thesis argued in postmodern texts attacks Eurocentrism and seeks to open knowledge practice to postcolonial experiences and to non-Western cultural codes and interpretations. The fifth thesis argues for a shift in research from time to space, from facts to interpretations, from grounded positions to narrative readings, and from testing propositions to mapping difference.

Perhaps the single most important characteristic of postmodern sensibility is an ontological shift from an essentialist view of one fixed reality, that is, reason as the controlling principle of the universe, to an antiessentialist view where reality constructs are seen to resist closure and where multiple and diverse truth claims become part of a continuous agonistic, or contested, struggle.

The central question of social change in the larger postmodernism debate is also at issue in the more recent debate in comparative education. That is, do contemporary developments—as postmodernists are prone to argue—mark a movement toward a distinct new form of social conditions characterized by nonmechanical yet complex relations that "appear as a space of chaos and chronic indeterminacy, a territory subjected to rival and contradictory meaning bestowing claims and hence perpetually ambivalent"?[4] Or, in contrast, as neomodernist texts are prone to argue, are contemporary developments best viewed as rational processes internal to the development of a global and reflexive "late modernity"?[5]

Before examining illustrative texts constructing positions in this debate, we might first note some foreshadowing of these exchanges during the earlier paradigm wars. In the 1977 "State of the Art" issue of the *Comparative Education Review,* edited by Andreas Kazamias and Carl Schwartz, for example, the cover pictures a broken house of knowledge, signifying, in my reading, the conflicted state of the field at that time (see fig. 1). Yet, note that the perplexed egghead professor remains whole and apart, a senior male in ivy league attire. This image suggests a material world in structural disarray, and it seems to question whether the power of rational professorial thought (i.e., theory) can rebuild the field's foundation.

In a contribution to this special issue, I proposed (see table 1) that comparative educators make a spatial turn and become more reflexive practitioners. I sought "to stimulate greater awareness of how individual views of social reality and social change tend to channel and filter perceptions and to look at alternative possibilities for representing educational change poten-

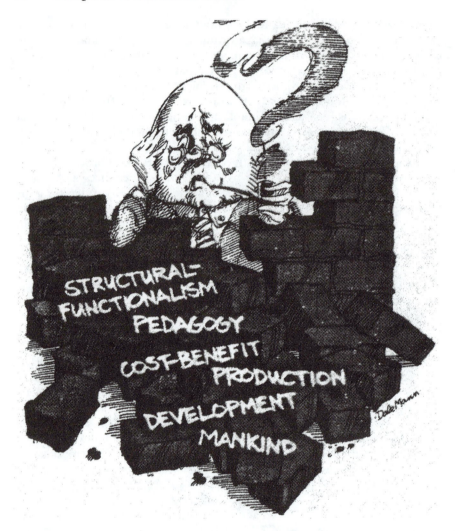

Figure 1: A late modernist cartoon portaying the once solid structure of comparative education after the paradigm wars of the 1970s and structural deconstruction. The question seems to arise regarding how we are to retain our modern identity yet deal with the crisis. Source: *Comparative Education Review* 21 (June/October 1977): Cover.

tials and constraints. To this end, I delineated the total range of theoretical perspectives that had been used to support educational reform strategies and to suggest how individual choice behaviors follow from basic philosophical, ideological, and experimental orientations to perceived social reality."[6] For the first time a phenomenological—albeit conflicted and static—portrait of how some 320 international texts constructed multiple educational reform realities appeared in a comparative education journal. In contrast,

C. Arnold Anderson, looking back to 1950, argued in this special issue for a continued orthodoxy of high modernity. To quote this founding father of the Comparative and International Education Society (CIES), "I continue to insist that traditional social science disciplines should remain the foundations for work in this field."[7] He advocated constructing theoretical models and formulating sound nomothetic conclusions, and he suggested avoiding fashionable ideologies and their semantics, clichés, and novelties. He advised comparative and international educators to produce solid scholarship by avoiding anthropology and ethnomethodology and embracing sociology and economics. In conclusion, Anderson offered guarded optimism for continued progress in CIES, but only if the field "avoids weary new panaceas" and works harder at the "identification of functional equivalents for the basic structures and functions of educational systems."[8]

My contribution focused on the space of texts in the literary construction of national educational reform debates and used what Foucault has called a genealogical approach to pattern texts as theoretical windows opening to multiple realities. Anderson's text, in contrast, argued for an orthodoxy of nomothetic research capable of generating hypotheses, covering laws, and following modernization theory based on the primacy of autonomous, professional actors measuring the way things really are. Editors Andreas Kazamias and Karl Schwartz stake out a third and more pragmatic position somewhere between my hermeneutical interpretivism and Anderson's patriarchal logocentrism. While firmly grounded in a realist ontology, the two editors chart a road ahead for the increasingly disputatious field of comparative education with their sensible call for a greater openness to cultural and critical approaches (my preference), for increased attention to pedagogical practice and teacher education (their preference), and for a view that sees social science (Anderson's preference) as "pluralistic, modest and open."[9]

Today, some twenty-two years later, in our more heterogeneous time, it is possible with exegetic analysis to identify at least five knowledge communities in comparative education discourse that are more or less favorable to, if not proponents of, postmodernist views. These are the sites of (1) postmodernist deconstructions, (2) radical alterity, (3) semiotic society, (4) reflexive practitioner, and (5) social cartography. All five tend to locate the emergence of postmodernism after the 1970s as a periodizing concept and, accordingly, as external to modernity. Communities defending the grand narratives of modernity, in contrast, while they may acknowledge the postmodernist critique, tend to situate, as with Jürgen Habermas, the postmodern debate as internal to and only comprehensible in terms of the notion of late modernity. In my close reading of the sixty or so texts selected, four modernist genres or positions in the debate emerged: (1) metanarratives of reason, emancipation, and progress; (2) rational actor gaming; (3) critical modernist appropriations; and (4) reflexive modernity adaptations. These sites can be characterized, mapped, and compared according to how they choose to understand reality and how they problematize practice. These differences are represented in figure 2, where we now turn our attention to the left, or postmodernism side, of the debate field.

TABLE I: Relations between Theories of Social and Educational Change/"Reform"

Social Change Paradigms and Theories	Illustrative Linked Assumptions Concerning Educational-Change Potentials and Process			
	Concerning Preconditions for Educational Change	*Concerning Rationales for Educational Change*	*Concerning Scope and Process of Educational Change*	*Concerning Major Outcomes Sought*
Equilibrium theories:				
Evolutionary	State of evolutionary readiness	Pressure to move to a higher evolutionary stage	Incremental and adaptive; "natural history" approach	New stage of institutional evolutionary adaptation
Neo-evolutionary	Satisfactory completion of earlier stages	Required to support "national modernization" efforts	"Institution building" using Western models and technical assistance	New "higher" state of education and social differentiation/specialization
Structural functionist	Altered functional and structural requisites	Social system need provoking an educational response; exogenous threats	Incremental adjustment of existing institutions, occasionally major	Continued "homeostasis" or "moving" equilibrium; "human capital" and national "development"
Systems	Technical expertise in "systems management." "Rational decision making" and "needs assessment"	Need for greater efficiency in system's operation and goal achievement, i.e., response to a system "malfunction"	Innovative "problem solving" in existing systems, i.e., "Research and Development approach"	Improved "efficiency" regarding cost/benefits; adoption of innovations

Conflict theories:

Marxian	Elite's awareness of need for change; or shift of power to socialist rulers and educational reformers	To adjust correspondence between social relations of production and social relations of schooling	Adjustive incremental following social mutations or radical restructuring with Marxist predominance	Formation of integrated workers, i.e., the new "Socialist Man"
Neo-Marxian	Increased political power and political awareness of oppresssed groups	Demands for social justice and social equality	Large-scale national reforms through "democratic" institutions and processes	Eliminate "educational privilege" and "elitism"; create a more equilitarian society
Cultural revitalization	Rise of a collective effort to revive or create "a new culture." Social tolerance for "deviant" normative movements and their educational programs	Rejection of conventional schooling as forced acculturation. Education needed to support advance toward movement goals	Creation of alternative schools or educational settings. If movement captures polity, radical change in national educational ideology and structure	Inculcate new normative system. Meet movement's recruitment, training, and solidarity needs
Anarchistic utopian	Creation of supportive settings; growth of critical consciousness; social pluralism	Free man from institutional and social constraints. Enhance creativity need for "life-long learning"	Isolated "freeing up" of existing programs and institutions, or create new learning modes and settings, i.e., a "learning society"	Self-renewal and participation. Local control of resources and community; elimination of exploitation and alienation

Source.–Rolland G. Paulston, "Social Educational Change: Conceptual Frameworks," *Comparative Education Review* 21 (June/October 1977): 372–73.

Note.–The table presents a phenomological comparison of how the international literature may be seen to construct national educational and social change/reform perspectives.

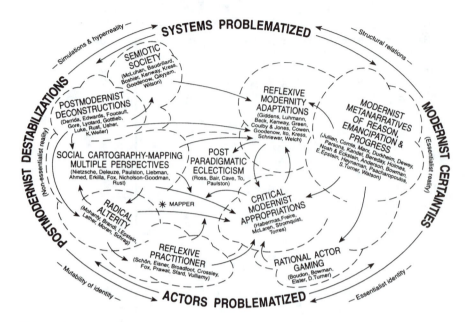

Figure 2: A metaphorical mapping of knowledge positions constructing the postmodernity debate in comparative education (and related) discourse. In this open intertextual field, arrows suggest intellectual flows and proper names refer not to authors, but to illustrative texts cited in the paper and juxtaposed above. In contrast to utopias (i.e., sites with no real place) much favored by modernist texts, this figure draws inspiration from Michel Foucault's notion of "heterotopias." These are the simultaneously mythic and real spaces of contested everyday life. Postmodernist texts favor heterotopias, as above, because they are "capable of juxtaposing in a single real place several spaces, several sites that are in themselves incompatible." See Michel Foucault. (1986). "Of Other Spaces." *diacritics* 16, no. 1 (Spring) p. 25.

POSTMODERNIST DECONSTRUCTIONS

With the publication of his presidential address in 1991, Val Rust opened CIES discourse to the debate on postmodern ideas, a far-ranging controversy that has energized and destabilized much of intellectual life in the academy since the 1970s. Rust introduced deconstructivist arguments of the French poststructuralists Jacques Derrida, Michel Foucault, and Jean François Lyotard, ideas that reject the basic language and realist assumptions of the modern age. Arguing that the comparative education community has played almost no role in this discussion, Rust selected four aspects of postmodernism that he considered to be crucial for a postmodern understanding of our field today: (1) the critique of the totalitarian nature of metanarratives; (2) recognition of the problems of the Other; (3) recognition of the development, through technology, of an information society;

and (4) an opening to new possibilities for art and aesthetics in everyday life.[10]

While Rust presents a compelling case for the utility of postmodern ideas in our era, his analysis remains strongly realist, even melioristic: "We comparative educators must discuss the opportunities of the incipient age. . . . We must define more clearly the metanarratives that have driven our field . . . we must engage in the critical task of disassembling those narratives because they define what comparativists find acceptable . . . we must increase our attention to small narratives . . . we must learn to balance high and popular culture."[11]

As Rust's text demonstrates, letting go of modernity's language, let alone its essentialist and instrumental vision, is more easily advocated than achieved. Despite the contradictions between his text and his message, Rust's pioneering call to move away from a universal belief system toward a plurality of belief systems remains timely and exciting. Unfortunately, it evoked little if any response in CIES discourse until 1994 when Liebman and I used Rust's critique to support our invitation to a postmodern social cartography.[12]

In contrast to the certainty of Rust's text about the instrumental utility of postmodern ideas, the British scholars Robin Usher and Richard Edwards, in their 1994 text, advocate a more ludic or playful approach so as better to avoid creating the monster of a new postmodern metanarrative. To quote their text: "Our attitude to the postmodern is ambivalent. We agree that to be consistently postmodern, one should never call oneself a postmodern. There is a self-referential irony about this which we find lucidly apt in encapsulating our relationships as authors to this text. At the least, we . . . have let the postmodern 'speak' through those texts [that] exemplify it."[13]

Building on Rust's earlier manifesto, Usher and Edwards problematize and deconstruct the very notion of emancipation in the project of modernity to show what they see as its oppressive assumptions and consequences, particularly in the field of education. In this, they side with Jacques Derrida in a desire to dissolve binary oppositions, to argue that education like power is neither inherently repressive nor liberatory, but perhaps both—or neither. Here, there is no Hegelian synthesis where opposition can be transcended by correct ideas or a more logical argument. Rather, they see, as did Friedrich Nietzsche, a continual and unresolvable tension and struggle of perspectives. Given this scenario, Usher and Edwards argue for an education of resistance to disrupt metanarrative power. Or to quote their accessible text, "it is in disrupting the exercise of power rather than in seeking to overcome it, that resistance can take form. The postmodern moment can enable us to transgress the boundaries of modernity rather than be contained within them. Resistance and transgressions, rather than emancipation, signify the possibilities for challenging dominant forms of power. It is analogous to Gramsci's war of maneuver rather than the war of attrition. And it is a war without end, a constant refusal of mastery, and of being mastered."[14] In this, they share James Whitson's contention that the postmodern is perhaps best seen as an attempt at the antihegemonic without being counter-hegemonic and thus risking incorporation as a relatively harmless rhetoric—as with much of critical pedagogy—into the dominant structure of control.[15]

RADICAL ALTERITY

The radical alterity battalions of the postmodernist forces apply Derriderian and subalterian ideas of the Other and seek to decenter and topple modernist control structures (i.e., hierarchy and patriarchy) with new possibilities opened by nonessentialist notions of body and identity. Where modernist texts see science, morality, and art as stubbornly differentiated, advocates of a radical alterity see the self after postmodernity as both a construct of multiple forms of speech, diverse language games, and variegated narratives, and as action-oriented and self-defined by the ways in which it communicates. As Calvin Schrag puts it, the self after postmodernity is open to understanding through its discourse, its actions, its being together in community, and its experience of transcendence. In contrast, "the modernist grammars of unity, totality, identity, sameness, and consensus find little employment in postmodernist thinking."[16] Instead, texts of the radical alterity community take up Lyotard's warning that forced consensus does violence to the free play of language games and that our new interpretive categories of heterogeneity, multiplicity, diversity, difference, and dissensus are now available to interrogate and deconstruct modernist views of the autonomous Cartesian self (as represented by the professor in fig. 1) along with all of its traditional metaphysics and epistemological games.

Radical alterity texts are, understandably, most often found in the discourse of ethnic and gender movements seeking to oppose the hierarchies and exclusions of modernity. These are often angry texts seeking to shock, challenge, and defy. I have found only three examples in our field's journals. Perhaps the best is a 1994 book review by Diana Brandi, then a doctoral student at the University of Pittsburgh, which appeared in the *Comparative Education Review*. Brandi's text, in my reading, is first and foremost a personal attack on the book's three senior author/editors, well-known and respected advocates of emancipatory modernity. She characterizes their representations of comparative education as it has emerged in the 1990s as a rehash of Marxist, functionalist, and structural functionalist perspectives. She finds this uniformity of content, perspective, and analysis not only troubling, but also puzzling. She claims that the chapters lack diversity, are self-referential, and lack a rich range of theoretical choices and multidisciplinary approaches, and that the book's structuralist orthodoxy precludes any critical reflection on whose views the research reflects or how comparative education can support transformative change for a more humane world.[17]

Brandi concludes that the central emerging issue for comparative education in the 1990s, and an issue the book virtually ignores, is the need to challenge the dominant hierarchies that continue to marginalize and silence the greater proportion of humankind. She contends the editors neglected more pluralistic discourses that challenge international development education and its service to structural adjustment, to militarism, and to the structural violence now being critically analyzed in other fields and disciplines. Here Brandi also challenges our field to open space for voices of the Other, antiessentialist voices that will attack and reject our modernist certainties of order and progress, if not of emancipation.

One year later, Irving Epstein, in a more conciliatory vein, also argued the desirability of realigning comparative studies from the seemingly innocent practice and critique of educational planning and policy to an opening up of space for cultural studies of contested local knowledge, of ethnicity, gender, disability, and the body. These issues of the Other are, Epstein complains, rarely addressed in comparative education discourse, despite a proliferation of just such studies in the academy after the 1980s.[18]

SEMIOTIC SOCIETY

The semiotic society perspective builds upon ideas of Canadian Marshall McLuhan and Frenchman Jean Baudrillard. In his pioneering 1964 study, *Understanding Media*, McLuhan interpreted modernity as a process of differentiation, as a virtual explosion of commodification, industrialization, mechanization, and market relations. These differentiations produce "hot" media. In contrast, television, as a "cool" medium, is a site of implosion of all boundaries, regions, and distinctions between high and low culture (i.e., "the new global village"), between appearance and reality, and between the binary oppositions maintained by traditional modernist philosophy and modernization theory.[19]

After first rejecting McLuhan's thesis during his neo-Marxist phase, Baudrillard has more recently accepted and extended McLuhan's "implosion of meaning" argument. Baudrillard's text now argues that the seemingly endless proliferation of signs and information obliterates meaning through neutralizing and dissolving all content. This leads to both a collapse of meaning and the destruction of distinctions between media and reality, creating what he terms a hyperreality. In Baudrillard's most recent texts, political economy, media, and cybernetics are seen to coalesce to produce a semiotic society far beyond the stage of capitalism described by Marxism. This is the time of postmodernity in which simulation models come to constitute the world and finally devour representation. Society thus is seen to move from a capitalist productivist orientation to a neocapitalist cybernetic order that aims at total control. Much like in television programs, models and codes come to constitute everyday life and social relations.[20] As in Brandi's text, Baudrillard's analysis sees a society subject to growing cybernetic control, where critiques that claim to be oppositional, outside, or threatening to the system become patterned into a society of simulations (i.e., copies without originals) as mere alibis that only further enhance social control.

Disneyland is Baudrillard's prime example of a hyperreality, that is, not the unreal but the more-than-real. In such a universe, there are no explosive contradictions, crises, or even oppositions because everything is designed and controlled. There is no reality, or even potentiality, in the name of which oppressive phenomena can be criticized and transformed because there is nothing behind the flow of signs, codes, and simulacra. In this nightmare hyperreal society, not even social critique or critical art are possible. For Baudrillard, "a cool universe of digitality . . . has absorbed the world of metaphor and metonymy. The principle of simulation wins out over the reality principle of pleasure."[21] This is Baudrillard's unsettling fantasy world, and it presents an extreme form of postmodern nihilism.

In a recent special issue on postmodernity and comparative education—the first in our field—in the British journal *Comparative Education*, three texts (none of which cite Baudrillard) address a number of more practical aspects of the so-called cyberspace challenge. Ronald Goodenow examines how the emergence of global communications networks, most notably the information superhighway, have created a new world of cyberspace. Issues of ownership and power, of how knowledge and services are defined and distributed, and of how technological have-nots gain access to networks now become major policy issues. Goodenow also stresses that educators will need to become more interdisciplinary and knowledgeable of trends and debates in many areas.[22]

Gunther Kress's text more specifically asks how the constitutive principles of postmodernity, for example, diversity, multiple reality, alterity, and paralogy, suggest the need for new representational approaches. Today our theories of meaning making, or semiosis, are largely grounded in late nineteenth-century notions of stable social systems (e.g., Emile Durkheim and Talcott Parsons), stable signs communicating stable meanings (e.g., Ferdinand de Saussure), and assumptions of an abstract reified formal appearance (e.g., C. Arnold Anderson). But now postindustrial societies are struggling to construct new forms of information-based economies responsive to cultural difference, change, and innovation. Kress challenges comparative educators to join in the creation of new modes of thinking about meaning and how we might jointly make and remake our systems of representation "in productive interaction with multiple forms of difference."[23] But one wonders how Kress would interact with Baudrillard's destabilizing notions of hyperreality.

Jane Kenway's text sounds a cautionary note in warning that educators and students need to question the cyberspace claims of both Utopians (i.e., the likes of Bill Gates) and Dystopians (i.e., the likes of Baudrillard). While granting the inevitability of the digital revolution, she draws attention to the way we produce and consume the new technologies and to associated issues of politics and justice. Teaching students about the consequences of technology is, she notes, perhaps even more important than teaching them how to operate the machines.[24] Mary Wilson and colleagues do exactly this in a later political economy study of the World Wide Web. Their text contends that an overwhelming American presence on the Web renders "the American perspective" the norm, or center, while the rest of the world becomes periphery. They argue that cyberspace, with its lack of boundaries and connection to geographical place, conceals U.S. dominance, and that astute educators need to recognize these factors and work to circumvent them.[25]

REFLEXIVE PRACTITIONER

The two remaining camps favorable to a postmodern reading of our time and our field are the reflexive practitioner and the social cartography textual genres. Both favor a hermeneutics of affirmation, and both are closely linked with the burgeoning qualitative research tradition in education. The reflexive practitioner genre especially has deep roots in Western humanism and in the romantic movement. In education, it has resisted scientist and technological efforts to objectify and commodify the world. During the paradigm wars of the 1970s and 1980s, the strongly humanistic reflexive perspective successfully defended *Verstehen*, or insight, as a key concept and goal for individual learning and knowledge work. An influential text of that time legitimating reflexive approaches in education is Donald Schön's *The Reflective Practitioner*.[26] Schön explored the crisis of confidence in professional knowledge and advocated a solution of moving from technical rationality to reflection in action. In comparative education, I made the same argument seeking to recognize the value of both imagination and technological reason in 1990, but to seemingly little effect.[27]

Today, postmodern attacks on modernist ways of knowing grounded in essentialist views of reality have helped to open a larger space for reflexive perspectives. For many, a reflexive perspective view of actors and systems offers a reasonable alternative to either the demanding perspective of radical postmodernity with its hermeneutics of despair or the perspective of a nostalgic, rule-bound modernity. For example, Patricia Broadfoot of the University of Bristol chooses this ontological middle ground in her foreword to *Qualitative Educational Research in Developing Countries*. Her introduction recognizes both postmodern influences, that is, a plurality of belief systems, a recognition of multiple realities, and the influence of culture and context, yet retains a clear concern for social scientific research and "the progress to which it will lead."[28] Variations on this recognition of multiple viewpoints and diverse interests by scholars in the eclectic center are also becoming increasingly evident in the educational research literature. Elliot Eisner, for example, advocates a multiplicity in data representations that welcomes artistic, linguistic, and visual alternatives along with more traditional positivistic choices. But he also warns that an interpretive multiple perspectives approach may introduce dangerous ambiguity and a potential backlash: "A genre of work can stand alone without an interpretive context when those reading, seeing, or hearing it bring that context with them. When they do not they are likely to be lost. Few people like to be lost. When the terrain is new, we need context. We also need to be sure . . . that we are not substituting novelty and cleverness for substance. In other words, we need to be our own toughest critics."[29]

SOCIAL CARTOGRAPHY

Texts clustered in the social cartography genre also share a number of defining characteristics, perhaps best captured by Foucault's notion of heterotopia. In contrast to the totalizing utopic (i.e., no-place) space of modernity, heterotopic spaces are the simultaneously mythic and real spaces of everyday life capable of juxtaposing in a single place a great variety of different sites which in themselves may be incompatible. As William Blake noted, modernist texts favor idealistic rational utopias of general good. In contrast, postmodernist texts favor heterotopias of situated difference and local knowledge. Figure 2 above illustrates just such a heterotopic mapping of difference. Here, within an intertextual field, all viewpoints producing a text in the CIES postmodernity debate find space and relation to other similar or totally different ways of seeing. As such, this tangled and interconnected mapping, or Deleuzian rhizome, of knowledge positions and relations can be seen as a metaphor of the debate, as a heuristic approach, and as a real site of paralogy and postmodern process. It can also be seen as a useful new spatial tool specifically created to give visual form to the growing complexity of knowledge work today. Where Pablo Picasso with analytical cubism made it possible to represent many sides of an object at the same time, social cartography also creates something in the very act of depiction. This is not simply a fragile synthesis, but a new way of looking at the world and, equivalently, a new aspect of the world at which to look.[30]

The ideas behind heterotopic mappings of perspectival difference began to take form in my paper "Comparing Ways of Knowing across Inquiry Communities," presented at the CIES annual meeting in Pittsburgh in 1991. A number of doctoral students at the University of Pittsburgh then joined the project, and together we worked to create a social cartography able to visualize and pattern multiplicity, be it multiple perspectives, genres, arguments, or dreams. In this heuristic, the field is also defined by the outlying positions. In modern, positivistic representations, in contrast, the opposite is true, that is, the intention is to plot a central tendency where outliers, such as the Other, simply disappear.

On the surface, discourse mapping appears to be a fairly simple, if demanding, process of reading and juxtaposing ways of seeing in texts. I proceed in the following "cookbook" fashion, much to the horror of my postmodernist colleagues: (1) Choose the issue or debate to be mapped. (2) Select the widest range possible of texts that construct this debate and, with close reading, translate their defining rhetorical characteristics, ideas, and worldviews. (3) Identify the range of positions in the intertextual mix. In figure 2, for example, these positions are presented on the horizontal axis as the ontological poles of "postmodernist destabilizations" and "modernist certainties." On the vertical axis, the poles chosen are "actors problematized" and "systems problematized." (4) Identify the textual communities that share a way of seeing and communicating reality; locate them within their space and interrelate communities of vision with space, lines, arcs, arrows, or the like. While resisting all modernist urges to box in or lay down a grid, locate coordinates outside the field to allow for a less restricted space of intersubjectivity, movement, and choice than provided by table 1. (5) Field test the map with the individuals or knowledge communities involved. Share the conflicting interpretations and remap as desired.

As an oppositional postmodern strategy, social cartography translates across interacting sites of material inscriptions, avoiding the idealist totalities of utopian modernity. This process of mapping and translating seeks to open up meanings, to uncover limits within cultural fields, and to highlight reactionary attempts to seal borders and prohibit translations. In this lies postmodern mapping's contribution to an antihegemonic critique.

Social mapping may also be seen as an emergent methodology from within the hermeneutic mode of inquiry that acknowledges that worlds are constructed and interpreted both objectively and subjectively, that is, that within fields of study or sites of knowledge, a dialogue is always taking place that involves meaning systems that are illusive. These meaning systems are formed by those who elaborate them, and an open, intertextual field is created by the dialogue. For this reason, the comparative researcher and the reader alike serve as translators within this mode of interpretive inquiry. But, as Eisner warns, the researcher now has a three-fold obligation to explicate what point of view is being utilized in the study, to disclose the interrelations of the field or site itself, and to convey something of the personal or professional experiences that have led her or him to choose a particular point of view.

As our social cartography project at the University of Pittsburgh took form, several dissertations and books mapped situated areas of the theoretical and operational landscapes of comparative and international education. Martin Liebman's thesis, for example, expands our understanding of metaphorical analysis in comparative method.[31] Zebun Ahmed's study maps how village women in rural Bangladesh view their nonformal educational experiences with Western nongovernmental organizations.[32] Kristiina Erkkilä maps positions in the entrepreneurial education debates in the United States, the United Kingdom, and Finland.[33] Katsuhisa Ito is currently critiquing the project from a human geography viewpoint, Michel Rakatomanana is mapping the debate on new information technologies and educational development, and Mina O'Dowd is mapping how multiple knowledge perspectives can be seen to construct a longitudinal research study in Sweden.[34] In our 1996 project book, *Social Cartography*,[35] a number of leading U.S., Canadian, and international scholars collaborated to demonstrated mapping applications in research practice (i.e., Christine Fox, Esther Gottlieb, Thomas Mouat, Val Rust, Nelly Stromquist, among others) or to critique and counterargue the book's contention that social mapping is a useful tool for comparative analysis today. Carlos Torres and John Beverley, for example, propose critical modernist and subaltern studies positions that are antithetical to social mapping. Patti Lather interrogates mapping from a radical feminist view, and Joseph Seppi from a traditional positivist position. If, indeed, all knowledge claims are now problematic, then opposing views will need to be consciously incorporated and juxtaposed in any credible argument or analysis. As we shall see in the following section on modernist orthodoxy, this will be a hard pill for many true believers to swallow.

MODERNIST METANARRATIVES

On the far right side of figure 2, I pattern illustrative modernist texts in comparative education discourse that oppose, in one way or another, the postmodern challenge within three broad areas: (1) utopian texts that largely reject postmodernist ideas and explicitly counterattack to defend a core modernist metanarrative (i.e., universal reason, or progress), (2) critical pedagogy texts that seek to preserve the modernist metanarrative of emancipation with the selective appropriation of postmodernist and/or feminist ideas, and (3) performativity texts that seek to elaborate a new narrative of reflexive modernity for our time of risk (i.e., what they call "late modernity") when the old modernist master stories of certainty and technological progress have less and less credibility.

In the counterattack category, Erwin Epstein's chapter "The Problematic Meaning of Comparison in Comparative Education" presents a spirited defense of totalizing modernist reason and a rejection of what he calls the "challenge of relativism."[36] His text, however, does not recognize postmodernism and its complaints, although that debate was raging then (1988) at a feverish pitch in the social sciences and the humanities. Instead, his targets are phenomenological and ethnomethodological additions to the literature and especially my study (summarized in table 1). These two perspectives share a nonessentialist understanding of ontology with postmodernism, and they view reality as a variously situated construct. In a masterly comparison of what he claims to be incomparable, Epstein's text contrasts examples of relativist (i.e., cultural interpretation and phenomenological readings) and realist (i.e., positivist theory-development) perspectives in comparative education. He rightly concludes that they are incommensurable in their assumptions, procedures, and aims. His text fails, however, to address the core difference of ontology or how reality is variously seen. His either/or approach, while seemingly evenhanded, has a strong essentialist bias:

"Generalizations across societal boundaries define . . . the comparative method for positivists. For cultural relativists, comparison is a process of observing the distinctiveness of individual cultures. These positions are to be sure incompatible, but they both rest on a procedure that requires multicultural analysis and therefore can said to employ some concept of 'comparison.' This is not so for phenomenological approaches, which carry relativism to a nihilistic extreme that allows only for interpretation of highly idiosyncratic interactions within severely limited contextual boundaries.

Within such parameters, not even culture is sufficiently contextually delineated to constitute a basis for analysis."[37]

Thus, from an extravagant logical positivist viewpoint that in Pascal's term "will admit only reason," Epstein's text contends that one who chooses a phenomenological approach (as in my table 1 and fig. 2) cannot be a comparativist, and he argues that the challenge of relativism is a threat not only to the metanarrative of reason, but also to the viability of comparative education as a field. "Only nomothetic explanations—or the discovery of underlying trends and patterns that account for whole classes of actions or events [i.e., covering laws] can support comparison capable of theory development and general laws."[38] Epstein's essentialist text is notable for its epistemological certainty and faith in the positivist story of social progress with the discovery of universal regularities—alas, as yet to be seen.

An anti-Enlightenment position might well counterargue Epstein and claim that only relativists can be comparativists because they alone are open to the indeterminacy of being. But that would be a modernist either/or argument. Postmodernists would open to all positions and, as illustrated in figure 2, turn to a spatial representation of "the order of things" that moves us a bit beyond the limitations of opaque language. This would also be my choice, but I must leave it to the reader to assess the comparative utility of figure 2 and Hayden White's claim that "the macroscopic configuration of formalized consciousness uncovered in language" might be translated into a spatial visual mode of representation.[39]

A more focused rejection of postmodern ideas, at least as they are present in our work on social mapping, can be found in Keith Watson's recent British Comparative and International Education Society (BCIES) presidential address and in his review of *Social Cartography*. These two texts warn the reader of the intellectual temptations of such dangerous postmodern ideas as pluralism, multiplicity, and uncertainty—or what Watson erroneously disparages as "New Age Thinking." His text sees postmodernist views as fatally flawed because they do not offer testable hypotheses, or criteria for decision making, or parameters for interpretation. Such "wooly thinking" is, he complains, written by enthusiasts who are so excited by the novelty of what they are saying that they do not see the weaknesses. Yet, at the same time, he also makes the odd claim that "these overly enthusiastic postmodern cartographers are [only] putting into diagrammatic form what most sociologists . . . have always recognized."[40]

But Watson's text sees a flaw in heterotopic mapping more serious than intellectual excitement and enthusiasm. Watson warns that most administrators and aid agency officials may well see social cartography as yet one more example of "esoteric comparative education" that is irrelevant for them. While acknowledging that postmodern mapping can indeed represent the micronarratives of all the players, whether they hold power or are on the margins, his text dismisses the need for such knowledge, claiming that educational planners and policy makers require only "hard data" for rational decision making.[41] Here the term hard data is repeated as a mantra and is not defined, nor are any data provided to support Watson's exclusionist claims.

Watson's text would seem to confuse the postmodern social cartography as practiced in figure 2 with traditional scientific or mimetic modeling, where the image is assumed to reflect a positive reality that can be known empirically, or ideologically. But with our postmodern mapping of metaphors, the map, like the self, can also be portrayed as in a state of Dionysian dispersal that, as with Foucault's notion of heterotopia, reconstitutes diversity as a provisional unity.

RATIONAL ACTOR

The rational actor, or game-theory, position can be seen as a close relation of Anderson's and Watson's modernist metanarrative of progress. Here, texts seek to develop nomothetic models able to explain and predict economic and educational behavior in universal terms. Raymond Baudon divides these efforts into two types, that is, the "determinist" and "interactionist."[42] Mary Jane Bowman's model of 1984[43] is cited by David Turner to illustrate the former because it seeks to explain school attendance rates in terms of prior events and to support the discovery of uniform covering laws. Using an analysis of variance, a deterministic approach would suggest that every individual is driven by "the programming that the social structure imposes on him."[44] In this, modernization and Marxist theories share the same certainty and reductionist view. But Turner's text problematizes actors, not structures, and argues that the determinist model is simplistic and fails to recognize features of free will and capriciousness in human behavior. Social theories and ultimately social laws are, Turner contends, still attainable, but only with the use of an interactive model based on empirical studies of student risk-taking behavior. Only with the scientific study of individual agents and educational demand, and not just formal structures, Turner's text argues, will progress in educational reform be made.

CRITICAL MODERNIST

Texts choosing the critical modernist perspective characteristically maintain a strong commitment to the modernist metanarrative of emancipation while seeking to breathe new life and credibility into the Enlightenment project. They do so by selectively appropriating postmodern ideas from antiessentialist reality positions to shore up their own essentialist foundations. Clearly, this is a difficult—if not confused—task and requires a good deal of qualification and rationalization. A recent text by Peter McLaren presents a prime example of such ontological fancy footwork: "While I acknowledge the importance of recognizing the conceptual limits of Marxian analysis [i.e., Marxist universal] for reading certain aspects of the postmodern condition, I believe that the main pillars of Marxian analysis, remain intact, i.e., the primacy of economics and the identification of contradictions and antagonisms that follow the changing forces of capitalism. It is important that critical educators not lose sight of these foci [i.e. modernist foundations] in their move to incorporate [antifoundational] insights from . . . postmodernism."[45]

Here McLaren's text shares the yearning of positivists for certainty in the form of hard data: "we need to be able to stipulate in specific contexts which effects are oppressive and which are productive of social transformation. I believe that to defend emancipation . . . we must make certain that not all voices are celebrated."[46] Where Erwin Epstein's counterattack excludes relativism as the enemy of Enlightenment reason and true comparison, McLaren's text would, like Watson's, silence the ideological Other. In order to avoid just this sort of silencing, I invited Carlos Torres to provide a concluding chapter for our *Social Cartography* book using a critical modernist perspective antithetical to the book's uncertainty thesis. This practice of incorporating oppositional views into intertextual constructions is seen by pluralists and postmodernists not as masochism, but as paralogy where science opens up from an Apollonian program of testing and verification for truth value to also include a Dionysian process of paralogical deconstruction and a recycling of all knowledge claims. In this way, we seek to create a spirited conversation and vouchsafe its continuation.[47] With mapping, as in figure 2, Torres's self-privileging metanarrative claim is recognized and reinscribed into the intertextual field/map, not as a master narrative of "general good," but as another contending mininarrative, that is, as perhaps useful "minute particulars" to be assessed in practice.

Torres also recognizes the utility of postmodernist critiques of representation, but only when they avoid what he sees (but does not illustrate) as the pitfalls of extreme relativism and solipsism. Torres's text sees the greatest danger of postmodern views in their claim that language constructs reality. His text sees this postmodern shift from hard data and "correct" ideology to metaphor, multiple perspectives, and methodological pluralism as antithetical, even subversive, of the theoretical integrity of his privileged modernist metanarrative of emancipation. His text defensively calls for a linguistic hygiene, that is, that "metaphors . . . should have no place in social sciences if they substitute for social theorizing including metatheory (or epistemology), empirical theory and normative theory."[48] Here, Torres's text seems to be deeply suspicious of any but a scientific, analytical method whose goal is not the recovery and confirmation of its own ideological origins. While Torres, like McLaren, acknowledges that postmodern ideas may help to make Marxist class analysis less totalizing and deterministic, his text continues to demand a so-called reproduction of the concrete situation in conformance with his ontological choice of theoretical realism and his claims of a universal truth system.[49]

REFLEXIVE MODERNITY

Texts representing the reflexive modernity position share common origins with critical modernist texts. They have, however, been better able—at least superficially—to let go of fading modernist certainties and master narratives. They seek to survive the poststructuralist storms by selectively adapting useful interpretations, stories, and vocabulary from the postmodern literature and choosing the metaphors of late modernity and reflexive modernity.[50] Texts from this burgeoning community retain modernist notions of a unitary and ideal space of a society that is mapped onto the body of a population along with territorial claims of a nation state and a national educational system. At the same time, they seem to have lost all hope for certainty and selectively attempt to incorporate and adopt postmodern ideas of fragmentation, polymorphous identity, and discontinuous thought spaces.[51] In the West, and especially in western Europe, the reflexive systems view recognizes a politics of voice and representation that often seeks to displace a welfare state held to be inefficient and paternalistic. Central to this view, and in marked contrast to the certainties of critial modernist texts, is the idea that to know how to act we need to know "what's happening." For this we need to develop a language and a space in which to engage our present willingness to let most, if not all, knowledge perspectives contend and compete.

In comparative education, this reflexive systems view is well illustrated by Robert Cowen's recent text, where he claims that Lyotard's 1979 analysis of the postmodern condition continues to offer the most accurate assessment of society—and of universities—as they move into "the post-industrial age and as culture moves into what is known as the postmodern age."[52] Lyotard's argument is that today knowledge is subject to "performativity," or the optimization of system efficiency. Knowledge has become a technology, that is, a marketable commodity subject to performativity as well as truth tests. Cowen perceptively argues that these changes define a different kind of comparative education predicated not on the tired old modernist meta-narratives of certainty, but on the recognition of a crisis of legitimacy. Where the modern comparative education of John Dewey and Talcott Parsons et al. focused largely on citizen preparation and equality of educational opportunity, in late-modern educational systems the strongest pairing is seen to be between the international economy and efforts to gird educational systems for global competition. Today, Cowen contends, we comparativists will need "to specify the patterns of muddle in specific national contexts of transition to late-modern education. [Today] the common sense categories of analysis—i.e., school management and finance, administrative structures, the curriculum, teacher education—are now dangerous. Even if we could deduce determined rules from them [as advocates of modernity would have us do] the rules would be a reading of the wrong world."[53]

CODA

To conclude, Cowen cites Zygmunt Bauman's observation that we are no longer legislators, that we should first look to our interpretations.[54] I can only concur and further suggest that as comparativists we are, from the look of things, also well positioned to become social cartographers, able to translate, map, and compare multiple perspectives on social and educational life. And as our intertextual traveling in this study suggests, while our collective work is becoming more postparadigmatic and eclectic, we are, as individuals, also aware of "sweet spots" or favored sites in knowledge work where we encounter more allies, resources for practice, and options for movement.[55] At the same time, we are learning to recognize and include views of the Other, thus enlarging the scope of our vision and the diversity, or minute particulars, of our representations.

So is there, perhaps, something akin to a general good, writ small, to be found in the opportunities arising from comparative education practiced as comparative mappings of disparate world views? This is our challenge today, to understand William Blake's belief that truth is particular, not general, while we move beyond his either/or formulation into a more heterotopic space of critically reflexive understanding—as shown in figure 2—open to the essentialist texts of late modernity, to the antiessentialist texts of the postmodernists, and to all the texts that have yet to claim their agonistic spaces.[56]

NOTES

1. For those interested in the intricacies of new social science ideas and terminology in education after modernity, see, among others, Rosa Nidi Buenfil-Burgos. (1997). "Education in a Post-Modern Horizon," *British Educational Research Journal* 23, 97–107; and Fenwick W. English. (1998). "The Postmodern Turn in Educational Administration: Apostrophic or Catastrophic Development?" *Journal of School Leadership* 8, 426–63. For an accessible introductory textbook on popular culture and the postmodern condition, see Walter T. Anderson. (1990). *Reality Isn't What It Used To Be.* San Francisco: Harper & Row.

2. See Isaiah Berlin. (1980). *Against the Current: Essays in the History of Ideas.* New York: Viking, esp. pp. 1–24. Berlin identifies the three central ideas of the anti-Enlightenment as (1) populism, or the view that people can realize themselves fully only when they belong to rooted groups or cultures; (2) expressionism, or the notion that all human works are above all voices speaking or forms of representation conveying a worldview; and (3) pluralism, or the recognition of a potentially infinite variety of cultures, ways of seeing, and systems of values all equally incommensurable with one another, rendering logically incoherent the Enlightenment belief in a universally valid master narrative or ideal path to human progress and fulfillment. Berlin identifies leading exponents of the anti-Enlightenment as Niccolo Machiavelli, Giambattista Vico, William Blake, Johann Herder, Alexander Herzen, and others, including Georges Sorel and Friedrich Nietzche.

3. A more detailed exposition may be found in David Owen, (ed.) (1997). *Sociology after Postmodernism.* London: Sage, pp. 1–22. Owen suggests that postmodern "theory" seeks to shift the work of social science from theorizing truth claims to representing new social and intertextual terrains in constant flux. For a useful guide to exegetic textual analyses as "close reading," see chap. 6 in Joseph Francese. (1997). *Narrating Postmodern Time and Space.* Albany: SUNY Press, pp. 107–54.

4. Zygmunt Bauman. (1992). *Postmodernity.* London: Routledge, p. 193. Earlier, Foucault, perhaps anticipating the cyberspace revolution, argued that today there has indeed been a fundamental change of consciousness from time to space: "the great obsessive dread of the nineteenth century was history, with

its themes of development and stagnation, crises and cycle, the accumulation of the past, the surplus of the dead. Our own era, on the other hand, seems to be that of space. We are in the age of the simultaneous, of juxtaposition, the near and the far, the side by side, and the scattered. A period when the world is putting itself to the test, not so much as a great way of life destined to grow in time but as a net that links points together and creates its own muddle [as in table 1 and figure 2]. It might be said that certain ideological conflicts which underlie the controversies of our day take place between the pious descendants of time and tenacious inhabitants of space." See Michel Foucault. (1986). "Of Other Spaces." *diacritics* 16, no.1, p. 23.

5. For useful discussions of the reflexive modernity—or late modernity—worldview, see Ulrich Beck, Anthony Giddens, and Samuel Lash. (1994). *Reflexive Modernization*. Cambridge: Polity.

6. Rolland G. Paulston. (1977). "Social and Educational Change: Conceptual Frameworks." *Comparative Education Review*, 21 (June/October) pp. 370–71.

7. G. Arnold Anderson. (1977). "Comparative Education over a Quarter Century: Maturity and New Challenges." *Comparative Education Review*, 21 (June/October) pp. 406–7.

8. Ibid., p. 416.

9. See Andreas M. Kazamias and Karl Schwartz. (1977). "Intellectual and Ideological Perspectives in Comparative Education: An Interpretation." *Comparative Education Review*, 21 (June/October) pp. 175–76.

10. See Val D. Rust. (1991). "Postmodernism and its Comparative Education Implications," *Comparative Education Review*, 35 (November) pp. 610–26.

11. Ibid., pp. 625–26.

12. Rolland G. Paulston and Martin Liebman. (1994). "An Invitation to Postmodern Social Cartography." *Comparative Education Review,* 38 (May) pp. 215–32. Here the authors introduce social cartography to comparative educators as "a new and effective method for visually demonstrating the sensitivity of postmodern influences for opening social dialogue, especially to those who have experienced disenfranchisement by modernism" (p. 232). Their social cartography text contends that spatial juxtapositioning provides a new way to seek a more situated truth in a cyberspace era. Now truth is not necessarily grounded in measurable fact alone; it is also predicated on the acquisition of a generosity of vision composed of many truths, that is, what postmodern texts call a "multiplicity of witness" and a "democracy of perception." By opening comparison in this way, postmodern social cartography helps actors move outward from subjective truth toward a reintegration of the self into a new social fabric/space composed of multiple voices and stories. This view is labeled "postmodern multiperspectivism" by Francese (n. 3 above) who advocates its utility as a safeguard against "any excessively strong, exclusionary reading of the past: the univocal truth that suffocates all others and quickly transmogrifies into reified myth" (p. 130).

13. Robin Usher and Richard Edwards. (1994). *Postmodernism and Education*. London: Routledge, p. 3.

14. Ibid., p. 224.

15. See James Whitson's (1991), somewhat quixotic "Post-structuralist Pedagogy as a Counter-hegemonic Praxis." *Education and Society*, 9. pp. 73–86. Texts advocating or applying a postmodern deconstruction perspective can also be found in Kathleen Weiler. (1996). "Myths of Paulo Freire." *Educational Theory*, 46 (Summer) pp. 353–71; Allan Luke. (1995). "Text and Discourse in Education: An Introduction to Critical Discourse Analysis," *Review of Research in Education*, 21 pp. 3–48; and others, including Esther E. Gottlieb. (1989).

"The Discursive Construction of Knowledge: The Case of Radical Education Discourse." *Qualitative Studies in Education*, 2, no. 2, pp. 132–44.

16. Calvin O. Schrag. (1997). *The Self after Postmodernity.* New Haven, CT: Yale University Press, p. 7. For the subaltern perspective, see, e.g., Chandra T. Mohanty. (1991). "Cartographies of Struggle." in *Third World Women and the Politics of Feminism*, ed. Chandra T. Mohanty et al. Bloomington: Indiana University Press, pp. 1–49. For an application of the radical alterity perspective to probe the trope of space in feminist studies, see Matthew Spark. (1996). "Displacing the Field in Fieldwork." in *Bodyspace: Destabilizing Geographies of Gender and Sexuality*, ed. Nancy Duncan (London: Routledge, 1996). pp. 212–33.

17. Diana Brandi. (1994). Review of *Emergent Issues in Education: Comparative Perspectives.* ed. Robert F. Arnove, Philip G. Altbach, and Gail P. Kelly, in *Comparative Education Review* 38 (February) pp. 159–62. Brandi claims that the book's structuralist orthodoxy silences questions of how research reflects the views of those under consideration and whose voices and what questions direct the evolution of the field (p. 160). She also contends that the inclusion of feminist theories on structural adjustment and phenomenological studies of local perspectives would better help oppressed people improve their quality of life.

18. Irving Epstein. (1995). "Comparative Education in North America: The Search for the Other through the Escape from Self?" *Compare*, 25, no. 1. pp. 5–16. In contrast to what Epstein's text sees as my purported optimism for the field, I see my viewpoint more akin to Isaiah Berlin's curious combination of idealism and skepticism. Epstein's text also makes an argument for measured skepticism in evaluating the field's future possibilities. The problem, as Epstein sees it, is that limited understanding of self restricts the scope and possibility of knowledge work within the comparative education field. But is our lack of reflexive self-knowledge, our naïveté, our bane? If so, could it not be viewed as an educational problem that might be treatable with heterotopic mapping? A third radical alterity example problematizing actors in comparative education texts can be found in Patricia J. Moran. (1998). "An Alternative Existence." *CIES Newsletter* 117 (January) pp. 1, 4. Moran compares two life histories, her own and that of Gail Paradise Kelly, with painful honesty and introspection. Her narrative account of one woman's struggle with the rules of patriarchal modernity provides a valuable pioneering contribution to comparative education, to date a largely logocentric male discourse repelled by the very radical alterity sensibilities that construct Moran's story.

19. Marshall McLuhan. (1964). *Understanding Media.* New York: McGraw-Hill.

20. See Mark Poster, (ed.). (1988). *Jean Baudrillard: Selected Writings.* Saint Louis: Telos.

21. See the neo-Marxist critique of Baudrillard's arguments in Douglas Kellner. (1989). *Jean Baudrillard: From Marxism to Postmodernism and Beyond.* Stanford, CA: Stanford University Press, p. 152. While Kellner seems to be fascinated with the brilliance and originality of Baudrillard's ideas, he nevertheless sees him trapped by "the absence of a theory of agency and mediation [by] . . . the impossibility of any sort of agent of political change . . . by the metaphysical triumph of the object over the subject" (p. 216). And yet Kellner concludes "the appeal of Baudrillard's thinking might suggest that we are [indeed] living in a transitional situation whereby new social conditions are putting into question the old orthodoxies and boundaries" (p. 217).

22. Ronald Goodenow. (1996). "The Cyberspace Challenge: Modernity, Postmodernity and Reflections on International Networking Policy." *Comparative Education*, 32, no. 2, pp. 197–216.

23. Gunther Kress. (1996). "Internationalization and Globalization: Rethinking a Curriculum of Communication." *Comparative Education*, 32, no. 2, pp. 185–196, quote on p. 196.

24. See Jane Kenway. (1996). "The Information Superhighway and Postmodernity: The Social Promise and the Social Price." *Comparative Education*, 32, no. 2, pp. 217–232.

25. Mary Wilson, Adnan Qayyam, and Roger Boskier. (1999). "World Wide America: Manufacturing Web Information." *Distance Education* 1999.

26. Donald Schön. (1983). *The Reflective Practitioner: How Professionals Think in Action*. New York: Basic. For a perceptive examination of different traditions in reflexive thought today, see Jonathan Potter. (1996). *Representing Reality: Discourse, Rhetoric and Social Construction*. London: Sage, pp. 88–96, 228–32. For two imaginative literary attempts to move beyond the tendency of most modern intellectual production to "state, qualify, and conclude," see Elizabeth Deeds Ermath. (1992). *Sequel to History: Postmodernism and the Crisis of Representation*. Princeton, NJ: Princeton University Press, and Rolland G. Paulston and David N. Plank. (2000). "Imagining Comparative Education: Past, Present and Future." *Compare*, vol. 30, no. 2, (2000).

27. Rolland G. Paulston. (1990). "Toward a Reflective Comparative Education?" *Comparative Education Review*, 34 (May) pp. 248–58.

28. Patricia Broadfoot. (1997). Introduction to *Qualitative Educational Research in Developing Countries*. ed. Michael Crossley and Graham Vulliamy. New York: Garland, pp. xi-viii.

29. Elliot W. Eisner. (1997). "The Promise and Perils of Alternative Forms of Data Representation," *Educational Researcher*, 26, no. 6 (August/September) pp. 4–11, quote on p. 9. Anna Sfard, in a related study, warns that the struggle for a conceptual unification of research is not a worthwhile endeavor and that too great a devotion to one particular metaphor can lead to theoretical distortion and undesirable practical consequences. Instead, she rejects Torres's stricture (see n. 48 below) and advocates a discursive approach of "metaphorical mappings" and metaphorical pluralism for conceptual renewal and improved practice. See her 1998 study, "On Two Metaphors for Learning and the Dangers of Choosing Just One." *Educational Researcher*, 27, no. 2 (March) pp. 4–13.

30. Foucault, p. 3 (n. 4 above). In making his shift from time to space in social analysis, Foucault graciously acknowledges his intellectual debt to Gilles Deleuze with the words "perhaps one day, this century will be known as Deleuzian" in his 1977 *Language, Counter-Memory, Practice*, trans. D. F. Bouchard and S. Simon. Ithaca, NY: Cornell University Press, p. 76. For their original and fecund ideas on concepts seen as territory and on the necessity of cartographics as a strategy to examine discourse with spatial analysis, see Gilles Deleuze and Felix Guttari. (1980). *A Thousand Plateaus*, vol. 2 of *Capitalism and Schizophrenia*. trans. B. Massumi. Minneapolis: University of Minnesota Press. For the cubism analogy, see Alexander Nehamas. (1985). *Nietzsche: Life as Literature*. Cambridge, MA: Harvard University Press, p. 59. I thank Professor Eugenie Potter for pointing out this relationship.

31. Martin W. Liebman, "The Social Mapping Rationale: A Method and Resource to Acknowledge Postmodern Narrative Expression" (Ph.D. dissertation, University of Pittsburgh, 1994). In postmodern mapping as in postmodern narrative, the effort at estrangement moves in two directions simultaneously: one magnifying the subjectivity of perception, the other diminishing any sense of mimetic connection between that subjectivity and the world that seemingly remains intact and apart. Liebman excels in producing this sense of estrangement as a distortion of scale and perception. In the words of Vladimir Nabokov, the

objective is to find "a kind of delicate meeting place between imagination and knowledge, a point, arrived at by diminishing large things and enlarging small ones, that [like social mapping] is intrinsically artistic." See Vladimir Nabokov. (1970). *Speaking Memory: An Autobiography Revisited*. New York: Capricorn, p. 167.

32. Zebun Ahmed. (1997). "Mapping Rural Women's Perspectives on Nonformal Educational Experiences: A Case Study in a Bangladeshi Village." (Ph.D. dissertation, University of Pittsburgh). Ahmed demonstrates how a mapping of women's stories from the margins can, indeed, provide valuable evaluative data for educational planners-if they will only look and listen.

33. Kristiina Erkkilä. (2000). *Mapping the Entrepreneurial Education Debates in the United States, the United Kingdom and Finland*. New York: Garland 2001.

34. See Katsuhisa Ito. (1998). "The Social Cartography Project at the University of Pittsburgh: A Geographer's Assessment." (Paper presented at the Western Regional Comparative and International Conference, University of British Columbia, Vancouver, June); Michel Rakotomanana. (1999)."Mapping the Debate on New Information and Communication Technologies (NICTs) and Development: Implications for Educational Planning in Francophone Africa." (Ph.D. dissertation, University of Pittsburgh, June); Jorge M. Gorostiaga. (1999). "Mapping Debates on Educational Decentralization: The Case of Argentina in the 1990s." (Paper presented at the Comparative and International Education Society [CIES] annual meeting, Toronto, April); and Mina O'Dowd. (1999) "Mapping Knowledge Perspectives in the Construction of Swedish Educational Research." (Paper presented at the CIES annual meeting, Toronto, April).

35. Rolland G. Paulston, ed. (1996). *Social Cartography: Mapping Ways of Seeing Social and Educational Change*. New York: Garland. The interested reader is also directed to a companion project volume by R. G. Paulston, M. Leibman, and J. V. Nicholson-Goodman. (1996). *Mapping Multiple Perspectives: Research Reports of the University of Pittsburgh Social Cartography Project, 1993–1996*. Pittsburgh: University of Pittsburgh, Department of Administrative and Policy Studies.

36. Erwin H. Epstein. (1988). "The Problematic Meaning of 'Comparison' in Comparative Education." in *Theories and Methods in Comparative Education*. Jürgen Schriewer and Brian Holmes (ed.) Frankfurt am Main: Verlag Peter Lang, pp. 3–23. Variations on this metanarrative can be found in George Psacharopoulos. (1990). "Comparative Education: From Theory to Practice." *Comparative Education Review*, 34, no. 3 (August) pp. 369–80; and Stephen Heyneman. (1993). "Quantity, Quality and Source." *Comparative Education Review*, 37, no. 4 (November) pp. 372–88.

37. E. Epstein, p. 6.

38. Ibid., p. 22.

39. See Hayden White. (1978). "Foucault Decoded: Notes from Underground." in *Tropics of Discourse: Essays in Cultural Criticism*, ed. Hayden White. Baltimore, MD: Johns Hopkins University Press, pp. 230–60, quote on p. 239. White concludes that the key to understanding Foucault's method of "transcription" is to be found in how it is used to reveal the inner dynamics of the thought process by which a given representation of the world in words is grounded in poesis: "to translate prose into poetry is Foucault's purpose, and thus he is especially interested in showing how all systems of thought in the human sciences can be seen as little more than terminological formulations of poetic closures with the world of words, rather than with the things they purport to represent and explain" (p. 259).

40. Keith Watson. (1998). "Memories, Models and Mapping: The Impact of Geopolitical Changes on Comparative Studies in Education." *Compare*, 28, no. 1, pp. 5–31. Watson echoes C. Arnold Anderson's earlier modernization agenda for comparative education: "above all, the work undertaken should have purposeful reformist and practical goals and should be used to inform and advise governments" (p. 28). In his text, Watson offers by way of illustration two structural functionalist figures, one of "the determinants of an educational system" (p. 22) and the other of "international influences that shape educational systems" (p. 27). However, it is not clear how these representations meet his criterion for "hard data," especially the latter figure, which is coded using world systems ideology and presents a soft critique of international capitalism, in, for example, the "Role of Stock Markets, e.g. Tokyo's Hang Seng" (p. 27). But as every Hong Kong schoolboy knows, the Hang Seng stock market is not in Tokyo, and even supposedly "hard data" may become a bit fuzzy now and then. The Nikkei is, in fact, Tokyo's stock exchange.

41. See also Keith Watson. (1998). Reviews of *Mapping Multiple Perspectives* by R. G. Paulston, M. Leibman, and J. V. Nicholson-Goodman; and *Social Cartography*, R. G. Paulston, ed. in *Comparative Education*, 34, no. 1, (March) pp. 107–8. While statistical analyses may indeed be useful in technical work, balanced educational assessment requires an alternative practice of formulating judgments not only on assigned numerical ratings, but also on the characteristics of performance in context. Watson's text sees useful knowledge from a rather narrow modernization theory viewpoint (i.e., articulated in simple, essentialist, and mechanistic terms). My view is broader and also welcomes a perspective that sees knowledge as individually and socially constructed and as reflected in particular contexts and discourses that can be mapped and discussed and remapped. See Genette Delandshere and Anthony R. Petrosky. (1998). "Assessment of Complex Performances: Limitations of Measurement Assumptions." *Educational Researcher*, 27, no. 2 (March), pp. 14–24.

42. Raymond Baudon. (1982). *The Unintended Consequences of Social Action*. London: Macmillan, pp. 155–59.

43. Mary Jean Bowman. (1984). "An Integrated Framework for the Analysis of the Spread of Schooling in Less Developed Countries." *Comparative Education Review*, 2 (November), pp. 563–83.

44. David A. Turner. (1988). "Game Theory in Comparative Education: Prospects and Propositions." in *Theories and Methods in Comparative Education*. Jürgen Schriewer and Brian Holmes, ed. Frankfurt am Main: Verlag Peter Lang, p. 158.

45. Peter McLaren. (1994). "Critical Pedagogy, Political Agency, and the Pragmatics of Justice: The Case of Lyotard," *Educational Theory*, 44, no. 3 (Summer) pp. 319–40. See also the related studies by Judith Butler. (1992). "Contingent Foundations: Feminism and the Question of 'Postmodernism.'" in *Feminists Theorize the Political*, ed. Judith Butler and Joan W. Scott. New York: Routledge; and Nelly P. Stromquist. (1995). "Romancing the State: Gender and Power in Education." *Comparative Education Review*, 39, no. 4, (November) pp. 423–54. Stromquist suggests that critical gender issues can be appropriated from feminist discourse to support a more liberating "manipulation of gender identities through schooling and the mass media" (p. 454). In this genre, see also Greg Dimitriadis and George Kamberelis. (1997). "Shifting Terrains: Mapping Education within a Global Landscape." *Annals of the American Academy*, 551 (May) pp. 137–50.

46. McLaren, p. 338. In contrast to McLaren's call to base critical pedagogy on neo-Marxist theory updated with selective postmodern appropriations, Jennifer Gore advocates Foucault's strategy of leaving specific tactics and strategies of resistance to those directly involved in struggle at the precise points where

their own conditions of life or work situate them. Here the shift is made from a master narrative of emancipation owned by intellectuals to the mininarratives or small stories arising from situated experiences and actual power relations. See Jennifer Gore. (1993). *The Struggle for Pedagogies: Critical and Feminist Discourses as Regimes of Truth.* London: Routledge, pp. 65–66.

47. For a valuable study seeking to situate, or map, various contradictory versions of constructivist theory in educational psychology, see Richard S. Prawat. (1996). "Constructivisms, Modern and Postmodern," *Educational Psychologist,* 31, no. 3, pp. 215–25. Prawat uses textual analysis and conceptual mapping, as in this study, to identify and compare different ways of seeing. This is a fine example of a reflexive practitioner viewpoint at work.

48. Carlos Alberto Torres. (1996). "Social Cartography, Comparative Education, and Critical Modernism: Afterthought." In *Social Cartography: Mapping Ways of Seeing Social and Educational Change,* ed. R. G. Paulston. New York: Garland, p. 430. A major problem with the moralistic approach found in many critical modernist texts is that it often leads to a dead end of author self-centering where the marginalized get marginalized still more. Nast puts it like this: "Guilt that centers merely on the existence of . . . inequality and not on how inequality can be transformed is . . . unproductively paralyzing." See Heidi Nast. (1994). "Opening Remarks on 'Women in the Field.' " *Professional Geographer,* 46, no. 1, pp. 54–66.

49. For a variety of ideas on opening new space for radical critique in a postmodern era, see Herbert W. Simons and Michael Billig, (eds.) (1994). *After Postmodernism: Reconstructing Ideological Critique.* London: Sage. I found Richard Harvey Brown's chapter "Reconstructing Social Theory after the Postmodern Critique" (pp. 12–37) especially helpful in its advocacy of self-reflexive talk-about-talk and its advice on teaching debates.

50. See introduction to Beck et al. (n. 5 above).

51. See, e.g., Anthony Welch. (1998). "The End of Certainty? The Academic Profession and the Challenge of Change," *Comparative Education Review,* 42 (February) pp. 1–14. Here Welch worries that disruptive postmodern ideas will be used as a stick to drive performativity efforts in the academy. While this, indeed, seems to be under way, his call to reassert a universal ideal of Western democracy as an opposing criterion of judgment, as an absolute standpoint to judge the truth, sounds a bit Eurocentric and nostalgic. For a serious attempt to rethink political space today, that is, the "hyperspace" of politics in the "global village" in which we all now live, see Warren Magnusson. (1996). *The Search for Political Space: Globalization, Social Movements, and the Urban Political Experience.* Toronto: University of Toronto Press.

52. Robert Cowen. (1996). "Performativity, Post-Modernity and the University," *Comparative Education,* 32, no. 2, pp. 245–58, quote on p. 247. For related work framed in this perspective, see also David Coulby and Crispin Jones. (1996). "Post-Modernity, Education and European Identities." *Comparative Education,* 2, no. 2, pp. 171–84, and, by the same authors, *Postmodernity and European Educational Systems.* Stoke-On-Trent: Trentham. See also Arnold W. Green. (1994). "Postmodernism and State Education." *Journal of Educational Policy,* 9 pp. 136–49; and Jürgen Schriewer. (1988). "The Method of Comparison and the Need for Externalization." In Jürgen Schriewer and Brian Holmes, eds. Frankfurt am Main: Verlag Peter Lang, pp. 25–83, where the text ambitiously advocates a "science of comparative education" based on styles of reasoning, or *Denkstile,* in "divergent types of theory *viz,* scientific theories and reflection theories" (p. 30).

53. Cowen, p. 167. In a related study, Peter Jarvis uses the concept of "late modernity" to situate performativity concerns of non-Western cultures consuming

educational knowledge that can now be packaged and marketed globally. See his 1996 "Continuing Education in a Late-Modern or Global Society." *Comparative Education*, 32, no. 2, pp. 233–43.

54. Zygmunt Bauman. (1987). *Legislators and Interpreters: On Modernity, Postmodernity and Intellectuals.* London: Cambridge University Press, Title.

55. Heidi Ross, Cho-Yee To, William Cave, and David E. Blair. (1992). "On Shifting Ground: The Post-Paradigmatic Identity of U.S. Comparative Education, 1979–1988." *Compare*, 22, no. 2, pp. 113–32. As in the study presented here, the authors report finding a "fragmented field constituting chaos for some, and for others a mosaic of diverse and sometimes competing goals, theoretical frameworks, methodologies and claims" (p. 113). In 1988, they found that CIES members by and large "placed their hopes in the multiple possibilities of diversity and defended the field's eclectic stance as a widening rather than an absence of identity" (p. 127). I locate this view as the "postparadigmatic eclecticism" position in the center of figure 2. It is, perhaps, still the favored perspective of most comparative education practitioners, but a followup study is long overdue. For a perceptive review of our *Social Cartography* book from this eclectic perspective, see John Pickeles. (1999). "Social and Cultural Cartographies and the Spatial Turn in Social Theory." *Journal of Historical Geography*, 25, no. 1 (January) pp 93–98.

56. Nigel Blake also addresses this challenge in his perceptive 1996 study, "Between Postmodernism and AntiModernism: The Predicament of Educational Studies." *British Journal of Educational Studies*, 44, no. 1 (March) pp. 42–65. Blake sees postmodernists resisting the use of a criterion of validity, as advocated here by Watson (i.e., "hard data") and Welch (i.e., "western democracy"), to settle a usage (see nn. 40 and 51). This would foreclose other stories and represent a claim to universal assent for one criterion. As such, postmodern theory impugns the value of all inquiry frameworks that make an a priori claim to universal validity. Indeed, it is one of postmodernism's most salient intellectual characteristics to repudiate the notion of uniquely valid or valuable perspectives on itself, or on anything else (p. 43). Here Nigel Blake reiterates the profound skepticism found in anti-Enlightenment and postmodern texts about the universal validity of any single master narrative or grand theoretical story. See Jean-Franciois Lyotard. (1984). *The Postmodern Condition: A Report on Knowledge.* trans. G. Bennington and B. Massumi. Minneapolis: University of Minnesota Press, where, with no little irony, the text might well be read as advocating as a master narrative the rejection of metanarratives. Social cartography, as practiced here, seeks to avoid this temptation by recognizing and interrelating all texts and arguments claiming space in knowledge debates.

CHAPTER 3

Mapping Rural Women's Perspectives on Nonformal Education Experiences

Zebun N. Ahmed

I think, underneath, all women are feminists. It's just a matter of time and encouragement.

—Susan Faludi, 1991

THE KNOWLEDGE PROBLEM

This study explores how rural women in Srefultoli, a Bangladeshi village, describe from their own point of view their experiences with out-of-school, i.e., nonformal education (NFE). Various studies, particularly feminist research, (Antrobus, 1989; Bhasin, 1991; Stromquist, 1988) show that the existing NFE programs in developing countries give women predominantly traditional knowledge, that is, knowledge of family planning, nutrition, and health care and tend to address primarily the short-term by emphasizing the need to meet women's practical needs. Feminists' texts argue that such a narrow developmental focus does not deal with the need to increase women's awareness of their own oppression and exploitation. Many critics of educational planning and policy, including Bovinic (1984), Leacock et al., (1986) and Stromquist (1988), showed that when NFE projects for women failed, that failure was often related to the exclusion of women in the design as well as in the implementation of the project and that planners did not consider women's perspectives. When attention was given to women, women's strategic needs were not addressed, and they were treated as "vulnerable groups" whose basic needs were confined to the domestic sphere (Stromquist, 1996). Fregeau's (1991) and Duza and Begum's (1993) research indicates that rural women are conscious of their strategic needs as well as their practical needs and, further, that women can identify their needs.

In feminist discourse, a recognition of women's voices and needs are seen to be integral to the processes of social critique and transformation. Feminist research also focuses on the need to empower women in all aspects of life in order to abolish existing inequalities in the family and in society. This discourse contends that education can empower poor women by providing them with opportunities to understand their own situations. Feminist texts also contend that NFE valorizes local knowledge and "works collectively toward producing knowledge by starting from where people are situated and working to develop a broader understanding of structures and how they can be transformed" (Walters, 1998, p. 440). Through education women in poverty can understand that the cause of their oppression is not necessarily a consequence of their own ignorance and/or laziness but of the oppressive and exploitative system under which they live. Understanding the reason for their disenfranchisement, feminists believe, will free women to learn to develop a critical consciousness of why and how social transformation is necessary for their own liberation. This will then allow them to work as agents of social change. In addition, they can learn new skills to help them along to better understanding and self-sufficiency.

In this study, I examine whether the current NFE programs in a rural village in Bangladesh give women new knowledge about their current situation in society and in the family and whether these rural Bangladeshi women are conscious of their strategic as well as their practical needs. I further examine whether the voices of the rural women, i.e. the intended beneficiaries, are considered during the planning stage and the implementation process of these educational projects. I believe that women need to know that they have the right to be in control of their own bodies, e.g., that they have a right to determine the number of children they can have. They need to know that they have a right to challenge tradition when it is seen not to be in their best interests. They need to know that it is within their power to bring about change in their own lives. They need to know that they can identify and develop their own projects rather than accept projects handed down by others in the traditional top-down approach. My personal experience as an urban Bangladeshi woman with these rural Bangladeshi women convinces me that women need to understand their own situation and position in society and in the family; they particularly need to have better knowledge about their subordinate condition. I chose to examine village women's voices/experiences in the specific, historical, and social contexts within which these women live and work, i.e. the village of Srefultoli. The recognition of different ideas and multiple realities, I believe, provides a plurality and richness to development analysis. The need is put to show how comparativists can include village women's voices in the ongoing development debate.

My research poses questions which seek to extend the scope of rural development studies. Since the purpose of this study is to explore rural Bangladeshi women's perspectives on their NFE experiences, I need to hear their own "voices" and need to look at their daily activities. I believe that rural women have a different interpretation from that of most educational policy planners about the objectives of NFE programs. On the basis of this belief, I have developed the following three basic research questions:

1. What are the rural women's expectations for nonformal education activities?
2. How do the rural women assess their nonformal education experiences?
   a. What aspects are seen to be the most relevant and beneficial to their lives in the village?
   b. What activities do they want to change?
3. In the specific case of Srefultoli, what obstacles do rural women see that keep them from participating in NFE programs?

Individuals' needs develop out of the social, cultural and economic contexts in which they live. So, it is appropriate to examine women's NFE needs from the perspective of women in the communities where they live. After thorough consideration, I have chosen an ethnographic approach as the most appropriate and comprehensive means of answering my research questions. Stacey (1991) suggests that ethnography fits many of the criteria feminists call for in research methods. It emphasizes an experiential reality and focuses on how people live everyday lives (Stanley and Wise, 1983). The way in which I conducted my research was influenced by my wish to frame my study in the feminist perspective which states that relationship between researcher and "subject" should not be oppressive, manipulative or hierarchical. Most of the interviews were conducted with women while performing their household duties.

The ethnographic narrative is shaped by the nature of its textual organization (Johannsen, 1992). There are many different possibilities for organizing a text, including, but not limited to: mediating on the dilemmas of events, rituals, practices or concepts; recording the progress of an activity; and, interviewing and observing actors or groups over a period of time (Marcus and Cushman, cited in Johannsen, 1992). In organizing my text, I employ the following primary methods of data collection: (1) participant observation; (2) in-depth interviews; (3) group interviews; and (4) document analysis pertaining to NFE programs. Important data came from my own observations derived from my six months stay in the Bangladeshi community of Srefultoli (located in Faridpur district); and through in-depth interviews with twenty women from that village who unveiled their life histories to me, not only as a researcher but also as a fellow countrywoman.

New themes emerged as I collected and sorted the data into domains (Spradley, 1979) covering what the participants expressed as important, the literature on women in developing countries, and the relationship of women's roles to women's needs in nonformal education. I found myself drawn to the radical humanist perspective as I interpreted the data, particularly at the nexus of the feminist and critical theorist perspectives where the two have recently merged. Recently, feminist writers are also using mapping and spatial metaphors to challenge and expose what they see as patriarchal representations and to develop new social maps grounded in feminist experiences (Paulston, 1996). For my study, I mapped the women's different perspectives and the map serves as a conventional symbol for "the way things are," or perceptions of truth (Paulston, 1993; Price-Chalita, 1994). This map may open a new space for rural women in Bangladesh. This new space will appear to provide a self-grounding reality for identity. In fact, the map does not simply itemize the world: it fixes it within a discursive and visual practice of power and meaning and, "because it naturalizes power and meaning against an impassive and neutral space" (Pile and Thrift, 1995, p. 48). Price-Chalita (1994) states, "Maps can be used as fluid guides for reworking and resisting established power relationships" (p. 243). In this sense, my maps become guides to possible worlds, rather than fixed, definitive statements of the known world.

WOMEN AND NONFORMAL EDUCATION IN BANGLADESH

In Bangladesh, the knowledge women receive through the education programs is limited (Islam, 1982). Most women's education has been carried out by the formal education system which is limited to middle and upper-class women and whose main role is the support and maintenance of the existing patriarchal system. Poor rural women have been almost totally excluded from formal education. Instead, they are recruited as a cheap unskilled labor force utilized in the industrialization of Bangladesh. Studies (such as Duza et al. 1993; 1992; Islam, 1982) have identified several factors which prevent women in Bangladesh from attending schools. The factors are: 1) Discriminatory Attitudes of Parents towards Women's Education; 2) Social Taboos and Traditional Beliefs; 3) Low Social Status; 4) Early Marriage; 5) Parents' Education; 6) Poverty; 7) Religion; 8) Content of Curriculum; 9) Unavailability of Schools; 10) Inconvenient Class Schedules.

While the government of Bangladesh has initiated some NFE programs for the purpose of increasing educational opportunities and improving the conditions of poor women, these NFE programs, like the formal education programs, help to reinforce women's subordinate position in society. Traditional NFE programs, and particularly the government-offered nonformal development programs for women, do not address the long-term, strategic needs of women and they overlook women's existing socioeconomic and domestic roles (Islam, 1982). Studies of NFE programs in Bangladesh show that literacy programs offered by nongovernmental organizations (NGOs), particularly offered by women's run organizations, raised the consciousness of women regarding their situation in society and in the family (Kabir, et al.; 1993; Kabeer, 1994; Lovell, 1992; Rahman, 1994). Rahman (1994) showed that literacy programs, which apply a participatory approach, enabled women to gain "some voice" and women were also organized against domestic violence through a NFE program in one village in Bangladesh.

The conditions of poor women in Bangladesh have drawn the attention of many conscientious educators and intellectuals, particularly women educators and intellectuals. These female professionals in Bangladesh have set up educational projects for rural women with the aim of helping them not only to critically analyze their oppressive situations, but also to become more self-sufficient by providing these rural women with the knowledge with which to increase their basic skills and to develop a functional literacy. Due to the innovative and radical nature of these female-centered NFE projects, however, these NGOs face powerful oppositions from the government and from orthodox rural Muslims.

In this study, I selected Srefultoli where three NGOs, Saptagram, BRAC (Bangladesh Rural Advancement Committee) and Palli Progati, had ongoing NFE projects already in place. Within these three, Saptagram and Palli Progati offer adult education classes along with other development programs. BRAC offers loan and different training programs for women. Saptagram is an organization run by women for women, whose primary objectives are to bring together women, both landless and land-poor, to fight for the right to define their own priorities and to better the conditions of their existence (Kabeer, 1994). Conscientization through adult education classes in an important component in Saptagram's approach. This organization teaches that conscientization takes place through a learning-teaching format in which literacy is taught, not through the convention of using words that have little relevance to the everyday lives of poor people, but rather through a dialogue of words and themes that have a deep resonance. In their NFE syllabus, they not only include many issues of particular interest to women, such as dowry, divorce, oppression, exploitation, family laws, etc. but also they utilize practical life stories and experiences of women. The Palli Progatis' program, in contrast, does not have any gender-based curriculum. This organization encourages the teacher for NFE classes to discuss various socio-cultural issues and problems which are seen to hinder women's development.

WHAT IS SOCIAL MAPPING?

Over the past several decades, scholars such as Paulston (1992, 1993, 1998, 1999) and Burrell and Morgan (1988) have tried to capture the increasingly diverse and fragmented ways that knowledge is constructed through mapping knowledge perspectives. Such maps are a distinct mode of visual representation that use space to represent space. Paulston (1993) sees the development education field moving from paradigm wars to a disputatious community as the use of knowledge becomes more eclectic and reoriented by new ideas and new knowledge constructs, such as interpretations, simulations, translations, probes, and conceptual mapping. Knowledge has become more textual. The metanaratives of modernity are no longer seen as universal "truth," but simply as privileged discourses that deny and silence competing dissident voices. From this view, there is no overarching grand meta-narrative to explain the world, only a multiplicity of competing perspectives and fragmentations.

Regardless of whether they hold power or are on the margins, the role of social mappers in this postmodern world is to map how actors see relationships and their interactions with other actors in society. According to Kirby (quoted in Paulston, 1996), social mapping provides a way of understanding how sliding identities are created, and how the multiple connections between spatiality and subjectivity are seen to be grounded in the contested terrain between discourse communities.

The advantages of social mapping are: 1) It aids decision-makers by pointing out ideological choices in research methods and theories, 2) Because of their openness to multiple orientations, social maps offer a strong ground or basis for new research and for new maps resulting from the knowledge generated by the research. Researchers will not be frozen into one perspective, 3) Since maps represent knowledge as integrated forms of culture, they have significant potentiality to provide new frameworks for understanding the world and for countering hegemonic claims. Readers may also benefit by seeing society and culture from multiple perspectives, and from discovering how social theories are interrelated, 4) Social maps have the potential for representing the total area of a large space within a smaller space, so that maps can help overcome the philosophical argument of inclusion and exclusion (Paulston, 1993).

According to Paulston, social mappers do not argue about validity because they understand that others are encouraged to question the spatial relationships of mapped social realities. As such, social maps are imaginative constructs of patterned relations, they are not mathematically correct representations. From this perspective, the social world is not measured, but rather experienced, reported and compared (Paulston, 1996).

FEMINISM AND MAPPING

Given the collapse of the cold war with its totalizing stories and the emergence of provocative new ways of seeing in post structuralist, post modern feminist and post colonial studies, the time seemed alive with opportunities to rethink our world, to sail off our brutal old maps.

(Paulston, 1996, p. xvi)

Marchand and Parpart (1995) argue that the modernist struggle for universal knowledge has largely been abandoned. Instead, a search has begun to hear previously silenced voices, and to see the specificity and power of language(s) and their relation to knowledge, context and locality. Usher and Edwards (quoted in Paulston 1996, p.16) also strongly argue that knowledge is no longer viewed only as positivist data but as integrated forms of culture open to the play of difference in meaning. In fact, in the last few decades feminist discourses have helped to illuminate the importance of multiple perspectives and multivocality. Most feminist researchers and scholars have rejected traditional positivistic way of knowing and doing research when studying women. This is especially true for studies of women of color and of lower socioeconomic status (Etter-Lewis, 1991; Fonow and Cook, 1991; Reinharz, 1992). Feminist research argues, as in this study, that women must be the subject rather than the object (i.e. the Other) of analysis. Feminist researchers also celebrate postmodernism's "emphasis on iconoclastic questioning rather than predetermination, on openness rather than pre-empting closure, on plurality rather than essentialism" (Slater, 1992, p. 311). Feminist writers have used social mapping and spatial metaphors to expose and challenge what they see as patriarchal representations and to chart new social relations grounded in feminist knowledge and experience (Ardner, 1981).

As a consciencitized female educator I also see that society is composed of diverse views and interests, and believe that it is not appropriate to use "totalizing" categories within the diversity of interests and views today. Stromquist (1996) views that "totalizing categories do exist in society and are often used by dominant groups for the purpose of exclusion. To combat this oppression, one must create counterhegemony or alternative views." Social mapping offers a new way of mapping the validity of women's multiple voices to oppose dominating ("totalizing") ways which repress their world views. From the review of the literature and from my own knowledge and experience, I see that there exists an inequality between men and women in virtually every sphere of society. These inequalities must be addressed at the time of development planning and of doing research on women. Being mindful of this pervasive dichotomy, I show how social mapping methodology can be utilized "to enhance the understanding of feminism as a new social movement" (Ibid.).

According to Paulston and Liebman (1996), the map is the product of its maker. Its contains some part of that person's knowledge and understanding of the social system. In the process of mapping meaning, the subject is seen to be mobile and constituted in the shifting space where multiple and competing discourses intersect. The maps I drew for my study (Figure 1, 2, 3, 4, and 5) are mainly conceptual maps representing a world view I observed from the "insider" point of view. In these maps, the women's voices, which had never before been heard in society, have been made visible. No texts were privileged, and all texts (women's views) were treated equally, i.e., each woman's story was given equal recognition on this map. I also situated myself in this debate and reveal my position by placing myself as the mapper on the map. In this way, my mapping work may be seen not only as counter-hegemonic but, in a larger sense, as anti-hegemonic as well.

MAPPING SREFULTOLIAN WOMEN'S PERSPECTIVES

From the life stories of women in Srefultoli, I have found that more or less all the participant women have similar backgrounds and similar socioeconomic, educational and cultural experiences. Based on the women's

Text	Observation/ Perspective	Textual Characteristics/Advocacies
Reshma bibi	Leader, Organizer	Outspoken, energetic, cooperative, friendly: asks for nontraditional work for women/ change social system.
Rahela	Happy wife	Open minded, cooperative & outspoken, friendly: abolish female oppression, dowry, patriarchal relationship, divorce / need income generating activities.
Mukul	Oppressed woman	Shy: wants women's liberation & education for income.
Roqshana	Hard life	Outspoken, cooperative: abolish class divisions in society / should not have any division of labor / education should be both for girls & boys / education for income generation / women can do many things.
Fatema	Happy farmer & mother	Cooperative, energetic: need for more agricultural training for women/ more agriculture extension workers, & education for income generation.
Minara	Semi-Liberated woman	Outspoken: women should have more voice against 'oppression'/ abolish the dowry practice / women need vocational education & training.
Amina	Active voice	Intelligent: women need education & money to get respect & voice / Practical: should add Islamic studies in NFE programs.
Seuli	Obedient wife	Cooperative: need vocational education for women.
Masuda	Happy family	Open-minded: need courses for agricultural management & training / need Islamic studies in the NFE curriculum to attract more women / need education for income.
Jasmine	Firm determination	Hard worker: need education for men and women/women need education for a good job / women can change their lives & society by themselves / women need money for freedom & speech; practical.
Jakia	Dedicated to family and organization	Soft but outspoken: education makes women conscious/ women should be united against social injustice / need to include history of famous women / need low cost medicine for domestic animals / need income generating activities.
Sakina	Hard and unhappy life	Quiet tone: women are insecure / women need real protection / education for girls is a must / without education women are like the blind / men treat their women as slaves.

Figure 1: Summation of Participant Women's Stories and Views

Text	Observation/ Perspective	Textual Characteristics/Advocacies
Shirin	Leader	Outspoken and a leader: veil should be in the mind, not outside / early marriage should not be encouraged.
Monica	Liberated, learner and teacher	Active voice, firm determination: education for mothers is more important than fathers / emancipation of women and men / religious leader's work seen as an impediment to women's progress.
Maya	Proud business woman	Smart and determined woman: education and earnings give women their own "voice" and hope for structural renewal.
Firoza	Self made woman	Pragmatic and open-minded, hard working, firm determination: if women do not earn anything, they will not get respect from the family / change social system.
Dina	Single and widow	Shy, soft spoken: women's education is urgently needed to secure employment.
Suriya	Happy wife, nationalist	Critical: the rich exploit the poor/exploitation and discrimination of women are very common in society and need to change / NFE curriculum should include a history of the war for liberation in Bangledesh.
Munira	Frustrated	Shy: self advancement is important.
Beauty	Oppressed woman	Shy, soft: men leave their wives in village and take other women in the town / women must know the marriage and divorce law / rural women need basic education.

Figure 1: Continued

narratives, a summary matrix (Figure 1) has been prepared to highlight my observations regarding the personal attributes, perspectives, and advocacy-strategy characteristics of the participant women's texts.

The detailed discussion and summary matrix of the characteristics of the texts are again transformed into a map (Figure 2) to project the individual participant's location within the broad perspectives defined by their personal attributes and choices of advocacy-strategy measures. Here, Munira, for example, a woman who has experienced very few successes in life exhibits attributes and expresses views that can be best described as an idealist-humanist perspective. Whereas, women like Firoza, Jakia and Jasmin represent a group that, compared to Munira, can be identified with rather different and somewhat opposite characteristics. This is a group in transition, from radical humanism to radical functionalism, exhibiting very firm views regarding the value and need of NFE in improving the status and conditions of women. Their views hinge on pragmatic and action-oriented advocacies. They are quite clear about how to transform women's lives.

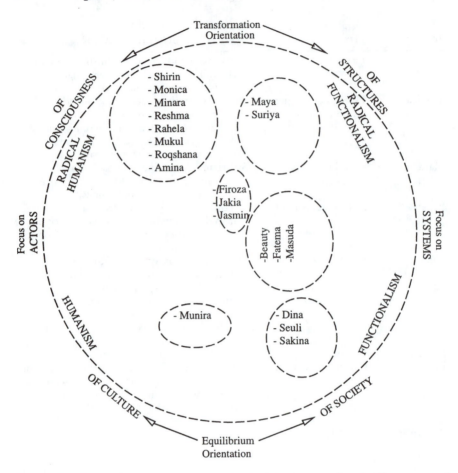

Figure 2: This map situates women in Srefultoli according to the space of their life histories and their world views.

Then, there is a group of eight women (Shirin, Monica, Minara et al,) on the upper left corner of the map, whose texts I have read and located as notable for their forceful feminist views. To them women's liberation from oppressive laws, customs, and practices should be the cornerstone of women's advancement strategies as well as NFE strategies.

Thus, an elaborate discussion on the texts, a summary matrix of the participants' personal attributes and choice of advocacy-strategy modes, and a map locating the belongingness of texts within the broad theoretical perspectives, summarize sequentially the findings of my in-depth interviews and case studies.

The participant women's views on NFE programs are separated from their life histories because some women did not want to disclose their names because of personal reasons and because of social constraints. In the following section I discuss participant women's experiences and perspectives from the world views that construct their texts.

NONFORMAL EDUCATION: THE WOMEN'S EXPERIENCES AND PERSPECTIVES

The participant women in Srefultoli were highly critical of the local NGOs programs, projects and of their existing activities. They freely expressed views of the local NFE programs offered by NGOs. From their stories and interviews I developed eight domains in which to categorize their various perspectives on and experiences with nonformal education: No experience, no opportunities; Agriculture projects; BRAC; Palli Progati; Saptagram; Samity (Women's groups); Sewing/ crafts/ cottage industry; and, Curriculum.

NO EXPERIENCE, NO OPPORTUNITIES

All the participant women in Srefultoli realize now that without education, there will be few if any opportunities for them and for their children. These women are also concerned about the lack of formal education for their children, particularly for their daughters. The high cost of materials and transportation are responsible for many young girls dropping out of their village elementary schools. Although primary education is free for all, books and other education-related materials and transportation costs must be provided by the parents, so it becomes difficult for many to pay the costs. Poverty is one of main reasons that many parents do not send their children to school. The family's demand for female child labor to take care of siblings and to do household work is another reason why girls drop out of school.

Sometimes women who are willing to attend the NFE training classes do not participate because the courses and programs are not seen to be financially beneficial to them. Sometimes, when women ask for a particular course or training related to earning income, their requests are denied. Rahela, one participant, stated, for example, that "The training courses offered by some NGOs are not worth anything. Food preservation or how to take care of domestic animals is not what women needed." She also added that women in Srefultoli needed some productive training or courses which would prepare them to earn some cash money. All participant women supported this view. When some NGOs refused to offer any sewing courses because they viewed that it would not be cost effective, the participant women replied that "Without opportunity and experience, how can we come to that conclusion?" These women want to be challenged.

Some women complained also that when NGOs offer any training, either they are not informed or classes are scheduled at a time when they have to do their household work. Women need to know in advance about the training so they can prepare themselves for that. Some women miss the training which they think is important for them. "We could never attend any training, but we would love to," they added.

AGRICULTURE PROJECTS

Most participant women in Srefultoli have experience in agricultural work. They help their husbands during the harvest time. However, these women's involvement in agricultural work did not provide any extra opportunity to participate in agricultural projects offered by the government or NGOs.

Women participants in this study who were directly involved in agricultural work expressed interest in agricultural training programs. They expressed their desire to learn more innovative techniques and processes in agriculture that would save them time and energy and could help their husbands more. Some participant women also argued that they do not have sufficient space for growing vegetables on a large scale, therefore, these groups prefer to keep domestic animals.

Some informants stated that the organization, particularly Saptagram, supplied crop seeds but the supply was irregular. They also pointed out that irrigation was a problem in Srefultoli especially in the winter season when the water dries up. These participant women suggested that providing them with some foot pump machines at a low cost would solve their irrigation problems and at the same time, help to fulfill the NGO's objectives.

BANGLADESH RURAL ADVANCED COMMITTEE (BRAC)

BRAC is the NGO that has the most contact with the rural people in Bangladesh, and was the most commonly criticized agency among the participants. One of my informants complained to me that, "BRAC's loan policy is very tough. If you cannot pay your installment, the agency people will force you to pay back your loan. They do not care how you are paying. They care only about money like Grameen Bank [a bank which gives loans to landless rural people, mostly rural women, outside the usual banking rules and procedures and rescue them from village money lenders who traditionally supplied about four-fifths of the total rural credits]. If you cannot pay your installment, the field officer will come to your house and wait [a] whole day for money."

Some participants believe that all agencies are the same: they give loans to those whom they like or to those who are rich and can pay them back. They also add that, at first, this organization gave loans to all women according to their needs, but later, the BRAC people began to show preferences to some groups or certain women.

These women also view that BRAC should offer adult education courses which are practical for meeting women's needs, such as courses for agricultural management training and job training courses.

PALLI PROGATI (VILLAGE DEVELOPMENT)

It seems to me from my conversation with some participants who were involved with this organization that they were happy with it because this organization provided *tins*, a silvery white metal used for roofing houses, and latrines, at a very low cost. This organization offers sewing training to women. After training, these women either look for jobs or sometimes Palli Progati places them in a garment factory in the main city if the women show an interest.

Palli Progati supplies plants for women to make their own nurseries. One of the participants said, "This agency has good policies but they do not have enough funds. This organization also plays a considerable role in the lives of rural people in this village. They are the only organization here in Mrigi *mauza* [defined area] where you can think of making a nursery." She also thinks that the adult education they offer is also good. "They talk about women and women's oppression, which I believe is part of our life," she added.

SAPTAGRAM NARI SWANIRVAR PARISHAD (THE SEVEN VILLAGES WOMEN'S SELF-RELIANCE MOVEMENT)

Saptagram Nari Swanirvar Parishad, in short, Saptagram is the most popular NGO program among the rural women in the Faridpur area. Through educational programs, this organization gives credit to women. Most of the informants are, to some degree, happy with this organization because of their flexible loan repayment policy. All my informants said that they have got their voice through Saptagram because, before going to their NFE classes, they did not know how to talk to other people. Now, however, they can express their views and opinions.

Rahela, Reshma, Minara, and Monica, are the few among many who informed me that they have established their rights in their families. They have a voice because of their education and the knowledge provided by this organization. They discuss family planning with their husbands, and decide about future children. Now they feel that the women have become stronger and more confident. They all informed me that they have overcome some domestic problems, such as their husbands' abusive behavior. For example, their husbands used to beat them without any reason and could divorce their wives without any valid reason. So, these participants think that they now know what they should do if their husbands try to commit any of these offenses again. Also, they believe that through NFE classes, they know well the value of civil marriage registration [without registration, a husband can divorce his wife at any time without any reason due to the lack of proper documents or conditions of marriage]. Before, marriage was performed by the local *imam* (priest) but now they are aware of the consequences of that kind of marriage. According to them, they have more control over their own body and mind than before.

Some also expressed their frustrations and angers with Saptagram and demanded tube-wells from this organization. They complained that this organization promised to give them tube-wells soon but did not keep their promise. The participant women also expressed their frustrations regarding their education program. These women think that with their current level of education, no woman could generate any income, therefore, they demanded vocational education in addition to their existing curriculum.

Some informants, particularly those who are from middle-class families, believe that the education this organization offers is anti-Muslim and anti-men. These women think that NFE education teaches rural women not to follow *purdah* (veil), but other informants protested that statement. They informed me that NGO people had taught them (which they believed) that purdah is a state of mind and need not exist outside one's mind.

SAMITY (WOMEN'S GROUPS)

Many organizations prefer that women work in groups in order to receive credit or take part in projects. Credit is one of the main motivations for forming *samity* (groups). Women's groups are seen to be very successful in the rural area of Bangladesh. Ranging from getting a loan, to planning protests against women's oppression, or simply to help each other, women are now organizing themselves for different needs and purposes.

One of the group members said, "We organized all the group members to protest different women-related issues. We organized and demonstrated against a rape case, and the *talaq* (divorce). We can organize women anytime when needed." Another group member told me that she was attracted to the group not because of the loan, but because she could learn so many things about women's problems and world news. She felt that all women are equally oppressed and exploited.

Firoza, one participant, was not very optimistic about the samity. She said that women do not work well in groups. They fight. But immediately one participant, Maya, protested, "Sometimes there are some conflicts within the samity because of men. Some men send their wives to school just for getting a loan and they cannot repay, or sometimes it happens that one group gets a loan from the agency but another group does not because they could not pay off their previous loan." Maya added that men often put pressure on their wives to get a loan or leave the samity. But through the group, they were doing many projects. For example, they bought land with their loan money and cultivated that land, and "whatever we get, that is our profit," she said. Most participants prefer to receive an individual loan rather than a group loan through the samity.

SEWING/HANDICRAFT AND COTTAGE INDUSTRY

"What we need in this village is a teacher to teach women handicrafts and sewing and agricultural skills. We have different samities. All the women want to earn money. They all are willing to do work." Roqshana expresses the needs of all the women in Srefultoli.

All participants I interviewed wanted education and training to provide them with skills to earn an income which would free them from their dependence on men and would give them the ability to adequately support their families. Minara expressed her feelings this way, "I strongly feel that without money, we can not earn any freedom. Women will be oppressed all through their life if they do not earn anything." These participants wanted to learn sewing and handicraft work, so they could work at home or in a nearby center. They wanted to work in any industry such as cottage or garment or sericulture industry, which would be near their village. They demanded vocational education besides their existing curriculum. They also thought that the NFE programs of Saptagram or some other organizations could attract more women and men if they offered sewing or some other handicraft courses useful for income generation.

Some participants made it clear to me that if any organization offers any potentially lucrative income generating program or training, they will join them. They do not care about whether that organization gives credit or not.

CURRICULUM

All the participant women in this study valued the curriculum of the Saptagram's NFE program because they viewed it as relevant to their own daily life. A typical topic discussed would be "Ajmat Bibi's Life Story." It is the story of an oppressed woman who was abandoned by her husband and how she changed her life. Participants believe that this kind of story is for the most part real. They believed that they were not only learning basic skills through Saptagram but also being exposed to different issues concerning women which every woman should be aware of in order to establish her rights in society and in the family.

Some suggested the inclusion of a history of famous women's lives and contributions in the curriculum in order to increase women's self-esteem. One informant indicated that women should know the history of Bangladesh in very short and easy language, particularly about the liberation war. Few women have any knowledge of the war for liberation and some participants believe that if women learn this history, it will increase their social and political knowledge.

PROBLEMS IDENTIFIED AND
SOLUTIONS SUGGESTED

It is a standard policy for development organizations to formulate or design programs for poor, uneducated villagers from the top down, using an educated "expert." However, such experts rarely give consideration to rural people, particularly to women and their interests and needs. The assumption is that rural women do not understand their own needs. Experts believe that they are better able to identify and solve rural women's problems than the rural women are. However, I believe that my interviews with the rural women in the village of Srefultoli reveal just how capable rural women are of identifying their own problems and of suggesting relevant solutions to those problems.

As a result of this research I have categorized the problems and needs identified by the women into six different areas, including: Cultural and religious issues; Girls' education; Conscientization of men; Project financing; Women's own inferior perception; and Other social problems.

CULTURAL AND RELIGIOUS ISSUES

Culture and religion have long played an important role in subordinating women in Bangladesh. Village people are more orthodox and follow religious traditions more closely than people living in urban areas. Most of the rural people misinterpret the religious traditions.

One of the participants expressed her feelings thus:

> There are deep cultural problems in a village. Men always think they are superior and women should be under their feet. Women here are the most marginalized in all respects. Men do not want their wives to go outside for work. It seems that it's a matter of male prestige. They want their wives to follow *purdah*. If anybody does not follow *purdah*, she will go to hell. But we believe that purdah is in our mind, not external.

Reshma Bibi, the leader, thinks that most women here depend on their husbands for income because of their traditional attitudes. Those women are obliged to do what their husbands say.

All the women informants reported that their husbands were concerned about the curriculum because the topics of this education covered many social issues for women such as women's oppression, women's liberation, women's equal rights, dowry, the divorce system, etc., along with the more traditional basic education classes. Most men in Srefultoli thought that this education would take their women out of their houses and would make them revolutionary and that consequently, their marriages were going to end. They thought that such an education would encourage women to abandon *purdah*, which would deny their culture and religion. That's why some participant women suggested that the NGO should introduce some religious studies beside their academic curriculum. It will also help to attract both men and women and might also clear up some misunderstandings about religion as well. In Masuda's words, "When the agency staff talk about irrigation system, training, or family planning system, the rural people who do not have any education think that these are anti-veil systems. Since it is not easy to change our system overnight, the agencies should introduce something which is related to religion."

NEED FOR GIRLS' EDUCATION

"We want our children to be educated, so we can have good leaders to keep our society good. I know also that it is best to have only two children." A participant, Beauty, strongly believes this as well as the importance of educating children, particularly girls. In general, almost all women agreed with Beauty regarding education for their children, especially for their daughters. Young and middle-aged women feel the necessity of education for their daughters because they do not want to see their daughters become dependent upon their husbands as they feel themselves to be.

They identified lack of girls' schooling as a major problem in Srefultoli. Since there is no school for girls nearby, if they want to send their daughters to school, girls need to walk a couple of miles. One informant added that she was very interested in sending her daughter to school, but her daughter of fourteen/fifteen years could not walk by herself because the young men bothered her by chasing after her and asking to marry her.

CONSCIENTIZATION OF MEN

The participants strongly argue that no education or opportunity will change their status without a dramatic, substantial and basic change in the attitudes of men. Therefore, these women in Srefultoli believe that if men can be educated to change their outlook about women, they will value women's education. They need to be taught to take equal responsibility for their children and recognize that women have the same rights as men. All informants expressed their desire for better understanding between men and women, and they believe that in order for that to happen, men should be re-educated. The women participants, like feminists, (Leacock et al., 1986) recognized patriarchy as perpetuating their subordination. Some participants think that since men's attendance is low in the adult education class for men [offered by Saptagram], more men should be encouraged to attend classes. They add that the reason for the low percentage of men attending is their dislike of Saptagram's curriculum. All participants strongly believe that the consciousness of men must be raised for the general social well being. Monica, the learner teacher, expressed her views: "The emancipation of women is only part and parcel of the emancipation of society as a whole. So in order to emancipate women, we [women] need to emancipate men, too."

PROJECT FINANCING: LOANS OR CREDIT

Since most loans or credit are usually given to a group instead of being given to an individual woman, a lack of money is the major problem for those participants who want to be involved with a project independently. All the participants in this study have ideas about doing some kind of business that could earn them a living, but they are all facing serious financial problems. All the women participants indicated that if they would get personal loans, they could start doing some kind of personal project. "I think that it [i.e, a personal loan] will also be good for keeping personal relationships. If someone is unable to pay, it is her responsibility and the organization will not put pressure on the other committee members for that," Maya adds.

WOMEN'S PERCEPTIONS OF INFERIORITY

These women's perceptions of a "woman's status" are still affected by numerous daily practices, often based on taboos, superstitions, religious beliefs, or even misinterpretations of religious tenets, that continue to have a stunting effect on their personal development, assertiveness, and participation in the life around them. Some informants discussed how the attitude of women is sometimes negative. Jasmin added that one of the problems of women in this village is that women feel that they are inferior—that they cannot be like men, that their brains are not good as men's brains. Reshma and Roqshana state that timidity is also a problem, that they have a fear of speaking. But once women become aware that they have the same brain as men and that they can have the same education, then they get back some of their self-confidence.

Monica suggests that the traditional male dominance, the tenet of male superiority, is the most disabling custom of all. Restricted mobility, inferiority, and total economic dependence are but a few of the factors created by a patriarchal culture/society that demands women and girls be submissive. She suggests that women can overcome these problems if they know their legal rights and get an education. NFE programs for women are helping women to overcome some of these problems. She adds that women must also have the opportunity to gain more autonomy and self-confidence.

OTHER SOCIAL PROBLEMS

The participants identified some problems women face in the village in general and in the Srefultoli area in particular. There are as follows: (1) dowry; (2) bad condition of the roads; (3) lack of security; (4) scarcity of tubewells; (5) lack of electricity; (6) lack of information; (7) no recreational facilities; and (8) lack of employment. Srefultolian women also have identified some obstacles which most women face in attending nonformal education and training programs: the negative attitudes of men towards NFE programs; overloaded household responsibilities; a lack of time; poverty; lack of a day-care system; lack of interest; and age.

Figure 3 shows how women in Srefultoli see the impact of NFE programs on their lives. From this figure, we see that the NFE's impact on women in two ways: gradual/incremental and radical. From the incremental perspective, women are becoming social which give them some mobility (women's mobility was always restricted). These women share their sorrows, pain, and

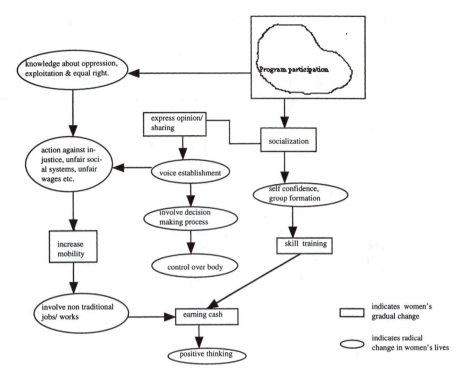

Figure 3: This diagram shows how women in Srefultoli see the impact of NFE programs on their lives and bodies.

ideas with each other. Additionally, they support each other as they become wage earners. From the radical change perspective, we see women talk about their rights, know about basic family laws, become involved with decisions about family planning and the family budget. This has increased their confidence regarding their own lives, and their children's lives. NFE gives them a voice against social and family injustice enabling them to participate in the village court which was quite unthinkable for these women only a couple of years ago.

EMERGING THEMES

When a woman gives her love, as most do generously, it is accepted. When a woman shares her thoughts as some women do graciously, it is allowed. When a woman fights for power as all women would like to, quietly or loudly, it is questioned.

—Hillary Rodham Clinton, 1995, Beijing Conference

Based on the data and insights gained from the various qualitative techniques that I employed, certain themes emerged in response to the research questions posed. Now, I will discuss the themes which emerged from my partici-pants' stories, views, and perspectives, present my own observations, and also assess the reviewed literature and development issues. I will determine which programs my informants view as most appropriate to the development of women, in general, and in Srefultoli. I also explore the needs that women be-lieve must be met by the nonformal education programs in Bangladesh.

The four themes that emerged are; (1) "Men control everything in this society" (gender); (2) "The rich exploit the poor" (class); (3) "Knowledge is not enough" (needs); (4) "If women are united, they can solve many prob-lems" (voice).

Gender : "Men Control Everything in This Society"

(a) Men want to preserve their power

All the women participants in this study believe that men control everything in the society. Men hold onto their traditional beliefs which perpetuates their domination and protects their ego. They want to preserve their power by any means. As an example, women in Srefultoli were introduced to dif-ferent kinds of nontraditional work such as construction work, digging and cutting earth and carpentry activities, tasks which are usually reserved for men in Bangladesh. Some women are also engaged in small businesses, teaching or other work. The participant women expressed that men (i.e., husbands) did not like to see their "women" engaged in nontraditional work. The men thought that these were areas of work which men should dominate in Bangladesh. Therefore, women should not be involved in these sectors. Women participants also believed that men felt their power and egos were threatened.

(b) Patriarchy obstructs women's development

The female participants thought that patriarchy still dominates society, although the society has progressed during the course of their lifetimes. All the participants echoed that social constraints, resulting from patriarchy, are the major reason why women are obstructed from participating in NFE programs.

Their life histories show how the patriarchal social system does not allow women to participate in formal schooling. Indeed, these women see them-selves as trying to free themselves from this dominant patriarchal system by gaining knowledge through the NFE programs. Still, they say, they remain trapped in traditional and subordinate positions. A majority of the women said that they experience great disquiet as a result of trying to liberate their oppressed voices. Most husbands do not want to accept the participation of "their" wives in educational or public spaces. But these women believe that the next generation of women will be better educated to fend for themselves and that they will understand better that they need not accept oppressive re-lationships.

(c) Men need to change their attitudes towards a woman's place in society

All the women I met and interviewed reported that their husbands raised many obstacles when they tried to attend NFE classes and training or do any nontraditional work. They also reported that their husbands' negative attitudes towards their education reflected a deep-rooted fear that education would lead them (women) to become independent and "uncontrollable."

The participant women believe that the only way to change men's attitudes and beliefs is for the government and NGO people to provide progressive education for men which will teach them women's rights, various family laws and other rules and customs in society. This, they hope, will ultimately teach men to value women, their work, and their place in life. The women contend that if the education programs would teach men that women are their partners and not their subjects, men will better realize women's contributions and rights, allow them to go to school, and engage in nontraditional work.

Therefore, most of the participant women recommended NFE not only for women but also for the men, and that schooling should take place in mixed groups. By "mixed groups," the participants meant that if husbands and wives came to class together and exchanged their ideas while learning the same things, it would help to clear up the misunderstandings between men and women. Men might begin to see that women are partners rather than just "wives," or subordinates.

(d) Religious leaders work as an impediment to changing gender roles

The villager's activities in Bangladesh sometimes are based on misleading religious beliefs, superstitions, or taboos, and even misinterpretations of religious tenets and "passive Muslims thoughtless obedience to the *Imam* (Muslim priest)" (Mernissi 1992, p. 26). Since the religious leaders play an important role in making decisions and conduct all religious ceremonies about various matters in the village, including marriage, the villagers respect and depend on the religious leaders.

All of the female participants in this study and the NGO workers reported that they met resistance from the *Imam* when programs were begun in Srefultoli and when the women wanted to join in the NFE programs. The *Imam* wanted to keep women in actual *purdah*, while they were being taught that *purdah* is really a state of mind and need not exist outside one's mind. Such teachings are against the *Imams'* belief. The women added that the *Imam* also did not want women's involvement in the *salish* (village court). Their concern is a reaction to the fear that boundaries are being broken down and threatening the security of the social order. This is the same fear behind the movement to keep women veiled and secluded (Mernissi, 1992). According to women participants, the religious leaders tried to legalize wrongful acts against women in- and outside of marriage. These women believe that these *Imams* are the enemies of women's development.

Class: "The Rich Exploit the Poor"

Shirin, along with other informants, said that "the rich cause our poverty and the rich people exploit the poor." The participant women say they got this notion from the NGO workers. They added that the NGOs' information seemed a reality, so the women were very attracted to the NGO's non-formal education programs.

Before joining NFE programs, women in Srefultoli used to give thumb prints, or tips, in order to get a loan. These uneducated poor women did not know what they had signed (thumb tips are considered to be one's signature) nor what was written on the paper. Sometimes, they were asked to and did sign on a blank sheet. Later, according to my informants, if they failed to return the money on time, the rich took their land whose value was more than the borrowed money. If they protested, the rich people showed their thumb tips as an evidence of contract.

(a) Middle-class women do not get involved in NFE programs

Not all of the women I interviewed showed a positive attitude towards the existing nonformal education programs and training offered by Saptagram or Palli Progati and BRAC. For example, some women dropped out of the NFE programs and some women did not join at all. These women have different perspectives on NFE programs. Some of these women stated that they did not join any NGOs because they believed that it would not solve any of the women's problems, because they have no time, because they are not interested, because the curriculum is anti-religion, because their husbands would not allow them to join, or, because they believe that women will be oppressed all through their lives, no matter what organizations say or teach. Since the nonparticipating women are mainly from middle- and lower-middle-class families that have some economic solvency and who are orthodox Muslim, it would seem that economic solvency and religious beliefs of some middle-class families make them less likely to be involved in nonformal education.

(b) "People on top" (policymakers) never consider the women

Although all the NGOs in Srefultoli seem much concerned about the involvement of women in NFE projects, there is slender evidence of any efforts to involve women in the project planning process. One informant remarked sadly that village women are always considered to be poor and illiterate, since "the people on top" (meaning the policymakers) were males and never considered women's views or needs.

One participant expressed that opinion in this way,

> Men think that women do not have brains and they [men] are the only persons who have them. As long as men do not change their understanding of women's roles, situations and expectations, it will be difficult to introduce any innovative agricultural project for women. Although women have the potential to apply farming knowledge if they are trained properly, unfortunately most planners, agriculturists, workers and leaders are mainly men who do not expect a lot from women.

They also strongly believe that there are some needs and problems which only the women in the village can identify, so if their own problems are not addressed, what would be the value of education? The participant women in Srefultoli proposed that rural women's perspectives must be considered in planning and implementing development of nonformal education in order for such education to fulfill the needs of rural women.

Women's Needs: Knowledge Is Not Enough

Many feminist texts argue that useful NFE programs for women must provide them with the mix of knowledge and skills that will allow them to be emancipated from unequal labor and social relations (Stromquist, 1994). Women in Srefultoli believe that the knowledge and the training that the NFE programs give women is not enough to emancipate women from their subordinate condition in society and in the family.

(a) Knowledge that brings income and freedom to women

"With this education no woman can generate enough income," said one participant. Like that participant, all the poor women and their husbands in Srefultoli expressed a need for some kind of activity which would generate income. The income from selling milk and eggs or from vegetable gardening is not enough to maintain their families. Some participants even said that the training courses being offered are not worth anything. Since there are no day-care facilities and since husbands tend to have a conservative outlook, many women cannot go outside for work. These women said that they would prefer microenterprises where women can work in or near their homes and in which the children can help if necessary.

All the women who participated in the study wanted to receive an education that would provide them with the skills to earn enough income to free them from dependence on men. To them, education and skills are inseparable. Those income-generating courses which the women, themselves, requested from the NGOs were refused on the basis that they were not cost effective. At the same time, these women also say that they value the consciousness raising education which, they believe, helps them counter the exploitation of employers.

Voice: Women Discover Their "Voices" Through Nonformal Education

Literacy is a part of liberation only when it is consciously linked with the process of "rupturing colonial domination, recovering democratic life, or revolutionary triumph." The potential for adult NFE to achieve its full liberating effect is often not realized. Stromquist (1994, p. 263) argues that "Yet circumstances can be created to provide the adult educational experience with an opportunity to re-examine old knowledge and produce new wisdom."

Most of the women participants believed that now they can express their feelings and frustrations to each other. Since women share each other's experiences, these women can mobilize other women for protesting social injustices against women. These women in Srefultoli have started going to the *salish* (village court) to establish their voices. Here are different ways the women described to me how they found their "voices" through the NFE programs.

(a) NFE empowers women to use their voices: Feelings of empowerment

I use Stromquist's (1993) definition and dimensions of empowerment for the analysis of women's feelings of empowerment in Srefultoli through their training and experiences with NFE programs. Stromquist defines empowerment as "a process to change distribution of power, both in interpersonal relations and in institutions throughout society" (Stromquist, 1993, p. 2). Her main thesis is that empowerment is a four-dimensional process, and that to act as equal participants in development, women have to be empowered in these four dimensions: cognitive, psychological, economic and political.

Figure 4 graphically represents the relationship between NFE and women's empowerment as revealed by my study of certain women in the village of Srefultoli. This map utilizes Stromquist's (1993, 1996) four dimensions of empowerment, but goes beyond the original ideal schema to examine the process-product relationship in various dimensions that affect the lives of women in the Srefultoli context. NGOs, particularly Saptagram consider different themes in their NFE programs such as literacy, dowry, domestic violence, women's right to control over their bodies, patriarchy, family laws, and different social injustices towards women. As a result of their programs in these areas, the women in Srefultoli have developed their critical con-

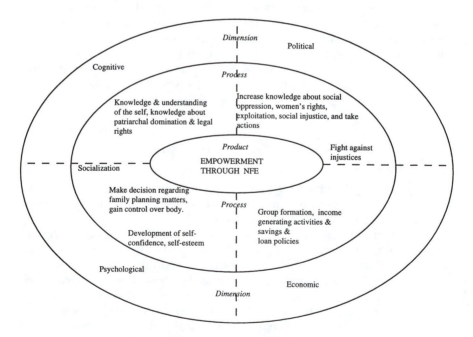

Figure 4: This concept map presents an idealized view of how NFE empowers participant women in the village of Srefultoli, Bangladesh. Adaptation of Stromquist (1993, 1996), "four dimensions of empowerment."

sciousness and become empowered in the dimensions of cognitive, psychological, political and economic empowerment.

1) *Cognitive empowerment* involves understanding the subordinate conditions and their causes at both the micro and the macro level of life. Cognitive empowerment calls for the knowledge and understanding of the self and the need to make choices that may go against cultural and social expectations. Knowledge about patriarchal control of the female body including sexuality and abuse, and knowledge and understanding of women's legal rights are key concerns. 2) *Psychological empowerment* is concerned with women's feelings and the belief that they can change their situation themselves. Psychological empowerment involves reversing the patriarchal order of doing things. This dimension calls for competence in making decisions and the development of self-confidence and self-esteem. 3) *Economic empowerment* involves the ability of women to engage in income-generating activities that will enable them to have access to independent income. Although involvement in income-generating activities increases the work burden that the women already shoulder, the economic independence they gain is motivation for them to participate. 4) *Political empowerment* entails the ability to analyze situations politically and to mobilize for social change. Collective action has been identified as an important prerequisite to any meaningful political or social change (Freire, 1972; Friedman, 1992). Through engaging in collective action, women will be able to raise cultural awareness among men and other women and therefore influence change at the social level.

All of the women participants have demonstrated some form of empowerment in these four dimensions. However, the levels of empowerment they demonstrate vary by individual and by dimensions. Most of the women display the greatest sense of empowerment in the cognitive realm followed by political empowerment, then psychological empowerment. The lowest level of empowerment the women have achieved is in the economic realm because of the very limited economic opportunities for them in Srefultoli.

(b) Nonformal education gives women "Voice" against social and political injustice: Collective action

All the participants reported that they are now very conscious about social and political issues in the village. The women participants believe they are gaining knowledge and becoming empowered as a result of joining the NFE programs of Saptagram.

Although their conversations reveal that they think that politics is an important issue, they do not want to be concerned with politics in the beginning of their own struggles. They know who is in power, who the opposition party leaders are, and who will be the best leader in future national elections.

With the inspiration of NGO workers and the lessons learned from the education programs, the participant women in Srefultoli have determined that collective action is important for social and personal change. As Dighe and Jain (1989) put it, "From a state of powerlessness that manifests itself in a feeling of 'I cannot,' empowerment contains an element of collective self-confidence that results in a feeling of "we can" (p. 87). These participant women have also developed a "we feeling" among themselves in Srefultoli. These women have protested many social injustices collectively such as unfair wages, wife beating, divorce cases, women's harassment, etc. These participants indicate that because of their collective actions, they have been successful in removing some traditional but illegal systems and prejudices from this society. An example of this is "*hilla*" (In this practice, a husband divorces his wife but then wants to take her back. In this situation the ex-wife has to get legally married to another man for one night and then get a divorce from that man the next day, after which her first husband can remarry her). Another example of injustice is "*talaq*" in which if a husband can utter three times the word "*talaq*" [which means "divorce"], she will be automatically divorced from that man. Also these women have been successful in encouraging women to register for marriage rather than just going to the Muslim *Imam*. These women also participate in the village "*salish*" (village court), which would have been quite impossible to believe just a few years ago. They feel that they have established their "voices" in the village salish system, through their participation and decision making there regarding various women's issues.

(c) "Women will have more freedom when they have more education and more knowledge": Empowerment for self-confidence

Empowerment for self-confidence can also be seen as a type of psychological empowerment. In order to overcome women's perception of themselves as powerless, women need to build up their self-confidence and self-esteem. Since women's theory of self is traditionally limited to a culture of silence (Freire, 1970) because of poverty, patriarchy, domestic violence and other difficulties, critical NFE seeks to break this culture of silence and give them their own space where they have respect, confidence and determination.

Women participants in Srefultoli claimed that the NFE provided by Saptagram, in particular, has helped them to redefine their concepts of themselves. The lessons that they learned about counteracting power within the organization provided them with vital models for their own lives. They have learned that their voices count and that they are worthy of being heard. They have also learned that women need to put "fire on their own candle."

The participant women believed that, through NFE, women were able to participate by sharing experiences and learning from each other. Some have changed their attitude towards domestic violence and are no longer willing to accept the myths that "heaven lies under the feet of her husband." These women now tend to respect other people's views because now they know what it is like to be ignored.

(d) "Now I know what is right and what is wrong. I know my dues": Increased consciousness and awareness regarding women's rights and oppressions

Increased consciousness and awareness in one's life of what is going on around them are the first steps to empowerment. According to the participants, NFE programs have increased their knowledge about their rights and the truth about their oppressive conditions. They have become conscious of their individual rights. They expressed the view that the curriculum of NGOs, particularly Saptagram, its teaching methods, dialogues with groups and discussions of women's daily experiences, have helped them to "think as a human being rather than 'just a *mahila*'" (woman). One informant stated that, "We were blind, and we thought that the world was like what we thought. But it is not the reality. It is something different. Women have a right to imput into their families and society."

Women think that they were often denied their rights by the society and by the family. They now understand that they are vulnerable when they are forced to be economically dependent on men, and that they are "being kept underfoot," even though sometimes they have more education than their husbands. Women now consider themselves as workers while some others consider themselves as breadwinners. The statement of Reshma reflects her confidence, her awareness and her rights in the family: "It is my turn, Apa, ('Apa' means sister) to go out. Let him cook." The majority of these women who have experienced the NFE programs are confident, saying that there is no gender difference in jobs and that women can do what is considered men's work. They say that several years ago, they did not think this way. "Men's earning ability gives them power over women. But women now work like men," Jasmin adds.

(e) "Income gives women 'Voice'": The impact of the acquisition of knowledge and skills on earning power

"I can go anywhere, anytime now, because I am the breadwinner in my family. My husband does not say anything about that" (Reshma), "I decide my family budget because my husband does not work" (Roqshana), "I do not beg my husband to buy anything for me because I earn." These statements of different women participants in my study reflect that their earning capabilities have given them "voice." The women I interviewed said that their earning capabilities have changed their lives. Now they make decisions with their husbands in planning the family matters and planning for future investment.

In terms of economic empowerment, most participants claim that they are earning some money, but it is not really sufficient. But a few years back they did not earn money by themselves. At least they have some earning sources now. These women firmly believe that the formation of women's groups that encourage savings and establish loan policies, and above all, the NFE programs guide them to become self-sufficient and help them learn how to utilize the loan money properly.

Women in the village believe that they have improved their literacy, numeracy and networking skills, and have gained skills in reflection and critical analysis. Women started with traditional economic activities and slowly they have shown an interest and confidence in taking up nontraditional employment such as brick making/construction work, carpentry, running small businesses, teaching, working as village doctors and making low-cost latrines. Some women also have taken up nontraditional agricultural activities such as ploughing and applying fertilizer. These women say that their self-confidence has increased tremendously. Such empowerment clearly demonstrates the active role some women are taking in respect to gaining control over issues that concern their financial well-being, as well as challenging the barriers of sexual inequality.

Figure 5 is a conceptual map patterning the various perceptions of participant women in Srefultoli regarding their NFE experiences as interpreted within certain theoretical paradigms. This figure gives us the understanding that women also have different cognitive space and beliefs and they are not stagnant in one position. There is a greater sharing of cognitive spaces. There is a fluidity of ideas between the various paradigms that results in the "opening of a new world space" (Stromquist, 1996, p. 245) with changing socioeconomic and political structure as well as changing women's potentials. Stromquist (1996) argues that mapping is useful to identify moments at which these spaces are crossed, how they are crossed, or why they are seldom crossed.

CONCLUSIONS

It is not likely that women-run NGOs, or NGOs in general, can push hundreds of years of patriarchy out of parliamentary chambers or homes. Women's subordination is deeply ingrained in the minds of both men and women in Bangladesh. One cannot dictate self-confidence and self-esteem; one can only provide conditions in which such new attitudes and behavior

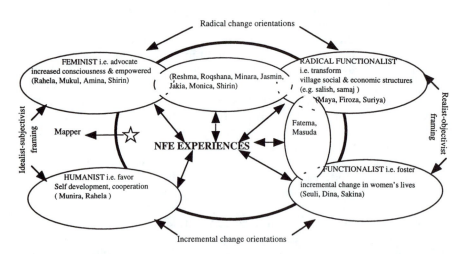

Figure 5: This map situates the participant women in Srefultoli according to their ways of seeing NFE experiences, i.e., Functionalist, Radical Functionalist, Humanist or Feminist. Adaptation from R. Paulston's Mapping Knowledge Perspectives in Studies of Social and Educational Change, 1993, p. 24.

may emerge and flourish. If NFE seeks the empowerment of women, it must involve women in all stages of NFE project from defining the problems, to identifying proposed solutions, applying solutions, and in assessing project processes and outcomes. Women need opportunities to assert themselves, even to make mistakes. In the long run these women, through their participation, will be able to take steps for themselves and for the sake of others.

Income-generating programs are desperately needed, but they are difficult to implement because they are risky, time-consuming and expensive. In terms of economic gain, these women's economic status might not change dramatically, but they need to earn something and gain a degree of financial independence. Yet, because the needs are overwhelming, it is not possible for only one or two NGOs to meet all the economic needs of the village women. The participants' basic and strategic needs can be fulfilled only by utilizing a variety of educational approaches, and being flexible with programs. If the government and other organizations work together, they could better address the needs of rural women in Bangladesh. It would be helpful if NFE curriculum provided women with some kind of job market analysis and analysis to help women make more realistic choices about job training.

At the nexus of the critical and feminist discourses is the view that women's voices and needs should be understood as an integral input in social transformation. In this study, women themselves knew better than outside "experts" what types of education would benefit them most. For both practical and equity reasons, women should have a voice in their own development. Accordingly, all organizations in Bangladesh which focus on women should respect the knowledge, views, and perspectives that these poor women bring with them to educational and developmental activities. The mapping of these rural women's stories/discourse will provide a greater understanding of the rich diversity of perspectives in rural settings. Women's knowledge and experiences should be recognized as valid in designing the plans for NFE projects. Such consideration would result in the beneficiaries feeling closer to the program and feeling that they have a stake in their own development. "If you give women the chance, they can do many things and would take over." Here Roqshana's statement shows her confidence in changing social position and status. If women are given the chance to talk about themselves and analyze their positions from their own experiences, a collective awareness will develop. As a consequence, the women will be better able by themselves to organize and mobilize for social transformation. The aim of offering NFE from the feminist perspective is to increase women's consciousness which will ultimately transform society and the social system. NFE can become liberating when "it helps the group [women] articulate their problems, dreams, and strategies for action" (Paulston, 1980, p.16).

My study reveals that some NGOs are trying to change gender roles through increasing the economic participation of women. But changing gender roles through consciousness raising without economic participation

has not been fruitful. Education and income are inseparable. The participants' demand for a NFE program that would increase male consciousness
may bring some solutions to certain problems, but solutions need to be
found to the participants' economic problems which continue to hold
women within the subordinating patriarchal systems. Stromquist argues that
literacy becomes a felt need after women gain some confidence in upgrading
their skills to improve their earning potential but "nothing of this would be
sufficient if women are not made to realize that they live under conditions
of subordination" (Stromquist, 1994, p. 265).

My study concludes that certain more participatory nonformal education
programs can bring meaningful changes in women's lives, and that rural
women, themselves, can best identify their own needs. In a rural community
(such as Srefultoli) where socio-cultural norms and attitudes exert a strong
influence on women's lives, NFE programs for women need to be designed
to address women's basic and strategic needs. Nonformal education programs need to be designed to foster the growth of self-awareness for women
as well as to foster an awareness of the socio-cultural reality that influences
and shapes their lives. Such awareness would enable them to analyze and
map their own situation, identify their needs, and develop the ability to
transform their own reality. Women should organize and recognize their
common needs and goals and draw upon what Faludi (1991) calls their
"vast and untapped vitality" to create a more just world.

REFERENCES

Antrobus, P. (1989). Women and Development: An Alternative Analysis. *Development*, (1), 26–28.

Ardner, S. (ed.) (1981). *Women and Space: Ground Rules and Social Maps.* London:
Croom Helm.

Burrell, G. and Morgan, G. (1988). *Sociological Paradigms and Organizational
Analysis.* London: Heinemann.

Buvinic, M. (1984). *Projects for Women in the Third World: Explaining Their Misbe-
havior.* Washington, D.C.: International Center for Research on Women.

Duza, A. and Begum, H. (1993). *Emerging New Accents: A Perspective of Gender
and Development in Bangladesh.* Dhaka: Women for Women.

Etter-Lewis, G. (1991). Black Women's Life Stories: Reclaiming Self in Narrative
Texts. In S. Berger Gluck and D. Patai (eds.), *Women's Words: The Feminist
Practice of Oral History (pp. 43–58).* New York: Routledge.

Faludi, S. (1991). *Backlash: The Undeclared War Against American Women.* New
York: Crown.

Finn, J. D., Reis, J., and Dulberg, L. (1982). Sex Differences in Educational Attainment: The Process. In G. P. Kelly, and C. M. Elliott. (eds.), *Women's Education in the Third World: Comparative Perspectives (pp. 107–126).* Albany: State
Univ. of New York Press.

Fonow, M. M., and Cook, J. A. (eds.) (1991). *Beyond Methodology: Feminist Scholarship as Lived Research.* Bloomington: Indiana University Press.

Fregeau, L. (1992). Perspectives of Rural Costa Rican Women on Nonformal Development Education: An Ethnographic Case Study of Coto Brus, Costa Rica.
The PhD Thesis. The Pennsylvania State University.

Freidman, J. (1992). *Empowerment, the Politics of Alternative Development.* Cambridge: Blackwell Publishers.

Freire, P. (1970). *Pedagogy of the Oppressed.* London: Penguin Press.

Freire, P. (1972). Education: Domestication or Liberation? *Prospect,* (2), 173–181.

Islam, S. (1982). *Women's Education in Bangladesh: Needs and Issues.* Dhaka: The Foundation for Research on Educational Planning and Development.

Johannsen, A. M. (1992). Applied Anthropology and Postmodernist Ethnography. *Human Organization,* 51(1), 71–81.

Kabeer, N. (1994). *Reversed Realities: Gender Hierarchies in Development Thought.* New York: Verso.

Kabir, M., et al., (1993). *Impact of Women in Development Projects on Women's Status and Fertility in Bangladesh.* Dhaka: Development Researchers and Associates.

Leacock, et al., (1986). *Women's Work, Development and the Division of Labor by Gender.* Amherst, MA: Bergin and Garvey Publishers, Inc.

Lovell, C. (1992). *Breaking the Cycle of Poverty: The BRAC Strategy.* Connecticut: Kumarian Press.

Mernissi, F. (1992). *Islam and Democracy. Fear of the Modern World.* New York: Addison-Wesley Publishing Company Ltd.

Nasrin, T. (1992). *Nirbachito Colum.* Calcutta: Ananda Publisher.

Marchand, M. and Parpart, J. L. (eds.) (1995): *Feminism/Postmodernism/Development.* London & New York: Routledge.

Paulston, R. G. (1992). *Comparative Education as an Intellectual Field: Mapping the Theoretical Landscape. Paper presented at the Eighth World Congress of Comparative Education, July 8–14, Prague, Czech Republic.*

Paulston, R. G. (1993). Mapping Ways of Seeing Educational Studies. *La Education,* 114, 1–18.

Paulston, R. G., and Liebman, M. (1996). Social Cartography. A New Metaphor/Tool for Comparative Studies. In R. G. Paulston (ed.), *Social Cartography: Mapping Ways of Seeing Social and Educational Change (pp. 7–28),* New York: Garland Publishing, Inc.

Paulston, R. G. (1998). *Mapping the Postmodernity Debate in Comparative Education Discourse.* Occasional Paper Series. Department of Administrative and Policy Studies. School of Education. University of Pittsburgh.

Paulston, R. G. (1999). Mapping Comparative Education After Postmodernity. *Comparative Education Review,* 43(4), 438–463.

Pile, S. and Thrift, N. (1995). Mapping the Subject. In S. Pile and N. Thrift (eds.), *Mapping the Subject: Geographies of Cultural Transformation* (pp.13–51), London and New York: Routledge.

Price-Chalita, P. (1994). Spatial Metaphor and the Politics of Empowerment: Mapping a Place for Feminism and Postmodernism in Geography. *Antipode,* 26(3), 236–254.

Rahman, A. N. S. H. (1994). The Impact of Adult Literacy Among Women. *The Daily Star,* Sept. 8.

Reinharz, S. (1992). *Feminist Methods in Social Research.* New York: Oxford University Press.

Slater, D. (1992). "Theories of Development and Politics of the Post-modern." *Development and Change,* 23(3), 283–319.

Spradley, J. P. (1979). *The Ethnographic Interview.* New York: Holt, Rhinehart and Winston, Inc.

Stacy, J. (1988). Can There Be a Feminist Ethnography? *Women's Studies International Forum,* 11(1), 21–29.

Stacey, J. (1991). Can There Be a Feminist Ethnography? In S. Berger Gluck and D. Patai (eds.), *Women's Words: The Feminist Practice of Oral History (pp. 111–119).* New York: Routledge.

Stanley, L., and Wise, S. (1983). "Back Into the Personal" or, our attempt to construct "feminist research" in G. Bowles and R. D. Klein (eds.), *Theories of Women's Studies (pp. 192–209)*. Boston: Routledge and Kegal Paul.

Staudt, K. (1982). Bureaucratic Resistance to Women's Programs: The Case of Women in Development. In E. Boneparth (ed.), *Women, Power and Policy*. New York: Pergamon Press.

Stromquist, N. (1988). Women's Education in Development: From Welfare to Empowerment. *Convergence*, 21(4), 5–16.

Stromquist, N. (1990). *Challenges to the Attainment of Women's Literacy*. Paper presented at the symposium Women and Literacy: Yesterday, Today and Tomorrow. Sponsored by the Nordic Association for the Study of Education in Developing Countries (Sweden, June, 1989).

Stromquist, N. (1993). *The Theoretical Basis for Empowerment*. Paper presented at international seminar on Women's Education and Empowerment. Hamburg, UNESCO Institute of Education.

Stromquist, N. (1994). Education for the Empowerment of Women: Two Latin American experiences. In V. D'Oyley, A. Blunt, and R. Barnhardt (eds.), *Education and Development: Lessons Learned from the Third World (pp. 263–282)*. Vancouver: Detelig.

Stromquist, N. (1996). Mapping Gendered Space in Third World Educational Interventions. In R. G. Paulston (ed.), *Social Cartography (pp. 223–248)*. New York and London: Garland Publishing, Inc.

Walters, S. (1998). Informal and Nonformal Education. In N. P. Stromquist (ed.), *Women in the Third World: An Encyclopedia of Contemporary Issues* (pp. 436–443). New York and London: Garland Publishing, Inc.

CHAPTER 4

Imagining Comparative Education: Past, Present, Future

Rolland G. Paulston

ABSTRACT   *The study is organized around three questions, i.e. (1) how have compar-ative educators, and related scholars, used their creative imaginations to construct new knowledge and understanding about ways of representing changing educational phe-nomena and relations? (2) what genres and forms of representation have been appropri-ated or elaborated and how have these code choices influenced ways of seeing and think-ing? and (3) can this self-reflexive history of imagination in practice be patterned as an intertextual field of difference, as a comparative cultural map that may help to open new vistas into the past and the future? In this, my desire is to move beyond the sterile po-larities of modernist rule-making and poststructuralist nihilism in knowledge work. Here I should instead like to privilege a hermeneutic of imagination with its power of disclosure, which I believe marks our basic ethical ability to imagine oneself as another. Two figures and two tables help to visualize my argument and summarize findings.*

Comparative research begins, in my view, with a destabilization of self—with a felt need for encounters with difference that invite one to imagine alternatives. While we would not want to abandon the efforts to generate theories and concepts that transcend cultures, we also want theories that address real human experiences. Culture nearly always entails en-counter with the unexpected. . . . To imagine culture, then, and at the same time to *culture* the imagination, is the task of comparative education in the next century. (Hoffman, 1999)

I still hope that there is room in the field for those scholars whose work is driven by intellectual curiosity and playfulness, because as in the natural sciences, the serendipi-tous outcomes of such endeavors may have substantial long-term policy implications. (Foster, 1998)

Imagination is more important than knowledge. To raise new questions, new possibili-ties, to regard old problems from a new angle, requires creative imagination and marks real advance in science. (Einstein, 1993)

Introduction

As a historian, the invitation to address "the future of comparative education" gives me pause, for where are the data? Also important is my desire to argue that our future as well as our past may be understood better if viewed through a lens of hermeneutical imagination with its power to enter into and bear witness to "exemplary" narratives of the past and present. The notion of hermeneutics is used here to denote the study of understanding, of interpretation, and of how meaning can be borne out of existential uncertainty.

To develop this argument, I have organized the study around three questions, i.e.:

- How have comparative educators, and related scholars, used their imaginations to construct new knowledge and understandings about ways of representing changing educational phenomena and relations?
- What genres and forms of representation have been appropriated or elaborated and how have these choices influenced ways of seeing and thinking?
- Can this self-reflexive history of imagination in practice be patterned as an inter-textual field of difference, as a comparative cultural map that may help to open new vistas into the past and the future?

I should, perhaps, also share a third concern. This is my desire to move beyond the sterile polarities of modernist rule-making and poststructuralist nihilism in knowledge work. While there is certainly space for both rules and irony in comparative studies, in this paper I should like to privilege the narrative imagination with its power of disclosure which I believe marks our basic ethical ability to imagine oneself as another. Here I join the authors of the three opening quotes to argue for a re-empowered imagination to help us move beyond our present aporia of the deflated sovereign subject. More specifically, I seek to suggest how a radical hermeneutic of imagination may help us reanimate what is valuable, if nascent, in modernity by re-inscribing its betrayed promises.

Where the pre-moderns tended to see the image as a *mirror*, and the moderns as a *lamp*, the postmodern model of the image is akin to a circle of *mirrors* where each viewpoint reproduces the surface images of all the others in a play of infinite multiplication. Recent attempts to break out of this so-called postmodern mirror play of simulacra, i.e. reproductions without originals, propose a hermeneutic of imagination that relocates the crisis of creativity in a world refigured or prefigured by our imaginings. This does not mean that the imaginary must return to a foundational ontology of being or a realist epistemology of knowing, or to grand ideological utopias which would yearn to anchor our images in their arrogant categories. Rather, a radical hermeneutics of imagination seeks to re-establish the link between text and history (Gerhart, 1979), to recognize the possibility of an intermediary course between the extremes of humanism—where imagination, as in Blake (1794), rules supreme—and postmodernism where imagination, as in Lyotard (1992), floats as just another signifier in a giddy play of signs. Today, as we look ahead to the new century, I believe we require more than ever the power of imagining to recast other ways of being in the world, other possibilities of existence and to wager once again that imagination lives on (Kearny, 1998).

EARLY VARIETIES OF IMAGINATION

Beginning with the earliest Western texts, imagination has been portrayed in terms of good and evil. Biblical commentary identifies imagination, as in the Adam and Eve story, with the human potential to convert the given confines of the here and now into a more open horizon of possibilities.

Buber (1952), for example, sees a dualistic tendency in how the biblical tradition of commentary and the early Greeks viewed image making:

> Imagination is seen as good and evil, for in it man can master the vortex of possibilities and realize the human figure proposed in creation, as he could not do prior to the knowledge of good and evil . . . it offers the greatest danger and greatest opportunity at once . . . To unite the two urges of the imagination implies to unite the absolute potency of passion with the one direction that renders it capable of great love and great service. Thus and not otherwise can man become whole.

Plato and Aristotle recognized imagination, i.e. the making of images, as a uniquely human attribute, but warned that humans can only mirror truths of the omniscient gods. Imagination may under the strict supervision of reason and revelation be used to instruct the faithful, but nearly all early and pre-modern texts share a deep suspicion that imagination threatened a natural order of being. Thomas Aquinas puts it well in his caution that imagination has the potential to make everything "other than it is."

But before our examination of earlier and current imaginative practitioners and their texts, it may be helpful to organize my narrative using an outline borrowed from Michel Foucault (1970). Foucault sought to identify in texts the major epistemic episodes, or discursive modes, of Western European thinking. His intertextual comparison, despite its gross insensitivity to diversity, will serve my purpose of organization via visual display equally well. It should be noted, however, that neither of us seeks to construct a matrix or table where reality is boxed according to some timelessness and universality of determination, i.e. as in a modern discourse of the Enlightenment. Rather, I offer my interpretation in Table I below as a heuristic where reality is seen to take a linguistic turn; i.e. to take on aspects of the linguistic mode in which it is presented to consciousness (White, 1987), and where the texts selected are read as modes of representation prevailing at a given time and place (Foucault, 1970).

While I include the early historians Herodotus and Ibn Khaldun in Table II below as exemplary practitioners of narrative imagination and cultural comparisons, it is not until the Renaissance and the age of humanism that imagi-

Table I. My visualization of Michel Foucault's poststructuralist comparison of how the imbricated epistemes, i.e. the rules, or codes, of European scientific discourse have changed over time. I have taken the liberty to add a fourth epistemic episode, i.e. the "Postmodern," that was, perhaps, only incipient at the time of his study.

Imaginary Era	Episteme	Focus On	Favored Representations	Comparative Education
Renaissance	Humanism: unity	Man, resemblance	Translations and pictures, the analogical	Erasmus (1512), Comenius (1628)
Classical	Rationalism: order	Natural history, nomenclature, comparison	Statistics and grids, the taxonomic	Berchtold (1789), Condorcet (1792), Basset (1808), Jullien (1817)
Modern	Realism: progress	Time, differentiation, functions	Nomothetic explanations and scientific models, the mimetic	Durkheim (1895), Dewey (1929), Holmes (1958), Husén (1967). Bowman (1984)
Postmodern	Pluralism: reflexivity	Space, complexity, performativity	Networks and mapped simulations, the ironic	Foucault (1970, 1986). Usher and Edwards (1994), Coulby and Jones (1995), Paulston (1999)
?	?	?	?	?

Source: Adapted from Foucault (1970).

Table II. A comparison of types of imagination and products of representational practice constructing comparative and international education discourse over time.

Types of creative imagination	Textual products	Illustrative texts
Narrative imagination:	Chronicles and stories of educational customs and practices: histories of educational ideas	Herodotus (B. C. 550); Ibn Khaldûn (1378); Dewey (1929); Hans (1959); Brickman (1960, 1966); Paulston (1968, 1980); King (1999)
Statistical imagination:	Methodologies for the numerical representation of educational data and practices; measurement	Berchtold (1789); Basset (1808); Jullien (1817); Roselló (1960); Husén (1967); Fuller et al. (1999)
Scientific imagination:	Positive models for representing educational functions and systems: iconic realism	Condorcet (1793); Correa (1963); Tinbergen & Bos (1965); Davis (1966); Bowman (1984); Seppi (1996)
Analytical imagination:	Causal explanations of social and economic relations and outcomes: theories	Marx (1867); Durkheim (1895); Schultz (1963); Carnoy (1974); Bernstein (1975); Bowles & Gintis (1976); Beck et al. (1994); Archer (1995)
Ethnographic imagination:	Thick descriptions of cultural processes and world-making; transformations, appropriations and personal witnessing *(testimonio)*	Geertz (1973); Modiano (1973); Turner (1974); Foley (1991);Rockwell (1996); Ahmed (1997); Torres (1998)
Rhetorical imagination:	Translations and deconstructions of literary texts and discursive practice: poetics	Erasmus (1512); Foucault (1970); Gottlieb & LaBelle (1988); Gottlieb (1989, 1996); Paulston (1993); Nicholson-Goodman (1996)
Spatial imagination:	Metaphorical mappings of diverse ways of seeing and nets of relationships: heterotopias of intellectual space	McLuhan (1964); Deleuze & Guattari (1980); Paulston & Liebman (1994); Liebman (1996); Paulston (1996, 1999); Erkkilä (2000)
Pictorial imagination:	Visual displays and image-making: pictures	Comenius (1659); Blake (1794); Freire (1970); UNICEF (1994); Yoh & Yanasi (1996); Paulston (1997)

nation came to be seen as a powerful human attribute, as a lamp projecting light from a single source of creativity—the human soul (Bowra, 1961).

THE RENAISSANCE IMAGINARY

I have chosen two "exemplars" of the Renaissance imaginary, i.e. selected historical texts of Erasmus Reterodamus (1467–1536) and of Jan Amos Comenius (1592–1670). Both men can be seen as early practitioners of international education in a European context. The Dutch humanist and peace advocate Erasmus imagined a liberal, classical education to replace the rote learning of medieval scholasticism. His new Latin school was "liberal" in that it was based on free will, which even children were seen to possess, and belief that the tutor had the wisdom and skill to use persuasion and gentleness, not the imposition of precepts and dogmas. His methods and pedagogical aims were shaped by the literary imagination, i.e. training in literary invention, the acquisition of a personal style by studying different classical writers (i.e. Plato or Cicero *et al.*), and the adoption of a critical approach to all literary texts. Erasmus achieved great success with his international project. His translations and pedagogical works spread throughout Latinate Europe via the trade fairs. He remained a Catholic priest and did much to humanize the Roman church. He eventually broke with his friend Martin Luther, who without humor called him an *errans mus,* or "roving rat" for spreading his powerful ideas that a liberal and humane education offered man's best hope for freedom, cooperation, and possible salvation. In contrast, Luther argued that humans are slaves of sin, and only God's grace—and not education—can deliver them from their fundamental misery (Margolin, 1993).

Comenius, a bishop of the Protestant Czech Moravian Brotherhood presents a second towering example of the Renaissance imaginary. Working "on the run" during the turmoil of the Thirty Years War, Comenius's metaphysics drew heavily on the medieval scholasticism inspired by Aristotle. Yet in espousing Francis Bacon's (1561–1626) inductive "science," he also looked ahead to the emerging rationalism of the seventeenth century. Comenius was the first to conceive of a full-scale science of education, which he saw as the means to achieve his even more ambitious philosophical project of a universal Pansophism. This highly original and imaginative philosophy sought "to teach all things to all men" and is detailed in his *The Great Didactic (Didactica Magna)* first published in 1628 in Leszo, Poland where Comenius taught as a refugee pedagogue. Something of the scope and daring of his imagination is indicated in the foreword to this astonishing work: "We venture to promise a *Great Didactic* . . . the whole art of teaching all things to all men, and indeed of teaching them with certainty, so that the result cannot fail to follow. Finally, we wish to prove all this a priori, that is to say, from the unalterable nature of the matter itself . . . that we may lay the foundations of the universal art of founding universal schools" (Comenius, 1896).

While his attempt to create a unique synthesis of nature and man through education had little if any institutional impact, Comenius's ideas promulgating international education, world peace, and the pedagogical utility of images (he produced the first educational textbook completely composed of pictures in his *Orbis Pictus,* 1658) have made a powerful and lasting impression. The European Union along with the World Court, UNESCO, IIEP, the IBE *et al.* have all embraced, at one time or another, his humanistic and scientific imaginary as their true forerunner (Rosselló, 1943; Piaget, 1993). Today even the postmodernists would, perhaps, look kindly on (and then deconstruct) his pansophic principle that "everything . . . from all points of view, must be put in, and that nothing is to be left out."

This he argued would mean that:

> . . . the slower and the weaker the disposition of any man, the more he needs assistance. Nor can any man be found whose intellect is so weak that it cannot be improved by culture. (Comenius, 1896)

Or, with regard to his fair and farseeing view on the education of girls:

> Nor can any good reason be given why the weaker sex should be excluded altogether from the pursuit of knowledge . . . They are endowed with equal sharpness of mind and capacity for knowledge . . . Why therefore, should we admit them to the alphabet, and afterwards drive them away from books? (Ibid.)

THE CLASSICAL IMAGINARY

For exemplars of the Classical imaginary with its *idée fixe* of reducing moral, political and educational questions to problems in mathematics—or a *Mathesis Universalis*—we move from Holland and Moravia to France. Leading this highly imaginative project, the Marquis de Condorcet (1743–1794) attempted to promulgate one rational law to govern a republican France and another to create a secular national educational system. His scheme sought to abolish the traditional geographical divisions of France in favor of a geometrical grid. Today he would most likely be enchanted with GIS, or geographical information systems (Mendelsohn, 1996).[1] While Condorcet's classical imagination may have found form in foundational grids and tables, his concern to use reason and logic to design one educational system seemingly without dogma for children of different religious beliefs, cultures, and futures so as to produce at least the minimum of loyalty and knowledge needed to secure the unity of the state is no less alive and pressing today. In his *First Memoir on Public Instruction* (1970) Condorcet warned against what he saw as a new evangelistic trend where the cult of the Nation, Nature and the Liberty Tree had begun to replace citizenship, science and personal responsibility. He pointed out that schools, now secular, had new high priests in disguise, a scathing remark against the revolutionary political class. Robespierre, the principle target, never forgave him.

Where Condorcet's classical imagination brought rationalism and the grid to national educational planning, it was the comparative educators Count

Leopold Berchtold, César Basset and Marc-Antoine Jullien who first sought to apply statistical imagination in support of practical educational policy recommendations (Fraser, 1964). Jullien also looked to related fields advocating comparison as scientific method. In 1795, for example, Goethe published his *Introduction to Comparative Method;* Cuvier, a leading French scientist and educator, brought out his *Lessons of Comparative Anatomy* in 1799; Bopp published his *Comparative Linguistics* in Berlin in 1816; and Villemain, a Sorbonne professor, published a text on comparative literary studies in 1826. In this context, Jullien argued in his *Plan for Comparative Education* (1817) that "Researchers on comparative anatomy have advanced the *science of anatomy.* In the same way the researchers of *comparative education* must furnish new means of perfecting the science of education" (Fraser, 1964).

As an applied form of mathematics, statistics along with cartography skills and comparative method began to claim scientific objectivity in the early Classical era. Edward Tufte (1983) has linked statistics and graphics at this time in a most intriguing manner. Speaking of the invention of data maps, Tufte contends that:

> It was not until the late seventeenth century that the combination of cartographic and statistical skills required to construct the data map came together, fully five thousand years after the first geographic maps were drawn on clay tablets. (p. 20)

The English political economist William Playfair (1759–1823) dramatically exhibited the links between statistics (and their service to the state), mapping (and its discoveries), and economics (an emerging science). The economy as a new concept was now seen to act in the world; it caused events, and created effects. To "see" the economy—or society, *et al.*—statistical data and representational mapping were needed to shift the point of view so that modern theorists could see the whole as if from the outside, in a way that allowed them, from a specific position inside, to find their bearings and begin to imagine and theorize relations and causality. Navigational and data maps were proto-typical and led the way: positive theoretical mapping of education, society and the economy would soon follow the outgrowth of these classical representational techniques (Mazlish, 1998).

By the early mid-nineteenth century, modern scholars had the conceptual tools—and the arrogance[2]—to begin writing the grand theories, or metanarratives, of scientific reason (Comte), social progress (Durkheim and Dewey), and economic and human Emancipation (Marx and Freire). This imaginary also saw the emergence of comparative education as an academic field, as may be seen in Table II above.

THE MODERN IMAGINARY

Although the episode of modernity saw a profusion of creative imagination across the types presented in Table II—with the possible exceptions of the rhetorical, spatial and the pictorial, the creative imagination of modernity *par excellence* has been the scientific and analytical (Jay, 1993). Where Jullien earlier proposed a static and descriptive comparative education modelled on comparative anatomy, modern imagination as in Auguste Comte's proposal for a "science of society" had nomothetic ambition for lawmaking. A science capable of explaining social processes and structures in a way that would help to nip any future French revolutions in the bud could provide no less. Emile Durkheim (1859–1917) also had a vision of a positive sociology of society and education grounded in "social facts." His vision also followed from experience with the trauma of social revolution. In Durkheim's case it was the failed Paris Commune (March–May 1871), the first but not the last civil war following the rise of a brutal industrial capitalism and the worker's movement. The modern imaginary might most accurately be characterised as obsessed with Similitude, i.e. the belief that the essence of a thing could be revealed by the discovery of the word which truly signified it (White, 1987). With such true words, or signs, Durkheim would gain access to the underlying phenomena to be investigated. This happy combination of realism and empiricism would be the key to a modern social science thought able to realize progress in human understanding and relations (Durkheim, 1895).

Viewing society as a living organism made up of organs (structures) fulfilling functions, Durkheim's conservative theoretical imagination saw the educational system as critical for the peaceful evolution of this modern, efficient social body (Durkheim, 1956). His "scientific" approach and structural-functionalist framing continues to be influential in modernization theory and in its numerous variants, i.e. in the statistical imagination (i.e., Husén, 1967), in the scientific imagination, (i.e. Correa, 1963; Bowman, 1984) and in the analytical imagination (i.e., Schultz, 1963; Archer, 1995), among others, in our field and in the social sciences in general.

In creating his grand theory in *Capital*, Karl Marx (1818–1883) also imagined a pure science of modernity. But for Marx, "science" would explain how the capitalist mode of production worked through invisible structures susceptible only to ideological critique. For Marx the relation between the visible and the invisible could be imagined as inverted, as in the *camera obscura,* i.e. the hidden truths of production were simply an inversion of the visual truths of social life. Marx's science accordingly would be ideological and dialectical, not positivistic and empirical—even if it shared the Enlightenment belief in the accessible truth of a real world (Zizek, 1994).

The Marxist imaginary in practice saw class struggle as the means to overthrow bourgeois democracy and replace it with socialist society. Accordingly, as a critique of the status quo it largely remained, and remains, outside of institutions controlled by the bourgeois class. Today, the Marxist imaginary "with no concrete final ends . . . is operationally empty" (Offe, 1996), yet it continues bowed if not broken in earlier forms of dialectical materialism, and more widely in analytical, critical, and even rational choice variations.

A serious problem with these "schools" is seen by Terrel Carver to be their claim to reflect the truth of the real Marx. Trapped in assumptions of normative universalism, they largely fail to see themselves as narrators-in-a-context. In denying their own plurality, they deny the possibility of a pluralist Marxist story needed because the problems of injustice are plural (Carver, 1998). In seeking to make Marxist critique more reflexive, or self-knowledgeable, Carver's imaginative reading of Marx's thesis *Capital* reformulates ideology as a protocol of interpretation. He claims that the hermeneutics of Gadamer and Ricoeur, Derridean deconstruction, and the Cambridge "contextualists" have all profoundly altered the way that reading a text is conceived, and that interpretive work on Marx today needs to catch up with and not simply reject the postmodern intellectual age. Using techniques of textual and narrative analysis on Marx's writings, he even finds a mild form of postmodernism in Marx's extensive use of metaphor, in his imagery, concepts, and stories. In sum, he finds multiple Marx with continuing utility to question problems of possessive individualism (Torres, 1998), Disneyism and global capitalism (Castoriadis, 1997), and how we might confront and critique all manner of exploitation, including socialist exploitation (Outhwaite, 1983).

The long sequence of social and educational texts over the Classical and Modern eras exhorting the creation of a "science of education" and "a scientific comparative education" would seem to have culminated in 1969. In that year Noah and Eckstein published their argument that: ". . . systematic, empirical testing appears to offer the best hope for the progress of comparative education . . . [that] the hypothetico inductive approach . . . offers the researchers of one generation the hope of building securely on the work of their predecessors [and] . . . point[s] the way to an influential, intellectually cogent and elegant science of comparative education" (Ibid.). Yet, curiously, their text offers little if any serious scientific proof to support their plea for a scientific choice. They fail to test their own hypothesis. Instead, the reader finds a profusion of whimsical quotes from *Alice In Wonderland,* and a somewhat puzzling conclusion that "hidden factors" will always threaten to make their hypothesis testing method problematic, and at best only a useful "heuristic" (Ibid.). Today, aside from occasional exhortations for more "hard data" or a "correct critical analysis," scientific calls for a positive or dialectical social science of education and society seem to have run their course.

IMAGINING COMPARATIVE EDUCATION TODAY

Today the tropes of difference, multiplicity, space, community, and risk, are ever more evident and influential in comparative education discourse. These figures of speech are most often present in the postmodern imaginary (Paulston, 1993, 1999). While I may see them as shaping a new cultural code, or "episteme" in Foucault's terms, others may find refuge in the continuation of many, if not all, earlier knowledge communities with their codes of shared meaning. Here, clearly, where you choose to stand will play a large part in what you see to be the past, present, and future of our field (White,

1987). But today, the choice is ours to consider, to situate, and compare (Stafford, 1996).

In Figure 1 below, I present a synchronic view of how perspectives or interpretations may be patterned to figure or reconfigure our field today. Figure 1 maps my reading of the positions of major knowledge communities, or standpoints, in the current "debate" on postmodernism. All points of view in this debate, including the mapper's, are identified in the discourse and located in the intertextual field. In this way, it is possible to construct a new more open and heterotopic representation of ongoing knowledge work in our field capable of offering equal space to all verbal and visual texts constructing a debate (Erkkilä, 2000). Utopian representations of modernity, in contrast, seek an orthodoxy of vision where difference is made into the

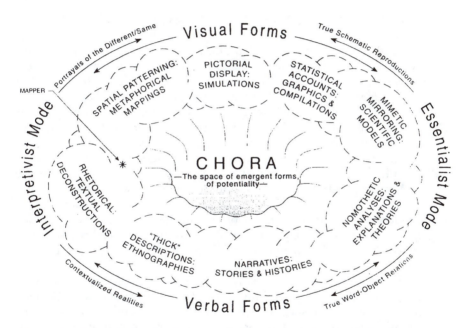

Figure 1: A web-like metaphorical mapping of knowledge positions and communities constructing the postmodernity debate in comparative education (and related) discourse. In this visualization of an open intertextual field, arrows suggest intellectual flows, and proper names refer not to authors, but to illustrative texts cited in the paper and juxtaposed above. In contrast to utopias (i.e. sites with no real place) much favored in modernist texts, this figure draws inspiration from Michel Foucault's notion of "heterotopias" (Foucault, 1986, p. 25). These are portrayed as the simultaneously mythic and real spaces of contested everyday life. Postmodernist texts favor heterotopias, as above, because they are "capable of juxtaposing in a single real place several spaces, several sites that are in themselves incompatible." Is the future of comparative education to be seen in the notion of heterotopia, or utopia, or perhaps in both, or neither? (Paulston, 1999, p. 445)

Same, or when this is not possible, the Other is made invisible (Correa, 1963; Davis, 1966; Bowman, 1984). Simply put, the postmodern imaginary is now working at full tilt to make visible that which modernity made invisible, i.e. differences of race, class, gender, ideas, dreams. In this work, the postmodern imaginary seeks to encompass an agonistic panorama of the whole, and to zoom back in order to take up any viewpoint within it. This holistic imagination, as seen in Figures 1 and 2, spatializes its patterns and visualises its concepts, so it can guide and inform thought in the imaginative modes of free spontaneity, material possibility, panoramic perspective and figurative visibility. Here the power of imagination is linked with the power of images to provide an immediate and unresolvably ambiguous intuition of simultaneous significance that is anathema to modernity's insistence on linear certainty and univocality (Jay, 1993; Stafford, 1996).

IMAGINING A FUTURE COMPARATIVE EDUCATION

How then, looking both back and ahead, might we imagine a future comparative education? True Believers, be they realists or relativists, will project an orthodoxy, rather a perceived orthodoxy or metanarrative, to the end of time. As a pluralist, my view ahead sees the possibility of heteroglosia and multiple futures limited only by our ability to imagine and craft new worlds (Dorling & Fairbairn, 1997). Certainly, the rules for world-making have never been more open—or dangerous (Lernert, 1995). Where modern thought has been largely shaped by notions of progress and scientific rationality, Anderson (1990) argues that powerful new and unsettling ideas are at this moment permeating our consciousness, and our work.

Changes in thinking about thinking: explanations of reality are increasingly understood as human constructions. The ability to become social cartographers, i.e. to reflexively step out of or into different reality constructs or ways of seeing while remaining a whole person will, as in Figure 1, facilitate future comparison.

Changes in identity and boundaries have been quickened by technological change, i.e. the emergence of notions of cyberspace and virtual reality, and by emergent global society with its pressing problems of human rights and global environmental deterioration. Comparative educators will also need to situate their knowledge work in heterotopias of difference (i.e. as "translators" and "facilitators"), as well as in their favored intellectual communities of shared culture and dreams, as both colleagues and advocates (Paulston, 2000b).

Changes in how we choose to represent our separate "truths" will require us to be less parochial and more self-knowledgeable in comparing contested realities. As information becomes ubiquitous and, perhaps, degraded, craft skills in visualizing and mapping oceans of conflicting data (as in Figures 1 and 2) will become more demanding and rewarding (Böhme, 1997). Problems of how to compare and pattern difference and spatial relations will, over time, override more traditional efforts in knowledge work to discover truth through testing "hard data" (Kaplan, 1992). Those comparative educators who learn to negotiate (navigate?) the new spaces of knowledge, i.e. the multiple "scapes" of reality construction work mapped in Figure 2 below will have unprecedented opportunities to imagine and help to shape an interactive postmodern comparative and international education beyond our understanding today.

Clearly, new opportunities and dangers for representing conflicting views of reality have emerged with the recent withering away of the modern imaginary and its grand stories of Progress and Utopia (Antonio, 1998). Today, heterogeneity and a spatialized ontology in all spheres of human activity open new opportunities for border crossing and comparison that, as in Figure 1, accept and attempt to pattern the space of difference in its own terms, i.e. as an open exchange or debate of conflicting interpretations or perspectives (Nietzsche, 1966; Paulston, 1996). This challenge will require that comparative educators go to work and master the ideas and craft required by both the linguistic, the spatial, and the pictorial turns, the three emerging cultural forms of our postmodern time, forms that enable and shape Figures 1 and 2. These representations of the rhetorical, spatial and pictorial imaginations have too long been neglected in our discourse. They will serve well as additional guides to knowledge work and representation in the next century as cultural forms part company with ascriptive positions to make possible greater cultural options for comparative educators, more possibilities for nonlinear meaning-creation and anti-hegemonic critique (Delanty, 1999).[3]

In sum, future efforts to represent and compare the growing complexity of socio-educational phenomena will require a generosity of spirit and a deepening of self-understanding that may leave many behind. The belief that epistemological research genres, such as the scientific text, have "real" objects and events, which provide a warrant for the knowledge-value of such "scientific" texts, is today highly problematic. What is increasingly recognized is that claims to absolute knowledge cannot be proven and that attempts to achieve hard data and objectivity all too often result in dilemmas of exclusion, circularity and infinite regress. A hermeneutical approach helps us realize that objects and events are inseparable from the process of apprehension (i.e. the imaginative process) within which they are formed. So if we are to fruitfully analyze and compare how things in the world take on meanings, it will be necessary to understand better the diverse imaginative enactments that produce meanings. As I have attempted to illustrate here using a critical pluralist perspective, imaginative work is not simply an act of disembodied consciousness, but also consists of historically developed practices that reside in the conflicting styles and forms in which statements are made (Shapiro, 1988). It is now time for comparative educators (perhaps using Figures 1 and 2?) to question how our choice of ideas and forms of representation influence our views of how reality is constituted and construed, how meaning and value are created and imposed on an otherwise unruly world.

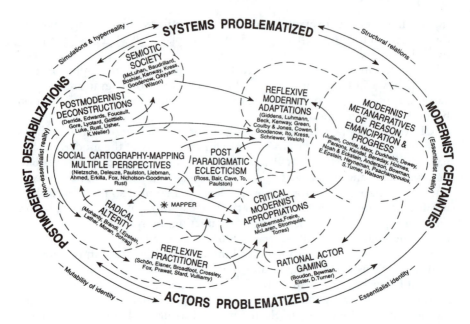

Figure 2: An intertextual mapping of the eight representational genres/forms presented in Table II. On the far right side of this non-linear tool I pattern the Apollonian forms of modernist rationality (as Nietzsche said, ". . . hardened into Egyptian rigidity"). On the far left side, we find what Foucault and I favor, i.e. a Dionysiac "revel of forms." Using the two axes of comparison, the eight genres may be seen to constitute a spatial patterning of the different forms of textual representation constructing our field, or space of imagination, over time. Plato (1977) used the idea of "chora" as the fertile space of emergent forms in his *Timaeus*. Anti-essentialist feminists (Gibson-Graham, 1996) have appropriated the notion of "chora" to explain how knowledge work has until recently been dominated by "male forms" (i.e. the right sides of Figures 1 and 2). They seek to reclaim all "fertile space" as feminine (Walkerdine, 1989; Grosz, 1995). My visualization or mapping in Figure 2 of chora avoids such either-or gender binaries and sees all representational forms available as practical choices. This spatialized ontology re-invisions comparative work as an effort to verbalize and visualize a plurality of forms and perspectives, an effort able to disengage itself from and to question its own imaginative creations. (Robinson & Rundell, 1994)

NOTES

1. In this line, Condorect's most famous publications are his *Essay on the Application of Mathematics to the Theory of Decision-Making* (1785) and *A General View of Social Mathematics* (1793). Condorcet's plan of 1792 for a universal comprehensive and secular educational system composed of five instructional levels (i.e. "elementary," "secondary," "the institute," "the *Lycée*," and the "National Society of Science and the Arts") was rejected by the National Assembly as unadventurous and overly liberal. He died in prison under mysterious circumstances on March 28, 1794.

2.   The privileging of counting nouns as *the* way to truth by William Thompson, Lord Kelvin (1824–1907) is a case in point: "When you cannot measure it, when you cannot express it in numbers, your knowledge is of a meager and unsatisfactory kind" (Mazlish, 1998).
3.   Both Figures may also serve to illustrate the postmodern notion of performativity, where verbal or visual discourse is called to enact what it describes, i.e. a subtle and complex refining of positions. Figures 1 and 2, for example, are not merely constitutive or argumentative, but also seek to exemplify the textual forms and features they are discussing. (Howells, 1999).

REFERENCES

Ahmed, Z. (1997). Mapping Rural Women's Perspectives on Nonformal Education Experiences: A Case Study in a Bangladeshi Village. Doctoral dissertation. University of Pittsburgh.

Anderson, W. T. (1990). *Reality Isn't What It Used To Be*. New York: HarperCollins.

Antonio, R. J. (1998). Mapping the Postmodern Social Theory, in: A. Sica (ed.) *What is Social Theory? The Philosophical Debates*. Boston: Blackwell.

Archer, M. (1995). *Realist Social Theory: The Morphogenetic Approach*. Cambridge: Cambridge University Press.

Beck U., Giddens, A. and Lash, S. (1994). *Reflexive Modernization*. Cambridge: Polity Press.

Bernstein, B. (1975). *Class, Codes and Control: Theoretical Studies Towards a Sociology of Language*. New York: Schocken Books.

Blake, W. (1794). *The First Book of Urizen*. Lambeth, London: Privately printed.

Böhme, G. (1997). The Structures and Prospects of Knowledge Society. *Social Science Information*, 36(3), pp. 447–468.

Bowles, S. and Gintis, H. (1976). *Schooling in Capitalist America*. New York: Basic Books.

Bowman, M. J. (1984). An Integrated Framework for the Analysis of the Spread of Schooling in Less Developed Countries. *Comparative Education Review*, 28(3), pp. 563–583.

Bowra, C. M. (1961). *The Romantic Imagination*. Oxford: Galaxy.

Brickman, W. W. (1960). A Historical Introduction to Comparative Education, *Comparative Education Review*, 3(1), pp. 6–13.

Brickman, W. W. (1966). Prehistory of Comparative Education to the End of the Eighteenth Century, *Comparative Education Review*, 10(1), pp. 30–47.

Buber, M. (1952). The Good and Evil Imagination, in: M. Buber (ed.) *Good and Evil*. New York: Scribner.

Carnoy, M. (1974). *Education as Cultural Imperialism*. New York: David McKay.

Carver, T. (1998). *The Postmodern Marx*. University Park: The Pennsylvania State University Press.

Castoriadis, C. (1997). *World in Fragments: Writings on Politics, Society, Psychoanalysis, and the Imagination*. Stanford: Stanford University Press.

Comenius, J. A. (1896). *The Great Didactic*. London: Adam and Charles Black.

Comenius, J. A. (1658). *Orbis Pictus*. Nuremberg. Reprinted by Oxford University Press, London, 1968.

Correa, H. (1963). *The Economics of Human Resources*. Amsterdam: North Holland.

Coulby, D. and Jones, C. (1995). *Postmodernity and European Education Systems*. Stoke-on-Trent: Trentham.

Daston, L. (1998). Fear and Loathing of the Imagination in Science. *Daedalus* (Winter), pp. 73–95.

Davis, R. C. (1966). *Planning Human Resource Development: Educational Models and Schemata.* Chicago: Rand McNally.

Delanty, G. (1997). *Social Science: Beyond Construction and Realism.* Buckingham: Open University Press.

Delanty, G. (1999). *Social Theory in a Changing World: Conceptions of Modernity.* Cambridge: Polity Press.

Deleuze, G. and Guttari, F. (1980). *A Thousand Plateaus,* trans. B. Massumi. Minneapolis: University of Minnesota Press.

Dewey, J. (1929). *Impressions of Soviet Russia and the Revolutionary World: Mexico, China, Turkey.* New York: New Republic.

Dorling, D. and Fairbairn, D. (1997). Representing the Future and the Future of Representation, in: *Mapping: Ways of Representing the World.* Harlow: Longman.

Durkheim, E. (1895). *Les régles de la Méthode Sociologique.* Paris: Presse Universitaires de France.

Durkheim, E. (1956). *Education and Sociology.* Glencoe: Free Press.

Einstein, A. Quoted in G. Morgan (1993). *Imaginization: The Art of Creative Management.* London: Sage.

Erkkilä, K. (2000). *Mapping the Entrepreneurial Education Debates in the United States, the United Kingdom and Finland.* New York: Garland.

Foley, D.E. (1991). Rethinking School Ethnographies of Colonial Settings: A Performance Perspective of Reproduction and Resistance. *Comparative Education Review,* 35(2), pp. 532–551.

Foster, P. J. (1998). Forward, in: H. J. Noah, and M. A. Eckstein *Doing Comparative Education.* Hong Kong: Hong Kong Comparative Research Center, the University of Hong Kong.

Foucault, M. (1970). *The Order of Things: An Archeology of the Human Sciences.* New York: Pantheon.

Foucault, M. (1986). Of Other Spaces. *Diacritics,* 16(1), pp. 22–28.

Fraser, S. (1964). *Jullien's Plan for Comparative Education, 1816–1817.* New York: Teachers College, Columbia University.

Freire, P. (1970). *Pedagogy of the Oppressed.* New York: Herder and Herder.

Fuller, B., *et al.* (1999). How to Raise Children's Early Literacy? The Influence of Family, Teacher, Classroom in Northeast Brazil. *Comparative Education Review,* 43(1), pp. 1–35.

Geertz, C. (1973). Thick Description, in: *The Interpretation of Cultures.* New York: Basic Books.

Gerhart, L. (1979). Imagination and History in Ricoeur's Interpretation Theory. *Philosophy Today,* 23(1), pp. 51–68.

Gibson-Graham, J. K. (1996). *The End of Capitalism as We Knew it.* Cambridge: Blackwell.

Gottlieb, E. E. (1989). The Discursive Construction of Knowledge. *International Journal of Qualitative Studies in Education,* 2(2), pp. 131–144.

Gottlieb, E. E. (1996). Mapping the Utopia of Professionalism, in: R. G. Paulston (ed.) *Social Cartography: Mapping Ways of Seeing Social and Educational Change.* New York: Garland.

Gottlieb, E. E. and Labelle, T. J. (1988). Consciousness-raising Theory and Practice: How Discourse Constructs Knowledge. Paper presented at the AERA Annual Meeting, New Orleans, LA.

Grosz, E. (1995). Women, *Chora,* Dwelling, in: S. Watson and K. Gibson (eds) *Postmodern Cities and Spaces.* Oxford: Blackwell.

Hans, N. (1959). The Historical Approach to Comparative Education. *International Review Of Education,* 5(3), pp. 299–309.

Hoffman, D. M. (1999). Culture and Comparative Education: Decentering and Re-centering the Discourse. *Comparative Education Review,* 43, p. 488.

Holmes, B. (1958). The Problem Approach in Comparative Education: Some Methodological Considerations. *Comparative Education Review,* 2 (2), pp. 3–8.

Howells, C. (1999). *Derrida: Deconstruction from Phenomenology to Ethics.* Cambridge: Polity Press.

Husén, T. (ed.) (1967). *International Study of Achievement in Mathematics.* Stockholm: Almqvist and Wiksell/John Wiley.

Issawi, C. (1958). *An Arab Philosophy of History: Selections from the Prolegmena of Ibn Khaldun of Tunis (1332–1406).* London: John Murray.

Jay, L. (1993). *Downcast Eyes: The Denigration of Vision in Twentieth-Century Thought.* Berkeley: The University of California Press.

Kaplan, S. J. (1992). A conceptual analysis of forms and content in visual metaphors. *Communication,* 13(3), pp. 197–209.

Kearney, R. (1998). *Poetics of Imaging: Modern to Post-modern.* New York: Fordham University Press.

King, E. J. (1999). Education Revised for a World in Transformation. *Comparative Education,* 35(2), pp. 109–117.

Lemart, C. (1995). *Sociology after the Crisis.* Boulder: Westview.

Liebman, M. (1996). Envisioning Spatial Metaphors from Wherever We Stand, in: R. G. Paulston (ed.) *Social Cartography: Mapping Ways of Seeing Social and Educational Change.* New York: Garland.

Lyotard, J. F. (1992). *The Postmodern Explained to Children: Correspondence, 1982–1984.* London: Turnaround.

Margolin, J. C. (1993). Erasmus. *Prospects,* 23(1), pp. 333–352.

Mazlish, B. (1998). *The Uncertain Sciences.* New Haven: Yale University Press.

Mcluhan, M. (1964). *Understanding Media.* New York: McGraw-Hill.

Mendelsohn, J. (1996). *Educational Planning and Management and the Use of Geographical Information Systems.* Paris: UNESCO/IIEP.

Mills, C. W. (1959). *The Sociological Imagination.* Oxford: Oxford University Press.

Modiano, N. (1973). *Indian Education in the Chiapas Highlands.* New York: Holt, Rinehart and Winston.

Nicolson-Goodman, J. V. (1996). Mapping and Remapping Discourse in Educational Policy Studies. In: R. Paulston *et al. Mapping Multiple Perspectives: Research Reports of the University of Pittsburgh Social Cartography Project, 1993–1996.* Pittsburgh, PA: Department of Administrative and Policy Studies.

Nietzsche, F. (1996). *On the Geneology of Morals,* Essay 3, trans. W. Kaufmann. New York: Modern Library.

Noah, H. J. and Eckstein, M. A. (1969). *Toward A Science of Comparative Education.* New York: Macmillan.

Offe, C. (1996). *Modernity and the State.* Cambridge, MA: MIT Press.

Outhwaite, W. (1983). *Concept Formation in Social Science.* London: Routledge and Kegan Paul.

Paulston, R. G. (1968). French Influence in American Institutions of High Learning. *History of Education Quarterly,* 8(2), pp. 229–245.

Paulston, R. G. (1980). Education as Anti-Structure: Non-Formal Education in Social and Ethnic Movements. *Comparative Education,* 16(1), pp. 55–66.

Paulston, R. G. (1993). Mapping Discourse in Comparative Education Texts. *Compare,* 23(2), pp. 101–114.

Paulston, R. G. (ed.) (1996). *Social Cartography Mapping Ways of Seeing Social and Educational Change.* New York: Garland.

Paulston, R. G. (1997). Mapping Visual Culture in Comparative Education Discourse. *Compare,* 27(2), pp. 117–152.

Paulston, R. G. (1999). Mapping Comparative Education after Postmodernity. *Comparative Education Review,* 43(4), pp. 438–463.

Paulston, R. G. (2000a). A Spatial Turn in Comparative Education? Constructing a Social Cartography of Difference, in: J. Schriewer (ed.) *Discourse Formation in Comparative Education.* Frankfurt am Main: Peter Lang.

Paulston, R. G. (2000b). Comparative Education as Heterotopia? in: J. Bouzakis (ed.) *Historical-Comparative Perspectives: Fetschrift for Andreas M. Kazamias.* Athens: Gutenberg.

Paulston, R. G. and Liebman, M. (1994). An Invitation to Post Modern Social Cartography. *Comparative Education Review,* (38)(2), pp. 215–232.

Piaget, J. (1993). Jan Amos Comenius. *Prospects,* 23(1), p. 2.

Plato (1977). *Timaeus and Critias,* trans. D. Lee. Harmondsworth: Penguin.

Robinson, G. and Rundell, J. (eds) (1994). *Rethinking Imagination: Culture and Creativity.* London: Routledge.

Rockwell, E. (1996). Keys to Appropriation: Rural Schooling in Mexico, in: B. A. Levenson, *et al.* (eds) *The Cultural Production of the Educated Person: Ethnographies of Schooling and Local Practice.* Albany: Suny Press.

Rosselló, P. (1943). *Marc-Antoine Jullien De Paris, Père de l'éducation comparée et Précurseur du Bureau International D' Éducation.* Genève; Portnoir.

Rosselló, P. (1960). Comparative Education as an Instrument of Planning. *Comparative Education Review,* 4(2), pp. 3–12.

Schultz, T. W. (1963). *The Economic Value of Education.* New York: NY: Columbia University Press.

Seppi, J. (1996). Spatial Analysis in Social Cartography: Metaphors for Process and Form in Comparative Education Studies, in: R. Paulston (ed.) *Social Cartography: Mapping Ways and Seeing Social and Educational Change.* New York: Garland.

Shapiro, M. J. (1988). *The Politics of Representation: Writing Practices in Biography, Photography, and Policy Analysis.* Madison: The University of Wisconsin Press.

Stafford, M. (1996). The Visualization of Knowledge from the Enlightenment to Postmodernism, in: *Looking Good: Essays on the Virtues of Images.* Cambridge, MA: Massachusetts Institute of Technology.

Tinbergen, J. and Bos, H. C. (1965). *Econometric Models in Education: Some Applications.* Paris: OECD.

Torres, C. A. (1998). *Education, Power and Personal Biography: Dialogues with Critical Educators.* New York: Routledge.

Tufte, E. (1983). *The Visual Display of Quantitative Information.* Cheshire: Graphics Press.

Turner, V. (1974). *Dramas, Fields and Metaphors: Symbolic Action in Human Society.* Ithaca: Cornell University Press.

UNICEF (1994). *I Dream of Peace: Images of War by Children of Former Yugoslavia.* New York: HarperCollins.

Usher, R. and Edwards, R. (1994). *Postmodernism and Education.* London: Routledge.

Walkerdine, V. (1989). *Counting Girls Out.* London: Virago.

White, H. (1987). *The Content of the Form: Narrative, Discourse and Historical Representation.* Baltimore: The Johns Hopkins University Press.

Zizek, S. (1994). *Mapping Ideology.* London: Verso.

CHAPTER 5

Comparative Education Redefined?

Ronald F. Price

The outsider, looking at comparative education, is perhaps surprised at the extent to which the insiders have been worried and have indulged in self-criticism and soul-searching during the past decades. The anxiety to be recognized by the rest of the academic community[1] as a real social science with a recognized methodology has resulted in a considerable literature. One example was the volume of *Comparative Education Review* devoted to "The State of the Art: Twenty Years of Comparative Education" (1977). More recently we have had Erwin Epstein's plea for the recognition of "ideology" by practitioners, first as the Presidential Address to the US Comparative and International Education Society's annual meeting of 1982 and then again in *Compare* of 1987 on the occasion of honoring Brian Holmes. This is to cite a only a handful of the large literature devoted to the genre. While adding to this literature is not to my taste I am compelled to do so by the concern I feel, not so much with comparative education but with the state of the world in general and education in particular, and by the desire I feel that the work to which I have devoted a considerable slice of my life should be of more than personal satisfaction. This would certainly classify me among those whose aim Epstein regarded as "practical" (he comments that "we display almost an obsession over the need to achieve some practical benefit from comparative study" [1983]) and I freely confess to being "ideological" in some of the rather many meanings he gave that term (cf. Holmes, 1983).

I am encouraged to write in this vein by two things. Firstly, during the last seventeen years I have found a majority of students taking comparative education courses have done so in the hope that they will learn about a better way of living and learning. Many have chosen to study China, Sweden or the USSR with that hope in mind. Of course they have been naive and their ideas have been ill-defined and diffuse. But they have been sincere and anxious, as young teachers-to-be, to do a better job than was done to them. They have been altruistic! That their study of comparative education has only served to disillusion them is a sad comment on our predicament, but it is also a challenge I have sought to take up.

Secondly, I am encouraged by a long tradition of writers in comparative education who have put before us the need to contribute to solving, in the words of a recent writer, "the great problems of our epoch" (M. Pecherski in Dilger *et al.*, 1986). Of course, all too many writers in the field have followed too narrowly the precept put forward by Jullien in 1817, that "education should become a positive science" and that "facts and observations . . . should be ranged in analytical tables, easily compared, in order to deduce principles and definite rules" (cit. in Hans, 1958). Nicholas Hans himself, writing in London in 1947, saw his book as being of interest not only to teachers, but also to "the general reading public" because he considered "educational reforms" (i.e. reform of schooling) to be "intimately connected with politics, with problems of race, nationality, language and religious and social ideals" (Hans, 1947), i.e. "the great problems." He chose as case studies England, the US, France and the USSR because "both in the past and in the present" he considered they had been "leaders of humanity in building up a new democratic society and supplied the ideas which later became the property of all nations and all races" (324). His book looks to the past as a means of understanding his present and and as a guide to the future. That his ideal was, as he put it, "that grand ideal of culture générale" (325) rather than a recognition of the real problems of the liberal democracies he admired, does not detract from the value of his general approach. He was concerned with values and the possibilities of human life and accepted it as a function of the educated to see life whole and to make judgements rather than to adjust to narrow interest and temporary political or economic order. A recent writer from the same European Enlightenment tradition is Bogdan Suchodolski of the University of Warsaw. Writing in a Festschrift for the German Comparativist, Oskar Anweiler, he calls for "a vision of a new, a different future." Recognizing that schooling is largely a conservative and adaptive force he invokes organizations like UNESCO and the Club of Rome as providers of an alternative vision (Dilger *et al.*, 1986). He refers to the "growing threat of total catastrophe," both through irreversible pollution of the environment and through the consequences of the unprecedented level of arms production (Dilger *et al.*, 1986). Other writers in this Festschrift look in a similar direction. I have already referred to Mieczyslaw Pecherski who, like Suchodolski, refers to the Club of Rome's "no limits to learning" and to the "creation of a new and rational society" (Dilger *et al.*, 1986). He counterposes "the destruction of the world" and "the improvement of life on earth" (Ibid) but does not offer us any real guidance in how comparative education might help. A number of contributors to the Festschrift, however, do offer, either explicitly or implicitly, a focus for comparative education studies which I believe could help, and there are other similarly directed writings to which I shall refer. But first let me define what I see as the "threat" and the alternative.

Like many others I am, as Epstein might say, "obsessed" with the contrast between the wealth devoted to war and the profit of big corporations and the poverty and unemployment which afflicts so many human beings. I am "obsessed" by the threat to human and other life posed by polluting industries which put short-term profit before the social good. Put differently, how can we establish a genuinely democratic, cooperative society which would finally eliminate the absurdity of poverty in the midst of plenty (which has been the general lot of humankind) and solve the ecological crisis: the threats of soil depletion, water poisoning, destruction of the ozone layer, loss of genetic variety and the like. In my "ideology" there is a direct connection between a political economy which puts commodity exchange and the accumulation of monetary capital first and the widely recognized threats to human, and an ecologically sustaining, life. The educational problem is not so much that the problems are not recognized, nor even that the connection I have just stated is not widely made. It is that problems are perceived in isolation and the means for their solution are not clear. It is, perhaps, here that comparative education could make a small contribution.

There is a previous question to any consideration of comparative education, which is the way in which academia fosters the exploration of what is and the extrapolation of future trends rather than the consideration of questions of what might or what ought to be. The various disciplines, therefore, too often become a rationalization, a justification of the status quo, rather than a critical exploration of the problems which face humankind. This is particularly so where the institution and/or the discipline is closely linked with particular interests. The links may be administrative, where the research school is government-funded and controlled, with, perhaps, the research topics determined in more or less detail by the government. Governments may say, as does the Australian government in its 1988 White Paper on Education, that it wants a higher education system which will not fail to "criticize the society in which it operates" (Dawkins, 1988). But when it comes to it few will pay for radical criticism, and it would be naive to expect otherwise. Comparative education, in seeking to become a tool of government advising is forced into a conceptual framework where criticism is unlikely to be radical and, I would add, where the focus is likely to be on the wrong problems. However, it is more a question of internal definition of disciplines and the methodologies they employ than of external influence. The "great problems" find themselves divided, and lost, between the disciplines of Philosophy, Psychology, Economics, Physics, to mention but a few. It is here that comparative education, drawing on all of these disciplines but bound by none of them, offers the opportunity to discuss the real world as the whole that it is. To those who have argued the difficulty of being familiar with more than one or a few disciplines I would counter with the difficulty of breaking out of conceptual frameworks once learned and the identification and avoidance of the game-playing nature of so much of academic disciplinary activity.

The search by Comparative Educators for an ideal methodology faces another problem which the destructive nature of much of modern technology is bringing increasingly to the fore. A broad range of people are expressing doubts about the attempt to apply universally the methodology developed by Newtonian Physics. This narrow mechanism, or reductionism as it is referred to by such writers as Steven Rose, is seen as unsuitable for the natural sciences today, as well as for the so-called social sciences and humanities.[2] Therefore I consider much of the discussion which has diverted comparative educators over the years, in part an attempt to fit our discipline into that mechanistic frame, to be doubly unhelpful. Not only has the object been too narrowly conceived, but the methodological debate has been one-dimensional.

There are other common features of academia which make the handling of the "great problems" difficult. Within the institutions the ladders to the clouds to a great extent predetermine what kind of research and teaching is done. The constraints of examinations is an old story, often retold. The concept of what a master's or a doctoral thesis is; the difficulties of accepting group research reports; the problems of finding examiners for genuinely new topics; all these factors make for a conservative pattern and encourage the careful treading of already marked-out paths. There is a rhetoric of new, creative and critical, but the reality is somewhat different. Promotion and tenure, increasingly a problem for younger staff, depend on acceptance of traditions rather than critical excursions into the unestablished. These last two are also often dependent on relations outside the institution. Then it is necessary to "publish or perish," and this again requires conformity to existing patterns. The established, and therefore acceptable, journals draw their referees from those established in the discipline and have an established editorial set. It may be difficult to find a publisher for an unusual topic or for an approach radically different to the norm. A socially significant example of this is the difficulty which those working on the danger of low radiation for human health have in getting their papers published in mainstream journals (Chowka, 1980). An example in comparative education is one from my own experience. With a colleague I am currently studying the teaching of science in Chinese schools. But comparative education journals and journals of Chinese Studies tend to publish broad, policy-type articles. Journals specializing in science education tend not to publish papers on foreign curricula problems. Papers which attempt to illuminate wider problems through detailed examination of curricula and school textbook materials are hard to place. This has, of course, been said many times. The knowledge is widespread, but the will to solve the problems is vitiated by particular interest.

TOWARD A NEW FOCUS

In 1981 Ludwig Liegle of the University of Tübingen made a number of suggestions for a change of perspective in comparative education which anticipated those I made in my *Marx and Education in Late Capitalism* in 1986. These were: (1) the shifting of central attention from the schools and pedagogic ideas to the subjects of education, children and youth; (2)

putting in the foreground out-of-school groups like the family, adults, neighbors, the local community, the work-world and the learnings of free-time and from the media; (3) thematizing this "environment-education": learning through participation and action, through interaction and communication, through observations, etc.; (4) studying the effects of the "hidden curriculum" of competition and striving for achievement, of feelings of anxiety and aggression and of the expression of youth cultures and generation-conflicts; and (5) the shifting of focus from only cognitive education to the development of values and political culture, and to those psychological structures on which the reproduction and change of society depend (Dilger *et al.,* 1986). Liegle's account of developments in the study of socialization in the USSR in his Festschrift contribution, where these suggestions were repeated, and where I first read them, fails to bring out the real value of his proposals (Dilger *et al.,* 1986). To me this lies especially in where he speaks of "the development of those psychological structures which serve the reproduction (or also the change and putting in question) of society" (Dilger *et al.,* 1986). I would only remove the brackets!

It is, of course, not new to recognize that learning, and important learning, takes place outside the school, and that this has important consequences for the learnings which occur within the school. What is new is the attention being given to these processes by educators who in the past have devoted their attention too one-sidedly to the schools and to teaching within them. A nice example of this is the Eighty-fourth Yearbook of the National Society for the Study of Education which was devoted to *Education in School and Nonschool Settings* and had chapters devoted to such "other educational settings" as families; workplace; museums; religious institutions; youth-serving agencies; media and technology (Fantini and Sinclair, 1985). However, we must distinguish here those who look at the whole range of teachings and learnings which occur in these different, but interacting agencies, and those who concentrate on their role as intentional teachers. An example of the latter is the book, *Maverick of the Education Family: Two Essays in Non-Formal Education,* a book which describes the diverse teaching provided by organizations of many kinds in Botswana (Townsend Coles 1982). So far as "the great problems" are concerned, the unintended learnings and teachings are at least as important as the intended, and, of course, much more difficult to theorize.

Let us try to put these aspirations and suggestions for a change of focus together and see what it might mean for comparative education. Taking first the suggestions of Liegle, I would not restrict the shift of focus to "children and youth," his first point, but include people of all ages. My focus change would be on the content of the learning-teaching processes in which they are involved, a content which includes knowledge, skills, beliefs, values, attitudes and feelings. I agree completely with his second point, that the focus needs to be shifted to the out-of-school situation, and with his third point, the need to thematize this. But I would like to do this through clarification of "the great problems" as identified by significant groups in different societies. In *Marx and Education in Late Capitalism* I particularly discussed the women's movement, the peace movement and the trade unions as significant educational groups. The ecology movement should certainly be added to that list. But my point is that comparative education studies could reveal which groups were significant, where, in what ways, to what numbers and kinds of people. Thematization through "great problems" would bring together learnings and teachings in and by different groups. For example, the important questions of the use of nuclear fission processes, whether "for war" or "for peace," are differently expressed in the peace movement and the ecology movement. A holistic understanding requires that the teachings of both these movements are considered, as well, of course, as the more obvious governmental, industrial and academic sources. Such examination requires careful analysis of the logical skills taught: of question formulation, the selection of evidence and its evaluation; the clarification of values involved; and the clarification of the interests of the parties concerned.[3]

What does this all mean for the aims of comparative education? It is not suggested that it should become a political movement! It will continue to be an academic discipline, a study of, among other things, political movements. The aim, as I believe it should be of all studies, will continue to be understanding. But that understanding will be more clearly focussed on those learning-teaching processes within which, as I put it elsewhere, "human beings learn the lessons which determine their being and their becoming" (Price, 1986). With that focus the school will find its rightful place, central for some people and peripheral or absent for others. Such a focus I would expect to assist us by clarifying the visions which different groups have of "a new and different future" (Suchodolski) and the means by which it might be achieved. More than that an academic discipline cannot hope for. More requires practice, but practice in part guided by the understanding which comparative education could help provide.

I would like to conclude this essay by examining some comparative education and other studies in the light of the focus I have been outlining. I shall suggest that there already exist many studies which can be built upon.

WORK WORLD AND WORLDVIEW

One way or another educators of all persuasions have seen work in some form as important for education. Writing in 1929, Pinkevitch, then president of the Second State University of Moscow, outlined the ideas of educators towards "labor in the school." He classified educators on a scale ranging from "reactionary bourgeoisie" (Neuendorf) to "Proletarian-communists" (Kalashnikov, Blonski) (Pinkevitch, 1929). Naturally he gave John Dewey careful attention. The interesting Soviet contemporary of Pinkevitch's, Shul'gin, is cited as saying: "To us labour . . . is the best method of teaching children how to live the contemporary life" (Pinkevitch, 1929; Fitzpatrick, 1979; Price, 1984). Today governments and employers are looking to the schools to solve problems of unemployment or to help with "modernizing" the economy, as in China. The difficulty of looking at the work world in a different way is shown very clearly in the contribution of Marvin Feldman, President of the Fashion Institute of Technology, NY, to the already cited book on *Education in School and Nonschool Settings* (Fantini and Sinclair, 1985). Writing about "The Workplace as Educator" Feldman begins: "The modern corporation does everything schools do, and more" (Fantini and Sinclair 1985: 102). He mentions instructing, motivating, athletics and other "interest groups," medical treatment and prevention, and (in Japan) company songs! When he writes "Clearly the experience of working is itself a learning experience" (Fantini and Sinclair, 1985) one's hopes are raised, only to be dashed when one quickly finds he is speaking of employers' requirements of work experience. Feldman is not talking about learning a world view. Again one's hopes are raised when he goes on to speak of "unresolved ethical, political, and pedagogical questions" and to ask "to what extent should schools shape students to the requirements of the workplace and "to what extent should educators ignore the requirements of the workplace (thus, perhaps, making their graduates less employable) and insist on a more balanced and broadly liberal learning experience?" (Fantini and Sinclair, 1985). But he does not spell out what he sees as value contradictions or just what these ethical, etc. problems are. As for the possibility of a different type of economic system, this appears to be unthinkable? We are only told: "The school, however, is the steward of a community's larger educational responsibility. The school must bring to contractual arrangements a sense of the noncommercial values that must nourish any true educational effort" (Fantini and Sinclair, 1985). Above all, like so many other writers today (Jones, 1982) he gives a very misleading impression of the general economic trend. He sees "our whole economy [as] converting to a new, dramatically different technological base" in which "everybody in the system" is going to be "pushed up a notch" in the social hierarchy (Fantini and Sinclair, 1985). Far from understanding the capitalist nature of current technological developments, i.e. their function in furthering the production of surplus value and capital accumulation rather than the social good, he sees it in abstract technological-social terms, in terms of a change of skills for which schools and industry alike must train people. For a more realistic view of modern capitalism, indeed the whole current world economy, one must turn to such writers as Joyce Kolko (1988). The volume edited by Rachel Sharp (1986) is also valuable for its attempt to answer the question: whether there are common elements in the structuring and restructuring of the forms of capitalist schooling which relate to the underlying logic and dynamic of the capitalist mode of production as analyzed by the framework of historical materialism. (Sharp, 1985)

The accounts of the various national economies and the changes in schooling provide a basis for the kind of examination I am suggesting, even though the version of Marxism Sharp et al. offer is inadequate for that task. For realism about the so-called "information society" Webster and Robins (1986) are also helpful.

For an understanding of the work world in terms of teachings and learnings there already exists a large database in sociology. Some of the seminal papers have recently been collected together by R. E. Pahl under the title *On Work: Historical, Comparative and Theoretical Approaches* (1988). Studying this topic with education in mind might help to more usefully relate questions about conceptualizing the economy,[4] conceptualizing work (Pahl, 1988), and the actual experience of work of different kinds. Studies of workshops from the inside like those of Burrawoy give some insight into learnings as well as teachings (Pahl, 1988; cf. Pfeffer, 1979). Others, particularly those which give an overview of the ongoing changes in the nature of the workforce, throw light on teachings. Important here are the division between the so-called "permanent" labor force and the "flexible" (Pahl, 1988) and the redivision of societies with the dirty, dangerous and usually lowest-paid jobs going to "women, the young, and migrants" (Murray in Pahl, 1986; cf. Davis, 1986). Accounts like that of Wallraff, who posed as a Turkish worker in Germany in order to expose conditions there, present a close-up of one of these migrant groups (1988). But what should one expect of an examination of the work world in terms of education? To many it may appear a lesson in disillusionment, in defeated aspirations and retreat into cynical individualism: "I'm all right Jack!" No doubt for many that is the lesson learnt. But examination of the needs and aspirations of people in the concrete conditions of their working lives (including the conditions of those denied work by the present system) and comparison of these with the possibilities offered by the present technical-scientific knowledge available, I believe, suggests disillusionment is a partial picture. A more thorough understanding of the present distribution of knowledge, beliefs and values, and of the barriers to its wider distribution could help change this, preparing the way for practical change.

Returning to a consideration of the school, the question of what is taught by and learnt within the real world of work is a very different one from that of the teachings/learnings that have occurred in the various experiments known variously as Radical Education or Open Schooling. Comparative education has not yet usefully evaluated these experiments, either by conceptualizing them or locating them in the social contexts in which they took place. One of the few recent Comparative writings on more general aspects of "radical education" is that by Knaup and Wompel on "Openness as an educational-political category in centralized systems: Poland and France" (Dilger *et al.*, 1986). While they testify to the persisting interest in the concept of "openness," to recognition and use of teachings and learnings in and through other institutions than the school in both Poland and France, they do not explore the nature of these in any depth. But they make the interesting point that in Poland, where the concept has been part of official educational policy for longer, out-of-school institutions are used to reinforce official "socialist" teaching, whereas in France, where the school has traditionally been cut off from society outside, openness takes more varied forms and pays more attention to changing relations on a personal-social level (Dilger *et al.*, 1986). The authors appear to recognize the need to relate their study to the wider out-of-school situation, but it is not clear in what sense they would do this.

At the beginning of this section I referred to Pinkevtich and Shul'gin and the latter's ideas on labor as teacher. The arguments of Soviet educators and

Communist Party officials over "polytechnical education" have been often told.[5] In the more recent past the term became simply a halo word (Price, 1977). My attempt to categorize the various uses of this term and the wider concept of "linking education with productive labor" as used in the USSR and China in a way which could be used to evaluate different experiences has not been followed up. Writers continue to accept current Soviet usage unanalyzed. Muckle's very useful recent study makes the mistake of regarding Khrushchev's reforms as "making (polytechnical education) compulsory again," when the essence of them was monotechnical; and then fails to distinguish between the Marx-Krupskaya tradition in which polytechnical education was to teach a critical understanding of society, and that of Stalin-Gorbachev which is that of adjusting the student to the current social norms and work world (Muckle, 1988). In any case, what is needed is studies which show the relation between what is taught and the lessons of the world of work outside the school.

The concepts polytechnical education and "combining education with productive labor" belong to the wider concept of moral-political education, and to this I will now turn.

MORAL-POLITICAL EDUCATION

One recent definition is that of Roberta Sigel: moral-political education is "the process by which people learn to adopt the norms, values, attitudes and behaviors accepted and practiced by the on-going system" (Price, 1986). But this is to neglect the problem posed by the gulf between what is accepted in words and in deeds, or by different groups within a society, and the equally important learning, the rejection or simple ignoring of those norms. In many cases one might wish to argue the need for the last! Have not our present set of values come about historically through people rejecting the teachings of their times? But the schools and those studies based on them do not often discuss this, confining themselves to conformity and adaptation. One clear example of this is the set of common themes prepared by the International Civic Education Committee for the IEA Civic Education study (Torney and Oppenheim in Price, 1986). Under "Behavioural Content" we find "willingness to obey the law, pay taxes" and the like, propositions which seem at variance with society's real problems.

In the school it is widely recognized that moral-political education takes place in all subjects, being especially explicit in literature, history and the social sciences. Muckle notes that for Soviet educators "[p]olytechnism is a spirit which is meant to permeate the whole of education" (36). At the same time there is a long tradition of special subjects in schools. If one goes back to beginnings, whether in China or Christian Europe, one must recognize that the early curriculum was almost entirely moral-political in subject matter. But in modern times, while occupying a less overt position and putting aside religious teaching, there have been many varieties of moral-political courses (Price, 1986). Most recently a number of new courses have appeared with names like Peace Studies, Women's Studies, Global Education, the Humanities Curriculum Project (Schools Council/Nuffield), or World Studies. These have led to a new controversy about Controversial Issues in the Curriculum, to use the title of a recent book (Wellington, 1986). But the discussion appears to revolve around problems of "indoctrination" and the best methods of teaching such subjects, if they are to be taught, rather than around the substantive nature of the issues and the skills required for judgements. Two expressions of this kind are:

> Pike and Selby: "There remains, for instance, something essentially 'unpeaceful' about the teacher who lectures on peace issues from the front of the class." (Wellington, 1986)
>
> Aspin: "The teaching methods adopted will be, one imagines, much less likely to succeed if they are predicated upon the confrontational or the heavily authoritarian model still favored by some teachers in this area." (Wellington, 1986)

One of the promising lines of study for our purposes is that of content analysis. Because of the overt nature of moral-political teaching in the USSR, and more recently China, there have been a number of studies of the content of teaching in the schools of these countries. Some of these, like *The Making of a Model Citizen in Communist China* (Ridley, Godwin and Dooley, 1971) and the more recent *Was Maos Erben in der Schule lernen* (Bos and Straka, 1987) attempt to be "scientific" by the use of elaborate attempts at "objectivity," counting and statistical juggling. In the process the content of the teaching is reduced to banalities like the number of times something is referred to, or complex passages are reduced to vague terms like "order," "patriotism" or "friendship." Better are such "subjective" accounts as *What Ivan Knows that Johnny Doesn't* (Trace, 1961), or T. Scrase in this volume, where the approach is clear but the detail provided allows readers to make their own judgement.[6] More studies along these lines, combined with the approach of Bronfenbrenner's (1974) *Two Worlds of Childhood (US and USSR)* might bring us nearer the goal I am suggesting. But one further step is required. Bronfenbrenner's world is that of childhood. Much more attention needs to be given to the adult world, the world of work and unemployment, and the ongoing and inter-acting teaching-learning processes of adults, youth and children.

CONCLUSION

I have tried to argue two things in this essay: that the focus of research and teaching in comparative education should be shifted more towards the learning and teaching about the "great problems" which humankind faces today; and that comparative education, because of its embracing the various disciplines is in a unique position to do this. I have shown that I am not alone in making this call for a shift of focus, and that there is already a precedent for it. I have also drawn attention to the existing demand for such a focus from many who choose to study comparative education at the post-graduate teacher training level. Such a reorientation could pave the way for a similar and much-needed reorientation in schooling at other levels.

So far as teaching is concerned, it is not difficult to show what is taught, where, how and to whom (by class and number). What is difficult is to say anything worthwhile about learning. Here we are faced with definitional and psychological problems: the nature and interrelations of knowing, understanding, believing, and, a jump, behaving. The last is what is visible but is it congruent with intentions, feelings, beliefs? What about the possibilities, perceived and real? It is doubtful to what extent comparative education can help us in these difficult areas. But it may at least be able to clarify some of the questions.

NOTES

1. Community is a much misused word. In reality, the academic world is more often mean and competitive than it is cooperative and supportive.
2. Needham's position has been often repeated. Best seen in his *Science & Civilization in China,* it is also shortly expressed in his contribution to Hilary and Steven Rose, *The Radicalization of Science.* See also Rose, Lewontin and Kamin, *Not in Our Genes,* and Levins and Lewontin, *The Dialectical Biologist,* Musschenga and Gosling, *Science Education & Ethical Values.*
3. Much of the heart-searching about impartiality and neutrality would be unnecessary if there was more clarity about what is meant by a value, and more attention were paid to the logical skills I have outlined. It should not be a question of "support[ing] alternative points of view equally" (Bridges in Wellington, 1986:31), but of making judgements about the evidence presented in favor of this or that proposition.
4. Gershuny's "formal and informal economies" and his calculations of a time-based system of accounts (Pahl, 579–97), discussions of the limitations of the measurement of Gross National Product and alternative ways of measuring the contribution of economic activities (Ekins, 128–66) and Marxist approaches which focus on concepts of exploitation and the form of production and appropriation of a surplus are useful here.
5. Perhaps the best is that by Oskar Anweiler (1964). Fitzpatrick is excellent. Regrettably Zepper's study of Krupskaya does not appear to have been turned into a book and there remains a dearth of good studies of, or even translations into English of her writings.
6. I recently completed a study of Moral-Political Education in Chinese Schools (1988, manuscript) which cites heavily from Chinese textbooks and teachers' materials.

REFERENCES

Anweiler, O. (1964). *Geschichte der Schule und Pädagogik in Russland vom Ende des Zarenreiches bis zum Beginn der Stalin-Ära.* Heidelberg: Quelle and Meyer.

Bos, W. and Straka, G. A. (1987). *Was Maos Erben in der Schule lernen: Ergebnisse einer vergleichenden Inhaltsanalyse von Grundschultextblichern der VR China.* Münster: Waxmann.

Bronfenbrenner, U. (1974). *Two Worlds of Childhood: US and USSR* (1970). Harmondsworth: Penguin Books.

Chowka, P. B. (1980). "A Tale of Nuclear Tyranny." *New Age,* August, pp. 26–35, 68–9.

Davis, M. (1986). *Prisoners of the American Dream: Politics and Economy in the History of the US Working Class.* London: Verso.

Dawkins, J. S. (1988). *Higher Education: A Policy Statement* (The White Paper). Canberra: Australian Government Publishing Service.

Dilger, B., Kuebart, F., and Schäfer, H-P. (eds.) (1986). *Vergleichende Bildungsforschung: DDR, Osteuropa and interkulturelle Perspektiven (Festschrift für Oskar Anweiler zum 60. Geburtstag).* Berlin: Arno Spitz.

Ekins, P. (1986). *The Living Economy: A New Economics in the Making.* London: Routledge and Kegan Paul.

Epstein, E. H. (1983). "Currents Left and Right: Ideology in Comparative Education." *Comparative Education Review* 27(1): 3–29.

Epstein, E. H. (1987). "Among the Currents: a Critique of Critiques of 'Ideology in Comparative Education.'" *Compare* 17(1): 17–28.

Fantani, M.D. and Sinclair, R.L. (eds.) (1985). *Education in School and Nonschool Settings.* (84th Yearbook of the National Society for the Study of Education). Chicago: University of Chicago Press.

Fitzpatrick, S. (1979). *Education and Social Mobility in the Soviet Union, 1921–1934.* Cambridge: Cambridge University Press.

Hans, N. (1958). *Comparative Education: A Study of Educational Factors and Traditions,* 3rd ed. (1949). London: Routledge and Kegan Paul.

Holmes, B. (1983). "Commentary on Epstein." *Comparative Education Review* 27(1): 42–5.

Jones, B. (1982/86). *Sleepers, Wake! Technology and the Future of Work.* Melbourne: Oxford University Press.

Kolko, J. (1988). *Restructuring the World Economy.* New York: Pantheon Books.

Levins, R. and Lewontin, R. (1985). *The Dialectical Biologist.* Cambridge, MA: Harvard University Press.

Muckle, J. (1988). *A Guide to the Soviet Curriculum: What the Russian Child is Taught in School.* London: Croom Helm.

Musschenga, B. and Gosling, D. (1985). *Science Education and Ethical Values.* Washington, D.C.: Georgetown University Press.

Needham, J. (1954–ongoing). *Science and Civilization in China* (especially vol. 2). Cambridge: Cambridge University Press.

Pahl, R. E. (1988). *On Work: Historical, Comparative and Theoretical Approaches.* Oxford: Basil Blackwell.

Pfeffer, R. M. (1979). *Working for Capitalism.* New York: Columbia University Press.

Pinkevitch, A. P. (1929). *The New Education in the Soviet Republic* (ed. George S. Counts; trans. Nucia Perlmutter). New York: John Day.

Price, R. F. (1977). *Marx and Education in Russia and China.* London: Croom Helm.

Price, R. F. (1984). "Searching for a Marxist Education: the Soviet Union and China." *Slavic and European Education Review* 1982 (2)–1984 (1, 2): 7–20.

Price, R. F. (1986). *Marx and Education in Late Capitalism.* London: Croom Helm.

Price, R. F. (1988). *Moral-Political Education in Chinese Schools* (manuscript, p. 253).

Ridley, C. P., Godwin, P. H. B. and Doolin, D. J. (1971). *The Making of a Model Citizen in Communist China.* Stanford: The Hoover Institution Press.

Rose, H. and Rose, S. (1976). *The Radicalization of Science.* London: Macmillan.

Rose, S., Lewontin, R. C. and Kamin, L. J. (1987). *Not in Our Genes: Biology, Ideology and Human Nature.* (1984, Pantheon). Harmondsworth: Penguin Books.

Sharp, R. (ed.) (1986). *Capitalist Crisis and Schooling: Comparative Studies in the Politics of Education.* Melbourne: Macmillan.

Townsend Coles, E. K. (1982). *Maverick of the Education Family: Two Essays in Non-Formal Education.* Oxford: Pergamon Press.

Trace, A. S. (1961). *What Ivan Knows that Johnny Doesn't.* New York: Random House.

Wallraff, G. (1988). *Ganz unten. Mit einer Dokumentation der Folgen* (1985). Köln: Kiepenheuer and Witsch.

Webster, F., and Robins, K. (1986). *Information Technology: a Luddite Analysis.* Norwood, NJ: Ablex Publishing Corporation.

Wellington, J. J. (ed.) (1986). *Controversial Issues in the Curriculum.* London: Basil Blackwell.

Zepper, J. T. (1960). "A Study of N. K. Krupskaya's Educational Philosophy." Unpublished Ph.D thesis, University of Missouri.

Part Two

Equity and Education

CHAPTER 6

Education and Muslim Identity: The Case of France

Leslie J. Limage

ABSTRACT *The French republican principles upon which public education is based include strict separation of religion from schooling. At the same time, public funds subsidize a large number of private schools, over 90 percent Catholic. Virtually no recognition or public support is provided for Muslim or Jewish schools, nor is there any public or group demand that it do so. This article examines the complex and changing context in which Muslim identity has evolved in France for and by second and third generation immigrants of Muslim origin from the Maghreb (Algeria, Morocco, Tunisia) or to a lesser degree from ex-Yugoslavia, Turkey or sub-Saharan Africa. The latest phase is the most confrontational as the Muslim origin population, regardless of its actual heterogeneity or length of stay in France, is affected by the waves of terrorism and fundamentalism flowing from the Algerian civil war. Ill-informed French public opinion frequently amalgamates all Maghreb or Machrek individuals and communities when faced with the threat of violence. This article situates the official discourse which proclaims that the state and its schools promote a secular and equal opportunity for all and at the same time makes no allowance for cultural, linguistic, religious or socioeconomic diversity. It examines more recent attempts by French governments to address the longer term needs and aspirations (especially religious) of immigrant populations of Muslim origin as it becomes clear that these populations are massively becoming French citizens and have no further plans to return to countries of origin. The article concludes with reflections on the specificity of the French approach to religious and cultural diversity. Above all, it emphasizes a certain unity of view across political parties and communities that this specificity, although in crisis, does not require major change of the traditional republican approach.*

Introduction: The Heritage of
the French Revolution 1792

To offer all individuals of the human race the means to see to their needs and ensure their well-being, to know and exercise their rights, to know and fulfill their obligations; to offer everyone the possibility of improving his skills so as to be capable of fulfilling the social responsibilities for which he may be called upon, to develop all potential talent received by nature and to establish equality of condition between citizens and real political equality recognized by law: these should be the first goals of a national system of instruction (schooling); and seen from this perspective, this goal is a duty of justice for the state (public power) . . .

Since the first condition of all instruction is to teach only truths, institutions established by the state (public power) must be as independent as possible of any political authority . . . that independence is best ensured by the assembly of representatives of the people, because it is the least prone to corruption . . . and the least likely to be an enemy of enlightenment and progress than any other power . . .

Thus, instruction should be universal . . . It should be distributed with all the equality which available resources allow . . . No public institution should have the authority or even the possibility of preventing the development of new truths, the teaching of theories which contradict its particular policies or its short term interests . . .

LIBERTY, EQUALITY, FRATERNITY:
A CENTRALIZED SCHOOL SYSTEM INTENDED
TO PROMOTE EQUALITY

The highly centralized French school system has always been perceived as offering the best means of promoting equality and national unity. The notion of the state in the Enlightenment sense began to take form with the French Revolution in 1792 (Furet, 1978). The France of the late eighteenth century was a linguistically and culturally diverse collection of regions and divergent interests. And the France of 2000 remains fundamentally diverse in spite of two hundred years of centralization, imposition of the French language and enormous efforts to promote a unified notion of equality in a single state, administered in a superficially equal manner (De Certeau & Revel, 1975).

It has long been thought that only a highly centralized system could and would effectively redistribute the nation's wealth to reduce regional disparities and special interests. This view extends, of course, well beyond France and in centralized countries/systems of schooling, is only marginally challenged from within. While globalization, the expansion of multinational corporations and the movement towards a more politically and economically united Europe proceeds at one level, the basic principles upon which the French state was founded, and the school system which it built to support those principles, continue fairly untouched by outside influence.

Social science research of the 1960s and 1970s, such as that of Pierre Bourdieu, demonstrating the social reproduction role of this centralized system has had virtually no long-term impact on how French schools are administered, how French teachers teach or how schooling is organized. Other research demonstrating that the school system straightforwardly contributes to wastage and underachievement by arbitrarily creating failure at an early age *(échec scolaire)*, such as that of Baudelot and Establet (1989), still has little impact on how equality of opportunity is best defined. Even very recent studies about the actual disparities between resources allocated by the central state school system to different regions have little effect on philosophical debate about the role of schooling. The fact that schools in Paris have better qualified teachers than those of other cities, that conditions of teaching and learning at a material level vary from one part of the country to another, that, in spite of basic principles, inequality of resources actually dominates school provision in France, has little impact on how decision-makers, intellectuals, trade unions and the school administration see matters. Parents and pupils are rarely heard (Gurrey, 1997; Fernoglio & Herzberg, 1998).[2]

A recent definition of equality and the never concept of positive discrimination by a member of the National State Council *(Conseil d'Etat)*, François Stasse, states the position as cleary as possible (Stasse, 1997). Stasse finds the origin of the notion of equality before the law in the "Declaration of human rights and those of the citizen" of 1789 in the statement that "all men are born free and equal and remain so under the law." The notion of equality progressively comes to mean that all citizens confronted by a similar situation should be treated *identically* under the law. This means that no distinction can be made between citizens on the basis of race, religion or national origin.

This critical definition has a basic weakness. The concept of equality before the law has had little impact on reducing economic, social and cultural inequalities in France (or elsewhere). The State Council recognizes the weakness of the simple principle of equality before the law and begins to address equality of opportunity as a form of social solidarity. Most of the social welfare measures of the post-World War II period and those currently under debate or criticism today have been developed with this second concept in mind. And even more recently, equity as equality of condition enters the arena of political debate. The implications for schooling are critical but the response is extremely hesitant. On the one hand, the overriding principle that equality should mean providing everyone with the same instruction or knowledge (with respect to schooling) does little to address the issue of inequality of ability or interest to take advantage of that body of knowledge or instruction. The French school system was founded in the latter part of the nineteenth century on the principle of equal access to the same education for all at the first stage (primary school). But it has taken nearly a century for the notion of positive discrimination to gain any ground. Educational priority areas *(zones d'éducation prioritaires)* based on the British model have been developed with the rationale that more educational resources (numbers of teachers, ancillary staff and necessary security personnel or building repairs) need to be provided in particularly disadvantaged areas.

But these measures are seen as temporary and fraught with the risk of further stigmatizing or marginalizing the populations they are meant to serve. The argument in France remains that special measures must lead back to the mainstream view of equality, the ability to participate on the same footing with all other young people, regardless of socioeconomic origin, with the same access to the same body of knowledge.

An understanding of this philosophical position is critical to understanding why and how French schools actually operate and the parameters of the debate about schooling. It plays a critical role in the experience of children of immigrant origin in French schools and frames the discourse concerning "integration" of populations of differing religions, geographic origins, socioeconomic status, etc.

A TEACHING FORCE WHICH IS PART OF THE CIVIL SERVICE AND UNACCOUNTABLE BEYOND HIERARCHICAL RELATIONS

Most teachers in France are civil servants. It has long been a corollary of the basic principle that the state is responsible for providing equal instruction for all, that the best way to ensure that responsibility is through a civil service. The civil service is viewed as the best status for teachers to ensure that they remain independent of outside pressures, be they of passing political views, the voices of families or children or religious positions. The French primary school teacher of the late nineteenth century was seen as a moral authority to promote the republican ideas of liberty, equality and fraternity in an atmosphere of secularity and complete neutrality. And if we return to the quotation from Condorcet at the beginning of this article as he addresses the National Legislative Assembly in 1792, it can be seen that the roots of this view of teachers are already present. Condorcet refers to a system of instruction free of all outside influence in which all have access to a body knowledge based on the truth as it is understood in a specific historic context. There is no doubt that there is a single truth to instruct, nor that truth will evolve over time. But the school system and its teachers will remain the best neutral judges of what is best to include in the body of knowledge to be conveyed.

French teachers fairly readily agree with this view and have done so consistently over time. It frequently makes it difficult for those from decentralized systems and for Americans, Canadians, Australians and perhaps Israelis to understand why French teachers do not behave in the same way nor value the same priorities as they do.

The history of the French unionization of teachers reflects this very particular perspective. Initially, teachers did not have the right to organize but as they did begin to do so, many tendencies of a political nature arose to distinguish between different views of what it meant for civil servants to unionize. While this article cannot go deeply into the history of unionization of French teachers, a few critical points need to be made. According to Robert (1995), early forms of organization were simply intended to protect and promote better conditions of service rather than question in any way the content of education or its transmission. This was not a difficult decision since a strong distinction has long been made between what constitutes school-based knowledge and instruction, and a larger role which has not been that of the school, namely to educate.

French teachers have rarely questioned the basic principle that they hold the knowledge to be transmitted and that knowledge is based on official instructions and decisions about what is to be taught, where and how. French teacher unions of all tendencies question salary and working conditions, allocation of positions in different parts of the country, violence and lack of security in schools, attempts to ask them to take on additional non-purely instructional tasks and any non-formalized contact with parents or pupils. They do not, with few exceptions, take on pastoral care or organize clubs, etc. as do teachers in many other countries.

The two principle parent associations in France are the *Parents d'élèves publiques* (PEP) (fairly conservative) and the larger *Fédération des conseils des parents d'élèves* (FCPE). In both cases, however, parent associations are welcomed solely to support teachers in their demands for better conditions of service and are no way considered as partners in what goes on within the classroom. Parents and teachers, as well as pupils, have been united in major demonstrations in very recent times on maintaining a secular school system (in the 1980s a confrontation between greater control over private essentially Catholic schools, and in the mid-1990s, against an attempt by the conservative government to allow state resources to be spent on improving private school buildings (again essentially Catholic in France)). In 1995 and again in 1997 and 1998, teachers, parents and pupils went on strike to protest about violence in schools. During the same period, a similar solidarity, but of a more complex nature, surrounded the restrictions placed on Islamic girls whose families wished them to wear a head covering in school. The great debate about the *foulard islamique* led to the exclusion of children who insisted on or were obliged to wear this head covering. The basic principle of French schools as free of such religious symbols or pressures also made for unanimity across teacher, parent and student organizations (Allaire & Frank, 1995; Glenn & de Jong, 1996). This issue will be taken up in some detail later in this article.

In several surveys and analyses of the teacher union press and policy statements by Robert (1995), teacher preoccupation remains resolutely the same over time. No teacher union asks for or considers parent or pupil participation in any classroom issue. Teachers "instruct"; parents "educate." Pupils receive, successfully or otherwise, "knowledge."

Teachers are accountable only to their hierarchy, as is the case in most civil service contexts. There is virtually no possibility of a teacher being censured except for the most flagrant abuse of pupils and even these cases are very difficult to prosecute. Children's poor results in examinations or performance in class is resolutely the child's fault or due to the parents' lack of support. Teachers are in no way accountable.

A very recent consultation held by the current Minister of Education, Claude Allègre (Blanchard, 1998a) asked teachers and pupils separately for their views on a range of educational matters. A direct consultation by questionnaire has no precedent. The resultant response about pupils by teachers, especially at secondary level, was precisely the same response that has been given for over a century (well-recorded in Baudelot and Establet's study of 1989, "Le niveau monte. Réfutation d'une vieille idée concernant la prétendue décadence de nos écoles," [The standards are rising. A denial of the old idea about the so-called decadence of our schools]. Teachers reported that pupils are lazy, do not have any intellectual curiosity, do not have the level or standards of former times, are not motivated, come to secondary school with limited reading and writing skills, are unable to assimilate the large body of knowledge which they are expected to cover in lower secondary school *(collége)* or one or other form of upper secondary school. The only indication that schools (not teachers) might have some responsibility in the matter comes out in the replies when teachers refer to overcrowded classrooms, lack of material resources or violence overflowing into the schools from disadvantaged neighborhoods.

This same Minister of Education has managed to alienate virtually the entire teaching and national education administration community as well as a number of intellectuals. M. Allègre began his administration as Minister by denouncing teacher absenteeism and by threatening to reduce the size of the administrative apparatus of the national school system. He referred to the sacred *Education nationale* as a mammoth that needed to be put on a diet *(dégraisser le mamouth)*. He immediately became unpopular across the board with teacher organizations while official reports were produced that teachers are responsible for the loss of pupils' classroom instruction by up to about 10 percent of the annual hours, but that it was not actually their fault. Teachers were simply not replaced when absent for illness, maternity leave or further training in very many instances. (All in-service training for teachers takes place during classtime thus creating a real problem for pupils to achieve continuity in their schooling.)

An interesting recent criticism of M. Allègre's efforts to undertake what are viewed as decadent American reforms—more parent participation and consultation of pupils, opening the school to the community, etc.—came recently from a famous left-wing intellectual Régis Debray, comrade of Ché Guevarra and revolutionary movements in Latin America in the 1960s. M. Débray denounced M. Allègre for attempting to let the vox populi (meaning parents and children) into discussion of what should be taught and how. He denounced the very notion that anyone other than teachers might decide what should be taught and how. His discourse places him in the mainstream of the very long tradition of what schooling is all about (Debray, 1998).

SCHOOL-BASED KNOWLEDGE EXCLUSIVELY THE DOMAIN OF THE STATE AND ITS TEACHERS

Since school-based knowledge remains exclusively the domain of the state and it is "transmitted" by teachers, there are only highly formalized means for including new or alternative issues, events and changes in French society. History and civics education are the content areas in a highly compartmentalized system of disciplines which are of particular interest in this context. The syllabus for each year of schooling is strictly decided by the Ministry of Education and teachers' choice is limited to selecting the books that their pupils must purchase for their classes (books based on a national syllabus are free at primary and lower secondary level but still selected by teachers).

For the past fifteen years or so, successive Ministers of Education, from Jean-Pierre Chevènement to François Bayrou, wanted to give civics education a real place in secondary school programmes. At present, civics education is hidden at lower secondary level in a short course on the institutions of the Fifth Republic and general moral principles of the secular French system of government. But the content of a renewed and enlarged program has beaten each minister.[3]

Initially, Jules Ferry, founding father of obligatory state primary schooling, saw civics education as inculcating respect for the values of the republic in children from an early age. These basic principles, according to Ferry, were attachment to secularity, respect for public institutions, and active and responsible citizenship in full knowledge of one's rights and responsibilities. The current Minister, Claude Allègre and the Minister for Schools, Ségolène Royal, are presently proposing that civics education has a place throughout all schooling and that it be based on the principles of tolerance, responsibility, respect for rights and obligations, secularity, solidarity and courtesy. Since no one can be opposed to these generalities, the problem lies in how one takes the step from general principles to a syllabus. The shadow of political pressure or non-neutrality remains omnipresent to each minister (ministers being political nominees while the civil servants of the National Ministry of Education remain as guarantors of this 'impartiality').

Civics education has consistently been the content area most difficult to define in French schooling for these reasons. There is no question of "social studies" or "current events" periods, American style. There is certainly no place for examination of cultural, religious or linguistic diversity or tolerance. The only content which has appeared non-controversial has been the study of the institutions of government in a fairly formalized manner. Another major stumbling block is already inherent in the institutional context of schooling. There is no space for the practice of democracy in the school as an institution, the classroom in particular. Parent bodies, as already mentioned, are outside the school and negotiate from the exterior. Parent representation on school councils, which meet several times a year, only exists as such since the Haby Reform of 1975. These councils in no way allow parents or their representatives to discuss pedagogical matters. Similarly, student representatives on these councils and student organizations are simply formally present to ask polite questions and receive decisions taken by teachers about their classmates. They are not the site of dialogue.

The practice of democracy and participation has virtually no place in the institutions where children spend so much of their time from the age of three to sixteen (if not longer). In schools, pupils receive sanctions which vary from one teacher to another. It is quite customary for teachers to insult their pupils of all ages with vague accusations of how stupid they are and how incapable. Traditionally, French school report cards are frequently annotated thus: "doesn't have the level (*niveau*); lazy, unmotivated, incapable, needs to make a greater effort" and teachers are not accountable for these vague comments which follow a pupil throughout his or her school career. Again, the impunity of teachers and the school administration makes it very difficult to envisage a civics education based on a shared view of individual and collective responsibility. The imbalance of power is too flagrant. The only response possible to many young people is to retreat into indifference or insolence (Gurrey, 1997).

EQUALITY THROUGH EXAMINATION-BASED SELECTION

Another major constraint to developing a sense of individual and collective responsibility in French schools has to be mentioned although it is not fully developed in this article. The French system is an examination-oriented system of education. Although overt selection after primary schooling has been eliminated, orientation and instruction at secondary level are bound and structured by the examination pupils will take in different forms of post lower secondary schooling. While the syllabus for all schooling is decided centrally, so too, the examination system dictates what will be taught and how it will be taught. As long as a particular form of writing is critical to success in the philosophy examination at the baccalaureate examination or another in the French language examination, all instruction focuses on those formalized rituals.

In terms of equality the goal remains to offer pupils equal opportunity to learn how to express themselves successfully in terms of a highly codified means of expression at oral and written examination time. The form of expression is considerably more important than the content, and outside knowledge which has not been transmitted by the teacher (or acquired in the families of middle-class households) is anathema *(hors sujet)*.

PRINCIPLES OF SECULARITY, NEUTRALITY AND EQUALITY AND PRIVATE SCHOOLING

While the philosophical foundations of French society and schooling are intended to offer equality before a body of knowledge, they in no way allow for diversity. There is little acknowledgement of the cultural and linguistic diversity which make up the school populations of France and French society in general. Since the French Revolution, the effort to impose the French language on all other dialects and languages has been seen as the best way to convey republican principles and develop national unity. Hence, the languages and cultures of immigrant populations of first, second and third generations, as well as the regional languages of France, have little place in schools. For a very long period, the latter were actually forbidden even on the school playground. The terms "multiculturalism" or "preservation of cultural identities" have no place in schools, other than the exceptional look at recipes or songs or folklore of other cultures at primary level. Foreign language instruction at secondary level is usually restricted to traditional English, German, Russian, Spanish, possibly Greek, Latin, Portuguese. Students wishing to take Arabic or less often spoken languages may do so, with special authorization, by taking outside or distance education courses only (Limage, 1984, 1986).

Respect for secular *("laïc")* schooling is perhaps the strongest normative pillar of French political philosophy. The historic attempt to separate church and state has deep roots and awakens passionate response whenever it is perceived as being threatened. The long negotiations with the Catholic Church over nearly two centuries have culminated in a delicate balance which can easily be upset. Any attention to populations of Islamic origin, the focus of this article, has to begin with this critical contextual background. The historic battles between the Catholic Church and successive French governments have been referred to as *guerres scolaires* quite literally. With respect to more recent "battles," an attempted reform in the early 1980s under Minister of Education, Alain Savary, to create greater state control over Catholic schools, led to such protest by Catholic families and politicians that the Minister was forced to resign and President Mitterand had to withdraw the proposed legislation. Even more recently, teachers, parents, students and politicians committed to secular education took to the streets to protest against a proposed law allowing state monies to be used by the regions to repair and improve Catholic school buildings under contract with the state. That proposed law was not enacted.

The major piece of legislation which defines the role of private (essentially Catholic) schools, the Debré Law (*Loi Debré*) was enacted in 1959 after World War II. The Catholic Church under the Vichy government had literally removed all elements of secular schooling during that period: exclusion of Jewish children, obligatory catechism and prayer as part of the larger "return" to national values. The argument used by the then Minister of Education, Jacques Chevalier, was that the French had lost to the Germans essentially because of the weaknesses of the system of public schooling. He closed the former secular teacher training colleges, opened the profession to priests and provided public funds for Catholic schools. In the post-World War II period, the Debré Law (finally adopted after long negotiations with the Catholic Church and the powerful pro-church groups in France) became a compromise. The state funds teachers' salaries in the religious schools but in exchange, the schools should be open to all pupils in the area and should respect the freedom of religious conviction of each individual. The state also determines, as with secular public schools, the basic syllabus. The Debré Law was weakened by two later pieces of legislation. Under Minister of Education, Olivier Guichard, in 1971 the state entered into a simple contract with Catholic schools and committed greater funds to teacher training. With the Guermer Law of 1977, further advantages were granted to Catholic schools without a demand for reciprocal responsibilities (Allaire & Frank, 1995).

In spite of the major concessions made to religious schooling in terms of Catholicism, the overriding discourse concerning French public schooling remains more than ever committed to a secular and neutral system. The most recent reaffirmation of this commitment is contained in the Circular of 12 December 1989 signed by then Minister of Education (and current Prime Minister), Lionel Jospin, as a result of the State Council's verdict concerning the wearing of head scarves in school by girls of Islamic origin. The actual conflict will be looked at in some detail later in this article, but it is important to cite the introduction to this ministerial circular to emphasise basic principles:

Secularity, a constitutional principle of the French republic, is one of the pillars of the public school. At school like elsewhere, religious beliefs are a matter of individual conscience and freedom. But since all children come together in school without any form of discrimination, the exercise of freedom of belief with the public service's responsibility for respect for pluralism and neutrality, means that the entire educational community should be protected from any form of ideological or religious pressure. (Introduction to the Circular of 12 December 1989 signed by the Minister of Education, Lionel Jospin, cited in Allaire and Frank (1995).[4]

PARENTS, CHILDREN AND THE OUTSIDE WORLD

While parents are not simply intruders in the French school system, they are not partners either. Their role is to support teachers to improve the material conditions in which they and their pupils work, and to assist them in protecting the school environment from outside influence. A child is a "pupil" or "student" in the school and relates as such to the teacher, and vice versa. The child is "educated" by its parents and community and "instructed" by its teacher. Outside knowledge, experience and aspirations stop at the school door. Other concepts of the school's responsibility to respond to the "whole" child are simply not relevant to the prevalent French philosophy of schooling/instruction. Political debate or practice of democtatic institutions do not find their place in French schools. And yet, France has one of the liveliest and most diverse political, social and cultural arenas of any country in the world. There is very real diversity of political affiliation and activism in French society, but it is still perceived to be the school's responsibility to ensure that the school remain as "neutral" an environment as possible.

While the economic situation has continued to degenerate across Europe, new forms of solidarity still based on the activism of a democratic society have sprung up in France. Most recently, associations of the unemployed have taken to demonstrating and acting in an organized fashion to demand a minimal living standard for all. On the other hand, most other countries have not simply reduced social spending but begun to call once more for charitable bodies and so-called "partnerships" with private industry to take up the challenge, as in the nineteenth century. The current Minister of Education, Claude Allègre, is at his most controversial in relation to intellectuals and teachers' unions alike when he appears to try to "privatize" on the American or International Monetary Fund/Organisation for Economic Cooperation and Development/World Bank model and talks of "partnerships" with industry, etc. (Roux, 1998; Vuaillet, 1998).

There is a very real sense of commitment to basic principles when these challenges are denounced. At the same time, there is a very real inability to take a step towards an acceptable form of dialogue between all "social partners." The school needs to recognize the "new truths" of the start of the twenty-first century but it still wants the monopoly, on identifying those truths through its civil service and the state. In this context, it is possible to attempt to understand the place of immigrant children in French schools and in particular, children and youth of Islamic origin.

IMMIGRATION IN FRANCE: AN OVERVIEW

France has a long history of political and economic immigration. The pace and scale of immigration from former colonies and other countries of the Mediterranean basin accelerated after World War II. Each group, depending on its origin, motivations for emigration and similarity to French cultural norms and practices has had a different experience. It is misleading to consider central and eastern European immigrants or Spanish, Italian and Portuguese alongside immigrants from north Africa or sub-Saharan Africa. It is also quite misleading to assume that all immigrants holding some Islamic cultural heritage have come to France under similar conditions or with similar expectations or have found a similar response to their needs and aspirations. An impressive research-based literature has developed, especially since the late 1960s, concerning immigration to France and other western European countries. (A selected bibliography is included with the references to this article.)

France's declining demographic situation since the turn of the twentieth century, however, made it a more likely destination for both political and economic immigration than many other western European countries. The need for an enlarged workforce led to both a continuing growth of clandestine as well as official immigration until the early 1970s. Across nationalities and at the risk of oversimplification, however, economic immigration usually meant that immigrants had a plan to return to their countries of origin once their material conditions allowed. Among immigrant groups who have maintained this plan as a dream or concrete project, Portuguese, Spaniards and Italians have been found to be most likely to foresee a possible return. Political and economic refugees from central and eastern Europe have been least likely to consider return migration. In an earlier period, North African (Tunisian, Moroccan, Algerian) and sub-Saharan African immigrants came with plans to return and forwarded earnings to families left behind. As economic conditions and in many cases, political conditions have deteriorated, both in Europe and in the countries of origin, the plan to return has seemed less and less likely.

With the onset of economic crisis in the early 1970s, most European countries drastically limited immigration. France was among the last to place such restrictions and confined further immigration to family reunification (especially among north Africans and to a lesser extent, to sub-Saharan Africans from former colonies). France has also been seen, when compared with other European countries, especially Germany, as one of the most open to, firstly, immigration and, secondly, the possibility of acquiring citizenship. Germany has always been seen as the country with the most restrictive immigration policies, calling economic immigrants *gasterbeiter* or "guest workers," reinforcing the temporary nature of their stay and welcome. Sociologists in the 1970s and 1980s easily discovered that immigrants were most likely to seek permanent residence in countries which welcomed them (at least at an official level) and least likely to do so where both the reception and conditions of stay were most restrictive (Germany) (Granotier, 1970; Limage, 1975, 1981, 1984, 1985; Charlot *et al.*, 1978; Cesari, 1997a).

Both countries of origin and countries of immigration have attempted to regulate movements of populations with varying degrees of success. As it has become clear that the political and economic conditions on a global scale have continued to deteriorate, these attempts have taken the form of incentive measures (sums of money to encourage voluntary departures) and more spectacularly in very recent times in France with forced departures for clandestine immigrants or those whose residence and work permits have expired. Countries of origin have long sought ways to maintain contacts with their expatriate populations without encouraging return migration. These means have included formal agreements with the host country (France in this case) to organize language and culture classes *amicales* or associations for mutual support and celebrations and to some extent, assistance in developing places of worship. These measures will be discussed in some detail with respect to populations of Islamic origin.

IMMIGRANTS OF ISLAMIC CULTURE: DIVERSITY OF POPULATIONS, DIVERSITY OF ASPIRATIONS

Before looking at the educational response to immigrants of Islamic origin, it is essential to recognize the diversity this sub-title actually represents.

Moroccan and Tunisian immigration is more recent than that of Algerians. Moroccans came to France essentially during the 1960s until about

1973. Tunisian immigration began in the mid-1960s and also ended around 1973. It has always been on a much smaller scale. Tunisian immigration has also a fairly specific socioeconomic character. Tunisians have been more likely to run small businesses and shops. Similarly, Moroccans have also been more likely to arrive with a small amount of capital with which to start a business. Algerian immigration, on the other hand, has been on a much larger scale over a much longer period of time and with a much larger impact on French society (Geisser, 1997).

It has taken considerable time, however, for official French society to recognize that impact fully. Each North African country had a particular relation to France. Only Algeria was considered as an integral (if unequal) part of France under the colonial period and recognized as a *département*. Large numbers of Algerians volunteered in both World War I and World War II to fight alongside the French. But it has only been in 1998 that the President of the Republic, Jacques Chirac, has publicly acknowledged the contribution of Algerians to the protection of the *metropole* during both world wars.

The category "French from Algeria" or *Maghrébins français* covers even greater diversity. For the purposes of this article, reference is made to all categories, but only those of Islamic origin are further discussed. First, a large French population settled in North Africa, Algeria in particular, over several generations and when forced to return to France at each country's independence has constituted a group known as *pieds noirs*. A second category of north Africans of Jewish faith were readily granted French citizenship and immigrated massively at the time of independence of each North African country. While these two groups have had some privileged treatment when compared with other North African immigrants, they have nonetheless encountered difficulties in integration or assimilation. Berber populations (non-Arab) of Algeria (Kabylie) and Morocco have distinct migration patterns. The repression of their languages and cultures by the Arab élites has not contributed to bringing them closer to other Arab immigrants in France. Nonetheless, the French public does not necessarily note the difference.

Probably the group which has encountered the greatest amount of misunderstanding and disappointment has been the *harki*. Even the term *harki* covers a wide range of people and is used frequently in a pejorative sense. The North African, mainly Algerian, populations who constituted the administration, officers and soldiers working for France before Algeria's independence are known officially as RONA *(Rapatriés d'origine nord-africaine)*. With either title, they have found little sympathy both in Algeria and in France. Their various motivations for working with the colonial power and then seeking asylum in France after being perceived as traitors by the victorious Algerian independence forces (FLN) have been the object of less publicity and even less justice in France (Hamoumou, 1994; Geisser, 1997). Hamoumou documents the diversity of motivations and backgrounds of Algerians who worked with the colonial power in some way, in many cases with no particular political attachment. The Algerian war of independence was undoubtedly the most violent on all sides and has left both

Algeria and France with lasting bitterness, along with lasting and current concerns over an equally brutal ongoing civil war. The Muslim populations who sought protection from the retreating French (for whom they had worked) were widely betrayed and those who eventually reached France were placed in camps. Most of these camps were in isolated areas and remained home to these populations for more than twenty years. Their children grew up in these camps and attended separate/segregated schools for the most part rather than being integrated with the rest of the French population and the children of other immigrants including Algerians. Recent attempts by children of *harkis* to claim their rights as French citizens and to dissipate the dishonor attached to their parents by both French and Algerian officialdom have been largely unsuccessful but not necessarily vanquished. Demonstrations by children of *harkis*, starting on 9 May 1998 in various parts of France, have been intended to draw attention to their bitterness over thirty-six years of French governmental indifference across political parties. Unemployment among this population is estimated officially at 42 percent of the active population (and as high as 62 percent by those concerned), whereas official French unemployment is estimated at approximately 12 percent (Hamoumou, 1994; Cesari, 1997a, b; Etienne, 1989).

Other immigrants of Muslim culture and Algerian origin who have immigrated over the past fifty years must also be distinguished by period of immigration, generation, and nationality. There is a considerable number of Muslims of Algerian origin who immigrated prior to the war of independence, i.e. before 1962. They have, for the most part, taken French nationality and are difficult to count. Similarly, second and third generation Muslims of Algerian origin with French nationality are not considered as "foreigners," although they may feel some attachment to cultural roots. Each generation is also characterized by a socioeconomic background. The discovery of the 1960s and early 1970s was that of "slums" or *bidonvilles* (Hervos & Charras, 1970). The discovery of the 1980s and the 1990s was that of decaying suburbs or *banlieues*. Multiple factors have led second and third generation Muslims of Algerian origin to develop new identities and a certain pride. *Beur* culture is a combination of distant ties to north Africa and current search for identity between an "official" French society and the reality of disadvantaged suburbs characterized by insecurity, violence, unemployment and new forms of solidarity in gangs or community-based associations.

North African immigrants who have come as university students, intellectuals and artists seeking freedom of expression or wider professional possibilities constitute élites which apparently find it easier to assume both their origins and their status in France. A recent study by Geisser (1997) of how north African élites act politically as they take French nationality and participate, particularly in local government, has shown that the vast majority give priority to French republican ideals and processes and seek to mediate between the larger Muslim origin community and the French state. Geisser comes to the conclusion that these political élites are actually unable to serve the mediation role assigned to them. It is especially interesting that both Geisser (1997) and Cesari (1997a, b) have found a very complex political scene. While integration of Algerian immigrants (and other north Africans) has occurred essentially through trade union movements, the attempts by the Socialist and Communist parties to include and promote French Muslim culture have been less successful than those of the more Conservative parties and recent governments. It is beyond the scope of this paper to speculate why this seems to be the case, but a considerable part of the response appears to be linked to the more Conservative French government's recent attempts to create and control a distinctly French Islam with representative institutions (Etienne, 1989; Cesari, 1997a, b).

Before examining more closely the contours of what French political scientists and sociologists . . . and government officials . . . call "French Islam" *(Islam français)* and the actual recent history of the practice of Islam in the country, the discussion returns to the reception and experience of immigrants of Muslim culture in French schools and the special measures taken by the countries of origin to provide a context for the discussion of this possibly provocative concept.

RECEPTION IN FRANCE: EDUCATIONAL RESPONSES TO IMMIGRANTS IN SCHOOL

After the eruptions of *"mai '68"* (May 1968) in France and student and worker uprisings across Europe and North America, the French left wing discovered the most disenfranchised population: the immigrant worker and in some cases, his family. Numerous associations and solidarity groups were created to "accompany" and encourage this heterogeneous population. With respect to adults, the entire movement for adult literacy (called *alphabétisation de travailleurs migrants)* quickly developed to promote access to what was, in fact, French as a second language. This discovery of literacy issues among the immigrant population created both a service and a disservice. For the next ten years, all literacy difficulties were officially associated with immigrants, especially north Africans, and no attention was given to the broader French public (Limage, 1975, 1986). The service was the creation of networks of training for adult immigrants to acquire rudiments of spoken and written French. Initially, the French Ministry of Education took some responsibility, but quickly returned that responsibility to nonprofit and profit associations. The finance for most of these programs came from the *Fonds d'Action Sociale* (FAS), a fund composed of social welfare benefits, withheld mainly from male immigrant workers whose families had not rejoined them in France. The FAS continues its work today, although it has broadened its clientele if not its resources. In her doctoral dissertation of 1975, the author identified over two hundred associations offering some form of adult basic education called adult literacy or French as a second language (Limage, 1975).

As family reunification became the main source of official immigration from the mid-1970s onward, immigrants' countries of origin entered into bilateral agreements with France to offer instruction in "mother tongues" or official first languages of immigrants' children. The French Ministry of Education resolutely insisted that these classes were not their responsibility and governments of the countries of origin, eager to demonstrate their continued links with their expatriate populations, financed teachers and rented space in public schools in order to provide such instruction outside class time (Limage, 1980; OECD-CERI, 1983). Thus, children whose families wished them to maintain some form of contact with the languages and cultures of origin, attended classes, which took place outside regular school time with no cooperation from French teachers nor any participation of indigenous French children. In the 1970s, some effort was made to make French teachers more aware of the backgrounds of immigrant pupils in their classrooms through in-service training. The number of teachers applying for such training (voluntary at the time) was minimal. For the most part, the response of the French school system to the linguistic and cultural diversity of its pupils has been rather homogeneous: grade repetition, placement in special education classes (when the issue is lack of language skills rather than individual handicap) and in some cases, special reception classes for special French language instruction. But, as the first section of this article describes, the entire thrust of the French system is to define equality through the offering of the same knowledge by the same means to all. If an individual pupil is unable or unwilling to keep pace, the individual is a "school failure" an *échèc scolaire* (Limage, 1980, 1990).

By and large, children of immigrant origin appear to have received the same treatment but to an even greater degree than indigenous French children. The public school maintained its primacy concerning legitimate knowledge and the means to transmit it in the name of republican ideals of neutrality, secularity and equality. The notion of individualized instruction or cooperative learning or making the school more responsive to the child have met with little response as diversity remains an out-of-school matter.

THE FRENCH GOVERNMENT AND THE DEVELOPMENT OF A "FRENCH ISLAM"

Diversity of Backgrounds and Aspirations

Islam as it is practiced in a multitude of ways according to national origins and family or personal inclinations, had always been a highly private matter in France until the 1980s. Some students of religion, sociologists and political scientists in France have seen this invisibility linked to the immigration process. In the first instance, men and some women have immigrated alone. As Islam is a religion more based on traditions and cultural context than institution-based rites, individual Muslims saw no particular means of carrying out the social behavior. For the most part, social relations between men and women, children and parents have been based on traditions pre-dating Islam. In France, the family was incomplete and in any case, compromise was necessary owing to the very different socio-cultural norms. The four ritual pilars of Islam (the profession of faith *(shada)*; daily prayer *(al-salât)*; the pilgrimage to Mecca *(haj)* and fasting during the month of Ramadan) could be practiced if faith dictated, without a high degree of visibility, so as not to conflict with French customs and norms.

At another stage of the migration process, that of family reunification, some Muslims felt the need to establish modest places of prayer or meeting close to their homes. Again, the emphasis in Muslim practices from north Africa did not include institutions beyond the immediate local group. Indeed, the cultural practices of Muslims vary greatly according to origin, region, the degree to which these practices are maintained and the aspirations of new generations of young people. Also, being a religion without a hierarchy and priesthood, and not a major institution like the Catholic Church with which the State has had the greatest official exchange, it attracted little notice before the 1980s in France.

Origins of Interest in Islam in France: Dilemmas of Republicanism and Fear of Foreign Influence

The attempt to regulate or institutionalize relations between the French government and Islam in France has been a completely new experience for everyone concerned. Muslims are discovering that they constitute a "minority," while French officialdom takes note of the impact of Islam in its many forms on French society. This process is evolving and it would be extremely difficult to do other than trace the distance covered to date. As mentioned above, the first sign of an Islamic presence occurred when small groups of individuals sought and set up rooms in which to hold prayers and meetings, either within their apartment buildings in distant suburbs or nearby. A second phase involved the creation of various associations with differing motivations and goals, often in competition with each other. The most recent phase, the intervention of the French government in the 1990s, has marked a turning point without clear direction.

INITIATIVES, POLICIES AND COUNTER RESPONSE

A law passed in 1981 removed obstacles to foreigners creating associations of their own and led to the creation of groups to support prayer rooms of a modest nature. These initiatives began solely as the prerogative of local groups neither supported nor hindered by outside, let alone foreign, influence. In a second phase, associations sponsored by north African governments have indeed offered financial or spiritual support. In the case of Algeria, the Mosque of Paris *(Mosquée de Paris)*, officially sponsored by that government, has made a concerted effort to extend its jurisdiction over local prayer groups and associations by offering temporary *imams* or spiritual leaders, or through the consulates by offering Arabic language teachers.

Local prayer groups either supported by outside associations or limited local assistance tend to become community meeting places as much as places of prayer. They have also progressively taken on the educational role of language instruction or religious instruction. It is their educational role which seems to have had a soothing effect on local authorities. A great variety of prayer groups exist, very dependent for their activities on the personalities and ages of those who lead them. Young and educated Muslim community leaders are more ambitious and their centers offer classes in calligraphy, music, literature, help with homework for children and sports and leisure activities.

After a number of years, the popularity of such prayer rooms and community centers has led to their inability to fulfill all that is expected of them. In the later 1980s and especially in the 1990s, in specific cities in France with high concentrations of Muslims, a demand to build actual mosques emerged. This stage has been an extremely delicate one with local sensitivities finally discovering the visibility of Islam. According to Cesari (1997a), the mosques in France today are located in Paris, Mantes-la-Jolie, Roubaix, Evry, Lille and Lyon, with approval having been given for construction of another in Paris. Other proposals for mosques are examined by local authorities with considerable reticence. For the most part, however, the architectural plans have attempted to ensure that the distinguishing features of the mosque blend in with the local architecture. And compromises have been made so that neighbors do not hear the ritual call to prayer five times a day. Nonetheless, some of the French cities with the largest Muslim populations, such as Marseilles or Toulouse, for example, have presented the greatest opposition to the construction of mosques.

Many will argue that it is high time that Islam and its practice in France be allowed the same guarantees of religious practice as those of other faiths. One area of controversy is in fact entirely fallacious. The argument that local or national tax money will be spent on the construction of mosques if they are allowed is actually untrue. The state cannot finance religious construction. That is why most mosques built over the last ten years have had financial assistance from other Arab countries, especially the Gulf States and Saudi Arabia. There is no real evidence that funding from outside France leads to control by the funding source.

On the other hand, there has been an effort over the past ten years to create some federation of Muslim associations, community centers and mosques. A considerable number of the parties in this struggle are too diverse in their goals to work together. It is, however, possible to distinguish the role of countries of origin as well as that of the French government. First among the parties in this struggle is the Paris mosque, sponsored by the Algerian government. Given the size of the population of Algerian origin, as well as the long history of close links with the country, it is not surprising that the French government has leaned towards the Paris mosque and its spiritual and managerial leaders. This pre-eminence has led to a long history of conflict. Most recently, however, in 1992, a rector of French nationality was named for the first time, Dalil Boubakeur. Until this nomination, the rectors have been Algerian.

A small number of fairly vocal federations of associations also exist which, while disagreeing among themselves on many matters, do advocate an autonomous Islam in France, especially an autonomy in relation to the Paris Mosque. The best known of these federations include the *Fédération Nationale des Musulmans de France* (FNMF) and the *Union des Organisations Islamiques de France* (UOIF). The former was created in 1985 through the initiative of a Frenchman converted to Islam, Daniel Youssouf Leclerc. After a rather tumultuous period, the organization seems to be under Moroccan influence. The latter, the UOIF, was created in 1983 by Tunisian intellectuals. It favors fairly strict obedience to Islamic rituals and customs while engaging in cautious dialogue with other religious groups in France. Other associations with other orientations are also growing and developing with the support of external sources.

The French government has been fairly indifferent to the practice of Islam in the country and to facilitating dialogue with its organization. That position has changed rapidly in very recent years. As the visibility of religious practice in prayer rooms *(salles de prières)* became more evident and also the financial backing for further growth, educational initiatives and building increased, various parties in the French government and in the competing associations and federations of associations representing the different interests surrounding Islamic cultures, sought ways to effect dialogue in a more traditional manner. In the first instance, the French government attempted to compare the means of dialogue which developed with the French Jewish community through the *Conseil Représentatif des Institutions Juives de France* (CRIF). The long history of French Judaism is beyond the scope of this article. It should be mentioned, however, that it has never seemed truly feasible to create the same institutional arrangements for the Islamic communities in France. In addition, international crises and internal security fears have created a more confused image of the reality of Islamic communities in France, further complicating policy positions based on anything more solid than temporary responses to immediate situations.

Until the early 1980s, the French government generally saw the extremely heterogeneous community of Islamic culture as an immigrant worker issue (as with the educational measures discussed earlier in this article). In 1976, Paul Dijoud, the Secretary of State for Immigrant Workers, took several initiatives to encourage the creation of prayer rooms in large factories or businesses in which Islamic workers were employed and encouraged flexibility with respect to observance of Islamic holy days. Later, in 1982, television and radio programs for the Islamic public were created.

International events in the early 1980s around the creation of the Islamic movements of the Machrek and the Maghreb in other countries led to a new focus on domestic Islam. A false parallel was drawn between situations abroad and those in France. Nonetheless, official interest in French Islam began to be mainly a security preoccupation. After the successful negotiation of freedom for French hostages in Lebanon by Algeria, the French Minister of the Interior, Charles Pasqua, announced that the Paris mosque issue was settled: it remained under Algerian jurisdiction.

In 1988, Pierre Joxe, Minister of the Interior and also Secretary of State for Religious Affairs created a commission *(Conseil de Réflexion sur l'Islam en France* CRIF). This commission was intended to act as a source of advice and communication between the government and the Islamic communities on any and all issues which might be of mutual concern. In fact, this commission marked the start of the French government's serious concern with Islamic affairs in France in a formal manner. The role of the government and its capacity for dialogue with a responsible and responsive partner seemed all the more urgent after the fatwa was declared upon Salman Rushdie and the rise of the head scarf issue in French schools. Also, as the issue of Islamic communities wishing to obtain planning and construction permission for mosques in various cities in France became more and more problematic when left to mayors and city councils, the government felt obliged to step in (Cesari, 1997a, b; Bruno, 1997; Geisser, 1997).

It is interesting to note how the French government justified this intervention in religious matters. Initially, it was pointed out that the majority of Muslims in France were, in fact, French. On the other hand, the majority of *imams* or religious leaders and teachers were foreign. There was no facility in France for the training of *imam*. Hence, virtually all of them came from abroad. Nonetheless, the CRIF gave every sign of representing a legitimate partner for the government holding little credibility among the actual Islamic communities in France. In fact, with a change in political majority in the French National Assembly in 1993, this commission was disbanded. The alternative solution became a simple return to giving the Paris mosque (still under Algerian tutelage), priority. The rector, Dalil Boubakeur, in turn, created another consultative body composed of the most prominent associations and individuals in the Islamic communities *(Conseil Consultatif des Musulmans de France)*. This new phase led to a long crisis in the Islamic communities which refused to accept the authority of the Paris mosque under Algerian hegemony. Nonetheless, Charles Pasqua, the Minister of the Interior, gave the Paris mosque authority for the ritual killing of animals intended for consumption *(halal)*. The council also developed a "Charter" for Muslim practice in France although the actual text was written by the Paris mosque leaders. Since this document was intended to reconcile the Islamic communities with their French nationality and provide for their religious aspirations, the controversy was focused on the hegemony of the Paris mosque rather than on the content of the charter.

Amidst much debate and controversy, another body was formed on 16 December 1995: the *Haut Conseil des Musulmans de France*, somewhat on the model of the Jewish CRIF. The debate, however, continues and no unified voice appears to emerge from the various temporary alliances among Islamic leaders and intellectuals in France. Alliances occur over specific issues, but re-form or disintegrate on the longer term concept of a single body speaking for Islam in France. The French government continues to take initiatives which provoke further debate. For example, since 1996, a policy concerning the construction of regional mosques (Evry, Lyon) has led to further dissension in the communities intended as beneficiaries.

The very notion of the French government attempting to create a unified Islam in France, either through councils or by giving priority to the Paris mosque (backed by Algeria), is a novel and problematic position for a society based on secular, neutral and equal relations by its institutions with the public. Theoretically, some of the issues actually to be treated by the government with the Islamic community already have precedents in terms of the Jewish community: ritual animal slaughter for making meat kosher, charitable organizations and activities, special food considerations, holy days. Even the creation of private Islamic schools is not an insurmountable problem, although only one actually exists at this stage (in Saint Denis-de-la-Réunion; another may open in Lille under the auspices of the Islamic cultural centre of the city). The obstacles are actually more political within the highly diverse Islamic origin communities (Etienne, 1989; Cesari, 1997a).

INTERNAL ISSUES: THE STATUTE OF IMAMS IN FRANCE

The role of the *imam* is not comparable to the Catholic priesthood. The *imam* is more a teacher and prayer leader. At present, the vast majority are trained abroad in the famous religious centers of Tunis or Egypt. Similarly, the specialists in religious law (*oulémas*) are also trained in these two countries for the most part. There is both a political and a practical issue here for the French Islamic communities. These foreign trained religious leaders are ill-prepared to act in the local communities to advise, mediate and guide, as they are rarely familiar with local conditions, practices, and the specific problems of the diverse communities to which they are sent. They rarely have training to take on the pastoral duties of a religious guide: visits to hospitals, prisons, leading funerals or weddings. Also, there is no official census of how many are practicing throughout France in one way or another. Very often they live solely on the charity provided by the community and can lose their residence permits if they show any sign of speaking out politically.

One of the major associations mentioned earlier, the UOIF, took this major problem seriously. In 1991, it created a European Institute for Social Sciences at Château-Chinon which includes an institute to train *imams* and educators. This institute is still seen as rather inadequate for offering satisfactory training. Other initiatives include an Institute for Islamic Studies opened by a Frenchman converted to Islam, Didier Ali-Bourg, in 1993 in Paris, thanks to a subsidy by the Gulf States. Another initiative was undertaken by the Paris mosque the same year to create an institute for the training of *imams*. Each of these initiatives has had very limited success. One obvious reason is that the main centers of intellectual and religious orthodoxy and prestige are all located outside Europe in Asia, the Middle East and north Africa. There is no convincing proof that Islam in France, with its diverse communities, has any reason to cut itself off from these sources of legitimation. The challenge remains to accommodate the very real links of Islam in France with its sources and inspiration abroad, while ensuring respect for republican principles. Further, as Islamic practices are frequently perceived as more cultural than ritual, it is these practices which actually produce conflict. An apt illustration of this dilemma is the head scarf affair of 1989 which still has its echoes in France in 2000.

REAFFIRMATION OF SECULAR PRINCIPLES:
THE FOULARD ISLAMIQUE AFFAIR

Since 1989, the reaction of school authorities, parents, pupils and the larger community in France to the wearing of head scarves in lower and upper secondary school by a handful of girls of Muslim origin has created both a political and a sociological debate. That debate remains unresolved, although the courts of France continue to hand down decisions concerning various appeals by families whose daughters have been excluded from school for wearing the scarf. The various cases and arguments are summarized here.

As the entire first part of this article has emphasized, the French state and its public schools are seen as the repositories of neutrality, secularity and equality before the law of all citizens. Schools are intended, rightly or wrongly, to educate pupils to become responsible citizens through access to the same knowledge. There is no question of any outside influence by parents, community groups, political or religious organizations. Religion is considered a very private matter and proselytism is absolutely forbidden in the institutions of the French republic. Teachers and other civil servants are bound to adhere strictly to these republican values.

Thus, when a handful of adolescent girls in several cities in France began wearing head scarves to school at the instigation of their families, the reaction was immediate. In addition to wearing the head scarves, many of the girls refused to participate in physical education activities and in some instances, they were supported in their initiatives by Islamic organizations or associations. The reaction of *proviseurs* or principals and teachers alike was to request the removal of the head scarves and to insist that the girls participate like all other pupils in the obligatory classes of the school program. The refusal to remove head scarves and/or participate in compulsory activities led, in most instances, to the girls being sent home. In a few cases, they were grouped in school libraries temporarily. The first demonstrations for and against this sign of "religious" practice were tense and remain so, in spite of the legal decisions taken to date.

In the first instance, the State Council *(Conseil d'Etat)* rendered a judgement which reminded the French public that it is the civil servants of the state who must remain neutral in all their official responsibilities, not the clients or, in this case, the pupils. Religious affiliation may be discreetly displayed as long as there is no attempt to convert or disturb the public in any way. The State Council left it to the Minister of Education to advise schools how to deal with this phenomenon. The Minister of Education reaffirmed the principles of neutrality and the secular nature of the school system. However, he asked each school principal and the teaching staff to treat the cases on an individual basis. He advised discussion and consultation with the girls and their families and an attempt to find a negotiated solution.

Unfortunately, French school administrators, especially principals, are unused to exercising authority over the teaching staff in French schools, let alone dealing with sensitive issues of cultural and religious conviction (Gruson, 1978; Allaire & Frank, 1995). The decision-making responsibility had, however, been handed back to them. This has meant that over the past ten years a number of cases in which girls have been excluded for wearing head scarves have reached the courts. By and large, the courts have overturned these exclusions unless the wearing of the head scarf has been accompanied by a refusal to attend physical education classes or been associated with protest by outside organizations (demonstrations, meetings, etc.) (Kessler & Bernard, 1997).

This continuing conflict is perceived from two perspectives in France. The first issue, that of religious neutrality and secular public space, is fairly understandable. The other and perhaps overriding issue is more sociological. The status of women in Islamic countries and cultures pre-dates Islam and reflects a strong patriarchal social order. International crises, especially the civil war in Algeria where women and children were the victims of rape, massacre and humiliation, have a very strong influence on French public opinion. The wearing of the head scarf is interpreted as a sign of girls' and women's lack of equal rights with men in Islamic societies. Above all, it appears as a potential threat to hard-won human rights for women, as for the most part, north African women have been less frequently veiled, cloistered or subjected to purdah than Islamic women in countries of the Machrek, Sudan and sub-Saharan Africa. Nonetheless, all three Maghreb countries still maintain the family code based on the Sharia or Islamic code of conduct in which women have a clearly secondary status.

It is thus difficult for the French public to engage in cultural relativism with respect to young women living in France and probably of French nationality. It is obviously an impossible task to decide whether the young woman is wearing the scarf voluntarily, because of religious conviction, under duress, or as a sign of expressing her complex cultural identities. What strikes public opinion most forcefully is the fact that head scarves were not an issue in earlier years. It is the rise of a stronger Islamic identity around the world and its associated conflicts and aspirations which seems to create fear and suspicion. France, of course, is not alone in this reaction. It cannot, however, reach a critical distance on the civil war in Algeria which has led to terrorism and bombings on French territory and daily reporting of the slaughter of women and children there. It cannot reach a critical distance on the events in ex-Yugoslavia, either Bosnia or Kosovo, let alone Iraq, Iran, etc. The only critical distance occurs when market priorities simply obscure human-rights issues.

CONCLUDING REMARKS: CRISIS OF THE REPUBLICAN MODEL AND THE WELFARE STATE

This article has focused on the principles which have framed the creation of institutions and policies in France for two centuries and the response to the evolution of Islamic presence in French society. The picture is not complete, however, unless at least passing reference is made to the crisis of the French state regarding the provision of equality and solidarity, as official discourse has promised since the end of World War II. High levels of unemployment and growing levels of poverty in France and across Europe, coupled with reduced public spending and alternating attempts to turn France into a basically market economy, and then to redress the situation, have taken their toll. The centralized state has not led to redistribution of wealth and resources, notably for public schools. The current strikes and demonstrations led by teachers and parents of Paris suburbs and other secondary schools around France continue to make headlines as the disrepair, danger and inadequacy of schools in disadvantaged suburbs remains problematic. The northeastern suburbs of Paris, as of a number of other major French metropolitan areas, are heavily populated by disadvantaged groups, including a very large proportion of immigrants of north African/Muslim origin. It is also the home of non-Muslim and non-Arab populations of Berber origin from Kabylie and a smaller number of Turkish origin, along with the full range of French of Mediterranean basin background.

Dissatisfaction turned to despair and then to violence has led a very small minority to join forces with what appear to be ways to express revolt and anger. It has been such young people who have turned to assisting the few "fundamentalists" or terrorist groups which have, in fact, carried out attacks in Europe. The response, however, by the French government has been framed as a security issue (as it has elsewhere, of course). The educational response to Islamic culture and Islamic ritual is still being sought by French people of Muslim and non-Muslim origin alike. It remains to be seen whether the extreme right wing (National Front and associates) will continue to gain votes in France or whether, as recent reactions in French politics have indicated there is still hope for the republican model. In the most recent regional elections, most conservative parties whose candidates won office with the votes of the extreme right wing were ordered to stand down and did so. A considerable effort of solidarity was required by the left wing (Socialists, Communists, Greens, etc.) to stand down and allow their votes to go to the conservative candidates to help a joint stand against the spread of neo-Fascism. Perhaps that is an optimistic sign. Another sign of optimism, again not directly related to the education of and with Islamic populations, but very relevant, was the seven-month trial of Maurice Papon, a high-level civil servant in the Vichy government, for complicity in crimes against humanity. This trial has been noteworthy for many reasons. Perhaps the one of greatest relevance to the discussion in this article is the notion of individual responsibility in the civil service. It has been demonstrated as a public civics lesson that it is not all right to say: "I was simply obeying orders" (*Le Monde* Supplement, March 1998).

In conclusion, a focus on France, schools and Islam in this article has raised issues of:

(1) religion as a private matter and the republican ideal of neutrality and secularity in the public sphere;
(2) equality as the same treatment for all;
(3) the nature of what constitutes legitimate knowledge; and above all,
(4) the clash of credibility of current institutions to hold the monopoly for resolving the major social issues of the end of the twentieth century.

It has only introduced these issues from a particular perspective. The search for solutions and more adequate analysis remains a critical priority.

NOTES

(Extracts from the Report on the General Organization of Public Instruction presented by Condorcet, Deputy from the Department of Paris, 20 and 21 April 1792 to the National Legislative Assembly. Quoted in Allaire and Frank (1995, pp. 25, 26). Author's translation.

1. Original French version of Condorcet's speech to the National Legislative Assembly of 21 April 1792:

    Offrir à tous les individus de l'espèce humaine les moyens de pourvoir à leurs besoins, d'assurer leur bien-être, de connaître et exercer leurs droits, d'entendre et de remplir leurs devoirs; assurer à chacun la facilité de perfectionner son industrie, de se rendre capable des fonctions sociales auxquelles il a le droit d'être appelé, de développer toute l'étendue des talents qu'il a reçus de la nature; et par là établir entre les citoyens une égalité de fait, et rendre réelle l'égalité politique reconnue par la loi: tel dois être le premier but d'une instruction nationale; et sous ce point de vue, elle est, pour la puissance publique, un devoir de justice . . .

    La première condition de toute instruction étant de n'enseigner que des vérités, les establissements que le puissance publique y consacre doivent être aussi indépendants qu'il est possible de toute autorisé politique . . . il résulte du mênte principe qu'il faut ne les rendre dépendants que de l'assemblée des représentants du people, parce que de tous les pouvoirs, il en est le moins corruptibles . . . il est dès lors le moins ennemi du progrès des lumières . . .

    Ainsi, l'instruction doit être universelle . . . Ells doit être répartie avec toute l'égalité que permettent les limites nécessaires des dépenses . . . Enfin, aucun pouvoir public ne doit avoir ni l'autorité, ni même le crédit, d'empcher le développment des vérités nouvelles, l'enseignement des théories contraires à as politique particulière ou à ses intèrêts momentanés . . .

2. When this article was originally written and again when it was revised, teachers, parents and pupils of one of the most disadvantaged *départements* of France, actually a northern suburb of Paris, the Seine-Saint-Denis, were on strike and demonstrating in the streets of Paris to denounce the conditions in their schools and community. In the autumn and winter of 1998 and 1999, many schools were closed in the Paris region and elsewhere in France while reachers went on strike over issues of their work conditions and terms of employment and the inadequacy of means for dealing with violence in and around schools. Secondary school pupils throughout France were on strike unilaterally in the autumn protesting against violence and lack of security in schools, oversized classes and lack of concern by teachers for their well being as individuals. Their demands, however, remain based on traditional requests for more teaching posts and financial resources to make school buildings safe, in good repair and well supplied with teaching/learning materials (books, etc.). Parents support teachers in their demands but do not question the objectives of what is done in the classroom or whether there might be other ways to approach teaching and learning. Many teachers and teachers' unions demand greater use of grade repetition to combat what they see as heterogeneous ability grouping and "school failure" by pupils. They do not see heterogeneous age groups as a problem in spite of considerable evidence to the contrary. They consistently refuse to question their own teaching practices and the lecture approach to lower and upper secondary schooling *(collège* and *lycée)*. See references to other newspaper articles in the reference section.

3. There is certainly no question of developing a module or unit on intercultural relations, human rights education, international understanding, etc, let alone a critical look at French history in terms of colonial practices, or most recently, the role of the Vichy government under German occupation (in spite of the widely covered trial of a high-level civil servant, Maurice Papon, for crimes against humanity in the deportation of Jews from the Bordeaux area). See *Le Monde* (Special Supplement, March 1998).

4. Original French version of citation: *"La laïcité, principle constitutionnel de la République, est un des fondements de l'école publique. A l'école comme ailleurs, les croyances religieuses de chacun sont affaire de conscience individuelle et relèvent done de la liberté. Mais à l'école ou se retrouvent tous les jeunes sans aucune discrimination, l'exercice de la liberté de consciences, dans le respect du pluralism et de la neutralité du service public, impose que l'ensemble de la communauté éducative vive à l'abri de toute pression idéologique ou religieuse." (Circulaire du 12 décembre 1989, signé par Monsieur le Ministre de l'Education, Lionel Jospin, cité en Allaire et Frank (1995, pp. 246–247).)*

REFERENCES

Allaire, M. and Frank, M. -T. (eds) (1995). *Les Politiques de l'éducation de la France de la Maternelle au Baccalauréat.* Paris, Collection: Retour aux textes. La documentation Française.

Allègre, C., Ministre de L'education (1998). Ce que je Veux. *Le Monde,* 6 February, pp. 1 & 14.

Baudelot, C. and Establet, R. (1989). *Le Niveau Monte. Réfutation d'une Vieille Idée Concernant la Prétendue Décadence de nos Écoles.* Paris: Editions du Seuil.

Blanchard, S. (1998a). Les Profs Jugent le Lycée. *Le Monde,* 6 March, pp. 1 & 13.

Blanchard, S. (1998b). Huitième Manifestation des Collèges et Lycées en Grève. *Le Monde,* 25 April, p. 8.

Bréchon, P. (ed.) (1994). *Le Discours Politique en France. Evolution des Idées Partisanes.* Paris: La Documentation Française.

Cesari, J. (1997a). *Etre Musulman en France Aujourd'hui.* Paris: Hachette.

Cesari, J. (1997b). *Faut-il Avoir Peur de l'Islam?* Paris: Presse de Sciences Po.

Charlot, M., Lauran, A. and Ben Dhiab, A. (1978). *Mon Avenir? Quel Avenir? Témoignages de Jeunes Immigrés* Paris: Casterman.

Citron, S. (1998). Et les Collèges, Monsieur Aliègre?, *Le Monde,* 18 February, p. 14.

Coquillat, M. and Sellier, G. (1998). Et les Filles?, *Le Monde,* 18 February, p. 14.

Debray, R. (1998). A Monsieur le Ministre de l'éducation. *Le Monde,* 3 March, pp. 1 & 14.

De Certeau, M. J. D. and Revel, J. (1975). *Une Politique de la Langue. La Rèvolution Française et les Patois.* Paris: Gallimard.

De Queiroz, J.-M. (1997). Ecole, Laïcité, Citoyenneté. *Cahiers français,* Numéro Spécial (May–June) Citoyenneté et Société pp. 58–63.

Etienne, B. (1989). *La France et l'islam.* Paris: Hachette.

Fernoglio, J. and Herzberg, N. (1998). La Seine-Saint-Denis Peine à Émerger, Après Trente Années d'abandon and Enquête sur la Seine-Saint-Denis, le Département le Plus Défavorisé. Chômage, Pauvreté, Insécurité etc.: un Concentré des Maux de la Société Française. *Le Monde,* 25 April, pp. 1,8,9.

Ferreol, G. (ed.) (1994). *Intégration & Exclusion dans la Société Française Contemporaine.* Lille: Presses Universitaires de Lille.

Furet, F. (1978). *Penser la Révolution Française.* Paris: Gallimard.

Geisser, V. (1997). *Ethnicité Républicaine, Les Élites d'origine Maghrébine dans le Système Politique Français.* Paris: Presse de Sciences Po.

Glenn, C. L. and Jong , E. J. (1996). *Educating Immigrant Children. Schools and language Minoritiés in Twelve Nations.* New York: Garland Publishing.

Granotier, B. (1970). *Les Travailleurs Immigrés en France.* Paris: Editions François Maspero.

Gruson, P. (1978). *L'Etat Enseignant.* Paris: Mouton/Ecole des hautes Etudes en Sciences Sociales.

Gurrey, B. (1997). Introuvable Éducation Civique. *Le Monde,* 2 December, pp. 1 & 20.

Gurrey, B. (1998). Ecoles Riches, Écoles Pauvres, les Écarts ne Cessent de S'aggraver, *Le Monde,* 12 February, p. 8.

Hamoumou, M. (1994). Les Harkis: Une Double Occultation: in G. Ferreol (ed.) *Intégration & Exclusion dans la Société Française Contemporaine.* Lille: Presses Universitaires de Lille, pp. 79–104.

Hervo, M. and Charras, M. A. (1971). *Bidonvilles.* Paris: Editions François Maspero.

Kastoryano, R. (1986). *Etre Ture en France. Rèflexions Sur Familles es Communauté.* Paris: CIEMI/L'Harmattan.

Kessler, D. and Bernard, P. (1997). Le Conseil d'Etat et le "Foulard Islamique", *Cahiers français,* Numéro Special (May–June) Citoyenneté et Société, pp. 63–64.

Le Monde (March 1998). Special Supplement. Condamné et Libre. La Cours d'assises de la Gironde a Condamné le 2 Avril 1998 Maurice Papon à Dix ans de Réclusion Criminielle Pour Complicité de Crimes Contre L'humanité.

Lequin, Y., Bauberot, J., Gauthier, G., Legrand, L. and Ognier, P. (1994). *Histoire de Laïcité.* Besancon Centre Régional de Documentation Pédagogique de Franche-Comté.

Limage, L. (1975). Alphabétisation et Culture. Cas d'études: L'Angleterre, le Brésil, la France et le Viet Nam. Unpublished doctoral dissertation, Paris.

Limage, L. (1979). *Education for Linguistic and Cultural Minorities. The Case of France. Study Prepared for the OECD-CERI Project on the Financing, Organization and Governance of Education for Special Populations.* Paris: OECD-CERI.

Limage, L. (1980). Illiteracy in Industrialized Countries. A Sociological Commentary. *Prospects,* XI, pp. 155–171.

Limage, L. (1981). *The Situation of Young Women Migrants of the Second Generation in Western Europe. Working paper prepared for the UNDP/ILO European Regional Project for Second Generation Migrants.* Geneva: ILO.

Limage, L. (1984). Young Migrants of the Second Generation in Europe: Education and Labor Market Insertion Prospects. *International Migration,* XXII, pp. 367–387.

Limage, L. (1985). Policy Aspects of Educational Provision for Children of Migrants in Western European Schools. *International Migration,* XXIII, pp. 251–261.

Limage, L. (1986). Adult Illiteracy Policy in Industrialized Countries, *Comparative Education Review,* 30, pp. 50–72.

Limage, L. (1990). Illiteracy in Industrialized Countries. On Myth and Misunderstanding. *Literacy Lesson,* Geneva: International Bureau of Education.

Minces, J. (1973). *Les Travailleurs Étrangers an France.* Paris: Editions Seuil.

OECD-CERI (1983). *The Education of Minority Groups. An Enquiry into Problems and Practices of Fifteen Countries.* Paris: OECD.

Ozouf, M. (1984). *L'école de la France. Essais sur la Révolution, L'utopie et L'enseignement.* Paris: Gallimard.

Robert, A. (1995). *Le Syndicalisme des Enseignants. Series: Systèmes Educatifs.* Paris: La documentation Française.

Roux, J.-P. Secrétaire Général de la Fédération de L'éducation Nationale (1998). Ce Que is Démocratie Exige de L'école. *Le Monde*, 11 February, p.13.

Stasse, F. (1997). Egalité et Discriminations Positives. *Regards sur l'actualité*, (232), June, pp. 19–25.

Vuaillet, M. Secrétaire Général du Snes, and Paget, D., Secrétaire Général, Adjoint du Snes (1998). Ecole: Sortir des Idées Reçures. *Le Monde*, 25 February, pp. 14 & 15.

Withol de Wenden, C. (1988). *La Citoyenneté*. Paris: Edilig/Fondation Diderot.

CHAPTER 7

The State, Adult Literacy Policy and Inequality in Botswana

Frank Youngman

Adult literacy programs in the Third World are widely regarded as promoting equality by extending educational opportunity to sections of the population who have failed to benefit from school education. However, the question of adult literacy in the capitalist countries of the Third World needs to be reconsidered in the context of the relationship of the state to the inequalities in the wider society. In this chapter I suggest that literacy programs tend to reproduce class, ethnic and gender inequalities and serve to legitimate the unequal social order, which the state seeks to uphold. Although the organizations of civil society, such as trade unions, church groups, peasant associations and community projects, often run literacy activities (some of which counter the hegemony of the state, such as the "popular education" movements in Latin America), most of their work remains on a small scale. In the Third World it is the literacy programs sponsored and controlled by the state which reach most adults. Analysis of such programs must therefore be based on a theory of the state and education.

The work of writers such as Apple (1982) and Carnoy and Levin (1985) has helped to clarify the relationship between the state and education from the position of critical theory, and recently Torres (1990) has extended this analysis to adult education. In essence, it is argued that in the class society characteristic of capitalism, the dominant classes exert control over state institutions so that the state's activities such as legislation, public investment and social policies serve to promote the conditions necessary for maintaining capitalist accumulation and the political power of these classes. However, it is emphasized that this control does not go uncontested and the subordinate classes often exert pressure in their own interests so that the activities of the state become an area of conflict. For example, at times when the working class is strong, it may succeed in getting favorable trade union legislation and social welfare measures passed, or if the alliance of dominant classes requires peasant support, land reforms may be enacted. Thus the contradictions between the classes in society are reflected in the state, and its activities will tend towards the management of these conflicts in order to preserve the capitalist social order, by consent if possible, by coercion if necessary.

Education, as an institution of the state, shares this dual character. To a large extent, public education serves to reproduce the division of labor and the disparities of power within society (between classes, sexes, races and ethnic groups) and to generate ways of thinking which legitimate the existing social order. Also, given that the capitalist state is controlled by dominant classes within society, education helps to meet the state's own needs to mobilize consensus and to be regarded as legitimate by the population as a whole (Welch, 1991). But the provision and expansion of education also represent possibilities of social mobility and political democratization, and education can provide people with knowledge and skills that will enable them to question the patterns of domination in society.

In the capitalist countries of the Third World, the state has specific characteristics resulting from historical developments which have been explored by writers such as Alavi (1972, 1982) and Thomas (1984) in considering the "postcolonial state" and the state under "peripheral capitalism." Two relevant characteristics can be mentioned here. First, the state "directly appropriates a very large part of the economic surplus and deploys it in bureaucratically directed economic activity in the name of promoting economic development" (Alavi, 1972, 42). Thus the state tends towards a relatively high degree of intervention, an interventionism justified by ideologies of "development." Second, there is extensive external involvement in the production systems of these countries, and international capital exerts significant influence on the activities of the state through a variety of means, varying from the use of aid to shape domestic policies to the physical presence of expatriates in the state bureaucracies. Thus educational policy in the Third World is articulated within the discourse of its role in "development" and educational activities are massively influenced by external factors.

The approach to the state and education outlined above assumes that in capitalist society there are different classes with different interests. Based on this assumption, the state is viewed not as a neutral body promoting the "common good" of all citizens, but as a structure through which the dominant classes try to maintain the mode of production and their position in society, often in the face of resistance by the subordinated classes. The educational activities of the state, such as adult literacy programs, therefore have a class character. It is within this framework that I present in this chapter a critical perspective on the state, adult literacy policy, and inequality in Botswana, focussing particularly on the first ten years of the National Literacy Program (1980–1989).

THE POLITICAL AND ECONOMIC CONTEXT*

When Botswana became independent from Britain in 1966 it had few apparent resources and was reliant on Britain for grants to cover even its recurrent governmental budget. It was classified as one of the world's twenty-five poorest countries. However, after the discovery of diamonds in the late 1960s the country experienced a long period of uninterrupted economic growth and its annual performance of 11.4 percent growth in the 1980s was exceeded only by Oman. By the end of the 1980s it was categorized by the World Bank (1990) as a "middle-income oil importer" and it was one of the few countries in Africa that had avoided the crisis of economic stagnation and decline. Its economic growth was based mainly on the export of diamonds, but also on exports of beef. Diamond revenues provided capital accumulation for use by the state, while the cattle industry provided possibilities for individual accumulation. Since independence, the capitalist mode of production has become dominant within the social formation of Botswana.

The ruling bloc of dominant classes (namely, the bourgeoisie, petty bourgeoisie and rich peasantry) improved its own situation significantly in this situation of economic expansion. It used its control of the state to pursue policies which advanced its economic interests, following a development strategy which used state intervention to provide the conditions for private enterprise and foreign investment (Ministry of Finance and Development Planning, 1985, 2). But the ruling bloc also used the available surplus to maintain the standard of living of other classes, in particular the working class in the formal sector, for whom there was a minimum wage and protection from inflation through regular increases. Of course, not all classes benefited equally from the growth in GNP and the situation of the poor peasants in the rural areas and of the unskilled urban workers deteriorated, so that a government document in 1985 concluded, "It is clear that the majority of Botswana's households are poor" (Ministry of Finance and Development Planning, 1985). However, revenues accruing to the state were used to provide social services on a large scale, for example, in the health and education sectors. In particular, the growing immiseration of the rural poor during the drought of 1981 to 1987 was ameliorated by the provision of a safety-net of drought relief and feeding programs which covered more than half the population (Ministry of Finance and Development Planning, 1985). This welfare dimension of the development strategy served to reduce possible social tensions. The main potential area of tension arose from the slow rate of employment creation in the formal sector (the mining industry, for example, is very capital intensive) which led to high levels of unemployment, especially among school-leavers. This problem was exacerbated by the steady decline in the numbers of labor migrants to South Africa.

The ruling bloc sustained its hegemony after 1966 because economic expansion enabled it not only to meet its own class interests but also to main-

*This section is based on Gaborone, Mutanyatta and Youngman 1988, 359–60.

tain the standard of living of other classes. It promulgated an ideology of "social harmony," and class conflict was muted, allowing political stability and the continuance of a pluralist parliamentary system in which, however, the same party held power from 1966. The bloc saw an identity of its own domestic interests in a capitalist social order with those of international capital, and within the geopolitics of Southern Africa Botswana acquired significance to the West as a model of a capitalist, nonracial democracy, attracting high levels of foreign aid as well as investment.

To summarize, it can be said that from 1966 the state acted in the interests of those local and foreign classes which stood to gain from the expansion of the capitalist system of production within Botswana. However, the state claimed legitimation from the population as a whole formally through regular elections and informally through social programs which took into account the welfare of the peasantry and working class. The resources made available to the state by rapid economic growth enabled it to undertake a variety of legitimation strategies. Thus the essential contradictions inherent in the increasingly class-divided society were ameliorated and a substantial degree of consent to the economic and political order was secured. It is within this context that policies on adult literacy were developed.

THE DEVELOPMENT OF LITERACY POLICY

Adult literacy activities in Botswana since Independence have been dominated by the government and therefore it is appropriate to analyze the development of literacy policy within a framework which focusses on the state and public policy formation (Torres, 1990). In general terms, as noted above, state intervention in Botswana's political economy since 1966 can be viewed as having been directed towards promoting the conditions for capitalist expansion and also to legitimating the accompanying class relations and social order. In particular, since the mid-1970s the development strategy has been based on mineral-led economic growth, with the mineral revenues being used by the state to create a modern capitalist economy and to improve rural welfare (Parson, 1984). The key documents which have presented government policy, in the context of a macro-economic analysis, an articulation of objectives and priorities, and a specification of projects, are the *National Development Plans* produced by the Ministry of Finance and Development Planning at approximately five-year intervals.

The formation of policy on adult literacy has had a number of different dimensions. There have been the technical and political arguments put forward by civil servants in the bureaucracy and by government politicians. The basis of these arguments has largely been shaped by the "modernization" theory of development, with literacy being viewed as an instrument for the development of a "modern" society and improved productivity. Policy has seldom been a response to expressed demands from the clientele for literacy, but indirectly the significance of the rural population as the basis of the ruling alliance's political support has had weight. Economic determinants have had great significance, particularly with the enormous increase in government resources that became available in the late 1970s (Parson, 1984). Finally, an important set of influences, as for most Third World countries, has been foreign donors and organizations, and developments in international policy debates.

When Botswana became independent in 1966, approximately 75 percent of the adult population of 543,000 was illiterate (Kann and Taylor, 1988). However, the legacy of colonial neglect in formal education was so extreme (for example, only four secondary schools offered grade 12) that the dominant concern of educational policy was the expansion of secondary and tertiary education to meet the demands for "skilled manpower" of the public service and the formal sector. The portfolio responsibility for literacy within the government structure lay with the Department of Community Development, but it gave priority to self-help projects for rural construction and, as evidenced in *National Development Plan, 1970–1975* (Ministry of Finance and Development Planning, 1970), it regarded literacy as a small-scale activity undertaken by community groups to whom the department would simply supply materials and training assistance.

In 1972, a UNESCO consultant proposed a national work-oriented literacy program to reach a quarter of a million people in an eight-year period, using the extension staff of various ministries (Brooks, 1972). The government rejected the proposal for a variety of reasons. The mass campaign approach was regarded as too ambitious and too demanding of existing extension services. Influential (expatriate) civil servants held negative views of literacy work based on their experience working elsewhere in Africa in the 1960s, in countries such as Kenya. Also there was a change of personnel in the local United Nations Development Program (UNDP) office which had sponsored the consultancy. Above all, adult literacy lacked priority at a time when government resources were scarce (1972–1973 was the first year in which the recurrent budget was balanced without British grants). This low priority was reflected in the *National Development Plan, 1973–78* (Ministry of Finance and Development Planning, 1973), which only expressed the intention of examining the feasibility of functional literacy programs on a local and national scale.

Thus in the first decade after independence there was no policy commitment by the government to dealing with the problem of adult illiteracy. The only literacy activities were small-scale programs undertaken by nongovernment bodies such as the University of Botswana, Lesotho, and Swaziland and the Botswana Christian Council. A number of reasons can be advanced for the lack of priority given to adult literacy. These include the preoccupation of educational planners with secondary and tertiary education and the skepticism noted above of civil servants concerned with rural development about the value of literacy, which was reinforced by the failures of UNESCO's Experimental World Literacy Program, 1965–1975 (UNESCO and UNDP, 1976). It can also be postulated that from the perspective of the dominant classes mass adult literacy lacked utility both to the model of economic development followed in the early 1970s and to strategies of hegemony in a period of political quiescence.

In 1975, the government initiated a major review of the education sector, establishing a National Commission on Education which reported in 1977 in a document entitled *Education for Kagisano*. The commission derived its goals for educational development from the government's stated national objectives of democracy, development, self-reliance, and unity, which are synthesized in the "national" philosophy of *Kagisano* (which means *social harmony*). In fact, the notion of "national" values is an ideological one, suggesting interests which transcend the divisions within society, and this is reinforced by the concept of "social harmony," which promotes the idea that there is consensus rather than contradiction between the different classes and other groups in society. *Kagisano* provided a Setswana concept which is consistent with functionalist sociology. This paradigm in sociology (Welch, 1985; Alavi, 1982) views society as a stable, well-integrated system in which there is a value consensus, such that all members of the society agree on its value system, and the functionalist conception of social development as a unilinear evolutionary process provided the basis for the "modernization" theory of development which prevailed in Botswana's development planning. Within this theoretical framework, education has a significant role in promoting the value system, including the attitudes and values required to develop a "modern" society. The commission's report, by emphasizing *Kagisano*, gave powerful support to the dominant ideology.

The commission conceived out-of-school education, like school education, as furthering *Kagisano* and stated, "It may be expected to contribute to the individual's development and to the promotion of social welfare" (National Education Commission, 1977). The commission identified literacy as a priority for out-of-school education:

> A fully literate population is an important long-term objective if Botswana's other national objectives are to be met. We do not emphasize literacy as a separate program, because experience in other countries indicates that literacy should not be pursued in isolation from other development programs as an end in itself. It is best acquired in the context of efforts to achieve greater productivity, health or control over one's environment; and indeed it will itself contribute to achievement of these objectives. (National Education Commission, 1977)

The report gave literacy high priority within out-of-school programs but its concept, as indicated in the above quotation, was vague. The commission seemed to argue against a literacy program "as an end in itself" and for some form of functional literacy activities provided in the context of other programs, such as agricultural extension or health education. Although it appeared to give adult literacy great significance, its rationale was general and it made no operational proposals—indeed, literacy was not included in the extensive list of specific recommendations at the end of the report.

It is therefore not surprising that the government paper, *National Policy on Education,* which was the government's response to the commission's recommendations, simply stated, "Consideration will be given to literacy programs" (Republic of Botswana, 1977). Senior civil servants and politicians remained lukewarm towards adult literacy programs, although a group of (mainly expatriate) professionals within the adult education section of the Ministry of Education ran two pilot projects in 1977 and 1978, explicitly to influence policy and demonstrate possible approaches (Botswana Extension College, 1977).

In 1978, the Ministry of Education implemented one of the commission's recommendations and established a Department of Non Formal Education. It appointed as Chief Education Officer an expatriate who was a UNESCO expert with a background in adult literacy. He proposed a national approach to the eradication of illiteracy led by the Ministry of Education and he succeeded in convincing influential civil servants (especially in the Ministry of Finance and Development Planning) and the Minister of Education (Townsend Coles, 1988). At a speech to a planning meeting to consider the proposal held in early 1979, the Minister referred to the international context of rising illiteracy rates and the World Bank's linkage between illiteracy and other development problems, such as malnutrition and poor living conditions. In respect to Botswana, he articulated the reason for concern with literacy in these terms:

> For the great majority of people, if life in modern society is to be lived to the full, they must be released from the bondage of illiteracy if they are to make their best contribution to their families, their communities and their nation. For them basic literacy, with which numeracy is involved, is an essential requirement. If the lot of ordinary people is to be improved, and the quality of their lives raised, then they must be given the chance of learning to read and write. For these are two of the skills needed to help them play their full part in national development. (Morake, 1979)

The rationale for eradicating illiteracy was therefore made in terms of the modernization of society, extended educational opportunity and the individual's contribution to the nation's development objectives, such as democracy and self-reliance.

The operational strategy for the proposed program was subsequently presented in September 1979 in an important document entitled *The Eradication of Illiteracy in Botswana: A National Initiative: Consultation Document.* The objective of the program was very briefly stated despite the fact that this was a document seeking support from politicians and civil servants for a major new policy:

> To enable 250,000 presently illiterate men, women and youths to become literate in Setswana and numerate over the six years 1980–1985. The teaching shall be undertaken in the context of development issues of relevance to the participants and concern to the respective Districts and the nation. The term "literate" shall be interpreted to imply that a person can comprehend those

written communications and simple computations which are a part of daily life (Ministry of Education, 1979).

The objective contained an ambitious target of approximately 40 percent of the population over ten years old (Kann and Taylor, 1988) and a limited time frame, so that the proposal was actually similar in scope to the one made by the UNESCO consultant in 1972. The document specifically avoided the concept of a "campaign," which had connotations of literacy work in socialist countries (Townsend Coles, 1988). It located literacy content in the context of development topics but avoided linking literacy acquisition to other skills because of the lack of success of UNESCO's Experimental World Literacy Program, which had promoted "functional literacy" as a means to training in productive skills (Jones, 1988). It therefore took the opposite view to the one suggested by the National commission on Education. Furthermore, the conception of literacy was very narrowly defined and consciously avoided the politicized, Freirean conception which had gained prominence in the mid-1970s, for example, in the Declaration of the International Symposium for Literacy in 1975 (Bataille, 1976).

The document laid the basis for what became the National Literacy Program, which has been the largest sustained program in any area of adult education in Botswana since independence. It began with a pilot program in 1980, and in mid-1981 it was officially launched as a nationwide program by the Minister of Education, who once again stressed its modernizing purpose: "If a person is to be able to make their fullest contribution to the modern society we are building here, the ability to read and write are essential skills" (Morake, 1981).

The adoption of a nationwide, large-scale literacy program at the end of the 1970s marks a major policy development (and contrasts with the rejection of a similar program proposal in 1972). There are a number of microlevel factors, including a persuasive and experienced advocate in a key position as Chief Education Officer, more sympathetic (expatriate) educational planners, receptive donor agencies such as the Swedish International Development Agency (SIDA), and the social demand revealed by the 1977 and 1978 pilot projects. But the more important determinants were the changes in the political economy that had taken place during the 1970s. These changes have been well documented by Parson (1984), who shows the transformations which took place in the economy and the associated processes of class "formation," with widening opportunities for wage labor and an expansion of the petite bourgeoisie. The political consequence was that the "class divisions generated during the period of growth began to require much more direct management than formerly" (Parson, 1984). The state had expanded resources for addressing this problem: "Botswana's increased ability to generate external aid combined with the country's increased diamonds and customs revenue led to a dramatic increase in available resources" (1984, 81). It can be argued that the provision of social programs, such as the National Literacy Program, was now necessary for the "management" of problems implicit in the increased class divisions, while it was also made possible through the state's access to greater resources. The modernization paradigm now underpinning the state's development strategy also provided the ideological basis for the literacy initiative.

Despite its comparatively large scale, the National Literacy Program was unable to reach its original goal of making 250,000 people literate by 1985. Thus its continuation was included in the *National Development Plan, 1985–1991*. The goal of literacy was restated—"A literate population is essential for the successful implementation of the country's ambitious development program" (Ministry of Finance and Development Planning, 1985)—and a new strategy was proposed with stronger linkages to primary education for young literacy graduates and with a program of basic education and skills training for income-generating activities for older graduates. This role for literacy was articulated within the wider objectives of nonformal education policy, namely, "to increase educational opportunities and to reduce inequalities in access to education" (Ministry of Finance and Development Planning, 1985). The equity dimension of this policy reflected, among other things, the influence of Swedish aid to the education sector and to the National Literacy Program in particular, while the new emphasis on integrating nonformal and formal education reflected international thinking in bodies such as UNESCO (Jones, 1988). It marked the beginning of a shift in the discourse about literacy to a broader concern with access to basic education.

This became clear during 1989 and 1990 when policy statements on literacy were framed within the context of the World Conference on Education for All. These statements argued that Botswana's commitment to universal junior secondary education (to grade 9) in conjunction with the National Literacy Program constituted an existing Education for All policy and program (Republic of Botswana, 1989). Increasingly, literacy was being conceptualized as part of a comprehensive provision of "basic education" within formal and nonformal education, and emphasis shifted to the postliteracy component, as indicated in the Ministry of Education's draft chapter for the *National Development Plan, 1991–1997*:

> A strategy will be developed . . . that will encompass both literacy and post-literacy activities as a continuum with the main focus on the post-literacy component. Emphasis will be on systematic organization of learning and action programs geared towards the social, cultural and occupational needs and interests of the newly literate. (1990, 47)

It is likely that future policy development will continue to be influenced by international activity related to the concepts of basic education for all and equity through expanded opportunities.

IMPLEMENTATION OF THE NATIONAL LITERACY PROGRAM

The policy decision taken in 1979 to undertake a national approach to the eradication of illiteracy was implemented during the 1980s through the

National Literacy Program (NLP) run by the Department of Non Formal Education (DNFE). Just as the process of policy formation described above involved the interplay of different interests, so the process of implementation has involved continued contradictions, particularly over the nature and resourcing of the program.

The NLP began with an experimental year in five districts in 1980 and moved to national coverage in 1981. It was initially conceived as finite and it was envisaged that it would end in 1986. It was considered as a "development project" rather than an item of recurrent government expenditure, and funding was sought primarily from foreign donors. Expatriate planning personnel in the government had close links with donor agencies and secured commitments from two German government organizations (the German Agency for Technical Cooperation—GTZ—and Credit for Reconstruction), the Swedish and Dutch governments, and UNICEF. The use of donor funds was normal for development expenditure (Parson [1984, 74] notes that 60 percent of development expenditure in 1980–1981 was from external sources) but this dependence certainly had an impact on the program. For example, the agreement with the German Agency for Technical Cooperation enabled the appointment from 1982 to 1985 of a German as the literacy coordinator, one of the main program managers in DNFE.

The operational and pedagogical system of the NLP which was established in 1980 remained substantially unchanged during the first ten years of the program. The country's nine districts were the main unit of administration, with a District Adult Education Officer who was a member of DNFE in charge of the program. Each district was divided into areas in which a cluster of ten to twenty literacy groups was supervised by a Literacy Assistant, who was a full-time (though temporary) member of DNFE's staff with a minimum of grade 10 schooling. The literacy groups themselves, consisting of approximately fifteen learners, were taught by a Literacy Group Leader. These leaders normally had grade 7 schooling and taught two or three groups. Their work was conceived not as "a salaried appointment, but rather a part-time act of service to the community, for which a small token honorarium is paid" (Townsend Coles, 1988). The groups met for an hour or two up to five times a week and undertook a free program of study based on five primers in Setswana. Reading was taught through the analytic method based on key words, many of which were related to topics on health, agriculture and other development issues. The key words provided the basis for a syllabic approach to learning how to construct words and sentences. Additional reading material was provided through a monthly broadsheet, and regular broadcasts on the government-controlled radio provided a radio magazine for all involved. An annual cycle of events was established involving the recruitment of Literacy Group Leaders and learners, staff training, materials production and distribution, group instruction and supervision, and reports to the National Literacy Committee.

The scope of the program during the 1980s is indicated in Table I. The interpretation of this data in Table I in terms of the NLP's coverage is problematical because the statistics on participants only indicate enrolments and

Table I: Data on the National Literacy Program, 1980-1989

	1980	1981	1982	1983	1984	1985	1986	1987	1988	1989
Participants	7976	23630	18779	27935	36068	38660	35354	20999	26200	33226
Literacy Groups	696	1779	—	2942	2945	1901	2403	1509	2038	2996
Literacy Group Leaders	—	1427	1188	1559	1633	1480	1221	907	1136	1466
Literacy Assistants	28	105	104	133	133	134	137	143	144	133

Source: Department of Non Formal Education (1990) *Annual Report on the National Literacy Program: 1989.* (Gaborone: Department of Non Formal Education, p. 9.)

it is not possible to differentiate new enrolments from existing cumulative enrolments (Gaborone, Mutanyatta, and Youngman, 1987). However, one estimate based on extrapolation from the sample of learners tested in 1986 suggested that there were 70,000 new learners between 1980 and 1986 (Gaborone, Mutanyatta, and Youngman, 1988). It is also not possible to calculate the success rate, that is, the number of learners who can be defined as having become literate in terms of successful completion of the primers. An informed estimate by Kann and Taylor (1988) is that the literacy rate of the population aged fifteen and over had increased from 54 percent in 1981 to between 61 and 65 percent in 1987.

Although the overall system changed very little during the 1980s, there were developments relating to the nature and funding of the program. In 1983 an internal evaluation was undertaken. This evaluation exercise (Ministry of Education, 1984) led to some incremental changes within the NLP's operation. In response to pressure from learners, it also focussed attention on the need for postliteracy activities and emphasized the demand for follow-up reading materials and access to skills training for income generation, which it called the "functional component." But above all the report crystallized the view that the program should be institutionalized as a regular activity of DNFE and a recurrent item of expenditure, with the Literacy Assistants becoming a permanent cadre of "Extension Educators" with wider responsibilities for adult learning.

It was clear by 1985 that the initial numerical target of the NLP would not be reached and the Ministry of Education decided to include the continuation of the program in the forthcoming development plan, for the period 1985–1991. This decision raised issues about the future direction and funding of the program. These questions were also being raised by the two main donors. GTZ expressed dissatisfaction with the program's management, its inability to reach its objectives, and its lack of forward planning, and in early 1986 the agency made future funding conditional on an evaluation and a management consultancy. The Swedish International Development Agency in its annual review at the end of 1985 also indicated that it would like to see improvements to the program and a greater proportion of the costs coming from the Ministry of Education's recurrent budget.

The National Literacy Committee therefore commissioned an evaluation by the University of Botswana, which senior officials in the Ministry of Education viewed as a means for securing continued donor funding and for gaining internal support (particularly in the Ministry of Finance and Development Planning) for a transition to an institutionalized program. Ministry of Education officials acknowledged that the lack of committed domestic resources indicated a relatively low priority and argued that although politicians saw benefits from the NLP, the public perception of the program was that it was less significant than, say, the need to expand junior secondary schooling (Youngman, 1987). From the perspective of these officials, the main purpose of the evaluation was accountability and policy justification, while its potential to assist in program improvement was secondary.

The evaluation report submitted in March 1987 provided a comprehensive analysis of the NLP (Gaborone, Mutanyatta, and Youngman, 1987). The findings in the report were generally positive. In particular, the results of a literacy and numeracy test administered to a national sample of NLP learners revealed a remarkable level of performance, with 81 percent scoring the equivalent of passing the grade 4 attainment test in the schools. Additionally, by making a series of detailed recommendations, the report suggested that improving the program was a manageable task in technical terms. The report's overall effect on the donors was positive, and it strengthened the arguments for a transition to a permanent program going beyond literacy to a comprehensive provision of adult basic education.

The NLP in practice has been an adult-education program which is large scale within the context of Botswana. It has remained a low-key operation without high-level political commitment. For example, the launching in 1981 was done by the Minister of Education rather than the President—and without popular mobilization. It has not met its original target of eradicating illiteracy although it has reached a significant number of adults, and it has promoted very few postliteracy activities. However, because it has had the political advantages of providing a social service to rural adults during a period of long-term drought and the collapse of the rural economy, and because in a period of resource availability it has not competed with other programs, the NLP has been sustained by the state and donor agencies for a decade at a similar level of operation and resource allocation.

LANGUAGE POLICY AND PRACTICE WITHIN THE NLP

An important aspect of adult literacy policy is the choice of the language of instruction. Decisions on language reflect wider conceptions and ideologies about the nature and purposes of literacy and have an impact on its equity potential. Because the NLP was run by the Ministry of Education, the issue of language was influenced by national language policies. The government's language policy since Independence has been that English is the "official language" (of Parliament and government administration) while Setswana, the language of the politically dominant and most numerous ethnic group, is the "national language." Thus English and Setswana are used in the education system (the transition to English as the medium of instruction takes place in grade 5) and in the state-controlled radio and newspaper. The use in formal political, administrative, or educational situations of the mother tongue of minority-language speakers is discouraged by the state although these speakers comprise at least 20 percent of the population. For example, minority languages may not be spoken on the state radio and language-related questions may not be included in the national census data (Nyati, 1989). A number of the minority languages (especially in the remote western areas of the country) are not written languages and even in Setswana there is a relative lack of written materials apart from school textbooks and bureaucratic documents.

The reasons given for discouraging the formal use of minority languages are that a single national language is a force for national unity against "tribalism" and that the costs of producing materials are prohibitive.

During the planning of the NLP in 1979 there was discussion on the language or languages to be used. It was recognized that choices had to be made in relation to minority languages, Setswana, and English. The professionals involved favored the use of mother-tongue instruction on pedagogical grounds and also thought that consideration should be given to the use of English, especially in urban areas. However, as the Chief Education Officer of the time records, the decision was taken to provide literacy in Setswana:

> It was at this juncture that political rather than educational or functional considerations carried most weight. To achieve national unity, there had to be the submergence of local, tribal, languages; this was the practice in formal education and this example had likewise to be followed in non-formal education despite the fact that this seemed likely to decrease the motivation of some of the potential learners. (Townsend Coles, 1988)

The effects of implementing the Setswana language policy for minority-language speakers have been documented in a number of reports. A progress report on the NLP in mid-1982 drew attention to the problems of teaching Setswana literacy to non-Setswana-speaking groups and recommended that Literacy Group Leaders be given skills in teaching Setswana as a second language (Department of Non Formal Education, 1982). DNFE subsequently encouraged the leaders to use translation in the classroom as an aid to learning, but no minority language materials were produced. The 1984 evaluation report included interview data from non-Setswana speakers who were still in literacy groups and those who had dropped out. The data suggested that the problem of having to learn another language created difficulties when also having to learn how to read and write. For example, 50 percent of the drop-outs stated their reasons for leaving related to language. However, the study concluded "The majority of non-Setswana learners actually want to learn Setswana. For many this is the rationale for joining the Literacy Program" (Ministry of Education, 1984). The results of the literacy test recorded in the 1987 evaluation report suggested that for those who manage to remain in the program and do not drop out, there is very little variation in performance between Setswana speakers and those whose mother tongue is not Setswana (Gaborone, Mutanyatta, and Youngman, 1987). There is little evidence of wide-scale pressure from learners to alter the policy of Setswana as the medium of instruction and it seems that for some minority-language groups learning literacy in Setswana is perceived as giving them increased access to the dominant language, thus extending their possibilities for participation in society and the economy.

The issue of access to the English language has been very different because, from the beginning of the NLP, learners have requested English tuition. The field staff of DNFE reported in 1981 and 1982 that the new literates wished to learn English, and learners' letters to the literacy broadsheet reinforced this. A study by a foreign consultant was commissioned in 1982 on the feasibility of a course in English as a second language for new literates. The study confirmed that learners saw English as significant, especially in relation to employment, quoting a group of learners as follows:

> They said they want to learn English because English is the important language in the whole world. They say they can't get better work in towns if you don't know how to speak English. (Alley, 1982).

The consultant concluded a special course in English was desirable and feasible and produced some materials. However, DNFE's response to the consultant's proposals was slow and although a draft English primer was produced in 1985, it was only used unofficially by a few interested Literacy Group Leaders. Policy statements in 1985 in *National Development Plan, 1985–91* and in 1986 in DNFE documents referred to a nonformal course in English as part of the postliteracy strategy, but in practice nothing was implemented. The survey of literacy learners recorded in the 1987 evaluation report found that two-thirds of the respondents wanted to learn English. The major reasons given for wanting to learn English were "to communicate" (54.4 percent) and "to get employment" (28.5 percent) (Gaborone, Mutanyatta, and Youngman, 1987). However, no large-scale English Language tuition was carried out.

The demand for English articulated by the learners represents their realistic perception of its significance as a language for opening up economic opportunities and for giving access to a wider sphere of social, educational, and political participation. This expression of demand was able to influence the policy of the NLP, which from 1985 has had a specific commitment to providing English in the postliteracy phase. However, the pressure from learners was not strong enough to lead to policy implementation. The blockages to the introduction of the English course may be partly attributed to the inherent problems of implementation, such as finding teachers with appropriate language competence. But it can also be postulated that the lack of priority given to introducing English reflects differing conceptions of the purposes of the NLP. For the majority of learners (three-quarters of the respondents to the questionnaire recorded in the 1987 evaluation report), the main reason for joining the NLP was to get employment. Access to English would obviously enhance that possibility. From the viewpoint of the government, although development plans since 1979 stressed employment creation, the expansion of formal-sector jobs could not take place on a scale which could absorb all literacy graduates. Hence while literacy policy was articulated in vague terms of "modernizing" society, its implementation focussed narrowly on reading and writing in Setswana as an end in itself, with some postliteracy assistance to the establishment of income-generating groups. A large-scale demand for employment would have exacerbated problems already being experienced by the pressure from secondary school-leavers.

The demand for English thus exposed an inherent contradiction in the literacy policy, insofar as widespread adult literacy would have raised expectations of further economic participation which could not have been met. The existence of the NLP helped politically to legitimate the state by demonstrating its concern to provide services to the rural and urban poor. But its extension beyond a minimum level would have been dysfunctional in terms of the nature of the economy and the existing labor market: hence the very limited commitment to the NLP in general, and the lack of urgency given to the particular issue of teaching English.

THE NATIONAL LITERACY PROGRAM AND THE SOCIAL ORDER

The central question here is the extent to which the NLP during the 1980s served to reproduce the existing patterns of inequality in society, thereby reinforcing and legitimating the inequitable social order characteristic of capitalism. The major determinant of the structure of social inequality is arguably that of production, with differences in access to and control over productive resources providing the basis of class divisions. But the disparities derived from the system of production intersect with and reinforce other divisions within society, such as those of ethnicity and gender. The role of the NLP in reproducing these disparities within the social order is underresearched, but it is possible to consider the outcomes of participation in relation to class, ethnicity and gender.

The period since independence has seen the expansion of the capitalist mode of production within Botswana's social formation. The rapid economic growth that has taken place has been accompanied by growing inequalities in the distribution of wealth and income and by persistent poverty. The processes of class formation have created the class structure typical of capitalist societies in the Third World. There is as yet a very small class of indigenous large capitalists but the petite bourgeoisie has become increasingly strong, using its role in the management of the state to consolidate its class position. Formal-sector employment has expanded and there is a growing working class whose income is derived solely from wage income. An important group remains which is partly dependent on wage labor but which retains involvement in agricultural production, including the migrant mine workers (a group called by Parson, 1984, the "peasantariat" to suggest their dual location). The peasantry, engaged primarily in agricultural production within the household, is internally stratified, with both a proportion of rich and middle peasants and a mass of poor peasants, the last group owning few means of production and often having to work for others. The rural class structure also includes capitalist farmers and rural wage laborers, as well as an underclass of the unemployed and underemployed. There is thus a clear class hierarchy of dominant and subordinate classes, and this is the class context in which the NLP takes place.

There is very little reliable data on the class composition of the NLP participants. The 1984 evaluation report recorded the following information on the occupational background of learners in 1983 (Table II):

Table II: Data on the Occupational Background of Sampled Learners, 1983

Housewives	36%
Farmers	21%
Herdsmen	12%
Maids	9%
Drought Relief Program Participants	5%
Others (mostly skilled workers)	17%

Source: Ministry of Education (1984) *How Can We Succeed?* (n.p.: Department of Non-Formal Education.)

The categories are obviously imprecise, as "farmers" gives no idea of location within the stratified peasantry and "housewife" gives no evidence of class position. However, it can be deduced from observational evidence and other information on Botswana's social structure that the majority of participants came from the poor peasantry in the rural areas, while in the urban areas unskilled workers and the unemployed predominated. This is substantiated by the perception of most learners that the NLP would help them enter into wage labor in the formal sector—the 1987 evaluation report records three-quarters of the learners questioned giving employment as their main reason for joining the NLP (Gaborone, Mutanyatta, and Youngman, 1987). The aspiration of most learners was probably to enter into the working class, with few envisaging a process of greater social mobility. Given the advantages of membership of this class in the period of prolonged economic growth (particularly in relation to the poor peasantry during the drought of the 1980s), this represented a reasonable aspiration, even though the working class was subordinate within the overall class structure. However, although the NLP might have raised this expectation, it did not itself provide employable productive skills, and the restricted growth of the formal sector, coupled with competition from school-leavers, meant the objective likelihood of paid employment for literacy graduates was small. Participants were aware of this: "When we see literacy graduates roaming the streets without a job to do . . . one wonders if one has made the right choice in joining the NLP" (Gaborone, Mutanyatta, and Youngman, 1987).

It can be postulated that the social outcome of the NLP in relation to class was that a small proportion of literacy graduates did enter or consolidate their position in the working class. A small proportion of others were enabled to become petty producers on their own or in income-generating groups, while some may have advanced their situation within the strata of the peasantry. But it seems likely that the overall impact of the NLP was to enable very little upward mobility within the existing class structure. The NLP therefore in effect reproduced class divisions, and even the aspirations for advancement of the learners were articulated within the existing class hierarchy. There is no evidence to suggest any activity within the program (at the level of policy or practice) that called into question the class divisions within the social order. However, it may be that the inability of the NLP to help participants meet their expectation of employment might have begun to generate a consciousness of the inequities in control over the productive resources of society.

One dimension of social inequality which intersects with class is that of ethnicity. At least 20 percent of the population belong to minority ethnic groups, most of which have a subordinate position in society. During the nineteenth century, the numerically dominant Batswana established political and economic control over other ethnic groups in the country. A precolonial class structure emerged in which those groups with the greatest cultural and linguistic distance from the Batswana experienced a degree of economic exploitation and social subordination, akin to serfdom (Datta and Murray, 1989). While the Kalanga in the northeastern part of the country retained access to land and other means of production and the Ovaherero in the west retained cattle herds, most of the ethnic groups in the west were increasingly dispossessed and drawn into agricultural labor, mainly as cattle herders on the ranches of Boer settlers or for cattle-owning Batswana. Today the dominated ethnic groups of the western areas form a rural underclass which is unemployed or working for irregular payments in cash or kind (Wilmsen, 1988).

The political and economic dominance of the Batswana has been accompanied by cultural hegemony, articulated in the postcolonial era in terms of the ideology of nationalism, which regards assertions of cultural identity by ethnic groups as negative expressions of "tribalism" and identifies "the idea of the nation with Tswana culture" (Datta and Murray, 1989). Some of the ethnic minorities have written languages but, in the face of official discouragement, they have seldom undertaken adult literacy in these languages. (An exception is the Adult Education Centre run by the Lutheran Church in Sehitwa which taught literacy in the Tjiherero language in 1985–1986). For the majority of the ethnic groups in the western areas, such as those labelled the Basarwa, their languages are unwritten and their literacy levels are very low. One study of households in the western region of the Central District in 1977–1978 found less than 1 percent literacy (Hitchcock, 1978).

The information on participation in the NLP by different ethnic groups is sparse, as there are no statistics on the ethnic background of the learners. The 1984 evaluation report (Ministry of Education, 1984) recorded the different language groups amongst the non-Setswana speakers interviewed (50 percent spoke Ikalanga) but it gave no indication of the proportion of non-Setswana speakers to Setswana speakers. The 12 percent of learners categorized as "herdsmen" in Table II certainly included a high proportion of people from ethnic minorities. However, a later study of the remote areas where most ethnic minorities other than the Kalanga reside concluded that:

> The National Literacy Program has not been very successful in [these] settlements. The Literacy Group Leaders find it difficult to recruit learners and even more difficult to keep them in the groups. (Kann, Hitchcock, and Mbere, 1990)

The study recommended greater efforts should be made by the NLP to provide literacy skills as these would enable greater political and economic participation (for example, in relation to benefitting from the special government Economic Promotion Fund for these areas).

It is suggested that participation in the NLP had contradictory outcomes for Botswana's subordinated ethnic groups. The acquisition of literacy in Setswana, as noted in the previous section, may have enabled their fuller participation in the mainstream of society. But the terms of that participation were likely to involve reduced cultural identity and greater incorporation into the hegemonic culture. Also, though this literacy may have reduced the extremes of economic exploitation experienced by some ethnic groups, it was likely to provide little advancement within the overall class structure. Thus any transition from marginality to incorporation which was facilitated by literacy would not have significantly altered the pattern of social inequality, and may indeed have served to legitimate it, by reducing the visibility of ethnic discrimination.

In relation to gender, it is important to consider to what extent the NLP reinforced women's inequality in society. The nature of Botswana society is such that women hold a subordinate position in the division of labor and this inequality is buttressed by a strong patriarchal ideology. The majority of women live in the rural areas and are primarily engaged in subsistence agriculture. They represent only a quarter of those in formal-sector employment, where they work mainly in areas such as domestic service, nursing, and teaching. Their participation in significant areas of economic and political decision making is low (for example, only two of the thirty-eight M.P.s are women). In the private sphere, cultural practices and social norms embody male superiority (Mannathoko, 1991).

Issues of gender within the NLP have not been adequately researched, apart from some pioneering work by Gaborone (1986, 1989). In order to elucidate the interconnections of knowledge, power, and gender in the context of literacy practice, considerable ethnographic analysis would be required. However, it is possible to make some initial comments based on available information. The starting point must be the fact that almost two-thirds of the learners in the NLP during the 1980s were women—for example, the figure in 1989 was 62.1 percent (Department of Non Formal Education, 1990). The reason for this high rate of participation can probably be found in the large numbers of female-headed households (almost 50 percent of those in the rural areas), with women disproportionately represented amongst the poor, unemployed, and unskilled adults who are the potential clientele for literacy. Unfortunately there is no evidence on the comparative drop-out and success rates of women learners in relation to men.

To some extent it is apparent that participation in the NLP served to reinforce women's social position and their place in the sexual division of labor. For example, one purpose of literacy that often appears in official statements is to learn how to read and write letters. The significance of this is that many women in the rural areas are on their own because men have migrated to Botswana's towns and to South Africa for wage labor, so that letters are an important form of communication. In this sense, the NLP may well have reinforced the status quo of migrant labor and women's marginalization. Additionally, a major element of postliteracy provision is home economics, and most of the income-generating groups that DNFE promoted amongst literacy graduates were involved in traditionally female occupations, such as knitting, sewing, weaving, basketry, and baking (Department of Non Formal Education, 1990). Furthermore, there is some evidence of men being reluctant to allow women to join the program (Gaborone, Mutanyatta, and Youngman, 1987), and of female participants going to great lengths to conceal their participation from their partners (Gaborone, 1986).

However, the implication of emancipatory possibilities suggested by the men's reluctance indicates that, to a certain extent, the acquisition of literacy may be a step for individual women towards exerting greater control over their own situation. Gaborone (1986) quotes one participant as follows:

> My partner used to keep two bank accounts, one for us and the other for girlfriends. And because I was unable to read and make sense of this, he used to leave information lying about. I did not know how much he earned or his wage. But I now know and make him account for every thebe he spends.

Much more research is required on the personal effects of the NLP for women learners, but it is likely that these effects were contradictory. Participation in a postliteracy sewing project may have given a small cash income that provided material benefits and a greater degree of personal autonomy, while simultaneously entrenching the individual in the lowest levels of the capitalist production system in stereotyped women's work. However, what is certain is that the NLP had no policy commitment to promote forms of consciousness and collective social action that would enable women to free themselves from economic exploitation and patriarchal oppression. Indeed, it is interesting to note that the organizational system of the program had an important gender dimension. The 1987 evaluation report records that 94.2 percent of the Literacy Group Leaders surveyed and 82.2 percent of the Literacy Assistants who responded were female (Gaborone, Mutanyatta, and Youngman, 1987). Thus the employment pattern of the program itself reinforced the situation of women in low-paid, insecure, stereotyped jobs. One can conclude that the NLP in many respects reproduced the gender inequalities in society while at the same time interacting with the latent contradictions in unequal male-female relationships, in ways which have the potential to bring these disparities into question.

CONCLUSION

In this chapter I have sought to provide an analysis of policy development in adult literacy within the specific context of Botswana in the twenty-five years since the country became independent in 1966. I have tried to show how the educational policy of the state in the area of adult literacy relates to the structure of inequality in the wider society. The focus of my discussion has been on public policy formation and on the social outcomes of the National Literacy Program in its first ten years of operation. I have not considered the NLP in terms of its curriculum, pedagogy, and evaluation. However, I believe an analysis at this level would reveal that its form and content embodied an approach and an ideology which reinforced the status quo. For example, its methods in practice involved authoritarian teachers and passive learners, and its approach was explicitly antagonistic to the notions of empowerment associated with people like Freire. It is recorded that the planners of the NLP in 1979 took note "of the conscienstisation approach of Paulo Freire, and . . . the political element in the method was not seen as being appropriate to Botswana" (Townsend Coles, 1988). The literacy practices of the NLP supported legitimation and domination rather than transformation and emancipation.

The case study I have presented has centered on adult literacy as a social service provided by the state, and I have looked at the provision of literacy as a means of dominant classes' securing their legitimacy within society rather than as an opportunity for individuals to acquire particular skills. I have done so in order to explore the question of who benefits from literacy in relation to the interests of classes and other groups in society rather than those of the individual. The argument I have made is that the capitalist state promotes a particular kind of literacy (Lankshear and Lawler, 1989) for two purposes: first, to legitimate its own role in maintaining the conditions for capitalist accumulation and the political power of the dominant classes; second, to legitimate the existing unequal distribution of power in society between classes, sexes, and ethnic groups. The National Literacy Program in Botswana in the 1980s can be seen to have served these purposes.

I have focused on the state provision of adult literacy rather than nongovernmental initiatives because I believe analyzing the role of the state is crucial given its dominance over literacy programs in most Third World countries. However, the particularities of the Botswana case must be borne in mind because of the strength of the state and the weakness of civil society (Molutsi and Holm, 1990). The domestic and foreign resources available to the state during the economic boom of the 1980s enabled it to pursue a number of legitimation strategies, including large-scale social expenditure, of which the NLP is an example. In general terms, the latent conflicts within an increasingly class-divided society were successfully managed, and there was little evidence of political or cultural struggles over the state's concept and practice of adult literacy.

Botswana has not yet experienced the economic problems and accompanying crisis of the state which have occurred in many other parts of Africa. However, economic growth in the 1990s has slowed down significantly, and reduced government revenues could lead in the future to a crisis of legitimacy for both the state and the capitalist social order it upholds. This in turn could lead to different policies in the sphere of adult literacy and to different responses from literacy's clientele. However, in the absence of major changes in the economic and political situation, it is likely that the National Literacy Program would continue to provide a steady incremental increase in the levels of adult literacy whilst contributing to the legitimation of capitalist development and inequality in Botswana.

REFERENCES

Alavi, H. (1972–1979). "The State in Post-Colonial Societies." In H. Goulbourne (ed.), *Politics and the State in the Third World*. London: Macmillan, pp. 38–69.

Alavi, H. (1982). "State and Class under Peripheral Capitalism." In H. Alawi and T. Shanin (eds.), *Introduction to the Sociology of "Developing Societies."* London: Macmillan, pp. 289–307.

Alley, E. (1982). *English as a Second Language—An Investigation into the Feasibility of a Course Suitable for People Who Have Just Learned to Read and Write Setswana*. Gaborone: Department of Non Formal Education.

Apple, M. W. (ed.) (1982). *Cultural and Economic Reproduction in Education*. London: Routledge and Kegan Paul.

Bataille, L. (1976). *A Turning Point for Literacy*. Oxford: Pergamon.

Botswana Extension College. (1977). *Functional Literacy Pilot Project: Draft Plan*. Gaborone: Botswana Extension College.

Brooks, K. (1972). *Proposal for a National Work-Oriented Literacy Programme in Botswana*. Paris: UNESCO.

Carnoy, M. and Levin, H. (1985). *Schooling and Work in the Democratic State*. Stanford: Stanford University Press.

Datta, K. and Murray, A. (1989). "The Rights of Minorities and Subject Peoples in Botswana: A Historical Evaluation." In J. Holm and P. Molutsi (eds.), *Democracy in Botswana*. Gaborone: Macmillan, pp. 58–73.

Department of Non Formal Education. (1982). *How Can We Succeed? Evaluation of the National Literacy Programme: A Progress Report: August 1982*. Gaborone: Department of Non Formal Education.

Department of Non Formal Education. (1990). *Annual Report on the National Literacy Programme: 1989*. Gaborone: Department of Non Formal Education.

Gaborone, S. (1986). Unpublished Notes on Fieldwork Undertaken for the Evaluation of the National Literacy Programme.

Gaborone, S. (1989). *Gender and Literacy: The Case of Botswana*. Paper. Symposium on "Women and Literacy—Yesterday, Today and Tomorrow." Stockholm.

Gaborone, S., Mutanyatta, J. and Youngman, F. (1987). *An Evaluation of the Botswana National Literacy Programme*. Gaborone: Institute of Adult Education.

Gaborone, S., Mutanyatta, J. and Youngman, F. (1988). "The Botswana National Literacy Programme—Progress and Prospects." *Prospects*, 18(3), pp. 352–62.

Hitchcock, R. K. (1978). *Kalahari Cattle Posts*. Gaborone: Republic of Botswana.

Jones, P. W. (1988). *International Policies for Third World Education: UNESCO, Literacy and Development*. London: Routledge.

Kann, U. Hitchcock, R. and Mbere, N. (1990). *Let Them Talk*. Report submitted to the Ministry of Local Government and Lands and the Norwegian Agency for Development Cooperation, Gaborone.

Kann, U. and Taylor, D. (1988). "The Adult Literacy Rate in Botswana." *Botswana Notes and Records,* 20, pp. 135–41.

Lankshear, C. with Lawler, M. (1989). *Literacy, Schooling and Revolution*. New York: Falmer.

Mannathoko, C. (1991). *Profile of Women and Development in Botswana*. Brussels: EEC-ACP Foundation.

Ministry of Education. (1970). *National Development Plan 1970–1975*. Gaborone: Ministry of Education.

Ministry of Education. (1979). *The Eradication of Illiteracy in Botswana: A National Initiative: Consultation Document*. Gaborone: Ministry of Education.

Ministry of Education. (1984). *How Can We Succeed? Summary Report from the Evaluation of the National Literacy Programme*. N.p., Department of Non Formal Education.

Ministry of Education. (1990). *Draft Chapter 14: Education and Manpower Development*. Gaborone: Ministry of Education.

Ministry of Finance and Development Planning. (1970). *National Development Plan: 1970–75*. Gaborone: Republic of Botswana.

Ministry of Finance and Development Planning. (1973). *National Development Plan: 1973–78*. Gaborone: Republic of Botswana.

Ministry of Finance and Development Planning. (1985). *National Development Plan: 1985–91*. Gaborone: Republic of Botswana.

Molutsi, P. P., and Holm, J. D. (1990). "Developing Democracy When Civil Society Is Weak: The Case of Botswana." *African Affairs,* 89(356), pp. 323–41.

Morake, K. P. (1979–1988). "Speech Delivered at the Opening of the Meeting on the Eradication of Illiteracy in Botswana." In F. Youngman (ed.), *Documentation on the National Literacy Programme, Vol. 1, 1979–1982*. Gaborone: University of Botswana.

Morake, K. P. (1981–1988). "Draft of Speech by the Hon. Minister of Education on the Occasion of the Commencement of the Botswana National Literacy Programme." In F. Youngman (ed), *Documentation on the National Literacy Programme, Vol. 1, 1979–1982*. Gaborone: University of Botswana.

National Commission on Education. (1977). *Education for Kagisano*. Gaborone: Republic of Botswana.

Nyati, L. (1989). *The National Language and Education for Democracy*. Paper. Symposium on Educational Research in the SADCC Region—Present and Future. Gaborone: University of Botswana.

Parson, J. (1984). *Botswana*. Boulder, CO: Westview.

Republic of Botswana. (1977). *National Policy on Education*. Gaborone: Republic of Botswana.

Republic of Botswana. (1989). *Education for All—Meeting Basic Learning Needs. Botswana Country Paper*. Gaborone: Republic of Botswana.

Thomas, C. Y. (1984). *The Rise of the Authoritarian State in Peripheral Societies*. London: Heinemann.

Torres, C. A. (1990). *The Politics of Non Formal Education in Latin America*. New York: Praeger.

Townsend Coles, E. K. (1988). *Let the People Learn*. Manchester: University of Manchester.

UNESCO and UNDP. (1976). *The Experimental World Literacy Programme*. Paris: UNESCO.

Welch, A. R. (1985). "The Functionalist Tradition and Comparative Education." *Comparative Education,* 21(1), pp. 5–19.

Welch, A. R. (1991). "Knowledge, Culture and Power: Educational Knowledge and Legitimation in Comparative Education." In R. Burns and A. R. Welch (eds.), *Contemporary Perspectives in Comparative Education*. New York: Garland.

Wilmsen, E. N. (1988). "The Political History of Minorities and Its Bearing on Current Policy." In A. Datta and K. King (eds.), *Botswana—Education, Culture and Politics*. Edinburgh: University of Edinburgh, pp. 31–52.

World Bank. (1990). *World Development Report, 1990*. Oxford: Oxford University Press.

Youngman, F. (1987). Unpublished Notes on Fieldwork Undertaken for the Evaluation of the National Literacy Programme.

CHAPTER 8

Juvenile Delinquency and Reformatory Education in China: A Retrospective

Irving Epstein

Introduction

In 1983, in the midst of a publicized spiritual pollution campaign, I traveled to China to investigate educational programs for juvenile delinquents in reformatories and work-study schools. Having spent the previous year and a half pursuing language study and comparative research on the same topic in Hong Kong and Taiwan, I understood that it would be difficult under any circumstance to complete a comprehensive study given the sensitive nature of the topic. I was also aware of the limitations placed upon the visitations I conducted: no repeat visits were permitted, public security and reformatory officials were present when questions were asked, and difficult questions remained unanswered due to feigned ignorance on the part of those who were being interviewed. In short, the use of true ethnographic methods was not possible at the time, although this work was definitely qualitative by nature. I still believed that it was beneficial to see with one's own eyes what one had read about in print, and used the visitations as a means of confirming the veracity of published material I had collected. Fifteen years afterwards, I think it is useful to reflect upon the assumptions I made in conducting research on delinquency and reformatory education, and critique those assumptions in light of the changing nature of Chinese education as a field of study. The fact that my research was not explicitly ethnographic in an interesting way highlights issues concerning the strengths and weaknesses of that method in a comparative sense, and it is hoped that this discussion will add to the discourse focusing upon the broader methodological concerns that are expressed throughout this volume.

JUVENILE DELINQUENCY IN CHINA:
THE NATURE OF THE PROBLEM

At first glance, juvenile delinquency in China appears to differ little from its counterparts in other regions of the world. Chinese delinquents are primarily male and engage in deviant behaviors including burglary, theft, murder, rape, arson, and gang activity. Delinquency is primarily an urban phenomenon, although rural violence has increased during the past decade and a half. Female delinquents are more likely to be incarcerated for sexually promiscuous behavior, theft, and activities less violent than those committed by males, contributing to a double standard that occurs internationally. Chinese scholars have described delinquents as being less educated and less intelligent than normal youth; they are more likely to have come from families where parental conflict has been present and have relatives who also have engaged in deviant behavior. Two important behavioral characteristics that have been attributed to delinquents include their plasticity and their eagerness to embrace a "cult of brotherhood." In the former case, they appear to be hardened individuals on the outside, but are emotionally quite fragile and easily shattered. In the latter case, they often commit crimes in groups rather than as individuals and seek peer support common during adolescence.[1]

During the early 1980s, specific attributions made about delinquents could be excessively romantic or often quite harsh and unflattering. They were in various publications depicted as "blossoms in the dust," ignorant *(yumei)*, muddle-headed *(hutu)*, tyrannical *(chengba)*, despicable *(xialu)*, impetuous *(jizao)*, crazy *(feng kuang)*, vain *(xurong)*, conceited *(zifei* or *kuangwang zida)*, reckless *(lumang)*, rotten *(fuxiu)*, and savage or inhuman *(miejue renxing)*. Females, it was noted, were particularly difficult to reform because, once incarcerated, they saw themselves as irreparably ruined, like a vase that once broken could not be put back together *(po guan po shuai)*.[2] Certainly such categorizations reflected a traditional Confucian reluctance to separate an understanding of the nature of deviance with the ethical implications of its occurrence. What was even more striking to the westerner, though, was the use of unicausality in explaining why delinquency even existed in the People's Republic of China.

Official explanations that sought to account for delinquency's occurrence included the effects of the Cultural Revolution, poor parenting, unsympathetic teaching, unhealthy peer group influences, and susceptibility to the dangerous influences resulting from increased contact with Western media. Certainly the effects of the Cultural Revolution received prominent attention as scholars sought to explain the embarrassing existence of delinquency that remained visible during the post-Mao era. It was commonly pointed out that as a result of the Cultural Revolution, youth born during that time failed to obtain a clear understanding of right and wrong, as authority relationships between children and parents, as well as between citizens and government officials, were easily and regularly compromised. A significant number of youth who later got into trouble had parents who themselves were incarcerated or detained during the Cultural Revolution; certainly the political factionalism that encouraged relatives to inform on one another weakened traditional family ties.[3] But with direct reference to criminal behavior, it is clear that it was the surreptitious reentry of sent-down youth into China's cities in the latter years of the Cultural Revolution, without benefit of residence documentation, that had a significant effect upon increased social dislocation and disorder in the late 1970s.[4]

It should be stressed that it was easy to overemphasize the importance of the Cultural Revolution in contributing to Chinese delinquency, and the political expedience of doing so during the early years of post-Maoism is clear. Scholars in the 1970s and 1980s conveniently forgot or underplayed the fact that waves of delinquency (reported as outbreaks of hooliganism) were reported in the press during the 1950s.[5] It is clear that the eradication of criminal deviance of all types held important political capital for the regime, as evidenced by the publicity given to campaigns aimed at eliminating prostitution in Shanghai and curtailing drug use in Southern China during the early years of the People's Republic.[6] In 1983, although it was no longer possible to deny that the growth of crime generally and juvenile delinquency in particular had become an important social problem, it was imperative that government officials set blame in such a way so as to deny personal culpability; the use of the Cultural Revolution, as an umbrella explanation, served that purpose.

Other explanations for the existence of juvenile delinquency contained important elements of truth but were similarly general and unidimensional. Poor parenting, for example, was attributed to the use of both overly authoritarian and overly indulgent disciplinary methods, although the negative effects of parental socioeconomic disadvantage upon one's ability to adequately perform child-rearing responsibilities were also acknowledged as a contributing factor. In a similar vein, teachers were criticized for their overly harsh disciplinary methods and their emotional distance from youth. One published example told of the inconsiderate teacher who berated the female student in front of the class, comparing her with excrement that deserved to be flushed down a toilet. The incident, it was claimed, provoked the student into committing delinquent acts. In all of these cases, the longstanding Confucian emphasis upon the power of role modeling, whereby the authority figure is normally responsible for shaping the behavior of the underling, is simply assumed as being an operative dimension of social relationships.[7]

The fear of Western "sugar-coated bullets" corrupting Chinese youth was also popularly expressed at this time and was a key issue in the general spiritual pollution campaign. Again, it was reported that when they came in contact with pornographic videos or other media produced in the West, Chinese youth were negatively influenced into conducting the very crimes that the media sensationalized. Beyond the xenophobia that belies such explanations was what many Western scholars have labeled a form of moral panic, whereby a general fear for the future direction of the society in light of de-Maoification was expressed through an ambivalence toward the independence and ethical character of the country's children.[8] The contradiction between viewing delinquents in such negative terms as were previously noted, as opposed to seeing them as powerless innocents, subject to the manipulation of external prurient forces from the West, can best be understood through appreciating the sense of moral panic that characterized the decade.

CULTURAL BAGGAGE BROUGHT TO A STUDY OF CHINESE DELINQUENCY

I, of course, came to my study of juvenile delinquency in China with my own set of assumptions, many of which were grounded in Western views of Chinese society. Deeply influenced by the writings of Whyte (1973), Whyte (1974), Parrish and Whyte (1978), and Whyte and Parrish (1984),[9] I viewed urban Chinese society as consisting of a set of interlocking institutions working to control individual behavior in the neighborhood, workplace, and in schools. The use of informal mechanisms for maintaining social control had its historical origins in the *bao-jia* self-policing system, first established during the twelfth century, but perfected during the Qing dynasty. Thus, the manipulation of local social institutions to informally maintain social control had some historical resonance. Reformatories could logically be categorized as institutions that ideally contributed to social control in a more formal manner, and were to be evaluated on those terms. Having read and been impressed with Etzioni's (1961) categorization of institutions such as prisons and reform schools as being normative-coercive, I viewed my task as one of evaluating the effectiveness of these institutions in light of the ideological shifts that occurred after their initial development.[10] A key question to answer was whether the normative value claims that rationalized coercive treatment of offenders could continue to be effective during the post-Maoist era.

The entire notion of coercion was of obvious interest, and in reading both Donald Munro's view of Mao's belief in the malleability of human character[11] and Bao Ruo Wang's (Jean Pasquale's) description of labor camp life,[12] it became clear to me that the degree to which institutional coercion occurred was often tied to one's participation in the self-criticism process and one's corresponding willingness to confess to wrongdoing. Confession was a necessary precondition to character reformation, but at least there was the theoretical possibility of achieving rehabilitation. Indeed, upon reading *Prisoner of Mao*, it became evident that much of the physical maltreatment that was inflicted upon Chinese prisoners was due to widespread poverty and economic deprivation that affected everyone, rather than an intentional effort to inflict pain on the prisoners. Accounts of life in prisons and labor camps also emphasized the importance of labeling and social stigma, and their effects upon offenders as well as their relatives. The necessity of divorcing one's incarcerated spouse in order to keep one's employment, let alone maintain minimum external social contact, impressed me as being extremely significant. I, of course, understood that issues of stigma, labeling, and coercive institutional practice commonly occurred in the United States and in other Western countries too. But it was the closed nature of Chinese urban life, the lack of privacy, the reliance on connections (*guanaxi*) for advancement, and the relatively low degree of mobility that made these issues especially compelling.

CHINESE PENAL INSTITUTIONS

Chinese penal institutions include prisons, reform and reeducation through labor camps, reformatories, work-study schools, and work-study classes. Although the latter institutions were designed specifically for juveniles, offenders can be sent to reform and reeducation through labor camps and prisons too, depending upon the nature of their offense. There is a pecking order throughout the penal system, an institutional hierarchy based upon coercive purpose. Thus, delinquents who are not placed in reformatories are more likely to be sent to labor camps, but within the labor camp system, they are likely to enter reeducation through labor camps that house political prisoners and offenders guilty of moderate offenses rather than those camps that house hardened criminals. By Western standards, any form of incarceration that places juveniles with adult offenders is a violation of children's basic rights. Yet in the Chinese case, it is important to note that the term "youth" refers to those from the age of eighteen up to the age of twenty-five. Juveniles supposedly include those aged fourteen through eighteen, although here, too, clear-cut distinctions between juveniles and youth are often compromised. Juveniles between the ages of fourteen and sixteen who commit serious crimes (homicide, bodily injury, robbery, arson, etc.) bear full criminal responsibility, although the severity of punishment is mitigated and the death penalty is only inflicted upon those aged eighteen and above.[13]

The two institutions that are specifically designed for youthful offenders are reformatories and work-study schools. The former hold relatively large numbers of youth who have been judged guilty of major offenses, and are well-established components of the criminal justice system. Work-study schools, which hold fewer offenders who have committed less severe offenses, were established during the 1950s.[14] They were eliminated during the Cultural Revolution, ostensibly because of their ineffectiveness, but were resurrected during the late 1970s. In 1979, they received widespread publicity as an important solution to combating growing delinquency. A long-held suspicion that remains is that they cater largely to cadre children and children of privilege who have gotten into trouble. Hooper reported that some work-study schools for girls served as little more than homes for pregnant teens.[15] In Guangzhou, two work-study factory classes, gender segregated, were established as local alternatives to the work-study school. Although work-study schools are usually operated under the jurisdiction of the municipal education bureau, these factory classes were operated with the support of the municipal government in conjunction with the public security bureau.

The range of penalties within the criminal justice system can include control (*guanzhi*), criminal detention (*juyi*), fixed-term imprisonment, life imprisonment, and the death penalty. *Guanzhi* refers to public security efforts to control criminal behavior prior to incarceration. In the case of juveniles, they continue to go to school and perform normal functions of everyday behavior, but are required to report to public security regularly and inform upon their actions as well as those of friends. In the case of *juyi* (criminal detention), offenders are actually housed in a confined setting for a period of fifteen days to six months.[16] Juveniles who are sent to work-study schools and factory classes would generally fall under this type of mandate although the length of their incarceration and conditions for their release are quite broad. Offenders given fixed-term imprisonment can be incarcerated from six months to fifteen years and, when combined with multiple offenses, even longer. Generally, offenders housed in reformatories are punished according to this category. One informant told me, though, that some of the offenders I saw at a particular reformatory would simply be transferred to labor camps upon their eighteenth birthday; their chances of ever being released from incarceration were quite slim.

PERSONAL OBSERVATIONS[17]

Upon visiting the principal reformatory serving Guangdong Province and one of the two work-study factory classes in Guangzhou during the spring of 1983, I had the following reactions. The Guangdong Juvenile Reformatory Institute at Shijing housed 520 offenders aged fourteen to eighteen, twenty of whom were female. Briefly closed during the Cultural Revolution and turned into a factory, the facility was reopened in 1972 and had operated continuously since then. Its physical plant, equipment, resources, and so on, seemed outstanding, and when I later visited the work-study factory class, officials there apologized for their comparative dearth of resources. The reformatory was a model institution whose affluence was exceptional, but it was, nonetheless, a typically coercive penal institution.

Immediately upon entering, offenders were fingerprinted, issued uniforms, and given haircuts. They were then divided into 150 member groups that were subdivided into cells of ten. Two leaders were elected for each cell; their jobs included leading political study sessions and reporting peer behavior to cadre supervisors. This process, known as collectivist education (*jiti jiaoyu*), played a major part of the offenders' political education. They were pressured into repenting during self-criticism sessions, and insofar as their lack of understanding of appropriate rule-governed behavior was blamed for their willingness to engage in deviance, they were taken to People's Courts and were given lectures by public security officials. At the same time, it was extremely important that they demonstrate publicly their willingness and ability to be rehabilitated. To that end, offenders would be forced into engaging in service activities including construction, street sweeping, and other visible group service activities.

The academic component of the curriculum included instruction in basic skills as well as manual labor in the broadest of terms. Offenders were given four forty-five-minute classes per day with ten-minute intervening rest periods and a two-hour rest period after lunch. The subjects taught included Chinese, mathematics, history, and music (communal singing) with normal class size set at a 50:1 ratio. Some classes were divided into a 20:1 ratio for purposes of remediation, although ability grouping was an exception rather than the rule. The national language (*Putonghua*) was used as the language of instruction as it was noted that the Cantonese youth could at least understand teacher instruction.

Offender manual-labor activities included work in the automotive shop, fishing, growing beans and peanuts, gardening, pursuing flower cultivation and arrangement, and completing construction work. Girls would pursue light manual labor such as sweeping and dusting, but were prohibited from engaging in automotive repair or construction work. These activities are noteworthy for their general rather than technical nature, as well as their collective rather than individual orientation. Since over half of the offenders came from urban environments, the transferability of some of the work conducted at the reformatory to their native settings was questionable. It certainly was unconnected to the institution's academic program.

Offender punishment included forced participation in self-criticism sessions and documentation of repeated offenses for one's permanent record. It was claimed that 5 percent of the offender population left before their sentences were completed but 2 to 3 percent of the offenders had their sentences lengthened. Although it was admitted that incarcerated offenders were subjected to physical punishment during the Cultural Revolution, it was claimed that this no longer occurred, although the use of solitary confinement from one-half to three days in length was acknowledged. Officials were proud of the fact that the facility did not include visible physical structures that would directly impede escape; however, as 1983 progressed, offender escape did become a national issue, penal institutions were criticized for their laxity, and public executions of criminals became a popular alternative to institutional incarceration.

In viewing the Guangdong Reformatory Institute at Shijing, my main reference points included previous visits to similar institutions in Taiwan and Hong Kong. The Guangdong facilities were impressive, but what was most noteworthy was that its institutional rituals did not explicitly condone the coercive treatment of offenders. Such was not the case in Taiwan, where the largest reform school on the island was run by a superintendent who was proud of his military background as a former army officer, where offenders as young as twelve were held in shackles and leg irons, where one's uniform number was displayed prominently, and where the mass haircut was quite visible. Offenders there were required to sit in silence with their hands on their knees for one-half hour after they had completed eating; they regularly marched in unison from building to building. Such rituals, which are supposed to teach internal discipline and self-regulation, have the effect of degrading one's individuality, and were surprisingly absent during my visit to the Guangdong Reformatory. The use of the group for purposes of controlling individual behavior and fostering compliance was much more noticeable though.

The work-study factory class at Fangcun, one of two institutions operating in Guangzhou, served two hundred males. The other institution served females who were charged with theft and prostitution. I was not allowed to visit it because the matter of female delinquency was considered too sensitive for a foreigner to observe and presumably comment upon. The Fangcun institution was first established in 1973 as a series of political and work-study classes for mildly delinquent males. In 1975, its permanent factory component was initiated, and in 1980, it officially became a work-study factory class with an increase in the number of courses and a strengthened education program. Three part-time primary level-education teachers were contracted from the municipal education bureau to operate the program; other staff came from the factory itself.

Students attending the work-study factory class were between ages fifteen and twenty-five; some were sent from their regular schools, while the others were factory workers or those who were unemployed. The environment could easily accommodate both recalcitrant workers and students, unlike the more restrictive environment of typical work-study schools. Most had previously attended a primary or junior-middle school, but none had attended a senior-middle school. Over 75 percent of the offenders were guilty of theft; other offenses included quarreling, hooliganism, minor gang activity, and gambling-offenses considered too minor for prosecution. Offenders typically stayed at the factory class for six months, but they were allowed to return home on Sundays. Ten percent of the offenders left before their sentence had been completed because of good behavior; 6 percent were required to stay longer because of poor behavior and attitude. Authorities admitted to a 15 percent recidivism rate within one year of release.

Since it was claimed that the purpose of the work-study factory class was to educate rather than punish offenders, a rewards system was instituted to encourage behavioral change. Offenders were assessed marks on a scale of one to ten for their behavioral and academic performance; upon receipt of eighteen hundred points they were able to leave, and each individual's score was posted on a blackboard outside of the classroom for all to see. Self-criticism sessions occurred on a regular basis, but corporal punishment was no longer used. Authorities noted that there had been seven escapes within the previous eight years; when offenders neglected to return to the facility on Sunday evenings, home visitations were made to ascertain the reasons for truant behavior.

Political education at the work-study factory class included legal and health education, but the teaching of factory discipline was especially emphasized because it was presumed that these students, at best, would be future factory workers. As was true of their counterparts in the Guangdong reformatory, they were taken to public courts and trials to see personally the consequences of criminal behavior. However, as their clothing complemented that worn by regular factory workers and as their haircuts, which were given by teachers or parents, were enforced unsystematically, they were not stigmatized by their appearance and blended in well with their larger external environment. They had access to the factory clinic if they fell ill, and were given a food allotment that included at least one meat and one vegetable dish per day.

The academic program included instruction in *Putonghua* and mathematics, with rudimentary literacy skills along with some history and geography included. The language of instruction was Cantonese as opposed to *Putonghua*; students were divided into primary, lower-middle, and middle school levels, and were grouped by ability within those levels into remedial, average, and above-average categories. Class size was approximately 50:1, and it was claimed that general curricular content paralleled that offered at ordinary public schools.

Vocational training was offered in arc welding, model making, wine making, and photographic machine operation and repair, with factory engineers specifically enlisted to teach the students how to repair electrical equipment. Most of their time, however, was spent engaging in general factory work of a menial nature, ostensibly to teach adherence to factory discipline and a respect for the rhythms of factory work. The parent factory at Fangcun produced diesel engines, though it would be unlikely that a work-study factory-class graduate would obtain employment there. Indeed, it was admitted that 70 percent of the offenders were unemployed after their release.

My impressions of the work-study factory class were positive, as I viewed the facility as a less coercive institution than its reformatory counterpart, which was not surprising since it dealt with offenders who had committed less serious crimes. It was clear that there was some jealousy between officials at the respective institutions, with the work-study class cadres viewing their own institution as lacking in prestige and positive publicity. Thus, my visit as an outside international observer was useful to them in buttressing their stature, and my positive reactions to the facility were reported in an edition of the local newspaper.

Overall, I concluded that juveniles in China faced more conflict outside of institutional walls than within them. The pressures of overcoming social stigma were intense. Indeed, the Chinese national press had reported on a delinquent's suicide as a general case, caused by the offender's despondency over a lack of parental contact while incarcerated. For offenders housed at both the reformatory and work-study factory class, institutional release did not mean starting anew. These youths were regularly required to report to public security officials, to play the role of informant, and to give details of the activities of peers and friends. Thus, their place within the criminal justice system reverted to stage one, *guanzhi*, as it was never expected that they would ever be free of contact with the system. My conclusion was that the use of stigma, negative labeling, and guilt by association, although informally communicated, was nonetheless extremely powerful outside of institutional walls. As essentially Maoist institutions, the juvenile justice facilities themselves communicated quite effectively to offenders the informal terms through which social control was to be exercised in their future lives. Those terms included engaging in manual labor as a means of fostering self-discipline and character reformation, submitting to the authority of the group during self-criticism sessions, publicly displaying remorse for one's actions, and accepting formal authority through a nominal academic routine. The emphasis upon rewarding individual behavior in an effort to promote substantive change was noteworthy, but, overall, the goal of authoritarian collectivism was constantly being reinforced within the institutional settings.

JUVENILE DELINQUENCY IN THE 1980s AND 1990s

Throughout the 1980s and 1990s, juvenile delinquency and youth criminality increased significantly in China. In 1980, for example, 61.2 percent of all criminals were youths and juveniles; by 1989, the percentage had increased to 74.1 percent.[18] This is part of a larger trend where crime increased markedly, from 54 cases per 100,000 filed by public security officials in 1987 to 181 per 100,000 by 1989.[19] The extent of youth and juvenile crime as a percentage of overall crime has become one of the highest in the world. With specific reference to juveniles (as opposed to youths), there has been a significant increase in the number of juvenile criminals and the rate of their criminal activity, although there has been a decline in the absolute number of juvenile criminals relative to other criminals. Still, criminals are getting younger. The total crime committed by fourteen- to eighteen-year-olds increased from 7 percent in 1980 to almost 20 percent in 1989.[20] More and more students are committing crimes while they still are in school, as many attend vocational middle schools and technical/worker schools, institutions with relatively low prestige[21] that are seen as offering no chance for social mobility.

As crime has increased in China, it has grown in urban areas and coastal regions, mirroring the uneven economic development in the country. Juvenile and youth crimes have correspondingly increased with respect to theft, burglary, robbery, hooliganism, rape, and violent criminal activity.[22] The latter category includes bombing, kidnapping, and hijacking as well as homicide, assault, and battery.[23] Crimes are increasingly brutal as firearms become easier to obtain. Gang activity has increased during the 1980s; gangs are larger and more brazen in their activities. Similar to the tongs of old, gangs have become more secretive, better-organized, and less spontaneous.[24]

During the 1990s, drug activity increased significantly and has had an impact upon juvenile and youth crime. Drug cases solved by police in Guangzhou in 1994, for example, were three times greater than those of 1981 through 1990 combined, while within Guangdong Province, 80 percent of drug users are under the age of twenty-five.[25] Yunnan Province traditionally has been a source of drug cultivation and smuggling, and its prominence has increased as social and political controls have decreased. As a result, drug trafficking has been accompanied by increases in gun smuggling, child kidnapping, and prostitution, with youth gangs playing a prominent role in these activities.[26] All of these trends have occurred within a general environment that has sanctioned widespread corruption on the part of government officials. From 1988 to 1993, 1.2 million cases of cadre corruption were acknowledged by the Chinese press, with 170,000 cases being reported for 1993 alone.[27]

Authorities have reacted to these trends in a number of ways. They have benefitted from gaining increased access to technology, which has been used to enforce greater social control. Thus, public security bureaus now use automobiles for motor patrol and make better use of telephones and electronic equipment to solve crimes.[28] Other responses have included improving legal education within schools, offering support for mediation, and using residence committees to assist in crime prevention and neighborhood surveillance. With specific reference to reformatories and correctional institutions, efforts have been made to enhance supervision in order to prevent escapes. It was reported that in Shanghai, for example, that inmate escape decreased from 0.05 percent in 1981 to 0.02 percent in 1991.[29] In addition, reward systems have been implemented at a number of facilities (not unlike the system used at the Fangcun work-study class), goal setting and evaluation procedures have been initiated, and some effort has been made to tailor the type of manual work offered to the specific nature of the inmate's offense.[30] At the same time, it should be noted that certain reformatories, as with the larger penal system, continue to force juvenile offenders to make goods that are sold for export in the West, which contributes income to China's prison labor system.[31]

Situ and Liu generally see a shift from reliance upon informal mechanisms of social control to use of professional organizations to maintain social order. Factories and places of employment are now training their own security divisions, and joint defense brigades, whose members come from various work units, patrol recreational areas and public places.[32] This is occuring within a general professionalization of the entire legal systems as more lawyers are being trained, along with participants involved in criminal justice.

Still, the ratio of 1 police officer for every 1,400 people remains one of the highest ratios in the world, where the average is 1:50;[33] and the reliance upon the mass campaign to expeditiously identify and punish criminals remains quite strong. Dutton and Lee argue that this type of informal policing allows for flexibility and gives a sense of security to the population. However, in 1996, over one thousand people were executed within a two-month span during China's "*yanda*" (Strike hard) campaign, the most violent of its type since 1983. The offenders were quickly tried, convicted, and executed without benefit of appeal. Mass trials attended by up to twenty thousand people were also held, and convicts were paraded in public before being sent off to be shot.[34] It is therefore fair to conclude that in spite of some efforts to professionalize law enforcement generally as well as reformatory education specifically, a reliance upon informal mechanisms for delivering justice remains strong in China.

It is tempting to associate the increase in juvenile delinquency in China during the past two decades with the material affluence that has accompanied swift economic change. However, such an attribution would be excessively simplistic if it failed to take into account increasing urban unemployment rates (officially acknowledged to be about 2.9 percent in 1997), increased urban and coastal migration, diminished control over residential mobility patterns, and structural changes within the educational system. In the latter case, authorities have successfully restricted the number of students with aspirations for attending university, so that in 1997 only 2.84 million high school graduates will take entrance examinations for 1 million available places in the country's colleges and universities.[35] The "cooling out" process begins much earlier, however, toward the end of primary school, when decisions are made as to the type and quality of middle school one can attend. At the senior-secondary level, further stratification occurs as students enter regular academic and "keypoint" high schools, secondary specialized schools, vocational high schools, and technical schools.[36] Although many delinquents do not advance this far through the system, their future aspirations are leveled at increasingly early stages of their development.

Thus, responses to increased youth crime and delinquency can be classified as both progressive and traditional. Progressive responses have contributed to a professionalization of the criminal justice system through the enhanced training and education of corrections officials, as well as through increased data collection and analysis. Chinese authorities joined Interpol in 1984, an event that has encouraged the sharing of information along with enhanced international cooperation, particularly with regard to drug trafficking. Although there is some evidence of professionalization within juvenile correctional institutions, the evidence for a radical change of institutional culture is more mixed; these still are organizations that profess strong ideological beliefs in the redemptive value of manual labor, the importance of character reformation in a general sense, and the need to respect collective authority. Outside of institutional walls, the use of the mass anticrime campaign to address rising crime rates with expediency, swiftness, and harshness continues unabated. And the official response to increased residential mobility and unemployment lies in continued reliance upon residence committees and street offices (whose functions were first formally articulated in 1954) to work with public security and correctional officials in preserving social order and preventing crime.

RECENT WESTERN RESEARCH ON CHINESE DELINQUENCY

Since my own research on delinquency was conducted, scholars have relied upon additional firsthand accounts[37] as well as survey questionnaire research[38] to gain a broader understanding of the topic. Zhang relied upon the assistance of Communist Youth League and public security officials to administer his questionnaires, which were distributed to 369 delinquents housed in reformatories, reeducation-through-labor camps, and prisons, and to 443 youths from the general population. Liu's sample included 403 middle-school students in Shenzhen. In addition, Marvin Wolfgang of the University of Pennsylvania has undertaken a long-term study of a 1973 birth cohort from the Wuchang district of Wuhan, and it is expected that his study will be expanded to include the entire city by the year 2000.[39] Generally, the authors conclude that Western criminological theories are applicable to the Chinese case. Wolfgang's preliminary results indicate delinquent/nondelinquent differences in levels of education, unemployment, susceptibility to school discipline and punishment, dropout rates, and learning attitudes. Others have discovered positive relationships between family deviance and child-rearing practices and delinquency status,[40] and have noted the salience of labeling theory for predicting friendship estrangement but not family ties.[41] There is some disagreement regarding the importance of social control factors over internal personal control factors in explaining delinquency potentiality,[42] but for the most part, all of the research assumes that criminological paradigms refined in the West are operational for the Chinese case.

Although the use of survey research in China is a testament to the growing importance of the social sciences there, it should be stressed that the results of these surveys should be treated with caution. Whenever one relies upon the local Communist Youth League director and accompanying correctional officials to administer one's questionnaire (as was the case with Zhang), it is difficult to see how, in spite of pledges of confidentiality, those administering the instruments would be viewed by delinquents as neutral parties. Further, the use of residence committee and school officials to record information while conducting the personal interviews (as pursued by Wolfgang and Liu) presents a similar if less extreme dilemma. Given the nature of their situations, reasonable questions can be raised regarding issues of informed consent and the freedom of delinquents to refrain from participating in such research. Their answers to particularly sensitive questions regarding their attitudes and value orientations must therefore be viewed with skepticism until the political implications of their participation in the research are better understood. Thus, I think that it is at least arguable as to whether the use of quasi-experimental survey research models, postulating cause-effect relationships between various delinquency factors, has been any more valuable in adding to our understanding of Chinese delinquency than the observational research that I and others conducted previously.

A REEVALUATION

When I began my dissertation research, a number of Chinese friends commented that it was strange for one to spend so much time investigating the conditions of youth who obviously would never contribute to society. Given the fact that the educational system had so many problems, in their eyes it would have made more sense for me to investigate policies that might beneficially affect a larger group of individuals who would be in a better position to enhance China's educational development. My response to my friends was twofold. First, I argued that I could better understand the nature of Chinese society by analyzing what was happening to its outcasts. Second, I argued that issues of opportunity and fairness were important in all societies and those issues deserved to be articulated and discussed. There is an arrogance to that response that I believe has colored not only my own research but also that of others pursuing work in Chinese education and Chinese studies generally. Such a response assumes that comparative social and cultural interactions can be understood totalistically. It assumes that observers can unobtrusively use their authority as outsiders to give voice to a group they view as marginalized and impotent. But more important than the naïveté that accompanied these assumptions is their negative impact upon one's ability to grasp the fundamental nature of the research being pursued. In this case, the result was an inability to appreciate the dynamics of social change, a tendency to falsely dichotomize social practices into extreme categories, and a failure to sufficiently control for Western bias in my analysis.

Comprehending the pace and importance of changing social relationships in a foreign context is extremely difficult, particularly when one's research is short-term and significant limitations are placed upon one's access to documents, human subject interviews are conducted while party officials are present, and follow-up visitations to the same facilities subject to initial observation are not possible. Nonetheless, in viewing juvenile correctional institutions as largely closed systems, self-contained organizations expressing their normative-coercive missions in traditionally Maoist terms, I neglected to appreciate either the external or internal pressures that might lead to significant institutional change. It was easy to see how internal and external conflicts might arise. The emphasis upon collectivist education, although a perfectly logical assumption on the part of authorities given the group-based nature of Chinese society, could easily foster gang affiliations that might be openly expressed upon release, since it placed offenders in constant small-group contact. Attempts to maintain contact with offenders themselves after their release, as well as with their street and residence committee officials charged with supervising their behavior and maintaining local order, would have been exceptionally difficult for reformatory officials, given the varied residences and geographical backgrounds of the offenders. Given these actual and potential conflicts, I neglected to comprehend how they would be reconciled or how the pressures for their reconciliation would be addressed. Instead, I viewed these institutions as doctrinaire and inelastic, because that is how I also viewed the ideological principles that governed their operation.

Certainly, I tended to dichotomize the practices I observed into extreme categories. I viewed reformatory education as little more than a form of enforced socialization that legitimized the coercive function of these institutions to the society at large. In so doing, I saw socialization as unidirectional, imposed upon the offenders without their consent, and largely ineffective in changing their value orientations. In truth, it is clear that correctional institutions of all types depend upon their inmates in order to function effectively, given that offender-staff ratios are so large.[43] The question for offenders is not one of their submission or resistance to authority, but how effectively can they minimize institutional constraints and negotiate conflict so as to maximize their individual power and influence. For obvious reasons, I was not in a position to obtain direct information about the actual social dynamics of the offender-guard relationship, but I was certainly remiss in making assumptions about that relationship in the absence of useful information.

A second problem concerned my view of the treatment of released offenders, as I believed that the social stigma offenders confronted upon their release, informally administered, was quite harsh and was of greater long-term consequence than the treatment they received within institutional walls. Here, too, the dichotomies of formal (institutional) versus informal offender treatment were simplistically constructed. In the West, for example, issues of offender stigma certainly are evident in spite of efforts to professionalize probation and after-care treatments. Unemployment rates remain high, as do recidivism rates. Recent Western efforts that rely upon community approaches to policing and emphasize informal preventative intervention strategies, which are implemented before delinquent behavior becomes severe, further blur the distinction between formal and informal approaches to crime prevention and the eventual disposition of criminal cases.

With regard to the Chinese case, in focusing upon the importance of social labeling as a function of social control, expressed through the activities of informal organizations such as mediation, street, and residence committees. I again failed to comprehend the internal dynamics of those organizations. Impressed with the importance of group affiliation and the lack of individual privacy that was afforded individuals living in urban China. I neglected to appreciate how individuals were able to maximize their status not only within group settings, which was a traditional pattern, but above and beyond them as well. In short, the use of *guanxi* to maximize one's interests implied a reciprocity with respect to individual relationships on a one-to-one basis that I had underestimated. Released delinquents, I believed, without access to strong group support lost the personal ties necessary to successfully reintegrate within the society, and as a result, their stigma was informally codified. What has occurred over the past two decades, though, has been an erosion of group loyalty throughout many aspects of urban Chinese life due to increased individual entrepreneurship, residential migration, and a tolerance for higher unemployment levels generally, as the government has retreated from its traditional paternalism. Instead, one sees a decrease in the social stigma of having engaged in illegal or quasi-legal activity and a significant increase in corruption on an individual basis at all social levels. My analysis failed to foresee this trend.

I previously noted that I viewed the Maoist ideological principles that played an important role in the articulated mission of reformatories and correctional institutions to be doctrinaire and inflexibly administered. Insofar as I viewed ideology as performing only a conservative rather than a progressive function, I believe that I allowed Western bias to color my perspective. Certainly, I failed to challenge the ideological assumptions of carceral bureaucracies such as those in prisons or other coercive institutions, as they have evolved in the West; nor did I critique the notions of professionalism that these institutions promote. In truth, ideology can be transformatory as well as restrictive, and in the Chinese case, its Maoist variant served many by giving a sense of direction to the future without renouncing the collective past. For all of the abuses and excesses that occurred within and beyond re-formatory walls in the name of ideology, it is certainly arguable as to whether Chinese delinquents are better off today in a less overtly politicized environment, or whether delinquents in Western environments have ever fared better than their Chinese counterparts did two decades ago.

The basic question that remains unresolved is whether such weaknesses are indicative of the limitations of more general research patterns, and, if so, whether ethnographic approaches have the potential for redressing these weaknesses in ways that other research methods fail to achieve. Certainly, we see the growth of collaborative research and the use of survey research in the study of Chinese delinquency and criminology over the past two decades, and these trends are representative of what has occurred within Chinese studies generally. It is arguable, however, whether those advances in them-selves help in our understanding of Chinese society. If I erred in my own work, through emphasizing the cultural uniqueness of Chinese social inter-action with respect to social control and labeling practices—depicting them totalistically and in dichotomous terms—more recent studies of delinquency have denied the importance of cultural context completely, and have instead attempted to use the Chinese case as evidence for the viability of their pre-conceived Western theories. Neither perspective does justice to the subjects of cross-cultural investigation.

Can the use of ethnographic methods make a difference? I believe that it can under certain conditions. To the extent that critical ethnography em-ploys a reflexivity that calls into question the fundamental nature of the sub-ject (researcher)-object relationship, the tendency to totalize the foreign in the name of cultural distinctiveness or use the foreign to superficially reaf-firm the primacy of Western paradigms can be checked. At the same time, a critical ethnographic approach holds the possibility of our exploring more honestly the ramifications of the politics of access and the use or censorship of information to control social behavior, issues that have traditionally con-fronted scholars pursuing social research in China. It is doubtful, for exam-ple, that foreigners or natives would ever be granted the access necessary to complete a full-bodied ethnographic study of a Chinese correctional institu-tion because to Chinese officials, the political sensitivity of the environment would outweigh the usefulness of any information that might be gathered and shared through intensive observation and analysis. But in examining the operations of schools and their relationships to family, work, and neighbor-hood, the critical ethnographer has the opportunity to gain insight into the nature of normalcy and deviance, personal motivation and leveled aspira-tion, self-interest and collective loyalty, open and closed opportunity struc-tures—in short, the fundamental conflicts that characterize so many aspects of Chinese life on a daily basis for those who are successful, as well as for those who are marginalized and dispossessed.

Chinese educational and correctional facilities share more than the most common of institutional characteristics. If correctional institutions rely upon very basic educational programs to legitimize their coercive practices, coercion, even if its appearance is less overtly visible, is regularly used within educational settings to enforce school policies as well. As Foucault so convincingly argued, the relationship between curricular discipline and the formal as well as symbolic exercise of power upon the individual has had strong historical resonance in the West,[44] and there is no reason to think that a similar relationship does not exist in contemporary China. Indeed, when the operation of work-study schools and factory classes for delinquent youths has been assigned to municipal education bureaus, such a relationship has been made more explicit and more formalized for those judged mildly delinquent. Traditional views of mainstream schools highlight their reliance upon remunerative characteristics (such as the distribution of grades and other symbolic rewards) that are supported by a modest degree of coercion (enforcement of compulsory attendance). For the Chinese case, however, the relationship between normative, remunerative, and coercive institutional goals is complex and in a state of flux, particularly as larger numbers of students have become increasingly disenfranchised, due to the imposition of rigid status hierarchies among and within schools, and their corresponding culling-out policies. The necessity of reevaluating the nature of authority patterns within schools is clear. And if such a reevaluation were to occur, the relationships between teachers, students, parents, administrators, and community members would be analyzed in terms that did justice to their complexity. Scholars would do more than simply identify the extent to which common practice corresponded to official policy. Instead, they would begin to investigate the ways in which instructors use various pedagogies in their efforts to assume control over students' private space and physical movement, while concurrently asserting authority over knowledge dissemination and production. Although the terms through which such authority is expressed are more harsh and visible within correctional institutional settings, they are no less salient to the culture of educational institutions and deserve to be scrutinized.

The usefulness of applying Basil Bernstein's notions of strong and weak framing systems (pedagogical relations between teacher and student) and classification codes (collection of curricular material on the basis of disciplinary boundaries) to Chinese educational settings has been noted by Western scholars.[45] But because the reformatory and work-study factory class cases highlight how strong framing systems and weak classification codes can coexist in unexpected and contradictory ways, it is even more imperative that scholars investigate the pedagogical and curricular similarities and differences that exist in more traditional educational settings. Certainly, delinquency studies highlight the importance of examining the nature of peer interaction within and outside of school boundaries more intensively; and this, too, is an area that has been neglected by mainstream Chinese educational scholars.

Nonetheless, the pursuit of ethnographic research in educational domains holds particular promise because the terms of the discourse easily transcend cultural boundaries and are inherently familiar and personal to all of us. It is because our educational experiences have been crucial to the formation of our own identities that we understand that the terms through which those experiences are expressed in cross-cultural situations are so important. Although it is arguable whether critical ethnographic approaches to the study of Chinese education have to this point fulfilled their ultimate promise, researchers committed to the method are asking the appropriate questions, a necessary precondition to enhancing our understanding of Chinese society.

NOTES

1. Irving Epstein. (1987). "Psychological and Behavioral Attributes of Juvenile Delinquents in the People's Republic of China." *Asian Thought and Society*, 12, pp. 267–269.
2. Ibid. pp. 268, 271–272.
3. Ibid. p. 267.
4. Thomas Bernstein. (1977). *Up to the Mountains and Down to the Village*. New Haven: Yale University Press. pp. 93, 261, 313–314.
5. "Rascals and Juvenile Delinquents Rampant in Shanghai." *Survey of China Mainland Press* 1576 (July 24, 1957) pp. 30–31; "Don't Overlook the Work Concerning Teenagers." *Survey of China Mainland Press*, 2675 (February 9, 1962), pp. 18–19; "Don't Let Your Children Do Small Business." *Supplement to the Survey of China Mainland Press* 105 (March 14, 1963), pp. 44–45.
6. Xiong Bo. (1982). "Jiefang chu Shanghai liumang gaizao jilue." ["Introduction to Remoulding Shanghai's Hoodlums during the Initial Post-Liberation Period."] *Shehui*, 2, 29; Zhou Yinjun, Yang Jiezeng, and Xue Suzhen. (1981). "Xin shehui bagui bien chengren: Yi Shanghai gaizao changzi shihua." ["The New Society Turns Ghosts into Human Beings: A Talk on the History of Reforming Prostitutes in Shanghai."] *Shehui*, 1, pp. 46–51.
7. Epstein. "Psychological." pp. 268–270.
8. Heidi Ross. (1991). "The 'Crisis' in Chinese Secondary Schooling." in *Chinese Education: Problems, Policies and Prospects*, ed. Irving Epstein. New York: Garland, pp. 109–144; Delia Davin. (1991). "The Early Childhood Education of the Only Child Generation in Urban China." in *Chinese Education: Problems, Policies, and Prospects*, ed. Irving Epstein. New York: Garland, pp. 42–65.
9. Martin K. Whyte. (1973). "Corrective Labor Camps in China." *Asian Survey*, 13, pp. 253–269; Martin K. Whyte. (1974). *Small Groups and Political Rituals in China*. Berkeley: University of California Press; William Parish and Martin K. Whyte. (1978). *Village and Family Life in Contemporary China*. Chicago: University of Chicago Press; Martin K. Whyte and William L. Parish. (1984). *Urban Life in Contemporary China*. Chicago: University of Chicago Press.
10. Amatai Etzioni. (1961). *A Comparative Analysis of Complex Organizations*. Glencoe, IL: Free Press.
11. Donald Munro. (1977). *The Concept of Man in Contemporary China*. Ann Arbor: University of Michigan Press.
12. Bao Ruo Wang. (1973). *Prisoner of Mao*. NY: Coward, McCann and Geoglican.
13. Guo Jianan *et al.* (1993). *World Factbook of Criminal Justice Systems: China*. Washington, D.C.: U. S. Department of Justice, Bureau of Justice Statistics, www.ojp.usdoj.gov/bjs/abstract/wfcj.htm.

14. Daniel J. Curran and Sandra Cook. (1993). "Growing Fears, Rising Crime: Juveniles and China's Justice System." *Crime and Delinquency*, 39, pp. 309–310.
15. Beverly Hooper. (1985). *Youth in China*. Victoria, Australia: Penguin.
16. Guo *et al.* 1993. *World Factbook*.
17. The following information comes from Irving Epstein. (1984). "Juvenile Delinquency and Reformatory Education in Chinese Society." (Ph.D. dissertation, University of California, Los Angeles); Irving Epstein. (1986). "Children's Rights and Juvenile Correctional Institutions in the People's Republic of China." *Comparative Education Review*, 30, pp. 359–372; Irving Epstein. (1986). "Reformatory Education in Chinese Society." *International Journal of Offender Therapy and Comparative Criminology*, 30, pp. 87–100.
18. Hang Hangwei. (1991). "Jinnian lai woguo qingshaonian fanzui de jiben zhuangkuang he tedian." *Qingshanian fanzui yanjiu*, trans. as "The Basic Conditions and Characteristics of Youth and Juvenile Crimes in Our Country in the Last Five Years." *Chinese Education and Society*, 26, pp. 88; Curran and Cook. "Growing," pp. 300–301.
19. Situ Yingyi and Liu Weizheng. (1996). "Comprehensive Treatment to Social Order: A Chinese Approach to Crime." *International Journal of Comparative and Applied Criminology*, 20, p. 97.
20. Curran and Cook. "Growing." p. 301.
21. Hang. "Basic." pp. 97–99.
22. Ibid. p. 92.
23. Ibid. p. 93.
24. Ibid. pp. 96–98.
25. Liu Weizheng and Situ Yingyi. (1996). "The Causes, Control, and Treatment of Illegal Drugs." *CJ International Online*, 12, no. 5, www.acsp.uic.edu/ OIJC/PUBS/ Cji205.htm.
26. Michael Dutton. (1997). "Translation: The Basic Character of Crime in Contemporary Cina." *China Quarterly*, 149, pp. 161–177.
27. Joe C. B. Leung and Richard C. Nann. (1995). *Authority Benevolence: Social Welfare in China*. Hong Kong: Chinese University Press, p. 161.
28. Situ and Liu. "Comprehensive," pp. 106–107.
29. Ibid. p. 104.
30. Ibid.
31. D. Lee, R. Neff, and J. Barnathan. (1991). "China's Ugly Export Secret: Prison Labor." *Business Week*, (April 22), pp. 42–43, 46.
32. Situ and Liu. "Comprehensive," p. 105.
33. Michael Dutton and Tianfu Lee. (1993). "Missing the Target? Political Strategies in the Period of Economic Reform." *Crime and Delinquency*, 39, p. 327.
34. Amnesty International. (1996). "China: One Thousand Executed in 'Strike Hard' Campaign Against Crime." *Amnesty International Homepage*, www.amnesty. org (July 5).
35. "Competition Rate 3 to 1 in College Entrance Exams" (1997). *China News Digest-Global GL 97–099.* (July 14) p. 3.
36. C. Montgomery Broaded and Chongshun Liu. (1996). "Family Background, Gender, and Educational Attainment in Urban China," *China Quarterly*, 134, pp. 53–86.
37. Curran and Cook. "Growing."
38. Zhang Lening. (1994). "Peers' Rejection as a Possible Consequence of Official Reaction to Delinquency in Chinese Society." *Criminal Justice and Behavior*, 21, pp. 387–402; Zhang Lening. (1995). "Consequences of Official Reactions to Delinquency in Chinese Society." (Ph.D. dissertation, State University of New York at Albany); Zhang Lening and Steven F. Messner. (1995). "Family

Deviance and Delinquency in China." *Criminology*, 33, pp. 359–387; Zhang Lening and Steven F. Messner. (1996). "School Attachment and Official Delinquency Status in the People's Republic of China." *Sociological Forum*, 11, pp. 285–303; Liu Weizheng. (1994). "Perceptions of Delinquency Among Junior High School Students in Shenzhen City of the People's Republic of China: A Control Theory Perspective." (Ph.D. dissertation, Indiana University of Pennsylvania).

39. National Institute of Justice. (1996). "Delinquency in China: Study of a Birth Cohort: A Summary of a Presentation by Marvin Wolfgang." Research Preview, http://www.ncjrs.org/txtfiles/china.txt (May).

40. Zhang and Messner. "Family."

41. Zhang. "Peers' Rejection"; and Zhang and Messner. "School Attachment."

42. For example, Zhang and Messner (1996) argue in favor of the importance of school attachment while Liu (1994) emphasizes value orientation and socialization.

43. Finn-Aage Esbensen. (1986). "Participant Observation in a County Jail." *International Journal of Offender Therapy and Comparative Criminology*, 30, p. 166.

44. Michel Foucault. (1977). *Discipline and Punish: The Birth of the Prison*. New York: Pantheon.

45. Irving Epstein. (1989). "Critical Pedagogy and Chinese Pedagogy." *Journal of Curriculum Theorizing*, 9, pp. 69–98; Ruth Hayhoe. (1999). *China's Universities and the Open Door*. New York: M. E. Sharpe.

CHAPTER 9

The Closing of the Gender Gap in Schooling: The Case of Thailand

John Knodel

ABSTRACT   *The results from the 1990 national census indicate that the long-standing gender gap in educational attainment favoring boys over girls has closed in Thailand at all levels. This occurred as responses to generalized questions on attitudes about schooling for boys and girls on nationally representative surveys are showing a substantial reduction in the preference for educating sons more than daughters, although some preference for sons persists. Qualitative data from focus group discussions in rural areas reveal that parental views on gender and schooling are complex and do not operate uniformly to favor one sex over the other. Moreover, the changing socio-economic context of schooling decisions in Thailand are likely to encourage parents to favor girls at least as much as boys in education. While gender inequality in schooling is no longer important, the socioeconomic level continues to influence starkly Thai children's chances for higher levels of education.*

Introduction

While formal education is increasingly valued by parents in most countries, differences often exist in the extent to which families deem schooling of equal importance for sons and daughters. These attitudes are often complex and involve a variety of contingencies but, on balance, they typically favor sons over daughters. Indeed, gender inequality in schooling favoring boys over girls is a common feature in much of the developing world (Smock, 1981; Kelly and Elliott, 1982; King, 1990; Sadik, 1990; King and Hill, 1991; Population Action International, 1993; United Nations Development Program, 1995). Despite the potentially important role culturally determined attitudes play in perpetuating this pattern, surprisingly little research has been conducted on

popular attitudes concerning the schooling of boys and girls and how they relate to educational attainment. The present study focuses on Thailand. It examines quantitative data on national trends in educational attainment by
gender and in attitudes towards whether sons or daughters should be favored
in schooling. It also explores qualitative data from rural parents on the underlying attitudes related to educating sons and daughters.

Thailand is a particularly interesting and instructive case for the study of
gender and schooling. As in most other developing countries, families have
traditionally expressesed some preference for educating sons over daughters
and this has translated into higher literacy and average educational levels for
men than for women in the adult population. Direct survey questions continue to elicit responses more favorable to educating sons than daughters although the extent to which this is the case has declined dramatically in recent years. At the same time, the gender gap in educational attainment has
closed. Analysis of in-depth qualitative data on parental attitudes, when interpreted in the context of recent educational policies, the changing socioeconomic environment brought about by the development process and the
more general cultural climate regarding gender preferences for children,
provides insights into how the closing of the gender gap in schooling could
come about.

Data for this study come from several sources. The 1.2 percent sample of
the 1990 National Census of Thailand provides quantitative evidence on the
trends in educational attainment by gender. The 1988 and 1993 Social Attitudes Towards Children Surveys provide nationally representative data on
general attitudes towards the education of sons and daughters. The 1987
and 1992 Children and Youth Surveys provide equivalent information on education, employment and pay. Finally, a series of focus groups conducted
with parents of current and past students in primary and secondary schools in
two rural districts of different regions in the country provide detailed qualitative information on the gender-specific education considerations of parents.[1]

THE THAI SETTING

Thailand is a tropical country in the Indo-Chinese peninsula of southeast
Asia bordered by Kampuchea and Laos to the east and northeast, by Burma
to the west and northwest and by Malaysia to the south. Unlike its neighbors, Thailand has never been colonized by a foreign power. A common religion is one of the most important factors contributing to the relative cultural homogeneity of the Thai population. According to the 1990 National
Census, 95 percent are Buddhists with most of the remainder (4 percent)
being Moslems who live predominantly in the south of the country. Much
of the dominant Thai value system and its associated behavior patterns derive from Theravada Buddhism, the predominant version of the religion in
Thailand. This is true despite the influence and practices of Brahminism and
animism which are readily evident and intertwined with popular religion as

practiced today. The teachings of this school of Buddhism are absorbed from early childhood and major precepts are recited in primary school. Many Thai males, particularly in rural areas, spend a short period (typically three months) as monks during early adulthood; this experience reinforces both Buddhist concepts and behavior patterns (Mole, 1973). The role of Buddhism and the nature of its influence in shaping gender relations in Thailand is still very much a matter for debate (see, for example, Keyes, 1987; Pyne, 1994).

Modern-day Thailand is in the midst of a social and economic transformation involving major shifts towards nonagricultural employment, increased urbanization, improving standards of living and increasing educational levels among its population. Indeed much of the developing world, particularly in East and Southeast Asia, have these features in common. Thailand is among the most successful, as measured by conventional indices of economic development such as the sustained high rate of economic growth during most of the last quarter century (Robinson *et al.*, 1991; Kulick and Wilson, 1992). It is also enviable in its achievement of almost universal literacy among adults and completion of primary school by recent cohorts of youngsters. Nevertheless, for a country at Thailand's level of development, the proportions of the population with more than a primary education is unusually low, at least within the present regional context of East and Southeast Asia (Keyes, 1987; Thailand Development Research Institute, 1989). Moreover, despite the ongoing socioeconomic transformation, Thailand still remains predominantly rural. According to the 1990 Census, only 29 percent of the population lived in urban or semi-urban areas and the remaining 71 percent in rural areas. Moreover, approximately one-third of the rural population was estimated to be living in absolute poverty (United Nations Development Program, 1994) and as development proceeds, income inequality is worsening (Robinson *et al.*, 1991).

Gender, Class and Education

Both today and in the past, education plays a crucial role in determining class distinctions in Thai society (Keyes, 1987, 1991). The current national system of education sharply "sorts" graduates according to the level of schooling they complete with the majority, until very recently, exiting before the start of even the lower secondary level. The sharp drop-off in the proportion who continue from one level to the next predetermines in a very real sense the access that graduates of the educational system will have to positions in either the extensive civil service or in the rapidly expanding industrial and technologically oriented service sector.

Although in the past education probably was of lesser economic importance, particularly in rural areas, it also played an important role in determining social class and prestige. Prior to the establishment of modern state-sponsored universal formal education, schools associated with local Buddhist temples existed in most communities with a monastic compound (Thompson, 1910; Keyes, 1991). The purpose of education at that time was to inculcate sufficient literacy to permit access to Buddhist religious texts. Instruction was intended primarily as preparation for becoming a monk. Nevertheless, the literacy gained as a result of attending such schools could also provide access to other texts and, hence, to a variety of knowledge that could earn respect and status in the community. Thus, not only monks but literate men in general were able to assume specialized roles and perform functions considered essential for social life, including those associated with religious ceremonies, calculating astrological influences or making medical preparations. In these ways, education served to differentiate men socially and illiteracy was typically associated with a low socioeconomic position within a community (Keyes, 1991).

Since only males could be ordained as novices or monks, girls generally did not attend the temple schools of the past. Although in some urban settings girls could acquire an education, literacy was largely restricted to men, particularly in rural communities. In some senses, education played less of a role in determining class for women in pre-modern rural Thai communities than it did for men. One reason was simply that schooling was almost universally lacking among women. Instead, women gained prestige through practical knowledge and skills that did not depend on textual learning and through "nurturing" monks by providing foodstuffs on a regular basis (Keyes, 1991). In the context of modern-day Thailand, where economic differentiation increasingly defines class and where formal schooling is of increasing importance for access to the opportunities for nonagricultural employment created by economic development, education is becoming equally crucial for both sexes.

The Modern Thai Educational System

Universal compulsory education was enacted into law in Thailand in 1921 but it was only in the 1930s, following the 1932 Revolution, that the law was implemented in most communities (Landon, 1939). Since then the educational system has undergone a number of changes. According to the present system, which has been in effect since 1978, primary education consists of a single, compulsory level of six years of schooling and secondary education is divided into a lower and upper level, each of three years' duration, and is not compulsory. Upper secondary education is divided into academic and vocational streams that are treated as equivalent for the purpose of the present analysis. According to the previous system, initiated in 1960, primary school was divided into a compulsory lower level of four years and an upper level of three years which was to become compulsory over a period of time on a locality-specific basis; secondary education was non-compulsory and consisted of a three year lower level and a two year upper level.

In practice, gaining a higher education within the Thai educational system involves a sequence of several critical transitions. The most important of these has been between the completion of the compulsory level and the start of the next level. In the context of the current system, this involves the transition from primary to lower secondary school. Since drop-out rates are low within a particular level, the second critical transition point occurs between the lower secondary and upper secondary levels (either in the academic or the vocational stream). Under the system that prevailed between 1960 and 1977, the transition between the lower and upper primary levels was the most critical because most students dropped out after completing the first four compulsory primary grades. During this period, however, the situation was changing as compulsory schooling was being extended through the upper primary level in increasing numbers of localities.

The national trends in educational attainment over the last six decades are represented in Fig. 1 based on the 1.2 percent sample of the 1990 Census.[2] The percentage completing primary grades 4 and 6 and starting lower and upper secondary school are shown for single year age groups. The measures are displayed only for persons at or above the age at which the large majority would have reached each particular level. Each age group corresponds to a birth cohort: the younger the age, the more recent the cohort. Thus, the trend towards increasing proportions receiving any given level of education with decreasing age signifies an increasing education over time (and over successive more recent birth cohorts).

Even though the large majority of persons who would eventually attain a particular educational level would have reached that level by the age of the youngest cohort shown, some "censoring" of the results is still present, because a small percentage of the youngest age cohorts shown were still

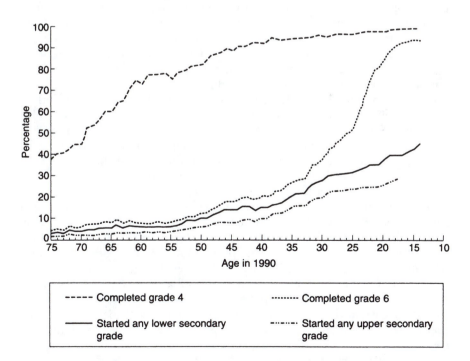

Figure 1:   Trends in educational attainment in Thailand in 1990.

attending grades below the index level and others who have already exited from the educational system could return through adult education programs.[3] Thus, the proportion completing any level of education is underestimated for the most recent cohorts shown. This is true even when the trend in proportions reaching a particular level displays a continuing increase through the youngest cohort shown.

The experience of the series of cohorts shown in Fig. 1 reflects the major recent changes in the Thai educational system. Persons aged around twenty-five years in 1990 would have been the first to be affected by the 1978 restructuring of the educational system in which compulsory schooling was universally extended to grade 6. In addition, the expansion of compulsory education from primary grade 4 to primary grade 7, that was taking place under the former educational plan, would have affected the birth cohorts immediately preceding it.

The percentage completing grade 4 is not directly affected by the changes in the compulsory level since grade 4 was within the compulsory range from the beginning. That this percentage has been high for quite some time reflects the Thai government's success in providing almost universal primary education to this level. Starting with cohorts that were aged forty-three years or younger in 1990 (who would have entered primary school in the mid-1950s), more than 90 percent completed grade 4; this has risen to more than 95 percent among more recent cohorts. In contrast, the percentages completing grade 6 show a recent sharp increase, rising from less than 30 percent among persons aged thirty-three years in 1990 to more than 90 percent among those in their mid- and late teens. This increase largely reflects changes in the compulsory level, first as increasing numbers of localities raised the compulsory level from grade 4 to 7 under the former educational plan and, more recently, as the nationwide change making grade 6 compulsory rapidly took hold from 1978 onwards. The levelling off for the most recent cohorts reflects data censorship, as mentioned above. For example, 1.9 percent of the fourteen-year-olds were still attending the lower grades (most of whom will eventually complete grade 6) compared with 0.7 percent of fifteen-year-olds. Thus, the final proportion of those aged fourteen years in 1990 who eventually complete grade 6 is likely to exceed that of the immediately preceding cohorts.[4]

The percentage starting lower secondary school (i.e. starting grade 8 in the earlier system or grade 7 in the current system) is not directly affected by changes in the compulsory level since secondary education has never been mandatory. The results show steady progress in the share of Thai children who start secondary school. Because of data censoring, the eventual rise in the percentage starting lower secondary school among the most recent cohorts is certain to be even sharper than that shown.[5] A slow but relatively steady increase in the proportion who attain upper secondary education is also evident although, as of 1990, only about one in four Thai youngsters were doing so.

The Thai Government has recently shown increased concern that the proportion of children continuing from primary to secondary school is low.

The high proportion of children who terminate education at the end of the primary level is seen as a serious impediment for upgrading the skills of the labor force and a source aggravating income inequality. The need to increase secondary education was explicitly mentioned in the Sixth Five Year Plan (for 1986–1991) and in the Seventh Five Year Plan (for 1992–1996) a specific goal was set to increase the continuation rate from primary to lower secondary to at least 73 percent by 1996. Moreover, plans are under way to extend compulsory schooling to nine years thus making lower secondary schooling (or its equivalent if the system is restructured) mandatory. In the meantime, two other programs have already been initiated by the Thai government to accelerate the increase in formal secondary education among children in rural areas.

One project, which started in 1987, involves waiving tuition fees, lending books and establishing branch schools at the subdistrict level, which after a short period are upgraded to independent secondary schools. The second project, known as the "Expanded Educational Opportunity Program," involves opening lower secondary level classes within existing village primary schools. Students attending such classes receive a free uniform, free textbooks and pay no tuition. The number of schools involved has become quite substantial in the few years since the program started (Knodel, 1992). Since the project started in 1990, it could not have affected the trends evidenced in the 1990 Census. The program does, however, bear on the views of villagers from which we collected qualitative data on the attitudes and opinions and perhaps on the attitudes expressed in the 1993 Social Attitudes Towards Children Survey.

GENDER DIFFERENCES IN EDUCATIONAL ATTAINMENT

Trends

The trends in educational attainment by gender based on the 1.2 percent sample of the 1990 Census are shown in Fig. 2(a)–(d), including the percentages completing at least some tertiary education (i.e. beyond the secondary level). While gender differences were pronounced in the past, they have entirely disappeared for the most recent cohorts. Gender differences in achieving at least a fourth grade primary education have been virtually nonexistent for more than a decade. For the proportions of students starting lower and upper secondary school, however, the convergence by gender is evident only for the most recent cohorts.[6] Moreover, the gender differential in tertiary education (shown in Fig. 2(d)) actually reversed during the last decade and a half.

Because of the wider range of ages during which tertiary education is initiated, data censoring is more severe for the younger age cohorts than is true at lower educational levels for which a clear lower age cut-off point can be determined. Thus, the declining proportions with tertiary education

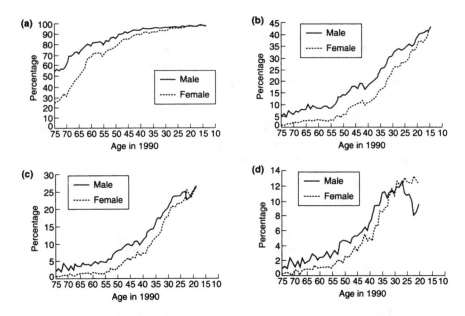

Figure 2: Trends in percentage by sex, of persons in Thailand, 1990 (a) completing at least four years of schooling, (b) completing at least some lower secondary schooling, (c) with at least some upper secondary schooling and (d) with at least some tertiary level education.

among younger Thais should not be interpreted as a reversal of the trend towards increasing tertiary education over time. This data censoring for the younger cohorts, however, is unlikely to affect the gender differences indicated in tertiary education, which is the focus of the present analysis.

A comparison of Fig. 2(b)–(d) reveals that for most of the cohorts shown, the gender gap favoring males has been greater in lower secondary than in upper secondary education and has been least pronounced, indeed for recent cohorts reversed, at the tertiary level. As shown in Table I, among all age groups, the ratio of the percentage of women to the percentage of men who reached the lower secondary level is lower than the equivalent ratio for the upper secondary level. Likewise, the ratio of the percentage of women to the percentage of men who reached the upper secondary level is lower than the equivalent ratio for the tertiary level. This effect comes about because, even though boys are more likely to enter lower secondary school than are girls, among children who do enter, girls are more likely than boys to continue to the upper secondary level. Similarly, among students who reach the upper secondary level, girls are more likely to continue to the tertiary level, thus further reducing the initial male advantage. Moreover, the progression rates from the lower to upper levels of education as well as from the upper secondary to tertiary level are consistently higher for girls than for boys for all age cohorts as shown in Table I. The difference in the progres-

Table I: Percentage reaching selected levels of education beyond primary school and percentage progressing from one level to the next, by age and gender

	Age in 1990 (years)				
	20–24	25–29	30–39	40–49	50 +
Percentage reaching given level					
Lower secondary					
Males	33.5	33.1	25.0	16.9	9.0
Females	31.4	26.6	16.8	9.5	3.1
Ratio (female to male)	0.94	0.80	0.67	0.56	0.34
Upper secondary					
Males	24.0	23.3	16.8	10.0	4.9
Females	23.6	21.0	13.0	6.1	1.7
Ratio (female to male)	0.98	0.90	0.77	0.61	0.35
Tertiary					
Males	9.3	11.6	10.4	5.7	2.8
Females	12.8	12.5	8.9	4.0	1.2
Ratio (female to male)	1.38	1.08	0.86	0.70	0.43
Percentage progressing from one level to next level					
Lower to upper secondary					
Males	71.5	70.5	67.1	59.1	54.2
Females	75.2	79.0	77.1	63.9	55.5
Upper secondary					
Males	38.7	49.8	61.9	57.4	56.7
Females	54.1	59.6	68.3	66.6	67.4

Note: The percentage progressing from one level to the next is determined by dividing the percentage of the cohorts with at least some education at the higher level by the percentage with at least some education at the lower level.

Source: 1990 Census (1.2% sample).

sion rate to tertiary education is particularly striking for the youngest cohort (those aged twenty to twenty-four years).

A greater self-selectivity among girls than boys among those who continued to the lower secondary level and gender differences in socialization which affect both study habits and interest in further education, probably account for girls' higher progression rates beyond the lower secondary school level. Given the general parental preference for educating sons over daughters, those girls who made it to lower secondary school have been more likely than boys to possess the characteristics important for academic success, including a self-inclination to continue schooling. Since decisions as to whether a child will continue at each juncture in the educational system also depends on the scholastic performance of the child, usually including the ability to pass an entrance examination, the girls who enter lower secondary school are likely to be more academically gifted than the boys, on average and, hence, do better subsequently.

Gender role differences among adolescents are also likely to favor girls. Their study habits and interest in school enables them to do well both in the classroom and in entrance examinations. As elsewhere, the socialization of boys and girls differs in Thai society. Adolescent sons are usually given more freedom and less responsibility than are adolescent daughters. While adolescent girls are more closely watched and are expected to do household chores, boys are given considerable license to go out and have fun (*paiteaw*) with friends (Rabibhadana, 1984; Pramualratana, 1992). As the focus group data presented below reveal, a relatively common perception exists among Thai parents that girls are more responsible and apply themselves more seriously in school than do boys.

Table II shows the types of tertiary education that each cohort received: general university, vocational, teaching and graduate nursing education. A clear shift in gender differences in the type of tertiary education took place at the same time that the earlier male advantage was reversed. Among the oldest women (aged fifty years and older), those who studied beyond the secondary level were substantially less likely than males to go to a general uni-

Table II: Percent distribution according to type of tertiary received, by age and gender

Current age and gender	Total	% distribution according to type of education (among persons with tertiary education)			
		University	Vocational	Teaching	Nursing
20–24 years					
Male	100	47.8	43.1	8.6	0.5
Female	100	51.7	32.1	12.2	4.1
25–29 years					
Male	100	45.0	36.2	18.3	0.6
Female	100	42.2	26.3	25.2	6.3
30–39 years					
Male	100	48.0	19.0	32.5	0.5
Female	100	41.2	12.4	42.1	4.2
40–49 years					
Male	100	51.2	18.3	30.0	0.5
Female	100	40.5	10.3	42.1	7.0
50 + years					
Male	100	59.6	12.8	27.3	0.4
Female	100	40.2	12.0	40.4	7.4

Source: 1990 Census (1.2% sample), original tabulation.

versity while among the youngest cohorts (younger than twenty-five years), the reverse is true. This reversal is part of a more complex shift in the type of tertiary education received by Thai men and women over the last several decades. Formerly, the largest share of women receiving tertiary education attended special teaching colleges. However, the share attending teaching colleges has declined substantially, particularly for women. At the same time, tertiary vocational education has increased its share substantially, particularly for men.

Data on the current attendance from the full 1990 Census (for the academic year 1989–1990; Thailand National Statistical Office, n.d.a.) confirm the feminization of tertiary education in general and the predominance of women in all but vocational schools. Overall, 54 percent of the students reported as attending school beyond the secondary level were women. This included 54 percent of the general university students, 69 percent of the teaching college students and 83 percent of the graduate nursing students. In vocational schools men predominated but even here 46 percent of the students were women.[7]

Socioeconomic Differentials

Numerous studies have documented substantial differentials in educational attainment in Thailand related to the socioeconomic background of the family of origin (Tan and Naiyavitit, 1984; Knodel and Wongsith, 1989; Thailand Development Research Institute, 1989). All the studies, for example, show a very striking difference according to rural-urban residence and economic status. Unfortunately, only a few socioeconomic characteristics are covered by the census and the information collected refers to an individual's or household's present status which itself is often influenced by educational background. For example, interpretations of rural-urban differences in educational attainment are complicated not only because people move but also because their changes of residence are often linked to schooling (given that both higher educational facilities and employment opportunities associated with better education are concentrated in urban areas).

Problems of interpretation associated with the fact that only the current socioeconomic characteristics are known from the census can be minimized by focusing on lower secondary education among fourteen- to fifteen-year-olds and the characteristics of the households in which they live. Most children of this age are unlikely to migrate independently of their family (in part because the legal minimum age of employment is fifteen years). Thus, the characteristics of the households in which they reside are likely to represent those of their family of origin.[8] Moreover, a lower secondary school attendance does not usually require a change in residence since (by the end of the 1980s) even most rural youths were within commuting distance of a lower secondary school. The gender differences in lower secondary schooling for fourteen- to fifteen-year-olds is also of particular substantive interest. Not only does the juncture between the primary and lower secondary schools represent the critical break between compulsory and non-compulsory education, but it is precisely for the fourteen- to fifteen-year-old cohorts (in 1990) that the long-standing gender gap in lower secondary education favoring boys has closed.

One rough indication of a household's economic status can be derived from census information on the type of dwelling and the material used for its construction. Previous studies in Thailand have used similar information effectively to measure wealth (Havanon *et al.*, 1992). The results in Table III indicate the percentage of fourteen- to fifteen-year-olds who had some lower secondary schooling according to sex, place of residence and type of housing, based on the 1990 Census. While there is little rural-urban difference in the gender gap for these youths, a very stark rural-urban difference in the percentage who continue to lower secondary school is quite apparent for both sexes. Note that since most Thais live in rural areas (e.g. 72 percent of the fourteen- to fifteen-year-olds), the much lower percentages of rural youths who progress to the secondary level of schooling carries a great weight in the national average. While the distribution of types of dwellings and their significance as indicators of wealth varies between the rural and urban areas, the results make it clear that in both settings, the substantial differences in lower secondary schooling are associated with dwelling characteristics. No doubt these differences reflect the important influence of a family's economic situation on the ability and/or desire to send children to school beyond the compulsory level. Generally, however, dwelling characteristics are not associated with major differences in gender equality for this young cohort in either the rural or urban areas. The main exception seems to be the noticeably higher percentages of urban boys than girls from concrete dwellings who continue to the lower secondary level. In this case,

Table III: Percentage of 14-15 year olds with at least some lower secondary schooling, by area of residence, gender and type of dwelling

	Urban (including semi-urban)			Rural		
	Total	*Boys*	*Girls*	*Total*	*Boys*	*Girls*
Total	68	69	67	32	32	32
Type of dwelling*						
Concrete (all or part)	80	85	75	53	54	52
Wooden shop house	73	71	75	61	59	64
Wooden regular house	63	63	63	30	31	29
From local/used material	37	37	37	16	15	16

*Excluding collective households.

Note: Urban and semi-urban refer to Bangkok, officially designated municipal areas and sanitary districts, while rural refers to all other areas.

Source: 1990 Census (1.2% sample), original tabulations.

however, the percentages are well above the urban average for both genders, reflecting the greater affluence of households that live in concrete dwellings.

POPULAR VIEWS ABOUT GENDER AND SCHOOLING

General Attitudes towards Education of Sons and Daughters

The nationally representative 1988 and 1993 Social Attitudes Towards Children Surveys provide evidence of popular attitudes towards the relative schooling of boys and girls. In both surveys, married women of reproductive age with children (or their husbands interviewed as a proxy) were asked identical questions about the level of education they hoped to provide for their children and whether or not their sons and daughters should have the same education.[9] The questions referred to their children collectively rather than to specific children.

The results in Table IV show that when children of one sex are favored, the respondents are more likely to favor their sons than daughters but that this tendency has declined dramatically between 1988 and 1993. Even in 1988, more than two-thirds of the respondents did not view gender as an appropriate basis for decisions about the level of education, with this group being equally divided between those who thought sons and daughters should receive equal schooling and those who thought schooling should depend on a child's ability. By 1993, the share who felt that gender was important for deciding on the level of schooling had declined to only 13 percent while the share reporting that ability should be the key determinant increased from one-third to over one-half.

In both rounds of the surveys rural parents were more likely than urban parents to favor sons over daughters explicitly, with parents in semi-urban areas intermediate in this respect. Nevertheless, very similar proportions of parents in all three residential categories responded that sons and daughters should be educated equally and only small proportions of all three favored daughters in either survey. The decline between the two surveys in the proportion indicating that boys should be favored over girls was a pervasive change in Thai society as indicated by the clear declines in all three residential categories. Likewise, the increase in viewing ability as the primary determinant of deciding how far to send a child to school was shared by all three sectors. In both surveys this attitude is most common in the urban areas and least common in the rural areas, although by 1993 more than half of even the rural respondents indicated that the level of schooling should depend on ability.

When attitudes are compared according to the educational background of the couple (based on the 1993 survey), only modest differences are evident.[10] In no educational group does much support exist for educating daughters more than sons. In addition, there are only moderate differences in the percentages who state that sons and daughters should receive equal schooling. The main variation is evident among the percentages who favor

Table IV: Percent distribution according to opinion about appropriate level of schooling for boys compared with girls, by selected characteristics of married women 15-49 years (or their husbands)

	Boys higher	Girls higher	Both equal	Depends on ability	Total percentage
Total sample					
1988	28	4	34	34	100
1993	10	3	32	55	100
Residence*					
Urban					
1988	12	3	34	51	100
1993	4	2	28	66	100
Semi-urban					
1988	24	3	35	37	100
1993	9	2	31	58	100
Rural					
1988	32	4	34	30	100
1993	11	3	33	52	100
Education of couple (1993 only)**					
One or both less than grade 4	14	2	35	49	100
Both grades 4–7	11	3	32	54	100
One secondary or more	9	2	29	60	100
Both at least secondary	4	2	35	60	100
Desired education for children (1993 only)					
Primary or less	10	4	57	29	100
Lower secondary	18	4	42	36	100
Upper secondary	17	5	37	41	100
Vocational	14	4	31	51	100
University	8	3	36	53	100
Other, unsure	6	1	19	74	100

*Urban refers to Bangkok and provincial municipal areas, semi-urban to sanitary districts and rural to the remainder.

**In cases where one spouse has less than 4 years of education and the other has secondary education or above, the couple is classified as "one secondary or above."

Source: 1988 and 1993 Social Attitudes Towards Children Survey, original tabulations.

educating sons more than daughters, which declines with greater parental education and in the percentage who believe that the appropriate education for a child should depend on ability rather than gender, which increases with the parents' schooling.

Attitudes towards gender equality in education are also related to the desired educational level for children. Again no substantial proportion of respondents categorized by educational desires favors educating girls more than boys. However, the parents whose educational desires for their children extend only to the compulsory primary level are most likely to express the view that sons and daughters should be educated equally, probably reflecting a recognition that all children, regardless of gender, are legally required to attain this minimum level. For parents who express a desire to educate children beyond the compulsory primary level, the percentage who explicitly favor boys declines consistently while the proportion indicating that the level should depend on ability consistently increases with the desired level of education. The largest group stressing ability is made up of those who did not express a specific desired level, undoubtedly because they believe that the level will be determined by the children's abilities.[11]

Parents wishing to educate their children beyond the compulsory primary level and who are concerned with their children's abilities more than with their gender probably recognize that success at higher levels of education requires abilities that are unlikely to be found more among sons than daughters. This reasoning probably underlies the pattern of association between attitudes about gender equality and rural-urban residence as well as the parents' educational level. Both urban and better educated couples emphasize a child's ability as a determinant of how much education to provide, probably reflecting the importance of ability for success at higher educational levels.[12]

In-depth Views towards Gender and Schooling

While sample surveys can document and quantify the prevalence of summary views on a variety of social issues, qualitative techniques are better suited for exploring respondents' concerns in depth and, thus, can lead to better informed interpretations, even if the data are not representative in any rigorous statistical sense. There is a variety of qualitative approaches that could serve this purpose (LeCompte and Preissle, 1993). The focus group technique is one such option. A focus group consists of a small group of participants selected from a target group and brought together to discuss a set of predetermined topics of interest to the researcher. The discussion is led by a moderator who follows guidelines developed for the purpose. The transcripts of the discussion serve as the data for analysis.[13]

The present analysis draws on transcripts of fifteen focus group discussions held in 1991 and 1992 in two rural districts of Thailand, one in the central region and the other in the northeast.[14] The decision to concentrate on rural areas was deliberate since the majority of Thais receive their primary education in village schools and the high drop-out rate between primary and secondary school is largely attributable to rural children. In each district, a similar study design was followed involving the purposeful selection of villages served by three different primary schools, two of which were relatively far from a regular secondary school and one of which was near such a school. In addition, in both districts, one of the two schools far from the secondary school was specifically chosen because it had recently started to offer lower secondary classes as part of the "Expanded Educational Opportunity Program" described above.

The focus groups varied in size from seven to eleven participants, purposely chosen from among parents of index children identified from the primary school records of current and past graduates. Each group involved participants who represented some particular target groups defined alternatively in terms of various combinations of criteria. These included the sex of the child, whether the index child was currently in primary school or had already graduated and, in the latter case, whether the index child terminated studies at the primary level, continued on to a regular secondary school or continued in an "expanded educational opportunity" school. In addition, the location of the primary school and the parents' socioeconomic status were selectively taken into account. In general, each group contained approximately the same number of mothers and fathers of index children divided equally among boys and girls. The design for the full set of focus groups is presented in Table V.

Discussions in the focus group sessions revolved around issues related to the education of children as specified in pre-set guidelines. Particular attention was concentrated on the determinants and consequences of continuing schooling past the primary level since this is the point at which the majority of rural Thai children terminate their education. The discussions provide general perceptions and attitudes related to education, reflecting not only the participants' own experience but their observations of others in the community. The discussions were tape recorded and transcribed. The transcripts (translated into English) serve as the data for analysis. Although no claim can be made that the groups from these two settings are representative of the larger population in any rigorous statistical sense, they provide in-depth qualitative data on the attitudes and opinions of a wide range of rural parents about various issues related to the role of gender as a determinant of the education of their children.

Non-relevance of Gender as the Predominant View

The views of the focus group participants are consistent with the national survey results with respect to whether boys and girls should be educated equally. Most participants either felt that boys and girls should be given a similar education or that the amount of schooling should depend on the ability and willingness of the child to study rather than on the child's gender.[15]

> Moderator: Between a boy and a girl, who should have more education?
> Prapha: I think they should have the same education.
> Namtha: It depends on each kid, whether he or she likes studying or not.
> (Parents of primary school students, central region, group 2.)

Table V: Design of focus groups with parents of index children (and group identification label)

	Central site (eight groups)	Northeast site (seven groups)
Parents of current students in primary grades 5 or 6		
Residents of village far from secondary school		
Better economic status	Group 1	—
Worse economic status	Group 2	—
Average or below economic status	—	Group 1/2*
Residents of village with 'expanded opportunity' primary school—average or below average economic status	Group 3	Group 3
Residents of village near secondary school—average or below average economic status	Group 4	Group 4
Parents of recent primary graduates		
Residents of village far from secondary school and village with 'expanded opportunity' primary school, child graduated from primary within last 6 years, continued to secondary school	Group 5	Group 5
Residents of village far from secondary school and village with 'expanded opportunity' primary school, child graduated from primary 3–6 years ago, child terminated education at primary level	Group 6	Group 6
Residents of village near secondary school, child graduated from primary 3–6 years ago, child terminated education at primary level	Group 7	Group 7
Residents of village with 'expanded opportunity' primary school, child is currently enrolled in grade 1 of lower secondary in the 'expanded opportunity' school	Group 8	Group 8

*This refers to one group and is the northeast equivalent of central groups 1 and 2.

Note: Groups generally include equal numbers of mothers and fathers and equal numbers of parents of sons and daughters.

> Sangdeun: In this high-tech age they (boys and girls) are the same.
> Pirom: You have to see each person for himself, whether girl or boy. Depends on who is interested. If the boy does well let him go on and if the girl is smart then she should get high education.
> (Parents of primary school terminators, northeast, group 7.)

The focus group participants viewed education beyond the primary grades as essential for making a decent living and for taking advantage of the changing work opportunities created by the rapidly developing Thai economy (Havanon, 1993). Generally this view was felt to hold true for both boys and girls. Most participants did not appear to believe that the value of education for the child differed by gender. A practical stance of investing in those children who are likely to benefit most, namely those with a sufficient aptitude (and desire to study), appears to be the most common strategy advocated, provided that the family has sufficient resources to fund the further study. There is also some sensitivity to recent "ideological" shifts emphasizing gender equality and this may influence views that children of both sexes should be given equal educational opportunities.

> Moderator: Comparing a boy and a girl, if both go to school, who will get more advantages?
> Chan: Now they have equal rights.
> Pra: It's the same for boys and girls.
> Moderator: The boys won't be more advanced later?
> Pra: No, not nowadays.
> Chorn: Today women can be soldiers.
> Chan: And police officers . . . No difference, equal rights.
> (Parents of secondary school continuers, central region, group 8.)

In several groups the opinion was advanced that now men and women can take the same jobs although not everyone agreed. The implication, at least among some participants, is that higher education has equal payoffs for boys and girls. Moreover, even if they were likely to take different jobs, girls could still make good use of their education, since virtually all the desirable jobs nowadays, whether gender specific or not, are likely to require schooling beyond the primary level.

Influence of Gender-specific Roles Later in Life

Although the predominant view of the focus group participants was that gender is not an important basis for determining the education of their children, as in the case of the survey results described above, a minority expressed views favoring education more for one sex (generally boys). Some of the reasons given were related to the future gender-specific roles parents envisioned for their children. Several participants emphasized that girls will have primarily domestic roles as wives and thus do not require much schooling, in contrast to boys on whom the main responsibility of supporting a family will fall.

> Pen: I want my sons to get higher education (more than my daughters). Boys who do farmwork will have a hard time when they have their own families. If they are educated, it won't be so hard for their wives and kids. For instance, my husband doesn't have any education, so my kids and I don't have an easy life. Therefore, I want my son to be educated so that the daughter-in-law will be happy.
> Moderator: And how about your daughters?
> Pen: If they get good husbands with knowledge and position, they'll be happy.
> (Parents of primary school terminators, northeast, group 6.)

The role of daughters as adult caregivers for their parents was also mentioned occasionally as a consideration relevant to determining how much schooling they should have. In Thailand, daughters, particularly the youngest, traditionally take care of their ageing parents (Knodel *et al.,* 1992). Usually, when this concern was mentioned in the focus groups, the attitude was voiced that the designated caregiver should not receive higher education since the child might then leave the parental village in search of employment opportunities elsewhere. Not all felt this way, however. Moreover, because there is some flexibility in whether the child who eventually stays with the parent is a son or a daughter, this concern does not always encourage favoring education for boys rather than girls.

> Pon: It's a tradition. Usually it's the responsibility of the youngest child (to stay with the parents) . . .
> Kiew: But on the whole we depend on daughters and not daughters-in-law . . .
> (The children) have to decide among themselves, otherwise we wouldn't have anyone to help at home. (Laughs) We'll ask to see who wants to stay. If we send them all (for further education) who will take care of us when we're sick? The ones who had the schooling won't visit us often so we have to choose who to send.
> (Parents of primary school students, northeast, group 3.)

A related issue involves parents receiving remittances from children living away from home. This is a common practice in Thailand, particularly for unmarried children who do not have a family of their own to support (Knodel *et al.,* 1987). A common perception is that daughters are more reliable providers of such an income than sons. Indeed, evidence from a 1986 national survey of the elderly indicates that non-co-resident daughters, particularly if single, are more likely than are sons to give money regularly to their parents (Knodel *et al.,* 1991). This could encourage parents to favor daughters in schooling if educated children are seen as being able to earn more and provide greater income.

> Sangkom: With the boys, if they have high education and work they'll drink and have fun when they have money and then the money is gone . . . Daughters are more responsible. They think more about family and parents . . .
> Somporn: For boys, if they're not married yet they send money to us but when they're married they have to be responsible for their wives. Girls, on the other hand, will take care of their parents.
> Tongpan: If they go to school, their pay is higher.
> (Parents of primary school students, northeast, group 4.)

Opportunity Costs

Sending children to secondary school involves not only direct expenses but opportunity costs that can differ according to the gender of the child (Hill and King, 1991). The focus group discussions make clear that for many rural families, the direct costs are a significant consideration and may deter parents from sending their children to schools which are outside the community. Survey data support this point as well (Knodel and Kaufman, 1993). However, such direct costs are unlikely to differ between sons and daughters and no comment was made during the focus group discussions to this effect.

Most groups indicated that the opportunity costs are minimal and are not a crucial consideration for the parents of children attending lower secondary school (children aged thirteen to fifteen years). Only a very few participants indicated that they had held back their children from studying in order to have them help with family work. Even for parents whose children terminated schooling at the primary level, the opportunity costs appear not to be very salient as a reason for not sending their child for further education. Most participants agreed that children at these ages are too small to do heavy work, such as helping in the fields and that without an official ID card, issued when a child reaches age fifteen years, a child cannot easily find work outside the family.

> Wanpen: (Children) do some work at home. They have to do something if they don't go to school. When they leave school they are not that big.
> Saneh: They don't do much really.
> Moderator: It's not like "I don't want you to go to school now because you have to stay home to work," is it?
> Wanpen: No. Usually we want them to learn but we don't have the money.
> Mun: Yes, short of money.
> (Parents of primary school students, central region, group 4.)

Hill and King (1991) pointed out that in a number of societies the opportunity costs of sending daughters to school can be greater than for sons, particularly where girls do more home and marketplace work than boys. The greater usefulness at home of young teenage daughters was mentioned occasionally in the focus group discussions and even once as a reason for why a participant did not allow her daughter to continue past the compulsory primary level. However this was an exception.

> Moderator: Would you send boys or girls to school?
> Noot: I'd send boys. I have two older boys, the youngest is a girl. I want her with me . . . Girls grow up in the household and they help their parents with the housework like getting water, cleaning and cooking . . . If you ask me I'd rather send boys to school. The housework is girls' responsibility.
> (Parents of primary school students, northeast, group 1/2.)

One reason why opportunity costs are not considered a major impediment to sending children to lower secondary school is that children can provide help even when they are still students. A number of parents mentioned that their children (mainly girls) help with housework after school and on weekends and some boys even help in the fields on the weekend and during vacation periods. How much children can help after school is contingent on how far school is from home; that is what time of day they return from school.

> Boonwat: If they have a school here the kids can even plough the field in the morning before they leave home.

Sangkom: They can take the cows to their parents and plough the field before they go.

Onsa: If we have a school nearby it will be a hundred times better. (Laughs) We can use them too. They can fetch the water and cook the rice, everything. (Parents of primary school students, northeast, group 4.)

In Thailand, a major change has been taking place over the last generation or two regarding the way parents view their children and their children's roles in the family economy. These changes are related to the spread of education and the change from having many to having few children (Knodel *et al.,* 1987). Many comments made during the focus group sessions suggest that parents now have considerably fewer utilitarian attitudes toward their children than they did formerly.

Sanga: It's because we see them as schoolchildren, that's why we don't ask them (to do work). "'That's okay dear, you don't have to do it,'" we'd say and we send them right up to age sixteen through lower secondary school. We never use them and then all of a sudden we want them to use the plough. We never used them since they were little.

(Parents of primary school students, central region, group 1.)

Gender-specific Issues Involving Children as Students

Although most participants did not explicitly state that gender was an overriding basis for deciding on the schooling of children, the focus group discussions made clear that the concerns of parents regarding the education of their children beyond the compulsory primary level often differed for sons and daughters. A variety of gender-specific considerations emerged from the discussions. Not all of these, however, favored educating boys more than girls. Several common themes arose.

(a) *Diligence and study habits.* One important perception that favors the post-primary education of daughters more than sons is that girls are more likely to take their studies seriously and to apply themselves in school than are boys. Adolescent boys are seen as more at risk of being distracted by their male peers with whom they spend time together, enjoying themselves in nonacademic activities. In some cases, this is seen to lead to truancy.

Wanpen: I think girls pay more attention (to their studies) than boys. When a father teaches them things, girls listen. Boys have their friends and they like to go out and hang around together. Girls don't go out much.

Kusuma: We tell them (girls) to read and they will read. But we tell boys that and they go to play.

(Parents of primary school students, central region, group 4.)

(b) *Exposure to bad influences.* A concern that arose in almost all the focus group sessions was the fear that attending secondary schools outside the village could result in children's adopting delinquent or otherwise worrisome behavior. Children could fall in with the wrong group of peers at the same time that parents' control over children is eroded by their being away from home. Moreover, such results could occur even if children were commuting to secondary school. Participants felt that as long as children remain in the village, parents and neighbors could more easily keep a watchful eye on them. While this concern was felt for children of both sexes, it differed in several aspects between boys and girls.

First, the participants generally believed that boys' nature makes them more prone to misbehaving than is the case for girls. Parents frequently mentioned boys smoking, drinking, sniffing glue and using other drugs; occasionally someone would say the girls can also adopt these bad habits but as noted earlier girls are perceived as more responsible and, hence, more likely to apply themselves in school.

> Moderator: Didn't you just say that you worry more about the boys? Why?
> Loy: Well, because when they go out of the house we don't know if they reach school or not. Say if they meet their gang, they can drink until afternoon and smoke too. But the daughters when they reach school, they will stay in school. They can't go anywhere.
> (Parents of primary school students, central region, group 1.)

Second, by far the greatest concern parents have about bad influences to which girls are susceptible when attending school outside the village is getting involved with a boyfriend and becoming sexually active. Such involvement could lead to premature marriage by elopement, with a resultant termination of studies or even to a non-marital pregnancy. Almost no-one expressed such concerns about boys.

> Buatong: Now boys and girls get the same schooling and that's good. But for sure I prefer boys to learn more.
> Moderator: Why do you prefer boys to learn more?
> Tongdum: Boys can't get pregnant.
> Kiew: When girls go out, parents think and worry but with the boys they can take care of themselves.
> (Parents of primary school students, northeast, group 3.)

> Moderator: And between girls and boys if they're to go on to secondary school will there be any difference?
> Onsa: (They are) different because one will be addicted to glue and the other to a boyfriend.
> (Parents of primary school students, northeast, group 4.)

Third, although the participants felt that girls were less likely to get into trouble than boys, the consequences for girls were usually deemed to be more serious, causing greater shame and other problems for parents. Thus, having a daughter who gets pregnant and brings a child home to be cared for by the parents was judged to be of greater concern, with more long-term consequences for daughter and parents, than having a son who sniffs glue or drinks.

Moderator: Talking about boys and girls, if they go the wrong way, who do you feel ashamed of more?
Sanga: I'm more afraid for the girls. I'm really afraid of their getting pregnant. Other things are not so bad.
(Parents of primary school students, central region, group 1.)

Pen: I'm not blaming my own sex. But bad boys can take care of themselves, while bad girls bring back their babies. And we have to take care of them all.
(Parents of primary school terminators, northeast, group 6.)

A number of the concerns expressed by the participants about exposure to bad influences could apply to any adolescents, away from the village for work or for school. However, most rural children of lower secondary school age, namely thirteen to fifteen years, who do not continue past primary school remain at home as they are considered too young to go off on their own to work and are legally prohibited from outside employment. Rural parents, who rarely have studied beyond primary school themselves, may also feel that they are less able to influence their children's behavior in the secondary school environment, which is foreign to them.

(c) *Threats to physical safety.* Another set of gender-specific concerns center around the physical safety of children who attend school outside the village. These concerns were usually raised in connection with girls, the most common concern being the risk of rape when boarding overnight away from home or when commuting back and forth to town to go to school. This concern was voiced in a number of the discussions and given sometimes as a reason for not sending girls to study beyond the village.

Manit: It's natural for parents to be worried more about their daughters than their sons.
Chorn: A boy never loses anything. They can go anywhere (laughs).
Manit: Simply put, nobody can rape a boy.
(Parents of secondary school continuers, central region, group 8.)

Although the safety of transportation was a concern for the parents of boys and girls alike, in some settings such a concern has a more negative influence on decisions to send girls to secondary school than it does for boys, particularly if commuting involved long bicycle rides or rough bus trips. As Hill and King (1991) pointed out, threats to physical and moral safety, posed by attending school away from home, are an issue that works differentially against girls in other developing countries as well.

The Effect of Having Schools in the Locality
The participants agreed that establishing a school nearby reduces their concern for their children's safety substantially. Opening a secondary school locally not only increases continuation for all children but apparently can make an even bigger difference for girls than for boys. Since girls, when studying away from the village, are perceived to be exposed to risks, more

serious and of worse consequence than for boys, the availability of secondary school classes in the home community reduces the "psychological" costs of sending daughters more than it does for sons.

> Pon: (Parents) are afraid that the girls will get involved (with boys) . . . They are worried so they only send boys.
> Umporn: And if it's a long way to school, then it might be dangerous for them (girls).
> Several participants: If they're near home the parents need not worry. If there is a school near home then everyone can go.
> (Parents of primary school students, northeast, group 3.)

As noted earlier, having a school nearer home also reduces students' travel time and, hence, increases the time during the day when they are available to help with family chores. If the burden of such chores falls more heavily on daughters than sons, the reduction in opportunity costs brought about by having a school nearby could also conceivably favor girls.

DISCUSSION

The results from the 1990 Census indicate that the long-standing gender gap in educational attainment, favoring boys over girls, has closed in Thailand at all levels. Moreover, this occurred as responses to generalized attitudinal questions on surveys indicated a continued but sharply diminished preference for educating sons more than daughters. To account for these changes, several interrelated points must be considered. First, as the trends derived from the census data show, the extent of the gender gap in schooling has been rather moderate in scale in Thailand for some time compared with many other developing countries (Hill and King, 1991; United Nations Development Program, 1995). Prior to the 1930s, when formal education was limited sharply to that provided by monks in Buddhist temples and oriented towards preparation for the monastic life, the gender differentials in literacy or formal education were indeed stark. However, since effective secular compulsory primary education has been implemented, the situation has improved greatly and for decades the gender gap has been relatively modest. As a result, the gap has been easier to close than had it remained wide.

Second, son favoritism is not a strong element of Thai society. Thai parents clearly value both sons and daughters although not necessarily for the same reasons. The results from numerous demographic analyses of fertility preferences document a strong desire to have a child of each sex and only a weak preference for having sons. This desire reflects the relatively favorable position of women in Thai society compared with many other parts of the developing world. Most observers of Thai society would agree that female autonomy is relatively high, inheritance practices are gender neutral, coresidence with the wife's parents is more common than with the husband's and conjugal relations are reasonably egalitarian (Knodel *et al.*, 1987). This situation undoubtedly conditions the impact of social and economic development in a different way than would be the case if favoritism of sons were deeply ingrained in an array of societal institutions (Greenhalgh, 1985).

Third, although Thai parents are more likely to say that they favor giving more education to boys than to girls than they are to say the reverse, they predominantly favor gender equality or gender neutrality in education. Moreover, a general question on a survey as to whether boys or girls should be favored in education elicits only the "net result" of a more complicated set of considerations on the part of most respondents. As the focus groups illustrate, such considerations can be many and varied and do not uniformly favor educating one sex over the other. Instead, they involve a number of contingencies whose importance can change as the social, economic and physical setting in which educational decisions are made alters. Indeed, in Thailand the setting has been changing rapidly and substantially.

Increased Accessibility to Schools

One contingency that the focus groups made clear is that changes in school accessibility can affect gender differences in educational attainment. Undoubtedly the closing of the gender gap has been influenced by the increasing accessibility to schools, promoted by the Thai government through the two programs described in the section on the Thai educational system. Even without such special programs, school accessibility has been effectively increasing as a result of general development processes at work in Thailand. Continuing improvement of local and provincial roads and the increasing availability of public transportation (including special arrangements to transport village children to secondary schools in the district or subdistrict town) brings schools closer in terms of travel time and ease of travel, even if not in literal distance. While these improvements benefit children of both sexes, given the greater parental concerns about sending daughters to schools outside the village, it could benefit girls differentially. For example, a collective means of transportation such as school buses or vans servicing commuting students from a rural area might be seen as affording girls greater safety from the risk of sexual attacks than bicycle or motorcycle commuting.

Rapid Economic Expansion

A second important factor that has influenced the trend towards attaining formal education beyond the primary level is the rapid economic expansion that has characterized Thailand during the last decades (Robinson *et al.*, 1991; Kulick and Wilson, 1992). Not only have employment opportunities expanded substantially in the modern, non-agricultural sector, but employers are increasingly insisting on secondary education as a minimum entry requirement for jobs (Beach *et al.*, 1992). As Hill and King (1991) pointed out, a changing economic environment not only alters parental views on the need for education but can also influence gender-specific considerations.

The focus group discussions make clear that rural parents are keenly aware of the rapidly changing situation with respect to education and employment opportunities (Havanon, 1993). The participants in virtually all the sessions viewed education beyond the primary level as essential for their children to reap benefits from the changes taking place in the Thai economy and society. Indeed, the most frequently mentioned value of secondary education was the access to good jobs that it afforded. Parents repeatedly mentioned that they want their children to have better lives than they themselves have as farmers. Invariably this meant obtaining some form of modern sector or government employment that requires formal schooling beyond the compulsory level. Villagers recognized that other children were increasingly attending secondary school and believed that their own children must do likewise to be competitive in the current day non-agricultural job market.

The results from the 1992 Children and Youth Survey, which are shown in Table VI, help to put some of the perceptions of the villagers about education, employment and gender into perspective. Among Thais aged eighteen to twenty-four years who were no longer in school, men are more likely than women to be working, both generally and specifically for pay. This difference, however, mainly reflects the exit from the workforce by some women to marry and bear and rear children (Knodel and Kaufman, 1993). If only single men and women are compared, the gender differences in the proportions working disappear. Indeed, single women are slightly more likely to work for pay than single men.

Given the keen concern of Thai parents in having children obtain modern sector jobs in a rapidly expanding economy, the associations between education, employment and salary are of particular interest. The same survey shows that education past the primary level is clearly associated with greater chances of working for pay, particularly for women. Moreover, for those who are educated at least to the upper secondary level and particularly for single persons, women are more likely to be working for pay than are men. Among eighteen- to twenty-four-year-old Thais with paid jobs, an increased education is plainly associated with higher pay for both sexes. Overall, women in paid jobs earn less than men. The differences are negligible, however, among those with at least upper secondary schooling.

These survey results suggest that, in some respects, the payoff to parents for educating daughters may be better than for educating sons. This is particularly so if the daughter remains single in which case, as other evidence suggests, she is more likely than her brothers to remit part of her earnings to their parents. A clear trend towards a later marriage age is under way, further reinforcing the value to parents of educating daughters. For example, the percentage of single women aged twenty to twenty-four years increased from 43.5 to 48.2 percent between 1980 and 1990. [16] As the focus group discussions indicate, the economic advantages of educating both sons and daughters past the primary level is clearly recognized by parents. Given that the economic value of post-primary education is increasing as opportunities for work in the modern sector expand in Thailand, it makes increasing sense to parents to send children of both sexes to secondary school.[17]

The focus group discussions suggest that parents' decisions about their children's schooling are based as much on concerns about the children's welfare as they are on the returns they foresee for themselves (Havanon,

Table VI: Percentage working, percentage working for pay and average monthly pay, by gender, marital status and educational attainment, among 18–24 year olds who are no longer in school

	% working		% working for pay		Average monthly pay in Baht (if working for pay)	
	Males	Females	Males	Females	Males	Females
All 18–24 year olds						
Primary or less	79	62	48	32	2104	1827
Lower secondary	84	69	58	46	2709	2527
Upper secondary or above	78	75	59	61	3693	3714
Total	79	64	51	36	2417	2213
Single 18–24 year olds						
Primary or less	77	76	43	44	2047	1853
Lower secondary	82	84	54	58	2647	2547
Upper secondary or above	74	80	55	65	3872	3766
Total	77	77	46	49	2421	2331

Source: 1992 Children and Youth Survey, original tabulations.

1993). Parents are largely motivated to educate their children because increasingly they see schooling as critical for their children's well being. The relatively equal desire among couples to have a child of each sex, as noted above, probably contributes to the lack of a strong preference for schooling sons rather than daughters. Parents are concerned that both their sons and daughters do well in the future. One way, perhaps the main way, to influence this outcome in the context of the current socioeconomic reality is by sending children for as much education as the family resources and child's ability permit. And this holds equally for sons and daughters.

CONCLUDING REMARKS

Despite the disappearance of gender differentials in educational attainment in Thailand, the gender-specific concerns of parents related to the schooling of their children continue to play a part in educational decisions for both boys and girls. Discussions of gender and schooling, not just in Thailand but in the developing world generally, often overlook the multidimensional nature of these concerns and focus instead only on their perceived net outcome, namely the disadvantage of girls relative to boys. The current efforts by international agencies to heighten awareness of women's issues in developing countries and to promote the empowerment of women serves to reinforce this tendency by completely ignoring gender-related issues that serve to inhibit boy's education (Population Council, 1995; Sadik, 1995; United Nations Development Program, 1995). As the present analysis shows, at least in the case of Thailand, the concerns of ordinary villagers about their children's education clearly reveal gender-specific barriers to education for boys as well as for girls. In most settings, addressing the full range of such gender-specific concerns would better serve government efforts to foster education than a more narrow emphasis on gender inequality and its focus on impediments to girl's schooling alone.

Thailand is by no means unique in the developing world in having closed the gender gap in schooling. At a regional level, recent international statistics on school enrolments indicate virtually no gender gap in schooling in Southeast Asia and the Pacific, nor in Latin America and the Caribbean and relatively modest ones in East Asia and sub-Saharan Africa; only in the Arab States and South Asia are girls grossly disadvantaged in school enrolments (United Nations Development Program, 1995). Moreover, virtually everywhere that girls receive significantly less schooling than boys, the gender gap is in the process of diminishing. In some cases, this is occurring so rapidly that a strong policy emphasis on closing the gap, as broadly advocated by the United Nations and other international development organizations, seems almost unnecessary.

The foregoing analysis for Thailand suggests it is important to keep in perspective the influence of gender on education. The census data cited above, as well as previous studies, make clear that the socioeconomic background of a family exerts a major influence on the chances that a Thai child of either sex will continue education past the compulsory primary level. Even in prior decades, when gender differences in educational attainment still existed, they were modest compared with the differentials that have persisted with respect to rural-urban residence, the parents' education or the family's economic status.

Not only in Thailand, but probably in all developing countries, socioeconomic inequality deprives both boys and girls of adequate schooling and to an extent that is likely to far exceed the gender gap in all but the most extreme settings of female disadvantage (Knodel and Jones, 1996). It is noteworthy in this connection that the results of a recent extensive study of educational attainment in Vietnam closely resemble those of Thailand. While the gender gap in schooling in Vietnam has closed or reversed at all levels, very substantial differences in the schooling of both sexes, with respect to household wealth level and parents' education, are evident (Anh *et al.*, 1995). Thus, in both socialist and non-socialist countries, disadvantaged socioeconomic backgrounds can be very important impediments to schooling. Unbalanced attention to gender inequality in education by international development organizations detracts from the attention accorded these other dimensions which are often more pronounced. It would be unfortunate to lose sight of the typically powerful effect of socioeconomic disadvantage on educational opportunities in the pursuit of promoting gender equality in schooling.

ACKNOWLEDGMENTS

Part of the research for the present study was conducted while the author was a consulting senior associate of the Population Council. Chris Wheeler provided helpful comments on an earlier version of this paper. Napaporn Havanon and Boonreang Kajornsin collaborated in previous analyses from which the present study has benefited. All the opinions expressed in the present paper, however, are solely those of the author.

NOTES

1. The results from the 1990 Census sample, the 1988 and 1993 Social Attitudes Towards Children Surveys and the 1992 Children and Youth Survey are based on original tabulations from the data tapes. The census sample involves almost 500,000 cases. Each of the subsets selected for analysis from the surveys involve over 10,000 cases. For additional descriptions of these sources see Thailand, National Statistical Office, n.d.a, 1990, n.d.b and 1994.
2. The estimations of completed education take account of the fact that completed education as recorded in the census does not reflect the schooling attained in the school year that terminated just prior to the census date.
3. The effect of adult education on the formal educational attainment of the cohorts shown is likely to be quite small judging from the proportion of adults who are reported as being enrolled at different levels of schooling in the 1990

Census. For example, among twenty- to twenty-nine-year-olds, 0.5 percent were reported as currently studying (presumably in adult education classes) at the primary level, 0.1 percent at the lower secondary level and 0.7 percent at the upper secondary level.

4. For example, if we assume that all the children who are in primary grades 1–5 in 1990 in each of the cohorts shown will complete grade 6, the total percentage of fourteen-year olds compared with sixteen-year-olds who would complete grade 6 would be 93.2 versus 92.1 percent, instead of 91.5 percent of fourteen-year-olds versus 91.4 percent of sixteen-year-olds, as indicated in the 1990 Census.

5. For example, if we assume that the same proportion of those children who are still in primary school in 1990 in each of the cohorts will start lower secondary school as observed among the members of the same cohort who already had completed primary school, the total percentage of fourteen-year-olds compared with sixteen-year-olds who would be starting lower secondary would be 45.8 versus 40.1 percent rather than 43.2 percent of fourteen-year-olds versus 39.5 percent of fifteen-year-olds.

6. The fact that the percentages achieving a particular level is slightly underestimated for the most recent cohorts shown, as explained above, is unlikely to affect the gender differentials to any substantial extent since children who were still in grades below the given level were only moderately weighted towards more boys than girls.

7. Calculated from Table 19 in Thailand, National Statistical Office (n.d.a), 1990 Population and Housing Census, Whole Kingdom.

8. Information in the census on the relationship to the household head indicates that among fourteen- to fifteen-year-olds, 82.5 percent are children of the head (including step- and adopted children). In addition, 6.8 percent and 5.3 percent are grandchildren or relatives of the head, respectively (whose households may also include one or both parents of the child).

9. Answers to the latter question were pre-coded into five categories: sons should receive more education, daughters should receive more education, both should have equal education, education should depend on ability (rather than gender) and other responses. Since few respondents fell into the fifth category, it has been combined with the fourth for purposes of presentation.

10. Given the uncertainty of the extent to which the responses by husbands actually represented their wives' views, it seems more appropriate to examine the response patterns with respect to the joint education of the couple rather than the education of either the wives only or the particular respondent.

11. The same patterns described in relation to the education of the couple and the desired education for children is evident in the 1988 survey (results not shown).

12. This is supported by an analysis of the association between the proportion saying education should depend on ability and both rural-urban residence and the couple's education, in which educational desires are statistically controlled. Using multiple classification analysis, the associations in both cases (for both rounds of the survey) are substantially reduced while the association with educational desires is little affected (results not shown).

13. Although the focus group concept emerged half a century ago in a relatively fully developed form as a special type of group interview, the technique was rarely utilized outside of marketing and evaluation research until the last decade, during which it has increasingly been used as part of basic social science research. For an up-to-date review of the status of focus group research within a social science framework see Morgan (1996). The issues of design and analysis of the focus group studies are addressed in Knodel (1993).

14. The focus groups used in the present analysis were undertaken as part of the Determinants of Post-primary Education Study, conducted by the graduate School of Srinakharinwirot University, Bangkok under the direction of Professor Napaporn Havanon.
15. In the quotations from the discussions that follow, the target population from whom the participants were drawn (as designated in Table V) is indicated. Sometimes the comments are extracted from a longer discussion, leaving out the intervening statements for the sake of brevity.
16. The percentage of single people is also rising among males (from 66.4 to 70.6 percent for twenty- to twenty-four-year-olds between 1980 and 1990). Marital status has less impact on employment for males, although it probably has an important effect on remittances sent to parents.
17. This is clearly evident from a comparison of the 1987 and 1992 Children and Youth Survey results. For example, the share of out-of-school eighteen- to twenty-four-year-olds who were working for pay increased from 40 to 51 percent for men and 29 to 36 percent for women. Moreover, these increases were far greater among those with at least some secondary education than for those with only primary or lesser schooling. In addition, earnings are increasing substantially for those who work for pay, as indicated by the fact that the average monthly pay reported in 1992 was 69 percent higher for men than in 1987 and 85 percent higher for women. While these figures are not adjusted for inflation, given the relatively low inflation rates in Thailand during the intervening period, they clearly represent an increase in real income.

REFERENCES

Anh, T. S., Knodel, J., Huong, L. and Thuy, T. T. T. (1995). *Education in Vietnam: Trends and Differentials*. Ann Arbor, MI: Population Studies Center, University of Michigan.

Beach, K., Schwille, J. and Wheeler, C. (1992). "Transition to School, Transition to Work: A Review of Studies and Data on Primary School Leavers and the Workplace in Thailand." (Unpublished paper).

Greenhalgh, S. (1985). "Sexual Stratification: The Other Side of 'Growth with Equity' in East Asia." *Population and Development Review*, 11(2), pp. 265–314.

Havanon, N. (1993). "Learning from the Grassroots about Continuation Past Primary Schooling." In *Reflections from the Grassroots: Issues and Options for Increasing Educational Opportunity*. Bangkok: Graduate School, Srinakharinwirot University.

Havanon, N., Knodel, J. and Sittitrai, W. (1992). "The Impact of Family Size on Wealth Accumulation in Rural Thailand." *Population Studies*, 46(1), pp. 37–51.

Hill, M. and King, E. (1991). "Women's Education in the Third World: An Overview." In E. King and M. Hill (eds) *Women's Education in Developing Countries: Barriers, Benefits and Policies*. Washington: The World Bank. pp. 1–42.

Kelly, G. and Elliott, C. (eds) (1982). *Women's Education in the Third World: Comparative Perspectives*. Albany: State University of New York Press.

Keyes, C. F. (1987). *Thailand: Buddhist Kingdom as Modern Nation-state*. Boulder: Westview Press.

Keyes, C. F. (1991). "The Proposed World View of the School: Thai Villagers' Entry into a Bureaucratic State System." In C. F. Keyes (ed.) *Reshaping Local Worlds: Formal Education and Cultural Change in Rural Southeast Asia*. New Haven: Yale University Southeast Asian Studies. pp. 89–130.

King, E. (1990). *Educating Girls and Women: Investing in Development*. Washington: The World Bank.

King, E. and Hill, M. (eds) (1991). *Women's Education in Developing Countries: Barriers, Benefits and Policies*. Washington: The World Bank.

Knodel, J. (1992). *Fertility Decline and Children's Education in Thailand: Some Macro and Micro Effects*. New York: The Population Council, Research Division.

Knodel, J. (1993). "The Design and Analysis of Focus Group Studies in Social Science Research." In D. Morgan (ed.) *Successful Focus Groups: Advancing the State of the Art*. Newbury Park, CA: Sage. pp. 35–50.

Knodel, J. and Jones, G. (1996). "Post-Cairo Population Policy: Does Promoting Girls' Schooling Miss the Mark?" *Population and Development Review*, 22, pp. 683–702.

Knodel, J. and Kaufman, C. (1993). *Work, Pay and Educational Attainment Among Thai Youths: Results from the 1987 Children and Youth Survey*. Population Studies Center: University of Michigan.

Knodel, J. and Wongsith, M. (1989). "Monitoring the Educational Gap in Thailand: Trends and Differentials in Secondary School Enrollment. *Asian and Pacific Populuation Forum*, 3(4), pp. 1–10, 25–35.

Knodel, J., Chamratrithirong, A. and Debavalya, N. (1987). *Thailand's Reproductive Revolution: Rapid Fertility Decline in a Third World Setting*. Madison: University of Wisconsin Press.

Knodel, J., Chayovan, N. and Siriboon, S. (1991). *Familial Support and the Life Course of Thai Elderly and Their Children*. Ann Arbor: Population Studies Center, University of Michigan.

Knodel, J., Chayovan, N. and Siriboon, S. (1992). "The Familial Support System of Thai Elderly: An Overview." *Asia-Pacific Population Journal*, 7(3), pp. 105–126.

Kulick, E. and Wilson, D. (1992). *Thailand's Turn: Profile of a New Dragon*. New York: St. Martin's Press.

Landon, K. P. (1939). *Siam in Transition*. Shanghai: Kelly and Walsh Ltd.

LeCompte, M. D. and Preissle, J. (1993). *Ethnography and Qualitative Design in Educational Research* (2nd edn). San Diego: Academic Press.

Mole, R. L. (1973). *Thai Values and Behavior Patterns*. Rutland, VT: Charles E. Tuttle.

Morgan, D. L. (1996). "Focus Groups." *Annual Review of Sociology*, 22, pp. 129–152.

Population Action International. (1993). *Closing the Gender Gap: Educating Girls*. Washington, DC: Population Action International.

Population Council. (1995). *The Unfinished Transition*. Population Council Issues Papers. New York: Population Council.

Pramualratana, A. (1992). "The Impact of Societal Change and Role of the Old in a Rural Community in Thailand." In: B. Yoddumnern-Attig, K. Richter, A. Soonthorndhada, C. Sethaput and A. Pramualratana (eds). *Changing Roles and Statuses of Women in Thailand: A Documentary Assessment*. Bangkok: Institute for Population and Social Research, Mahidol University. pp. 44–54.

Pyne, H. H. (1994). "Reproductive Experiences and Needs of Thai Women: Where Has Development Taken Us?" In G. Sen and R. C. Snow (eds). *Power and Decision: The Social Control of Reproduction*. Boston: Harvard Center for Population and Development Studies. pp. 19–41.

Rabibhadana, A. (1984). "Kinship, Marriage and the Thai Social System." In A. Chamratrithirong (ed.) *Perspective on the Thai Marriage*. Bangkok: Institute for Population and Social Research, Mahidol University. pp. 1–27.

Robinson, D., Byeon, Y. and Teja, R. with Tseng, W. (1991). *Thailand: Adjusting to Success: Policy Issues*. Washington, DC: International Monetary Fund.

Sadik, N. (1995). *The State of the World Population 1995.* New York: United Nations Population Fund.

Smock, A. C. (1981). *Women's Education in the Developing Countries: Opportunities and Outcomes.* New York: Praeger.

Tan, E. A. and Naiyavitit, W. (1984). "The Distribution Flow of Education in the Formal School System: An Analysis on Distribution of Educational Attainment." *Journal of the National Research Council of Thailand,* 16(2), pp. 19–43.

Thailand Development Research Institute. (1989). *Literature Review of Demand for Education in Thailand.* Bangkok: TDRI.

Thailand, National Statistical Office. (n.d.a). *1990 Population and Housing Census, Whole Kingdom.* Bangkok: NSO.

Thailand, National Statistical Office. (n.d.b). *Report: The Social Attitudes Towards Children Survey, 1993.* Bangkok: NSO.

Thailand, National Statistical Office. (1990). *Report of the Social Attitudes Towards Children Survey, 1988.* Bangkok: NSO.

Thailand, National Statistical Office. (1994). *Report of the Children and Youth Survey, 1992.* Bangkok: NSO.

Thompson, P. A. (1910). *Siam: An Account of the Country and the People.* Bangkok: White Orchid Press. (Reprinted 1987).

United Nations Development Program. (1994). *Human Development Report 1994.* New York: Oxford University Press.

United Nations Development Program. (1995). *Human Development Report 1995.* New York: Oxford University Press.

CHAPTER 10

Peace Education and the Comparative Study of Education*

Robin J. Burns and Robert Aspeslagh

> We think you ought to know our opinion of some things in your civilization. Because you seem to think that we look upon the European world as our ideal. It is not always there that we have found true education, and we know that you must think the same thing. True education is not the exclusive property of those who have the advantage of books; it is found as well, among the people upon whom a majority of the white race, convinced as it is of its own excellence, looks down with disdain. (Kartini, 1976)

The young Javanese high-born girl, Kartini, wrote these words to a Dutch friend in 1902. She herself longed for the book-learning that she hoped might enable her to become a bridge between the world of her people and that of the colonizers. Denied it, she turned to the people and to an attempt to understand and change the effects on their lives of the limitations of their situation. On the one hand, she recognized the possibilities for practical good that were available, for example, through European medical knowledge, and the more intangible benefits of communication through learning of other languages and of contact with a diversity of people and ideas. On the other hand, she was acutely aware of power and of the one-sided relationship established between those with certain kinds and amounts of formal schooling, and those without it. While identifying the latter with the status of "child," she perceived that it was racial rather than formal educational differences which prevented the Europeans from finding any merit in the knowledge of the "brown" people. This same racial difference and senti-

---

*This appears as the introduction to the larger work, *Three Decades of Peace Education Around the World: An Anthology* edited by R. J. Burns and R. Aspeslaugh. (1996). NY and London: Garland Pub. Inc.

ment also determined how much access, if any, her people would have to European knowledge.

Kartini is cited here because her concerns continue to puzzle and to occupy those who long for a better future, and who seek a solution through education. In these decades-old writings, we find hope for the future expressed through education: hope both through the opening up of ideas and the acquisition of skills to enable the individual to have more control over her or his life, and through changing the position of a group, race or culture whose situation has been defined as low in relationship to a dominant group. Thus education is posed both as hope but also as a major basis for maintaining inequality since the dominant group not only defines what is valued knowledge, but controls access to it. The hope for a better future waxes and wanes, and the image of it changes. While human beings have this capacity for hope and for imagining a future which does not merely reproduce the present, key features of the image vary at different times, in different places, and according to the situation and aspirations of particular groups. Education plays a role in conditioning the imagination and providing or withholding means for the realization of particular visions, especially for minorities subject to educational institutions under the control of the power elites. Attempts to realize future visions through education are not just undertaken by idealists: they have to contend with other visions and motivations. It is argued that an understanding of the effects of the content and process of education, and proposals for change through education require some analysis of the mechanisms of power as they operate within and through education, in order to realize both potentials and barriers to change. For education is embedded within a culture and a social structure, and the latter limits the former (Carnoy, 1986). Thus, inequality can be based on and expressed through differential educational opportunity, which affects access, and through that, the position of the individual and the group. The knowledge which different groups acquire is also hierarchically evaluated: it may be adequate for day-to-day functioning (Berger and Luckmann, 1967) but this will not change the position of the group (Apple, 1986).

However, short of total domination, resistance is possible, which may be expressed through failure to acquire the dominant modes of thinking and behaving, thereby leaving room for alternative ideas and visions. The deliberate cultivation of alternative ideas, and the attempt to spread them, is the substance of this work. While some may argue that it is sufficient to teach a new message, especially one of hope for a better future, it is argued here that some analysis of power is necessary in order to enable learners to act effectively for the realization of their hopes. Inequality is the outcome of the exercise of power, and through inequality we see the explicit and implicit distortion of resources, concepts and processes in the interests of dominant power-holders. When we consider the possibility for imagining and realizing a better future, for creating a peaceful culture which embodies relationships between people based on tolerance, justice and participation, within an ecologically sustainable environment, we need also to think of the sources of our present ideas about these things. In the context of this work, that means particularly the social and cultural, economic and political discourses that support the negation of peace.

Kartini implicitly recognized the significance of inequality and its basis in the exercise of power backed up by the universalization of certain characteristics of the power holders, so that what they possess is defined as "normal" and "desirable." Those who are advantaged within a particular system define the world in ways that continue to favor themselves, and their knowledge as the "correct" version of reality. Foucault advances the concept of knowledge/power to show the binary link between the two: power is exercised when particular knowledges are accepted as revealing "truth" (Foucault, 1980). This acceptance affords validity and legitimacy to such knowledges, making them a powerful tool for defining how the world is to be seen (Watson, 1994). The world is described in a particular way, which renders other ways illegitimate, and discourse is at the juncture between power and knowledge as the means whereby the two are brought to bear on the construction of social life.

An essential step in the understanding of power and its nexus with knowledge is to recognize that the way in which we describe and give meaning to the world is constructed. Those in power use their knowledge to determine discourse, and through that, the legitimation of their own worldview. A key advantage that holding power confers is this control of discourse. Examples of dominant discourse relevant to the subject of this work include ideas about the future, resources, the environment and the differential value of particular ideas, concepts and ways of life, and that war is inevitable in the struggle to retain power. The different discourses come from an underlying cultural discourse which is determined by those whose power interests are served by perpetuating such ideas (Mannheim, 1954). Domination also enables the powerful to determine the major features of social institutions such as education, thus spreading the ruling discourses and distributing rewards for adhering to them. Power implies a division into ruler and ruled, and one of the perquisites of being a ruler is the right to define who can become one, and by what means. To maintain power, it is also necessary to convince others of one's right, in other words, to successfully claim legitimacy for one's acts. The more people's consciousness is formed so that they accept the social order as legitimate, the less need there is for the use of physical force to maintain power, therefore control of public socialization processes is sought after by the powerful. Education is both a site of power, and of conflict by competing interest groups (Scotford-Archer and Vaughan, 1971), who try to use it for settling different legitimacy claims. Who gets various types and amounts of education, and the content of that education, is an ongoing part of the struggle for power and legitimacy. Those who wish to change consciousness for more "just" and more "enlightened" ends, are also part of the ongoing processes to maintain or change the socio-political, economic, cultural and educational status quo.

The "radical" educational thinkers show the ways in which education as cultural practice supports the hegemony of certain groups (Apple, 1979; Bernstein, 1977; Bourdieu and Passeron, 1977; Bowles and Gintis, 1975;

Carnoy, 1974; Connell, 1977; Flude and Ahier, 1974; MacDonald, 1977; Young, 1971). Further, how subordinates learn to accept the negative evaluation of themselves and their culture has also been investigated, especially under colonialism (Carnoy, 1974; Fanon, 1970; Mannoni, 1964). Such understandings can be applied to minority groups in general. Kartini recognized the process, and expressed it through her concern to gain Western education for herself and her people, for its intrinsic usefulness and for changing the negative evaluation and inferior position of her people. She intuitively understood the interplay between power and knowledge. Only through access to the European knowledge, she perceived, could the Javanese people take their place in the wider world. What this would do to their own culture, and the efforts to prevent equal access, is another story.

INEQUALITY: A METAPHOR FOR PEACELESSNESS?

If we take Eckstein's (1986) notion that educational paradigms are characterized by sets of metaphors, then the radical paradigm is a way of depicting the relationship between education and society as one which is mediated by power and the desire to control the individual and the culture. This paradigm can be applied comparatively in the study of education in different situations. This article does not explicitly address questions of access to education and the knowledge and discourses it distributes. However, the peace education paradigm which forms the basis for a number of the contributors, engages with the radical paradigm, at least indirectly through its critique of dominant discourses. It does this in two ways: through the critique of structures and processes which underlie the negation of peace, of which inequality is a central outcome, and through the analysis of education's role in sustaining this culture, which is a "war culture." As Haavelsrud shows the radical solution is transformation, the other option being reform, which is an older paradigm in which peace education was founded and which continues for some today.

Concern about inequality and justice, as metaphors for radical peace education, are integral to the change program which is bound up in peace education. Change of culture, structures and consciousness alike will only enable the realization of the participatory and just visions of the peace educators and their companions, when constructed categories such as race, creed, gender, affluence or age cease to be the basis for the distribution of educational opportunities, in turn releasing the possibility of empowerment through education. And further, the world for which peace educators act, is one which addresses the issues of inequality, so that they must at some level be concerned with access to knowledge and the kind of knowledge which they, too, are transmitting. Perhaps the major difference between the transformative or radical and the reform paradigms for peace education today is the extent to which the program for change is directed at a structural program or one of individual change. And as several contributors suggest, a shift to an emphasis on culture is taking place, which may re-order the components of society and the individual in such a way that new resolutions can emerge. How these can be translated into, and brought about at least partially by educational programs, is also suggested in the contributions.

A COMPARATIVE PERSPECTIVE ON EDUCATION FOR PEACE

The present work is about knowledge for survival, in particular through the prevention of war and the promotion of peace. It is concerned with analyses of factors that allow war to be considered normal, with education to enhance people's consciousness of the mechanisms supporting a war culture, and with learning to challenge those mechanisms through empowering people for transformation. Our central thesis is that education, and the generation and transmission of knowledge which challenges dominant thinking and puts forward alternatives, can contribute to the realization of a peaceful, just and sustainable future. In order to examine this thesis, we have chosen to use the framework of comparative education as an approach to presenting the different ways in which peace education is framed and practiced.

Peace education, like other forms of educational ideas and practices, emerges in concrete settings at particular times, through the interaction of past and present. The influence of certain groups and their ideas is also a matter of situational particulars. We may choose to define a situation in a narrow, localized way; or through the socio-political entity, the state, or in broader terms such as north and south. These considerations of extent include a temporal dimension, as well as a spatial one.

We have chosen to focus on peace education as it has developed over the past twenty-five years through the ideas of people who have worked together in an international setting, the International Peace Research Association (IPRA), especially through its educational study group, the Peace Education Commission (PEC). The authors write from concrete situations and specific experiences and practices, and have brought those to the wider discussions not only at conferences but through friendships, projects, and ongoing contact. It is argued that contact has given rise to some general conceptual frameworks which are then taken back by individuals to work out in the local situation, including modification in those settings. How this transfer takes place, and the outcomes, is an issue which is central to at least one major strand of the discipline of comparative education (Halls, 1990). Insofar as the substantive content is about peace, and the use of education to attain human and social ideals which promote peace, the larger book also deals with ideals and processes which were at the forefront of the educational movement which gave birth to comparative education (Taylor, 1970).

The book presents sections which deal with the issues at a general level, and ones which address specific situations or "cases." The field of comparative education is littered with case studies. Despite the fact that comparison of education has been described as both a method and as the object of study (Halls, 1990), many case studies lack a specific comparative focus or intent. The field is also littered with complications of a specific educational issue in the education systems of different nation-states, not always in conceptually coherent ways (Kelly and Altbach, 1986). Peace education has not often figured in either the case studies or the educational issues and content discussed by comparativists. The book is intended to enable comparative investigation to take place. It is an orientation to the ample material available on peace education, including some details of the field within particular national contexts (Bjerstedt 1988, 1990a and 1992a; *Bulletin of Peace Proposals*— special editions in 1974, 1979, 1981, 1984; *Convergence*, 1989; *Gandhi Marg*, 1984; Haavelsrud, 1976; *International Review of Education*, 1983; *Teachers College Record*, 1982; and Wulf, 1974). There is little written from a comparative perspective on the ideas and issues surrounding peace education and related concepts. Exceptions include Aspeslagh (n.d.), Burns (1979) and Tonkin (1988), each relatively inaccessible. There are some brief histories of peace education which deal with the subject globally, written by social scientists rather than comparative educators (Boulding, 1987; Haavelsrud and Borrelli, 1993; Hermon, 1988). It sometimes appears that each practitioner develops his or her own definition, and each group must distinguish itself from others. Unraveling these and their various relationships to traditions, philosophies, ideologies and popular movements, as well as to pedagogies, is an extremely complex task, not often undertaken by educationalists. The comparativist, for example, who wishes to take an approach to peace education which Halls labels "international pedagogy" and a branch of international education (1990), which in turn he subsumes within comparative education, is faced with a bewildering array of terms and concepts which vary not just between nations but between different approaches to peace. There are also few accounts of peace education from the point of view of pedagogy, as comparative studies or otherwise, though it will be seen in this volume that the Dutch peace educators in particular draw on pedagogical theory and educational philosophy in their development of practice.

If, as is argued here, peace education was intimately linked to the foundation of comparative education, and if comparative education provides a way to understand the development of educational ideas and their practice, in concrete settings (Burns and Welch, 1992; Welch and Burns, 1992), then a book on peace education approaches from a comparative perspective is timely for both fields. Further, a grid has been used to select contributions based on place, time, approach and educational level, which provides sufficient material for reflective analysis by readers of both the conceptual development and issues, as well as the changing substance and practice of peace education. This in turn is the basis for raising issues about the way in which comparison can throw light on the questions: How do we educate for survival? Can education lead to a more peaceful culture? And how can such education be implemented?

PEACE EDUCATION: A BRIEF
COMPARATIVE OVERVIEW

The educational ideas which are the subject of the larger book are presented from a comparative perspective. There is an initial general concern, subsumed in the term "peace." Most peace educators claim a supranational rather than national or sub-national sectional order as the basis for conceptualizing this. The claim is made in different ways, from a concept of world order to normative appeals to justice, a common humanity and survival of the planet. Survival is the key underlying concern, and the focus is on averting war, and on alternatives to war, which is considered a major threat to human life. And the advocates of education for peace see education as central to efforts to change actions and consciousness in order to stop war and to bring about a more desirable human and ecological state.

There is great diversity within this overarching set of ideas. Content as expressed through the work of peace educators will first be sketched, in relationship to changes over time related to social issues at different levels, and then the ways in which cultural and national priorities also affect peace education will follow. Since considerations of context are integral to a comparative approach to an educational area, these issues are dealt with in greater detail.

The Development of Ideas over Time, and in National Contexts

The *time element* can be seen almost in decades. As we enter the period covered in the book, the Vietnam War was still a central concern for activists in Europe, Australasia and North America. In the 1960s in which Cold War politics were dominant and colonial empires were giving way to "developing countries," there were two major issues. These hinged around nuclear issues and the specter of global nuclear holocaust, accidental through the spread of nuclear power or deliberate within the context of nuclear weapon stockpiling and the possibility of their use in regional conflicts on the one hand, and inequalities, neo-colonialism and the growing rich-poor gap on the other. By the end of the 1970s, disarmament education had grown specifically to deal with issues of nuclear weapons, which were seen as the greatest threat; other issues were being canvassed in response to inequality, especially that between rich and poor nations, more usually under the terms "development education" and "global development studies."

Largely through the interactions of educators within the International Peace Research Association (IPRA), formally constituted as an educators' group in 1972, a distinctive peace education emerged (Percival, 1989). The Norwegian peace researcher Johan Galtung's idea of "structural violence" as a way to analyze war, disarmament, peace, justice and human rights was very strong at this time (Galtung, 1971), as was the educational approach of the Brazilian Paulo Freire, who linked education to liberation from oppression through "cultural" action (Freire, 1972a and b). As the ideas developed, there were attempts to implement them within formal education systems.

Efforts to form a strong and positive peace education to overcome violence in its various forms built up in the early 1980s. Emphases differed and disarmament education was a distinct strand, but positive peace was more and more clearly enunciated as the goal: more than the absence of war, the attainment of certain forms of human coexistence. And from this position peace educators entered into dialogue with educators with related central concerns: development, human rights, international understanding, racism, sexism. Analysis of the underlying structural conditions and the social formations which affect human interaction was a common element of all these issue-oriented concerns and educational approaches. Peace education clearly emerged as a concern for "one world, or none," from its early concerns with personal peace to an overriding concern with societal peace issues.

Toward the end of the 1980s new orientations began. These grew in part from developments internationally and within nations, and changes in consciousness arising from disenchantment with decades of political action whose gains could be swept aside with new conservative governments and changing economic circumstances. These can be linked with broader cultural trends, in particular the move toward a postmodern approach to individual, cultural and political life. On the one hand, "new age" thinking brought up new issues, including a way of expressing global awareness in terms of "holism," which can link the individual directly, rather than through stages, to the wider environment (Zohar, 1991). In this framework, individual change is directly related to global or universal change, and brought with it amongst peace educators a new concern with personal peace and with psychological approaches to helping individuals acquire a more peaceful way of being. On the other hand, the postmodern disdain for structures and groundplans has filtered into peace education as an emphasis on local action, diversity of approach and—resonating with "new age" thinking—an individual focus. The peaceful individual who can withstand outer turmoil is the image for this approach. A move from societal peace to peace culture is central. A third element is based in part at least on pedagogical issues, in which peace educators struggle with the process as well as the content of peace education. In recent years, these issues have brought together a number of earlier concerns—with engaged action as well as cognition in the formation of young people for the future; with "relevance" of subject matter to students' lives and with the "hidden curriculum," or making the environment in which learning takes place into an example of the desired social change and interaction processes, especially regarding power relations. Examples of such programs address conflict in schools and neighborhoods, twinning projects which address issues of "enemy images" and the effects on students' lives of various oppressions—poverty, family violence, unemployment and racism. Individual learning and skill development for action, rather than analysis, is a key objective.

The changing *cultural and national priorities* are harder to sketch and present in overview form. They involve national issues such as who determines the curriculum, the importance of the academic disciplines, the room for teacher and student involvement in curriculum decision-making and design, and historical and cultural factors affecting attitudes, ways of approaching issues, and the starting points for the development of peace education and its cousins. One factor which has played some role in peace education in particular places is the role of peace and related movements.

Liberation movements have been more influential than peace movements in forming the ideas of peace educators at the international level. At the national level, however, in the 1980s in particular, "Teachers for Peace" groups were formed in many countries, fairly directly related to the dominant peace movement, and they have formed an international network. The concerns of particular peace movements have been more likely to be reflected in national and local peace education efforts, than those of a more remote group of internationalized pedagogues. For it is at the level of implementation that the encounter with opposition, and the manipulation of the art of the possible, takes place, and this is done within a national-political and cultural context, as any comparative educator would acknowledge. A number of the contributions to the larger volume therefore can be seen as case studies, not just of the way peace education is conceived at a particular time, but of the way it is conceptualized and practiced in a particular setting.

Balancing the Centripetal and the Centrifugal in Education for Peace?

If peace education is practiced at a local level, what is the possibility for a concerted effort, and for a vision of a peaceful global society? In the post-war decades, as the need to ensure a lasting peace and to deal with regional conflicts accelerated, peace educators seemed to be global in their ambitions and approaches. The nuclear threat in Europe gave rise to the "third wave" of peace movements this century, and also gave it a particular direction, with disarmament and environmental issues to the fore. In the United States, disarmament has been a dominant theme, given the great power status and consequent threat, through disarmament action has had some different elements in the United States than in Europe. Where do other regions fit in? Struggling with issues of North and South, of racism and sexism, of human rights and global environmental scenarios, has been left to some extent to the peace education "internationalists," especially the North-South concerns. We have been faced with the issues in our attempts to work together. The second European Educators for Peace conference in 1988 provided one approach to the issues: think globally, act locally. What this means in concrete terms, and approaches to it, are exemplified in this volume. The global-local dilemma is at the interface not only between peace movements and other movements working for a more humane future, especially development, environment and human rights ones. It summarizes the political-personal tension, and with it, the tendencies to see action for change versus deconstructed consciousness and enhanced individual choice as the aim of peace education. It is also at the interface of different rationales for peace education, especially those that stress universal ethical principles versus enlightened self-interest as the bases for program development (Lindholm, 1975). Understanding and dealing creatively with diversity may well be the way to solve this issue, a new way to pose the problem which averts the dichotomizing of perspectives, and feminist theory is at present leading the way to this outlook (Weedon, 1987). Will it, however, satisfy those in the South, for example, who could well see in such an approach a rationalization for enlightened self-interest which leaves their concerns largely untouched? This is a dilemma which peace educators approach, walk beside, but often barely grapple with. Through working internationally, and through a comparative perspective on peace education efforts, the extent of the issues and their diversity is concretely encountered.

Both comparative education and peace education have their origins in a notion which can be summed up as world education (Scanlon, 1960). Peace education has a place within this, alongside a sometimes confusing proliferation of other "educations" and perspectives. The contributions selected for the larger volume have been chosen in part to illustrate the extent to which various approaches maintain an international perspective, since it is argued that peace is not an issue that can be solved by one group alone, while walking the tightrope of avoidance of a totalizing set of ideas and practices.

From Content to Process

The foregoing focuses largely on the content of education for a different future and for the solution of particular problems related to ongoing conflict. Content is not the only relevant consideration in the assessment of its capacity to change human action and interaction on a global scale. As Kartini discovered, who is educated, and by whom, which ideas are legitimated, and the effects on the people whose knowledge is not considered of any value, affect the outcomes of an educational process. Pedagogy has been as much an issue as content among the international peace educators and has also been an issue in some national settings. The issues are incorporated into the exploration of education for peace in this work. In so doing, they address an area of comparative education which has received relatively little attention.

THE COMPARATIVE STUDY OF EDUCATION FOR PEACE

The larger book provides the raw material for the comparative examination of peace education and related educational concepts. In the selection of contributors, we have also engaged in a comparative task through the inclusion of work which illustrates approaches within different geo-political regions (recognizing however that the concepts East, West, South, North which have been used to describe the major divisions of the world are not fixed, the East–West changes in the 1990s being a dramatic example). It also includes different approaches to the subject matter, conceptually and at different educational levels and sites. We have selected for inclusion different ideas and visions, different interest groups promoting particular ideas and visions, and different educational philosophies and approaches to policy and to investigation of the issues. And there is some historical perspective, from 1975 to the present.

From a comparative educational perspective, a comprehensive comparative study of peace education might have the following form:

Charting the Field

Basic concepts and their educational manifestations: peace education, peace and conflicts studies and disarmament education. Addressing the issue of basic survival would be considered first. This would then be considered in the light of related educational ideas, such as global and international education and humanitarian imperatives, and internationalized education, which considers both expanding content and issues of the individual, the labor market and the nation-state. Other sets of relations are with race, ethnicity, gender and class issues, or how does education deal with human difference and structured inequalities? Development, social justice, human rights and the environment form another set. Two underlying educational agendas might then be considered from which central concepts about content can be deduced. One such agenda deals with the question of political literacy (Jones, 1988; Macklin, 1985; Porter, 1983; Torney-Purta and Schwille, 1986) or what people need to learn in order to participate actively in society at different levels, and how they learn it, while the other is concerned with cultural transformation, also a question of both what is learned, and the impact of the learning methods and environment. These two agendas are keys both to proposals for change, and as ways to examine present educational programs and their outcomes. Both of these agendas are considered together, and a framework suggested for conceptualizing the different sets of education which address major themes.

Policies and Praxis in the Field

Approaches to educational policy-making and curriculum can be presented through first considering the process of generation of knowledge, its selection and organization for transmission, and the evaluation of both learning and learners. Such an examination raises questions of the ways in which particular sorts of educational knowledge and pedagogies are legitimated. Policy and praxis can be studied through case materials, but it is argued that a framework is needed, such as the one outlined in the foregoing, in order to theorize the ways in which such knowledge and pedagogies are formed. This in turn, provides the basis for change (Holmes, 1981). Further analytic studies might include ones which problematize the control of educational resources and examine the roles of interest groups.

Interpreting the Field

Two major approaches can be elucidated. One focuses on the substance of the ideas which underlie different educational framing of the issues. This in turn has two elements: the values and worldviews especially regarding the preferred future world, and the pedagogies which are associated with the different contents. This gives rise to a comparative discussion of future worlds and the means to reach them. A complementary approach looks in greater detail at the political sociology of educational knowledge, and uses the framework of pragmatic, normative and conceptual approaches to the solution of the problem: what shall be taught about the world, and how shall it be done in different educational settings?

The Way Forward

If we can put together the different questions and frameworks, then we can address issues which might provide the basis for showing how particular ideas can be introduced into educational settings with certain characteristics. This possibility to provide such a blueprint implies that comparative education can be predictive, and insofar as comparativists attempt to modify simple transference of ideas and practices from one system to another, it is assumed that we can have sufficient knowledge of processes to bring about planned change. On the questions which form the substance of the larger volume, however, we can only suggest, for the underlying values and concepts, hopes and concerns, are derived from the human capacity to imagine, invent and improve. The comparative study of the ways in which this is done through education, thus, can throw light on the way it has happened and provide new ideas and options.

This work is intended as one such attempt. In the vast array of issues and approaches to education about and for peace around the world, we can only take a small handful and present them, together with reflections about the issues and material. The outline above is better described as a collaborative research agenda, which is intended to challenge the reader to examine the scope both of the topic, peace education, and its manifestation around the world. While the book is not a detailed survey of the issues and practices of education for peace, it contains information about the development of particular practices and the links between individuals, groups and approaches. The background, concepts and major approaches during the period are considered in the larger volume. Also provided are perspectives from each of our particular backgrounds, the former putting a comparative and personalized face on the ways in which ideas are discussed, transmitted and implemented; the latter is also a personal account, showing how the search for a peace culture goes beyond idealistic utopian world-building and rather tries to implement steps toward the transformation of the non-peaceful present realities. The way in which it is written gives a foretaste of the complex interplay which we argue is the very nature of the issues and the realities they attempt to depict and change. There is change over time in the priorities and approaches;

there is also a circular process which returns to issues, bringing to bear on them some light from past experience, while the contemporary context throws out new perspectives, combinations and challenges.

OBJECTIVES

The following objectives form the basis for structuring the intent and scope of the complete book.

1. *To examine the ways in which the building of "a realistic basis for world peace" is interpreted as educational content.* This is presented from a comparative theoretical perspective so that the reader can examine questions about formal education as the interface between knowledge and identifiable social complexes. It also forms the basis for a comparative perspective on the role of non-formal education as an agency within and between nations for the transmission of knowledge, values and worldviews. The educational work of movements and non-governmental organizations is included under non-formal education.

2. *To present discussions of the processes of generation, selection, organization, transmission and evaluation of knowledge for peace and related goals, identified in the foregoing, looking at the political as well as the educational dynamics of these processes.* Such examination, it is argued, is necessary in order to show the socio-political basis for particular knowledge packages and educational processes. Thus, the notion of the legitimation of educational knowledge is suggested to provide conceptual insights into the ways knowledge is conceived and passed on.

3. *To bring together the fields of peace education and its like, and comparative and international education, in a way that is intended not only to provide a more productive way of conceiving and working with each, but to address some central issues of education and the future.* Thus, the book is about peace education; it is presented from a comparative and international education perspective. A comparative perspective, we argue, is valuable for the interpretation of the processes of highlighting particular educational contents, and devising educational processes and programs to transmit that content, at both the policy and educational institution or organization levels.

4. *To present these issues through the work of people within the Peace Education Commission of the International Peace Research Association.* While it is not an historical account of this organization, it uses contributors to the meetings and debates of that organization, which is an international association in substance, while also in the individual topics addressed dealing with practical peace education issues at the national or local level.

There are four parts. The first deals with *background, concepts and theoretical issues.* Following the chapter dealing with an overview of these, and a suggested framework for understanding different approaches to education for the future, the 1975 *Global Strategy for Communication and Consciousness-Raising* is reproduced. This came from a group of peace educators meeting within the IPRA Summer School. It incorporates several key elements of the work of PEC: a concern with analysis of underlying structural issues, which owes its origins to the work of Johan Galtung and Paulo Freire in particular, and development of a joint framework which could be applied in different settings while acknowledging the unique aspects of those. This is followed by Máire Dugan's and Dennis Carey's overview of peace studies. This term has come to be the way in which peace education is translated into formal education especially at the post-compulsory, mostly tertiary levels. Peace studies, like area, development and cultural studies, etc., tend to emphasize the dispassionate, often ostensibly "objective" process of intellectual inquiry, within a particular subject matter such as peace (that is, learning *about*). The article provides a broad background to the substantive issues of the nature of peace which have been integrally bound up with the development of both peace education as preparedness to practice peace, as well as to know about it in an essentially cognitive way. The relationship among peace education, peace research and peace action is a question which arises when "studies" are defined in particular, and separated from "education." Jan Maasen discusses the relationship in the larger volume, looking at the common roots of peace education and peace action and some problems of their interrelationship.

Robin Burns also considers the interrelationships. Haavelsrud and Burns each address issues underlying the problem of education, which is by definition concerned with change, given that those who hold political power have an interest which may be to reinforce the status quo, or reform it in minimal ways. Magnus Haavelsrud demonstrates the ways in which the presentation of an issue can dramatically affect how the key issues can be analyzed and comprehended, and that these ways are linked to an interest in social reinforcement, reform or transformation. Robin Burns uses the concept of the legitimation of educational knowledge to undertake a critique of formal education and the ways in which it affects the introduction of critical peace education, and suggests a preference for non-formal peace education.

Part III is headed *Perspectives on Peace Education: Substance and Impact.* It consists of examples, first, of ways in which the contents or substance is addressed. Betty Reardon's consideration of the relationship between militarism and sexism, and the ways in which both perpetuate readiness for war, is also a critique of the education system which reproduces structures and values which predispose to readiness for war. By implication, an alternative vision, one of a peaceful society, is needed and one way in which this has been derived is from women's visions. Related issues, racial justice and development, are taken up by David Hicks, who looks at underlying issues and themes and the ways in which they can be meaningfully related in classroom programs and projects. The issue of development is further elaborated and linked to other global issues by Toh Swee-Hin and Virginia Floresca-Cawagas, and exemplified in a detailed content analysis of the World Bank development education paradigms, their underlying values and the dramatically different futures to which each gives rise. Another issue, ecology, is the concern of Marianne Gronemeyer's chapter, which is linked through the concrete example of opposition to the siting of a particular nuclear power plant to an underlying analysis of social issues. In this case, people are mobilized to think about the issues through their experience, and are enabled to act non-violently for change through participation in an educational process.

The impact of the local situation on the possibilities for education and the issues which are central are found in the three chapters which focus on educational needs and possibilities. The first, by Samie Ikechi Ihejirika, deals with Africa, where a combination of colonialism, neo-imperialism and global militarism, grafted onto the local cultures, has created particular human imperatives which require a re-examination of the meaning of peace and the global context within which countries of the South are constrained. This is similarly the case in Lebanon, where violence has been the rule as different global power games are played out on its soil. Sanàa Osseiran puts the case for cultural action to overcome the ongoing violence, recognizing too that action is needed at the level of other countries and putting before the people of other countries material which presents the different viewpoints, not just one biased account. In post-communist Poland, Zbyszko Melosik argues, on the other hand, for international understanding as a basis for education, rather than yet another sectional approach which emphasizes the nation-state and so-called nationalist concerns. These studies each present examples of the ways in which knowledge of the local context enhances our understanding of the issues, and of the different forms which education for peace can take, in order for it to enable people to participate through education in dialogue and action for the future.

Approaches to the Process of Peace Education forms the fourth part, with examples from adult education as well as school-level work. Chad Alger, Eleanor Dionisio and Eva Nordland each stress the practical processes of peace building. Alger takes this up in the context of a community approach in a local context, Dionisio shows the way in which a student movement can address the mobilization of people through research and action and Nordland introduces a cooperative approach to peace-building through project work involving grass-roots participants from three different countries. These exemplify, again, different situations, and the ways in which those provide particular challenges and possibilities for adapting the methods of adult education, learning-through-action and cooperative project work. Kazuyo Yamane extends peace education to the public arena through her review of peace museums, showing how these may reinforce the heroic image of war, or overwhelm us with its horrors, but may also become the place where people discover their potential to imagine and to create peace, aware of the past but not overcome by it.

Most of the foregoing papers are from the late 1970s and 1980s. In a sense, peace education had a growing profile, nationally and in the work of international organizations during that time. The "balance of terror" presented by the image of the two giants, the United States and the USSR, ready to blow the world apart, and acting out their opposition in regional conflicts, was dominant. Some regional conflicts began to be solved in the late 1980s, and then the face of Europe began to change dramatically with the fall of most of the communist regimes. While we have not "solved" the issues which were seen as the most urgent when peace education "grew up," we have both new dominant issues and a new perspective from which to continue working through education. The last two chapters of this section deal with peace education into the 1990s and take up issues of change. Robert Aspeslagh focuses on the vision of a pluralist society, at different levels, and at cultural relations as a new theme in international relations. Peace education can be at the center of this, since education is the core of cultural transmission. Peace education can shape the conditions for a peace culture. He illustrates this through educational work which has been done between countries in Europe, but cautions that transfer from particular projects cannot automatically take place directly into national educational systems. Lennart Vriens also centers his discussion on culture as a human activity and looks at the ways in which some philosophers of education depict culture as a filter between education and the world. Currently, postmodernism provides a radical critique of culture, especially the grand narrative of enlightenment and progress through science. New issues are thereby raised about the nature of culture and of the individual, especially issues of identity, and he proposes that the peace movement and peace research can surpass postmodernism in their search for a peace culture based on ethical premises. This in turn can be the basis for renewal in education.

Finally, in the epilogue, the editors each offer their personal perspectives on peace education. These are presented in the form of reflections on the work of PEC, and through it on the work of many educators around the world who are struggling to find ways to renew education in order to achieve a vision of a sustainable, livable future. Both have a long involvement in work in peace education and related fields, and each has been the executive secretary of PEC (Aspeslagh, 1979–1983; Burns, 1983–1988). Each tries to show a way to make some sense of the issues and actions, ideas and educational programs, which form the complex, sometimes contradictory and confusing, and often visionary work of peace educators.

The nineteenth-century pioneers of the field of comparative education contended that the school was the only agency capable of advancing education across national boundaries (Scanlon, 1960; Taylor, 1970), and set about establishing an organization to promote education as an agent of peace. How education, including non-formal education, has interpreted this task through a major focus on peace issues in the last twenty-five years is the subject of the book. We invite you, the reader, to bring your own perspectives and concerns, skills and experiences, to this task, as you consider the issues and contexts presented here, and dare to envisage and work for a future world.

REFERENCES

Apple, M. W. (1979). *Ideology and Curriculum*. London: Routledge & Kegan Paul.
Apple, M. W. (1986). "Ideology, Reproduction, and Educational Reform." In Philip G. Altbach and Gail P. Kelly, eds. *New Approaches to Comparative Education*. Chicago and London: University of Chicago Press, pp. 51–72.

Aspeslagh, R. (1987). *Een Olifant in Het Onderwijs. Over de Spanning Tussen Eenheid en Verscheidenheid Bij Opvoeding en Onderwijs Over Wereldproblemen.* [*An Elephant in Education. About the Tension between Wholeness and Diversity in Education about World Issues*] Antwerp: International Peace Information Service (IPIS) Dossier 9.

Berger, P. L. and Luckmann, T. (1967). *The Social Construction of Reality.* New York: Doubleday Anchor Books.

Bernstein, B. (1977). *Class, Codes and Control,* 2nd ed. London: Routledge & Kegan Paul.

Boulding, E. (1987). "Peace Education as Peace Development." *Transnational Associations/ Associations Transnationales* 39(6), pp. 321–26.

Bourdieu, P. and Passeron, J. C. (1977). *Reproduction in Education, Society and Culture.* London: Sage.

Bowles, S. and Gintis, H. (1975). *Schooling in Capitalist America.* New York: Basic Books.

Burns, R. J. (1979). The Formation and Legitimation of Comparative Education with Particular Reference to Australia and Sweden. Melbourne: La Trobe University (unpublished Ph.D. dissertation).

Burns, R. J. and Welch, A. R. (1992). "Epilogue." In Robin J. Burns and Anthony R. Welch, eds. *Contemporary Perspectives in Comparative Education.* New York: Garland, pp. 401–15.

Carnoy, M. (1974). *Education as Cultural Imperialism.* New York: David McKay.

Carnoy, M. (1986). "Education for Alternative Development." In Philip G. Altbach and Gail P. Kelly, eds. *New Approaches to Comparative Education.* Chicago and London: University of Chicago Press, pp. 73–90.

Connell, R. W. (1977). *Ruling Class, Ruling Culture.* Cambridge and New York: Cambridge University Press.

Eckstein, M. A. (1986). "The Comparative Mind." In Philip G. Altbach and Gail P. Kelly, eds. *New Approaches to Comparative Education.* Chicago and London: University of Chicago Press, pp. 167–78.

Fanon, F. (1970). *Black Skin, White Mask.* St. Albans: Paladin [transl. C. L. Markman].

Flude, M. and Ahier, J., eds. (1974). *Educability Schools and Ideology.* London: Halstead.

Foucault, M. (1980). "The History of Sexuality." In C. Gordon, ed. *Power/Knowledge.* London: Harvester Press, pp. 183–93.

Freire, P. (1972a). *Cultural Action for Freedom.* Harmondsworth: Penguin [transl. M. B. Ramos].

Freire, P. (1972b). *The Pedagogy of the Oppressed.* Harmondsworth: Penguin [transl. M. B. Ramos].

Galtung, J. (1971). "A Structural Theory of Imperialism." *Journal of Peace Research,* 8, pp. 81–117.

Haavelsrud, M., ed. (1976). *Education for Peace: Reflection and Action.* Guildford: IPC Science & Technology Press.

Haavelsrud, M. and Borrelli, M. (1993). *Peace Education within the Archipelago of Peace Research, 1945–1964.* Tromsø: Arena.

Halls, W. D., (ed.) (1990). *Comparative Education: Contemporary Issues and Trends.* London: Jessica Kingsley, in association with UNESCO, Part 1.

Hermon, E. (1988). "The International Peace Education Movement, 1919–1939." In C. Chatfield and P. van den Dungen, eds. *Peace Movements and Political Cultures.* Knoxville: University of Tennessee Press, pp. 127–42.

Holmes, B. (1981). *Comparative Education: Some Considerations of Method.* London: George Allen & Unwin.

Jones, B. (1988). "Developing Political Literacy: The Dimensions of the Challenge." Melbourne: Victorian Association of Social Studies Teachers. *Ethos Papers,* (May).

Kartini, R. A. (1976). *Letters of a Javanese Princess*. Hong Kong/Singapore/Kuala Lumpur: Heinemann Educational Books (Asia) [transl. A L. Symmers].

Kelly, G. P. and Altbach, P. G. (1986). "Comparative Education: Challenge and Response." In Philip G. Altbach and Gail P. Kelly, eds. *New Approaches to Comparative Education*. Chicago and London: University of Chicago Press, pp. 309–27.

Lindholm, S. (1975). *Conjoining-Identity-Meaning*. Stockholm: Department of Education, Stockholm University, Animation Project Report No. 1.

MacDonald, M. (1977). *The Curriculum and Cultural Reproduction*. Milton Keynes: Open University Press.

Macklin, M. (1985). "Political Literacy in School." Melbourne: Victorian Association of Social Studies Teachers. *Ethos Papers*, (March).

Mannheim, K. (1954). *Ideology and Utopia*. London: Routledge & Kegan Paul [transl. P. Kecskemeti].

Mannoni, O. (1964). *Prospero and Caliban. The Psychology of Colonization*. New York: Praegar [transl. P. Powesland].

Percival, M. (1989). An Intellectual History of the Peace Education Commission of the International Peace Research Association. New York: Teachers College, Columbia University (Ed.D dissertation).

Porter, A. (1983). "Social and Political Education: Some Principles for Curriculum Planning." Melbourne: Victorian Association of Social Studies Teachers, *Ethos Papers* (September).

Scanlon, D. G., (ed.) (1960). *International Education. A Documentary History*. New York: Teachers College, Columbia University, Bureau of Publications Classic in Education No. 5.

Scotford-Archer, M. and Vaughan, M. (1971). "Domination and Assertion in Educational Systems." In Earl Hopper, ed. *Readings in the Theory of Educational Systems*. London: Hutchinson, pp. 56–70.

Taylor, H. (1970). *The World as Teacher*. New York: Doubleday & Company (Anchor Books).

Tonkin, C. B. (1988). "World Perspectives in the Social Studies, A United Kingdom-Australia Comparison." Melbourne: La Trobe University (unpublished Ph.D dissertation).

Torney-Purta, J. and Schwille, J. (1986). "Civic Values Learned in School: Policy and Practice in Industrialized Nations." *Comparative Education Review* 30(1). pp. 30–49.

Watson, A. (1994). Women's Identities. Melbourne: La Trobe University (mimeo).

Weedon, C. (1987). *Feminist Practice and Poststructuralist Theory*. Oxford: Basil Blackwell.

Welch, A. and Burns, R. (1992). "Introduction." In Robin J. Burns and Anthony R. Welch. eds. *Contemporary Perspectives in Comparative Education*. New York: Garland, pp. xi–xiv.

Young, M. F. D., (ed.) (1971). *Knowledge and Control*. London: Collier-Macmillan.

Zohar, D. (1991). *The Quantum Self*. London: Flamingo/HarperCollins.

Part Three

Education, Development and Policy Planning

CHAPTER 11

Development Studies and Comparative Education: Context, Content, Comparison and Contributors

Angela Little

ABSTRACT   *This article reviews Comparative Education over the past twenty years, explores the parallel literature of development studies and identifies future directions and challenges for comparative education. Using Parkyn (1977) as a benchmark, an analysis of articles published between 1977 and 1998 suggests that only a small proportion appear to meet his criteria for comparative education. Parkyn's purpose for comparative education, to increase our understanding of the relationship between education and the development of human society, is shared by development studies. Educational writings within development studies have explored the meanings of development and underdevelopment and have raised important questions about the unit of analysis for comparative education. Several reasons are advanced to explain the separate development of these literatures. The contemporary challenge of globalization presents fresh opportunities and challenges for both literatures. A shared commitment to understanding the role of education in the globalization process and the reasoned response to it could form the heart of a shared effort in the future. Globalization also highlights the need for more effective dialogue between comparative educators in different corners of the globe.*

Introduction

The purpose of this article is three-fold: to provide a brief review of the journal over the past twenty years in terms of criteria it has set for itself; to identify concepts which have emerged from development studies over the past twenty years which can contribute to and enhance comparative education; and to conclude with suggestions about the future development of the field of comparative education.

REVIEW OF THE JOURNAL

The benchmark for this review is Parkyn's (1977) contribution to the Special Number, entitled "Comparative Education Research and Development Education" (Grant, 1977). Parkyn reflects on an issue which exercised a number of academics in the 1970s, the similarities and differences between comparative education and development education, and the potential contribution of the former to the latter. For Parkyn, the purpose of comparative education was: . . . to increase our understanding of the relationship between education and the development of human society by taking into account factors that cannot adequately be observed and understood within the limits of any particular society, culture, or system, but that transcend particular societies and have to be studied by comparative methods applied to societies, cultures and systems . . .

Parkyn uses the term "development" to refer to all societies that are undergoing change. He does not confine the use of the term "development" to "developing" countries. The purpose of development education,[1] by contrast, was: . . . education aimed at the modernization of . . . technological activities in order to provide better for their material and cultural needs, and at the adaptation of their political machinery and other societal institutions in such a way as to make possible the most effective use of this modernization in the satisfying of those needs.

Despite the association in the minds of many of the term "development education" with "less developed" countries, Parkyn was at pains to point out that the fundamental distinction between comparative education and development education was not one of geography. The distinction was one of purpose. The purpose of comparative education was understanding and analysis, the purpose of development education was action and change. Comparative education could and should be undertaken in the countries of the North and the South. Wherever it is practiced, development education should rest on a foundation of comparative education.

Wherever in the world it was undertaken, the purpose of comparison was to explore the influence of system-level factors on the interaction of within-system variables. This definition of intellectual purpose in turn led to Parkyn's critique of comparative education in the 1970s.

The inadequacy of many studies purporting to be comparative, and superficially appearing to be comparative, is, in the last analysis, to be found in the fact that those which concentrated on within system variables or cultural contexts have often lacked information on across-system variables, while those which have dealt with across-system variables have often failed to show their different interaction with within-system variables in different countries. (Parkyn, 1977) So how has the field, as represented by studies published by *Comparative Education*, fared over the past two decades? Does the journal include a good representation of so-called "developing countries," in support of Parkyn's proposition that geography is not a defining characteristic of comparative education (context)? Does the journal include a good representation of articles addressing the fundamental question of comparative education, the relationship between education and the development of human society (content)? Does the journal demonstrate an understanding of the intellectual purpose of comparison (comparison)?

The review classifies the titles of articles published by *Comparative Education* between 1977 and 1998 (Volumes 13–34). A total of 472 articles were classified by country context (Table I), content (Table II) and comparison (Table III) by the author and Dr. Felicity Rawlings, working independently. While acknowledging that a title is only an indicator of an article's content, a classification based on a full reading of all 472 articles fell beyond the scope of the present review.

Context

Table I indicates the countries mentioned in the titles of articles. The authors of some 68 percent (320/472) of articles made explicit reference to one or more countries in the titles of their articles. Seventy-six countries were mentioned, just over one-third (34 percent) of the 224 countries listed in UNESCO's *Statistical Yearbook 1998*. A few countries have featured in the titles of a large number of articles, for example the UK (43), China (31), Japan (28), Germany (21), the USA (20), France (20) and Australia (16). Some thirty-four countries warrant mention in the title of only one article in twenty years. The number of countries that have at least one title published was compared with the total number of countries in the same region, as listed in UNESCO's *Statistical Yearbook 1998*. In Africa, some seventeen countries appeared in the title of at least one article, compared with some fifty-six countries in the Africa region, or 30 percent. Asia, South America and Oceania achieved similar percentages. The countries of Europe achieved the highest representation of 56 percent, while those of North America were under-represented, at 16 percent. The apparent under-representation of titles from North America may be accounted for by the propensity of authors on North American education to contribute to our important sister journal, *Comparative Education Review*, based in North America. The similar levels of representation of countries in the other four continental blocs—Africa (30 percent), South America (36 percent), Asia (35 percent) and Oceania (30 percent)—is a significant achievement for a journal established in London and run from the UK, and publishing (currently) only in English.

A comparison of the number of articles whose titles refer to one or more countries, by continent, presents a different picture. The total number of countries referred to in titles is 362. Just over half of this total refers to countries in Europe or North America (Europe 40.1 percent; North America 10.5 percent). A further 29.6 percent refer to Asia. Articles focusing on

Table I: Articles by country context noted in title and region 1977-1998

Africa		Asia	
Botswana 1	No. countries	Bangladesh 1	No. countries
Burkina Faso 1	published = 17	Cambodia 1	published = 19
Comoros 1		China 31	No. titles = 107
Ghana 1	No. titles = 41	Hong Kong 9	
Kenya 4		India 7	No. countries in
Mali 1	No. countries in		Asia = 52
Nigeria 9	Africa = 56	Indonesia 2	
Sierra Leone 1	% countries in Africa	Iran 1	% countries in Asia
Somalia 1	published by	Israel 5	published by
South Africa 7	CE = 30%	Japan 28	CE = 35%
Tanzania 4		Macau 1	
Togo 1		Malaysia 3	
Tunisia 1		Nepal 1	
Uganda 1		Pakistan 2	
Zaire 1		Philippines 2	
Zambia 3		Saudi Arabia 2	
Zimbabwe 3		Singapore 4	
		Sri Lanka 3	
North America		Taiwan 1	
Canada 9		Thailand 3	
Greenland 1	No. countries = 6		
Grenada 1	No. titles = 38	**Europe**	
Mexico 5		Austria 2	No. countries = 22
Nicaragua 2	No. countries in	Belgium 1	
	North	Bulgaria 1	No. titles = 145
United States 20	America = 37	United Kingdom 43	
	% countries in North	Cyprus 1	No. countries in
	America published by	Denmark 2	Europe = 43
	CE = 16%	Erie 1	
		Finland 2	% countries in
		France 20	Europe
		Germany 21	published by
		Greece 2	CE = 56%
		Hungary 5	
		Italy 4	
		Malta 1	
		Netherlands 5	
		Norway 6	
		Poland 2	
		Spain 9	
		Sweden 7	
		Switzerland 1	
		USSR 8	
		Yugoslavia 1	

Table I: Continued

South America		Oceania	
Argentina 1	No. countries = 6	Australia 16	No. countries = 6
Brazil 2		Cook Islands 1	
Chile 1	No. titles = 7	New Zealand 2	No. titles = 24
Columbia 1		Papua New Guinea 3	
Ecuador 1	No. countries in	Solomon Islands 1	No. countries in
Venezuela 1	South America = 14	Vanuatu 1	Oceania = 20
	% countries in South		% countries in
	America published		Oceania
	by CE = 36%		published by
			CE = 30%

countries in Africa, South America and Oceania account for 11.3 percent, 1.9 percent and 6.6 percent respectively. If one excludes Australia and New Zealand from the Oceania bloc, the percentage falls to 1.6 percent.

A classification by "developed" and "developing" country, using the 1998 UNESCO classification, presents an even sharper picture. UNESCO's *Statistical Yearbook 1998* classifies 53 (24 percent) countries as "developed" and the remaining 171 (76 percent) as "developing." Some 224 (62 percent) of our articles refer to "developed" countries, and 138 (38 percent) to "developing countries."

To the extent that a large number of developed and developing countries attract the attention of authors, Parkyn's proposition that geography is not the essential characteristic of comparative education appears to be borne out. At the same time, it is clear that over the past decades comparative educators have attended disproportionately on educational issues in the countries of Europe, North America and, to a degree, Asia.

Content

Table II presents the content of articles, as indicated by title, using the classification of journal aims published in 1978.

The relationship between education and the development of human society, education and development for short, appears to lie behind forty-four of the articles, or 13 percent of the articles classified by the 1978 scheme. Titles here include, for example, "Persistence and Education: A Formula for Japan's Economic Success" (Blinco, 1993) and "Asia's Four Little Tigers: A Comparison of the Role of Education in their Development" (Morris, 1996). These titles appear to address one aspect of Parkyn's definition of comparative education purpose, the relationship between education and the development of human society. Whether, simultaneously, they account for "factors that cannot adequately be observed and understood within the limits of any particular society" (Parkyn, 1977) requires a more careful reading of the text than has been possible in this brief review.

Table II: Content themes 1978, by the number and percentage of articles, 1977-98

(The aims of the journal are to) present up-to-date information and significant trends throughout the world, interpreted by scholars in comparative education and related disciplines, but expressed in a straightforward way for the general reader as well as for professional teachers, researchers, administrators and students . . . The . . . Board recognize important changes of commitment and partnership in comparative studies of education—with particular reference to developments in cognate disciplines and to problems of decision-making or implementation. These considerations bring closer interactions with studies of government, management, sociology—and indeed technology—both generally and on particular points of decision. A comparative perspective is now integral to any study affecting public policy, and the educational ingredient in all such studies is now more formative than it ever has been . . . the Board invites contributions . . . dealing with international or analytically comparative aspects of the following themes.

	No articles	%
Educational reform and problems of implementation	58	17.6
Education and socio-economic or political development	44	13.3
Relationships between education and a working life	24	7.3
Post-compulsory and "young adult" education	24	7.3
Part-time, recurrent, or alternating education/training	6	1.8
New structures/operational patterns in higher education	26	7.9
The "management" of educational systems and of the learning process	25	7.6
Teacher preparation and reorientation	35	10.6
Questions of access to education and of its diffusion	13	3.9
Curricular content, and the learner's experience	20	6.1
Innovation in educational and community interaction	4	1.2
Significant aspects of comparative research	35	10.6
Implications of international co-operation/experimentation	16	4.8
Total	330	100%

Other: exams/election 6, colonial schools/education 9, girls and women 11, diversity/cultural pluralism 12, pedagogic and philosophical theory 11, minorities 11, international organizations 8, language policies 5

A further 17.6 percent of articles address educational reform, including the internal problems of reform and the influence of societal development on the reform of education. The latter may be viewed as the inverse of the category noted above, the relationship between education and the development of human society. Titles here include Gu Mingyuan (1984) on "The Development and Reform of Higher Education in China," La Belle and Ward (1990) on "Education Reform When Nations Undergo Radical Political and Social Transformation," and Mitter (1992) on "Educational Adjustments and Perspectives in a United Germany."

Around 10 percent of articles may be classified under the heading "significant aspects of comparative research." This has been interpreted to include discussions of (i) comparative method; (ii) comparative theory; and/or (iii) comparisons drawn across a set of individual country papers. More than one hundred articles could not easily be classified under the 1978 headings. Of these, twelve addressed cultural diversity and pluralism, eleven pedagogic and philosophical theory, eleven the education of minorities and five language policy.

Comparison

Table III presents the geographic scope of comparisons made. It distinguishes titles that refer to single countries, two or more countries, regional groups, the "world," and those from which such reference is absent. This classification does not enable us to judge whether studies have identified the interaction between system-level and within system level factors, Parkyn's intellectual purpose of comparison. However, the very large number of studies, some 248 (58 percent), that focus on single countries, would suggest that Parkyn's criterion has not been met in more than half the cases. A smaller number, some 72 (15 percent), explicitly make comparisons across two, and less often, three, four or five countries. A further 11 percent indicate in their titles that the study draws on/makes reference to countries within a particular region (e.g. "developing" countries, "Europe," the Pacific, Africa). A very small number, some 3 percent, focus on globalizing or internationalizing trends, or on agencies (e.g. the World Bank) which have a global remit. Some 18 percent of titles omit reference to country focus.

Among those which focus explicitly on a single country, some 145 (58 percent) focus on "developed" countries and 103 (42 percent) on developing. Of the titles that indicate comparison across one or more countries, the majority involves two-country comparisons. Of these, 42 (68 percent) are comparisons between two developed countries, 12 (19 percent) are comparisons between two developing countries, and the remaining 8 (13 percent) make comparisons between developed and developing countries. The fairly sizeable percentage of articles that omit a reference to country (18 percent), are of many types. They include articles of the kind included in this Special Number, reviewing generally the state of the field and/or raising theoretical or methodological questions. Or they may focus on a particular country, but do not consider this focus to be sufficiently important to mention in the title.

Among those that draw explicit comparisons across countries, the majority do so across developed countries. The majority of studies drawing comparisons across two countries, and all those across three and four, focus on developed countries. Those that draw comparisons across five countries include four developed countries and Singapore. The studies whose titles make a regional or global reference are difficult to classify further without detailed analysis of the content of the articles.

It would appear then that only a small percentage of articles published by *Comparative Education* since 1977 have adopted an explicitly comparative approach. The majority of articles focus on single countries. Authors are contributing to a body of educational knowledge drawn from diverse educational settings. This is not to imply that the studies lack a comparative "dimension." Many authors locate their studies in relation to the more general comparative education literature, and indeed are encouraged to do so by the journal. However, the primary focus of the study is a single country context.

Table III: Articles by nature of comparisons, 1977-1998

Geographic scope of comparison.	No.	%
Single country	248	53
North	120	
North (Soviet)	25	
South	103	
Across specified countries	72	15
Across 2 countries	62	
North-North	42	
North-South	8	
South-South	12	
Across 3 countries	4	
All North	2	
All South		
South and North	2	
Across 4 countries	3	
All North	3	
All South		
South and North		
Across 5 countries	3	
All North	3	
All South		
South and North		
Regional	56	11
"Developing" countries	13	
"Industrialized" countries	1	
Europe	17	
Latin America	3	
English-speaking world	1	
OECD	1	
Nordic	1	
Asian tigers	1	
Pacific	9	
Africa	4	
Southern Africa	1	
South East Asia	1	
British Colonial Dependencies	1	
Gulf states	1	
Europe and North America	1	
Global/World	16	3
Not specified	84	18
Total	472	100

Context, Content and Comparison

The above analysis indicates that the articles published in *Comparative Education* cover a very broad range of context, content and comparison. Parkyn's criteria are met by only a small proportion of articles. Geography is clearly not the defining characteristic of comparative education, although the representation of articles on countries in the "South" is not yet as high as it should be. The breadth of content areas covered goes well beyond Parkyn's prescription. And the "comparative" approach adopted by authors varies considerably.

Breadth has the considerable advantage of bringing together readers with different and shared foci. Several of the Special Numbers of *Comparative Education* take a single country as their theme. Within this shared focus, authors address the specific issues of curriculum, teachers, management and employment. Other Special Numbers focus on a single topic, for example, post-compulsory education (Williams, 1994). Authors address this issue from a range of countries. Both of these approaches are valid, and encourage a two-stage approach to comparative-education knowledge. In the first stage, country or topic specialists presented contextualized knowledge. In the second stage, comparative specialists synthesized and located context. The guest editor of the Special Number usually executes this second stage. In principle, if not always in practice, the guest editor can identify the interaction between system and within system factors, thus meeting Parkyn's definition of "comparative" purpose. Indeed, Parkyn's criterion of comparative purpose may be best handled through this two-stage approach. Well-contextualized knowledge about education is a necessary, and complex, first step in the process of comparison. Much comparison neglects context and renders itself superficial and meaningless.

However, breadth of context, content and comparison has the disadvantage of dilution and a loss of focus for a field of study. In view of the number of articles that can be published each year, and the invitation for contributions from several disciplines, the potential for a loss of overall focus for the field of study increases greatly.

DEVELOPMENT STUDIES

I turn now to the field of development studies and explore the impact it has had on comparative education. Development studies emerged in the 1950s and 1960s, in the wake of the processes of reconstruction and decolonization after World War II. Key questions for development studies include: What does is mean to say that a society is developing or developed? What is the role of societal processes and institutions (such as education) in the process of development? What are the social and economic conditions that facilitate or impede the development of society? Thus, the fundamental questions of development studies with respect to education and those of comparative education, following Parkyn's definition, converge.

Modernization

Theories of economic and social modernization became central frameworks for the analysis of economic growth and societal development, and became influential also in determining national economic and social policy and policy implementation, as countries asserted their economic and political independence. Education was a central pillar of post-colonial social policy as countries sought to "modernize" and to replace expatriate highly skilled labor. Theories of development in developing countries, formulated largely by social scientists from the developed countries (although often working in developing countries), emerged alongside policies for development. From the outset economic goals formed the essential character of the "development project."

Education played an important part in development theory. The theory of "modernization" presented an optimistic model for development of those societies that were not yet modern and industrialized. Modernization theory attracted the attention of researchers from several social science disciplines. Economists focused attention on the application of technology to produce growth in economic production per unit of input. Sociologists focused on the process of social differentiation that characterize societies which use technology to promote economic growth. Demographers focused on patterns of settlement that accompany urbanization, the impact of modernization on population size, growth and density. Political scientists focused on nation-building, on the bases for power and how power is shared, how nation-states achieve legitimacy and the extent and depth of national identity.

Research on the relationship between education and the modernization of society was also pitched at the level of the individual. For example, McClelland (1961) focused on the values held by the majority of people in a society and the implications of these for economic and technological growth. The value attached to and the motivation for achievement, were central to McClelland's explanation of modernizing societies. Where Max Weber (1930) had focused attention on the role of ideas and religion in setting the conditions for the rise of capitalism, McClelland focused on early socialization and child rearing practices. Inkeles and Smith (1974) drew from both sets of ideas. They accepted the logic of modern values leading to modern behavior, modern society, and economic development. In contrast to McClelland, however, they stressed the role of modern institutions such as the formal school and the factory in the formation of modern values and attitudes.

Human Capital

Education was also a central part of theories of development that focused on the economic imperatives and conditions for development. In one of the most influential writings on the role of education in development in the twentieth century, Theodore W. Schultz explored the idea of education as a form of capital and introduced the notion of education as a form of human capital (Schultz, 1961). The propositions of "human capital" theory were that the skills and knowledge which people acquire are a form of capital. This capital was a product of deliberate investment and had grown in Western societies at a rate faster than "conventional" (non-human) capital. Its growth has been the most distinctive feature of the economic system of the mid-twentieth century. Human capital theory formed an important part of the development studies discourse about the relationship of education to the development of countries in the South from the mid-1960s. It emerged much later, from the late 1970s, as part of the discourse about education in the countries of the North.

The role of education in modernization was the subject of several well-known collections. For example, the collection on "Education and Economic Development," edited by Anderson and Bowman (1965), drew together historians, economists, sociologists, educators and geographers. It explored the role of education in economic development in Russia, India, America, Ghana, Chile, England and Japan. Another, edited in the same year by Coleman, entitled "Education and Political Development" (1965), focused on the political dimension of modernization. Drawing on cases from the "developing areas" (former French Africa, Indonesia, Nigeria, Tunisia, Egypt and Brazil) and from countries where educational development has been "polity-directed" (Soviet Union, Japan, the Philippines), the book addresses the questions: What part can and does education play in the process of modernization? What is the real (sic) relationship between political policy and the educational process?

Dependency

By the late 1960s and early 1970s the conceptual frameworks of both modernization and human capital theory were coming to be challenged by a set of ideas which came to form the school of "dependency." Marxist ideas on exploitation of the proletariat by the bourgeoisie, and Lenin's writings on imperialism, were developed by Andre Gunder Frank (e.g. 1967) and Galtung (e.g. 1971). Dependency theory addressed the extent to which poor countries were dependent on rich countries and the mechanisms through which economic dependency was maintained.

The dependency perspective focused on under-development rather than development, viewing it as a necessary outcome of systematic exploitation and manipulation of peripheral economies by central economies (Frank, 1967; Cardoso, 1972; Dos Santos, 1973). Poor countries are conditioned by their economic relationships with rich economies to occupy a subordinate and dependent role that inhibits development by expropriating investible surplus. Indigenous élites, firmly wedded to the international capitalist system and rewarded handsomely by it, have no interest in giving up these rewards. Dependency theory accords overriding importance to the historical conditions that provide a context for development and to the international system of "global exploitation" managed by developed capitalist countries. Wallerstein (1974) presented an early formulation of a globalized economic system structured by world capitalism. The "dependency" perspective encouraged economists, political economists and sociologists to abandon the national economy, nation-state and national society as their central unit of analysis and to focus instead on the nature of relations between economies, states and societies.

Dependency was conceived as a cultural phenomenon also. The structure of dependent economic relations was asserted to create a "cultural alienation" in which values, norms, technology, concepts and art forms were inspired externally rather than internally (Carnoy, 1974). Formal schooling in dependent economies played a key role in the furtherance of a cultural and economic dependency of peripheral upon central economies. Carnoy's thesis focused largely on schooling in the "Third World":

> Western formal education came to most countries as part of imperialist domination. It was consistent with the goals of imperialism: the economic and political control of the people in one country by the dominant class in the other. The imperial powers attempted, through schooling, to train the colonized for the roles that suited the colonizer (Carnoy, 1974).

The dependency school altered the discourse on education and development in a number of ways. It drew attention not only to the post-colonial or neo-colonial relations between countries which persisted long after so-called political independence, but it also focused attention on the analysis of the constraints on development, on stasis and decline in economy and society. It focused on the role of education for domination rather than for development. It provided answers to the question: How does education impede the process of development? It focused on the "negatives" of development. These included increasing disparities of income between social groups and countries, the continuing and increasing role of multinational economic interests, the formation and co-option of transnational élite social groups, the divergence of values of different social groups, the creation and maintenance of underclass countries and groups. Education played a role in this through many social and cultural processes. These included the legitimation of élite social and economic status, through qualification systems, through curriculum and learning materials developed through international publishing projects, and through cross-national and international professional networks (Mazrui, 1975; Altbach and Kelly, 1978; Watson, 1984; Lewin and Little, 1984; McClean, 1984).

For those in the North, the dependency perspective was as challenging as it was uncomfortable. While it bore an intellectual relationship with emerging analyses of the role of education in the development of the US capitalist economy (Bowles and Gintis, 1976), it resonated most with those intellectual interests that lay in the colonized countries of the South or in the internally-colonized communities resident in countries in the North. As a set of ideas it bore closer links with the broader school of economic dependency than it did with the discourse of comparative education dominant at that time. It was substantially influenced by writers who appealed to notions of social equity in the perspectives they took on the processes of education and development. Thus, Carnoy acknowledges his particular intellectual debt to Raskin and Memmi, who wrote on colonialism and to Illich who promoted de-schooling in the developing countries and in the impoverished areas of developed countries.

COMPARATIVE EDUCATION AND DEVELOPMENT STUDIES COMPARED

Whereas the dependency perspective emerged as an intellectual response to modernization theory and the questions it posed about the role of education in development (defined as modernization), debates in comparative education in the late 1960s and 1970s concerned the methodology of comparative education. Questions included: What is the purpose of comparison? What types of question and evidence provide a legitimate basis for comparison? What is the appropriate focus for comparisons, as between systems and classrooms? What is the relative role of theory and practice in the generation of research questions? How is the comparative education method different from that of comparative sociology, comparative politics, comparative religion and philosophy, economic and social history, cross-cultural psychology?

While much of this debate was conducted with considerable vigor and intellectual sophistication, it had the unintended effect of distracting attention away from the content questions that could usefully be addressed by using the method(s) of comparative education. Method is valuable to the extent that its application provides new insights into a problem. What new insight could the comparative education method offer which comparative sociology, comparative social history, comparative politics or comparative social psychology could/did not?

The methodological debates of the 1970s passed many people by and had little lasting impact, with a handful of exceptions. While a number of articles in *Comparative Education* adopted an explicitly comparative approach, few justified or explained their comparative approach in relation to those set out in the earlier debates. Interchange with comparative educators from many countries suggests that these debates have had little impact on the understanding or use of the so-called *Comparative Education* research method. A similar view was reached recently and independently by Rust *et al.*, (1999) who reviewed almost two thousand articles appearing in *Comparative Education* (1964/95), *Comparative Education Review* (1957/95) and the *International Journal of Educational Development* (1981/95).

The fundamental question of comparative education, according to Parkyn (1977), is the relationship between education and "development." This question was fundamental also to those who wrote about modernization and dependency. However, questions of method and country context distinguished the two literatures. Those who engaged most actively in the modernization and dependency debates largely ignored the methodological debates in comparative education. Those who engaged most actively in the comparative methodological debates, drew their knowledge of educational context largely, although not exclusively, from the education systems of the North. Even those who designed the early IEA studies and drew inspiration from Noah and Eckstein's (1969) approach to comparative education addressed education mainly in the "developed countries." In the first round of the International Association for the Evaluation of Educational Achievement (IEA) studies of twenty-one countries, only four, Chile, India, Iran and Thailand were, at that time, classified as "developing countries." The driving question and problem behind the massive IEA research endeavor must be seen in the context of the Cold War and the race for supremacy in space. "Development" in this sense meant progress and world supremacy. It did not mean what it means for many of the "developing" countries—catch up, staying in the game, and basic survival. In short, the literatures addressing the fundamental question of the relationship between education and the development of human society have not been as integrated as they might have been. Two reasons for this less than optimal integration, suggested above, were the preoccupation of comparative education, through much of the 1970s and 1980s, with debates about method, and the tendency for contributors to the field to focus their intellectual efforts on particular groups of countries. Three further reasons for the parallel rather than integrated development of the literatures of comparative education and development studies include differences in (i) the scope of analysis; (ii) the practice of development; and (iii) the emphasis on economic and cultural goals of society and development.

Scope of Analysis

The dependency approach suggested that national systems of education did not necessarily provide the most appropriate point of comparison for comparative studies. The scope of analysis needed to include contemporary and historical relations (of domination and dependency) between countries. This was especially so in the case of the former colonies. In principle, then, comparisons between countries needed to include their contemporary and historical relations of influence with other countries. Although the call for an historical approach in comparative education is familiar, it did not resonate with those who, at that time, were stressing comparisons of a contemporary nature. Nor did it resonate with those who sought comparisons across nations. The national system, economy and society remained for most comparative educationists the focus or unit of analysis. The notion of a national system of education sitting within a national economy and national society provided a clear focus for research that was within grasp. The implication of dependency theory—to include an analysis of education within international economic and political relations—was largely ignored by those whose knowledge of educational contexts drew largely from "developed" countries whose education systems, with some notable exceptions (Phillips), had been largely immune from external influence.

Practice

The emergence of the education and development "business" contributed further to the parallel development of literature. Much of the early work on modernization and its economic parallel, human capital theory, was used by development agencies and international banks to justify financial investments in education in developing countries. Schultz's (1961) work was especially influential in the 1960s and 1970s among those who allocated money to development programs and those who promoted the growth of formal education worldwide. Significantly, many of these actors and agencies were external to the emerging states of the countries to be "assisted" or "aided." The production of an educated labor force was perceived by both economists and development planners as a means to the end of the growth of the national economy, and hence, development.

Not only did these ideas and writings bring the concepts and theories of economics to the center stage of thinking about the relationship between education and development, but they did so in a way which smoothed (and sometimes ignored) the intellectual transition from analysis to advocacy, from description to prescription, from single cases to universal trends. Thus, many wrote of the relationship between education and development and ignored the multiplicity of possible relationships conditioned by variations in economic, cultural, social and political contexts and histories. These writings were oriented towards policy recommendations for the present and the future. In other words the writings were guided as much by the need to generate advocacies for education, as by the need to generate an understanding of why and how education was related to development in specific settings. The project of development, buttressed by financial resources and controlled by agencies external to the "developing" countries, encouraged a definition of development as economic growth and a discussion of the role of education in achieving that end. It encouraged a concern with immediate policies and practices and a tendency to seek policy recommendations of a "one size fits all" nature.

Economic and Cultural Goals of/for Development

The relative emphasis on economic and cultural definitions and explanations of development also distinguished the literatures. Human capital theory promoted the idea of education as a form of economic capital in the quest for development, defined as economic growth. It rendered subordinate supplementary and alternative ideas about the goals of learning and education—education as empowerment, education as citizenship, education as enculturation, education as liberation.

The emphasis on economic development was accompanied by the notion that culture was separate from economy and impeded economic development. Culture was often invoked as an explanation of past failure rather than success, of present problems rather than achievements and of likely future difficulties rather than possibilities. Culture was treated frequently as a fixed and enduring endowment responsible for continuities and inhibiting change. This view was at odds with much that had been written on education and change in the "developed" countries of the North, where cultural analysis was more prominent.

THE WAY FORWARD

Aspects of the context of education and development in the so-called developed and developing countries have changed in ways which would have been unrecognizable to those who contributed to and read the 1977 Special Number of *Comparative Education* (Grant, 1977). These changes in turn present us with a fresh opportunity to reconstruct comparative education in ways that integrate rather than separate knowledge about education and development among the richest and the poorest social groups and countries.

Already, there are signals that many of the old divisions apparent in the literatures could be breaking down. In developed countries the discourse on education, modernization and economic competitiveness chimes uncannily with the discourse on human capital theory and modernization in developing countries two or three decades ago. The "business" of development is arguably also influencing the discussion of education and development in the North as the work of universities becomes more commercialized and more driven by the needs of short-term policies and practices. The interest in "lessons from abroad" on the part of education policy-makers in developed countries increased markedly in the 1990s as the East Asian Tiger economies of the 1990s, themselves developing countries of the 1960s and 1970s, demonstrated enviable rates of economic growth.[2] There is a growing awareness that many of the jobs which educated young people in "developed" countries have done in the past will, in the future, be taken over by educated young people in "developing" countries. The marginalization of large numbers of future generations—"social exclusion"—is a growing problem on the doorstep. Poverty is not confined to "developing" countries.

Globalization

Underlying these signs is an economic and technological process we term "globalization." As Giddens notes:

> The term may not be a particularly attractive or elegant one. But absolutely no-one who wants to understand our prospects and possibilities at century's end can ignore it (Giddens, 1999a).

Writers in *Comparative Education* are already addressing it and many comparative education conferences have adopted it recently as a central theme (*Comparative Education* Web Page www.carfax.co.uk/ced-ad.htm, Watson, 1996; Cowen, 1996; Little, 2000a). The literature attracts "skeptics" and "radicals."

The skeptics dispute the whole thing . . . Whatever its benefits, its trials and tribulations, the global economy isn't especially different from that which existed at previous periods. The world carries on much the same as it has done for many years . . . (the radicals, by contrast argue) . . . that not only is globalization very real, but that its consequences can be felt everywhere. The global marketplace, they say, is much more developed than even two or three decades ago, and is indifferent to national borders (Giddens, 1999).

For the radicals, the manifestations of so-called globalization are economic, political or cultural. The economic include stateless financial markets, a massive expansion of world capital and finance flows, a rising proportion of global trade and investment in developing countries accounted for by transnational companies; the domination of international technology flows by transnational corporations (Wood, 1994; Stewart, 1996). The political manifestations of globalization include a decline in state sovereignty (Ohmae, 1990); the reduced control of national governments over money supply and regulation of exchange rates; an increase in the power of global, sometimes stateless, organizations over national organizations; a definition of local issues in relation to the global as well as the local; and an increase in the ability of national and local issues to be played out on a world-stage. In the cultural arena the manifestations include a convergence of lifestyle and consumer aspirations among the better off, and the widespread distribution of images, information and values (Waters, 1995). The educational manifestations include the phenomenal growth in the flows of educational goods and services, in the revolution in modes of delivery of educational services, and in the definition of policy goals and curricula for education in developed and developing countries.

The manifestations of globalization are not the same as its underlying causes. For some (Wood, 1994) a major reduction of obstacles to international economic transactions constitutes the essential definition of globalization. Hitherto, these obstacles have included transport and transaction costs, trade barriers, financial regulation, and speed of communication. Their reduction, a function of both economic policy and technological advance, has led to a major increase in the volume of international financial transactions. At the same time, the technological advances that have increased the speed of communication have facilitated connections not only between financial markets worldwide, but also between people worldwide. This is why the manifestations of globalization are not simply economic; they are also political, social and cultural. They are personal as well as impersonal; they are "in here" as well as "out there" (Giddens 1999).

However, among those who acknowledge the phenomenon and consequences of globalization, are the "optimists" and the "pessimists." The optimists, like the development modernizers before them, concentrate on the positive consequences. The "pessimists," like the dependency theorists and the Marxists before them, concentrate on the negative.

Development Studies

For Grindle and Hilderbrand (1999) the heart of the mission of development studies has two aspects. Firstly, *an understanding of the impact of globalization*, and secondly, *a response to this understanding in ways that advance the positive and ameliorate the negative consequences of globalization*. Some of the current and projected "positives" and "negatives" of globalization between and within developed and developing countries are presented in Table IV.

The extension of these themes to education is inviting. The following questions, among others, emerge. How will different of forms of education, especially those supported by new information technologies, attain legitimacy and contribute to the improvement of living standards? How will education contribute to a heightened awareness of the need to provide economic, political and social opportunities for women and marginalized minorities? How will education contribute to democratic decision-making at national and local levels? How will education contribute to the functioning of international movements to improve institutions of governance, to counter corruption in public life and to adopt environmentally sound practices? How will differential access to education provision and quality contribute to the further marginalization of young people? How will sanctions for countries that fail to adapt economic policies affect educational provi-

---

Table IV: Positive and negative consequences of globalization

---

Consequences judged as positive

Improved living standards of large numbers of the world's people through increased numbers of jobs and incomes

Spread of ideas about ways to improve access to education, health and information

Heightened awareness of the need to provide economic, political and social opportunities for women and minorities

Spread of democratic decision-making at national and local levels

International movements to improve institutions of governance, to counter corruption in public life and to adopt environmentally sound practices

Consequences judged as negative

The further marginalization of those who do not, currently, have access to or benefit from an increased flow of goods, services, capital and information (especially the world's current (1999) estimate of 1.3 billion people)

Sanctions for countries that ignore or avoid adapting economic policies and regulatory regimes to new international standards, with the consequent distress for their citizens

Greater financial vulnerability because of increasing interdependence and spread of financial flows

Increased exploitation of poor workers and of children and women

Increased threats of environmental damage, disease, cross-border conflict, migration, political instability and crime

More conflict between those who benefit from globalization and those who do not

Heightening of ethnic, religious and cultural differences

Source: Adapted from Grindle & Hilderbrand (1999).

sion, especially for the poorest? How will different forms of education serve to legitimate and reproduce social and economic stratification? What will be the balance between local, national, international and global forces for educational decision-making?

But to these should also be added a number of questions that emerge from conditions only weakly connected with globalization, or from contexts where its particular effects are strongest. In many situations local and national influences will continue to be the most powerful in determining educational curriculum, control, resources, provision and outcomes. This requires sensitivity to and understanding of local and national contexts, and reinforces the earlier point about the need for comparative education to be grounded in an understanding of particular contexts. Such understanding will also generate issues common to regions and sub-regions. For example, at a recent Sub-Saharan Conference on Education for All, educators and researchers identified a number of priorities for research and action common to the Africa region and sub-region. These included the contribution of education to the alleviation of poverty, the impact of the HIV/AIDS pandemic on education and of education on its slow down, the provision of education in the context of emergency and post-conflict, and the contribution of education to the reduction of gender inequity and cultures of peace (Johannesburg Declaration, 1999).

Development studies captures the twin objectives of understanding and action, of analysis and advocacy, of policy analysis and policy prescription. It embraces the divide between "thinkers" and "do-ers." It places on those who reflect, analyze, theorize about and study a responsibility to act, to advocate, and to prescribe. Simultaneously it places on those who act, do, advocate, and prescribe a responsibility to think about and question their own actions and the advice they give to others, *especially in situations where power relations are unequal,* within a broad scheme of global, national and local influence. Understanding and action are both important and valuable. Each requires overlapping but separate skills. While each benefits from the other, neither can be reduced to the other (Little, 2000b).

The understanding of the role of education in the globalization process within the framework presented in Table IV and the reasoned response to it could form the heart of the both the development studies and comparative education effort over the next few decades in both the developed and the developing countries.

THE CHALLENGES

Marginalization, communication and access to information are key themes in the globalization discourse. As editors of *Comparative Education* we frequently discuss how to encourage contributors and contributions from a larger number and wider range of "developing countries." If we are to encourage a better understanding of the relationship between education and "development," both in terms of national and international development, then we need to find more effective means of promoting dialogue between comparative educators in different corners of the globe.

At the beginning of this article I provided a review of context, content and type of comparison employed in *Comparative Education* articles published between 1977 and 1998. A review of the authors' "address for correspondence" provides an indication of the communication and information challenge ahead. It also provides the final theme of the subtitle of this article. While "address for correspondence" is a perfect proxy for neither nationality nor country of residence or domicile, it does indicate authors' current location in non-virtual space. Some 609 authors contributed to 472 published articles. While the total number of countries mentioned explicitly in the title of articles was 76, the number of countries in which contributors were based was 50. Some 85 percent of the contributors were based in developed countries. Only 15 percent were based in developing countries. In other words, the country base of authors is more concentrated than the countries they study, and the underrepresentation of authors based in developing countries is even more marked than the underrepresentation of articles based on them.

Those of us who wish to inhabit a truly global and comparative field of study which can, in turn, make its own modest contribution to the cause of human progress, must create virtual and non-virtual space to encourage the participation of and exchange between educators from a much greater diversity of educational culture than hitherto. We must be sensitive to the diversity of educational and other contexts worldwide, achieve consensus on the fundamental questions of comparative education, and embrace in our comparisons local, national, regional, international and global spheres of influence. This is our collective challenge.

ACKNOWLEDGMENTS

I am grateful for assistance and comments on an earlier draft of this paper from Jane Evans, Felicity Rawlings, Chris Williams and members of the Editorial Board of *Comparative Education*.

NOTES

1. It should be noted that Parkyn's use of the term "development education" reflected common usage in the USA at that time. In England the term "development education" usually referred to the curricula of teaching courses, largely at school level, which aimed to increase school-children's knowledge and understanding of the problems of poverty in the countries of the South. In the 1970s the equivalent of Parkyn's usage in England might have been the practice (as distinct from the study) of education in developing countries.
2. The waning of interest in the wake of the end of the century crisis in those same economics illustrated the perils of cherry-picking and the importance of serious comparative analysis.

REFERENCES

Altbach, P. G. and Kelly, C. P. (eds) (1978). *Education and Colonialism*. London: Longman.

Anderson, C. A. and Bowman, M. J. (eds) (1965). *Education and Economic Development*. Chicago: Aldine Publishing Company.

Blinco, P. M. A. (1993). "Persistance and Education: A Formula for Japan's Economic Success." *Comparative Education*, 29(2), pp. 171–183.

Bowles, S. and Gintis, H. (1976). *Schooling in Capitalist America*. New York: Basic Books.

Cardoso, F. (1972). "Dependency and Development in Latin America." *New Left Review*, 74.

Carnoy, M. (1974). *Education as Cultural Imperialism*. London: Longman.

Coleman, J. S. (ed.) (1965). *Education and Political Development*. Princeton, NJ: Princeton University Press.

Cowen, R. (ed.) (1996). "Comparative Education and Post-modernity." *Comparative Education*, Special Number (18), 32(2).

Dos Santos, T. (1973). "The Crisis of Development Theory and the Problem of Dependence in Latin America." In H. Bernstein *Underdevelopment and Development: The Third World Today*. Harmondsworth: Penguin. pp. 57–80.

Frank, A. G. (1967). *Capitalism and Underdevelopment in Latin America*. New York: New York Monthly Review Press.

Galtung, J. (1971). "A Structural Theory of Imperialism." *Journal of Peace Research*, 8(2), pp. 81–117.

Giddens, A. (1999). *Runaway World*. Cambridge: Polity.

Grant, N. (ed.) (1977). "Comparative Education—Its Present State and Future Prospects." *Comparative Education*, Special Number, 13(2).

Grindle, M. S. and Hilderbrand, M. E. (1999). *The Development Studies Sector in the United Kingdom: Challenges for the New Millennium*. Report to the Department for International Development, UK.

Inkeles, A. and Smith, D. (1974). *Becoming Modern*. London: Heinemann.

Johannesburg Declaration of Education for All. (1999). Draft document tabled for discussion at the Sub-Saharan Africa Conference on Education for All, 6–10 December. Johannesburg: EFA Regional Technical Advisory Group.

La Belle, T. J. and Ward, C. R. (1990). "Education Reform when Nations Undergo Radical Political and Social Transformation." *Comparative Education*, 26(1), pp. 95–106.

Lewin, K. M. and Little, A. W. (1984). "Examination Reform and Educational Change in Sri Lanka, 1972–1982: Modernization or Dependent Underdevelopment." In K. Watson, *Dependence and Interdependence in Education: International Perspectives*. Beckenham: Croom Helm. pp. 47–94.

Little, A. W. (ed.) (2000a). "Globalization, Qualifications and Livelihoods." *Assessment in Education*, Special Issue (forthcoming, 7(3)).

Little, A. W. (2000b). "Post-Jomtien Models of Educational Development: Analysis vs Advocacy." In L-E. Malmberg, S-E. Hansen and K. Heino (eds) *Basic Education for All: A Global Concern for Quality*. Vasa: Abo Akademi University.

Mazrui, A. (1975). "The African University as a Multi-national Corporation: Problems of Penetration and Dependency". *Harvard Educational Review*, 45, pp. 199–210.

McClean, M. (1984). "Educational Dependency: Two Lines of Enquiry." In K. Watson, *Dependence and Interdependence in Education: International Perspectives*. Beckenham, Croom Helm. pp. 21–29.

McClelland, D. (1961). *The Achieving Society*. New York: The Free Press.

Mingyuan, G. (1984). "The Development and Reform of Higher Education in China." *Comparative Education*, 20(1), pp. 141–148.

Mitter, W. (1992). "Educational Adjustments and Perspectives in a United Germany." *Comparative Education*, 28(1), pp. 45–52.

Morris, P. (1996). "Asia's Four Little Tigers: A Comparison of the Role of Education in Their Development." *Comparative Education*, 32(1), pp. 95–109.

Noah, H. and Eckstein, M. (1969). *Toward a Science of Comparative Education*. New York: Macmillan.

Ohmae, K. (1990). *The Borderless World: Power and Strategy in the Global Marketplace*. London: HarperCollins.

Parkyn, G. W. (1977). "Comparative Education Research and Development Education." *Comparative Education*, 13(2), pp. 87–94.

Rust, V., Soumare, A., Pescador, O. and Shibuya, M. (1999). "Research Strategies in Comparative Education." *Comparative Education Review*, 43(1), pp. 86–109.

Schultz, T. W. (1961). "Investment in Human Capital," *American Economic Review*, 51, pp. 1–17.

Stewart, F. (1995). "Globalization and Education." Keynote address, *UKFIET Conference on Globalization and Learning*, New College, Oxford.

Stewart, F. (1996). "Globalization and Education", *International Journal of Educational Development*, 16(4), pp. 327–334.

UNESCO (1998). *Statistical Yearbook 1998*. Paris: UNESCO.

Wallerstein, I. (1974). *The Modern World System: Capitalist Agriculture and the Origins of the European World Economy in the Sixteenth Century*. London: Academic Press.

Waters, M. (1995). *Globalization*. London: Routledge.

Watson, K. (1984). *Dependence and Interdependence in Education: International Perspectives*. Beckenham: Croom Helm.

Watson, K. (ed.) (1996). *Globalization and Learning, Special Issue of International Journal of Educational Development*, 16(4).

Weber, M. (1930). The *Protestant Ethic and the Spirit of Capitalism*. London: Allen and Unwin.

Williams, V. (ed.) (1994). "Edmund King's Contribution to Post-compulsory Education: An International Review and Appreciation," *Comparative Education*, Special Number 16, 30(1).

Wood, A. (1994). *North-South Trade, Employability and Inequality: Changing Fortunes in a Skill-driven World*. Oxford: Clarendon Paperbacks.

CHAPTER 12

Qualitative Research and Educational Policy-Making: Approaching the Reality in Developing Countries

Kai-Ming Cheng

Introduction

This chapter demonstrates how qualitative research may help to inform effective educational policy-making and how the lack of such research may lead to distorted information and false conclusions in the policy formulation, implementation and evaluation process.

To begin with, the title of the chapter itself could be controversial and some remarks are necessary. The term *qualitative research* is now widely used in the literature, but many readers will realize that qualitative studies need not be confined to qualitative data alone. The term in its fashionable sense is frequently defined through being contrasted with statistical research and hypothesis-testing, which is inevitably quantitative. In this paper, the term *qualitative research* is used to mean research of which the primary purpose is to identify "native" perspectives (or local culture) so as to illuminate a policy issue. The general process in such qualitative research is to allow the researcher's thinking to be shaped by field data and to generate hypotheses, conclusions or theories therefrom.

The term *developing country* also deserves attention. First, the adjective "developing" is a polite form for "poor," and often assumes a unidimensional measurement of national development: the GNP or GDP. This assumption encounters challenge when other developmental dimensions, such as those favored by UNDP, are taken into consideration. Economic wealth is but one dimension of national development that includes health care, literacy, educational, spiritual and other social dimensions. Second, the developed-developing (or north-south) dichotomy is too broad a generalization that artificially polarizes nations in the world. It has difficulties in accommodating countries such as the newly industrialized economies (NIEs) in East Asia (Cheng, 1991b) and the newly converted nations of Eastern Europe. Third, much of the literature about developing countries, including that on education, is written by people in developed countries. There is, in this sub-field, often a tacit "donor-recipient" paradigm where the "wise" of the north explore the exotic south. This reflects the fact that the majority of known research projects in the south are supported by money and personnel from the north.

Problems with the word *reality* are even more fundamental. People may have totally different perceptions about their social reality and the nature of knowledge. At the one extreme, one may argue that reality is nothing but human creation. At the other extreme, one may believe in a reality which is external to the researcher and is fully accessible and comprehensible. In between, there are various ways of conceiving what reality is and of understanding the researcher's capacity to fully comprehend it. Lincoln and Guba (1985) present a useful discussion of these epistemological issues as do other contributors to this volume. Talking about reality is, nevertheless, always risky but, while it is not intended to pursue philosophical or epistemological issues in this chapter, it is essential to say that most policy-related research assumes that (1) there is an objective reality and (2) such a reality can be better understood by the policy-maker through research. By policy-related research here we mean "research for policy" rather than "research *on* policy." The former is meant to inform policy-making which demands realistic solutions to practical problems. Epistemological assumptions, however, may face challenges when research is about human organizations where policy is built upon interpretations of human perceptions. This is particularly an issue when the researcher works across cultures, and even more so when those from the developed world are looking at developing countries.

In the light of the above, it is the purpose of this chapter to address issues encompassed in the title by evaluating examples and problems in policy-related research; and to illustrate how qualitative methods may help improve our analyses. In so doing, the chapter draws upon experience from China and Hong Kong, the part of the world the writer is most familiar with. Following qualitative conventions, discussions that follow are illustrated by details of specific cases, and where examples are politically sensitive, pseudonyms are used to maintain confidentiality.

PROBLEM DEFINITION AND IDENTIFICATION

Rational policy-making comprises problem identification, solution searching or development and solution selection. Although rational processes are only one dimension of policy-making, problem identification is a useful and practical starting point for any policy process. A first question is then: whose problem are we dealing with? Problems so often have to do with what people expect. It is also argued here that problems, as identified, should reflect or acknowledge local perceptions. This is not always appreciated by researchers coming from outside the community in question. Often, outsiders identify problems, with considerable expertise, from their own frames of reference. In so doing, many ungrounded assumptions are made suggesting that there are universal yardsticks that can be used to measure or evaluate any education system. If visiting researchers are not conscious of their limitations as foreigners, and pay little respect to the local context, they are likely to identify problems which are foreign to the specific context, and their input may not serve the local community well.

By way of illustration, a mission team (of which the writer was a member) was recently sent by an international funding agency to the less-developed province of Shaanxi in China to identify target projects for a substantial loan. It was winter and children were seen shivering in thick clothes, with running noses, in classrooms at freezing temperatures. Heating was not available because the province was not in a region eligible for heating subsidy from the central government. The mission team thought this should become a priority project. Some calculation was done and it was found that for a heater to be installed in a classroom the cost would be around U.S. $71, including a simple stove and chimneys made of iron plates. This would last for three to five years. However, there were 145,579 classes in that province alone at the time of the visit. Heaters for all would cost over U.S. $10 million, and this was disproportionately expensive. This did not include the running costs for coal, and coal was expensive because it was not produced locally. In time the mission team decided to drop the idea of launching such a project.

Subsequent discussions outside the formal visit, however, revealed that the local educational planners and school administrators had been unenthusiastic about the heating proposal from the very beginning. "This is not *our* priority," said the local planners. "We have been learning under the same conditions for generations," said the teachers. "If we had money," both groups said, "we'd rather pay the teachers." Most of the teachers were community employees paid by the local community, and due to recent policies of decentralization, the underdevelopment of the local economy rendered many of them underpaid, or their paychecks were long overdue. However, because funding agencies are never attracted to support recurrent expenditure, the local educators and planners did not raise an initial objection to the heating project.

In this case, there was a marked difference between what was perceived as a problem by the mission team, and by the local educators and planners. There was a difference in expectations. The visiting team, given the brief to fund nonrecurrent items, and with their experience of heated environments back home in winter, naturally focused upon the temperature of the classrooms. The local people had taken the coldness for granted. Cold was expected of life there in any room in the locality. It was not that they did not want warm environments, but for generations they had realized that heating was an expensive item, and it was therefore not a realistic expectation. In other words, heating was not a problem to the local community and was not on their policy agenda, or it was low on the priority list.

Had the mission team tried harder to understand the local perspective by using a more qualitative approach to their study from the very beginning, they might have arrived at proposals more suited to local expectations. Unfortunately, this is not the usual convention with many funding agencies. Too often, international teams tend to regard developing countries as backward; backward not only in their economic conditions, but also backward in their overall development perspectives. In this context, there is a tendency for visiting researchers to "discover" problems for the local community, and this itself is regarded as a valid contribution. In other cases, visiting researchers negate problems that are identified by the local people, and identify policy priorities conforming to an imported framework that they have taken for granted, but which may be totally incompatible with local needs and perspectives.

HOW CAN PLANNING INDICATORS HELP?

Consultants who visit a developing country often have to rely on planning indicators of acknowledged international significance so that situations in the country in question can be assessed through comparison with those elsewhere. However, education is practiced differently in different countries and the same indicator may reflect very different stories. It is therefore argued that such indicators should be used with greater caution, or else they may prove deceptive and be misleading.

In the early and mid-1980s, for example, researchers who went to China were often amazed by the shortage of qualified teachers on the one hand, and the "over-generous" student/teacher ratios on the other. A World Bank report thus made the following observation:

> The student-teacher ratio has . . . gone down from twenty-seven to one in 1979 to twenty-five to one in 1983 (the median ratio for other LDCs is about thirty-five to one). The class size has been kept almost constant, at around thirty-four, which implies that teachers' weekly workload—by international standards, already a low twenty periods—has gone down further. (World Bank, 1985)

These policy analysts therefore concluded that there would be a general surplus of primary school teachers in the years to come if the existing policies were to be maintained. The World Bank subsequently recommended that the student/teacher ratio should be increased to thirty-four to one and there should be a gradual closing of some primary teacher training schools (Ibid.). Berstecher's (1986) case study of the province of Sichuan arrived at similar observations and comments:

From a student/teacher ratio of currently thirty-two to one, the plan framework for basic education proposes to go towards a ratio of eighteen to one by 1990. By any standards, this policy implies an amazingly generous use of precious and costly human resources. What is more, there is hardly any evidence to suggest that a massive lowering of student/teacher ratios will really pay off in terms of better educational achievements. . . . Thus, it is reasonable to ask whether Sichuan's plan to go all out for an improvement of student/teacher ratios in primary schools is really the best or the only alternative. Does it strike a proper balance between quantity and quality? (Ibid.)

These observations, criticisms and recommendations are sound as long as one stays at the macrolevel and looks at average figures. The picture becomes different when analysis moves to the microlevel. In a case study of two countries in the province of Liaoning (Cheng, 1991a), for example, the writer acknowledged a shortage of qualified teachers and an increasingly generous student/teacher ratio. Using a qualitative approach to research, however, it was possible to trace the planning process in greater depth and conclude for at least two reasons, the demand for teachers was not decided by a simple calculation of overall figures. First, rural classes were normally smaller than the standard class size of fifty and hence calculation by simple teacher-pupil ratio would arrive at very unrealistic results. Second, there were specialized teachers for Language and Mathematics in Primary 5 and 6. Hence, a simple class-teacher ratio, again would not lead to meaningful planning. The actual "planning" was done through careful school-by-school and subject-by-subject calculations. (Ibid.)

In this case, because of the policy of universalizing primary education, more but smaller schools were built to comply with the national norm of 2.5 km as the maximum student travel distance (or alternative requirements to guarantee neighborhood attendance). The net effect was that although there was a decline of population, there were more schools because of the sparse distribution. Indeed, there were extremely crowded classrooms in towns and cities (the largest of which held over one hundred pupils), but there were extremely small classes (of just a few children) in remote schools. Hence, although many of the rural teachers were unqualified, they were still very much needed in scattered small schools. Average figures at the national or provincial levels could not possibly reflect the huge disparity in sizes among classes, and greater depth of research in context was required.

The expensive reduction in the student/teacher ratio was also seen by local planners as a problem. However, it was inevitably brought about by the broader policy of compulsory education. The decline was not intended. But this is only one part of the story. The workload of twenty periods per week as identified by the World Bank should not lead to the conclusion that teachers share a light workload. Over the years, the writer came to understand that Chinese teachers lead a more demanding life than their counterparts in many other parts of the world. Given an opportunity to systematically study this issue in the province of Zhejiang, an in-depth case study of five sites was conducted (Cheng, 1996), and the following extract is taken from the forthcoming final report:

> The task facing a teacher in China is complex. First, teaching is formal and re-quires *formal preparation*. In all schools almost without exception, each lesson is taught with a detailed lesson plan. It has become a strong tradition consid-ered by teachers as part of the professional conduct. . . . The lesson plan is considered part of the teacher's performance. It is constantly inspected by the principal, read by peers and is part of the appraisal when it comes to promo-tion or awards. Even for very experienced teachers, teaching without a lesson plan is thought to be irresponsible if not inconceivable. Repeating last year's lesson plan is also considered as indecent. . . . Preparation of lessons therefore consumes a large part of teachers' time.
>
> Second, teaching is *target-oriented*. That is, students are expected to per-form according to targets. This is based on the Chinese tradition which trea-sures *effort* rather than *ability*. In practice, it means that the teacher is ex-pected to supervise the class of students to work towards some achievement targets. The tacit belief is that if students work hard, they can always achieve. The implication of this is that apart from classroom teaching, the teacher may spend enormous time to individually help students to pass examinations, for example . . . In the case of China, there is a requirement that over 80 percent of the students at primary 6 in rural schools have to pass their graduation ex-amination. The required passing percentage is 95 percent for cities. Appar-ently, these targets are actually reached . . . Hence, there is a basic assumption that teachers' performance is the predominating factor that determines stu-dents' performance. This significantly adds pressure to the teachers' workload.
>
> Third, the pastoral aspect of a teacher's job is again a heavy load. Most teachers in China are class teachers. . . . A class teacher in the Chinese context is the adviser to the class association which is a student organization. In prac-tice, the class teacher is responsible for the development of all the students in the class. The class teacher is therefore an organizer, a leader, a social worker, a counsellor, a remedial teacher and sometimes a private tutor to the academi-cally weak. In short, the class teacher is responsible for the comprehensive de-velopment of each student in his/her class. The general holistic approach to education has also made the class teachers' task more complex than their counterparts elsewhere. For example, home visit is a general routine of the class teacher. The usual practice is that the class teacher is expected to visit the home of each student in the class at least once per term in a two-term year. This really means that for a class of forty, the class teacher has to pay eighty home visits in the year. These are quite apart from the special visits paid to the family due to irregularities in the students' performance.

The rather lengthy quotation above illustrates how Chinese teachers are not underemployed or underutilized. The traditional expectations of each teacher are already very demanding. Moreover, these observations are fur-ther confirmed by quantitative data generated from the same study. Teachers, rural and urban alike, showed an average of 40.2 percent of their time in a day spent on work, 12.1 percent on housework, 14.0 percent on self-study/reading and 33.7 percent for rest/leisure.

From the above it is argued that pupil/teacher ratios and the number of teaching periods alone are not good indicators of the teachers' workload. Real workload can be better understood by qualitative studies of their actual lives. Consequently, policy suggesting a change in the number of active teaching periods may require an overhaul of the concept of classroom teaching and the role of the teacher if change is not to threaten real quality. Indeed, in recent years, some urban schools have achieved an "improvement of internal efficiency" by increasing teachers' contact time, but this has been done at the expense of home visits and the pastoral role of the teachers.

There are also factors in the larger educational context which limit the extent of change possible. Even if there was a will to change the pupil/teacher ratio, the employment system in China would make such a change extremely difficult. To date, with the exception of highly developed regions, what is practiced is still largely a policy of full employment. Schools are staffed with quotas that they are obliged to fill. Although there are national and provincial norms for pupil/teacher ratios, actual staffing is often governed by the requirement to fill the quota regardless of the student numbers. In practical terms, it is difficult to reduce the number of teachers in a school, although it is often equally difficult to increase the number. Such factors are not visible or understandable simply by looking at educational indicators from afar.

The lesson here is that statistical indicators that are convenient for international comparison may not serve effectively for national policy-making. Indicators may reflect factual data well, but education is more of a process. Statistical indicators are rarely meaningful for national policy-making unless the underlying educational processes are also revealed and studied. This is the strength of qualitative research. In pressing this case there is no intention to deny the value of quantitative research and associated indicators. Such data are often good starting points for in-depth inquiry that inevitably entails greater attention to qualitative methods.

THE POTENTIAL AND LIMITATIONS OF MATHEMATICAL MODELS IN POLICY RESEARCH

Mathematical models can be powerful tools for forecasts and policy simulations. Popular applications are estimations of school dropouts and forecasts for manpower supply and demand. The power of such models lies in their rigor in mathematical deduction that allows extrapolation of past trends into the future, or the collation of local trends to provide a global picture. However, there are two primary limitations with mathematical modeling. First, there are many assumptions underlying each model, and the validity of such assumptions is not always verifiable by the model itself. Second, mathematical models rarely take into account trends that are emerging, but which are not yet significant mathematically. Such emerging trends, however, may well be commonsense for those in the field, and can be identified through qualitative study. Without such contextualized study, mathematical modeling runs a very real risk of producing results that soon become obsolete.

An illustration of this can be taken from China, which, in 1983, launched the world's largest scale manpower forecast for the planning of education up to the year 2000. The manpower forecast was geared to planning higher and technical education. The forecasting exercise adopted a then novel bottom-up approach. Instead of starting from growth in national output and deducing manpower implications for various sectors, industries and work units, this exercise started from work units. For the purpose of manpower stock-taking, full population surveys (covering 99.5 percent of working personnel) were conducted in seventy-two industries in which work units were visited and their manpower structures studied on the sites. For forecasting, the collected data then underwent mathematical modeling in order to produce forecasts for the year 2000, for example, for the whole of industry in various regions. However, the planners, who had been used to statistical methods, were not content with a purely quantitative approach. The results of the forecast were then scrutinized by a modified Delphi approach such that over one hundred experts in each industry went through multiple back-and-forth "voting" to arrive at some consensus (Zhou, 1990; Cheng, 1991a). In hindsight, this multi-method forecast from 1983 provided a reliable broad outline of manpower trends in China and efficiently informed policy-making in higher and technical education in the following decade.

This type of combination of qualitative and quantitative methods clearly has much greater potential. Hong Kong, for example, has undertaken manpower, surveys in selected industries since 1973. The surveys are employer-oriented and the detection of manpower shortages is the prime objective. Conducted biennially, the surveys start with full-population site visits for manpower stock-taking in a particular industry, plus an element of employers' opinion survey for future needs. The latter is qualitative in nature. The data, together with earlier records, then undergo mathematical modeling in such a way that more recent data carry greater weight. This modeling provides only a family of curves showing the range of possibilities from the most optimistic to the most pessimistic scenarios. It is then up to the industry's Training Board to meet and decide qualitatively which of the possibilities is the most realistic (Cheng, 1985). Occasionally, qualitative "insider" knowledge of the industry persuades the Training Board to decide to select outside the range provided by mathematical modeling, for example, at times immediately after or before recession.

The two cases mentioned above suggest that while mathematical models may provide an essential basis for policy-making, in practice, many policies are made on the basis of more qualitative data and analyses. It is important not to equate rational decision-making solely with quantitative methods. This is particularly important in the developing world where context-free decision-making is far from unusual among research consultants visiting a new country for a short period.

The following example illustrates the case further. The writer joined an international consultancy team that was sent by a funding agency to look at basic education in a poor province in China. The official net enrollment ratio for the entire country was 97.4 percent in the year when the visit was done. This is an extremely high figure by international standards and naturally invites all sorts of skepticism among observers. The team visited a large number of villages. Among various things that the team looked at enrollment records were examined in most villages, and these sites were selected by the team not by the local officials. Questions were also asked about dropouts and repetitions in various villages. It was found, for example, that primary school dropouts were more common in some pockets, such as among girls in minority areas and in remote mountains. Otherwise, primary attendance was impressive and was an accepted part of the order of life. The province set down a ceiling of 5 percent for repetition at each grade, but with a few exceptions, teachers in most villages said this was often not met and not necessary. The team also noticed that at many sites the primary school principal, who was virtually the educational planner for the village, kept a "cultural registration" of all children born because these would be his future students. Fieldwork thus revealed healthy attendance in practice.

However, in the official consultancy report, it was concluded that 30 percent of the children who enrolled in schools never attended and that only about 50 percent of those who started school in the first grade ever reached the fifth grade (the final grade in these primary schools). None of these findings reflected field experience but the report admitted that these were estimations based upon models that had yielded effective results in Latin America!

Today, this report may easily gain the attention of readers who have no experience of the Chinese education system, and it may satisfy those who prefer to distrust official figures, particularly from China. However, these data present a picture which is far removed from reality and this has subsequently led to misconceived policy recommendations. The 30 percent non-attendance and 50 percent non-completion rates are inconceivable for anybody who has life experience in Chinese villages. In the majority of villages in China, non-attendance at primary school level has become socially unacceptable. There may be some distortion in the official figures, but the extent of the distortion should neither be overstated nor understated. This is not to say that mathematical modeling should not be used. Rather, if conflicts occur between statistical results and field experience, then the conflicts should be a starting point for more in-depth qualitative study to understand the reasons for this. If modeling data are inevitably to be given greater weight than information generated by field visits, then perhaps visits should not take place, and the resources spent in organizing them should be used to help improve schools.[1]

Secondly, much more in-depth but largely unacknowledged research has been done by local researchers on the issue of dropout and repetition. In a survey of this literature on rural education (Cheng and Paine, 1991), approximately thirty studies were thus identified and we concluded:

The studies in this area have seen a general trend of moving from impressionistic speculations based on limited data (Zhang 1985), to rather sophisticated approaches combining quantitative with qualitative techniques (Ma, 1984; Yang and Han, 1991). In the earlier studies, there were implicit assumptions of linear causality between dropouts and educational reasons (Zhao, 1987; Chen, 1988), hence attributing school dropouts to planning or instructional factors. Later studies include economic considerations (Shen, 1988), . . . The work by Zhou *et al.* (1987) is perhaps one of the earliest attempts to explore the reality in an intensive case study . . . with the preparedness to adopt multiple perspectives.

The more recent of these studies produced within country display a number of significant trends. First, a movement can be detected away from reliance upon statistical and macrolevel analyses. Second, multiple perspectives on policy issues are increasingly acknowledged and documented. Third, more descriptive and qualitative studies are being carried out and are gaining recognition.

In particular, Yang and Han (1991) conducted a valuable mixed-method study with a high degree of rigor that included questionnaires, in-depth case-study and focus group discussions. This report was submitted to UNESCO as a country paper. A useful study was also conducted by the Education Committee of Hebei Province (1990) which involved (a) a past trend analysis of thirty-nine years, and a statistical projection of future scenarios, (b) a full-population survey among a sample of nineteen countries and (c) a three-year backward tracer study of a random-sampled cohort of 103,887 primary students and 77,171 junior secondary students.

Many of these local studies were under way while the international consultancy visit referred to above was being made. Had the visiting team inquired into the Chinese literature and paid more respect to what was being done in country, their own report would have been more useful and more accurate. Indeed, the studies done by Chinese researchers arrived at conclusions that refute many of the results of the mathematical model developed in Latin America. In some cases the methods adopted are highly sophisticated and can stand any international scrutiny. The UNESCO-sponsored study, for example, followed a general framework defined for international comparison and the Hebei provincial tracer study was a large-scale cohort analysis combined with qualitative probing. Here it is pertinent to note that had the visiting team included a qualitative element (such as several case studies) in its own study, or surveyed the local literature, more realistic conclusions about dropouts and repetitions in Chinese primary schools would have been produced. Mathematical modeling might have been used in a more cautious way that compared initial results with real situations, as was done in Latin America when the model was first utilized. The team might thus have been in a better position to make use of their experience in the field to create a new model more appropriate to the situation in China. Then, and only then, could the conclusions and recommendations made by the team have played a more positive role in tackling the real problems of basic education in China.

CULTURE AND ENVIRONMENT

In educational policy-making, solutions to a problem can be viable only when the causes of the problem are correctly identified and understood. Problems may look alike in different countries and different parts of a country, but their causes and nature may differ considerably. Accordingly, solutions must often vary and problem identification should not stop at the discovery of discrepancies. It is essential to understand the processes by which such discrepancies are formed and the contexts or environments in which such processes take place (Crossley and Broadfoot, 1992). An understanding of processes and environments requires attention to the local culture; and the study of such processes, environments and cultures is a strength of a qualitative approach to educational research.

Illustrative of this point is a recent study of an ethnic minority area in China. In Miao villages, girls' attendance is exceptionally low. These are the "difficult spots" or, as mentioned above, what the planners call "pockets" where universal primary education was difficult to achieve. In a survey done in one of the prefectures (subdivisions of a province) that are inhabited by minorities (Wen, 1988) it was shown that although average female enrollment in the prefecture was over 70 percent, there were counties (subdivisions of a prefecture) where the enrollment rate was as low as 31 percent. Meanwhile, the boys' enrollment rate was almost 100 percent. In addition, only about 27 percent of the girls ever completed primary school. In some of the schools we visited, there were only one or two girls among a whole school of several hundred children. These are called the "monk" schools. Low attendance among girls has led to low output of female graduates, which in turn leads to a shortage of female teacher trainees and hence female teachers. This has become a rather stubborn vicious circle because parents are reluctant to send their girls to schools with only male teachers.

The same report identified four causes for the low enrollment: economic underdevelopment, parents' discrimination against girls and early marriage, high private cost for parents, and the irrelevance and low quality of schooling. Recommendations to overcome low enrollment are therefore reduction of private costs, expansion of the public schools sector, development of vocational education, and propaganda and education to discourage early marriage.

Home visits were paid to families as part of our research strategy and a general picture began to emerge from such fieldwork. Most importantly this revealed that girls in the Miao ethnic group are expected to take embroidery most seriously. Skills and knowledge of embroidery lore are a demonstration of their talents and hence an indicator of their social prestige. This in turn determines their future in terms of finding a good husband and explains the famous and splendid costumes the Miao girls wear. Each girl wears only costumes that are products of their own manual skills. Embroidery is therefore so important in their social life that girls learn embroidery as soon as they can hold the needle. At ages of twelve or thirteen, girls are expected to do embroidery for their future husbands, and a little later, they do pieces for their future children. Some of these girls become engaged as young as eight or nine years old.

Such qualitative research, within the local culture, revealed previously overlooked but important causes for the non-attendance of girls in school. In this context embroidery skills bear a much higher "economic" value than schooling. Indeed, girls who attend schools incur an opportunity cost which they cannot afford. There is a basic contradiction in the relations between education and the local economy. On the one hand, education is basic to the long-term development and well-being of the Miao communities. At the time of the research, the literacy rate for girls in the prefecture was just over 28 percent, in strong contrast to that of 71 percent for boys, and development in the local economy is inevitably hindered by low educational attainment. On the other hand, the social structures and lifestyles of Miao communities present formidable hurdles for the schooling of girls.

In this case, the local planners are aware of the situation and the embroidery issue is fully described in Wen's analysis. However, the difficulties generated by this were classified by external policy analysts as "discrimination against girls" and "backward traditions," hence the proposed solutions lay in "educating parents" and "promoting the Marital Law." The planners were thus thinking in the framework of universalizing basic education and hence anything that presented obstacles to such a course needed to be rectified and changed.

Qualitative fieldwork through the home visits, however, helped the writer not only to understand how the emphasis on embroidery skills had become a problem, but also to assess the importance of culture among the Miao communities. To the Miao parents and the Miao girls, schooling is something imposed on them because of an importance that is not felt within their community. Meanwhile, in order to attend schools, they have to put aside their embroidery exercises, and because of that they worry about their future. Schooling causes problems for girls with immediate effect. From a local perspective, it is therefore not embroidery that is causing problems, but compulsory education that is disturbing their normal lifestyle and culture.

This qualitative study has shed new light on the issue of girls' attendance in Miao communities. If social conditions and cultural expectations are not changed in these Miao villages, there does not seem to be an easy way to improve girls' attendance. The cultural issue that has to be given attention in order to make compulsory education possible is much greater than the problem of compulsory education itself. If the Marital Law (which permits legal marriage only after age eighteen) is difficult to implement in the villages, then the Law of Compulsory Education is a secondary issue. The question before policy-makers is then: is it realistic, and culturally acceptable, to ask such villages to achieve compulsory primary education in the near future? In recent years, some educators in China have advocated a reconsideration of the uniform target of nine-year compulsory education applied throughout the country. The Miao girls have further demonstrated the necessity for such a reconsideration. As a pragmatic measure, national policy has moved away from 100 percent coverage of compulsory education throughout the nation. The social situation in the Miao villages further challenges policy-makers with questions such as: if all girls in Miao villages can be helped to receive four (or even two) years of school education, is that not a significant target in its own right? What is the most realistic and culturally appropriate policy option?

Clearly, it is often legitimate for central government to make policies for parts of a country to comply with. In the case of compulsory education in China, for example, national policies have made essential contributions to the improvement of basic education in the past decade. In this sense, uniformity in national policies has been a positive factor in educational development. However, uniformity in policies inevitably encounters problems among diverse localities, and where national policy is not so relevant to local needs, imposition may bear little fruit—and in some cases may arouse resentment. Policies are thus viable only when they are realistic, but they are realistic only when they are seen as realistic by the local community. In other words, local perspectives are important in the policy formulation and implementation process. In this respect, qualitative research, which accesses and identifies local views in context can, and should, play a crucial role for policy makers.

MULTIPLE INTERPRETATIONS OF POLICY-RELATED CONCEPTS

Policy-related research often works with concepts that are attractive to policy makers. Concepts such as efficiency, equity and quality are particularly common in the literature and efficiency looms high on the policy agenda. Efficiency is also a priority of donor agencies and international organizations who are concerned about whether or not funding channeled to developing countries is used in the most economical way. The measurement of efficiency may seem unambiguous to planners. To many, efficiency is either measured by input-output analysis or cost-benefit analysis. Such concepts and procedures are, however, more appropriate to industrial enterprises and, when applied to other systems (including education), require more careful modification and application than is often the case in practice. Much research and evaluation is thus conducted at the expense of real understanding of the language with which the system operates.

Such problems were encountered in a project carried out in 1993 in three provinces of China to study the internal efficiency of basic education in rural villages.[2] The research team was drawn from a local research institute, the Shanghai Institute of Human Resource Development. During a preliminary discussion before the research the team arrived at the conclusion that, given the disparity among different parts of China, it was impossible to set a uniform measure for output of the school system. According to members' experience in various parts of the country, the expected output of primary schools may range from "attendance rate for the required years," "high passing rate at graduation" to "high enrollment rate in secondary schools." In each case, the expected rates again vary. Using any unified yardstick to measure educational output with such a variety of expectations did not seem to be sensible. The team therefore decided to adopt a notion of "minimum acceptable quality" as a benchmark of educational output in the various counties to be studied. This is a floating benchmark that is locality-specific. What this actually means had to be identified during each of the case studies. As such, the case studies were designed to include strong qualitative components. Apart from the collection of financial data and interviews with local officers and planners, each case study included in-depth interviews with school principals, focus group discussions with parents and observations of classroom teaching. The question to be addressed about output was: what is seen as the minimum acceptable quality in this locality?

Discussion about notions of output thus encouraged the research team to be more sensitive about local perspectives. With this preparation and orientation the team discovered a number of other issues that were beyond their expectation, but that were essential to understanding efficiency issues in the villages. First, local planners and educators were more concerned about inadequacy rather than efficiency. Some went as far as saying that efficiency is an issue only when funding is adequate. In a team meeting after the first interviews, members came to the consensus that for the local planners and educators, efficiency (xiaoyi) was taken to mean benefits. When they say a school is efficient, they mean the school can do a good job. A further analysis of the situation revealed that a reason for this local perception of efficiency was that the parties who received funds were different from the parties who spent the money. In other words, those who were responsible for the output and those who were responsible for the input never interacted. Not that they did not meet each other physically, but the two groups were not related in a dialectical way. When the input parties did not find enough to spend, they asked for more; when the output parties were asked for more, they tried to find more. This helps to explain why the notion of inadequacy prevails over efficiency. The research team concluded that this is a reflection of traditional thinking in operation in a planned economy.

Second, in addition to the separation of input from output, there was also a "compartmentalization" of funding. That is, all funds were earmarked for specific expenditures, and a convention in China is that different expenditures are taken care of by different sources of funding. In the case of primary schools in villages, the state is largely responsible for salaries of public teachers, educational levies are used for community teachers, and donations are sought for physical constructions (Zhou, 1992). In addition, schools may also generate income through school-owned factories or other economic activities. What was discovered in the research, even by those who had long been familiar with the basic conventions, was that because of the earmarking convention, school principals and local education officers were not given discretion for mixing available funds across budget categories.

They also never considered ways to mobilize funds from one "compartment" to another in order to maximize their utilization, largely because this was not expected under the planning system.

Accordingly, the research team made recommendations which pointed to reforms that would be fundamental to the system. Their recommendations included an increase in the discretion for principals in reallocating funds, freedom for schools to raise salaries in exchange for heavier teaching loads to create an incentive mechanism, creation of differential learning targets to motivate the largest majority of students, and the replacement of formal science experiments by low-cost life-related activities.

This is an example of how qualitative research may touch upon the crux of policy issues that are not always assessible through the collection of quantitative data and macrolevel information. The institute in charge of this research was well known for producing national annual reports of educational finance. They were not short of system-level information and they did make very insightful analyses based on the quantitative data. However, efficiency is something that is improved mainly through changes in practice in schools and by the people who work in them. As such, the team rightly emphasized qualitative aspects of the study and therefore began to better understand local perspectives (and misconceptions) of efficiency. This provided sound grounds for making more realistic policy recommendations.

If such recommendations were put into practice, it is argued there would not only be an improvement of efficiency in schools, but also a clarification of the notion of efficiency among local educators and planners. The benefits of the latter would be far-reaching in themselves.

CONCLUDING REMARKS

As argued at the beginning of this chapter, much educational research in developing countries is funded by development agencies operating from developed countries. Too many studies are either carried out by consultants from the north, or they are conducted by local researchers who have to shape their research agendas according to the expectations of the donor agencies. Very often, projects adopt a functionalist point of view, assuming a linear relationship between education and development and, often despite very good intentions, a deficit model of developing countries. Endeavors to identify strengths in education provision in developing countries are rare and only recent (Filp, 1993). Such tendencies often trap researchers in unhelpful intellectual and planning frameworks that result in findings which are unrealistic for the specific context.

To illustrate how preconceived ideas can predetermine analysis we conclude with a brief comparison of China and Japan. These two countries share a similar education tradition and are fairly close in their educational practices. If we examine research funded and published by the major aid agencies, research about Japanese education tends to highlight its strengths whereas, until recently, research about Chinese education tends to identify difficulties. One can argue that this is natural because research on China is used mainly to justify loans, which is not the case for Japan. There is a tacit functionalist assumption that Japan's economic strength is attributable to its sound education; while China's poor-quality education reflects its low level of economic development. It is, nevertheless, significant to note that publications that are based on qualitative research are often more realistic and fairer to educators in both countries (Lynn, 1988; White, 1987; Rohlen, 1983; Cleverly, 1991; Gardner, 1989; Ross, 1993). Qualitative research and evaluation, emphasizing an ethnographic approach, is thus a valuable mode of investigation for policy makers willing to challenge ethnocentric assumptions, and other preconceptions, that may limit the effectiveness and relevance of educational plans and proposals.

Moreover, our review of the literature produced by researchers visiting developing countries reveals little reference to findings of local research. Even when members of visiting teams have developing country origins, the fact that they are sent by a "northern" funding agency often locates the visit in a north-south relationship, and the study is likely to adopt a strong "donor-recipient" paradigm. Too often there is also tacit disrespect for whatever is generated by local research efforts. Indeed, acknowledging the existence of expertise in the host developing country may limit the future role of visiting consultants.

Under these circumstances, quantitative methods can provide a safe shelter for visiting researchers, and for international funding agencies. The mathematical model cited earlier, for example, had been successful in Latin America and became a convenient vehicle for visiting teams to fulfill their duties elsewhere. In this case there is multiple beauty. First, the model generates a considerable level of sophistication, requires high-tech skills and is seen as "scientific," and "impartial." Second, it has already proved successful in the developing world. Third, results point to a negation of official information about dropouts and so provide the visiting team with considerable legitimacy to maintain its expert position and deliver an authoritative report. How many students actually drop out from schools in China is perhaps less of a real concern for the team, or for the funding agency as a whole, than many would wish to acknowledge.

While this may be an overly cynical and provocative perspective, more criticism in this arena of policy research is required if we are to improve our chances of realistic policy formulation and successful implementation—and qualitative research and evaluation clearly has much to offer, especially in developing countries.

ACKNOWLEDGMENT

The writer would like to thank Mark Constas, his colleague, for reading through the text and making useful comments.

NOTES

1. In that particular visit, per evening per team member in a five-star Beijing hotel cost about U.S. $100. The visit report estimated that the per-student unit expenditure per year in that particular province was about U.S. $16.
2. The project, known as TSS-1, was sponsored by UNDP with the assistance of UNESCO. The writer was the external consultant.

REFERENCES

Berstecher, D. (1986). *Provincial-level Educational Planning and Management in China: A Case Study of Sichuan Province*. Paris: UNESCO/UNICEF Co-operative Program (Mimeograph).

Chen, H. D. (1988). "Bufada Dqu Shisi Jiunian Yiwu Jiaoyu de Xuezhi Wenti (The School System for Implementation of Nine-year Compulsory Education in Under-Developed Areas)." *Jiaoyu Yanjiu*, 6, pp. 10–12.

Cheng, K. M. (1985). *Forecasting in a Free Market: Manpower Survey in the Planning of Technical Education*. Paper presented in the Second Annual Conference of the Hong Kong Educational Research Association, November 16.

———. (1987). "Where are the Trainees?—Trainers' Plans Versus Students' Aspirations in Hong Kong." In E. D. Fortuijn, W. Hoppers and M. Morgan (eds.) *Paving Pathways to Work*. The Hague: CESO.

———. (1991a). *Planning of Basic Education in China: A Case Study of Two Counties in the Province of Liaoning*. Paris: International Institute for Educational Planning.

———. (1991b). "Challenging the North-South Paradigm: Educational Research in East Asia." In International Institute for Educational Planning and Institute of International Education, Stockholm University (eds.) *Strengthening Educational Research in Developing Countries*. Paris: International Institute for Educational Planning

———. (1996). *Quality of Basic Education in China: A Case Study of the Zhejiang Province*. Paris: International Institute for Educational Planning.

Cheng, K. M. and Paine, L. (1991). *Research on Education in Rural China: A Survey of the Literature*. Plenary paper delivered at the International Conference on Chinese Education of the 21st Century, November 19–22, Honolulu.

Cleverley, J. (1991). *The Schooling of China: Tradition and Modernity in Chinese Education* (2d ed.). Sydney: Allen & Unwin.

Crossley, M. and Broadfoot, P. (1992). "Comparative and International Research in Education: Scope, Problems and Potential," *British Educational Research Journal*, 18(2), pp. 99–112.

Filp, J. (1993). *The 900 Schools Programme: Improving the Quality of Primary Schools in Impoverished Areas of Chile*. Paris: International Institute for Educational Planning.

Gardner, H. (1989). *To Open Minds: Chinese Clues to the Dilemma of Contemporary Education*. New York: Basic Books.

Han, Q. L. (1990). "Woguo Zhongxiaoxue Xuesheng Lushi Zhuangkuang de Fenxi he Duice (The Analysis and Solutions for the Problem of School Dropouts in China)," *Jiaoyu Yanjiu*, 2, pp. 20–23

Hebei Education Commission, Office of Policy Studies. (1990). *Hebeisheng Xiaoxue Chuzhong Liushi Liuji Zhuangkuang de Diaocha Yanjiu Zonghe Baogao (A Comprehensive Report of the Study of Dropout and Repetition in Primary and*

Junior Secondary Schools in Hebei Province). (Mimeograph). Also reported in *Zhongguo Jiaoyu Bao (China Education Daily),* February 7, 1991.

Lincoln, Y. S. and Guba, E. G. (1985). *Naturalistic Enquiry.* Beverly Hills: Sage.

Lynn, R. (1988). *Educational Achievement in Japan: Lessons for the West.* London: Macmillan.

Ma, Y. Q. (1984). "Dangqian Nongcun Xiaoxue Liujilu Wenti Diaocha Yanjiu (A Study of the Current Rate of Grade Repetition in Rural Primary Schools)," *Jiaoyu Yanjiu,* 9, pp. 47–51.

Rohlen, T. P. (1983). *Japan's High Schools.* Berkeley: University of California Press.

Ross, H. (1993). *China Learns English.* New Haven: Yale University Press.

Shanghai Institute of Human Resources Development. (1994). *Internal Efficiency of Educational Finance in Rural Primary Schools in China: Report of a Research Based on Case Studies.* Prepared for UNDP and UNESCO. (Mimeograph).

Shen, G. M. (1988). "Sunan Nongcun Xuexiao de Liusheng Wenti ji Duice (The Problems of Dropouts and the Solutions in the Rural Schools in South Jiangsu Province)," *Jiaoyu Yanjiu,* 7, pp. 43–46.

United Nations Development Program. (Various years). *Human Development Report.* New York: Oxford University Press.

Wen, B. (1988). *Qiandongnan miaozu dongzu zizhizhou nu ertong ruxue zhuangkuang, wenti ji jianyi (Girls' attendance in the Miao and Dung Autonomous Prefecture of Southeast Guizhou: Situations, Problems and Recommendations),* Mimeograph.

White, M. (1987). *The Japanese Educational Challenge: A Commitment to Children.* New York: The Free Press.

World Bank. (1985). *China: Issues and Prospects in Education.* Washington D.C.

Yang, N. L. and Han, M. (1991). "Xiaoxue Chuzhong Xuesheng Cuoxue Liuji de Yanjiu (A Study on the Drop-out and Repetitions in Chinese Primary and Junior Secondary)," *Jiaoyu Yanjiu,* 3, pp. 45–57.

Zhang, J. Y. (1985). "Dangqian Nongcun Zhongxue Liusheng Wenti de Diaocha (A Survey of Rural Secondary Student Dropout)," *Jiaoyu Yanjiu,* 8, pp. 33–36.

Zhao, J. (1987). "Chuzhong Yanxue Xuesheng de Xingqu (An Investigation into the Interests of Junior Secondary School Students Who are Sick of Schooling)," *Jiaoyu Yanjiu,* 7, pp. 59–62.

Zhou, B. L. (1990). *Mianxiang Ershiyi Shiji de Zhongguo Jiaoyu: Guoqing, Xuqiu, Guihua, Duice (China's Education for the 21st Century: Situations, Demands, Planning and Decisions).* Beijing: Higher Education Press.

Zhou, N. Z. (1992). *Reinforce the Connections between Education and the Economy: Major Issues and Solutions in China's Education Reform.* Paper delivered at the International Conference on "Education, Social Change and Regional Development," June 23–25, Hong Kong.

CHAPTER 13

The Limits of Modern Education

William K. Cummings

"To enlighten the people is to destroy kings"

—Alexis de Tocqueville

Modern education, conceived in the late eighteenth to early nineteenth century to promote enlightenment and social equality, may finally be nearing its institutional limit. Over the past decade, following nearly a century of steady gains, there has been little further advance in the diffusion of modern education. The modern system has proved effective in serving the interests of the established core of contemporary society, but ineffective in "reaching for the periphery." This, in our view, is wrong and needs to be set right.

The core chapters of this work outline a set of strategic shifts that will enable education to reach the periphery. But as a first step, it is necessary to understand what constrains modern education. We propose here that modern education, despite its egalitarian rhetoric, was never designed to provide equal or even appropriate education for all.

EDUCATION FOR ALL

"Liberty, Equality, and Fraternity" is perhaps the most memorable slogan of the modern period, shouted as the citizens stormed the Bastille in 1789. The French Revolution symbolizes a worldwide process of reform that aspired to liberate all of the human race from bondage and slavery into a common condition of freedom, and ultimately to the status of equality and citizenship in a new world order. The reform movement of the nineteenth century gradually expanded the concept of citizenship to include first human rights, then political rights, and finally social rights.

Among these social rights was the guarantee of a basic education. Myron Weiner (1991), in a fascinating analysis of contemporary Indian attitudes toward compulsory education, notes that the debate over education is closely intertwined with the debate over child labor. On the ideological right are those who argue that the economy needs cheap child labor in order to be competitive, while on the left are those who argue that child labor is exploitative. In several of the early European cases, the balance was tilted by Protestant religious leaders who argued that young people needed a basic education so they could read the Bible and thereby discover the path to salvation (and, moreover, become more productive). With the French Revolution, this religious reform movement was adopted by progressive political leaders who insisted that the modern state should provide education for all.

According to Weiner, as early as 1524, "Martin Luther sent a letter to German municipalties insisting it was their duty to provide schools, and the duty of parents to educate their children" (1991). Protestant influence also was behind the early progress of mass education in Scotland and eventually throughout Europe. For example, in Sweden a royal decree of 1723 told parents and guardians to "diligently see to it that their children applied themselves to book reading and the study of lessons in the Catechism." Japan's modernizing Meiji government, only four years after overthrowing the feudal Tokugawa regime, issued the Fundamental Code of Education, which insisted "every guardian, acting in accordance with this, shall bring up his children with tender care, never failing to have them attend school" (Passin, 1965).

Thus by the turn of the twentieth century, education for all was a firm plank in the political fabric of most independent states. As other nations became independent, particularly following World War II, they usually adopted this plank, and introduced selective policies for its promotion. The United Nations Charter of 1946, with its declaration of the Human Right of Literacy, was another important symbolic step on the road of educational progress.

Particularly since the late fifties, universal education has become an important concern of the international donor community. A recent indication was the much-heralded World Conference on Education for All (EFA) that took place in Jomtien, Thailand, March 5–9, 1990. This conference, attended by chief ministers of education and delegates from over 130 nations, prepared a World Declaration on Education for All as well as a Framework for Action (UNDP, UNESCO, UNICEF, and World Bank, 1990). These documents once again affirmed the commitment of the world's educational leaders to the noble goal of universal literacy through a combination of national, regional, and international initiatives.

But neither these words nor the various actions that are supposed to follow will be enough. For what is envisioned in the current EFA campaign is more of the same: Modern education designed by the center to serve, first and foremost, the interests of the center. The Jomtien initiative, while using the phrase "for all," in fact only proposes to reach 85 percent of the world's young people by the turn of the century; and while it makes reference to such groups as the poor and the disabled, it nowhere suggests that these groups require preferential treatment, relative to the advantaged who reside in the societal center. Without setting educational policies on their head, without developing new strategies that favor the periphery over the center, it will be impossible to realize the dreams that inspired the modern educational revolution.

MODERN EDUCATION IS CREATED BY AND FOR THE CENTER

There is little reason to doubt the sincerity of the eminent national and world leaders who have promoted modern education, and who recently reiterated their concerns in the EFA Declaration. But we will argue that their efforts inevitably face an upper limit, simply because they, as representatives of the central institutions of the modern system, have proposed policies that favor the center, over the periphery.

To introduce this argument, it is useful to gain some understanding of the nature of the center, and of the centripetal forces in social interaction. Edward Shils (1975), who has perhaps done more than any other thinker to enhance understanding of the center-periphery relation, writes:

> Society has a center. There is a central zone in the structure of society. This central zone impinges in various ways on those who live within the ecological domain in which the society exists. . . . The central zone is not, as such, a spatially located phenomenon. It almost always has a more or less definite location within the bounded territory in which the society lives. Its centrality has, however, nothing to do with geometry and little with geography.
>
> The center, or the central zone, is a phenomenon of the realm of values and beliefs. It is the center of the order of symbols, of values and beliefs, which govern the society. . . . One of the major elements in any central value system is an affirmative attitude toward established authority. . . .
>
> The central values system thus . . . legitimates the existing distribution of roles and rewards to persons possessing the appropriate qualities which in various ways symbolize degrees of proximity to authority (Shils, 1975).

Shils then goes on to discuss the center's regard for those who are distant from the center. He note the center naturally "legitimates the smaller rewards received by those who live at various distances from the circles in which authority is exercised." The center, in his view, is inevitably disposed to look firstly after its own interests and only secondarily, if at all, after the interests of those who are distant from the center.

THE CONSOLIDATION OF CENTERS

Shils's generalizations refer to all societal units, regardless of scale, but in the development of his argument he observes a historical pattern of the consolidation of societal centers. At the height of the medieval period in Western Europe, there were as many as five hundred societal centers. With advances in transportation and particularly in military technology, a process of consolidation began which ultimately culminated by the mid-nineteenth century in a much smaller group of powerful centers, known as nation-states, which are essentially the same national entities that have prevailed down to the present day. The major question since that time has been the relative preeminence within this small group. Paul Kennedy (1989), in *The Rise and Fall of the Great Powers*, traces a shift from Great Britain to Germany to the United States.

As these nation-states gained ascendency, their leaders sought by various means to strengthen their position of authority vis-à-vis constituencies both within and outside their national boundaries. The development of military strength was one means, but particularly for the consolidation of national power the leaders placed considerable reliance on mass education to instill a sense of loyalty and civil responsibility. National systems of education were established and supported by funds, curriculum, teachers, and instructional materials provided primarily by the center. These national systems, which have since come to be called modern educational systems, sought to build national unity through controlling the influence of familial, community, and religious values in the educational process—particularly where these traditional influences were perceived to be hostile to the new state. The centrally devised control procedures have inevitably led to systems that favor the center, no matter how egalitarian the rhetoric espoused by the educational leaders. However, there is variation in the degree of the central bias.

THE MAIN PATTERNS OF MODERN EDUCATION

Common to all of the emerging modern nation-states was the concern to promote education so as to provide the members of society with a common educational experience that would reinforce the center's authority. But the particular approaches that emerged varied according to national circumstances. It can be argued that six distinctive patterns of modern education emerged. The first four, to be discussed below, were administratively more centralized, while the last two were more decentralized.

French or Continental Model

The French case is perhaps the most celebrated example, because of the abruptness of the change. Up to the time of the French Revolution, the Catholic church had commanded a virtual monopoly in the field of education in France, and used this pulpit to reinforce the legitimacy of both the church and the monarchy. The founders of the First Republic sought to cleanse education of what it considered to be the traditional and superstitious influence of the church. Robespierre told the National Convention he was "convinced of the necessity of operating a total regeneration, and, if I may express myself in this way, of creating a new people" (Blum, 1986).

Thus the First Republic declared an end to religious education, to be replaced by a new system of national schools. As Danton declared, "It is in national schools that children must suck republican milk. The Republic is one and indivisible; public instruction must also be related to this center of unity" (Pierre, 1881). But the Republic initially lacked the resources to establish a national system, and, moreover, many parents remained loyal to the church. Thus the progress of the new Republic in realizing these ambitious goals was staggered. It was not until the 1830s under Guizot that the Republic drafted a systematic plan for the delivery of republican education, and even then the major initiatives were in urban areas and at the secondary level. Only from the 1870s did the state fully assert its influence at the primary level by establishing a public school in every commune, regardless of whether it had a Catholic School or not. Jules Ferry, Minister of Public Instruction during this period, condemned Catholic schools as "establishments which are maintained as schools of counter-revolution, where one learns to detest and curse all of the ideas which are the honor and the purpose of modern France" (Legrand, 1961).

Thus we see in the French example a strong determination by the central state to impose a single pattern of education throughout the Republic. The central Ministry of Public Instruction established uniform guidelines on educational expenditures, which were to be jointly financed from local and central revenues. And it appointed officials in the administrative units of academies, departments and cantons to carry out its various policies on school construction, textbook utilization, teacher assignment and training, and instruction. Local participation in the educational process was limited, and little attempt was made to adjust educational approaches to take into account variations in local conditions.

The French approach led to universal primary education by the turn of the twentieth century—but there is much controversy concerning the uniformity of provision. A myth prevails that the system provided identical education throughout the nation and indeed throughout the French empire. But recent empirical research indicates a clear bias in this system to serve urban areas and particularly Paris. For example, the major *lycée* were located in the towns and cities, and most of the elite *grande école* were located in or around Paris. There was, and continues to be, a strong urban and upper-class bias in the composition of students admitted to these elite institutions. Thus the centralized French system was more favorable to those at the center than those in the periphery.

Prussia

While the French pattern, by virtue of France's imperial domination, has had an extensive global impact, it is important to recognize that many of its features were inspired by the nearby example of Prussia. Through much of the nineteenth century, France and Prussia were joined in intermittent conflict. The Prussians, after suffering defeat under Napoleon in 1807, concluded that education was the vehicle of future strength. And thus Prussia took even more vigorous steps than France to develop a national educational system. But in the case of Prussia, the King enjoyed a relatively harmonious relation with the Lutheran church and with other local religious groups; thus Prussia devised an educational approach where the central state incorporated rather than rejected religious education.

Prussia's educational successes were widely admired throughout the Continent as well as in the New World. Especially notable was the systematic approach in teacher education and the promotion of strong research-oriented universities. The speed of Prussia's industrial revolution as well as the impressive strength of its armed forces were attributed to the rapid progress in educational expansion.

Prussia also relied more on local participation in the finance and governance of schools than did France. Of particular interest in the Prussian case was an equalizing provision in the central funding formula to insure that local areas which had difficulty in generating their own founds would receive additional support from the center. However, in most particulars the two systems had strong similarities and can be thought of as exemplars of the Continental Pattern.

The main features of this pattern can be summarized as follows: The central government played a leading role, while requiring local governments to provide at least partial support for the schools in their areas. Principles of control varied from nation to nation, though the most common approach was a line bureaucracy setting the major guidelines on curriculum and exams, textbooks, teacher training and assignments. Public participation in the control of education was relatively limited.

Lowlands Pattern

The Lowlands (now extending to Scandinavia) provide an interesting exception to the Continental Pattern. The nations now known as the Netherlands, Belgium, and Denmark were not, as distinct in the early nineteenth century as they are today; and when the French Republican government proposed a centralized secular educational system, the leaders in these areas were inclined to follow the French example, but for a different reason. In these areas, the religious commitments of the people were quite diverse, preventing the state from favoring a particular religion; might it not be preferable for the state to divorce itself from all religions?

The National Assembly of the Batavian Republic (later the Kingdom of the Netherlands) in 1796 issued *General Reflections on National Education*, in which the advantages of a secular approach were outlined:

> Through education and propagation of (Liberal) "culture" among all classes the circle of citizens could be broadened and the basis of the state as well. On this course a homogeneous Dutch nation would come into being, and would naturally take on a liberal coloration. This is the political core of the liberal school policies. The school as *nation-forming* must not be divided among competing "sectarian schools" or left in the hands of an exclusive political or

church party. The Liberals considered themselves *algemeen* (that is, common, nonsectarian, nonpartisan) (Glenn, 1988).

This secular approach was attempted for a number of years, but it did not lead to acceptable results. So by the second decade of the nineteenth century, educational leaders proposed a shift to a religiously oriented school assisted by state subsidies. The eventual outcome was a system of independently managed schools, subsidized and loosely regulated by the central government to insure common coverage of certain subject matter. State regulation became relatively more rigorous at the upper grade levels. Thus individual school enjoyed considerable autonomy while receiving substantial state support.

Japanese

Distinctive approaches have also been set up in the socialist countries and in Japan, both drawing heavily on the centralized tradition of the European continent. However, particularly in the Japanese case, the social origins of the central leaders led them to develop special concern for the educational fortunes of children in peripheral areas. While the modern European states had gained ascendency on the wave of a bourgeoisie revolution, the modern Japanese state was formed by what is sometimes called an aristocratic coup. Lower- and middle-rank samurai from somewhat peripheral areas, fearful of the consequences of Japan's technological backwardness relative to the West, overthrew the tradition-focused center and replaced it with a new government that was committed to modernizing Japan. The new government was also more mindful of peripheral areas than had been its predecessor.

As in the continental case, the Japanese leaders promoted a centralized system and stressed a common curriculum that reinforced the legitimacy of the new government. But relative to the continental pattern, the Japanese system was exceptionally thorough in providing equal opportunities to children of the peripheral areas. For example, equalizing formulas were used to insure sufficient founds in impoverished local areas; and special incentives were developed to reward teachers who took up jobs in difficult settings. Also compared to the standard European model, the Japanese approach was more tolerant of private schools.

The Japanese system expanded much more rapidly than its European predecessors. It is generally regarded that the system achieved universal enrollment in basic education during the first decade of the twentieth century, or within four decades of the official commitment to compulsory education. In recent years, with increases in Japanese affluence and experience with democracy as well as a concern to foster national creativity, the Japanese system has encouraged more local control of education.

Socialist

The socialist approach was the last major system to emerge on the world scene. The first socialist system was developed in the former Soviet Union, while important variants were latter developed in China and Yugoslavia. Drawing heavily on the Continental model, it is perhaps the most centralized of all the extant models, with central prescription in virtually all policy areas and no tolerance for a private sector.

The egalitarian rhetoric is prominent in socialist education, and most socialist educational systems have an exceptional role in providing basic education to all citizens. However, the systems vary in their provision at the secondary and tertiary level. Some critics suggest the socialist system, at least as developed in the former Soviet Union, has a strong urban bias. In socialist systems that have been instituted in large nations such as China, provincial governments are accorded a role in educational finance and are also allowed to conduct some of the education in their local languages.

Anglo and American Patterns

In contrast to the prominent role of the central state on the Continent, in England and later the United States, local governments assumed a more prominent role, providing the great proportion of funding and enjoying considerable autonomy to develop distinctive local policies. In England, the state chose to subsidize worthy private schools whereas in the U.S. the state required private schools to be self-supporting.

In both of these decentralized approaches, local boards of education were established to assume responsibility for most educational policies in the local area. Individual schools and their executive officers were subordinate to district-level school superintendents who were in turn subordinate to these local boards. School-level discretion varied between localities.

However, the geographical scope of local boards as well as the funds they can access differ. In the U.K., which currently has a population of 55 million, there are approximately 106 local education authorities; whereas in the U.S., with a population of 240 million, there are approximately 15,000 school boards. The U.S. school boards are typically responsible for a smaller geographical area, and also draw the majority of their funds from this small area; if the area is poor, the schools tend to be poor, for the subsidies coming from other government levels are modest. Thus, particularly in the American system, there are enormous disparities between school districts. The best-funded are not in the "center" but rather in the suburban areas that encircle a major urban center. In the U.K., because of the larger districts, disparities between districts are not as marked.

While private schools are allowed in both systems, they occupy a more prominent place in the English system. In fact, a subset of the English private schools known as "public schools" are generally viewed as the appropriate vehicles for elite education. These schools do not receive much state funding, but they are generously funded through tuition and endowment. The success of these independent schools disposes U.K. (and, to a lesser degree, American) educational leaders to consider the merits of an educational system where the central government's role is sharply curtailed. Thus, in recent years in virtually all countries that have one or the other of these decentralized patterns, consideration is being given to a further devolution of control to the "self-managed school."

The development of new information technologies and the increasing professionalization of educational personnel has led educational policy makers to propose a reduction in district-level controls and an increase in the discretion of the heads of individuals schools. This shift to increased school-level discretion is associated with new systems of accountability, both to the parents of children and to the system of public finance. In the United Kingdom the approach is to directly empower individual schools, whereas in the U.S. the current preference is for fostering local school markets through offering parents the means to choose among diverse school options. These market reforms promise to stimulate much innovation at the school level, but they also are likely to further the inequalities that are already inherent in these decentralized systems.

In sum, while the modern educational revolution has generated several distinctive models or patterns for the delivery of mass education, all of the models tend to be biased towards the respective centers of these societies, and to be deficient in reaching for the periphery.

MODERN EDUCATION AND INEQUALITY

The central bias of the modern system was the focus of extensive research and policy reform in the sixties. In the early stages of the modern era, reformers focused on equality of educational opportunity. Every child should have a right to attend a school that had "inputs" of equal quality. One finding from the research of this period was that the quality of inputs varied widely between schools. In the United States, for example, suburban schools generally had superior inputs to both rural and urban schools. And the differences in inputs were tied to differences in outputs such as student achievement or school completion. So one reform objective was a leveling of inequalities in inputs.

However, the research made an additional finding of critical importance. Even when the inputs of schools in different areas were similar, children in more "central" schools did better than those in more "peripheral" schools. Indeed in some cases, even where the central schools had higher student-teacher ratios, older buildings, or poorer laboratory equipment, the children did better. Factors associated with the central setting such as parental support, peer group interaction, and opportunity to learn from the environment were associated with the superior performance of the central schools. This finding of the relatively low salience of school factors relative to environmental factors led to a new policy focus, striving for equal outcomes. Thus reforms such as the preschool Head Start, enrichment programs, busing, and other equalizing changes were initiated. But within a few years, many of these reforms were abandoned. The modern system was not really committed to equality of outcomes. Thus studies conducted twenty years later show little change in the level of center-periphery inequality.

THE GLOBAL DIFFUSION OF MODERN EDUCATION

Following World War II, a large number of new states were established as the great powers liberated their former colonies; most of these new states affirmed a commitment to compulsory education in their constitutions. Perhaps of greater significance for the educational expansion of the new states was the emergence of powerful international organizations to perform coordinating roles in the evolving world system. Thus parallel to the central role of the great powers in the centralizing impact of the services provided by the United Nations and its technical agencies, that of the World Bank, and various bilateral actors.

The emergence of new states has not, by and large, been accompanied by the emergence of new educational approaches. Rather the new states have tended to adapt the administrative models of the early modernizers. Cultural ties have played a major role in the process of replication. For example, countries in the Commonwealth tend to follow the English model, those once under French control, the French model. Most Latin American nations threw off the yoke of Spanish or Portuguese colonialism at the time the French Revolution was inspiring liberation movements, and thus most of the Latin American nations adopted the French model.

IMPLEMENTING THE MODERN MODEL:
THE CASE OF INDIA

The record of the new states in developing modern educational systems and especially in extending these educational services to the periphery has been checkered. Weiner's research on India, a nation where enrollment rates are pitifully low, reveals an interesting contrast between India's firm legal commitment to compulsory education (sixteen of the twenty-two states in India have laws on compulsory education) and a weak commitment to implementing these laws. Quotes from interviews with key political officials and policy analysts illustrate this reality:

A key senior official working on the National Policy on Education:

I think that by and large the people of India want their children to be educated, so we do not need coercive power to send their children to school. Besides, what right to we have to compel parents to send children to schools that are not worth much? The teachers aren't any good. Often they don't even appear at the school. We must first provide the country with schools that are worth something. Right now our schools are trash (Weiner, 1991).

The Director of the National Institute of Public Cooperation and Child Development:

Look at the tribal children, for example. They have a tradition of learning crafts at home, but once we put them into school they won't go back to their own culture to learn their crafts. This new culture we teach in the schools has given them nothing. They can't even get a job as a peon. The problem is that the schools pull the children out of their own culture. . . . If these low-income people had a chance, they would send their children to school to get degrees rather than learn the family craft. But that would be a mistake because then we would have more educated unemployed. Schools just add to the ranks of the unemployed (Weiner, 1991).

Chitra Naik, a leading educational researcher:

The majority of these children (children from tribal and poor, rural families) evade the compulsion laws simply by enrolling in a near by primary school, with hardly any intention to attend. The teachers usually connive at this stratagem since it is convenient for them to show large enrollments on paper and actually have a small attendance in class. This enables them to send to the "higher authorities" good reports on the spread of primary education, while their routine teaching load remains light. Such an arrangement is mutually convenient for everyone concerned, i.e., the children, parents, teachers, and even education offices where the "coverage" shown by enrollment statistics matters for the preparation of progress reports. The names of a few non-attending children are struck off the attendance register every now and then, thus satisfying the given regulation by token. The inadequate communication facilities in the tribal and rural areas prevent adequate personal supervision and lead to dependence on reports which cannot be easily verified (Weiner, 1991).

THE CORRELATES OF EDUCATIONAL EXPANSION

Clearly, at least in the case of India, there are major constraints that stand in the way of realizing education for all. Cross-national studies have identified several dimensions of modern societies that tend to complicate the efforts of national governments in providing social services such as education.

Class

Modern states were typically formed through the realignment of class relations. In Europe, modern states were formed though the urban bourgeoisie displacing rural landed elites, and the policies of these states thus came to favor the city over the country. In Japan it can be argued that a rural and peripheral aristocratic subclass displaced an urban and central elite; thus, the modern Japanese state has evidenced exceptional sensitivity in reaching out to the periphery. Nevertheless, even in Japan we find that the great universities are located in the leading cities, as are the most prestigious jobs. In Russia, urban workers were at the forefront and in China it was the peasant class. Hence, Soviet education is relatively well developed in urban areas, whereas in China there is a periodic rejection of the urban intellectual class—better red than expert. In sum, modern education favors the class that is preeminent in the modern state.

Affluence

While class dominance influences the pattern of distribution of social services, with increasing economic development it becomes possible for social services to be more equitably distributed, without sacrificing the interests of the dominant class.

Ethnicity

It is often the case that a particular national group is the primary force in national government; after all, the founding principle behind the current international order is the formation of states around particular nations. In a few nations, there is relatively little ethnic diversity. Cultural and religious barriers do not complicate the delivery of social services nor do they affect the government's will to provide these services to all. But mono-ethnic modern nations are a rarity. Where a nation is composed of multiple ethnic groups, there are a variety of options for structuring relations that can be more or less inclusive. But in most instances, it will be the case that one ethnic group is in the center of power, while others are likely to be neglected or even worse.

Language

Even where there is ethnic diversity, the delivery of social services can be eased by the command of a common language, as has come to be the case in many of the industrialized societies or in Indonesia or China. But in other contexts, the respective groups command different languages. Social services can either recognize this difference and be accommodative, or ignore it.

Geography

Possibly the most powerful force leading to peripheralization is national scale. The larger the scale, the more effort that is required in terms of serial communication and transportation to link the center with the periphery. Administrative modifications such as decentralization can ameliorate this condition, but it still remains the case that large nations tend to do the poorest job in providing social services to their entire population. In large nations, those in rural areas particularly remote from the capital are most likely to be peripheralized. The Indian subcontinent is somewhat of an extreme case; in India in 1981, 67.3 percent of rural young people aged fifteen to nineteen were illiterate compared to 34.9 percent of urban young people; in nearby Pakistan, the difference was even more extreme, 82.6 percent versus 53.1 percent. In rural Pakistan, 92.7 percent of rural females fifteen to nineteen years old were illiterate (Carceles, 1990). While physical distance from the center is a critical determinant of peripherilization, it is also often the case that large numbers of peripherilized can be found near the center, in shanty towns, townships, or as in the U.S., in urban ghettos.

Difficult Terrain

Aggravating national scale are such factors as low population density, which makes it difficult to reach sufficient numbers of people with standard approaches for the delivery of social services. Similarly, where a population is located in difficult terrain such as on islands or in mountains or jungles that lack roads, these difficulties are compounded.

GOVERNMENT STRUCTURE AND POLICY

The actual resolution of these different interests is shaped through the political-administrative process. Governments tend to reflect these other factors to some degree, but also it can be argued they have a life of their own. Our historical work has identified six different political-administrative patterns, that vary in terms of degree of centralization, inclusiveness of representation at the policy level, local control of revenues and services, and openness to private initiative. These are the Continental, Lowland, Japanese, Socialist, English, and American variants.

In our judgement, these structures vary in their attentiveness to peripheral areas in somewhat the following manner: The Japanese polity may be the most responsive to the periphery, simply because it does not acknowledge class, ethnic, or geographic differences. The socialist structures rank second in terms of attentiveness. The decentralized structures, while having the potential for incorporating various social and ethnic interests, often are dominated by a single ruling group, and thus seem to be least attentive.

Relative attentiveness is expressed through the various policies devised by the respective polities. One simple indicator is the relative equity in government expenditures by region and subregion down to the operational units for the delivery of social services. While the Japanese and socialist governments are relatively more attentive in reaching out to the periphery, we would argue that even they are deficient. The modern state, whatever the pattern, is ultimately committed to serving the center.

THE DIFFUSION OF MODERNISM AND PERIPHERALISM

While the modern century has focused on realizing the ideal of equality, it is remarkable that few official statistics have been devised to measure its progress in realizing this ideal. Indeed, only in recent years have scholars begun to probe this issue, and most of the indicators they have proposed (e.g. Gini indices of regional equality, of income distribution, of the distribution of social services) have yet to be adapted by national governments or international agencies. It is as if the modern state was committed to the rhetoric of equality but not the reality.

Turning to the scholarly work on equality and peripheralism, two patterns of analysis are evident. The first pattern relies on a straight count of the proportion of the target population that receives a particular service. In the field of education, this research often focuses on enrollment ratios, the proportion of the primary age group in a nation who attend primary schools or the proportion of the secondary age group who attend secondary schools. Data on these indicators tend to be widely available, and thus are more amenable to comparative analysis. Table I, below, which relates national differences in these proportions to various national characteristics, again shows that equality of provision is affected by national income level, degree of urbanism, extent of population concentration, national scale, ethnic homogeneity, government centralism, and even government tradition.

The second research tradition attempts to establish measures of the spread of services between geographical units of societies, that can then be compared across societies. Statistics such as Gini coefficients and coefficients of variation are typically employed.

The most extensive work has focused on income distribution, and generally finds a curvilinear pattern with relative equal income distribution in the least and most developed countries and greater inequality in the intermediate stages. However, while income is somewhat evenly distributed in advanced societies, between these societies there are wide variations that seem to be related to several of the factors we have noted above: greater ethnic and linguistic diversity, geographic dispersion, and political decentralization are all correlated with greater income inequality. Other studies which focus on the equality of government expenditures or equality in the provision of services tend to find a similar pattern.

In the field of education, research studies carried out largely in the more advanced societies suggest a consistent urban (central) bias in academic achievement, with elite (and often) private schools performing well above national norms. Regional and ethnic differences are also substantial. Some efforts have been made to compute indicators of degree of spread (typically

Table I: Cross-National Correlates of Enrollment Ratios, 1985

Correlate	Primary Enrollment Ratio	Secondary Enrollment Ratio
GNP Per Capita	.29	.67
Population	.16	.04
Population Density	.10	.20
Urbanization	.52	.81
Ethnic Complexity	−.36	−.45
Centralized Govt.	.37	−.53
Centralized Finance	−.20	−.40
English Tradition	−.09	−.04
French Tradition	−.30	−.46

Source: PIE Data Bank

the coefficient of variation in national scores, or ratios of urban to rural scores) and relate these indicators to national characteristics. Again, there is evidence suggesting that the more centralized and ethnically more homogeneous societies achieve greater equality.

In poorer countries, an even more fundamental concern than academic achievement is school enrollments. As noted above, the enrollment rates are comparatively low in India. However, in the state of Kerala, nearly all children enroll in the primary grades and 88 percent of the age cohort are enrolled in secondary schools. Thus Kerala has a literacy rate of 70.4 percent, or twice the national average (Weiner, 1991). So within nations, not only are there rural-urban but also important regional differences that require examination.

THE UPPER LIMIT OF MODERN EDUCATION

The biases of the modern state are less evident in good times when the economy is thriving, and the government can spare resources to accommodate various interests. But when the modern state faces hard times, it is liable to turn inwards and focus on its core interests and clients; the periphery becomes neglected.

For much of the period since World War II through the early seventies, most national economies enjoyed relatively stable growth and government enjoyed a steady expansion of revenues. Education benefited from this growth. Expanding government budgets resulted in an expansion of educational facilities, and in most nations in an increase in pupil enrollment ratios. Figure 1 provides a comparison of historical trends in primary-level pupil enrollment ratios by geographic region. In all of the major regions of the world, the ratios steadily increased through at least the early seventies. But African levels were initially lower and thus did not climb to the same level as the other regions. Latin America, Asia, Europe, North America (the latter two plotted together with the Middle East as EMENA) had relatively high levels from the beginning, and thus did not experience much change.

But the events surrounding the "oil shock" led to a major interruption of the upward trend. As governments faced a leveling of revenues, they had to make hard choices on priorities. According to one study, these choices more often than not involved a reduction in real expenditures for education (Lewin and Little, 1982). With leveling or declining educational expenditures and, due to population grown, an expanding number of school-aged youth, enrollment ratios tended to stabilize or even, in several cases, to decline. A recent UNESCO study indicates over the eighties that enrollment ratios for the primary level have decreased in twenty-six nations and have shown no advance in another twenty-three (Carceles, 1990). This pattern of stabilization has continued into the nineties, even as the world economy has begun to improve. Thus the cross-national educational gaps, which once seemed to be narrowing, became a new area of concern.

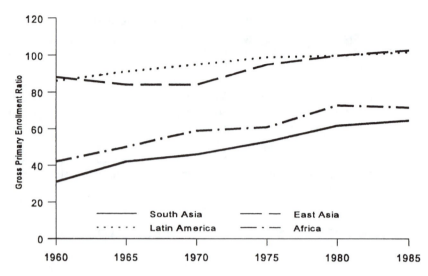

Figure 1. Growth in Educational Participation Since 1960
Source: Crouch, Spratt, and Cubeddu, 1992.

Aggregate national statistics are based on summations of local statistics. When national totals go down, it is often the case that some areas go down faster than others. In the recent downward shift in enrollment ratios, it turns out at least for some countries that the peripheral or rural areas have suffered sharper declines than the central or urban areas.

LESSONS FROM THE PRIVATE SECTOR

The strategies of nations may gain some insights from the experience of large business corporations, which also traditionally have attempted to reach diverse markets in dispersed localities with centralized management structures. For a time, large multinational corporations such as General Motors, Caterpillar, IBM, and Sony achieved considerable success with their centralized structures. But in recent years there have been major changes. Peters's and Waterman's *In Search of Excellence* (1982) tells how the most successful among these corporations have placed a new emphasis on "Getting Close to the Customer" and "Nichemanship."

This change can be illustrated by focusing on a common product such as a wristwatch. In the early stages of the new quartz watches, most of the multinational watchmakers concentrated on a small number of models which they mass-produced in large quantities and marketed throughout their national and even international markets. Low prices made these watches competitive, and, at least for the first few years, sales were impressive. But at a certain point, sales slacked off. Yet there were large numbers of potential clients who had not bought the new watches. The companies realized they had to get closer to the customer. And to do so they radically decentralized both marketing and production. Separate and largely independent units were established with the companies to focus on distinctive markets—young people, sports people, swimmers, joggers, musicians, classy dressers, casual dressers. The once uniform market was divided up into dozens of smaller niches, and unique approaches were developed that conformed to the needs of each of these niches. The considerable interest of employees in the small independent units in developing unique products resulted in continuing high-quality production, but with much greater diversity than had previously been possible. In this way, sales were once again invigorated and a near saturation of many markets was realized.

PUTTING THE PERIPHERY FIRST

In the production of watches, a fundamental realignment of corporate strategy was required. The corporate centers came to realize they did not or could not have all the answers; they thus streamlined the role of the center to the formulation of broad goals, and the development of standard of accountability for the various quasi-autonomous production/marketing units. Within the limits of this framework, the diverse units were granted the freedom to work closer to their clients. The successful corporation made a clear distinction between the center and the field—or what we call here the periphery.

In education, we think such a distinction is also required. We think it is important to recognize that the established programs favor those at the center, and slight those distant from the center, those in the periphery. A new approach is needed which will give more attention to the periphery.

The introduction of the concept of "Periphery" into the strategic vocabulary of educators can provide a point of departure for reappraising the limitations of established approaches and legitimizing the development of new strategies. Thus we believe that the recognition of the periphery is a critical first step towards starting the second half of the journey towards EFA. Our conclusions are not especially new, for there already is in the lore of education considerable recognition of nontraditional approaches, of nonformal education and so on. But it may be that these approaches do not have a forceful rationale, and for that reason were relegated to a secondary status in government strategies.

RATIONALE FOR A NEW STRATEGY

In earlier times governments may have been able to ignore the periphery or give it short shrift. But we would argue that those days are past. In part, yes, the argument is moral—governments should keep their promises. But there are also practical reasons. On the political front, it is now apparent that governments who fail to relate effectively to their peripheries fall apart—e.g., the former Soviet Union and possibly India.

And there is also a strong economic rationale as well. Whereas in the past, most individuals could make a reasonable livelihood through hard physical work or personal charm, this is no longer the case. As the world economy moves into a new stage where the processing of codified knowledge is the key to success, it is no longer justifiable on economic grounds to leave people unprepared.

THE ELEMENTS OF A NEW STRATEGY

While governments and international agencies have repeatedly issued calls to eradicate illiteracy and spread enlightenment, and in most instances have set up elaborate programs of public education, there are today far more people who cannot read than there were in 1789 or 1945. Clearly the established educational programs miss large proportions of the world's citizenry.

In thinking about what has gone wrong, we have reached the conclusion that the established programs may be incapable of making much further progress. They may have reached an upper limit. And the EFA initiative, channeled through international donors and central governments, offers little that is new. What are the limits of modern education, and what needs to be changed?

1. The established programs tend to be tailored to the standard situation, that found in the large cities and places of population concentration. To be specific, the established programs are based on:
   - A system of centrally funded instructional and infrastructure support that considers schools as the major unit for planning rather than the communities which they serve, and treats all schools as equal, independent of the school's resource base or the challenge it confronts;
   - A centrally devised curriculum, typically authorizing instruction in the metropolitan language; centrally produced textbooks;
   - A school premised on separate classes for separate grades;
   - Teachers trained for standard settings, and rewarded by a salary schedule and a promotion ladder that culminates in a central bureaucratic office;
   - Principals appointed from the center who have authority to operate independent of community will.

Modifications of these programs are often introduced to accommodate settings that differ from the standard. But these modifications on the "One Best System" are not enough.

2. Rather than seek modifications to central formulas, if the concern is to reach to the periphery, it will be necessary to encourage unique approaches for a diversity of unique local settings. These unique approaches may include multigrade classrooms, locally tailored curricula and learning materials, community involvement in decision making

and instruction, locally recruited and specially trained teachers, and instruction in the local language.

3. While the focus of central educational systems is on the schools established by the center, it should be on communities and their educational needs. Communities have legitimate leaders who can become partners in education, helping to identify priorities, mobilize local resources, propose approaches that fit local circumstances, and provide continuity.

4. Central support for schools tends to provide equal support for each educational administrative unit, based on the number of pupils that unit serves:
   - But these formulas provide equal funding for unequal conditions. Some areas are more challenging, because of difficult terrain, dispersed populations, and lack of pupil preparedness; these are the peripheral areas. A truly equal funding formula would provide support in direct ratio to the challenge.
   - These formulas do not take into account the differential ability of the pupils within the administrative units to support education. An equalizing formula favorable to the periphery would provide central support in inverse ratio to a local area's ability to support education.

5. Central funding, when channeled through local administrative units, can often lead to waste and excessive regulation. New approaches to funding need to be considered that are more equitable and that reward performance:
   - Central support to administrative units enables these units to allocate funds and other resources between schools, according to criteria decided by the administrators often with little concern for the differential need of schools. A more equitable approach would be to channel funds and resources directly to the schools.
   - Funding directed to schools might be provided in response to budget requests by schools, and allocated in such a manner as to provide incentives for those schools that are most prepared to help themselves. Alternately, funding might be provided in proportion to school improvement in academic or other areas of performance.

CONCLUSION

We have explored the concept of periphery and outlined some of the forces behind peripheralization. This seems important, because without understanding what is behind peripheralization, we will not know where to start in altering the situation.

But we see little diminution in the strength of these factors. Thus we reach the somewhat pessimistic conclusion that there is little objective evidence to suggest that the prevailing governments of the contemporary world are likely to improve on their record of promoting enlightenment until they face up to their limitations. However, as nations come to recognize the need to serve their peripheries, our analytical work suggests some handles on which to attach their efforts.

REFERENCES

Benavot, A. and Riddle, P. (1988). "The Expansion of Primary Education: 1870–1940. Trends and Issues." *Sociology of Education,* 61, (July), pp. 191–200.

Blum, C. (1986). *Rousseau and the Republic of Virtue: The Language of Politics in the French Revolution*. Ithaca, NY: Cornell University Press.

Carceles, G. (1990). "World Literacy Prospects at the Turn of the Century: Is the Objective of Literacy for All by the Year 2000 Statistically Plausible?" *Comparative Education Review,* v 34, n 1 (Feb.) pp. 4–20.

Carnoy, M. and Samoff, J. (1989). *Education and Social Transition in the Third World*. Princeton: Princeton University Press.

Crouch, L. A., Spratt, J. and Cubeddu, L. M. (1992). "Examining Social and Economic Impacts of Educational Investment and Participation in Developing Countries: the Educational Impacts Model (EIM) Approach." *BRIDGES Research Report Series* No. 12 (April).

Cummings, W. K. (1980). *Education and Equality in Japan*. Princeton: Princeton University Press.

Cummings, W. K., and Riddell, A. (1992). "Alternative Policies for the Finance, Control, and Delivery of Basic Education." HIID Occasional Papers.

Fuller, W. (1982). *The Old Country School: The Story of Rural Education in the Middle West*. Chicago: The University of Chicago Press.

Gildea, R. (1983). *Education in Provincial France 1800–1914*. Oxford: Clarendon Press.

Glenn, C. L., Jr. (1998). *The Myth of the Common School*. Amherst: The University of Massachusetts Press.

Kennedy, P. (1989). *The Rise and Fall of the Great Powers*. New York: Random House.

Legrand, L. (1961). *L'influence du positivisme dan l'oeuvre scolaire de Jules Ferry: Les origines de la laïcité*. Paris: Marcel Riviere.

Lewin, K., Little, A. and Colclough, C. (1982). "Adjusting to the 1980s: Taking Stock of Educational Expenditure." In International Development Research Centre (Canada), *Financing Education Development: Proceedings of an International Seminar*. Mont Sainte Marie, Canada, May 19–21.

Ministry of Education, Science, and Culture. (1980). *Japan's Modern Educational System: A History of the First Hundred Years*. Tokyo.

Passin, H. (1965). *Society and Education in Japan*. New York: Teachers College Press.

Peters, T. J., and Waterman, R. H. (1982). *In Search of Excellence*. New York: Warner Books.

Pierre, V. (1881). *L'Ecole sous la Revolution francaise*. Paris: Librairie de la Société Bibliographique.

Ringer, F. K. (1979). *Education and Society in Modern Europe*. Bloomington: Indiana University Press.

Shils, E. (1975). *Center and Periphery: Essays in Macrosociology*. Chicago: University of Chicago Press.

Tyack, D. B. (1974). *The One Best System: A History of American Urban Education*. Cambridge, MA: Harvard University Press.

UNDP, UNESCO, UNICEF, and World Bank. (1990). *World Declaration on Education for All and Framework for Action to Meet Basic Learning Needs.* Jomtien, Thailand, March 5–9.

Weiner, M. (1991). *The Child and the State in India.* Princeton: Princeton University Press.

CHAPTER 14

Improving the Quality of Basic Education? The Strategies of the World Bank

Rosa-María Torres

Introduction

An international bank, the World Bank (WB), has in recent years become the most visible institution in the education field on an international scale, to a great extent now occupying the space traditionally assigned to UNESCO (United Nations Organization for Education, Science, and Culture).[1] Financing is not the only nor the most important role of the WB in the education sector; it has become the principal agency providing technical assitance in education in developing countries and, in league with this, a promoter of educational research at the international level. In the WB's own words "The World Bank's main contribution must be advice, designed to help governments develop education policies suitable for the circumstances of their countries" (WB, 1995). This, in turn, responds to the view that "school administrators are faced with decisions on specific cost-effectiveness quality-improving investments and various tradeoffs. What they want are guides to specific investment choices" (Heyneman, 1995).

Rather than presenting a series of isolated ideas, the WB arrives with a compact proposal—a diagnosis of problems and a package of recommendations—aimed at improving access, equity, and quality of school systems, particularly at the primary level. This reform "package" includes a broad spectrum of recommendations dealing with financial, administrative, human resources, curricular, and pedagogical issues.

This chapter analyzes and discusses the WB's proposals for the reform of primary education in developing countries. We will argue among other points that: (1) although presented as the result of scientific research and lessons drawn from international experience, the policies and strategies recommended have serious weaknesses in fundamental conceptualization, data interpretation, and analysis; (2) the strategies proposed for "developing countries" in large part take Africa (and rural realities) as a paradigm of the "developing world," specifically sub-Saharan Africa, one of the poorest regions and with one of the most problematic educational situations in the world. In fact, most of the policy recommendations that have been made in recent years and that are made today (WB, 1995), were present in the regional study conducted by the WB in 1985 on thirty-nine sub-Saharan African countries. Ulterior information and research results have thus fundamentally served to reinforce those initial positions; and that (3) the reform package and the education model that underlies the WB's recommendations in the field of basic education, rather than contributing to changes in the said direction—improving educational quality and efficiency in the school system, and more specifically in the public school and among the poor—are contributing to reinforcing traditional tendencies in school systems. This is due not only to the nature and content of the proposals, but also to uncritical reception and application of these policies in borrowing countries.

Experience in some education reform projects financed by the WB in developing countries shows that, although originating from a homogeneous proposal, actual implementation can differ considerably from one country to another and can even "deviate" significantly from the original pattern. This is not only because each reality ends up adapting the proposal to its specific conditions, but also because there are margins in project definition and negotiation, margins that some country (and WB) officials utilize and others do not, and for which some national counterparts are capable of offering alternatives, while others are not.[2]

THE URGENCY OF EDUCATIONAL REFORM: THE WORLD BANK PERSPECTIVE

Although the visibility of the WB in the education sector is rather recent, the bank has been working in this sector for over thirty years, continuously amplifying its sphere of influence and action. Besides providing loans, WB's current activities in education include research, technical assistance to governments for the design and implementation of education policies, and mobilization and coordination of external financial resources. Since its first education project (in 1963 to Tunisia, for secondary education), total lending over the last thirty years amounts to nearly 20 billion dollars, through more than five hundred projects in more than one hundred countries (WB, 1995). The loans have covered all levels, from primary to post university, in addition to vocational and nonformal education.

The WB's position with respect to education, and primary education in particular, is neither monolithic nor fixed. Within its own documents and studies (and among the personnel and spokespersons of the organization for the distinct areas, levels, and regions of the world) exist important differences in focus, divergent and even contradictory conclusions, and criticisms of conceptual frameworks, methodologies, and results of other studies published or cited by the WB. Moreover, there are changes, movement, and even significant shifts in the trajectory and policies of the WB in the education sector.

Over the last three decades, the WB has been modifying its priorities and, consequently, its investment policies in this sector. In the 1960s, WB loans favored infrastructure and secondary education and, particularly, technical and vocational education. In 1973 Robert McNamara, then president of the WB, announced a shift in the policy of the organization: the WB would focus on the poor, attending to their basic needs in housing, health, food, water, and education. In this last area such a shift translated into the prioritization of primary education as the cornerstone in the strategy to "alleviate poverty." After 1970 there was a strong and sustained increase in investment for primary education—together with an increasing role of the WB in technical assistance—and a decrease in loans for secondary education. This focus on primary education has been reinforced since the World Conference on "Education for All" (Jomtien, Thailand, March 1990) convoked jointly by UNESCO, UNICEF, the UNDP (United Nations Development Program), and the World Bank. The conference proclaimed basic education as the priority for the present decade and primary education as the "cutting edge" to achieve the basic education goal.

PROBLEMS AND SOLUTIONS FROM THE PERSPECTIVE OF THE WORLD BANK

The absolute number of children in the world who receive no education at all is likely to increase in the next twenty years.

Only two-thirds of primary school students complete the primary cycle.

Adult literacy appears likely to remain a major problem, especially for women.

In part because of past success at the primary level, the demand for secondary and tertiary education is growing faster than many education systems can accommodate.

The educational gap between the OECD countries and the transition economies of Eastern Europe and Central Asia is widening (WB, 1995).

Major challenges remain: to expand access in some countries and, in many others, to increase equity, improve educational quality, and speed educational reform. The current systems of finance and management are frequently not well suited to meeting these challenges. Public spending on education is too often inefficient and inequitable. In view of the competition for and pressure on public funds, new sources of financing are needed (WB, 1995).

Most education systems are directly managed by central or state governments, which put a great deal of effort into dealing with such issues as teacher salary negotiations, school construction programs, and curricular reform. This central management, extending even to instructional inputs and the classroom environment, allows little room or the flexibility that leads to effective learning (WB, 1995).

This is the vision of the WB with respect to the main problems currently affecting school systems in developing countries, the necessity of education reform, the prioritization of its components, and the definition of its strategies.

School systems in developing countries, in the WB perspective, are confronted with four fundamental challenges: (1) access, which has been achieved in most countries, in the case of primary schooling. It remains as a serious challenge principally in Africa; (2) equity, fundamentally seen among the poor in general, and among girls and ethnic minorities in particular (the segregation of girls being especially problematic in the Middle East and South Asia); (3) quality, seen as a generalized problem that affects all developing countries; and (4) the lag between the reform of economic structures and that of education systems, today most noteworthy in the transition economies of eastern and central Europe.

In the view of the WB, education reform—limited in fact to school reform—is not only unavoidable but urgent. Postponing it would have serious economic, social, and political costs. The current package of reforms proposed by the WB to developing countries is characterized by a number of features:

Priority on Basic Education

Basic education is the top priority in all countries because it provides the basic skills and knowledge necessary for civic order and full participation in society, as well as for all forms of work (WB, 1995).

A complete basic education is normally provided free of fees, since it is essential for the acquisition of the knowledge, skills, and attitudes needed by society. The definition of basic education is country-specific, but it typically encompasses at least primary education and often lower-secondary education as well (although not always, as the example of Korea shows) (WB, 1995).

This basic level typically requires about eight years of schooling (Ibid.).

Since 1990 the WB has encouraged countries to concentrate public resources on primary education, seen as an essential element for sustainable development and to alleviate poverty. Also, it is asserted that "in low- and middle-income countries the rates of return to investments in basic (primary and lower secondary) education are generally greater than those to higher education. Therefore basic education should usually be the priority for public spending on education in those countries that have yet to achieve near universal enrollment in basic education" (WB, 1995), which is equivalent to saying in the majority of developing countries.[3]

It is necessary to pause and look more closely at the concept of basic education, given the variety of meanings of this term and its different uses within the WB (as also among other aid agencies and, of course, among the individual countries).

In the first regional study on the education sector conducted by the WB (*Education in Sub-Saharan Africa*, 1988), the term *basic education* was reserved for non-formal basic education for youths and adults.[4] Subsequently, basic education came to be equated with primary education. In the 1995 policy document basic education comprises primary and lower secondary education, it being estimated that the acquisition of knowledge, skills, and essential attitudes to function in an effective manner in society is achieved in school and requires about eight years of instruction. In this way, the notion of basic education, and education in general, is now firmly centered on formal education and on the education of children. Other aspects of education—and of the term basic education—such as the family, the community, the environment, work and the workplace, mass media, and so on, remain outside the margins of education policy considerations. Also outside are adult education, non-formal education, and other institutions and modalities (for example, Koranic education) not recognized within the parameters of official education. This is joined together with the emphasis placed on in-school factors (supply) to improve access, equity, and quality, while virtually excluding from the analysis and policy proposals nonschool factors (demand), which are major determinants of limited educational access, inequity, and poor quality. WB proposals thus deal with school policy rather than with education policy.

This concept of basic education diverges from the "expanded vision" of basic education that was agreed upon at the 1990 World Conference on "Education for All," one of whose supporters and organizers was the WB. This "expanded vision" of basic education includes children, youths, and adults; begins at birth and continues throughout life; is not limited to formal schooling nor to primary schooling nor to a specific number of years or levels of study; and is defined in terms of its capacity to meet the basic learning needs in each individual (see Table I).

Improving Quality and Efficiency as Pillars in Education Reform

The third—and probably most important—challenge [besides improving access and equity] is to improve educational quality; it is poor at all levels in low- and middle-income countries. Students in developing countries are neither acquiring the skills called for within their own countries' curricula nor are they doing as well as students in more developed countries . . . Improving quality is as important as improving access, but is even harder to achieve (WB, 1995).

Educational quality is equated with outcomes, and learning outcomes measured by achievement tests vis-à-vis the goals and objectives set by the school system (learning what is taught, being promoted to the next grade, completing the primary school cycle, etc.). The relevance of what and how it is taught and learned are not viewed as an essential dimension of educational quality. The main indicator of educational quality is the "value added of schooling," which consists of "learning gain and the increased probability of income-earning activity" (WB, 1995).

In the WB perspective, quality education results from the presence of specific "inputs." In the case of primary school, nine inputs are identified as

Table I: Competing Views of Basic Education

Restricted Vision	Expanded Vision (EFA/Jomtien)
• is aimed at children	• is aimed at children, youths and adults
• takes place at school	• takes place at school, at home, through the media, etc.
• is equivalent to primary education or a specific number of years defined as compulsory	• is not measured by the number of years or certificates but by what is actually learned
• is organized around predetermined subjects	• is organized around the concept of basic learning needs
• is limited to a specific period in the life of an individual	• begins at birth and continues throughout life
• is homogeneous—the same for all	• is differentiated because social and individual basic learning needs are different
• is static, remains relatively unchanged	• is dynamic—basic learning needs change over time
• is the responsibility of the Ministry of Education	• involves all Ministries and government departments responsible for education
• is the responsibility of the State	• is the responsibility of the State and the whole society, and as such requires partnerships and consensus building

Source: Torres (1993)

determinants of effective learning. These are, in order of priority (according to the proportion of studies that would reveal a correlation of positive effect):[5] (1) libraries; (2) instructional time; (3) homework; (4) textbooks; (5) teacher subject knowledge; (6) teacher experience; (7) laboratories; (8) teacher salaries; and (9) class size (WB, 1995). On this foundation, the WB bases its conclusions and recommendations for developing countries regarding which inputs to prioritize in terms of policy and resource allocation. While discouraging investment in the last three—laboratories, teacher salaries, and reduced class size—it encourages investment in the first ones and, specifically, in three of them: (1) increasing instructional time by lengthening the school year, increasing the flexibility of school scheduling, and assigning homework; (2) providing textbooks, seen as the materialization of the curriculum and relying on them as compensation for the low level of teacher qualification. The WB advises countries to leave the production and distribution of textbooks to the private sector, to train teachers in their use, and to develop teacher's guides for their more effective utilization; and (3) increasing teacher knowledge, especially by providing in-service training (rather than preservice training) and encouraging distance education modalities.

School infrastructure is no longer considered an important input either in terms of access or in terms of quality. In order to minimize construction costs it is recommended that: (1) education costs be shared by the family and the community, (2) school facilities be used in multiple shifts, and (3) school infrastructures be adequately maintained.

Focus on Administrative and Financial Aspects of Education Reform

Within the broader context of the administrative reform of the state, education reform tends to be seen as a primarily administrative and financial endeavor, with decentralization as a major reforming strategy. Specific measures proposed are: (1) fundamental restructuring of Ministries of Education, intermediate institutions, and individual schools; (2) strengthening information systems (especially emphasizing the collection of data in four indicators: enrollment, attendance, inputs, and costs); and (3) training of education personnel in administrative issues.

Curricular and pedagogical components of education reform are overshadowed by financial and administrative concerns. Financial resources tend to be seen as the critical factor that enables or hampers reform, while little attention is paid to the restrictions and potential of the human resources, those who ultimately conduct the reform and make it possible.

"IMPROVING EDUCATIONAL QUALITY" AS A PARADIGM

WB proposals for education are fundamentally made by economists, using economic analysis.[6] Cost-benefit relationships and rates of return make up the principal categories which underlie education policy recommendations, investment priorities in this sector (for the various educational levels and the various inputs to be considered), learning outcomes, and the quality of education provided.

Economic discourse has come to dominate the education field to the point that genuine educational discourse—the dynamic of schools and the education system as a whole, the relationships and teaching-learning processes in the classroom—and its primary actors (educators, pedagogues, education specialists) are scarcely included in the discussions. At both the national and the international level, education policy formulation is generally and principally in the hands of economists or professionals associated with financial or managerial aspects of education rather than with curriculum and pedagogical issues. Many of those who advise on what should or should not be done in the education sector, and make important decisions from the local to the global level, lack the necessary knowledge and experience to deal with the fields for which they take decisions such as basic education, teaching and learning in the classroom, child learning, teacher education and training, curriculum development, linguistic policies, child and adult literacy, textbook and instructional materials development, learning evaluation, and so forth. Few of them have any actual experience in front of students in a classroom. Few have children in the public school system for which they plan and design reform measures. The virtual absence of teachers and teacher organizations in the formulation and decision-making processes contributes to further seal this discourse developed by economists to be implemented by educators.

Despite the fact that current policies are recommended and applied in the name of learning, the world of school and the classroom remains a black box, and teaching-learning issues continue to be treated as if they were "technicians" or the "details" of educational thinking, decision making, and action. From the national and international macroviews and macroproposals, top-down approaches in the formulation and application of education policies are taken for granted. It is assumed that reforms will "land" in the classroom, through declarations, decrees and normative guidelines, textbooks, curriculum, institutional reform, and teacher training, all of which would, supposedly, be accepted and adopted by school administrators and teachers, parents, and students. This "landing," however, has not occurred and remains a critical factor in the perpetual education reform movement worldwide.

Education is currently analyzed with criteria and standards of the market, the school is viewed as an enterprise (rather than a social system), and teachers are considered inputs and manual workers (Coraggio, 1995; Gimeno Sacristán, 1992). Teaching and teachers' roles are oversimplified and misunderstood—teaching as the possession of, and capacity to select from, "a wide repertoire of teaching skills" (WB, 1995)—and learning as a predictable result of the presence (and "proper mix") of a series of inputs. Each input is evaluated separately and is prioritized on the basis of two criteria: its influence on learning (according to selected studies which demonstrate such influence) and its cost. In the light of these parameters, a series of binary policy options are identified for primary school reforms; for example, textbooks are prioritized (strong influence and low cost) over teachers (strong influence but high cost), in-service over preservice teacher training, and textbooks over school libraries.

WB documents on education show a precarious understanding of educational theory and of the accumulated research in the field. It is common to find in WB literature on education, including the 1995 policy paper, imprecision and even indistinct use of key educational concepts. These are education and training; education and schooling; teaching and learning; education and learning; education and teaching; education and instruction; schooling outputs and learning; curriculum and content; knowledge and skills; information and knowledge; pedagogy and teaching skills; pedagogy and methods; methods and techniques; textbooks and reading materials; initial education and preschool education; formal, non-formal, and informal education; adult, non-formal, and literacy education; class size and pupil/teacher ratio; and even primary education and basic education. Furthermore, there persists the association between "universal primary education" and "universal access to primary education," which ignores considerations of quality, retention, completion, and effective learning.[7]

Successive WB sectoral analyses continue to benefit little from advancement of educational research and from the contribution of related sciences (e.g., psycho- and socio-linguistics, anthropology, psychology, history) to the modern theories of learning. Education is perceived as a field that lacks specificity, antecedents, or history. It is an orphan of theoretical tradition and pedagogical discussion—a field of interaction of inputs rather than people.

It is in the curricular and pedagogical domain—the domain that essentially defines education—where the limitations of WB economists are most evident. The notion of curriculum that is used and underlies WB proposals is narrowly construed, basically understood as content (and content reduced to subjects).

The reduction of education to content (teaching as information to be transmitted and learning as information to be assimilated) underlies the traditional, transmissive, "banking" education model, and is consistent with the notion of "educational quality" reduced to "educational outcomes." This view also explains, in part, why textbooks are seen as repositories and ideal transmitters of the curriculum (the explicit content) while the central role of teachers in defining, developing, and implementing the curriculum in their interaction with students both inside and outside the classroom is ignored.

In the WB perspective, improving classroom instruction is essentially about curricular reform, not also about pedagogical reform. This responds to the traditional disassociation between content and methods, curriculum and pedagogy, and to the illusion of achieving education reform without a profound pedagogical reform and changes in the school culture as a whole.

In fact, the limitations and vices of this economics-dominated approach to education are beginning to be acknowledged and questioned by some of WB's chief staff:

> The bulk of economics research has been superfluous to making educational decisions. It has overemphasized rates of return to expansion by level, and under-emphasized the economics of educational quality, new subjects, target groups, teaching methods, and system reforms. (Heyneman, 1995)
>
> The field [economics of education] in general has been slow to ask the questions whose answers are necessary for educators to run education systems better, and has been quicker to ask questions generated by concerns within the academic economics community. (Ibid.)
>
> Economics is more successful in estimating production functions when there is a single product (e.g., rice), and when the influences on productivity are physical. The difference between a classroom and a farm is that soils do not depend upon motivation. What this implies is that a tone of humility would be in order when discussing results. (Ibid.)
>
> Educational officials are held publicly accountable for error. In general, economists are not. (Ibid.)

THE PRESENTATION OF PROPOSALS AS UNIVERSAL AND SUPPORTED BY SCIENTIFIC KNOWLEDGE

The WB's analyses and package of proposals for school reform appear supported by several studies—many of them promoted and financed by the WB—as well as by international experience, including the lessons drawn by the WB from its own activity in the education sector for over thirty years. Nevertheless, there are significant voids in the evidence used to support these policy recommendations, as pointed out by numerous authors (Coraggio, 1994 and 1995; Heyneman, 1995; Plank, 1994; Reimers, 1993; Samoff, 1995; Schwille, 1993; Torres, 1995b).

A Western and Anglophone Bias in Research

Most studies on which the WB bases its recommendations and which are cited in its publications (especially those dealing with basic education) refer to education in the Third World. However, the majority of such studies and publications are products of authors from the First World and from international funding agencies. There are few references to studies emanating from developing countries and/or conducted by specialists from such countries. Bibliographies that serve as a basis for policy formulation are principally anglophone, virtually ignoring important research produced in other languages. There is thus an abyss between the supposedly universal international discourse on education, and that produced at the national and regional level.[8]

On the other hand, the majority of publications cited are recent (1990s or late 1980s). This impedes a more dynamic and analytic vision of the education field and its evolution. The bibliographic selection gives priority to empirical and quantitative studies, capable of providing data and square conclusions on issues a priori identified as problematic. Conceptual or theoretical studies aimed at conceptualizing and deepening the understanding of a given subject, that pose questions and point out contradictions or dilemmas rather than providing unique and final answers, are rarely taken into account.[9]

Skirting the Difficulties that Underlie Contemporary Educational Research and Information

The "statistical problem" is widely recognized in the education sector throughout the developing world: much statistical information is not available and what is available is known not to be reliable.[10] On the other hand, educational research has arrived at a critical juncture: with the information available it is not possible to reach definitive conclusions on any specific issue. Research results exist now for practically all desires, to prove or to refute almost any thesis. However, the recognized problems of reliability and comparability that characterize current educational research and information, including that cited by the WB, is mentioned only briefly, if at all, in official WB literature. For methodological as well as ethical reasons, recognition of this fact should be clearly stated in any exposition intended to influence decision-making, priorities, and strategies in the education field.

Statements appear as monolithic and research results as conclusive, ignoring the lack of supporting evidence or, indeed, the existence of contradictory evidence demonstrated in other studies on the same research subject. Such omissions occur in numerous WB statements regarding textbooks (studies that do not find textbooks as an important input affecting the quality of learning, or that suggest a differentiated importance in different study areas, or that determine the impact of textbooks on educational quality to be a function of the presence of specific conditions); teacher training (studies that identify a positive correlation between years of teaching experience, quality of teaching, and student learning results; or studies that do not find the claimed strong comparative advantages of teacher in-service training over initial training); or instructional time (studies that find that increasing it, in and by itself, does not necessarily result in improved educational outcomes).[11]

A Strong Tendency to (Over)generalize

A number of postulates tend to be affirmed and understood to be universally applicable, when in truth they result from only a few studies conducted in specific countries and under specific conditions. Examples here are statements about basic inputs exerting a positive influence on learning—teacher knowledge of the subject, time of instruction, and provision of textbooks. Statements about types of teacher training and teacher knowledge affecting student outcomes were initially supported by studies conducted in four countries (Brazil, India, Indonesia, and Pakistan), using different theoretical frameworks and methodologies.

A strong assertion, like the following, has no foundation: "In low- and middle-income countries school and classroom characteristics account for only about 40 percent of differences in learning achievement; the remainder is attributable to individual and family-background characteristics not typically amenable to school-level interventions" (WB, 1995). The empirical foundations for many points are not made explicit or are extremely weak. To argue in favor of a specific policy option, the WB frequently resorts to citing one or more examples of experiences that demonstrate that such an option was adopted and had effective results, but does not describe the context—political, economic, social, historical, cultural, institutional—and the specific conditions that explain the success (or failure) of any given intervention.

In the realm of external aid agencies, it is the African (and rural) reality that, to a considerable degree, serves as the paradigm for "developing countries." In fact, the essential elements of the diagnosis and package of policy recommendations offered by the WB to developing countries in the 1990s were contained in the sub-Saharan Africa study conducted in 1985, in which thirty-nine countries were analyzed. The strategies that now constitute the heart of the WB reform package—priority on primary education, cost-recovery strategies, increasing class size, multiple shifts, central importance of textbooks, multigrade teaching, selectively recruiting teachers and reducing their salaries (or intensifying their work by organizing double shifts in schools), payment by results, in-service teacher training, among others—were recommended back then to such countries. "Strong research evidence" was already cited as the basis for these and other policy recommendations.

A Simplistic Treatment of Educational Innovations

"Success stories," "innovative programs," "best practices," or "effective schools" described in publications by the WB are often presented in boxes that are interspersed throughout the text. These boxes "bring reality" to the arguments and exemplify the strength of a specific policy recommendation. Nevertheless, the programs highlighted typically appear void of context, trajectory or movement; are described through exterior and superficial aspects; and are exempt from problems or limitations. Rarely found in such descriptions are accounts of what actually occurs in the programs, or the institution in question. The dynamic in the school or classroom, even in the cases of innovations that are specifically pedagogic in nature, is not discussed. The organizational aspects of education reforms, often critical factors in the success or failure of reform attempts, are generally absent from both the diagnosis of the problem and its proposed solution.

Instead of analyzing the factors that explain the contradictory nature, the potential advantages and disadvantages of a given policy option, the path of generalization is preferred. The "Asian Tigers" are presented as ideal models—examples of the importance of will and tenacity in achieving ambitious objectives, including those for education—ignoring the specificity of these processes and their irreplicability in different historical, cultural, and socioeconomic contexts. "Success" in some current education reform processes (the cases of Bolivia, the Dominican Republic, Ghana, Guinea, India, Jordan, Mauritania, Mozambique, Romania, and Thailand are mentioned in the 1995 WB report) is explained by the fact that "stakeholders have been involved in developing and implementing the reform," including teachers' unions (WB, 1995). A direct, in-depth knowledge of any of these reform processes, each very different and complex in its own right, would call into question the simplicity of such assertions.

In the context of policy documents, "success stories" serve a clear function: rather than explaining the dynamics and the complexity of innovative interventions or education reform processes, their purpose is to convince readers and, particularly, policy makers, about the proven effectiveness and the infalliability of what is being proposed. This inevitably leads to simplification, bias, and even distortion. Innovative programs and reform processes appear without a historical context, frozen in a time period chosen as the ideal moment of their realization. Given the low survival rates of many innovations, mention of the temporal dimension (when the program was initiated, how long it has been operating, etc.) is often avoided. Because the chronic difficulties of consolidating and expanding educational innovations are known, as well as the lack of evaluation of results and impact, numbers (coverage, population affected, etc.) are rarely provided. Finally, references to costs are absent. The "innovative" tends to automatically be considered "successful" and "success" is seen as devoid of problems. Few publications opt for diffusing innovative experiences making known both their pluses and minuses "despite the cultural conventions challenged by this public presentation of 'difficulties' " (Little, Hoppers, and Gardner, 1994).

Simplistic understandings of educational innovation and reform, and of what "works" and "does not work" in education, are not limited to the WB. This appears to be rooted deeply in the working logic of international agencies and Ministries of Education. However, such treatment by an international organization, and especially by the WB, takes on a particularly sharp profile when innovation is converted into just another marketing tool for "selling" policies and strategies to the developing world. As stated by Schiefelbein and Tedesco (1995): "A positive step in both educational reform and research would be an in-depth discussion of successful experiences."

A Manual Approach to Education

Despite addressing extremely complex subjects and decisions that admittedly require more information and analysis, particularly in the case of developing countries, the WB "makes few confessions of ignorance" (Schwille, 1993) in its policy recommendations. Rather than posing questions or suggesting paths for future research, and rather than permitting a glimpse of the still fragile nature of education theory and practice, everything appears to have an answer, a precise recommendation, a clear map of options and priorities. Individuals who are not knowledgeable on education issues or do not follow education's practical and theoretical development—the usual case for a large number of policy makers in this field, and at whom WB proposals and discourse are directed—may receive the impression that everything about education has been researched, discussed, and resolved.

As will be discussed below, instead of analysis and presentation of policy options addressing a variety of objectives, situations, and contexts, WB policy options are organized according to black/white dichotomies and presented as if they were binary tradeoffs: quantity versus quality, centralized versus decentralized, teachers versus textbooks, teacher training versus teacher salaries, in-service versus preservice teacher training, intended versus implemented curriculum, school breakfasts versus school lunches, and so on.

A Proposal that Dichotomizes Policy Options: Blind Alleys versus Promising Avenues

From studies and from its own history of investment in the education sector, the WB draws a series of conclusions about what does not work ("blind alleys") and what works ("promising avenues") in primary schools in developing countries (Lockheed and Verspoor, 1991), and these are then recommended as policies.

The possibility of drawing conclusions and generalizing proposals for "the developing world" is questionable, more so given the fragile information available on education in general and for each country in particular. On the other hand, no policy decision appears in reality as a binary option, but rather as a selection from a broad menu of possibilities and shades. Educational change is systemic and does not operate on the basis of discrete, isolated elements: good textbooks without competent teachers are often a fruitless investment; teacher training, in the absence of an overall revision of the status and condition of the teaching profession, ends up increasing teacher rotation in search of better remunerated jobs; increasing instruction time does not necessarily result in improved educational outcomes if curriculum and pedagogy remain unchanged, and so on.

Curricular Reform versus School Textbooks

In light of the acknowledged weaknesses and limited results of past attempts at curricular reform, the WB now proposes to concentrate on textbooks. If the decade of the 1970s was the decade of investment in school infrastructure, the decade of the 1990s is likely to be remembered as the decade of textbooks.

The WB confronts us with a false dilemma between the prescribed curriculum (also known as the official, intended, normative, or written curriculum, and usually condensed in the syllabus) and the implemented curriculum (that which is actually realized in the classroom, also known as effective or real curriculum). Curricular reforms aimed at modifying the prescribed curriculum are being discouraged, alleging their complexity, the fact that such reform attempts generate excessively high expectations, and finally, that they have not translated into improvements in the classroom: "Most curriculum reforms attempt to modify the intended curriculum by concentrating on the courses taught and the number of hours officially allocated to them. Such changes in the intended curriculum are small, ineffective, and resisted by parents and teachers" (Lockheed and Verspoor, 1991). Textbooks are presented as a substitute for curricular reform since they are considered in themselves the curriculum—"textbooks are the major, if not the only, definition of the curriculum in most developing countries (Ibid.), that is, they condense the content and guide the activities of both teachers and students. Based on this analysis, the WB has seen an important increase in budgetary expenditures destined for textbooks within its primary education projects. In many borrowing countries, textbooks have become the first or second most important rubric of expenditure within WB-supported primary education projects, with teacher training usually ranking third or fourth in order of priorities.

The proposed dilemma between curricular reform (associated with the prescribed curriculum) and textbooks (associated with the implemented curriculum) and its underlying assumptions raises numerous questions:

1. The curricular reform model that underlies the analysis and proposals of the WB is the centralized, partial and ineffective reform that has predominated in the past. Nevertheless, conditions currently exist to overcome that conventional, top-down reform model. There is no reason for curricular reform to be designed in a centralized and elitist manner, and for curriculum content to be prescriptive and homogeneous. The old as well as modern traditions of the reform package developed centrally by a small group of specialists have shown their weaknesses and limits, and rarely have succeeded in modifying practices and results in the classroom. But this does not refuse the necessity of curricular reform in developing countries. On the contrary, accumulated experience suggests the need to revise the model and carry out reform in an alternative manner (Torres, 1993).

Indeed, renewed school systems need not only a new curriculum but, most importantly, a new manner of conceptualizing and developing the curriculum, through more participatory mechanisms and searching for social consensus, overcoming the fragmentary, partial, and short-term vision of past curricular reform efforts. These were generally focused on content, ignoring instructional methods, and on superficial addition or subtraction operations, without perceiving curriculum as a totality and without a long-term vision. Many influential educators and policy makers still understand curricular reform as a document, a decree, or an eminently intraschool intervention, rather than as a complex social process involving profound cultural change within and beyond the school system (Torres, 1993). Above all, it is urgent to understand that it is impossible to carry out curricular reform without including teachers, not only as potential trainees and change implementers, but as partners and architects of the reform process.

Renewed and participatory approaches to the curriculum and to curricular reform are, in fact, contemplated in the "Education for All" initiative. Countries were urged to organize participatory and consultative mechanisms in order to identify the basic learning needs of children, youths, and adults (WCEFA, 1990). This is neither the vision nor the proposal of the WB. In the light of pragmatism and economic analysis, school textbooks appear as an easier and faster path (a direct manipulable variable) than the sustained information, participation, discussion, and social elaboration process that is required for effective curricular reform. Indeed, the 1995 policy document recommends maintaining curriculum design and development at the central or regional level, without local participation and without forming part of the package of functions to be decentralized.

2. The recommended prioritization of textbooks is based on two premises: (a) that textbooks themselves constitute the implemented curriculum, and (b) that textbooks are a low cost (when compared to a broad curricular reform) and a high incidence input affecting educational quality. In both cases what is in play, explicitly or implicitly, is another false option: textbooks versus teachers. From the WB economists' point of view, textbooks are a shortcut not only to curricular reform but to teacher preparation and professional competence.

The implemented curriculum is that which is effected in the classroom, with or without the mediation of textbooks, and fundamentally depends on the decisions made by the teacher (in fact, it is the teacher who decides whether, when, and how to use a textbook). Therefore, the surest and most direct manner of influencing the implemented curriculum is by addressing teachers, their motivation, preparation, and conditions. Both teachers and textbooks are fundamental for teaching, but there is no doubt that, if forced to choose, it is more important to have (good) teachers than to have (good) textbooks. Textbooks are educational tools; teachers are educational agents. It is the textbook that should serve the teacher, not vice versa.

The idea of the textbook as the implemented curriculum rests on the idea of a programmed, closed, normative, and self-contained text that orients teaching step-by-step and offers both the teacher and the students all the answers. This type of text, if highly esteemed and welcomed by the untrained or poorly qualified teacher, rather than alleviating the problem created by the continuous deterioration of teacher qualification and teaching quality, contributes to strengthen it by further disempowering teachers and perpetuating the classic (and growing) dependency of the teacher on the textbook. The need for an open and flexible curriculum, a tool of development rather than a straitjacket for teachers, is a contemporary concern, in tune with the "protagonist role," the "professional autonomy," and the "new teacher profile" proclaimed in modern educational discourse.

On the other hand, textbooks cannot be seen in isolation from the prescribed curriculum. Working on textbooks independent of the current curriculum (or that being revised) in a country implies promoting even greater internal disorder in the school system, possibly resulting in a plethora of disjointed, uncoordinated functions (e.g., a Division of Curriculum and a Division of Textbooks, each one with its own separate teacher training system), a situation which is already in operation in several developing countries. Moreover, as ratified by recent experience in many countries, this situation favors uncontrolled practices by private textbook publishers, who often end up defining the character and orientation of the reform (Coll, 1992; Ochoa, 1990; Torres, 1993).

3. While curricular reform is a complex issue, providing schools with good quality textbooks and assuring their effective use and positive impact on learning is no simple task, as acknowledged by the WB itself: "Throughout the world few individuals possess the expertise required for writing good textbooks, and most textbooks are therefore written by committees of experts" (Lockheed and Verspoor, 1991). Therefore, the textbook option often results in contracting international experts or importing foreign texts rather than stimulating and strengthening national capacities and institutions to develop and produce quality textbooks in the medium and long term.

4. In practice, experience reveals the extremely problematic nature of projects involving school textbooks. WB lessons learned in this area include poor quality of the texts, inadequate distribution systems, the inability to sustain production, inadequate procedures for purchasing textbook inputs, lack of coordination between curriculum and textbook development, lack of synchronization between new textbook publication and teacher prepara-

tion, and the inability to establish institutions that will continue producing good quality textbooks upon finishing the project (Verspoor, 1991).

Assertions about the central importance of textbooks in the improvement of educational quality and outcomes (and, concomitantly, about the limited impact of teacher salaries and initial teacher preparation) merit additional discussion. On one hand, there are studies that refute, or at least relativize, the importance of textbooks on educational outcomes vis-à-vis teachers and teacher performance. On the other hand, several studies, including some promoted or cited by the WB, reveal that the quality of learning depends not only on accessibility but on the quality and variety of reading material in general. In spite of the fact that, according to the proposed input prioritization scheme, in which school libraries score higher than single textbooks in terms of their impact on educational quality, it is the textbook—not the library—which receives priority in WB recommendations for developing countries. To sum up, in dealing with curricular reform issues, several points need to be stressed:

1. Curricular and pedagogical reform are the very heart of education reform. Unless the what and how of teaching and learning are modified, that is, the actual practices and relations in the classroom, all other aspects—administrative, legal, institutional—are meaningless.
2. Reforming the curriculum implies working with both the prescribed and the implemented curriculum in an integrated fashion, and in a manner distinct from what has predominated in the past.
3. Modifying the implemented curriculum implies working with all elements that intervene in the teaching-learning process. The teacher occupies a central, privileged role among those factors.
4. Modifying the implemented curriculum implies working both within and outside the school system, with parents, communities and society at large.

Initial versus In-service Teacher Training[12]

In general, teachers are an issue with which the WB is uncomfortable and over which it has maintained ambiguous, inconsistent, and even contradictory positions. Teachers tend to be seen as teacher unions, and these evoke intransigence, disputes over salaries, strikes, and political maneuvering. Teachers are currently seen more as a problem than as a resource; they are seen as a costly, complex, and difficult to manage educational "input." Indeed, teachers themselves, and not only teacher training, tend to be seen as a "blind alley."

Two issues are particularly thorny: teacher salaries and teacher training. Although the WB has its views and proposals on both issues, and studies that provide a basis for minimizing the importance of both, there exist discussion, diverse opinions, and important changes in WB discourse regarding these and other subjects related to the teaching profession. For example, there is increasing recognition of the importance of teacher knowledge as a determining factor in teaching performance and learning outcomes (the 1995 policy document even acknowledges that available studies on the relationship between teacher training and student learning outcomes do not show a clear pattern). Nevertheless, teacher training continues to be relegated to low status among WB priorities and proposed strategies for developing countries, ranking behind investment in school infrastructure, institutional reform, and textbooks. Also, teacher training continues to be viewed in an isolated manner, without considering the changes needed in other spheres (e.g., salaries, professional and living conditions, and overall status) in order to make teacher training a useful investment.

In the mid-1980s, a WB study (Haddad, 1985) concluded that preservice teacher training programs financed by the WB were not cost effective.[13] In recent years, other studies have started to show that teachers with more years of study and higher qualifications do not necessarily produce better student learning outcomes. Based on this, the WB has discouraged investment in initial teacher preparation and recommended in-service training. Also recommended are distance modalities, considered more cost effective than residential modalities. Finally, it is asserted that teachers' subject knowledge impacts student achievement more than the teachers' pedagogical knowledge. As will be discussed below, these (and other) traditional "hard" WB positions are being softened in recent times.

In reality, initial and in-service teacher training are complementary and different stages of a single learning process of teachers. Both are necessary and both are currently facing problems. In-service programs—proliferating over the last few years and yet to be evaluated in terms of their impact on actual teaching performance and learning processes and outcomes—are definitely not the panacea for the school problems and much less for the broader challenge of preparing the teachers required to deal with modern, complex education goals and objectives. Subject knowledge and pedagogical knowledge are inseparable in competent teaching, as finally recognized in the 1995 policy document, although with a limited understanding of pedagogy: "The most effective teachers appear to be those with good knowledge of the subject and a wide repertoire of teaching skills" (WB, 1995). Even more, as suggested by different studies, several of them conducted in Latin America (Filp, Cardemil, and Valdivieso, 1984), and confirmed by practical experience, teachers' attitudes and expectations can play a more important role in student learning than teacher knowledge of either subject matter or pedagogy.

Distance education is recommended as a low cost alternative for teacher training. However, experience with distance modalities for teacher training purposes in developing countries is still incipient, and there is insufficient information and evaluation to conclude that distance training modalities are in fact less costly and more effective than face-to-face, residential ones (Klees, 1994; Tatto, Nielsen, and Cummings, 1991). In fact, distance training programs promoted in the international literature in the last few years often have not achieved and the same level of acceptance in their own countries.

There is growing consensus that initial teacher education is undergoing a serious crisis, and that traditional institutions offering such teacher education, whether at the secondary or tertiary level, need major reform. The heavy emphasis placed on in-service training and the open discrediting of initial teacher education over the past decade has been of course a contributing factor to this crisis. However, as in the case of curricular reform, the solution is not to eradicate what does not work properly—whether it is education reform, teacher training institutions and practices, or the school system as a whole—but to identify why it has not worked, and to change or redirect it accordingly. It is not initial teacher education but the conventional teacher education model, whether preservice or in-service, that has not worked and needs major transformation (see Table II).

The importance of the school system, and of secondary education in particular, as a principal source in teacher preparation, was acknowledged in the sub-Saharan report (WB, 1988) and is further stressed in the 1995 policy document. Empirical evidence indicates that teachers tend to behave in the classroom based more on what they experienced as school students themselves than on what they learned in their formal preparation as teachers. Both initial and in-service training become merely compensatory and remedial strategies vis-à-vis a deficient general education provided by a low quality school system. A good school system constitutes indeed the best and most certain investment in teacher preparation.

Recognizing the importance of general knowledge for teacher performance and the importance of the school system in providing such knowledge, the WB's recommendations for teacher recruitment and development include: (1) ensuring quality secondary education, (2) complementing it with a short initial preparation focused on pedagogical aspects, and (3) hiring teachers based on proven knowledge and competence—national proficiency tests for teachers are suggested—with criteria and procedures similar to those utilized for hiring university professors. Points (2) and (3) were present in WB recommendations to sub-Saharan African countries in the mid-1980s. Obviously, to attract and fill this teacher profile in sufficient numbers implies a radical shift in the parameters under which both the school system and the teaching profession have been operating. Among others, such a shift supposes drastically revising teacher salaries and working conditions. On this point, the WB limits itself to insisting that teacher salaries be tied to performance and that this be measured through student learning outcomes. No analysis is provided on the viability and costs of this proposal.

Teacher salaries constitute the most slippery aspect of the entire reform package proposal. The WB's position is that increasing teacher salaries does not improve school outcomes. The argument—deceitful inasmuch as no education input, in and by itself, can affect learning outcomes—has been extended in many cases to conditioning WB loans to a nonincrease in teacher salaries.

Trapped in defense of its policy options and cost-benefit schemes, and confronted by practical developments of these policies in the borrowing

Table II: The Teacher Education Model That Has Not Worked

• each new policy, plan or project starts from zero	(ignoring or disregarding previous knowledge and experience)
• considers education/training principally as a need for teachers	(and not also for principals, supervisors and human resources linked to the education system in general and at all levels)
• views education/training in isolation from other dimensions of the teaching profession	(such as salaries, working and living conditions, promotion mechanisms, organizational arrangements, etc.)
• ignores teachers' real conditions	(motivations, concerns, knowledge, available time and resources, etc.)
• adopts a top-down approach and sees teachers only in a passive role of recipients and potential trainees	(does not consult teachers or seek their participation in the definition and design of the training plan)
• has a homogeneous proposal for "teachers" in general	(instead of adjusting to the various types and levels of teachers and their specific needs)
• adopts an operational approach to teacher training	(in-service training is viewed as a tool to persuade and implement a definite policy, program, project or even a textbook)
• assumes that the need for training is inversly proportional to the level of teaching	(thus ignoring the importance and complexity of teaching young children and in the initial grades)
• resorts to external incentives and motivation mechanisms	(such as scores, promotion, certificates, rather than reinforcing the objective of learning and improving the teaching practice)
• addresses individual teachers	(rather than groups or work teams, or the school as a unified whole)
• is conducted outside the work place	(typically, teachers are brought to the training sites instead of bringing the training to them and making the school the training site)
• is asystematic and limited to a short period of time	(not integral to a continuing education scheme)

- is centered around the event (the course, the seminar, the workshop, etc.) as a privileged—and even unique—teaching and learning tool (ignoring or marginalizing other modalities such as horizontal exchange, peer group discussions, class observations, distance education, self-study, on-site visits, etc.)

- disassociates *administrative* and *pedagogical* issues as content and as learning needs (pedagogical issues are considered the realm of teachers, and administrative issues are consigned to others, without an integral approach to both types of knowledge and skills)

- disassociates *content* and *method* (subject matter and pedagogy, knowing the subject and knowing how to teach it) and promotes the prior over the latter (ignoring the inseparability and complementarity of both types of knowledge, and the need for both)

- considers education and training to be formal, stern and rigid (denying the educational and communicational importance of an informal environment, of play, laughter and enjoyment)

- is focused on the teaching perspective (rather than on the learning perspective)

- rejects teachers' previous knowledge and experience (instead of starting from there and building on it)

- is oriented toward correcting mistakes and highlighting weaknesses (rather than toward stimulating and reinforcing strengths)

- is academic and theoretical, centered around the book (while denying the actual teaching practice as the raw material and the most important source for learning)

- is based on the frontal and transmissive teaching model (teaching as the transmission of information and learning as the passive assimilation of that information)

- is essentially incoherent and contradictory to the pedagogical model that is requested of teachers in their classrooms (teachers are expected to elicit active learning, critical thinking, creativity, etc., which they themselves do not experience in their own education and training process)

Source: Torres, 1995b

countries as well as by new information and knowledge available (providing much more varied conclusions than the WB's package is able to accommodate), the WB has reached the critical point of being forced to review some of its positions.

It is impossible to continue asserting that in-service training is more (cost) effective than initial teacher training when, at the same time, it is recognized that in-service training is only a remedial strategy when faced with a poor quality school system or poor quality (or nonexistent) initial teacher education, and that the latter is critical in ensuring teacher knowledge of subject matter, a fundamental variable in teacher performance: "Teachers' subject knowledge, an intended outcome of pre-service training, is strongly and consistently related to student performance" (WB, 1995). It is not possible to continue framing teacher education within the dichotomous pre/in-service scheme, while recognizing that the school system (and its improvement) is the surest source of solid general education for teachers. It is not possible to propose new parameters for teacher recruitment—the best and the most competent—while bypassing teacher salaries and professional development issues that are a condition for the adoption of such parameters in reality. Furthermore, it is impossible to continue advocating educational quality improvement without integrally addressing the teachers issue.

Reducing Class Size versus Increasing Instructional Time

Several studies quoted by the WB conclude that the number of students per class (when it is above twenty) has little impact on learning achievement. On this basis, since the 1980s, borrowing countries have been recommended not to invest resources in attempting to reduce class size—a clear tendency over the last few years, except for South Asia—and, on the contrary, to "save costs and improve learning by increasing student-teacher ratios. They would thereby use fewer teachers and would be able to allocate resources from teachers to other inputs that improve achievement such as textbooks and in-service teacher training" (WB, 1995).

Assertions about class size and the recommendations derived from them are among the oldest and most insisted upon by the WB, and also among the most controversial and resisted in borrowing countries. Conventional wisdom (and actual standards and practice in Western industrialized countries) suggests that smaller student-teacher ratios provide better conditions for learning. The assertion that "class size makes no difference" may be true from an economist's point of view but not from a teacher's point of view, and definitely not unless fundamental curricular and pedagogical changes are introduced in the regular classroom.

It is indeed necessary to rationalize the distribution of teachers within the school system. However, a homogeneous application of this policy would also be irrational and lead to increased inequality, inequity, and poor quality of school systems. If improving educational quality is a major goal, together with drastically reducing repetition and dropout rates in primary school, de-

veloping countries should on the contrary be explicitly recommended to reduce student-teacher ratios in the first grades, typically the most overcrowded and with the worst teaching and learning conditions of the entire
school system. In any case, the WB itself acknowledges that "in practice,
such savings (obtained by increasing student-teacher ratios) are seldom allocated to other inputs" (WB, 1995).

The other variable highlighted is instructional time: "The amount of
actual time devoted to learning is consistently related to achievement. Students in low- and middle-income countries receive fewer hours of classroom
instruction than those in OECD countries—a consequence of a shorter official school year, unscheduled school closings, teacher and student absences,
and miscellaneous disruptions" (WB, 1995). Measures recommended to increase instructional time include extending the official school years; permitting flexible scheduling to accommodate the demands of agricultural
seasons, religious holidays, and children's domestic chores; and assigning
homework. However, in practice, the establishment of multiple shifts and
multiple use of classroom buildings, which the WB has been recommending
as a means of minimizing construction costs and maximizing the labor of
the teaching force, results in reducing instruction time rather than increasing it. This is a clear example of how two policy recommendations can have
opposite effects and annul each other.

The subject of teacher absenteeism, as yet poorly documented and analyzed, is the expression of diverse and complex personal and work-related
factors (sickness, distances and transportation difficulties, additional jobs to
complement a meager salary, bureaucratic and lengthy procedures to collect
salaries, training outside the workplace, and many others) that cannot be resolved simply with coercion and control by either local or central authorities, parents, or communities. The feminization of the teaching profession
at the primary level, in the case of Latin America—a result of the fallen prestige and remuneration of teaching as a professional option—constitutes in itself a fundamental factor in teacher absenteeism; it implies having implicitly
selected a specific teacher profile (women; low-income women; housewives;
women that become pregnant, give birth, have and care for children; etc.),
without having concomitantly considered the consequences of choosing
such a profile and the measures necessary for combating absenteeism (child
care services, emotional support services, effective mechanisms for substitu-
tion or team teaching, revising traditional masculine and feminine roles at
home and in the school, etc.). In other words, the very conditions spawned
in the development of the teaching profession are conducive to absenteeism.

The most expressive and devastating form of teacher absenteeism has become the strike, which is on the increase all over the world. In Latin America, teacher strikes—each time more violent and more prolonged, sometimes lasting three or four months—have become common in the majority
of countries. Against this context, forcing an increase of a few hours or days
of class per academic years through ways that ignore the reasons causing repeated strikes is like trying to stop a hemorrhage by applying a Band-Aid.

The "savings" in teacher salaries and acceptable working conditions for teachers have a very high cost, both in terms of available time for teaching and learning and, more fundamentally, in terms of educational quality.

CONCLUDING THOUGHTS

Through both conceptualization and implementation, instead of improving the quality, equity, and efficiency of the school system, the World Bank reform package is actually helping developing countries to reinforce and to invest in the wider reproduction of the existing, conventional education model, at most disguised with new clothing and modern terminology.

Some of the characteristics of the conventional education model are the following:

1. It reduces education to school. It assumes that education policies are reduced to school policies, that formal schooling is the only source of learning, and that basic education (meeting the basic learning needs of children, youths, and adults) is resolved in the classroom, thus ignoring the important educational role of the family, the environment, play, work, experience, and mass media.

2. It has an eminently sectoral vision of education, understood as a monopoly of a ministry and specialized educational institutions. Sector analyses and interventions consider health, nutrition, production, employment, the economy, and so on, as extra-educational factors. Most importantly, poverty is treated as if it were extra-sectoral.

3. It lacks a systemic vision, a vision of the education system as a system: the different levels (initial, primary, secondary, and higher) are fragmented and lack coordination; educational change is attempted by addressing discrete, isolated factors (administrative, legal, curricular, teacher training, provision of textbooks, etc.) without understanding that change in education can only be systemic.

4. It is permeated by a dichotomous vision of education realities and policy options: quantity versus quality, child education versus adult education, basic education versus higher education, administrative versus pedagogical issues, contents versus methods, pre- versus in-service teacher training, supply versus demand, centralized versus decentralized, decision makers versus implementers, governmental versus nongovernmental, public versus private, teaching versus learning, teacher-centered versus learner-centered approaches, success versus failure, and so forth. Educational change and innovation are generally viewed in terms of pendular movements from one pole to the other.

5. It acts and reacts to the immediate and the short term, tied to political timing and administrative needs rather than to the needs of educational change and development, lacking a strategic and long-term

vision that sees beyond particular administration periods and overcomes the "project" mind set.

6. It is vertical and authoritarian, centralized in the decision-making process, with no tradition of public information or accountability in the use of resources, and with top-down approaches to education reform and innovation. It does not promote information, communication, and social debate about the realities and prospects of education, the results of the school system, or the education policies adopted. The "failure" of a specific policy or program is attributed to lack of will or incapacity of those who implement rather than to errors in policy conceptualization and design.

7. It grants priority to quantity over quality, results over processes, how much is learned over what is learned, how it is learned, and for what it is learned. Enrollment constitutes the main, if not the only, indicator to measure educational progress (or regression), equality, and equity (and even the concept of "universal primary education" is reduced to this sole indicator), while paying little attention to retention, completion, and effective learning. Education is measured and evaluated by the number of certificates, degrees, and/or years of instruction, rather than by what is effectively learned and the usefulness of such learning.

8. It disassociates demand and supply in education. Reform and improvement strategies focus on the supply side (intraschool factors) while ignoring the demand (parents, communities, and society at large) and the importance of empowering such demand (through public information, parents' education, training at the community level, etc.) as a fundamental condition to achieve meaningful community participation, a strong school system, and quality education for all.

9. It disassociates administrative and pedagogical issues, grants priority to the former, subordinates the pedagogical model to the administrative model, and assumes that changes in the latter will inevitably bring changes in the former. Pedagogy is considered marginal in both teacher performance and policy decisions and planning.

10. It prioritizes investments in things (buildings, supplies, textbooks, laboratories, computers, etc.) over investments in people (motivation, capacity building, professional development, working conditions) involved in the education sector at the different levels (students, parents, teachers, headmasters, administrators, intermediate cadre, specialists, educational journalists, etc.).

11. It is based on the supposition of homogeneity (for students as well as for teachers, for schools within a country, and for developing countries at the world level) and defines therefore homogeneous diagnostic and action frameworks for all of them. There is an inability to recognize, accept, and manage diversity, from the classroom level to the national and international policy level.

12. It does not differentiate between teaching and learning. It assumes that what is taught is learned, that modifications in teaching automatically produce modifications in learning, and that lack of learning is the fault of the student ("learning disabilities").

13. It views education as a process of transmission, assimilation, and accumulation of information, provided by teachers and textbooks, rather than as an active process of construction and appropriation of knowledge, skills, values, and attitudes that initiates well before, and goes far beyond, schooling.

14. It is based on a frontal and transmissive model of teaching, in which teaching is equated with speaking and learning with listening. This model applies to students in the classroom and to teachers in their own preparation and training. The model is extended to the relationship between advisors and advisees.

15. It has demonstrated misunderstanding and negligence in the management of teacher-related issues: Teachers are ignored as fundamental actors in educational provision, quality, and change; they are relegated to a secondary and passive role, and their advice and participation ignored as a fundamental condition in the design, implementation, and effectiveness of education policies, and of education reform in particular.

16. It shows a marked preference for the quick and easy fix, with little attention to effectiveness and sustainability of actions over time; the decree or the formal announcement as a substitute for systematic communication, explanation, and persuasion efforts; replicating innovative experiences rather than enhancing the capacity to innovate; top-down education reform packages rather than participatory reform processes; short in-service teacher training courses rather than a comprehensive teacher education strategy; improving textbooks or adding new areas (e.g., health, peace, environment, life skills, etc.) as a substitute for a thorough revision of the curriculum; distribution of supplies rather than capacity-building efforts; consensus building understood as signatures and formal agreements rather than as an active and sustained social dialogue among stakeholders; and so on.

17. It views parental and community participation in education in a unilateral and restricted manner (e.g., limited to the school, restricted to "nontechnical" matters, etc.) and usually, and increasingly, focused on monetary aspects. Participatory rhetoric is not accompanied by measures (e.g., information, training, financial, administrative) to make it a reality.

18. Finally, it perceives education policy development as always starting from zero, without a retrospective view; discarding what was done before rather than building on it; proposing new models, policies, and strategies prior to analyzing why previous ones did not work; and giving little attention to actual implementation conditions (political, social, cultural, and organizational).

NOTES

1. In this chapter I am using as a central reference for analysis the most recent education policy document by the WB, *Priorities and Strategies for Education: A World Bank Sector Review* (both the March and May 1995 preliminary drafts and the August 1995 printed draft), which will be abbreviated WB, 1995. This document synthesizes the principal studies on education published by the WB since the last documents on this sector: *Education in Sub-Saharan Africa* (1988), *Primary Education* (1990), *Vocational and Technical Education and Training* (1991), and *Higher Education* (1994). The objective of this document is "to assist policymakers in these [low- and middle-income] countries, especially those concerned with the education system as a whole and with the allocation of public resources to education" (p. xii).

2. The Bolivian education reform process offers some interesting lessons in this respect. See Anaya, 1995, for an account of such process "from within."

3. What is considered "near universal enrollment" is not specified. Latin America and the Caribbean, and the developing region with the highest enrollment rates at the primary school level, admit to an official average of 15 percent of school-age children out of school.

4. Basic education generally refers to instruction in literacy and numeracy skills for out-of-school youths and adults (WB, 1998, p. x).

5. See Fuller and Clarke, 1994.

6. For a critical analysis of the economic theory underlying WB education policies, see Coraggio 1994 and 1995.

7. The assertion that "in East Asia and Latin America and the Caribbean primary education is almost universal" (WB, 1995, p. 33) refers, obviously, to primary school *enrollment*. Both Asia and Latin America are far from having achieved the goal of universal primary education, if retention and completion also are considered.

8. The 1995 policy document includes 274 bibliographic references, all of them in English. The book on primary education in developing countries by Lockheed and Verspoor (1991) includes 446 references, of which 441 are publications in English. The remaining five are in French (2), Spanish (2), and Portuguese (1).

9. An example of this is the assertion (based on a few studies) that the provision of educational inputs has a comparatively stronger impact on school outcomes in developing countries than in developed ones. From this follows the conclusion and the recommendation that justifies large investments in inputs in the Third World, and other actions—presumably more qualitative in nature—in the First World.

10. Today it is difficult to find two statistical sources that coincide over data about the same indicator or phenomenon. There are often important differences between official data provided by each country and the data provided by international agencies. There may also be significant differences in information and statistics used among international agencies.

11. A study by Harbison and Hanushek (1992) in Northeast Brazil found that textbooks had statistically insignificant or even negative effects on student achievement. However, "the authors [were] not willing to give up on textbooks (Plank, 1994) because they argued that "we know [sic] from elsewhere [that textbook use] is a powerful component of educational performance (Harbison and Hanushek, 1992, p. 161).

12. A more comprehensive analysis of teacher education issues can be found in Torres, 1995b.

13. Between 1963 and 1994 the WB was financially involved in 110 training insti-
     tutions for primary school teachers (Haddad, 1985).

REFERENCES

Anaya, A. (1995). "Gestación y Diseño de la Efoema Educatiua Boliviana: Una
    Visión Desde Adentro". La Paz: CEDES, mimeo.
Arnove, R. (1995). "Neoliberal Education Policies in Latin America: Arguments in
    Favor and Against." Paper presented at the CIES annual conference,
    Williamsburg, VA. 6–10 March.
Arthur, L. and Preston, R., with Ngahu, C., Shoaib le Breton, S. and Theobald, D.
    (1996). *Quality in Overseas Consultancy: Understanding the Issues*. Warwick:
    International Centre for Educational Development, University of Warwick,
    March.
Bacchus, K., Aziz, A. A., Ahmad, S. H., Bakar, F. A. and Rodwell, S. (1991). *Cur-
    riculum Reform*. London: Commonwealth Secretariat.
Carron, G. and Govinda, R. (1995). "Five Years After Jomtien: Where Are We"?
    IIEP Newsletter 13(3), Paris: UNESCO-IIEP, July-September.
Coll, C. (1991). *Psicología y currículum*. Barcelona: Paidós.
———. (1992). *La Reforma del Sistema Educativo Español: La Calidad de la En-
    señanza Como Objetivo*. Colección Educación N° 4. Quito: Instituto FRONE-
    SIS.
Coll, C., Pozo, J. I., Sarabia, B. and Valls, E. (1992). *Los contenidos en la Reforma*.
    Madrid: Santillana.
Deble, I. and Carron, G. (eds.) (1993). *Jomtien, Trois ans Aprés. L'éducation Pour
    Tous Dans les Pays du Sahel*. Paris: UNESCO-IIEP/UNICEF.
Contreras, J. (1990). "El Currículum Como Formación." *Cuadernos de Pedagogía*
    184.
Coraggio, J. L. (1994). "Human Capital: The World Bank's Approach to Education
    in Latin America." In J. Cavanach (ed.), *Beyond Bretton Woods*. Washington,
    D.C.: IPS/TNI.
———. (1995). "Las Propuestas del Banco Mundial para la Educación: ¿Sentido
    Oculto o Problemas de Concepción?" *La Piragua* 11. Santiago: Consejo de
    Educación de Adultos de América Latina.
De Grauwe, A. and Bernard, D. (eds.). (1995). *Developments after Jomtien: EFA in
    the South-East Asia and the Pacific Region*, Paris: UNESCO-IIEP/UNICEF.
Espinola, V. (1989). "Los Resultados del Modelo Económico en la Enseñanza
    Básica: La Demanda Tiene la Palabra." In Juan Eduardo García-Huidobro
    (ed.), *Escuela, Calidad e Igualdad*. Santiago: CIDE.
Farrell, J. and Heyneman, S. (eds.). (1989). *Textbooks in the Developing World: Eco-
    nomic and Educational Choices*. Washington, D.C.: Economic Development
    Institute, World Bank.
Filp, J., Cardemil, C. and Valdivieso, C. (1984). *Profesoras y Profesores Efectivos en
    Chile*. Santiago: CIDE.
Frigerio, G. (ed.). (1991). *Currículo Presente, Ciencia Ausente. Normas, Teorías y
    Críticas*. Vol. 1. Buenos Aires: Miño y Dávila Editores.
Fuller, B. and Clark, P. (1994). "Raising School Effects While Ignoring Culture?
    Local Conditions and the Influence of Classroom Tools, Rules, and Peda-
    gogy." *Review of Educational Research* 64(1), pp. 118–158.
Gatti, B. (1994). "Avaliação Educacional no Brasil: Experiencias, Problemas, Re-
    comendações," *Estudos em Avaliação Educacional* 10 (July–December) Sao
    Paulo: Fundação Carlos Chagas.

Gimeno Sacristán, J. (1992). "Investigacíon e Innovación Sobre la Gestuón Pedagógica de los Equipos de Profesores." In UNESCO-OREALC (eds.), *La Gestión Pedagógica de la Escuela*. Santiago: UNESCO-OREALC.

Gimeno Sacristán, J. and Pérez Gómez, A. (1995). *La Enseñanza: Su Teoría y su Práctica*. Madrid: AKAL Editor.

Haddad, W. (1985). "Teacher Training: A Review of World Bank Experience." *EDT Discussion Paper*, No. 21, Washington, D.C.: World Bank.

Harbison, R. W. and Hanushek, E. A. (1992). *Educational Performance of the Poor: Lessons from Rural Northeast Brazil*. New York: Oxford University Press.

Heneveld, W. (1995). "Effective Schools: Determining Which Factors Have the Greatest Impact." *DAE Newsletter 7*, 3 (July-September).

Heyneman, S. (1995). "Economics of Education: Disappointments and Potential." *Prospects 25*(4), pp. 200–210.

Klees, S. (1994). "The Economics of Educational Technology." In T. Husen and T. Neville Postlethwaite (eds.). *The International Encyclopedia of Education*, (2d. Ed) Oxford: Pergamon, pp. 1903–1911.

Lagos, R. (1993). "Quality and Equity in Educational Decentralization: The Case of Chile." *The Forum* (May).

Little, A., Hoppers, W. and Gardner, R. (eds.). (1994). *Beyond Jomtien: Implementing Primary Education for All*. London: Macmillan Press.

Lockheed, M. and Verspoor, A. (1991). *Improving Primary Education in Developing Countries*. Washington, D.C.: Oxford University Press.

Lorfing, I. and Govinda, R. (eds.). (1995). *Development Since Jomtien: EFA in the Middle East and North Africa*, Paris: UNESCO-IIEP/UNICEF.

Ochoa, J. (1990). *Textos Escolares: Un saber Recortado*. Santiago: CIDE.

Peru, Ministerio de Educación. (1994). "Perú: Calidad, Eficiencia, Equidad. Los Desafíos de la Educación Primaria." Lima: División de Recursos Humanos del Banco Mundial, Ministerio de Educación, (mimeograph), (June).

Plank, D. (1994). Rev. of *Educational Performance of the Poor: Lessons from Rural Northeast Brazil*, by R. W. Harbison and E. A. Hanushek. *Comparative Education Review* 38(2) (May), pp. 284–289.

Prawda, J. (1993). "Lessons in Educational Decentralization: A Note for Policymakers." *The Forum* 2, 3 (May).

Reimers, F. (1993). "Time and Opportunity to Learn in Pakistan's Schools: Some Lessons on the Links Between Research and Policy." *Comparative Education* 29(2), pp. 201–212.

Samoff, J. (1995). *Analysis, Agendas, and Priorities in African Education: A Review of Externally Initiated, Commissioned, and Supported Studies of Education in Africa (1990–1994)*. Paris: UNESCO-DAE Working Group on Education Sector Analysis.

Schiefelbein, E. and Tedesco, J. C. (1995). *Una Nueva Oportunidad. El Rol de la Educación en el Desarrollo de América Latina*. Buenos Aires: Santillana.

Schwille, J. R. (1993). Rev. of *Improving Primary Education in Developing Countries*, by M. Lockheed and A. Verspoor, *Comparative Education Review* 37(4), pp. 490–493.

Tatto, M. T., Nielsen, D. and Cummings, W. K. (1991). "Comparing the Effects and Costs of Different Approaches for Primary School Teachers: The Case of Sri Lanka." *BRIDGES* 10.

Tedesco, J. C. (1991). "Estrategias de Desarrollo y Educación: El Desafío de la Gestión Pública." *Boletín del Proyecto Principal en América Latina y el Caribe* 25.

———. (1995). *El Nuevo Pacto Educativo: Educación, Competitividad y Ciudadanía en la Sociedad Moderna*. Madrid: Grupo Anaya.

Torres, R. M. (1993). "¿Qué (y cómo) es Necesario Aprender? Necesidades Básicas de Aprendizaje y Contenidos Curriculares." In *Necesidades básicas de aprendizaje. Estrategias de Acción.* Santiago: UNESCO-OREALC/IDRC.

———. (1995a). *Los Achaques de la Educación.* Quito: Instituto FRONESIS-LIBRESA.

———. (1995b). "Teacher Education: From Rhetoric to Action." Paper presented at the UNESCO/UNICEF International Conference on "Partnerships in Teacher Development for a New Asia." Bangkok, (6–8 December).

UNESCO-OREALC. (1993). *Situación educativa de América Latina y el Caribe 1980–1989.* Santiago: UNESCO-OREALC.

Verspoor, A. (1991). "Veinte Años de Ayuda del Banco Mundial a la Educación Básica." *Perspectivas* 21(3).

WCEFA. (1990). *World Declaration on "Education for All" and Framework of Action to Meet the Basic Learning Needs.* New York: WCEFA.

World Bank. (1988). *Education in Sub-Saharan Africa: Policies for Adjustment, Revitalization, and Expansion, A World Bank Policy Study.* Washington, D.C.: World Bank.

———. (1995). *Priorities and Strategies for Education: A World Bank Sector Review.* Washington D.C.: World Bank.

CHAPTER 15

Alternative Development and Education: Economic Interests and Cultural Practices in the Amazon

Sheila Aikman

This chapter is concerned with different perceptions of development according to different cultural and philosophical traditions. It examines a new education policy in the southeastern Peruvian Amazon that is expected to foster intercultural dialogue, participatory processes, human-resource development, and respect for the environment as a means of encouraging new alternatives for the development of the region. The chapter examines alternatives for development as they are expressed by different cultural groups in terms of their relationships with their environment and their aspirations for their children's education and their future. Despite its aims, the new education policy remains bound to an economic development discourse which fails to acknowledge that other cultural groups' aspirations for education are based on broader perceptions of development and qualitatively different relations with the environment.

THE NEED FOR A NEW EDUCATION POLICY

In September 1991, in Cuzco, Peru, the Incan regional government approved a proposal for a new education policy for the department of Madre de Dios, an area of tropical rainforest within the otherwise Andean Inca region. The education policy had been drawn up by state and civil organizations and included criticism of the exploitative nature of the development process in Peru, and Madre de Dios in particular, and the irrelevance of formal education for the peoples of the region (CAAAP, 1992).

The education policy states its aim as being to shape the potential of the youth of Madre de Dios to enhance the development of new, less ecologically destructive and more sustainable economic practices based primarily on the natural resources of the department. Moreover, it stresses the need for the development not only of a sound economic basis for the future but of an alternative approach to development based on more equitable relations between the diverse linguistic and cultural groups living there (CAAAP, 1992).

The education policy proposal reflects changing agendas not only within Madre de Dios but at continental and global levels. In the 1990s the governments of Mexico, Bolivia, Chile, the Dominican Republic, Ecuador, and Peru began a process of national consultation and cooperation with nongovernmental organizations, social institutions, and religious orders to promote the greater pertinence and relevance of educational programs, as well as to act as new sources of funding in a climate of economic recession and structural adjustment policies. At an intergovernmental meeting in Quito in 1991 it was agreed that, after the quantitative expansion of education in previous decades, new radical strategies were needed to respond to new demands for social equality, political democratization, and the transformation of production (Rivero, 1993). By the late 1980s several South American governments had legislated for intercultural bilingual education for the indigenous peoples of their countries to foster "unity within diversity" (Chiodi, 1990). Meanwhile, this was a time of preparation for the United Nations Conference on Environment and Development (the "Earth Summit") at Rio de Janeiro in June 1992, which produced Agenda 21, an intergovernmental blueprint for sustainable development.

THE MADRE DE DIOS: CULTURAL DIVERSITY AND GEOGRAPHICAL MARGINALIZATION

The Madre de Dios is a region of lowland tropical rainforest situated in the southeastern corner of Peru, bordering the Bolivian, Brazilian, and Central Peruvian Amazon to the north, south, and east and with the steep Andes mountains to the west, that provide a forbidding mountainous barrier between the Amazon and the Peruvian coast. The Madre de Dios remained largely isolated until the end of the nineteenth century, when its natural resources, particularly rubber, attracted the first wave of colonization. This colonization led to huge loss of life for the indigenous peoples who followed a hunting, gathering, fishing, and horticultural lifestyle in their respective territories. Today there are some ten thousand indigenous people in Madre de Dios belonging to seven different linguistic families and nineteen different ethnolinguistic groups.

The 1970s was a period of increasing gold mining activity on riverine and inland areas of alluvial deposits. By the end of the decade this "gold rush" reached its peak as the price of gold soared on the international market

(Gray, 1997). Much of the gold production, which still continues today, relies on cheap labor in the form of underemployed and landless *serranos* (predominantly highlanders from the Cuzco area, many of whom are monolingual Quechua speakers). The total population of the region today is estimated to be around 49,000, of which the majority is concentrated in the department capital of Puerto Maldonado. However, there are increasing numbers of permanent settlements along the banks of the main rivers. Today 70 percent of the gold exploitation is by transitory *serrano* and *mestizo* (mixed descent) migrants using artisan methods, and 30 percent by Peruvian and transnational companies using mechanization in the form of bulldozers and river dredgers (CAAAP, 1992).

The price of gold declined through the 1980s, forcing the migrants to search for complementary sources of income. Successive governments have promoted the Madre de Dios as an area of huge potential for colonization and agriculture in attempts to ease urban and rural poverty on the coast and in the Andes. This has been a widespread policy for the Amazon which, as living conditions in Madre de Dios testify, is not synonymous with "development" in the sense of material improvement. Migration from the Andean region to both the coast and the rainforest was fuelled by the failure of the land reform in the 1970s, increasing oppression by both the Shining Path guerilla movement and the military, and drug-trafficking-related violence.

Governments see the natural resources of Madre de Dios—timber, cattle, gold, and oil—as sources of revenue for servicing the international debt.[1] In 1996 Mobil began oil exploration in two areas of Madre de Dios, one inhabited by voluntarily isolated peoples and the other on the indigenous territory of the Arakmbut people.[2]

Increasing demand in rural areas throughout the 1980s led to a quantitative expansion in the provision of primary schooling in Madre de Dios, though secondary schools remained concentrated in the urban centers. The existing system is characterized by authoritarian and bureaucratic relations between levels of the educational hierarchy (e.g., inspectors/teachers and teachers-pupils/parents). The majority of teachers are mestizos who have a high turnover rate in rural areas where those with least experience are sent and often work in multigrade or single-teacher schools. They closely follow the national curriculum using standard textbooks which have an urban focus and make no reference to the rainforest in general or Madre de Dios in particular. Teaching methods are teacher-centered and learning very passive, with end-of-year grade promotion exams leading to a high rate of repetition and drop-out (Aikman, 1994).

In 1991, concern for qualitative improvement in education brought together a range of interest groups: the local education and health authorities; continuing education institutions, secondary schools, and health services run by Dominican Catholics; the Catholic lay-missionary education service for indigenous communities; indigenous and environmental support nongovernmental organizations; and the representative indigenous federation of Madre de Dios. They deplored the numbers of young people who were acquiring educational qualifications but were not being equipped for any of the jobs available in the region or who were without the appropriate training to allow them to benefit from the productive potential of the rich natural resources of Madre de Dios (CAAAP, 1992).

The new education policy calls for an education system that promotes education for work and intercultural dialogue. Education for work is interpreted as training for existing occupations in the region (such as mechanics, shopkeepers, or small-scale entrepreneurs) and the provision of competencies, skills, and attitudes to design and implement transformational industries. The policy calls for schooling that promotes communal dialogue, planning, and decision making so as to contribute to economic development and increased economic returns and investment in Madre de Dios. It is hoped that in turn this will have a positive effect on the quality and provision of social services and facilities. The policy appears to set great store by intercultural dialogue based on more equitable and democratic practices between the indigenous Amazonian, serrano, and mestizo populations (as well as between these and the state) and sees it as the key to an active and creative search for new alternatives for the economic development of the region (CAAAP, 1992).

THE NATURE OF DEVELOPMENT IN MADRE DE DIOS

Considering Madre de Dios in relation to Peru as a whole, the region bears many of the hallmarks of what Casanova and Stavenhagen term internal colonialism: "a metropolis-satellite structure within countries [that] constitutes a kind of internal colonialism which is strengthened by the political power structure and, in some nations, by the inter-ethnic relations between different segments of the population" (Kay, 1989). The relations between the resource extraction in Madre de Dios and the urban metropolis of Lima reflect the dynamics of internal colonialism, while the relations between social and ethnic groups are characterized by the "domination of one ethnocultural group by another largely through extra-economic coercion" (Kay, 1989). Social and economic relations in Madre de Dios reflect the ethnic hierarchical relations between mestizo, serrano, and indigenous Amazonians.

The serranos who form the main labor force for gold production, receive wages below subsistence level, have no political participation or labor rights, and have restricted access to health provision. Others are involved with non-capitalist forms of colonial relations: many of these laborers, or *peones*, become indebted to mestizo *patrones* (bosses) and find themselves enmeshed in debt bondage[3] (*enganche*). The indigenous Amazon peoples suffer discrimination, human rights abuses, the destruction of their territory by illegal settlers, gold panners, and loggers, and the consequent depletion of forest and river resources on which they depend. Their rights to their legally titled territories are flouted by serranos and mestizos alike and they are denied access to their rivers at gunpoint. They do some gold panning on their lands, but work in kin groups, not for *patrones*.

Of the economic wealth produced through primary resource extraction, little has been reinvested in the Madre de Dios. Thus development in Madre de Dios is hierarchical, authoritarian, and extractive, characteristics reflected in the education system. Fortunes have been made during the booms of natural resource extraction in Madre de Dios by people from outside who move in when economic opportunities abound and move out again when opportunities dry up. Similarly, the economically and politically powerful elites use the education facilities in Madre de Dios as they suit them. Those with the economic power "extract" their children from the local education system and send them for secondary and higher education to Lima, where it is considered of higher quality and status. For the people whose lives are rooted in Madre de Dios, the indigenous peoples and landless migrants, moving away is not an option; they must live with the consequences of the economic exploitation and with schooling which is nothing but a poor reflection of the urban, middle-class mestizo education provided in Lima.

DEVELOPING THE HUMAN-RESOURCE POTENTIAL OF MADRE DE DIOS

Today, destructive natural-resource exploitation continues, as do the abuses of human rights and indigenous rights and contraventions of the Peruvian constitution. Since the 1970s, however, there have been changes in the guise of the capitalism which promotes this "development." At the beginning of the 1980s, after a decade of revolutionary socialism, the Peruvian government embarked upon a trajectory of monetarist economic policy and free-market principles. Foreign bank lending and foreign and private investment soared, although raw material prices dropped (Poole and Renique, 1992).

Puerto Maldonado was a frontier town in the early 1980s; the main street was lined with timber-built stores selling sacks of rice, dried Andean potatoes (*chuna*), and picks and shovels. At that time the natural resources were exploited by a primarily serrano labor force. After an economic dip in the mid- to late 1980s, it is thriving again, as witnessed in the plastic-clad fast-food restaurants and growing numbers of hi-fi and computer shops. As a growing administrative center, it has a flourishing finance sector and both a fast growing urban middle class and fast growing slum areas inhabited by unemployed or underemployed mestizo migrants, a reflection of the dramatic influence on the poor of neoliberal public spending cuts. Today relations between different indigenous, ethnic, and social groups in Madre de Dios present a complex picture, although the exploitation of serrano *peones* by Quechua urban elites in gold production in the 1970s indicates that these were never clear-cut homogeneous groups and, conversely, that debt peonage and child slavery continue (CODEH-PA, 1983).

Over the last few years new alliances and relationships have been established between different sectors of civil society, for example, between indigenous and agriculturalists' organizations. The spread of municipal government has produced, on the one hand, new opportunities for democratic representation and, on the other, new levels of political corruption and hegemony. New horizontal relationships are being forged, for example, between indigenous and nonindigenous Brazil nut gatherers and rubber tappers, to fight a common exploitation and injustice.

The next section investigates the contributions of the mestizos, serranos, and indigenous Amazon peoples to the new education policy call for alternative developments. Their perspectives on education and development will be examined in terms of the way they perceive their relations with the natural environment, their vision for the future, and the place of formal education in their lives.

MESTIZOS–BRINGING DEVELOPMENT
TO THE RAINFOREST

Mestizo means "mixed" and is a residual category applied to people of mixed racial descent who do not consider themselves serranos (from the Andes) and are not indigenous to the rainforest. The mestizo population is ethnically heterogenous, but is predominantly urban based. While the mestizo middle and lower classes are growing rapidly in Puerto Maldonado, there is also an expanding mestizo migrant population of dynamic, individualistic, enterprising individuals who have been influential in establishing growing settlements in the "outback." These settlers see themselves as pushing forward the frontiers of a modern world in a pioneering attempt to build better futures for themselves and their families than seem possible in the economically depressed coastal towns of Peru whence they came. The success of the trading, agriculture, and timber extraction in which they are involved hinges on improving communications and achieving support for infrastructural facilities. In the municipal center of Boca Colorado, mestizo settlers are lobbying for a new road link with the main gold extraction area of Huaypetue in order to market agricultural produce, and for electricity, solid cement housing, sewage, sanitation, and running water to bring a permanence and dignity to their new settlement and lives.

They are "opening up" the rainforest, "bringing development" to the area. While central government lack of efficiency and local government corruption frustrates them, the majority support President Fujimori's neoliberal aims for the spread of a free market and foreign investment (Gray, 1997). Breaking the economic isolation of Madre de Dios from the rest of Peru is a priority for most mestizo inhabitants, be they urban or rural. Plans for a transamazon highway linking Pacific and Atlantic coasts has long been a goal of the main extractive companies and traders, a goal which may become a reality with outside investment. Consequently, mestizo development plans (be they individual settler, private sector investor, or government official) focus on the development of the economic extractive potential of Madre de Dios.

In Boca Colorado, schooling is one of a range of institutions that symbolize the arrival of development (civilization) to the rainforest and is considered an investment by mestizo parents so that their children can "improve themselves" and aspire to the urban middle-class values and material wealth promoted in the classroom. The hierarchy of the education system reflects the hierarchies in society; education is to help their children progress up the social and economic ladder, a meritocratic means to a better chance in life. To this end mestizo parents have clubbed together to supplement teachers' salaries and to contribute towards their board and lodgings to encourage them to stay in this insanitary settlement perched on the edge of the forest and river.

SERRANOS–COLONIZATION IN AN ANTISOCIAL JUNGLE[4]

The serranos' relationship with the environment is embedded in their relations as indigenous peoples with land and identity. The rainforest has always been part of the Quechua world; the Incas called it Antisuyu and there is evidence throughout history of a widespread trade between the Andes and the lowland forests. For the serranos in the Andes or the rainforest, the environment is sacred and animated and "frames life" (Skar, 1994). The serranos in the rainforest are part of a whole identity and wider territory that is bound together by ties of ritual kinship and shared identity. However, the rainforest is associated with wild, antisocial, subterranean forces competing with the orderliness of agriculture. The natural environment of the rainforest is something that has to be conquered and tamed because its natural forces sap physical strength and have a corroding effect on health.

In the Madre de Dios, serranos who manage to break free of *patrones*, or who arrive in the region independently in search of land, clear the forest to grow maize and tend some animals and perhaps pan some gold. Some clear land on indigenous titled territory, usually unaware of the status of the land or because they do not consider the *chunchos* to be farmers, but rather people who "live off the forest like animals" (Skar, 1994). Thus, the serranos define their lives in the rainforest in terms of their relationship with the sierra and mother earth, *Pachamama*. Their identity as Quechua comes from their relationship with their kin and their Andean highland environment, which is for them a sacred landscape in which agriculture is the epitome of a well-ordered and functioning world (Skar, 1994).

Many of the serranos have had no schooling and come originally from small isolated highland communities. In the Madre de Dios, they continue to live relatively isolated lives in small shacks along the river banks. If there is a nearby settlement, they may send their children to school there, but many consider the schools in indigenous communities as inferior (Wahaipe Pukiri, 1992). In general, there is not a great demand for schooling, because it is not seen as reflecting their Quenchua values or providing access to a useful body of knowledge. Moreover, those who can, send their older children to live with their extended families in the Andes and to attend school there.

THE INDIGENOUS PEOPLES—PROTECTING THE LAND FOR FUTURE GENERATIONS

One of the largest original peoples in the region, the Arakmbut provide an illustration of another relationship with the rainforest environment and aspirations for the future. The Arakmbut number one thousand and live in five communities situated at large distances from each other over their traditional territory. Their communities have legally titled areas of land for their hunting, gathering, and gardening pursuits, but the official piece of paper offers no protection from incursions by colonists or companies denuding the land of its profitable hardwoods, deforesting for cattle ranching, or from the work stations and depots of large national and international oil exploration companies.

The indigenous peoples are deeply troubled by the destruction of the rainforest because it implies not only a destruction and loss of resources such as wild meat (peccary, tapir, monkey, large rodents), fish stocks, building materials, and edible forest fruits and plants, but it signifies a breakdown of their relationship with a territory and its resources, both physical and spiritual. Hunting and fishing are fundamental activities for the Arakmbut, not simply in terms of the source of food they provide, but because of the relations that the hunters and fishers establish with the animal species and, through them, with the invisible world of the spirits (Aikman, 1994).

For the Arakmbut their territory (*wandari*) binds the visible and spirit worlds. For the Arakmbut it is not only the law which legitimizes their collective ownership of the land, but the invisible spirit world (Gray, 1996). The Arakmbut consider themselves the guardians of their *wandari*, which they hold in trust for future generations. They have no word for "development" and they do not talk of their children's futures in terms of "progress" or economic growth. They do not focus on productive activities without reference to their social and spiritual dimensions, dimensions which give gardening, hunting, and fishing meaning.

They want to be able to participate in the wider society and welcome formal education and Western medicine to help them combat change imposed from outside. They have schools that, above all, give them status in the eyes of the serranos, mestizos, and missionaries, and official recognition as "native communities" by the state. They see the schools as providing their children with Spanish, which they need in order to help defend their lands and to negotiate with traders. In order to have their own educated people (e.g., sociologists, economists), they have supported several youths in studies in Lima. They are supportive of the development of an intercultural education which is qualitative and relevant and provides them with access to higher tiers of formal education. But they want it also to respect and reinforce their own educational practices and processes (Aikman, 1994).

EDUCATION FOR DEVELOPMENT—CULTURAL PERCEPTIONS OF THE ECONOMY

The Arakmbut and indigenous peoples of the Amazon have a relationship with the environment that is intrinsically different from that held by both the mestizos and the serranos. We could discuss whether this indigenous relationship implies an "alternative development" by those on the periphery in search of visibility, participation, and justice (Hettne, 1992) or an "alternative to development" that rejects the entire development paradigm, is critical of established scientific knowledge, and focuses on local autonomy, culture, and knowledge (Escobar, 1995). However, the Arakmbut talk in terms of the need for their "self-development." This is a total phenomenon which cannot be defined only in terms of economics, politics, or culture. As with all indigenous sociocultural formations, indigenous self-development has to be seen as a whole, covering many different areas. Unless the terms of development are defined by the people themselves, then there is no self-development (Henriksen, 1989).

Indigenous Amazonian self-development is respectful of the environment and knowledgeable of its diversity and fragility. The spirit world regulates the use of its resources, bringing sickness to individuals, families, and communities if transgressed. Relations with the land and its resources are not governed by competition and individualism, but based on collective access and use. The Arakmbut are not "owners" of the land; they have legal communal title to their territory and maintain it as its guardians for future Arakmbut generations.

The serranos, trying to reproduce Andean agricultural patterns in the rainforest, do not present a model for sustainable development in Madre de Dios, nor do they relate to the environment in capitalist economic terms. As Gose (1994) explains, when a body is buried, energy is released from the soul, which travels to the mountains where it provides water, enabling crops to grow. Through the "death" or soul-loss that arises from hard labor, men provide the energy to plant or bury seeds irrigated by water from the mountains. Their relationship with the land is a complex spiritual relationship in which their identity is embedded. However, their taming of the lowland forest and its "wild antisocial forces" is ultimately destructive of the forest.

While we acknowledge the lack of attention to the heterogeneity of the category of mestizo, we can, nevertheless, identify in this group a broad adherence to capitalism, the inevitability of progress, and of economic development as the means of achieving it. From the company director or bank manager in Puerto Maldonado to the pioneer at Boca Colorado, "getting ahead" and "doing well" are common goals achieved, or at least aspired to, through the capitalist economic system. Economic development is the route to improved social conditions and material comfort.

The three relationships exemplified by the indigenous, serrano, and mestizo groups with the environment and its development can be termed self-development, dependency, and modernization, respectively. The mestizo modernization is an economic model in which formal education has an important part to play in terms of acquiring certificates and qualifications that allow access to higher rungs of the hierarchy. The new education policy's emphasis on education for work and developing local human resources, as well as greater local relevance of the curriculum, is completely compatible with their capitalist aspirations. The policy's focus on breaking hierarchical ethnic and social relations through participation and intercultural dialogue, however, is not a mestizo priority.

The serrano model of development is embedded in a structural shortage of land in the highlands and, for the *peones*, in an exploitative dependency in the rainforest. Formal education is not central to realizing their aspirations for the future or an understanding of their own philosophy of relations between the natural and spiritual world. Serranos in search of a humble subsistence are following a path that will ultimately lead to the destruction of the environment, the direct exploitation of which is at present the basis of their existence, and where the rainforest itself is seen as the problem to be overcome (Norgaard, 1990). Nevertheless, there are some nonformal educational efforts being directed at overcoming this contradiction. The federation of agriculturalists (FADEMAD) is providing training for serrano settlers to introduce them to alternative agricultural practices that are more suited to the rainforest soils than their traditional Andean horticulture. These practices use local crop varieties and are not aimed at monoculture for commercialization, but at using the biodiversity to facilitate a sustainable subsistence agriculture. The majority of land-seeking serranos aspire to a well-ordered and functioning subsistence agriculture, which is only possible in the rainforest through agricultural practices suited to the region.

Conversely, the indigenous peoples want formal education to facilitate and strengthen their participation and representation in institutions in mestizo society, but primarily to be able to use these institutions and processes to break their own dependency on outsiders and for their own ends, which are the realization of self-development and the future integrity of the rainforest. However, formal education alone will not lead to self-development. It is not taught in schools, but learned and practiced through informal indigenous learning practices and the knowledge of the elders.

TENSIONS BETWEEN ECONOMIC DEVELOPMENT AND CULTURE

The new education policy states that it rejects the authoritative and hierarchical education system oriented to the maintenance and preservation of a development that is exploitative of both the environment and people. On the contrary, it promotes equality, social justice, and participation and has a strong faith in the contribution that formal education can make to the development of appropriate skills and knowledge. Education is seen as the means of fostering a development for and by the people of Madre de Dios themselves.

But what kind of development is this? To what extent is it an alternative to the modernization paradigm currently prevalent and reinforced through the school system? The new education policy talks of respect for the environment, alongside maximizing economic growth which is potentially destructive of the same environment. What of the potential of intercultural dialogue for producing alternative developments? In a region rich in cultural diversity, the new education policy advocates intercultural dialogue, yet denies the possibilities for this to happen. The policy is based on a misconception that economic growth is the universal basis of all development. Economic development is taken unquestioningly as a neutral, culture-free baseline common to all societies and their philosophies, yet, as we have seen, the serranos and indigenous peoples have alternative relations with the land, that derive from very different epistemologies and not from an economic relationship with the environment based on individualism and profit-making. Both serranos and indigenous peoples have a multidimensional relationship with the land that cannot be reduced to economics and to economic exploitation. Neither are maximizing the land's potential and neither talk of progress. Consequently, there is no common ground for intercultural dialogue.

For the mestizos, the new education policy for Madre de Dios details proposals that are coherent with their perception of the role of education as improving human resources and economic activities within an encompassing capitalist growth model of development. The same policy, however, is limited in what it can offer the serranos, who do not confront the world around them in terms of maximizing production and progress. Nevertheless, like the indigenous peoples, the serranos are making increasing use of the formal education system embedded in a capitalist model in order to acquire skills and knowledge with which to break out of a dependency on neoliberal economic development. For the indigenous peoples the new education policy will remain ultimately subordinate to their own "informal" learning practices until they acquire the self-determination they desire to develop an intercultural education that addresses the nature of the intercultural lives they lead.

The serrano population did not participate in the education policy-making discussions, as they have no representative political organization in Madre de Dios. The indigenous peoples, with their representative organization, FENAMAD, did take part, and we may assume that references to the educational needs and situation of the indigenous peoples and the proposals for intercultural dialogue in the policy are, to some degree, a reflection of their participation. But what is the future potential of intercultural dialogue if it takes place in an unequal and hierarchical society in which neoliberal economics determine the distribution of power?

To consider the implementation of the new education policy, a seminar on "Methodology for the Design of an Alternative Curriculum" was convened in December 1991 in Puerto Maldonado. The meeting was organized and controlled by members of the Madre de Dios mestizo educational establishment. In the course of the three-day meeting, the indigenous representative organization, although represented and participating in the meeting, was sidelined and there was only one fleeting reference made to the educational needs and aspirations of the indigenous peoples.

CONCLUSION

This chapter has illustrated that in the Madre de Dios, people's aspirations for education are intimately bound up with the nature of the development in which they believe. Thus, for the mestizo population, development is perceived in terms of economic progress and improved social conditions, where education has an important role to play in access to higher social strata through qualifications and certificates. The serrano population provides a different perception of development, deriving from their complex and contradictory relationship with the land in the "hostile" rainforest environment. Formal education is not central to achieving their aims, which are to practice a well-ordered and functioning subsistence agriculture. However, without nonformal educational interventions in alternative agricultural practices, they are embarked on an ultimately destructive course. The indigenous peoples, on the contrary, are knowledgeable of the forest's diverse resources and base their self-development on collective access and use. Their own educational practices promote a respectful sustainable management of the environment, but they are increasingly in need of formal education that can support them in their struggle to protect the territories from the ravages of both mestizo maximizing exploitation and serrano agricultural practices.

This examination of the Madre de Dios education policy proposal has illustrated how education systems and their aims and objectives do not stand "above" theories of development. On the contrary, the new education proposal itself is embedded in a particular development theory; it calls for alternatives to an extractive development which is exploitative and destructive, but it limits new development possibilities to those available within a neoliberal economics discourse. For the proposal to lay the foundations for alternative developments in Madre de Dios, there must also be a recognition of the validity of alternative conceptions of education based on different ways of perceiving the relations with the natural environment and different epistemologies. Before the education system can be the focus for alternative developments, policy makers must be aware of the ideological and paradigmatical bases of the development discourse in which they are immersed. Alternative education practices and aims are thus intimately linked with different conceptions of development, not independent of them.

In Madre de Dios, alternatives to economic development are practiced by the least powerful groups in society, the serranos and the indigenous peoples. We are left pondering the possibilities for a meaningful participation of these peoples in future education policy-making processes, given that their alternatives hold no legitimacy in Madre de Dios discourse. The old internal colonial hierarchy has undermined the promise of intercultural dialogue and the monologue of economic development has swept away any real possibilities of an alternative development in Madre de Dios for the time being.

NOTES

1. The multilateral banks have played a key role in influencing the economic and political dynamics of development in rainforest regions by promoting cattle projects, capital-intensive agriculture, and colonization projects (Rich, 1990).
2. For details of the environmental effects of ranching, agro-forestry, cash cropping, and oil exploration in the Amazon, see Gelber, 1992; Johnson *et al.*, 1989; and Kimerling, 1993.
3. The form this takes in the Amazon can be termed *coercive peonage*, which relied on the existence of semi-autonomous pockets controlled by companies that scarcely acknowledge the national political regime, which allows abuses to go unchecked and unreported (Knight, 1988).
4. This section relies heavily on the work of Skar (1994), whose investigations into Quechua colonization in the rainforest, unlike many other studies, approaches an understanding of Quechua conceptualization of the rainforest.

REFERENCES

Aikman, S. (1994). "Intercultural Education and Harakmbut Identity: A Case Study of the Community of San Jose in Southeastern Peru." Unpublished Ph.D. thesis, University of London.

Aikman, S. (1995). "Territory, Indigenous Education and Cultural Maintenance: The Case of the Arakmbut of Southeast Peru." *Prospects* 25(4), pp. 665–681.

Centro Amazónico de Antropología y Aplicación Practica (CAAAP). (1992). *Propuesta de Politica Educativa: Sub-region de Madre de Dios*. Lima: Centro Amazónico de Antropología y Aplicación Práctica.

Chiodi. F. (compiler). (1990). *La Educación Indígena en America Latina: México, Guatemala, Ecuador: Perú, Bolivia*. 2 vols. Santiago: Abya-Yala.

Comite de Defensa de Iso Derechos Humanos de las Provincias Altas (CODEHPA). (1983). *La Selva y su Ley: Lavaderos de Oro*. Sicuani: Comite de Defensa de los Derechos Humanos de las Provincias Altas.

Escobar, A. (1995). "Imagining a Post-Development Era." In *Power of Development*, J. Crush (ed.). London: Routledge.

Gelber, G. (1992). "Land Rights and Land Reform." In *Poverty and Power: Latin America after 500 Years*, G. Gelber (ed). London: Cafod.

Gose, P. (1994). *Deathly Waters and Hungry Mountains: Agrarian Ritual and Class Formation in an Andean Village*. Toronto: Anthropological Horizons.

Gray, A. (1997). *Indigenous Rights and Development: Self-Determination in an Amazonian Community*, Oxford: Berghahn.

Gray, A. (1996). *Mythology, Spirituality and History: The Arakmbut of Amazonian Peru*. Oxford: Berghahn.

Henriksen, G. (1989). "Introduction." In *Indigenous Self-Development in the Americas*. Amsterdam: International Work Group for Indigenous Affairs.

Hettne, B. (1992). *Development Theory and the Three Worlds*. 2nd ed. Harlow: Longman.

Johnston, C., Knowles, R. and Colchester, M. (1989). *Rainforests: Land Use Options for Amazonia*. London: Oxford University Press and WorldWide Fund for Nature, UK, in association with Survival International.

Kay, C. (1989). *Latin American Theories of Development and Underdevelopment*. London: Routledge.

Kimerling, J. (1993). *Crudo Amazonico*. Quito: Abya Yala.

Knight, A. (1988). "Debt Bondage in Latin America." In *Slavery and Other Forms of Unfree Labor*. L. Archer (ed.). London: Routledge.

Norgaard, R. (1990). "The Development of Tropical Rainforest Economics." In *Lessons of the Rainforest*, S. Head and R. Heinzman (eds.). San Francisco: Sierra Club Books.

Poole, D. and Renique, G. (1992). *Peru: Time of Fear*, London: Latin American Bureau.

Rich, B. (1990). "Multilateral Development Banks and Tropical Deforestation." In *Lessons of the Rainforest*, S. Head and R. Heinzman (eds.). San Francisco: Sierra Club Books.

Rivero, J. (1993). *Educación de Adultos en América Latina: Desafíos de la Equidad y la Modernización*. Lima: Tarea Asociación de Publicaciones Educativas.

Skar, S. (1994). *Lives Together—Worlds Apart: Quechua Colonization of Jungle and City*. Oslo Studies in Social Anthropology. Oslo: Scandinavian University Press.

CHAPTER 16

Public Policies on Gender and Education in Paraguay: The Project for Equal Opportunities

Carmen Colazo

Introduction: The History of Gender Equity in Public Policy in Paraguay*

Paraguay is a small country sandwiched between Argentina and Brazil in the center of South America. It has experienced long periods of isolation, which have favored a nationalist culture with prolonged stages of authoritarian centralization. Historically, it has suffered under severe dictatorships, which have left rigid patriarchal patterns that are difficult to modify in the medium term.

Despite the rigid patriarchy, women reconstructed the country after the two great wars, which decimated the masculine population. First, after the War of the Triple Alliance (1870) with Argentina, Brazil, and Uruguay, where boys as young as twelve years old were killed. Later, in the war against Bolivia, or the Chaco War (1935), that leaves a recent memory of a country populated by women. But women never took advantage of these situations to take more power or protagonistic positions. They continued with their daily work, promoting men in public and visible leadership positions.

The periods of greater freedom for Paraguayan women coincided with historical stages of the advance of feminism internationally. There was a

---

*In the text; various articles from the National Constitution of the Republic of Paraguay have been cited. Official Edition, Spanish and Guaraní, June 1992.

large public campaign to win women's vote at the beginning of the century, and the campaign was finally won in the 1960s, under the dictatorship of General Alfredo Stroessner Matiauda. Finally, since 1987, women's organizations, as social movements, have been consolidating around working for legislative change, for quotas in decision-making positions, and for a Women's Secretariat at the ministerial level.[1]

For the first time since the coup on February 3, 1989, that overthrew the Stroessner dictatorship that lasted for more than thirty-five years, the country finds itself in a transition toward democracy that is not without difficulties. After General Andrés Rodríguez (1989–1993), Stroessner's son-in-law, was removed by force, the first free elections in years were planned and an electoral agenda was organized that included constitutional reform.

The country's first democratic constitution was passed in June 1992, and it included as many of the demands as the organized women could get included. Later, the country was run for the first time in decades by a civilian leader, Juan Carlos Wasmosy (1993–1998). Important gender issues were addressed within this emerging democratic framework. For the first time, during the government of General Rodríguez, a woman headed up a ministry when Cintya Prieto was the Minister of Health and Social Welfare from November 17, 1989, until 1993.

That government administration addressed women's issues within the National Development Plan, and women's organizations played an active role in the development of laws and the promotion of specific public policies. The First Civil Code developed by a feminist organization, the Women's Coordination of Paraguay, was passed in 1992, with minor modifications by the legislature. The women fought for a participation quota of no more than 60 percent for either sex in decision-making posts, but won only a 20 percent women's quota in the 1995 Electoral Code reform, by pressure from another organization: the Network of Political Women. This group also proposed the law to create the Women's Secretariat at the ministerial level, which was instituted under Law 34 of 1992.

The Wasmosy government formed the Women's Secretariat in 1993. The first minister was Cristina Muñoz, who, despite competing against the daughter of President Rodríguez, obtained the post because of her ability, her political involvement, her commitment to gender issues, and the support of an important sector of Paraguayan women. The Women's Secretariat has now been functioning for more than six years.

Through its Education Office, the Secretariat began to organize, coordinate, and monitor the country's gender equity policies. It was difficult, however, to get the Ministry of Education and Culture (MEC) to support the dissemination of these new contents and practices. Initially, it was practically impossible to work intersectorally in this area. The Women's Secretariat designed a project of equality of opportunities and results for women in education, emulating the Argentine Program of Equal Opportunities for Women (PRIOM). The idea was that MEC would implement the project and be one of its beneficiaries. The project was designed and structured with the advice and support of the former head of the Argentine PRIOM, Gloria Bonder, working with Carmen Colazo, the head of the Paraguayan Education Office of the Women's Secretariat.

This was the beginning of PRIOME, the Project for Equal Opportunities and Results for Women in Education, which embodied the primary political and strategic objective of the Secretariat, to work for interinstitutional gender equity policies in education. The Secretariat was aware that the educational reform, which had been in process since 1990, could not continue moving forward without broad, clear, and concrete support for gender, and the only institution that could do this efficiently was the Women's Secretariat, as the coordinator of the state's gender equity policies.

The educational reform was initiated by presidential decree 7.815 on November 26, 1990, with the formation of an Advisory Council. Of the twelve founding members of the Council, only two were women, and currently there is only one women member. None of the women have had experience in gender issues.[2]

The national educational reform incorporates equality of opportunity between men and women in its educational goals. But it does not speak of coeducation, nor does it mention gender as a broad-reaching component, but instead speaks of "family education." It has been conceived of and implemented from the Ministry of Education and Culture with criteria of complementarity between the sexes for marriage, the affirmation of the traditional role assigned to women, and other concepts and practices considered discriminatory from the feminist position.

This demonstrates that at the level of public policy, there is still a lack of understanding or acceptance of the significance of gender in education and its consequences for individual and social development. There is not an understanding of its true human and political dimension, or its support for the analysis of social inequalities and the value of its integration in the solution of social inequalities. The existence of this gender component in Paraguayan public policy is more linked to the people who are committed to gender and who find themselves in certain positions where they can push it. There is not a global concept at the state level or strategic criteria about gender.

It is common to find within national public policies that certain ministries, institutes, or state offices are given to certain party sectors, power factions, or pressure groups. This makes national policy a difficult puzzle to put together, with compartmentalized and sometimes even contradictory characteristics, which can be understood only by taking into account the complexity of the distribution and exercise of power.

The Catholic Church has had, and continues to have, significant influence in Paraguayan educational policies. The 1992 constitution, which for the first time separates church and state, and leaves behind the confessional church and official religion, also recognizes and expressly thanks the Catholic Church for its support of national culture. This institution has demonstrated its power both by holding posts in the Ministry of Education and Culture, by proposing people linked to the church for positions of minister and vice minister, as well as by participating in the formulation of educational policies. The Educational Reform Council, an autonomous consulting body, which is responsible for the reform's "philosophy," has a majority of members who are recognized in Paraguay for their contribution to education and close links to the Catholic Church. Several of them are, or have been, priests. The educational reform reflects the religious position of the Council and the Ministry, and reinforces the population's cultural traditions, which have visible feudal and patriarchal characteristics. These coexist with the modernizing tendencies of globalization and its demands. The reform has also had critical support from the World Bank and Harvard University, which have also influenced its tendencies to promote educational criteria emphasizing labor needs, in accordance with current neoliberal and globalization demands.

THE PRIOME PROJECT AND THE PRIOME PROGRAM

The PRIOME Project was designed within the Women's Secretariat, thanks to initial Swedish Cooperation and later support from the Spanish International Cooperation Agency (AECI), which helped to implement the project. An accord between the Paraguayan and Spanish governments established shared tasks to put into practice article 48 of the constitution, which addresses equality between men and women.

A Tripartie Commission was organized between the Women's Secretariat, the Spanish International Cooperation Agency, and the Technical Planning Secretary in order to decide on activities and budget. The PRIOME Project was the cornerstone from which the Women's Secretariat could initiate direct conversations with the Ministry of Education and Culture to initiate and Equal Opportunity Program for Women in Education, to develop four priority areas: (a) curricular reform with a gender component; (b) review and analysis of texts and materials from a gender perspective; (c) teacher training in gender; and (d) raising the awareness of public opinion around the importance of the inclusion of gender in education.

Thus began in the country an institutional process to slowly introduce a gender focus in education. It also introduced a different experience of working together through the gender specialist team within the country linked to the feminist movement and to nongovernment organizations, working together with state technicians and teachers.

The PRIOME Project initiated an Inter-ministerial Accord between the Women's Secretariat and the Ministry of Education and Culture, which initiated the program of the same name. The program became part of the Curriculum Department of the MEC, which designs the Ministry's basic educational policies, through an office that includes a technical operating unit with a director and two consultants, one a gender specialist and one an education specialist. The PRIOME Program has the specific function of fulfilling the cross-curricular component of gender in Paraguayan education, as expressed in the accord signed by the Minister of Women and the Minister of Education and Culture.

PRIOME PROJECT ACHIEVEMENTS IN SHARED WORK WITH THE PROGRAM

The project teams organized working plans around the educational reform implementation, to work with it and enrich it with gender support. The project's members worked with the Ministry of Education and Culture to build contacts with those responsible for the respective areas and to try to introduce suggestions for the curriculum, for teacher training with directors, teachers, and trainers, as well as for texts and materials. They developed analysis matrices in each of the project areas and theoretical documents addressing the areas, taking into account gender considerations and indicators. Listed below are the most important achievements of this part of the project:

1. Began to work interinstitutionally in order to establish gender across the curriculum in the educational system, within an education that is accustomed to speak in masculine terms to identify all people, and which has not taken into account dignity and equality of rights between men and women as a priority—and even less has considered respect for differences—in the context of a pluriethnic and multicultural country that has only just begun to weakly leave behind excluding nationalism.
2. Initiated a change in curricular images and content, giving suggestions to modify the absence of women from history and science, and in general, highlighting women's diverse contributions to culture, in contrast to the traditional and stereotyped image of woman as mother, daughter, symbol of the homeland, teacher, partner in procreation and patroness supporting great achievements of men.
3. Analyzed the transmission through educational practices of hatred, love, care, generosity, evil, activity, and inactivity. Identify who was assigned which roles and why, and what have been the cultural consequences; and develop analysis matrices so that teachers and others who work in nonformal or informal education can identify them and work to change them.
4. Collaborated in buying books and materials, reviewing them from a gender perspective, and making clear and concrete suggestions for change.
5. Structured and developed a gender module, together with another on sexuality, within the teaching training of more than fifteen hundred directors, teachers, workers in the educational system, and trainers from teachers training centers. During these modules, issues were addressed that were almost considered taboo within the traditionalist, stereotyped and rigid cultural structure as manifested in curriculum, texts, and so on.

6. Initiated a debate about sexuality—a taboo issue within Paraguayan culture, resisted in the education sphere—beginning with dialogue about gender and heterosexuality, and eventually talking openly and respectfully about different sexual identities. This motivated, on the teachers' part, the sharing of experiences within their educational practices, in terms of issues brought up by girls and boys about their homosexuality and with respect to other sexual identities, not in terms of the abnormal, the prohibited, the dirty, the ugly, but from the powerlessness of ignorance, perceived rejection, or the shame of teaching what they do not know enough about or about which they have their own preconceptions. There was a positive dialogue with teachers of both sexes around the reasons that there are statistically high levels of sexual confusion among young people and adults in a society that hides and prohibits free speech about these experiences. Participants also looked at why there is a problem with teenage pregnancy, as early as twelve years old in rural areas, as well as other problems in a world bombarded by media images of sex, without the possibility for children to dialogue with adults who can listen, understand, and help them.[3]

7. Wore down existing resistance to coeducation within the teaching force and to see how, little by little, interest was piqued in knowing more about it and putting it into practice.

8. Noted how the Guaraní have a hard time translating certain Spanish words that describe the reproductive apparatus, which leads to jokes in class, and how teachers would rather tear pages out of books than pronounce certain words to their students, and how understanding the language issues can help in understanding the problem and finding possible solutions.[4]

9. Debated why girls are not encouraged to study math and science, but are pushed to play with dolls, to practice domestic tasks and the roles of wife and mother. Why boys are at the top of the list and girls appear at the end, without using an alphabetical ordering that would be nondiscriminatory, but where all, both boys and girls, equally suffer the violence of a hierarchical and authoritarian system that in many schools is translated into physical blows against students "so that they will learn."

10. The project was able to plan the incorporation of gender in education for a five-year period and to organize instruments for monitoring and evaluation. At the same time, the project has also developed materials and texts to incorporate gender into education.

In sum, it was an achievement to have been able to address these issues with people from different social strata in the country, and to see how all of them participated in placing the intimate and daily into the public sphere. Throughout this process, international cooperation that is committed to incorporating gender into education has been critical, gambling on change and a future in democracy, providing experts and finance for the process.

OBSTACLES TO THE PRIOME PROJECT

One of the major obstacles that the project faced was the difficulty of changing ingrained bureaucratic MEC structures. This made it difficult for people from nongovernment sectors to understand certain indispensable hierarchical codes, like who writes a note and who signs it, and the power that these actions imply, which is often expressed in the outlook that expresses: What can they teach those of us who already know? All of this requires negotiations.

Another obstacle was the difficulty, for people from the private sector with their particular concept of work, of adjusting to the single preset schedule of officials who work in the public sector, as well as adjusting to their patterns and rhythms. For instance, the MEC did not have an annual plan, but organized activities throughout the year, which presented a major obstacle for the gender project work. Even the dress code seems to divide the two almost irreconcilable worlds: that of the formal world and that of the informal world.

It was also difficult for people to recognize the gender component as a questioner of women's traditional roles, within a socializing structure that considers mothers and teachers (second mothers) as almost sacred archetypes, and that understands women's classic role to be the best way to socialize boys and girls and to prepare them for future families. This attitude persists despite the articles in the constitution that speak of equality, no discrimination in education, and respect for different kinds of families (Article 46 on equality, Article 73 on education and culture, and Article 49 on the rights of the family).

At various times, the PRIOME team members faced a problem with dogmatic religious beliefs, whose proponents resisted the incorporation of the gender component. The team members even found that people within Family Education—the term used in the education reform—presented ideas of the complementarity of the sexes and antifeminism. They found these attitudes among authorities, teachers, and other people involved in the process. The most extreme example of these positions was found in the courses, where there were different opinions expressed that opposed the incorporation of a gender perspective in education, which are worth sharing.

Participants of both sexes offered reasons for not including the gender component in education. They said that the gender perspective goes against the Catholic religion and other religions for the following reasons: (a) it speaks of equal opportunities between men and women when men and women are not and should not be equal; (b) there cannot be equality because it goes against cultural norms established by religion; (c) the Bible expressly states that God the Father is male and that He created us, that Christ was also a man, and that Maria, his mother, had a specific role as woman-mother; (d) the Bible states that woman was made from the rib of man and thus is complementary to man, not superior to him; (e) women should remain in their places as wives and mothers and should not want to have other roles that would destory the family through their own fault, as is currently happening when mothers work outside of the home; (f) feminists are seeking women's superiority over men and they are foreigners and extremists who do not understand the country's culture; and (g) if girls and boys are educated with a gender focus, boys will become homosexuals when they do girls' activities, and girls will become tomboys when they do boys' activities. There was extreme fear that boys and girls would "become homosexuals" if nonsexist education was instituted.

Another interesting aspect for analysis was the teachers' difficulty in talking about sexual pleasure. It was noted that in almost all the images and concepts that are communicated in materials, texts, and classes about the genital organs, the feminine reproductive organs were not explained in detail because it was difficult to explain the functioning of some of the organs. There was fear that if teachers explained that the clitoris was an organ expressly for pleasure, this could imply that sex is pleasurable, which might provoke young people to engage in sexual relations and face serious problems of early pregnancy, "promiscuity," "immorality," and so on.

With respect to the debate that emerged around other sexual identities, there was also significant fear expressed by both men and women participants. They feared that they might influence the socialization process or push girls and boys into "premature" sexuality, or sexuality that is considered "abnormal" if they give them the opportunity to explore their sexuality with specific materials and texts.

The team also faced some resistance to the idea of interculturality. Participants questioned the fact that some consultants were of other nationalities. This occurred even though at the beginning of the course it was explained that international cooperation supported the project economically and it was also supported by the work of some experts at the Spanish Women's Institute and some young Spanish collaborators. At various times the participants insinuated that the gender issue was for other countries, not for Paraguay, and that is why foreigners had to come in to inculate them. However, not all people spoke this way, though a considerable number of teachers did.

We share these positions because they are the clearest expression of the reality that we confront when we introduce the gender component in Paraguayan education, and because they must be considered when analyzing the achievements and obstacles to incorporating into education feminism's beliefs in equal opportunity between men and women, respect for differences, and support of equitable human development.

LESSONS LEARNED AND FINAL CONCLUSIONS

The work carried out by me as the Women's Secretariat's leader, first as director of education, and later as a promoter for the PRIOME Program and designer of the PRIOME Project, offers some lessons that are worth sharing.

As we know, the incorporation of gender in education is an arduous task that will take many years. The educational system, as an agent of the socialization process, is generally structured to reinforce patriarchal and sexist cultural practices, not to change values, attitudes, and behaviors, and this is especially true in Latin America.

Public policies that seek to modify such entrenched cultural patterns are both necessary and revolutionary, but are strongly resisted by the dominant culture. The obstacles are powerful, and are expressed by the institutions or sectors with the greatest interest in preventing change, that is, by the most conservative elements of society.

The degree to which gender policies can be implemented, weakened, or disappear depends on the political-ideological sector holding state power at any one time. In Paraguay, this is fundamentally related to the state's religious or dictatorial commitment. The more the state tends toward religion or dictatorship, the more difficult it will be to implement gender policies, because: (a) the Church generally does not conceive of women as people with the same opportunities and rights as men, and they see in women's individual and social freedom the seeds of the destruction of the family because of the abandonment of traditional roles; and (b) Paraguayan populist dictators favor the preeminence of the military *caudillo* figure and strengthen classic feminine stereotypes that complement that image.

In addition, the degree to which schools are linked to religious or dictatorial criteria has a direct relation to their resistance to accepting gender concepts, even more so if we consider the possibility of inserting content that expresses people's right to have other sexual identities. Boys and girls who can feel, manifest, and/or define in themselves a different sexual identity will continue to be painfully discriminated against in this educational system, as are all those people who do not adjust to the norm.[5]

Another aspect to be pointed out is that international cooperation has generally favored the inclusion of the gender component and has almost obligated that it be included in order to get funding. However, when cooperation ends—since the funding is supposed to promote plans, programs, projects, but not to sustain them for many years—many of the programs will end. Efforts vanish and the people who implemented them get burned out.

That is why the PRIOME Project runs the risk of not having continuity if international cooperation ceases. The state does not appear to have emphasized its necessity and has not assigned the necessary budget to the program. But the strategy of organizing the national program and legitimizing it by an accord between ministries offers hope that not everything will be paralyzed and that work will continue.

Despite the insistence on and the training about the importance of incorporating a gender component in education to authorities and other involved sectors, the individuals and institutions involved did not internalize the idea that is part and parcel of the gender perspective, the sense of equity and social justice implied by gender. What is means, exactly, is that girls should have the same opportunities in the future as boys in Paraguay. We say that gender discrimination is cultural, and this ends up being an empty sentence.

Many strategies have yet to be considered, and much patience is needed to continue fighting against the trends: from avoiding conflict and seeking negotiation in order to avoid greater tensions, to standing firm behind certain ideas. It is important to continue the discourses, investigation, and compiling of statistics. It is important to plan, knowing that sometimes large steps are less effective than small steps that might go unnoticed in certain situations.

It is important to note the interest of many male and female teachers in gender once they begin to understand its transforming magnitude, and even their manifested desire to continue to receive training from this perspective. We could see interest in organizing gender projects in the different areas they were working in and how, little by little, they left behind prejudices and preconceptions to support this component and use its multiplier effect within the educational process, which requires the deconstruction of earlier patterns, to find a more human and democratic synthesis within the school, society, and the state.

I have also come to the conclusion that despite the fact that we are accustomed to saying that no one is irreplaceable, this is not always true. There are irreplaceable people in the gender issue, because when someone really committed to gender leaves a certain post, years of work can be lost in just a short time. The commitment of feminist women is invaluable, because they are committed to and skilled in a transforming ideology. It is always important to support women's organizations, and individual women, who share and support our work.

Gender equity in public policy in Paraguay has begun to be institutionalized, especially because of the existence of a permanent program, which now has clear priorities, and thanks to a pioneering project that is currently making plans for four more years of work. However, it must be recognized that, given the rapidly changing situations in our Latin American realities, that is no guarantee for the future.

Thus, now is the time to continue the project in its impact study phase, and to solidify new and better products, and it is also the time to design and implement new projects within the PRIOME Program. It is also the time to connect them to the National Plan for Equal Opportunities already designed by the Woman's Secretariat and to its operating plan, based on the Platform for Action endorsed in the Fourth International Women's Conference in Beijing, China, in 1995.

The PRIOME Program has great possibilities for future development, but it needs greater autonomy and a larger budget. It should focus on the modification of the "family education" component to incorporate gender criteria. It should work toward coeducation, and should be capable of arguing and defending itself to authorities, teachers, and society. It also needs a support team to implement training projects, which should be solidified in an accord with the NGOs that have the human resources and experience in this area.[6]

The PRIOME Program has the future challenge of designing ministerial norms in gender and education, designing the research that is required, working with all levels of formal education and projecting toward nonformal education, in coordination with interested organizations.

PRIOME can become a space where people can denounce incidents of sexual harassment, rape, and any other type of violence in the educational sphere, as long as there is no other specific body for that task. It can also connect to other organizations that work on that issue. PRIOME should establish agreements to fulfill and implement its Action Plan.

This program was supported by cooperation from AECI, which gambled on a pioneering project that will only see fruits in the long term. But it is also clear that the responsibility for its continuation in the national and international sphere must be supported by the political will of governments that are initiating cultural change toward a sustainable development with social justice. It is the people who have the national political decision-making power who should be valuing these tools and who should give them the budget support they need to achieve the required modifications.

It remains clear, finally, that only gender solidarity—such as the support for this work from the Women's Institute and from Argentine PRIOM, and support from individual women like Gloria Bonder, Pilar Gonzalez, Ana Manero, Concepción Jaramillo, Francisco Venegas, on the international level, and Cristina Muñoz, Esther Prieto, Graziella Corvalán, Line Bareiro, and Marta Melgarejo, on the national level, and so many others—will make possible the construction of different societies, if we remain committed to our work for a better world that is more just, more equitable, and more united.

NOTES

1. See: Line Bareiro, Clyde Soto, and others. (1996). *Alquimistas.* Asunción: Centro de Documentación y Estudios; Cecilia Silvera Alvarez. (1992). *Telémaco Silvera, Un demócrata Republicano (Vida y escritos).* Asunción: Editorial Saleciana; Esther Prieto (ed.). (1996). *"Igualdad ante la Ley," New Legislation in Paraguay.* Asunción: Presidencia de la República, Secretaría de la Mujer, Ediciones La Rural.
2. Fundación En Alianza. (1992). *Reforma Educativa. Compromiso de Todos, Informe de Avance del Consejo Asesor de la Reforma Educativa.* Asunción: Ediciones Koé-Yú.
3. See: María Victoria Heikel. (1996). *Ser Mujer en Paraguay. Situación Sociodemográfica y Cambios Registrados en el Período Intercensal. 1982–1992.* Asunción: Presidencia de la República, Secretaría Técnica de Planificación, Dirección General de Estadísticas, Encuestas y Censos, Fondo de Población de las Naciones Unidas [FNUAP]; Cándida Mereles and Angélica Roa de Beca. (1996). *Ahora Ya Saben Todo. Vivencia de la Sexualidad de las Adolescentes. Factores Socioculturales y Expresiones de una Conducta Sexual de Riesgo en Adolescentes de Zonas Urbano Marginales del Paraguay.* Asunción: Fondo de Población de las Naciones Unidas [FNUAP], QR Producciones Gráficas.
4. Throughout the project many teachers talked about tearing out page N52 from the third-grade book distributed by the Ministry of Education and Culture as part of the free materials from the educational reform. This book had been solicited, analyzed, and approved by the Ministry. The page spoke about the sexual act in technically simple terms, but it said that it was an act that gives

pleasure to those who engage in it. There was dialogue in the courses about this issue. Women and men teachers shared their difficulties with expressing that sexuality is pleasurable because of the fear of promoting "unleashed" sexuality, and they also talked about the difficulty of translating the terms used in the page into Guaraní, because in that language they are very "strong" and cause laughter.

5. Bejamín Arditti. (1989). *Circuito Norma-Diferencia*. Asunción: Centro de Documentación y Estudio. We clarify that when we speak of boys and girls we are referring to the age contemplated in the International Convention on the Rights of the Child, which identifies people as children until eighteen years of age.

6. Paraguay has been going through a difficult stage in its process of transition to democracy. In 1998, during the presentation before Parliament of a law dealing with violence against women by the Coordination of Women of Paraguay, a demonstration by military *caudillo* Lino Oviedo, supporter of the country's real power during the government of Cubas Grau—who just resigned after a period of impeachment proceedings by the Parliament supported in great measure by the population, and which cost the lives of six young demonstrators—called the women who accompanied the presentation "crazy feminists" and other offensive terms. Today, after a period of great national agitation, the country finds itself with a new government that is talking of returning to more respectful forms of interaction and that favors the continuation of programs and projects like PRIOME.

REFERENCES

Arditti, B. (1989). *Circuito Norma-Diferencia*. Asunción: Centro de Documentación y Estudio.

Bareiro, L., Soto C., *et al.* (1996). *Alquimistas*. Asunción: Centro de Documentación y Estudios.

Fundación En Alianza. (1992). *Reforma Educativa. Compromiso de Todos, Informe de Avance del Consejo Asesor de la Reforma Educativa*. Asunción: Ediciones Koé-Yú.

Heikel, M. V.H. (1996). *Ser Mujer en Paraguay. Situación Sociodemográfica y Cambios Registrados en el Período Intercensal. 1982–1992*. Asunción: Presidencia de la República, Secretaría Técnica de Plantificación, Dirección General de Estadisticas, Encuestas y Censos, Fondo de Población de las Naciones Unidas (FNUAP); Mereles, C. and Roa de Beca, A. (1996). *Ahora ya Saben todo. Vivencia de la Sexualidad de las Adolescentes. Factores Socioculturales y Expresiones de una Conducta Sexual de Riesgo en Adolescentes de Zonas Urbano Marginales del Paraguay*. Asunción: Fondo de Población de las Naciones Unidas (FNUAP), QR Producciones Gráficas.

Prieto, E. (ed). (1996). *"Igualdad Ante la Ley," New Legislation in Paraguay*. Asunción: Presidencia de la República, Secretaría de la Mujer, Ediciones La Rural.

Silvera Alvarez, C. (1992). *Telémaco Silvera, un Demócrata Republicano (Vida y escritos)*. Asunción: Editorial Saleciana.

Part Four

Teachers and Teaching

CHAPTER 17

Comparative Perspectives on Professionalism among American, British, German and Finnish Teachers

Reijo Raivola

Introduction

This chapter deals with the conclusion of a research report on the history of teaching. The development of teacher education in four countries—the United States, England, Germany, and Finland—is pursued in order to see if the proletarianization hypothesis can be corroborated (Raivola, 1989). In ancient times teaching was a respected profession, in authority next to the priesthood, or, in fact, interwined and embedded in it. However, as soon as teaching was separated from sacred ceremonies and became, instead, adopted for livelihood, the deterioration of the profession began.

First, the four countries are compared using the Hansian idea of *tertium comparationis*. In fact five different dimensions are utilized (Judge, 1988). Then the deprofessionalized status of teachers is discussed on a more general level.

THE FIVE CHARACTERISTICS OF A UNITED PROFESSION

National, Regional or Local Control

In the United States, the school and, accordingly, the teacher as part of the institution have traditionally been controlled by the neighborhood society (*gemeinschaft*). At the other end of the continuum lay Prussia, whose compulsory school had a clear political and national function. Finland adopted the German model. The school seemed to be controlled by local laymen, but in essence the teachers were civil servants and state functionaries, and the school educated the young for state citizenship. In England the chaotical conglomerate of schools was articulated into local systems towards the end of the nineteenth century.

National systems have quite early produced uniform contracts of service for teachers (salary, pension, and qualification requirements), national curricula, and final examinations. Teacher training is harmonized, especially for public institutions. Application for an office and conditions of employment are regulated in detail.

From a historical point of view, it is quite understandable that after the Reformation in Prussia and in Finland, the secular power and the clerical power shared an interest in educating a model citizen and an obedient member of the state church. Extreme examples are the oath of allegiance demanded from teachers and the banning of leftist teachers.

In England, on the other hand, the Catholics, the Anglicans and the Dissenters fought each other for the right to teach children. This rivalry was an obstacle in the birth of a widely accepted educational ideology. The parties opposed any interference by the state; it would have been interpreted as a pro-Anglican act. So, in a way, the establishment of a local administration of education was a compromise.

The construction of American states "out of nothing," individual settler attitudes and the vastness of territories compressed education into a local activity of the neighborhood. The teacher was made a trustee of society. This educational and training ideology of the early stage of the Industrial Revolution has been handed down until the post-industrial era. This is one of the reasons for the present mismatch between education and the wider society (Ringer, 1979).

Despite the differences, each nation had to guarantee the political reliability of teachers, i.e., their capability to preserve social order. That is why their training programs were very strictly regimented. Thus awakening of political and economic consciousness was hindered. By applying strict norms the maladjusted were screened out of the system. The curriculum consisted of moralizing and socializing content rather than of psychological and pedagogical skills. The final unprofessional subjugation was carried out by inspectors who mainly came from outside the teaching ranks, especially in England. The working conditions and the teacher-proof material made up the technical imperative that maximized discipline and order as a necessary condition, and even as an ultimate end, of teaching. In England, for example, the Revised Code was a reaction to the fear of a class upheaval. The school in Europe should mirror and support class society (Grace, 1985).

Stratification of the Profession

The United States did not inherit the European division of the educational system into common and academic schools. The medieval Latin school did not gain a footing in America. The democratic high school evolved from the elementary school. That is why the teaching profession shares approximately the same status irrespective of the stage of teaching. But the stratification of teachers in England, and even to a greater extent in Finland and Germany, was very clear until recently. The European secondary school teacher originated from the middle class, went to elite schools, and studied "subjects" in a university. Then he started teaching the same subject without any or with very limited formal teacher training. He was a member of a "learned profession." Hegel, for example, wrote some of his major works when working as a headmaster of a Nuremberg school.

The primary school teacher, on the other hand, originated from the common people. He, or increasingly often she, had to remain poor, diligent and faithful. Part of the teacher's authority has always come from the status of the parents whose children he or she has been teaching. So it is no wonder that differentiated training and different pupils produced separate teacher categories.

Müller (Müller et al., 1987) interestingly describes the sociologics that works up the structures of the education system and differentiates the teachers to correspond to the differing demands of a hierarchical society. He compresses his examination into the concept of systematization. A number of independent schools with relatively free admission and heterogeneous student body evolves into an articulated system of institutions. Each type of school has its own curriculum, recruitment population, and teacher body with specific qualifications. The system of education is a model example of a Weberian rationalization process. It differentiates into finer and finer subclasses along with the developing class or status society, thus legitimizing the hierarchical division of labor. The teaching profession also becomes hierarchical as an integral part of the process. The explanation seems to correspond to reality. The parallel school forms (the common school and the academic school) developed a third type in between them: Realschulen in Prussia, "technical" schools in England, and middle schools in Finland. Later on even the gymnasium differentiated into parallel forms in Prussia.

Müller's theory does not, however, explain development in England very well. Only one type of upper secondary school evolved (grammar school). Traditional public schools were not much affected by the new social divisions. In Prussia the centralized administration of education guaranteed the qualifications given by schools. In England the free competitive market did the same. But in both countries social hierarchies were converted into educational hierarchies—and back again. Although the curriculum in England did not symbolize the school's status as clearly as that in Prussia, in both countries the educational structure and the economic structure, present in emerging industries, were converging.

It is even more difficult to apply Müller's theory to the situation in the United States. Education had a democratic meaning in the construction of the new nation, not only in public speeches but also in reality. Since the days of the first presidents, a shared suspicion arose of those who tried to give birth to any kind of a new aristocracy. Andrew Jackson said that college was "a haunt of dandies" and "a protector of well-born and stupid" (Orr,

1987). Unlike the European situation, the public school had to assimilate diverse ethnic and cultural groups into an integrated nation. Education had to bring forth both enculturation and acculturation. Three basic principles have molded the American educational policy from the beginning: education must be universal (right to education); it must be independent of the political regime (decentralization); it must guarantee a common core of civilization to everyone (comprehensiveness). It was the number of years in formal education, not the type of an institution, that stratified people.

The universalistic interpretation of functionalism can be disputed on other grounds, too. In America the school did not earn the right to act as a gatekeeper to working life for a long time. It was not the only elector of people to status positions. In England there was a remarkable overlap between descending grammar schools and ascending primary schools. Grace (1985) shows that as opposed to functionalistic and deterministic reproduction theory, "the representatives of the employers' interests," the inspectors, acted openly and strongly against the Revised Code and for the rights of the teachers. Usually they were products of "Oxbridge" and famous public schools, which openly resisted the values of the competitive meritocratic society. Through their supervisory activities, these values were bound to reflect on the teaching profession, too. The teacher was not a servile follower of the will of his superiors, although Henry Bérenger at the turn of the century said that the souls of the intellectual proletrait were fatally inclined either to slavery or to rebellion. The trade union movement in England chose to rebel quite early.

One had to remember "the veto of the powerless." Even if the teachers in their hierarchical positions are objects and means of the use of power, they can always water down the will of their suppressors. Their pedagogical autonomy makes it possible.

The conflict theories of education come from the branch of social sciences that aims, besides producing new knowledge, at a pointed social criticism. The lack of equity and democracy is the target of criticism in education. But Jürgen Schriewer (Müller *et al.*, 1987) shows us that the analogy of reproduction comes from biology. The opposite of reproduction among organisms is not equity but extinction.

Autonomy of the Profession

Secondary school teachers, in particular, have enjoyed great autonomy in England. Curricula were born (often undocumented) at the level of a school or even in the mind of an individual teacher. The choice of teaching material was limited only by resources. The teacher as a state official in Germany was more strictly tied by numerous norms whereas the American teacher was the object of the parents' arbitrary will. However, through their right to collective bargaining, teachers have fought themselves, step by step, for more space and air to act independently. In many European countries, the democratic development has culminated in a kind of a paradox: an individual teacher's power of decision is restricted by the union rules! Teachers have never achieved the highest stage of professional decision making, i.e., collegialism.

In the United States, the school has always been managed by "neighborhood managers." Industrial and managerial ideas of efficiency have restricted teachers' autonomy. Efficiency is seen mostly as pedagogical, and it is measured by standardized achievement tests. Now, when resources allocated to education are decreasing, demands for accountability are intensified, not only in the United States but in England, too. It is not enough for a teacher to have graduated from an accredited college. She must be licensed, too. Sometimes she has to pass competency tests. She is paid by merit. Classroom responsibilities are identified in detail, and activities must be reported regularly. In England central government has taken on responsibilities for curriculum planning, resource allocation, etc. In countries such as Finland, where administration has traditionally been centralized, the opposite is occurring. Disentangling the norms and cutting down bureaucracy (deregulation) have delegated the right of decision downwards. Autonomy of Finnish teachers, or should we say Finnish schools, has increased.

Unity of the Profession

Unity of the profession is one of the central characteristics of professionalism. This does not mean that a profession cannot differentiate into specialities. After all, a physician is a physician whatever his special field is, be it surgery or pediatrics, for example. There have always been two categories in teacher corps: the teacher of the academic school and the teacher of the common school. The former has been the transmitter of codified knowledge and has selected his clients on a competitive basis. Teaching imparts thorough knowledge of the subject matter. Therefore teachers have been university graduates with no need for pedagogical qualities. The common school teacher, on the other hand, has been a substitute parent for young children. Custodial care and supervision have been the school's main functions. There was no need for its teachers to demonstrate their knowledge. What they needed was pedagogical and psychological control skills, because they made education in the proper sense possible (Lundgren, 1987).

The educational system has assigned teachers to status groups according to the level and track of education. The most essential divider was the question of whether the teacher was teaching a child or a subject. The higher level he/she taught, the less pedagogical training was needed. The more pedagogical qualifications were included in the training, the less highly the occupation was regarded. Even in the academic school, the teacher was valued according to the subject he/she taught.

Except in the United States, teacher unions are split according to the stage of the educational system. As for the United States, one of the main unions has included employers' representatives as members. In England, headmasters, women teachers, etc., have their own organizations. Subject teachers usually have their own pedagogical associations. In Finland, for example, legislation has prevented administrators from using a teacher, appointed to a particular office, on different levels or in different school forms. On both continents, the principal is no longer *primus inter pares*. He is a full-fledged administrator and the employer's representative.

The heterogeneity of the occupation has been an obstacle to the establishment of an official teacher register. The register, which includes every certified and licensed teacher, and only such teachers, constitutes a guarantee of skills and proficiency. The register is an assurance for clients and customers that the profession bears the full responsibility for its members' behavior and craftsmanship. Among teachers there have always been unqualified and untrained members. In many countries, for example England, these unqualified teachers have been appointed permanently in remote areas. They have formed a floating *underclass*, which is not supposed to honor the professional code of ethics or whose interests were not taken care of by unions. In England such teachers were excluded form union membership.

Teachers have always been a miscellaneous lot, differing by education, capabilities, and personal traits. Teacher training has been in a state of continuous change, thus producing wide intergenerational differences in qualifications and dividing teachers into different salary grades.

Various trends in professional, political, and union development have, however, brought different teacher categories closer to each other. The extension of compulsory schooling from seven to nine years has also contributed to the harmonization of primary and secondary teacher training and lowered the barriers between different school forms and categories of teachers. But now, the zeal for accountability and the concern for the quality of education have turned the wheel back towards differentiation. In the United States (and Japan), for example, there are plans to divide teachers into professional categories according to their training, experience, and demonstrated efficiency.

Unionism

In all four countries, it was clearly understood that especially the common school teachers on primary and elementary levels did not deserve full recognition or, by social contract, did not obtain the essential elements of a professional status. They had to resort to the labor movements, i.e., unionism. The first to radicalize was the English teacher at the end of the nineteenth century. The German teacher followed in the days of the Weimar Republic, the Finnish and the American teacher not until the end of World War II. From the point of view of professional ethics, unionistic radicalization can be, and in fact has been, detrimental to professional aspirations. Whether professionalism and unionism are incompatible by nature remains to be seen in a future research project. There is no doubt, however, that in addition to the continuous rise of the social import of schooling, teacher unions have tremendously improved teachers' economic position and their contracts of service. Allies have been sought sometimes among the political Left, as in England, sometimes among the state bureaucracies.

THE PROLETARIANIZATION HYPOTHESIS

One of the leading themes in this research project has been the proletarianization hypothesis. The project has dealth with the reasons, in classical antiquity and the Middle Ages, for the deterioration of teachers' original highly regarded status (Raivola, 1989). In the following section, those factors are discussed which are connected with the birth and development of modern educational systems. Metzger (1987) writes in his brilliant essay:

> that as the amount of knowledge increases, so too does the relative amount of ignorance, for each person can know only a decreasing fraction of what can be known; that knowledge, as it becomes more specialized, also tends to become more potent, more capable of being used for good or ill; that the growth and specialization of knowledge produce not a mass society but a lay society, a society in which everyone is at the mercy of someone more thoroughly in the know, that this state of mutural dependency grows more dangerous as knowledge, which has once been in the hands of holy men, kin and neighbors, passes into the hands of strangers. . . .

We are living in a world of specialists. If our televison set breaks down, we need a specialist to repair it. We can also live without it or buy a new one. TV mechanics are not vital to our well-being. They are not professionals. If we break our bones, we again consult a specialist. Only a medical doctor is able to and allowed to heal us, but he is not only a specialist but an expert and a professional. Teachers are neither! Many sociologists claim that teachers lack both special know-how and an expert's authority. Silberman (1970) says: "No one ever died of a split infinitive." Teachers have no monopoly on any knowledge area. Although they are university educated, they have no clear, undisputed scientific basis for their practical work. Educational sciences already had a bad reputation before they were incorporated in university curricula. Other fields of science had centuries-old traditions and established boundaries.

Education and psychology tore up the institution, its distribution of power and the mechanisms of resources allocation. When the rise of social sciences began, education wanted to be part of it. It claimed scientific independence. It wanted to be both a science and a provider of professional knowledge, both within the scope of one degree. Older sciences recognized neither of these claims. Education was placed as and remained the lowest discipline in the academic order.

The determinants of successful teaching are mastery of content, knowledge of children, and familiarity with methods. The subject teacher's mastery of content is only a necessary, not a sufficient condition for good teaching. All the prerequisite knowledge of teaching cannot be covered by one discipline. The scientific basis for teaching must be broad. If we consider upbringing instead of instruction, many philosophers see that as a normative activity it cannot be the object of science-indoctrination could be that. Good teaching is an art! A professional can be an intermediary between knowledge, service, and the client, but in education, science cannot generate direct instructions or directives for practice.

An expert uses knowledge in his work without sharing it with the client. Even a psychiatrist does not form a close and direct personal relationship with his patient. Expert authority maintains a knowledge gap between the layman and the professional. Pedagogical (anthropological) authority is used to narrow the gap. Whereas continuity of professions supposes that clients are dependent on experts, teachers should encourage pupils towards independence. In the classroom the teacher's main tool is his/her personality; the professional has his/her monopoly on knowledge (Dove, 1986; Schwebel, 1985; Silberman, 1970). To put it more bluntly: the expert is not interested in the client but in his problems.

The problem of legitimized knowledge must be seen in the historical context. An everlasting war prevails between the world of work and the world of education, between the promoters of science and the practitioners. No final solution is in sight, because the differences in opinion are caused by different epistemological understandings. But it is possible to adapt to each other. It takes several decades, however, before opponents are sufficiently adapted. For example, it was not until the 1930s that a university education was demanded for lawyers in court in the United States, and in the 1950s formal training finally displaced the apprenticeship system. Likewise, it took forty years before the Johns Hopkins model of medicine was adopted by the profession. On a global scale, university education of teachers has not been required yet. The state of ferment is mirrored, among other things, by the unusually common discontent of teachers with their initial training (Spring, 1980).

Teaching in the compulsory school has always been a constitutive mass occupation (Groothoff, 1982), which has had nothing to do with the training of a nation's political or economic elite. The common school teacher directed the young to factories, fields, and offices. Social qualifications were more important than technical ones. For that reason the teacher was to serve as a model for her pupils. Especially in the countryside, she lived like a fish in an aquarium. This pressure for conformity and living under strict moral surveillance made the teacher a second-class citizen, at least as far as his/her personal liberties were concerned. On the other hand, severe school discipline together with other structural characteristics of the school made the teacher a very authoritative figure for his/her pupils. Only the reform pedagogy took the school ". . . away from the authoritarian . . . and theoretically-oriented school to a more child-centered education . . ." (Wigger, 1986).

Appealing to caretaking and custodial obligations of the teacher, society saddled the school not only with moral education and instruction but also with an ever-increasing number of often-contradictory tasks of well-being and surveillance. The job description of teaching was blurred. The teacher became a jack of all trades.

In a profession, marginal tasks are delegated to assisting personnel. In classrooms the work has differentiated in the opposite way. Beside and, more often, above the teacher work different types of specialists: psychologists, curriculum experts, welfare officers, nurses, etc. Didactics made the teacher an applier of different techniques, when he/she tried to meet the efficiency demand by trying to achieve the objectives set by outsiders with minimum resources. Curriculum studies during initial training emphasized the development of technical self-understanding. Teaching strategy was modeled after the concept of technical work, and classroom tactics were chosen to solve the problems with contextual knowledge. However well the teacher did his/her work, it was never finished. The medical doctor heals the victim of an accident; the lawyer solves a legal problem; the priest promises the sinner an absolution. The teacher, year after year, has new raw material to shape, but he/she never sees his/her product as ready. The teacher is very much an institutional role figure; a representative of a power organization rather than the solver of acute human problems.

Conflicting hopes and expectations have always been directed to the school. The most essential question for the elite and academic school was whether it should be a producer or a reproducer of knowledge. Because the university started to change into a research institution as late as the nineteenth century, it is natural that its graduates delivered only the knowledge they themselves had acquired. Pieces of this knowledge, separated from the whole, were transferred into the curriculum, but they were blurred into rudiments and relics, which had very little to do with the everyday life of the students.

Even today the education of teachers and that of researchers are different. One reason for this can be that the teacher trainers' backgrounds, careers, identifications, and intellectual orientations differ from those of other university teachers. In the United States their salary and status are lower than those of the other faculty. The culture of teacher training differs from cultures of other programs, often in an unintellectual direction (Schwebel, 1985).

The first thesis in the Metzger quote on page 169 is also illuminating. Although our relative ignorance in the flood of information and in the world of specialists increases continuously, that does not apply to school. Knowledge of teaching has experienced no information explosion. At least it does not show in the organization of schooling. Functioning principles and even part of the curriculum are much the same as they were at the birth of the modern educational system. If new knowledge should happen to show in school activities (and of course it does), very soon it would be in "public domain delivery." Pupils and students have a wider experience of different teachers and teaching styles than teachers themselves, who very seldom know what is happening in other classrooms. Parents have often had more education than teachers. Everyone seems to be an expert on school and education. Teaching is difficult to mystify.

Whether a professional really knows more than lay people, whether he/she has expert knowledge or not, is not essential according to the symbolic interpretation of professionalism. What is essential is that those whose services are in demand believe and, what is important, want to believe in the superior knowledge of the professionals. Parents will not believe in teachers in this way, because they do not want to give up their rights over their children to the school. In many medical, legal or technical problems they feel they are at the mercy of experts, but in education they feel they are as expert as anyone else. They want to maintain their integrity in relation to the school.

Longer and more effective teacher education has undoubtedly produced teachers who are more skillful technicians, but a kind of one-sided contract cannot make them into professionals. If the structure and conditions of the job do not change, no training can make teachers into professionals. Teachers think that they are already at the professional level; the problem is that the general public does not see it. However, procuring objective, distinctive characteristics of professionalism is not the objective of education. They do not even exist. It is a question of a symbolic relationship between the suppliers of services and the clients. Laymen give professionals the power of attorney for taking care of their complicated problems, and professionals guarantee that the problems will be taken care of in a discreet and professional way. A professional status is given as much as it is taken.

The history, status, and working conditions of primary and elementary school teachers work against achieving a professional status (Spring, 1980). Working conditions have traditionally been wretched. Classes have been big. The teacher's energy has been depleted by keeping order rather than by teaching. Sykes (1984) mentions "the deal" American teachers make with difficult students in high schools: if you do not disturb me and my class, I won't disturb you either; if everything goes peacefully, I will give you a D in my subject. The salary has always been low. The social status of the common school teacher has been vague. She originates from among the common people, but does not belong to them anymore; the middle class and the intelligentsia are suspicious and do not accept her as a member.

The marginal conditions of teaching and its low social and economic compensation have frightened the most capable individuals away from the field, especially in times of general prosperity, when the economy has offered more dynamic alternatives for earning one's livelihood and for self-fulfillment. When the school, because of its internal mechanisms and inevitable functions, has not been able to keep up with social development, teachers have been blamed. Public criticism has caused many teachers to leave the field. The high turnover of teachers is even a bigger problem than their quality. The school has always been controlled by others rather than teachers: by the church until the first half of the nineteenth century, by the social structure for the next hundred years, and by the economy for the past forty years. Servants are not highly respected.

Teaching offers very few career prospects. To advance is to leave teaching: to move up is to move out. A tension prevails between career consciousness and role commitment. In the segmented school, the teacher is obliged to instruct syllabi in forms and levels of school for which she does not feel qualified. Good work is seldom rewarded. The automatically increasing salary (seniority bonuses) provokes routines. The concept of merit pay, as it is understood in the United States, is no solution, because its criteria are not agreed upon.

CONCLUDING REMARKS

Modern professions were born with the rise of the capitalistic form of production and with the scientification of universities. At the same time the need to create a state citizen and the change in living patterns brought about by the Industrial Revolution, formalized education into school systems. New professions close their ranks from minorities and women. Professions were occupational cartels controlled by the elite of the mainstream culture. The teacher served without discriminating against anyone. The quantitative demand for teachers was greater than the concern for the quality. First in England, then in the United States and finally in Finland and Germany, the occupation became dominated by a female majority. In present-day Europe, only Greece and the Netherlands have a male majority at the primary level. In twenty-four countries surveyed in 1983, the average percentage of women was 71 percent. In the former GDR, the proportion was the highest—87 percent. In general, 80 percent seems to be the ceiling; then men start to return to teaching (Braster, 1988).

As higher education has become more general among women, the number of women teachers in secondary and tertiary education has increased. However, the lower the stage of education, the greater the proportion of women among teachers (Braster, 1988), because preprimary education as a care occupation almost without exception was in the hands of women. Educative tasks attached to the gender became the women's responsibilities in school. As an indicator of wealth, GNP correlates negatively with the proportion of women as teachers. Further, it is an international fact that the number of women as teachers and the salary level as well as the length of training and the number of female teachers correlate negatively. During economic booms men enter more respected occupations, which leaves more room in the teaching profession for women. When the recession comes, there are no more vacancies in teaching left for men. The conclusion is that in patriarchal societies the female majority in the occupation has been an obstacle to social and professional status.

Organizationally it is easy to return to teaching after many years' absence, as if no break existed. Those who return are usually women. Teaching is often the first college-based job for racial or ethnic minorities or for those who yearn for social mobility. A medical doctor or a lawyer is perceived as an individual, while a teacher is seen as a representative of his/her occupation. Thus, the label of lower strata is linked to the occupational group.

The professional knows, when offering his/her services, what knowledge must be applied and in what way, whom he/she may consult for advice, what measures and how many operations are needed and what their costs will be, when and in what order operations must be executed and why. The teacher lacks collegial support. He/she is seldom cost conscious. His/her sociological and political understanding of the school's functions is limited. He/she teaches his/her pupils at the time and for as many years as some formal rule tells him/her to. The prefixed curriculum answers mainly "what" and "how" questions and only occasionally "why" questions. In all four countries the university education of teachers is justified by scientification of teaching. Theories are taught deductively: novices are acquainted with different theoretical approaches to teaching and then they try to apply some of them. If the basis of the teacher's work is practical, as it seems to be, theories should be built inductively as experiences accumulate. The vaccination theory has dominated teacher education until the 1970s: once vaccinated, always safe. If teaching is an inductive and practical activity, teachers are in need of continuing education.

My final question is, thus, whether teaching can be considered more art than science. If so, is there any reason for the vocation to strive for a professional pressure group ideology and status?

REFERENCES

Braster, J. (1988). "The Feminization of Teaching." In *The Social Role and Evolution of the Teaching Profession in Historical Context*, S. Seppo (ed.). Jyvuskylu: Joensuu.

Dove, L. (1986). *Teachers and Teacher Education in Developing Countries*. London: Croom Helm.

Grace, G. (1985). "Judging Teachers: The Social and Political Contexts of Teacher Education." *British Journal of Sociology of Education* 6(1), pp. 3–16.

Groothoff, H. H. (1982). *Funktion und Rolle des Erziehers*. München: Juventa Verlag.

Judge, H. (1988). "Cross-National Perception of Teachers." *Comparative Education Review* 32(2), pp. 143–158.

Lundgren, U. (1987). "New Challenges for Teachers and Education." Standing Conference of European Ministers of Education. 15th Session, Helsinki.

Metzger, W. (1987). "The Spectre of Professionalism." *Educational Researcher* 16(6), pp. 10–19.

Müller, D., Ringer, F. and Simon, B. (1987). *The Rise of the Modern Educational System*. Cambridge: Cambridge University Press.

Orr, J. (1987). "The American System of Education." In *Making America*, L. Luedtke (ed.). Washington: USIA.

Raivola, R. (1989). *Opettajan Ammatin Historia*. (The History of Teaching). Kasvatustieteen laitos A 44. Tampereen: Yliopisto.

Ringer, F. (1979). *Education and Society in Modern Europe*. Bloomington: Indiana University Press.

Schwebel, M. (1985). "The Clash of Cultures in Academe: The University and the Education Faculty." *Journal of Teacher Education* 36(4), pp. 2–7.

Silberman, C. (1970). *Crisis in the Classroom*. New York: Vintage Books.

Spring, J. (1980). *Educating the Worker-Citizen*. New York: Longman.

Sykes, G. (1984). "The Deal." *The Wilson Quarterly* 7(1), pp. 59–77.

Wigger, L. (1986). "Bericht vom XXII." Salzburger Symposion-Pädagogisches Rundschau 40, pp. 615–623.

CHAPTER 18

Classroom Management in Japan: Building a Classroom Community

Nobuo K. Shimahara

Definitions and patterns of classroom management vary, depending on the societal and cultural contexts in which they have evolved. Classroom management can be better appreciated when it is examined from the perspective of the culture where it is practiced. In this chapter, I will explore Japanese classroom management with particular attention to its premises or underlying beliefs, which reflect cultural practices embedded in Japanese society. In Japan, as in other cultures, there is a significant degree of isomorphism between the basic tenets of classroom management and the dominant cultural orientation. My discussion will focus on elementary school classroom management to explore that relationship, and I will incorporate materials on secondary school classroom management into the chapter when they are relevant to my analysis. I will triangulate various sources of data so that I may identify a dominant pattern of classroom management in Japan. These sources include my ethnographic studies on teacher occupational socialization and the culture of teaching, conducted in Japan from 1989 to 1996, including a project currently progressing in Osaka, Japan (Shimahara, 1996; Shimahara and Sakai, 1995), case studies conducted by Japanese researchers, official documents, and the Japanese literature in the field.

Classroom management is of central interest for classroom teachers, because it induces the classroom context where teaching and learning occur. Its theoretical and historical development is explored elsewhere (Sato, 1998). Japanese elementary classroom management is inclusive and emphasizes the process of building a classroom community where interpersonal relations and emotional bonding between teachers and students and among students are developed. Because teachers believe that classroom management is pivotal to children's lives in the classroom and to effective learning, they use a variety of strategies and devote considerable time to promoting it. The classroom is seen as a crucial environment where students develop an appreciation of group life and learn skills that enhance their participation in group activities. Teachers predictably insist that children's instrumental learning be embedded in that environment and not be separated from the social and emotional context of classroom community life. In other words, Japanese elementary classroom management represents a process of socializing children to the group, a fundamental social form of interface between individuals that Japanese learn to organize, from which they derive an expressive source of attachment, and in which they find a vital social anchorage. Elementary years are a critical time when children learn essential routines and habits requisite for adult social life with a focus on curiosity, spontaneity, energy, and collective activity. These years represent the crucial time when children gradually make the transition from family attachments to peer groups before taking on the challenge of individual attainment through academic competition in entrance examinations at the end of middle and high-school education. There is a significant shift in the landscape of learning, but it symbolizes a developmental process, not a break in the pattern of growing up.

In Japan, classroom management is largely an uncodified practice invented, transmitted, and re-created by classroom teachers. Multifaceted dimensions of classroom management will be addressed in this chapter. I will first discuss how Japanese elementary education is organized because this context is important to appreciating the nature of classroom management. Next will come an analysis of how cultural values are reflected in classroom management and an examination of its underlying premises. Subsequently, I will focus on what is known as *gakkyuzukuri* among classroom teachers, or building a classroom community.

EDUCATION FOR THE WHOLE CHILD: AIMING TO ACHIEVE BROAD GOALS

Japanese elementary education offers programs that foster the growth of the whole child, including cognitive, social, emotional, and physical aspects of development. Elementary education is conceived of as a broad arena in which child development is the major challenge. The close interface of socialization in the family and the school characterizes this period, in contrast to American elementary education, where the cognitive development of the child is the paramount concern (Shimahara and Sakai, 1995). In the United States, that concern is salient, beginning at the kindergarten level, whereas the primary goal of preschool education in Japan is the social and emotional development of the child with minimum academic training (Tobin, Woe, and Davidson, 1989; Lewis, 1995; Peak, 1993). Japanese classroom management plays an important role in enhancing education of the whole child. Before I focus attention on classroom management, however, I will explore common characteristics of education for the whole child. Every school in

Japan states its educational goals on the first page of its handbook; these vary in specifics but share a broad, common rationale. The themes of school goals are generally diffuse and symbolize the significance of education for the whole child. They typically include such goals as the development of:

- a robust and healthy child;
- a child who thinks deeply and is creative;
- an empathetic and cheerful child with a sensitive heart;
- a cooperative and diligent child; and
- a child who gets along well and helps others.

It is apparent that main themes encompass the cognitive, moral, expressive, social, and physical dimensions of students' development. The goals of schooling enunciated by Japanese elementary schools commonly place priority on cooperation, empathy, diligence, and a healthy body and mind, in addition to cognitive skills. The expression of these themes makes it clear that schooling is expected to promote children's growth holistically.

School goals are implemented through a variety of activities. The elementary curriculum is developed following the course of study issued by the Ministry of Education. For the reader who is not acquainted with Japanese education, it should be noted that Japan has a national curriculum and a uniform school system consisting of elementary schools, lower and upper secondary schools (middle and high schools, respectively), and colleges. The course of study spells out three major areas: academic subjects moral education; and *tokubetsu katsudo*, or special activities.

Moral education is thought to pervade all aspects of schooling. The official course of study stipulates that moral education be provided in a moral-education class (one period per week) and throughout all the educational activities of the school. It stresses that moral education is present in all dimensions of teaching and learning. There are nearly thirty moral themes to be covered throughout the year. Each school is expected to develop a plan to address these themes in all grades during a thirty-five-week period. Examples of these themes include the importance of order, cooperation, thoughtfulness, participation, endurance, hard work, character development, justice, and the like.

As the course of study enunciates, special activities are organized to strengthen the harmonious development of body and mind, individual students' awareness that they are members of a group, and the spirit of cooperation. Special activities include *gakkyukatsudo*, or classroom activities, clubs, school events, and *jidokai* (a student self-governing body). Moreover, one period per week is allocated to classroom activities, which are centered on handling such classroom issues as the division of responsibilities for classroom maintenance, improvement of interpersonal relations, and individual emotional concerns. To develop students' personal interests, one period is also allocated to clubs, in which students from fourth through sixth grades participate under the supervision of assigned teachers. Clubs range from popular sports to music, calligraphy, and science projects. *Jidokai* is a body of elected representatives from the fifth and sixth grades whose charge is to organize self-initiated activities on behalf of all the students of the school.

Every week a fifteen-minute special time slot is created for *jidokai's* presentation at a meeting of the entire student body. Schoolwide activities include ceremonial events, sports and art festivals, excursions, school theater, swimming programs, and mobile classroom (outdoor) programs, which expose students to nature. The underlying premise of school events is to foster students' sense of belonging, appreciation of communal life, and aesthetic and physical skills. Schools attach great significance to school events and devote considerable time to planning and implementing such events. In addition, one free period is provided to organize nonacademic activities. The schools I observed in Tokyo used this period to encourage upper-grade students' participation in a variety of committee activities related to school activities. Typically, each school organizes a dozen committees to provide students with a broad range of selections. For example, these committees include a broadcasting committee that creates a school broadcast program; a library committee which reviews library activities; an assembly committee which plans for *jidokai* presentations; and a newspaper committee which publishes a school paper. It is obvious from the above description of the four domains of schooling that Japanese elementary education is broadly structured. All in all, these domains make up part and parcel of Japanese schooling and complement the academic subject area.

The comprehensive nature of schooling is reflected in the weekly schedule of classes shown in Table I. The schedule reveals that reaching encompasses a gamut of activities in addition to academic instruction. At the sixth-grade level, for example, besides twenty-six academic periods running from Monday through Saturday, there are also clubs, classroom activities, moral education, morning assemblies, morning classroom meetings (*asanokai*), and afternoon reflections (*kaerinokai*). (Japanese schools started to close one Saturday per month on a trial basis in 1992; this was increased to two Saturdays per month in 1995. In a few years, the Ministry of Education will implement a five-day school week, eliminating Saturday attendance.) In addition, there are lunch periods and clean-up times, in which relevant tasks are performed by students under the supervision of classroom teachers. Longer recesses are scheduled between the second and third periods and after clean-up to allow students shared time for peer interaction and recreational activities. It should be noted that Japanese schools attach special importance to these long and short recesses because they offer students time and space within schooltime to play together in the playground or engage in other interactional activities. It is believed that such activities contribute to the students' development of both social skills and health. Teachers quite often join students in the playground during the twenty-minute recess, because they believe that playing with them will enhance bonding and amplify understanding of them, since formal relations of control typical in the classroom are absent. Beginning teachers especially are encouraged to play with their students, taking the opportunity to get to know them well. One of the beginning teachers who participated in my study, for example, said that because learning to know her children was her priority she played with them in a variety of situations.

Table I: Weekly Schedule of Classes for Sixth Grade

	Monday	Tuesday	Wednesday	Thursday	Friday	Saturday
	School Assembly		Sports Assembly		Student Assembly	
8:35–8:50	Morning Meeting	Morning Meeting	Morning Meeting	Morning Meeting	Morning Meeting	Morning Meeting
8:50–9:35	Japanese	Arts and Crafts	Social Studies	Physical Education	Science	Japanese
9:35–9:40	Recess	Recess	Recess	Recess	Recess	Recess
9:40–10:25	Math	Arts and Crafts	Music	Math	Math	Club Activity
10:25–10:45	Long Recess	Long Recess	Long Recess	Long Recess	Long Recess	Long Recess
10:45–11:30	Physical Education	Math Education	Japanese	Science	Japanese	Committees
11:30–11:35	Recess	Recess	Recess	Recess	Recess	Recess
11:35–12:20	Social Studies	Japanese	Math	Science	Music	Dismissal
12:20–1:10	Lunch	Lunch	Lunch	Lunch	Lunch	
1:10–1:30	Clean-up	Clean-up	Clean-up	Clean-up	Clean-up	
1:30–1:40	Recess	Recess	Reflection (1:30–1:45)	Recess	Recess	
1:40–2:25	Moral Education	Home Economics		Social Studies	Physical Education	
2:25–2:30	Recess	Recess		Recess	Recess	
2:30–3:15	Reflection (2:30–2:45)	Home Economics		Japanese	Classroom Activity	
3:15–3:30	Reflection	Reflection		Reflection	Reflection	

Japanese teachers also regard cleaning and lunch as meaningful educational activities—part of inclusive schooling—and devote a substantial amount of time to them. Cleaning is not viewed just as a task that needs to be completed, but as an opportunity to teach students cooperative skills and accomplishing a shared task. Cleaning helps to develop students' sense of ownership of and responsibility for their classrooms and schools. They clean not just their classroom, but also other parts of the school as an assigned responsibility. The handbook for beginning teachers in Tokyo recommends: "[It should] not be taken as a merely utilitarian exercise; the school-cleaning activity needs to be understood as an occasion to provide education; it is a valuable activity that affects the educational efforts of the school as a whole."

Hence, cleaning is required of all students from first through sixth grade and is done under the supervision of classroom teachers. Lunch time is a communal and most enjoyable part of student life in school, during which students and a teacher sit in small circles in their classroom. Students take full responsibility for setting up tables, fetching meals from the kitchen and serving them, and returning dishes and utensils to the kitchen after lunch is completed. The principal of a school I observed told me: "Children enjoy lunch time most. It helps students to learn eating habits and nurture desirable peer relations through eating together." During lunch time, the broadcasting committee usually announces nutritional elements of the meal and plays music on a loudspeaker installed in each classroom.

In Japanese education these nonacademic domains, including moral education, special activities, and school events, assume a large and important role in schooling. Japanese teachers regard these activities to be as essential as academic lessons. Education for the whole child integrates a diversity of children's experiences into the process of schooling and requires teachers' commitment to developing children's cognitive, social, physical, emotional, and moral skills.

CULTURAL UNDERPINNINGS OF CLASSROOM MANAGEMENT

We have observed that Japanese elementary education is organized to promote diverse activities that realize interpersonal connectedness, pupil participation in schooling, and the fulfillment of common goals. I will now explore cultural values that influence classroom management in order to make their implicit cultural rationality explicit.

Because social practices are grounded in culture, it is useful to understand their cultural formulation. The ways in which the Japanese differ from peoples in the rest of the world, especially Westerners, have become a recurrent topic of discussion in recent decades. For example, it is a well-known fact that the Japanese are group-oriented and place priority on bonding, while Americans are individualistic and emphasize options (Hsu, 1963; Dahrendorf, 1978; Nakane, 1972). In this sense, both Japanese and Americans represent what Lipset (1996) calls exceptionalism—uniqueness in their orientation toward society. These societies are situated at opposite ends of Dahrendorf's continuum of cultural orientation, ranging from ligature to option, or the Parsonian pattern variables (Parsons, 1951). The way in which the Japanese see themselves in relation to others is distinct and central to Japanese culture. Japanese exceptionalism is ubiquitously manifest in Japanese school and other social practices.

Why do the Japanese attach such great importance to the group? This question anticipates an examination of how the Japanese define themselves. The Japanese see themselves as part of a given network of human relations and pay specific attention to others' behaviors, feelings, and opinions. As Kiefer (1976) aptly states, "The Japanese tend to include within the boundaries of [the] concept of self much of the quality of the intimate social groups of which the individual is a member." This explains why the Japanese develop what Lebra (1976) calls social preoccupation, a tendency to be highly sensitive to social interactions and relationships.

School programs celebrate school activities as a component of group life even when they refer to development of individuality. In other words, individuality is viewed as developing from harmonious relationships between individual children and their peers within a context of social interaction. In this respect, as Smith (1983) suggests, "the identification of self and other is always indeterminate in the sense that there is no fixed center from which, in effect, the individual asserts a non-contingent existence." Put differently, there is a constant interplay between the self and others in the definition of the self.

Befu (1986) points out that it is personal interdependence and interconnectedness that determine who one is. For that reason he prefers the term "personhood" to "self" to identify the image of a Japanese person whose self is embedded in an interpersonal web. The Japanese do not see their selves as distinct from all others and immutable, as Americans do (Hsu, 1963). Personhood involves grounding oneself not only in a network of interpersonal relations in particular situations and organizations, but moral commitment to others, reciprocity of relational commitment, and extension of trust. A sense of interdependence is fostered through mutual trust and assistance. As will be seen later, Japanese classroom management is designed to develop such personhood.

Befu suggests that interdependence is mediated by self-discipline involving hardship, endurance, and self-exertion. It is very common in everyday interaction for Japanese to say to each other, "Make utmost efforts (*gambare*) and exert yourself to the limit (*isshokenmei yare*)." Likewise, teachers and parents frequently inspire children by resorting to these sayings, which suggest a moral benchmark for children's attitudes and behavior. This benchmark refers to the quality of personhood, a moral power enhancing one's ability to overcome hardship and willing dedication to the realization of ends. It is such qualities that earn trust. Young students, as well as adults, are thought to be unworthy persons or members of a group if they do not internalize the moral fundamental of self-discipline.

This brings us to the notion of "role dedication" of which De Vos (1973) speaks. The Japanese achieve social self-realization by fulfilling a role that they assume as part of an interconnected network. One's role links an individual to a web of interdependent individuals, and the actualization of his or her aspirations is attained within that social context. Instead of seeking self-actualization as an independent pursuit, as Americans do, the Japanese seek it through appropriate roles. They exhibit a disposition to perfect fulfillment of their perceived roles through dedication to them. In this respect, "role perfectionism" is an element of ideal personhood (Befu, 1986). For example, as is well known, Japanese bureaucrats and company employees typify this cultural phenomenon of role dedication through their devotion to their institutions, by subordinating their personal needs and family lives to the imperatives of their roles. Likewise, women are dedicated to their roles as wives and mothers whose personal needs are secondary to the needs of their children and, above all, subordinated to the pressing priority of children's education. Schoolchildren are socialized into various roles in the classroom, and through that socialization learn receptivity and the necessary skills to perform their roles.

The notion of Japanese dedication to role stems from the Confucian ideology dominant in premodern Japan, which deemphasized the individual as an end in himself or herself, emphasizing instead individual responsibilities and obligations (De Vos, 1973; Dore, 1987). Individuals were assigned ascribed roles, the performance of which was a virtue. That ideology remains potent in contemporary Japan and is the underpinning of what characterizes Japan as a role-oriented society (Azuma, 1994), in which individuals not only are dedicated to performing their roles but also identify themselves in terms of those roles defined in a particular institutional setting (see Nakane, 1972). For example, when the Japanese introduce themselves to others, they identify themselves by referring to their place of work, occupational status, and their relationships to particular individuals. School practices to develop students' sense of belonging and connectedness, fostered through special activities, reflect and adhere to this cultural ideology. Although roles are no longer ascribed to individuals in contemporary Japan, role performance remains a strong cultural tenet permeating school and other institutional domains.

The emphasis on role performance leads to another important concept—what Azuma (1994) calls "receptive diligence." The Japanese are socialized from infancy through adulthood to internalize socioemotional dispositions to adapt to external demands, expectations, and constraints. As applied to schooling, Japanese teachers encourage development of students' adaptive dispositions by relying on their diligence and receptivity to the demands of school and avail themselves of these dispositions for effective learning and teaching. Thus, in the words of Hess and Azuma (1991), "In Japan teachability is an internalized receptive diligence. . . . Overt control by the teacher is minimal. . . . Students perceive the situation, realize what is expected of them."

TENETS OF CLASSROOM MANAGEMENT

This section discusses salient beliefs about classroom management, a set of assumptions that leads to the embodiment of management activities in the classroom, paying attention to general tenets.

First, because Japanese schooling is considered a form of group life, a primary goal of classroom management is to socialize children to the group (Rohlen and LeTendre, 1996). Japanese teachers are conscious that there is tension between individual children and the group in various social contexts of classrooms. Classroom management aims to dissolve this tension in favor of developing congenial and trustful relationships among children that serve as the basis of a classroom community. It provides a process and a structure in which children learn to become members of a group. It is apparent from our earlier discussion that, given the Japanese notion that the self is nestled in an interpersonal web, the group is the most potent context for children's lives, a context in which cognitive and noncognitive experiential learning occurs. Elementary teachers I studied in Tokyo unambiguously pointed out that, unless students are smoothly socialized within the group, it is difficult to promote effective teaching and learning in the classroom. The detailed plans for classroom management of elementary schools in Tokyo that I collected enunciate the importance of:

- harmonious development of the heart, the body, and individuality through participation in desirable group life;
- fostering of active initiatives and attitudes to build a better life as a member of a group; and
- cultivation of activities and methods for developing group life appropriate to different grade levels.

Children are expected to develop emotional dispositions to group life and the skills to organize groups, to participate in their activities, and to learn appropriate roles in classrooms from preschool through elementary levels. Preschool children develop receptivity to group activities through shared routines, including plays and rituals of singing, dancing, greeting, and ceremonies, all of which provide opportunities for strengthening children's identities as friends in a familylike environment (Lewis, 1995). Elementary students learn the skills they need to participate in group activities through a wide range of formal opportunities.

Second, a critical task of classroom management is to create a classroom community where the heart, empathy, and emotional security of each child and trustful relations are promoted. Japanese socialization is potent, enduring, and pervasive in accentuating emotions throughout childhood (Hess and Azuma, 1991; Azuma, Kashiwagi and Hess, 1981; De Vos, 1973). As mentioned earlier, one of the salient goals of elementary schooling is to nurture rich hearts, or *kokoro*. Because of the paramount significance of this goal, the Ministry of Education (1986) issued a handbook on how to encourage the development of empathetic hearts. Anthropologist Takie S. Lebra (1976) offers a relevant interpretation of empathy: "Empathy is manifested in Ego's readiness to anticipate and accommodate Alter's need. Ego tries to optimize Alter's comfort by providing what Alter needs or likes and by avoiding whatever might cause discomfort for him."

This suggests that heart, or *kokoro*, is a central concept in Japanese education that occupies teachers' attention. My research participants in Tokyo at both the elementary and middle school levels spoke of *kokoro* as the basis of education. For example, a veteran teacher at an elementary school said: "My focus is on developing children's *kokoro*—an important concern throughout my teaching career. Another thing is to foster their ability to empathize with others. I have wanted to create a classroom environment where every child feels comfortable and relaxed." Appreciation of children's feelings by their peers and teachers is paramount—emotional commitment by children to their classmates and by teachers to children all lead to the development of bonds among children and between children and teachers. Teachers' use of the word *kokoro* suggests its ontological status, the child's state of being seen from an expressive perspective. The child's sense of well-being and relationships with the world—peers, teachers, and other humans—are revealed and controlled by the heart. Both elementary and middle school teachers referred to the heart as a window through which a student's universe unfolds. It follows that creating an emotionally supportive classroom is a fundamental priority for the classroom teacher.

Third, building a classroom community is in large measure predicated on children's participation in self-management. Consistent with the notion of education for the whole child discussed earlier, children's active involvement in building a classroom community is considered an important part of schooling. It is assumed that even low-grade-level students are capable of taking responsibility for ownership of their classroom and of governing their activities in the school. A priority in classroom management, therefore, is to build students' skills in self-management. Self-management involves setting goals for the class, assigning division of work, and performing such duties as cleaning, lunch service, and student monitoring. Students sign up for different kinds of activities, called *kakari*, such as library, assembly, physical education, bulletin board, treasurers for classroom activities, study coordination, and the like. Student monitor duties are rotated daily. Two monitors, a boy and a girl, are usually in charge of duties, including conducting a brief morning meeting and an afternoon reflection meeting; cleaning the chalkboard; writing entries in the class diary; and calling the class to attention at the beginning and end of each period. The teacher does not begin a lesson until the monitor quiets the class and makes students pay attention. When everyone is quiet, the monitor announces, "We will begin the math lesson," and when the lesson is over, the monitor again calls the class's attention, saying, "We will finish the lesson." This monitoring function is important, enabling students to take control and be orderly while engaged in lessons and lesson-related activities.

What is preeminent about self-management is that it is a shared experiential process in which everyone plays a part. Thus, part of classroom management is educating children to learn roles and develop the essential attitudes and skills to perform them. The classroom teacher is a participant involved in every aspect of student activities, enabling her to offer assistance and advice. It is common for teachers to participate in cleaning the assigned areas, discharging lunch duties, and writing the classroom diary. All in all, self-management provides students with a significant degree of control of the classroom—activities, space, and time.

Fourth, elementary school classroom management is an inclusive activity echoing the notion of education for the whole child. The classroom management plan typically includes instructional strategies, moral education, and special activities, some of which emphasize experiential activities. Among instructional strategies, for example, are procedures to use small groups with an emphasis on cooperative work and problem solving; nurture an emotionally bonded classroom environment, where children feel secure in participating in classroom activities, discussion, and recitation; and develop individual uniqueness within the context of group life, referred to earlier as social-self realization. Both teachers and administrators often attribute lack of student concentration on the task at hand, disruptive behavior, and lack of participation in discussion to a teacher's poor management.

For example, in 1989 I was invited to observe a Japanese language demonstration class held at a Tokyo school by an experienced teacher, which was organized as part of the in-service education program. Having observed that class, in which students were distracted during the lesson, the principal candidly attributed the problem to the teacher's ineffective classroom management, especially the lack of a trusting relationship between her and her students. Teaching and learning in schools, Japanese teachers emphasize, are inseparable from emotional and noncognitive aspects of human development. As Nancy Sato (1996) points out, "[Cognition and cognitive development] are just two of many areas of expertise in the fluid ownership patterns of knowing, teaching, and learning." A fifth-grade teacher in a Tokyo school insisted that the fulcrum of his efforts to induce students' concentration on the cognitive task and exhort them to show high cognitive performance in the classroom is grounded in understanding of them gained through trustful relationships and interactions with them. That understanding, in his view, is reciprocal: he wants his students to understand him just as much as he endeavors to know them. It is that mutual personal knowledge and the friendliness resulting from such relationships that enables him to build an enduring motivational foundation for the learning and teaching enterprise.

Fifth, improvement of classroom management results from a short but important part of the school day devoted to reflection. Reflection is carried out formally, built into the schedule in the form of a daily afternoon "reflection meeting," classroom activities, and moral education. Reflection is a critical element in building up bonding and trust, group life, and other aspects of the classroom community. Children in all grades reflect on their experience every day. The reflection period allows students to focus on their own shortcomings, growth, and contributions to the class. The practice of self-reflection is seen in other institutionalized settings in Japanese society, such as in the training of Zen monks, of apprentices in other occupations, quality control circles, present-day teacher internship programs, in-service education for teachers and corporate employees, and so forth.

BUILDING A CLASSROOM COMMUNITY: CLASSROOM MANAGEMENT PRACTICE

Having already discussed general tenets of classroom management, in this section I will look at particular practices, focusing on the elementary school. I have explored both cultural values, reflected in the classroom, and tenets of classroom management. Nonetheless, there is less uniformity in classroom management strategies than one would expect, because they invariably reflect teachers' different pedagogical beliefs and professional competence, and the leadership of the school. Classroom management by and large supports or enhances classroom culture, which is a dimension of the school's covert curriculum (Kojima, 1990), in contrast to the overt curriculum consisting of academic and other formal subjects taught at school. The school's overt curriculum is delineated in the course of study issued by the Ministry of Education and is uniform throughout the country, but classroom management is considerably influenced by the creativity of individual teachers and an individual school's culture of teaching. In short, strategies for classroom management reflect professional qualities of individual teachers and schools.

Moreover, definitions of classroom management also vary, including the following views (Kojima, 1990; Nagaoka, 1995). The first view is represented by scholars and practitioners, who define it as an approach to creating a classroom community. The second includes this approach and some nonacademic programs mentioned previously, whereas the third is most inclusive, addressing both academic and nonacademic aspects of schooling. The third view embodies strategies for promoting the classroom community and teaching. Given these variations in classroom management practices and definitions, the literature on the subject abounds, with a broad range of publications, including a number of books written by classroom teachers on their practices. Because classroom management is diffusely conceived and extensively embedded in teachers' personal knowledge and practice, there is wide latitude for exploration and creativity. Teachers share classroom practices not only through books and other publications, but also in citywide and prefectural meetings, in which many schools are represented. There is also a national organization of classroom management practitioners that meets once a year. In 1958, the Japan Teachers Union organized a national study group known as *Zenseiken* at a time when this powerful union enrolled nearly 90 percent of the teachers. *Zenseiken* became an influential group of teachers who explored a new approach to building a classroom community and student guidance (Zenseiken, 1990). Japanese teachers' commitment and interest in classroom management are extensive and widely shared among themselves, and teacher networks play an important part in offering opportunities for sharing support and collaboration in their field of practice.

Classroom management initiatives commonly involve both schoolwide and individual efforts. It is general practice for Japanese schools to decide on a study theme each year as the focus of yearlong commitment. Some schools concentrate on classroom management, encouraging teachers' concerted commitment to developing perspectives and strategies. These schools usually organize demonstration classes for observation, sharing, and critique to which practitioners from various schools are invited; they also publish monographs for dissemination. Experts are invited to offer advice to observed teachers. Incidentally, in-service education of this type is very popular and is held at most Japanese schools several times a year; it is widespread throughout the country. Other schools coordinate individual teachers' classroom management initiatives, which are compiled for administrative review.

Given the fact that Japanese classroom management centers on the creation of a classroom community, teachers' initiatives are critical for enriching its depth and breadth. In the pre- and post-World War II period, notably successful teachers often published their records of practice as books, some of which have been highly influential and offer useful examples for classroom practice (Nakano and Koguma, 1993). Those teachers also served as leaders of voluntarily organized circles of like-minded professionals. For example, Muchaku Seikyo (1951) led a movement to create a classroom community through sharing children's diaries that described their poverty-stricken lives in the immediate postwar years. His book, *School Echoing in the Mountains*, was followed by the publication of *Classroom Revolution* by Kenjiro Konishi (1955), who was influenced by Seikyo. Tadaharu Onishi, a middle school teacher in Shikoku, developed an influential approach to the creation of a classroom community and collectivism in education. He played a major role in the aforementioned *Zenseiken* and published a widely read book titled *A Classroom with a Core* (1963).

By way of illustration, I will now discuss a classroom management program currently implemented by Midorigaoka Elementary School in northern Japan, which is a relatively small school with two classrooms at each grade level. The school's campaign to articulate and enhance classroom management is supported by its entire teaching staff, who agreed to make their school a demonstration site in 1995. The school views classroom management as a framework to develop a broad educational plan. Its classroom management program, which includes each teacher's detailed classroom plan, delineates instructional goals and strategies, emphases in moral education, and special activities (the aforementioned three broad areas defined by the course of study). Special activities, which constitute an instrumental core of classroom management, aim to provide students with group activities to develop both social and physical skills for self-management and distinctive individual qualities and to build children's competence to contribute to group life and self-realization. Classroom management is designed to primarily promote three goals: (1) activities that are conducive to enhancing supportive and sympathetic human relations; (2) *fureai*, or interactions that contribute to nurturing a warm heart, and (3) self-awareness through *fureai* and a sense of attachment to the group. Midorigaoka staff want to permeate various aspects of schooling with these goals. (The term *fureai* is rich in cultural meaning. Although its English translation is "interaction" or "contact," neither translation conveys its full emotional subtlety. *Fureai* is best understood as emotionally supportive interpersonal contact.)

Midorigaoka emphasizes the development of individual children's distinct qualities in the three areas of schooling. The school enunciates these individual qualities and self-realization in the context of group activities. Because this enunciation appears to be self-contradictory, it calls for a further comment. Although the Japanese are fundamentally group-oriented in their behavior and emotional dispositions, they strive to be distinctive persons capable of displaying what they call *shutaisei*, or individual presence by a degree of independence, self-initiative, and some unique contribution. Put differently, they seek a harmonious balance of both group orientation and *shutaisei*. It follows that persons who are completely submerged in a group are considered unworthy. What is euphemistically stressed nowadays as individuality, a standard term in the current Japanese vocabulary, refers to active *shutaisei*. Present-day emphasis on individuality in the above sense reflects a new pedagogical orientation originating especially from Japan's school reforms in the 1980s, which stressed diversity and individuality in schooling by rejecting excessive traditional imposition of uniformity and conformity on students. Accordingly, the Ministry of Education revised the course of study in 1989 to reflect the new orientation in school programs and disseminated a handbook titled *Creation and Development of Curriculum Based on a New Vision of Academic Performance* (1993).

It is apparent that Midorigaoka is trying to align its classroom management strategies with the new pedagogical ideology. Teachers at the school emphasize a classroom climate conducive to the development of distinctive individual qualities and *shutaisei*. That climate promotes students' cooperation, encouragement of each other, cheerfulness, robustness, and mutual respect. These attributes of classroom culture, developed through classroom management, reflect qualities of interpersonal relations, what I earlier referred to as bonding. In this climate, classroom management seeks (1) shared expression of mutual concerns of teacher and students; (2) articulation of what students want to accomplish; (3) provision of space and opportunity by which students may engage in efforts to achieve their goals; and (4) the teacher's provision of appropriate assistance to students.

Midorigaoka teachers' strategies to develop students' distinctive qualities, which by and large reflect the national pattern of classroom management, involve a variety of formally organized settings and activities, to which I referred earlier. For example, they include:

- short morning class meetings,
- lessons,
- classroom duties, including student monitoring and play during recess,
- lunch time,
- reflection meetings and cleaning, and
- events, such as sports festivals, student theaters, and mobile class-rooms.

Meanwhile, *fureai* is promoted through related group-oriented activities and programs such as:

- activities that create classroom goals,
- classroom activities to share interests and concerns,
- games involving all students in the class,
- events, such as sports and art festivals, study trips, and mobile class-rooms,
- active use of "reflection" meetings managed by students,
- club and committee activities,
- cultivation of gardens and planting vegetables and flowers,
- volunteer activities, such as cleaning the school neighborhood, and
- sister-school events with a Canadian school.

These activities constitute part and parcel of the holistic education discussed and are common among elementary schools in Japan.

Midorigaoka teachers also seek to achieve classroom management goals within the instructional setting. They pay special attention to individual students' distinctive characteristics and interests during lessons, and they create opportunities to engage in cooperative learning for collaboration and emotional support. Their aim is to empower each child with the desire and interest to participate in the academic task at hand. That, they emphasize, requires the teacher to develop a holistic understanding of every child. Cooperative learning occurs in small groups in the classroom, which Japanese teachers customarily call *han*. Teachers at Midorigaoka adopt a combination of the whole class and small groups as teaching formats. Small groups consist of two types of *han:* groups for daily life management, which address various tasks to provide support for students' self-management, and groups for academic projects. Life-management groups are employed to facilitate collaboration and peer assistance during the class hour, while project groups are formed to promote projects in the academic area. The former groups are small support networks each consisting of about six students, which provide a social anchorage in carrying out classroom tasks. They are semipermanent groups, reorganized only once or twice a year. Both kinds of groups are organized not only in elementary but also in middle schools. At a middle school in Osaka attended by Japanese minority students, for example, life-management groups are used as a vehicle to enhance minority education.

Life-management groups induce cooperation between minority and majority students, encourage student autonomy, and a sense of responsibility for promoting classroom life. These small groups are selected by the students themselves, and the group leader is chosen by its members. Because groups do not function efficiently without effective leaders, teachers must help develop students' leadership qualities, including the ability to take the initiative and coordinate activities, fairness, and thoughtfulness.

Midorigaoka staff view classroom management as a cycle of four developmental stages: a planning phase (April–June), an operational phase (July–September), a mature phase (October–December), and a reflective phase (January–March). (The Japanese academic calendar begins in April and terminates in March.) Most critical to designing classroom management are the first three months of the planning stage, during which *gakkyuzukuri*, or the creation of a classroom community, starts. *Gakkyuzukuri* involves the development of classroom goals, the creation of small groups for life management, a decision on *kakari* or voluntary activities and classroom monitors, and plans for classroom activities. During the first and second weeks of the new academic year, each class devotes the classroom activity period to making decisions on these items of student self-management.

Classroom goals are inclusive, just as school goals are, but they differ in emphasis from classroom to classroom. Each class decides what kind of classroom community it wants to create. Like teachers in other schools, Midorigaoka staff consider classroom goals to be of great importance in nurturing classroom character. One of the sixth-grade classes, for example, devoted one classroom activity period to discussing its goals based on a survey questionnaire it conducted in which each class member was asked to describe the kind of classroom the class should develop. The class agreed on the following thematic goal: the creation of a classroom community characterized by a lighthearted and cheerful atmosphere, thoughtfulness, and perseverance, and inspired by its responsibility and pride as the highest grade level in the school.

Because self-management requires individual roles and their performance, each class at Midorigaoka discusses requisite roles and role allocation upon the advice of the classroom teacher. Requisite routines must be decided and incorporated into student life in the classroom, so that student self-management may occur smoothly. *Toban*, or duties whose performance is essential to the maintenance of the classroom, require rotation among students throughout the year. *Toban* duties are complemented by *kakari* activities distinguished from these duties at Midorigaoka, as at other schools. They include voluntary tasks that students can choose to further their interests.

Further observations on morning and reflection meetings draw on practices in other schools. The morning meeting conducted by student monitors is held for ten to fifteen minutes before the first class to familiarize class members with the classroom life for the day. It includes greetings, health and attendance check, the teacher's talk, an announcement of the activities of the day, and one-minute speeches by two or three students. Students may choose any topic pertaining to their experience for their one-minute speech, the purpose of which is to share their thoughts and experiences. This segment of the meeting may be replaced by the singing of a song or a brief oral book report. Reflection meetings also last fifteen minutes. Typical agenda items are reports from *kakari* groups, reflections on the day, the teacher's talk and health check, distribution of information, and a formal good-bye to each other. As these meetings are held every day, they tend to become ritualistic, causing students' interest to flag. The teacher's role is pivotal in helping to maintain interest by suggesting, for example, alternate topics or activities.

Another important aspect of classroom management is nonacademic classroom activities, for which, as mentioned earlier, one period is reserved per week. Members of the class are responsible for creating an activity program for the entire year. An elementary school in Tokyo, for example, has an activity program for sixth graders that includes the following selected monthly topics: discussion on a classroom community to be developed and creation of *kakari* activities for April; making plans for an athletic festival and developing cooperation between boys and girls for May; deciding a program for a mobile classroom; and organizing a display by the classroom newspaper *kakari* for June.

I will elaborate on the mobile classroom, which is based on the assumption that knowledge and skills are acquired in an experiential process with mental, emotional, moral, and physical components. It is offered in elementary schools throughout Japan and comprises one of the most memorable experiences for students. Students participate in an intense retreat for two days and one night at a distant, mountainous site. They gain knowledge from their exposure to nature, deepen their appreciation of communal activities, and learn social responsibility by participating in these activities. It is an exciting experience for students, contributing to their appreciation of interpersonal relations. In the special activities class, students construct a detailed retreat program featuring a campfire, games, meals, and an orienteering event. Each aspect of the program requires students to play particular roles or perform *kakari* tasks. The campfire, for example, involves a number of tasks necessitating performance of appropriate roles, and students must agree on the assignment of these roles.

Likewise, classroom activities practiced in middle schools play an important role in creating a classroom community, especially because the homeroom teachers' contact with students is relatively limited, since teaching is specialized, as in the United States. In a middle school in Tokyo I studied in 1994, classroom activities substantially contributed to promoting a sense of bonding among students in ninth-grade classrooms, where there had previously been little sense of mutual trust. Distrustful relations had resulted from widespread student rebellion against teachers, cases of bullying, and violence. A main concern of teachers at the school was to restore trustful relations with students and *fureai*. Classroom activities offered students an opportunity to organize events involving all students. One event was a classroom-based choral contest, combined with an art festival, organized by ninth-graders. They used the special activities period to make plans, rehearse for several weeks in addition to after-school time, and decide on a set of rules to be observed during the contest. Homeroom teachers regularly participated in rehearsals and helped students prepare for the art festival. Students displayed intense interest in the events and a spirit of unity throughout the entire process of rehearsal and preparation, which surprised the homeroom teachers. When the event was held on Saturday in a gym, it was a great success, testifying to 250 students' cooperation, self-imposed discipline, and desire to win. Not a single disruption occurred during the entire three-hour program.

Another relevant classroom management program at the middle-school level is club activities, which are very popular and contribute to the character development of students (Letendre, 1996). In each club there is a chain of command demanding that students learn to endure hardship for the sake of the group; clubs require students' intense, daily participation. The majority of teachers in most middle schools in Japan participate in club activities as advisors in the belief that they provide a unique space in the school program enabling them to develop close relationships with students. One teacher suggested that these activities significantly enhance the development of students' nonacademic interests and their ability to organize and promote their own activities. Teachers devote one to two hours to these extracurricular activities every day but Wednesday, when a staff meeting is held. Club activities are highly valued by teachers despite the fact that they contribute to intensification of teaching. Although club activities are not a classroom-based program, the personal knowledge of students that homeroom teachers gain from participation contributes to successful classroom management.

SUMMARY

A pivotal assumption of Japanese classroom management, especially at the elementary level, is that teaching and learning are closely connected with the emotional, social, and physical aspects of human development. The notion of educating the whole child requires inclusiveness in schooling. The centrality of classroom management lies in the belief that its main purpose is to socialize children to the group when they have a great deal of plasticity, curiosity, energy, and spontaneity. Japanese children's personal identity, social skills, and emotional balance are developed in the context of interpersonal interactions. Sensitivity to other people, qualities such as empathy, thoughtfulness, and kindness, are highly valued. The heart becomes a window to the self through which individuals reveal their qualities. However, those who are completely immersed in the group are considered unworthy; they are expected to build attitudes of *shutaisei*, or active subjectivity. These values are embedded in Japanese culture, and Japanese teachers strive to realize them through classroom management. The underlying philosophy of Japanese classroom management is different from the view that classroom management is primarily instrumental, intended to promote students' cognitive development, that is, teaching and learning in a narrow sense. Striving to achieve the goals of classroom management that have been discussed in this chapter is stressed more than discipline and the rules of behavior that students are expected to conform to in order to maintain classroom order. Emotional balance, exertion, robustness, participation, self-management, and an experiential process of learning are enunciated as goals, in contrast to the academic goals relevant to a purely cognitive view of education.

Gakkyuzukuri, or the creation of a community, is the overriding goal of classroom management. It is inclusive and reflective and enhances self-management. Students are expected to assume multiple roles to achieve self-management. A typical classroom management plan that Japanese teachers develop demands consideration of the following points (Nagaoka, 1995): goals (schoolwide, grade-level, and classroom); a classroom profile; an overall framework of classroom management; and strategies to promote classroom management (including the creation of a classroom community, particular instructional emphases, student guidance, physical environment of the classroom, and collaboration with parents). This chapter addressed the cultural and pedagogical rationales of classroom management and salient strategies to promote it.

Amagasa (1995) suggests a set of criteria against which the success of classroom management may be measured. I will cite some of these. The first is clarity of classroom goals. Practitioners must ask if they are concrete and specific, and if they are formulated on the basis of a clear understanding of students' characteristics. The second is ascertaining whether practitioners have a written classroom plan and concrete strategies to implement it, and whether the plan addresses the needs of individual students. The third is checking the process of implementation. Relevant questions pertaining to the implementation include: Are students enjoying an emotionally balanced classroom life? Do students enjoy receptive interpersonal relations conducive to mutual support and respect? Have students developed an awareness that they are living in a peer community? Are students' creative ideas reflected in special activities, including classroom activities and the self-management process? Do classroom teachers have a clear understanding of students as members of the group and as individuals? The fourth is openness of classroom management. In elementary schools homeroom teachers have nearly exclusive control of their classrooms, by virtue of the fact that their students are under their supervision for the entire day. Such exclusive control of students tends to lead to the development of a closed classroom, or what is often called a "classroom kingdom." Openness of classroom management, hence, becomes an important avenue of consideration. Classroom teachers are encouraged to check the extent to which their management draws on collegial consultation and superiors' advice.

I add a final comment. There is a tension between the Japanese pattern of classroom management, with its emphasis on bonding among students and a personhood embedded in the group, and recent pedagogical views that emphasize individuality. The teachers whom I interviewed are fully aware of this new emphasis on individualized teaching and learning and are interested in implementing it. Recent education policy and the literature in the field of teaching articulate the new approach. Yet whole-class teaching still remains a dominant method of teaching in the schools I have observed over the past ten years, regardless of classroom size—although the whole class is frequently broken into small cooperative groups, as discussed earlier. Japanese classrooms at elementary and middle school levels are heterogeneously organized and undifferentiated. Nowadays, the average class size at the elementary level is thirty students; there is a continued downsizing trend largely due to demographic changes. Of late I have seen several schools where class size ranges from fifteen to twenty. But teachers continue to adopt the whole-class teaching method, reflecting the traditional culture of teaching in Japan. Although Japanese teachers' approaches, recognizing individual differences in the classroom, display elements of pedagogical innovation, they are still modest in individualizing teaching and learning, which are more often than not confined within the accustomed pedagogical framework.

The absence of individualized teaching and learning is not simply a result of teachers' adherence to traditional pedagogy. Given their overriding interest in the creation of a classroom community, my research participants believed that differentiation and ability grouping would adversely affect it. Differences in student ability are recognized only in the context of the classroom community. Further teachers prefer a large classroom of thirty to a smaller one, because, in their view, the larger classroom is livelier and more active, promoting animated interaction among students, and not dominated by a few superior students. This suggests that these teachers experience a tension between their culturally grounded beliefs and the emerging trend.

Japanese teachers' unchanging dispositions, strongly affected by the culture of teaching into which they have been enculturated, and cultural forces that perpetuate the centrality of group orientation, are evident in many Japanese schools. Teaching in Japan is best conceived as a craft that is reproduced and refined by practitioners. During the process of occupational socialization, mentors, such as senior colleagues with whom beginning teachers interact, play a major role in the reproduction of teaching. Further, in-service educational programs organized at the individual school and citywide levels are largely reproductive and traditional, contributing only in limited ways to new views of teaching. Japanese teachers, however are being gradually exposed to a new orientation in teaching and classroom management that gives more prominence to individuality.

REFERENCES

Amagasa, S. (1995). "Planning and Evaluation of Classroom Management." In. J. Nagaoka and S. Okuda (eds.), *Classroom and grade-level management*. Tokyo: Gyosei.

Azuma, H. (1994). *Japanese Socialization and Education* Tokyo: University of Tokyo Press.

Azuma, H., Kashiwagi, K. and Hess, R. D. (1981). *Mothers' Attitudes/Behavior and Children's Intellectual Development*. Tokyo: University of Tokyo Press.

Befu, H. (1986). "The Social and Cultural Background of Child Development in Japan and the United States." In H. Stevenson, H. Azuma and K. Hakuta, (eds.), pp. 13–27. *Child Development and Education in Japan*. New York: W. H. Freeman.

Dahrendorf, R. (1978). *Life Chances: Approaches to Social and Political Theory.* Chicago: University of Chicago Press.

De Vos, G. A. (1973). *Socialization for Achievement.* Berkeley: University of California Press.

Dore, R. (1987). *Taking Japan Seriously: A Confucian Perspective on Leading Economic Issues.* Palo Alto: Stanford University Press.

Hess, R. D. and Azuma, J. (1991). "Cultural Support for Schooling: Contrast between Japan and the United States." *Educational Researcher.* 20(9), pp. 2–3.

Hsu, F. (1963). *Clan, Caste, and Club.* New York: Van Nostrand.

Kefed, L. "The Zandhi Zoku and the Evolution of Metropolitan Mind." In L. Austin, (ed.), (1975). pp. 279–300. *The Paradox of Progress.* New Haven: Yale University Press.

Kojima, K. (1990). *Between the School and the Classroom.* Tokyo: Gyosei.

Konishi, K. (1955). *Classroom Revolution.* Tokyo: Makishoten.

Lebra, T. S. (1976). *Japanese Patterns of Behavior.* Honolulu: University of Hawaii.

LeTendre, G. (1996). "Shido: The Concept of Guidance." In T. Rohlen and G. LeTendre, (eds.), pp. 275–294. *Teaching and Learning in Japan.* New York: Cambridge University Press.

Lewis, C. (1995). *Educating Hearts and Minds.* New York: Cambridge University Press.

Lipset, S. M. (1996). *American Exceptionalism.* New York: Norton Ministry of Education (Japan).

———. (1986). *Teaching Methods for Educating Empathic Hearts at the Elementary Level.* Tokyo: Ministry of Education.

———. (1993). *Creation and Development of Curriculum Based on a New Vision of Academic Performance.* Tokyo: Mombusho.

———. (1994). *Course of Study on Special Activities.* Tokyo: Ministry of Education.

Nagaoka, J. (1995). "What is Classroom and Grade-level Management?" In J. Nagaoka and S. Okuda (eds.), pp. 2–26. *Classroom and Grade-level Management.* Tokyo: Gyosei.

Nakane, C. (1972). *Japanese Society.* Berkeley: University of California Press.

Nakano, A. and S. Koguma (eds.). (1993). *The Japanese Teacher: Creation of a Classroom Community.* Tokyo: Gyosei.

Onishi, T. (1963). *A Classroom with a Core.* Tokyo: Meijitosho.

Parsons, T. (1951). *The Social System.* Glencoe, IL: Free Press.

Peak, L. (1993). *Learning to Go to School in Japan.* Berkeley: University of California Press.

Rohlen, T. and LeTendre, G. K. (1996). "Introduction: Japanese Theories of Learning." In T. Rohlen and G. K. LeTendre (eds.), pp. 1–16. *Teaching and Learning in Japan.* New York: Cambridge University Press.

Sato, N. (1996). "Honoring the Individual." In T. Rohlen and G. LeTendre (eds.), pp. 119–153. *Teaching and Learning in Japan.* New York: Cambridge University Press.

Seikyo, M. (ed.). (1951). *School Echoing in the Mountains.* Tokyo: Siedosha.

Shimahara, N. (1996). "The Culture of Teaching in Japan." *Bulletin of the National Institute of Multimedia Education.* 14, pp. 37–60.

Shimahara, N. and Sakai, A. (1995). *Learning to Teach in Two Cultures: Japan and the United States.* New York: Garland.

Smith, R. J. (1983). *Japanese Society: Tradition, Self and the Social Order.* New York: Cambridge University Press.

Tobin, J., Wu, D. and Davidson, D. (1989). *Preschool in Three Cultures: Japan, China, and the United States.* New Haven: Yale University Press.

Zenseiken (National Study Group for Guidance for Living). (1990). *Introduction to the Creation of a Classroom Community.* Tokyo: Gyosei.

CHAPTER 19

Reforms to Teacher Education in Indonesia: Does More Mean Better?[1]

H. Dean Nielsen

ABSTRACT   *In recent years, Indonesia has made serious efforts to improve the quality of its public schools through changes in teacher education. Since 1990, all new primary school teachers have had to be certified at the post-secondary level while practicing teachers have been urged to upgrade their credentials. In addition, extensive networks of in-service training and professional support have been constructed and new civil service laws for teacher career development enacted. Unfortunately, these structural changes have generally not exerted their desired influences on the quality of teaching since they are largely undermined by a bureaucratic environmental press which does not accord high priority to educational quality. Dominated by the agenda of the bu*reaucratic authoritarian state, *the bureaucratic environment has replaced lofty and sometimes, elaborate plans/mechanisms ("levers") for quality improvement with an emphasis on reaching quantitative targets of "deliverables," expanding the state bureaucracy and central control, and strengthening national security and political loyalty. Also, consistent with the theory of the bureaucratic authoritarian state is the government's heavy reliance on external technical assistance and interagency fragmentation and competition. Changes in the national bureaucratic environment will be required before quality improvements in teacher education can bear fruit.*

CHANGES IN EDUCATION POLICY: AN EMPHASIS ON QUALITY

During Indonesia's "First Period of Long Term Development" (1969/70–1994/95), the government of President Suharto made impressive progress towards "universalizing" basic education. Whereas the gross participation rate in primary education at the beginning of the period (1969/70) was about 41 percent, by 1995, it had climbed to over 100 percent! Participation in lower secondary education (grades 7–9) also increased dramatically over that period, from 15 percent to 48 percent. By the early 1990s, the government decided to expand its definition of Basic Education (that expected for all youths) to include lower secondary education (nine years in all). When the government's Sixth 5-Year Plan was launched in 1994, the universal attainment of nine years of Basic Education was one of its main social goals.

With the break-up of the Soviet Union in 1991, Indonesia became the *fourth* most populous country in the world. Thus, programs of national-level change in education are enormous in scope and complexity. For example, as of 1988/89, the number of primary school students in the country was well over 25 million and the number of primary school teachers more than 1.2 million. At that time, primary school teachers were trained in one of the 632 teacher training high schools (SPGs), 208 public and 424 private. As will be described below, by 1990, the SPGs were phased out in favour of diploma-level training (two years of post-secondary) at institutes or faculties of higher education. This latter form of training reaches school teachers through in-service education (near 1 million potential participants!). Clearly, the government had embarked on an immense task of educational change.

This emphasis on institutional growth and expansion has been accompanied by an unprecedented concern for educational quality. Studies conducted during the 1970s and 1980s revealed that outcomes of primary education were far below desired levels. For example, a national assessment in 1976 showed that, in general, primary school completers attained less than 50 percent mastery on achievement tests in science, mathematics, social studies and the national language, with rural students failing far below the national average. More recent analyses, using 1987 primary school leaving examination results, continue to show poor subject matter mastery: 50 percent of test takers in the National Capital Region earned scores below the minimal level in science and mathematics.

Therefore, in the government's Sixth 5-Year Plan, there is a serious commitment to improving educational quality—defined generally as the capacity of the schools to contribute to national development goals through student growth in the cognitive, attitudinal, and behavioral domains. In actual fact, educational quality improvement had already been articulated as a national goal by the government in its New Educational Policy (1988) and reemphasized for Basic Education in Law No. 2 on Basic Education (1989). To carry out these policies, the Ministry of Education and Culture (MOEC) initiated numerous projects, many with development agency support (e.g. UNESCO/UNDP, USAID, the Asian Development Bank, and the World Bank) to:

- revise the national curriculum (making it more *active learning oriented*);
- improve textbooks and textbook distribution;
- enhance the status and career patterns of teachers;
- create teacher support systems, involving administrative as well as peer support networks; and

- strengthen programs of teacher education, both pre-service and in-service.

This paper takes a close look at Indonesia's efforts to improve the quality of education through the strengthening of teacher training. It finds unprecedented levels of commitment to and investment in teacher development activities involving a wide range of projects having state-of-the-art quality improvement features. A critical examination of these project features will reveal a pattern of disappointing results in terms of actual quality improvement: more teacher education and professional development has, in general, not led to better teacher performance. To explain this shortfall, the concept of the *bureaucratic authoritarian state* will be invoked. It will be argued that no matter how much money is invested in teacher education or how sincere and talented teacher educators are, the country's efforts towards quality improvement will be undermined by a state bureaucratic environment which has pressed for goals and priorities fundamentally unsupportive of quality improvement.

TEACHER EDUCATION IN INDONESIA

The strengthening of teacher education programs became one of the centerpieces in the MOEC's quality improvement campaign. Its prominence was both a consequence of demonstrated deficiencies in teacher preparation and a strong faith buttressed by intenational research results (Fuller, 1986; Oliveira, Farrell and Etienne, 1988) that improved teacher education could make a difference.

During the period of rapid system expansion (1970s and early 1980s), Indonesia was chronically short of trained primary school teachers. During that period, several crash programs were instituted in order to supply enough teachers to fill tens of thousands of new classrooms each year. In the beginning, persons could be certified with scarcely more education than the students they were sent to teach (primary school and three years of secondary). These requirements increased until they stabilized in the mid 1970s at the SPG level-teacher training high school (or normal school), which amounted to six years of post-primary education. With the help of development agencies such as the World Bank, SPGs were established throughout the country. By the late 1980s, the teacher shortage had turned into a vast teacher surplus (in the early 1990s estimated to be as large as 250,000) (Nielsen and Somerset, 1992). The fact that huge cohorts of prospective teachers were coming on to the job market without a hope for getting a teaching job began to create an unfortunate backwash on people's perceptions about the desirability of teacher education. In fact, declining job prospects was cited as one of the main reasons for declining numbers and qualifications of teacher education applicants in the late 1980s (Somerset, 1988).

At about the same time, the Research and Development Office of the MOEC released a new study of teacher competence. The results were devastating: only 45 percent of a random sample of SPG-trained teachers could pass the science test given to the primary school completers. In addition, teachers appeared unable to use science equipment, claiming that they never were trained to do so and had no time to carry out experiments anyway (Jiyono, 1986). Another study, based on field observations in West Java, found teaching methods to be seriously flawed, asserting that the average teacher fails to employ basic pedagogical tools such as clarfying learning objectives, explaining new concepts clearly, giving examples, stimulating thinking through appropriate questioning, and providing feedback on test results (Djalil, 1988). The World Bank *Basic Education Study: Indonesia* concludes its section on teacher preparation at the SPG with the following grim assessment:

> Pre-service training has relied upon inappropriate lecture methods and has provided insufficient opportunities for students to practice teaching skills. Despite tremendous efforts in recent years to improve SPG curricula and materials, pre-service teacher training is isolated from the realities of primary classrooms and teacher trainers are usually not themselves trained in primary methods. (World Bank, 1989)

Despite this gloomy assessment, faith in the potential of teacher education to become a key factor in quality improvement has been buttressed by recent global studies as well as by the MOEC's own research. Two recent global reviews have placed teacher education and training among the crucial determinants of school effectiveness and student achievement (Fuller, 1986; Oliveira *et al.*, 1988). Furthermore, a large international study showed teacher factors to be more of a contributor to student achievement in low-income countries than in high-income countries (Heyneman and Loxley, 1983). Research conducted in Indonesia by the MOEC's Office of Educational Research and Development, supported under US AID's *Improved Policy and Planning Project*, was even more specific in its findings about the impact of teacher quality and subject matter mastery, as indicated by the following conclusions based on school samples from three diverse provinces:

> It appears that teacher quality and the length of instructional time in each subject are the strongest policy manipulable predictors of student achievement. Teachers' scores on subject content tests turns out to be most positively related to student achievement. This teacher capacity variable is the strongest not only among the teacher quality variables, but among all school quality variables included in the model. (Suryadi, 1992)

PROGRAMS FOR STRENGTHENING TEACHER PREPARATION AND PROFESSIONAL GROWTH

Sensing both the deficiencies in existing teacher preparation programs and potential of such programs to affect teacher subject matter mastery and teaching skills, the government of Indonesia made several bold moves in the late 1980s and early 1990s. First, it declared that as of 1990, all primary school teacher education would be conducted at the university level (as opposed to the senior secondary school level). This meant phasing out its 152 state SPGs and replacing them with two-year post-secondary diploma (D-II) programs in the country's teacher education institutes and faculties of education. At the same time, the Government decided to provide D-II upgrading opportunities to all practicing primary school teachers in the country (except those nearing retirement) through in-service education. Moreover, a new program of teacher support called Primary Education Quality Improvement Project (PEQIP) was initiated within the Directorate General of Primary and Secondary Education with the support of the World Bank in 1992, which was to use local teacher networks as a means of providing in-service training and other forms of professional support to teachers. Finally, the government decided in 1988 to change the Civil Service Laws, extending a "functional credit system" to primary school teachers that would allow them to earn faster promotions in the system, with the potential to rise to a civil service level comparable to that of a university professor while still remaining a school teacher.

The D-II teacher upgrading activities were eventually given additional project support through the initiation of a World Bank Loan to the Directorate General of Higher Education which began in 1992 and which became known as the Primary School Teacher Development Project. Since universities had never before had the task of producing certified teachers at the primary school level, the project included a large staff development component for primary school teacher educators (e.g. 175 fellowships for overseas graduate degrees) and substantial support for D-II program development, both pre-service and in-service. Based on findings showing substantial inequalities of teacher distribution (Nielsen and Somerset, 1992), the project also aimed to include an information and tracking system for identifying teacher shortage areas and a selective recruitment mechanism to help youths from those areas to become teachers.

QUALITY IMPROVEMENT ASPECTS OF CURRENT TEACHER DEVELOPMENT PROJECTS

Each of the interventions mentioned was designed to contain significant quality improvement features or "levers." These will be discussed under the following headings: Pre-service Teacher Education at the Diploma II Level; Diploma II Upgrading for Practicing Teachers; In-service Education and Professional Support through Teacher Networks; and A Functional Credit System for Teacher Career Development.

Pre-service Teacher Education at the Diploma II Level

Among the many quality enhancement features of the pre-service Diploma II (D-II) program is the fact that its candidates are drawn from among upper secondary school graduates. This means that its recruits have stronger backgrounds in school subjects (language, mathematics, science, social studies) than those who entered the lower level SPGs. It also means that the intake is more selective (there is a screening to get into upper secondary schools) and students are more mature (at least by three years) than those who entered the SPG. In addition, the program provides additions to subject matter knowledge and pedagogical training at the university level. It is also more classroom practice oriented than the SPG was, requiring students to visit and observe classrooms early on, and expecting them to spend an entire semester (one out of five) in student teaching.

One threat to quality enhancement in the program is the fact that institutes and faculties of education newly charged to implement it had never done primary school teacher education before. There has been a concern that the D-II instructors are providing training more suitable for secondary school teachers. The program is dealing with this threat by recruiting substantial numbers of former SPG teachers to work in the program. In addition, it has used World Bank loan funds to initiate a massive staff development and retraining effort: by 1996/97, up to 175 teacher educators were expected to have received advanced graduate training overseas (masters or doctoral) in fields related to primary school teacher education, and hundreds of others will have acquired second undergraduate degrees in subject areas where staff capacity has been weak (mathematics, science, special education, etc.). An additional quality enhancement feature of the program is the fact that enrolments were to be kept low—no more than seven thousand per year nationwide during the first few years to ensure that all graduates would find teaching jobs and to allow the program to concentrate on quality improvement measures such as staff training, curriculum revision, and learning materials development.

The selective recruitment feature of the program is a quality enhancement feature of a different sort. It is based on research findings revealing severe teacher shortages in some areas and high rates of teacher turnover (Nielsen and Somerset, 1992). To deal with the problem, the bank-supported *Primary School Teacher Development Project* provides funds for an information system for tracking teacher distribution problems and identifying teacher shortage areas. It is then expected to initiate selective recruitment efforts in those areas, admitting candidates without their need to take the national university selection examination, and providing scholarships, dormitory space and tutorial support, if needed. The project also includes support for periodic coordination forums with school system managers so that they can be involved in decisions about teacher recruitment and placement. These features are to produce university trained teachers who are willing to work and remain in chronic teacher shortage areas.[2]

Diploma II Upgrading for Practicing Teachers

This is one of the most ambitious quality enhancement programs ever mounted anywhere. It supports D-II upgrading for *all* current primary school teachers except those near retirement or already possessing post-secondary credentials, about 800,000 teachers in all. This is to be accomplished through the teachers studying modules prepared by the Indonesian Open University and attending weekly tutorials. The program is actually called D-II "equivalency," since it is not precisely the same as the pre-service program. For one thing, the curriculum is weighted towards subject matter mastery, under the assumption that teachers already have had basic pedagogy courses at the SPG and have learned many things about teaching practice through experience on the job. Veteran teachers can, in fact, receive some academic credit for their work experience. The main goal for the project is clear: to help primary school teachers overcome common deficiencies in subject matter mastery.

The modules for the upgrading were hastily written by university lecturers in the early 1990s since the project was asked to begin operations just nine months after it was annnounced. None of the learning materials were field tested. Therefore, resources were allocated in the *Primary School Teacher Development Project* for curricular revision and learning materials improvement. The intake into the program has been near forty thousand per year over the past five years, with approximately half of the teachers receiving full scholarships; the other half have been required to pay the Open University's modest tuition and fees.

In-service Education and Professional Support through Teacher Networks

This program of quality improvement is based on a successful experimental program mounted by MOEC's Curriculum Development Center with the support of the British Overseas Development Agency and the British Council (Tangyong, Wahyudi, Gardner and Haws, 1989). Often called the Cianjur Project (after the original project site in West Java), the program provides professional support by helping teachers organize "working groups." Such groups draw members from clusters of neighboring schools and convene several times a year. They become local forums in which teachers can discuss problems related to instruction and classroom management and receive in-service education initiated by the teachers themselves or by similar working groups of local school administrators. After the successful and highly visible piloting in Cianjur (the project site received thousands of visitors), the system was replicated in several locations throughout the country where it was also found to be effective. In the early 1990s, the MOEC therefore mandated that all primary schools be organized into clusters and all teachers into working groups. Fearing that this "bureaucratic take-over" would lead to a watering-down of the effectiveness of the teacher support system, the World Bank-financed PEQIP, initiated just prior to the *Primary School Teacher Development Project*, included this system as one of its main vehicles for quality improvement. In PEQIP, however, dissemination of the teacher support system would be gradual and deliberate, beginning with six provinces and involving program improvements and local adaptations along the way. The ultimate goal of the project is to overcome teacher isolation and to encourage cooperative efforts among teachers to solve problems and foster their own professional growth.

A Functional Credit System for Teacher Career Development

This system, developed by the National Civil Service Bureau in the late 1980s, is built upon the premise that teachers will be more likely to strive for professional growth and better performance if they receive "credit" for such efforts as civil servants. With the initiation of the functional credit system teachers can now accelerate movement up the civil service ladder through such activities as attaining a higher level certification, working long hours, teaching in remote areas, participating in in-service training activities, contributing to curriculum development, writing reports or articles, and performing community service. Those who accumulate the requisite number of cumulative credits towards a new civil service rank can, for example, receive a promotion in two rather than the conventional four years. In addition, there are no caps on the level to which they can rise: as long as they receive the requisite number of credits teachers can be promoted to the same civil service rank as a university professor. Thus, whereas the previous regulations provided automatic promotion after a certain number of years, irrespective of performance and salary/status caps for primary school teachers, this system is expected to encourage good teacher performance and to make staying in the classroom more attractive to teachers with high professional aspirations.

PRELIMINARY ASSESSMENT OF TEACHER QUALITY IMPROVEMENT EFFORTS

The above discussion shows that Indonesia has committed enormous resources to improving the quality of primary school teaching. In addition to the resources involved in program development and delivery, the government must pay the bill for teachers who enter or move to relatively high levels on the civil service pay scale. Perhaps, no nation in the world has designed a more comprehensive and far-reaching strategy.

Interestingly enough, however, the strategy does resemble in many ways strategies developed in other countries. For example, the four programs mentioned above have features similar to those of a major teacher professional development movement in the United States. In its book *Tomorrow's Teachers*, the Holmes Group (1986):

- calls for teacher education that is *more intellectually sound*—the Indonesian system emphasizes better grounding in the curricular subjects;
- calls for an orientation towards a teacher career ladder—the Indonesian "functional credit system" lengthens the career ladder for teachers

and makes movement contingent upon improved credentials and teacher performance;

- calls for more rigorous standards of entry into the profession—Indonesia just increased the standard from a normal school degree to a post-secondary diploma;
- calls for university-school partnerships—the new D-II program calls for much more field-based, hands-on training; and
- advocates preparing teachers for shared responsibilities and decision-making roles—the Indonesian teacher "working groups" put more responsibility for professional development and problem solving at the school level into the hands of the teachers.

Unlike the Holmes Group and similar movements in the United States which are voluntary and limited in their coverage (Glickman, 1993), the programs in Indonesia, however, are nationwide in their coverage. This means that the potential impact of the quality improvement measures is great indeed.

Given this potential, it is helpful to begin sorting out the extent to which this potential can or will actually bear fruit in terms of more effective teaching and learning in Indonesian primary school classrooms. Will more teacher education, more teacher working groups, and more career opportunities for teachers lead to improved instruction and better student outcomes? Will more mean better?

In principle they should, but there are some distressing signals from the field that suggest that they might not. This section will describe some preliminary observations that suggest that the quality enhancement features of the new programs are, at this point, falling short of their potential to leverage positive change. In the section that follows, I attempt to provide some reasons for the apparent shortfalls, and conclude with a few reflections on solutions to the current dilemmas.

Most of the quality enhancement efforts described above have not been formally and systematically evaluated. However, it is possible to make some preliminary observations about the way in which they are being implemented. This should allow some patterns to emerge and help us to formulate some cautionary signals. Each of the four quality improvement programmes will be discussed in turn.

Pre-service Teacher Education at the Diploma II Level

By mid-1995, the World Bank's mission to review the *Primary School Teacher Development Project* (World Bank, 1995) found that substantial progress had been made in placing teacher educators in undergraduate (domestic) and graduate (overseas) programs related to the task of educating primary school teachers. Progress towards revising the D-II curriculum and developing new learning-teaching materials for program instructors and students had moved much slower. Revisions had been made in response to various overseas study tours and the release of the new National Primary

School curriculum in 1994, but no new curricular guidelines had been written yet or learning materials drafted (major goals of the project). At current rates of development, it is now too late to carry out field trials of curricular guidelines and materials over a full four-semester period within the lifetime of the project. It thus appears that materials for all semesters will need to be tested at around the same time on different samples of students in a cross-sectional manner. This will sacrifice the project's capacity to test the sequencing and cumulative effects of its curriculum. In addition, the first three to five cohorts will have come through the D-II program, having been exposed to few readings and instructional materials, except those created by the Open University for the D-II equivalency program (an assessment of which appears in the next section of this article) and a combination of materials used by instructors in their secondary teacher education programs or in the SPGs.

This assessment applies to both textual materials and library materials. This situation suggests a heavy reliance on lecturing as a means of communicating new knowledge, subverting the project's hope of modelling active learning strategies.

Other parts of the review show that little has been done to set up an information system to pinpoint problems in teacher distribution. There has been selection of students through the special system which waives the national selection examination, the building of dormitories and the awarding of scholarships to students from remote and/or low income areas, but there is still no mechanism to determine whether candidates from shortage areas are getting access to the D-II program. In addition, numerous regional consultation forums have been held in which teacher needs have been discussed, but these have generally resulted in exaggerated projections, since personnel managers almost never acknowledge pockets of (sometimes, substantial) teacher surpluses. Until these deficiencies are addressed, it will be hard to identify where the real shortages are.

Finally, startling findings concerning placement of D-II graduates have been revealed. Among those in the first cohort, almost all graduates found teacher jobs; fewer than 25 percent of those in the second cohort found teaching jobs; and the placement of those from the third cohort is still in doubt. This has caused the MOEC to reduce intake for the 1995–96 cohort from the regular seven thousand to five thousand. Placement problems appear to be the result of a new "no growth" policy in the civil service; also, local teacher placement officers appear to be returning to the SPG graduate pool for many new hires, despite regulations to the contrary. The impact of market signals on the quality of the candidate pool has been significant and swift: at the Teacher Education Institute in Yogyakarta, the year when most students were placed was followed by an applicant pool so large that only 15 percent could be admitted. A large proportion of them were general upper secondary school graduates. In years following a poor placement record, applications have fallen and those applying have been predominantly former SPG graduates. If the program is to attract those with solid academic backgrounds, this problem with placement of D-II graduates will need to be solved.

Diploma II Upgrading for Practicing Teachers

Even before the *Primary School Teacher Development Project* was launched, there were some reviews of different aspects of the D-II upgrading or equivalency project. Most of the reviews focused on the curriculum and learning materials. A 1990 review noted that the courses are "far beyond the reach (and the needs) of the typical primary school teacher"(MOEC, 1990). It went on to say that "it is ironic that students will be asked to study trigonometry and calculus, when the average teacher has mastered only 45 percent of the primary school subject matter in science" (MOEC, 1990). Similarly, a recent content analysis of the modules (Nielsen and Somerset, 1992) further revealed their theoretical and irrelevant nature: "there is nothing in them that would suggest they are for primary school teachers." Indeed, the textbooks contained almost no examples from primary schools, very few ideas concerning how to teach the concepts to children, and nothing that connects the lessons to everyday life. Discussions with early managers of the D-II upgrading curriculum revealed a *bias* and a *flaw*: the bias was viewing equivalency as the need to provide exposure to the same subject matter content as other university students (as opposed to providing exposure to the content that would be useful to the teacher in his/her professional life). The *flaw* was in assigning single authors—usually a prominent professor in the field to write the text. Used to publishing books and journal articles and working with secondary-school teachers, these writers fell in to writing at that level. Working alone, they did not have access to others such as current or former primary-school teachers, who could help them keep their content relevant and appropriate. Thus, to date, over 200,000 teachers have gone or are going through upgrading in content that is, in many ways, irrelevant to their teaching tasks.

Resources for revising the curriculum and learning materials for the D-II equivalency course were included in the *Primary School Teacher Development Project* but so far (three years into a four-year project), none have been used for this purpose.

In-service Education and Professional Support through Teacher Networks

As the PEQIP nears the end of its initial five-year cycle, evaluations of its effectiveness are beginning to appear. Reports show that annual in-service education efforts have consisted mainly of twelve-day, residential workshops for trainers (experienced teachers, called tutors) at the national level, followed by twenty-four-day workshops at the province level in which tutors give training to large groups of project teachers. These workshops have been found to be largely ineffective: according to one monitoring report, "there has been little significant impact on teaching and learning activities from the training in the first three years." The main reasons for this assessment, the report continued, based on participant accounts, included the fact that "the training was largely theoretical and was largely given at the national level by trainers who had little or no primary classroom experience and little or no experience of modern teaching methods" (PEQIP, 1996a). Another report found local training to be ineffective too, mainly because it was conducted with groups that were too large (averaging 115 teachers), during a period that was too long (twenty-four days) by tutors who themselves had been inadequately or inappropriately trained (PEQIP, 1996b).

The professional support to teachers, provided through teacher working group activities and follow-up classroom visits by tutors, was also not as effective as expected. Evaluators indicated that teachers groups were generally functioning on a regular basis, but noted a tendency for tutors and advisory teachers to fall back on traditional didactic methods, even in the study circles, and noted few specific instances of teachers gaining new active learning skills from the meetings. Also, tutors' visits were less frequent and less intense than envisioned since schools have been reluctant to reduce the tutors' teaching load and tutor training had not included "mentoring" skills (PEQIP, 1996a).

Functional Credit System for Teacher Career Development

Even a surface analysis of this recent regulation reveals some of its flaws as a catalyst of teacher quality improvement. First, the system, as described above, is biased towards university teaching roles—primary school teachers, especially those in rural areas, are rarely in a position to develop curricula, publish papers and articles, and attend training workshops. In addition, the review process seems to get bogged down in the case of those outside the metropolitan areas. Discussions with rural teachers during the system's early years revealed that many teachers had not even had their starting credit level determined yet, something that should have been done for all before the system was launched. Finally, it seems clear that the system rewards being busy more than being effective. One reviewer found that teachers can even get credit points for teaching in more than one school; it was also noted that in-service training activities were often scheduled during regular school hours, which could mean leaving students unattended (MOEC, 1990). Ironically, nowhere in the regulations are there any credits for being in the classroom and for teaching effectively.

SOME EXPLANATIONS FOR APPARENT SHORTFALLS IN QUALITY IMPROVEMENT

In many ways, the failure of Indonesia's recent teacher education reforms to create significant breakthroughs in teaching quality is a perplexing puzzle. The various efforts have demonstrated no lack of vision about quality improvement; clearly, on paper at least, the reforms have adopted some of the international community's most widely accepted quality improvement strategies. Funding support has not been a problem either—government and Development Agency sources have contributed hundreds of millions of dollars to the effort.³ Furthermore, there is no lack of talent in Indonesia among teacher-education professionals. For example, during the 1980s, under an earlier World Bank-financed teacher-education project, 64 leaders from teacher training institutions received their doctorates, and 249 received their Masters degrees, all from respected institutions in North America, Europe and Australia. According to one tracer study of 134 doctoral and MA degree recipients, the returning lecturers indicated having made significant gains in professional knowledge and habits of work, and were judged by their supervisors to have strong program management and research skills (Huda, Ibnu and Raka Joni, 1989). This program created a virtual treasure chest of talent for implementing the reform projects of the 1990s.

There is a growing sense, launched already in the 1970s by Beeby's pathbreaking book, *Assessment of Indonesian Education* (1979), that the main inhibitor to educational quality improvement in Indonesia is the bureaucratic environment in which the reform projects have been implemented. In the 1970s, social scientists began to popularize the idea of environmental press (Lewin, 1936; Stern, 1970; Moos, 1976). The environmental press in the Indonesian educational establishment is particularly strong, and, as will be argued briefly below, tends to emphasize many goals in lieu of quality improvement. The press of the bureaucracy begins in Jakarta at offices of the Directors General and other civil servants but is not limited to the central bureaucracy. In fact, the environmental press of the bureaucracy radiates to all levels of public institutions—regional and local educational offices, institutions of higher education, and even the school and classroom. It effects the way supervisors oversee schools, lecturers organize instruction, and teachers conduct their lessons. It characterizes the culture of the educational system from top to bottom.

The Bureaucratic Authoritarian State

The Indonesian national bureaucracy, through its Ministry of Education and Culture, has exerted almost total control over the reforms and innovations described above. The Directorate General of Primary and Secondary Education has overseen the in-service training programs in the schools and the Directorate General of Higher Education has managed pre-service education and teacher upgrading programs (D-II). The Functional Credit System has been managed by the National Civil Service Agency. In recent years, a certain amount of autonomy has been granted institutions of higher education in developing and managing programs, but because the above programs of teacher education were new and dealt with manpower (teachers) serving important national integration functions, all reform efforts were tightly managed by Jakarta.

In describing the functioning of Indonesian bureaucracy under the current regime (President Suharto's *New Order*), a recent scholar has used the concept of the *bureaucratic authoritarian state* (Kuntjoro-Jakti, 1988). Based on the works of political economists such as O'Donnell (1979) and Hirschman (1981), this concept describes a pattern of heavy state intervention in countries experiencing "late industrialization." Kuntjoro-Jakti (1988) asserts that Indonesia, in the late 1980s, was experiencing "late, late, late industrialization" and portrays the main features of state intervention as follows. First, late industrialization, especially since the decline in Indonesia's oil revenues in the early 1980s, has followed the pattern of direct foreign investment. To ensure an attractive international investment climate, the government of President Suharto found it necessary to create conditions of economic and political stability in both the short- and long-term. This has meant a heavy emphasis on national-security goals and centralized control over all state-agencies, both through the bureaucracy and the military, which by the early 1970s, had adopted a policy of *dwifungsi* (dual functions: defence and development). To safeguard economic stability, the central government has relied on a cadre of brilliant US-trained "technocrats" (economists, planners and engineers), who have emphasized rationality (e.g. in trade and monetary policy), efficiency, and economic development (growth). The system's reliance on foreign investment has been mentioned, but more than just providing capital, this policy has also brought in new technology and expertise. Finally, the power elite have, as in the case of other authoritarian systems, tended to maintain their dominance by creating conditions of inter-agency competition and factional infighting.

Implications for Quality Improvement in Education

The Indonesian attempts to improve educational quality through reforms in teacher education, although well meaning and sincere, have been largely futile, given the bureaucratic environment of the reform efforts and its press for other outcomes. As mentioned above, each of the major interventions reviewed above contains quality improvement mechanisms or levers, which, if pulled, could yield significant progress; some of the reasons they have not been pulled are the following:

Emphasis on Rapid Growth and Quantitative Expansion

The technocratic culture in the bureaucracy has valued rapid growth of a quantitative nature—the numbers of years of pre-service training, the number of teachers upgraded, the number of teacher study groups formed, the number of functional credits accumulated. It has encouraged the mounting of a rapid succession of projects, all with ambitious quantitative goals. Attainment of these goals has been assumed to lead to qualitative change, but in some sense, they have undermined it. One reason is the *lack of absorptive capacity* in the bureaucracy. The number of senior administrators in Jakarta has been kept quite small, yet the number of projects they have had to supervise keeps expanding. Administrative capacity thus becomes spread thinner and thinner. The current situation is similar to that experienced by Indonesia twenty years ago during its major oil boom, when Beeby (1979) commented:

> the main constraint on further progress in education will not be finance but administrative capacity. If the additional funds made available for education over the past year or two can be held constant in real terms for the present,

and then expanded reasonably as administrative capacity improves, they should be sufficient to alter the whole face of education . . .

Lacking administrative capacity to pull the time-consuming and sometimes complex quality change levers, the bureaucracy has tended to resort to "goal displacement" (Wildavsky, 1987; Fullan, 1993): substituting goals that can be reached for those that cannot. Thus, we see hundreds of thousands of teachers going through an upgrading course that has been acknowledged to be poor in quality. Questioned about this at a Jakarta meeting, one senior bureaucrat replied, "The goal of this course is increasing teachers' qualifications, *not* improving quality."

Excessive Bureaucratic Centralization

As mentioned above, the movement towards university autonomy has not yet included teacher education and upgrading in any substantial way. All important decisions, and even most minor ones, are still made in Jakarta. This "one size fits all" mentality caters to bureaucratic efficiency and central control, but leads to many serious misfits at the local level. For example, teachers in remote area schools find it impossible to gather in school clusters for weekly "working group" meetings, have difficult access to upgrading (D-II) tutorials, and rarely get the information or opportunities they need in order to accumulate functional credits towards promotion. These teachers, mostly residing "off-Java," need locally crafted initiatives to their problems. Yet, educational assessments have repeatedly shown that "extreme centralization has tended to sap the initiative of teachers, pupils and supervisors and make them look to Jakarta for a lead" (Beeby, 1979).

Emphasis on National Security and Loyalty to the State

The New Order government has, over the past thirty years, taken seriously its nation-building mandate—the creation of unity, order, and stability. The school system has played a crucial role in this massive undertaking, teaching the national language, conveying the national ideology (*Pancasila* or "Five Principles"), and bringing the symbols and apparatus of the nation state to the remotest villages. Having succeeded in creating three decades of economic growth and political stability, the government is beginning to acknowledge the pressures and needs for more "openness" in public expression. Yet, at university campuses, where teachers are trained, there are still heavy constraints on intellectual activity and expression. As one leading Indonesian publisher, Gunawan Mohamad, has recently remarked:

> Universities are dead. Ideas are dead. The government's obsession with security is like a black hole swallowing all independent thought.
>   (Schwarz, 1994)

The emphasis on security also plays itself out when new teachers go to the field. As in many other countries, new teachers in Indonesia are probationary during their first year of teaching. However, instead of being evaluated on their subject matter knowledge and their competence in teaching and classroom management, probationary teachers are mostly assessed on their understanding of and adherence to the state ideology. Thus, the chance for the probationary period to act as a quality lever is lost.

Reliance on External Resources

As mentioned above, one feature of the bureaucratic authoritarian state is its reliance on external investment and its accompanying technology and expertise. Most of the teacher education initiatives described above have relied heavily on development agency support (mostly the World Bank, but also the Asian Development Bank and bilateral donors like ODA and USAID), both in their financing and in their design and implementation. The infusion of fresh ideas and state-of-the-art thinking into reform efforts would appear to be a viable path to overcoming local inertia and stagnation. However, issues of absorptive capacity also enter in this arena. Most project design efforts have involved teaming foreign consultants with local experts and managers. Unfortunately, given the over-extension of the local experts, this has often resulted in an uneven partnership. Thus, the meaning and nuances of the (often complex) quality enhancement levers in projects often end up residing more in the heads of foreign consultants than with local experts and project managers. The best thinking of local experts often does not even get articulated. This issue is further exacerbated by the fact that project managers in Indonesia are usually not the same persons as project developers, given bureaucratic constraints (e.g., persons having the rank of professor or equivalent cannot manage projects) and the problem of over-extension mentioned above.

The development agencies themselves also contribute to the deflection from quality improvement goals. Their own priorities are also geared toward attainment of quantitative targets and expansions, that is, bringing new projects on line. Thus, supervision of existing projects (quality control) suffers and quality enhancement goals give way to more easily quantified indicators such as the number of persons trained and the amount of funds dispersed.

Interagency Fragmentation and Competition

For decades in Indonesia, the work of public-school teachers has been handled by competing government agencies. Teachers in primary school have found themselves under dual management: the Ministry of Home Affairs (through the governor's office) does the hiring and placement of teachers and issues their paychecks, while the MOEC sets the curriculum for the schools and fields school supervisors. To complicate matters even more, since 1990 teachers have received their preservice training under the MOEC's Directorate of Higher Education, but are supported and further trained at the school level by officers of another Directorate General. The lack of coordination among these various agencies has become legendary. Both Beeby's book (1979) and the World Bank's *Basic Education Study* (1989) comment on how dual management negatively affects quality, given the frequent mixed messages from the two managers and the lack of coordination between those who manage funds and materials and those who are expected to look after quality. Another problem is the lack of coordination between those who produce teachers (institutes and faculties of teacher education) and those who hire and place them (the governor's office). The problem of placing new D-II program graduates mentioned above is an instance of this: by limiting D-II program output, the Directorate General of Higher Education felt certain that all graduates would find teaching jobs; however, the governors' offices had other agendas—they still had a huge background of unassimilated graduates from the former (SPG) program, many of whom had been working as volunteers in schools for many years. Under severe local pressure, the governors' offices have tended to hire the early graduates instead of the better-trained Diploma holders.

A third instance of fragmentation is that between the providers of pre-service and in-service education. The Directorates General who manage these two systems are so disjointed that there is little intersection between the two kinds of training. The D-II upgrading program created by the Open University has little grounding in the school; conversely, the school-based programs for teacher self-help and mutual support are often lacking in academic content. With some careful coordination, the two programs could fill one another's gaps, but given the traditional distance between the two Directorates General, there is little indication that this will happen.

CONCLUDING REMARKS

In Indonesia, massive efforts to improve the quality of basic education through changes in teacher education have been launched over the past decade. They have included elevating preservice education for primary school teachers to the level of higher education, providing post-secondary recertification opportunities for up to nearly 1 million practicing teachers, organizing teacher working groups for local in-service education and professional support, and providing a career ladder system in which teachers receive credits towards promotion on the basis of their performance. These are all "state-of-the-art" innovations, and in them, there are innovative and creative quality improvement levers. Nevertheless, their contributions to real quality improvements at the classroom level have appeared to be marginal at best. There have been some breakthroughs, to be sure, like widespread teacher involvement in weekly study group sessions. Moreover, a plentitude of funds and local talent has been made available. Nevertheless, crucial levers of quality improvement have been scarcely or poorly operated, resulting in disappointing project performance.

To explain these shortfalls, this article has used the concept of environmental press. It maintains that the bureaucratic environment, influenced by the demands of the *bureaucratic authoritarian state*, has pressed for goals and priorities inconsistent with quality improvement such as:

- an emphasis on rapid growth and quantitative expansion as indicators of quality improvement;

- excessive power and control at the central office level;
- a slant towards national security issues and unquestioning loyalty to the state's ideology;
- excessive reliance on external resources (funds, technology and expertise); and
- the promotion of interagency fragmentation and competition.

Since such environmental factors tend to subvert the success of quality improvement efforts, their identification and reduction becomes a crucial element in future strategies.

This is not to propose bureaucratic reform as a kind of panacea. The effort to improve school quality will still require action on a number of parallel fronts, for example, revising an overly-dense curriculum, developing and equitably distributing high-quality textbooks, increasing the number of effective hours of instruction, reforming the examination system, and increasing the pay and benefits of teachers and lecturers. Nevertheless, without bureaucratic reform, a fundamental change in the organizational culture of state-supported education, none of the other reforms will bear their expected fruit.

In recent months, there have been a few encouraging signs of institutional change, mostly initiated from outside of the govenment. A new round of basic education quality improvement projects is now being developed, with World Bank participation and support, at the provincial level with a suggestion that some decisions might even devolve to the district level. (There is still a question as to whether this will represent *real* devolution of decision-making power or simply another national program negotiated separately in each province.) In addition, the concept of university autonomy is beginning to take hold, at least in some fields, creating a precedent and an opening for some more local decision making in the field of teacher education.

On a broader scale, student and non-governmental organization (NGO) voices are beginning to be heard with more clarity and frequency, many pressing for more openness and liberalization in government. In addition, increased liberalization in trade and international business is beginning to bring with it the natural pressures for the creation of a civil society.

Optimistic views of these movements suggest that changes in the New Order are inevitable, and that the current fixation on security and the military's *dual function* which supports it, will give way to more democratic goals and processes. Such changes, coupled with Indonesia's growing prosperity, could have a salutary effect on the bureaucratic environment, especially if civil servants are rewarded such that they can focus on a single job and thus not have to be spread too thin. Freed to make use of their own creativity and initiative, and given the time to focus on a single project, mangers in a reformed bureaucracy would be in a position to develop and pull the levers of quality improvement that today's educational institutions require.

NOTES

1. An early draft of this paper was presented at the Western Regional Conference of the *Comparative and International Education Society* in Honolulu during January 3–5, 1996. The author has been involved in Indonesian educational development efforts since 1977 in a variety of research and development roles supported by UNESCO, USAID, IDRC, and the World Bank. During the past six years, he has contributed to two World Bank teacher development projects and two projects for improving the quality of basic education.
2. Studies had shown teacher education to be dominated by those with the Sl (B. Ed.) in educational sciences (pedagogy) or curricular studies. The "second degree" program has provided incentives for large numbers of these instructors to gain a new Sl in a subject-oriented field such as mathematics, science or language education.
3. Two recent World Bank loans to Indonesia for teacher education; one at the primary-school level and the other at the secondary level were themselves worth almost US $100 million ($36.6 million and $60.4 million, respectively).

REFERENCES

Beeby, C. E. (1979). *Assessment of Indonesian Education: A Guide in Planning.* Wellington: New Zealand Council for Educational Research and Oxford: Oxford University Press.

Djalil, A. (1988). Improvement of Primary School Quality in Disadvantaged Rural Areas through Better School Management and Teacher Professional Development. Working Paper prepared for the World Bank, September, 1988.

Fullan, M. (1993). *Change Forces: Probing the Depths of Educational Reform.* London: The Falmer Press.

Fuller, B. (1986). Raising School Quality in Developing Countries: What Investments Boost Learning? World Bank Discussion Paper No. 2.

Glickman, C.D. (1993). Mainstreaming Democracy in Public Education: Policies for Enduring School Renewal, Athens, GA: University of Georgia.

Heyneman, S. and Loxley, W. (1983). "The Impact of Primary School Quality on Academic Achievement in Twenty-Nine High and Low Income Countries." *American Journal of Sociology,* 88, pp. 1162–1194.

Hirschman, A. (1981). *Essays in Trespassing: Economics to Politics and Beyond.* New York: Cambridge University Press.

Holmes Group (1986). *Tomorrow's Teachers.* East Lansing, MI: The Holmes Group.

Huda, H., Ibnu, S. and Raka, Joni T. (1989). *The Reentry and Utilization of Overseas Training Program Returnees, Vol. 1.* The Second Indonesia—IBRD Teacher Training Project. Jakarta: Directorate General of Higher Education, Ministry of Education and Culture.

Jiyono. (1986). *Research on Teachers' Aptitudes and Instructional Materials in Physical Science at the Primary-School Level.* Jakarta: Office of Educational Research and Development, Ministry of Education and Culture.

Kuntjoro-Jakti, H. A. (1988). External and Domestic Coalitions of the Bureaucratic Authoritarian State in Indonesia. Unpublished Doctoral Dissertation, University of Washington.

Lewin, K. (1936). *Principles of Topological Psychology.* New York: McGraw-Hill.

Ministry of Education and Culture (MOEC). (1990). *A Review of Teacher Education Issues.* Jakarta: MOEC, Office of Educational and Cultural Research and Development.

Moos, R. (1976). *The Human Context: Environmental Determinants of Behavior.* New York: John Wiley & Sons.

Nielsen, H. D. and Somerset, H. C. A. (1992). *Primary Teachers in Indonesia: Supply, Distribution, and Professional Development.* Washington, DC: The World Bank.

Oliveira, J., Farrell, J. and Etienne, B. (1988). "The Costs and Effectiveness of Teachers in Developing Countries. Unpublished Manuscript.

O'Donnell, G. (1979). "Tensions in the Bureaucratic Authoritarian State and the Question of Democracy." In D. Collier (ed.), *New Authoritarianism in Latin America.* Princeton, NJ: Princeton University Press.

Primary Education Quality Improvement Project (PEQIP). (1996a). First National Monitoring Report. Jakarta, Indonesia: PT Manggala Epsilon Sigma, The British Council, and the Institute for International Research.

———. (1996b). Gtz-BTE: Special Report No. 2 (September). Jakarta: Ministry of Education and Culture.

Schwarz, A. (1994). *A Nation in Waiting: Indonesia in the 1990s.* Boulder, CO: Westview Press.

Somerset, H. C. A. (1988). *Quality Issues in General Secondary Education.* Jakarta: Ministry of Education and Culture.

Stern, G. (1970). *People in Context: Measuring Person-Environmental Congruence in Education and Industry.* New York: John Wiley & Sons.

Suryadi, A. (1992). *Improving the Educational Quality of Primary Schools: Assessment of School Quality and Students' Achievement in Indonesian Primary Schools.* Jakarta: Office of Educational and Cultural Research and Development, Ministry of Education and Culture.

Tangyong, A., Wahyudi, F., Gardner, R. and Haws, H. (1989). *Quality through Support to Teachers: A Case Study from Indonesia.* Jakarta: Office of Educational and Cultural Research and Development, Ministry of Education and Culture, and London: University of London Institute of Education.

Wildavsky, A. (1987). *Speaking Truth to Power: The Art and Craft of Policy Analysis.* New Brunswick, NJ: Transaction Publishers.

World Bank. (1989). *Indonesia: Basic Education Study.* Washington, DC: The World Bank.

———. (1995). *Aide Memoire: Project Review Mission, May 22–31.* Indonesia: Primary School Teacher Development Project.

CHAPTER 20

Education, Teacher Training and the Prospects for Economic Recovery in Cambodia

Stephen J. Duggan

ABSTRACT   *With the conclusion of 1994, Cambodia will have ended its first year of rehabilitation under a freely elected government. Since the 1993 elections, Cambodia has moved cautiously towards a modern era and there has been considerable international effort to ensure that all sectors of the economy achieve the improvements required to achieve political and economic stability towards 2000. The education sector has been a major focus. Cambodia is ready to move into the next stage of development of the education sector—reconstruction. With the non-governmental organizations (NGOs) having provided support in this sector for over ten years, the restoration of bilateral and multilateral aid will see a growing involvement of foreign governments and donor organizations in the restoration of the sector. This activity will need to be coordinated. Cambodia had a rapidly expanding education system before Pol Pot's Year Zero. Largely based on French colonial models and structures that system served a society very much in transition—a transition from colonial dependency to a possible so-called "new tiger." The current period will see a different "system" emerge; one that is neither French nor Western nor indeed "modern." The transition of the education system will be predicated on an overhaul of the existing bureaucracy, training regimes and school curricula before modernization processes are installed. This paper provides a historical backdrop for the current situation. It also examines current policy priority areas in education in Cambodia and the level of international assistance.*

INTRODUCTION

In June 1994, I held lengthy consultations with senior Khmer Ministry of Education staff to formulate a national education policy framework for Cambodia. This policy framework was meant to highlight priority areas of investment for reconstructing and restructuring that country's run-down education system. When discussing education priorities for Cambodia in the lead up to 2000, one senior member of staff claimed that in his view, there were going to be many problems in implementing internationally financed education projects. He was concerned that an international commitment to restructuring and modernizing the system could collapse under its own financial weight. Earlier in the year, we had been examining the complex of buildings that collectively housed the central ministry's key departments. Each department appeared the same: run-down buildings, no electricity and outdated office facilities, dysfunctional procedures, an absence of line-management and around 20 percent of each department's staff carrying out daily duties. An air of inertia prevailed and the hundreds of thousands of dust-bearing documents choking doorways and vacant rooms testified to the fact that documents were rarely filed and often not acted upon. By June, things were changing. International organizations including the World Bank, the Asian Development Bank, the United Nations Children Fund (UNICEF) and numerous non-governmental organizations (NGOs) were renovating these buildings with a view to accommodating increasing numbers of international consultants who, to meet operational requirements, would require modern office complexes and procedures.

One official held a concern for the immediate future of a country moving rapidly from a centrally controlled economy and bureaucracy to one driven by market forces. He said "Angkor, that is the problem. If you can understand Angkor, you can understand the problems with Cambodia now. The problems of today can be explained by those monuments. This is something you need to understand." The metaphor was not clear. Had Cambodia expended all of its energy or could it only compete with new international players if it could recreate a modern society and city equal to that of the Khmer past?

These sentiments reflected not so much resignation but concern that a Cambodia emerging from a long period of civil war and social dislocation would require considerable international financial resources and expertise to define its future. His vision was prophetic as just as Cambodia had stagnated under the excesses of the Khmer Rouge and later an impoverished Vietnamese-backed government and economy during the 1970s and 1980s, educational development had also been deemed to stagnate during the same period despite significant efforts by the government to modernize the system. External financial and technical assistance had not been able to affect this course of events. As he reflected on the potential failure of educational development in his country, education experts likewise expressed doubt about the capacity of financial institutions to improve the situation of education in developing nations (Psacharopoulos, 1989; Tilak, 1991, 1994b; Verspoor, 1993).

It has been a long-standing government policy in Cambodia to align economic and national development by strengthening the education sector. Since the early 1980s, teacher training and in particular in-service training has been regarded as pivotal for the qualitative improvement of the education sector. This policy priority emphasis on teacher training to bridge the knowledge gap created by the social dislocation of the 1972–1991 period has prevailed in Cambodia into the late 1990s. Since the early 1990s, major multilateral investors in education, namely the World Bank and Asian Development Bank, have also argued that strengthening the education and health sectors is a necessary precursor for strengthening developing economies (World Bank, 1993, 1994a). Teacher training is viewed as a most critical quality input to the process. Throughout Asia, UNESCO has estimated that the total teaching population numbers around 23 million. However, UNESCO has argued that this teaching force is inadequate to deal with the educational problems facing the region. Some 35 percent are either unqualified or inadequately trained or have received no training at all (Sharma, 1992). In Cambodia, unqualified teachers constitute some 85 percent of the active teaching force.

The purpose of this study is to review the recent history of education development in Cambodia. The objective is to provide a historical context underpinning the education system as it now stands. Since 1991, international interest in the restoration of the education sector has been significant. However, the system is riddled with problems restraining reconstruction. This paper discusses the past and present arrangements for education. It is argued that owing to the Pol Pot (Khmer Rouge) regime, when formal education in Cambodia, including plant, personnel, students and equipment was all but eliminated, Cambodia has maintained a strong focus on educational development. At the end of the regime in 1979, basic education and teacher training were raised as national priorities for Cambodia (as they had been in Vietnam since 1975). However, today, the majority of teachers remain untrained and few children receive a full basic education. Central to the discussion is the current and proposed concentration of investments in teacher in-service training as the key strategy for achieving a qualitative improvement in education and the economy.

THE BACKGROUND: EDUCATION IN THE PRE-WAR PERIOD, 1945-1975

During French colonization . . . rural children attended schools organised inside the temples offering an education which combined modern and traditional patterns . . . a small group of children entered the French school system. (Galasso, 1990)

Cambodia has experienced a troubled history since the demise of the Khmer Empire. It is not a well-known history when compared with Western knowledge of Cambodia's neighbors. Indeed, the image of Cambodia in Western thought roughly coincides with French intervention in Khmer affairs in the nineteenth century. William Shawcross' (1991) celebrated *Sideshow,* begins his comprehensive chronology of Cambodian history from 1864 when France imposed a protectorate over the kingdom of Cambodia, while Chandler's *A History of Cambodia* (1993) is more generous with just over half of the text devoted to the post-protectorate period. Unlike Vietnam, where the history of education can be divided into four major periods covering a thousand years (Thu, 1995), formal education in Cambodia is constrained to the independence period (1953–1973) and the post-Pol Pot period (1979–1995). It is this second period which is of most concern here.

The provision of education in Cambodia has been uneven. Unlike its neighbor Vietnam, where formalized schooling was treated as pivotal for national security and identity, education in Cambodia was largely restricted to royalty. With Thailand bordering to the west and Vietnam to the east, it seems that the people of Cambodia spent much of the time fully engaged in agricultural production during peace and defending its borders during war. Formal education for the greater majority of people does not seem to have been a priority. Today, there remains a deep suspicion of the Thais with ongoing concern about the territorial aspirations of Vietnam. It is difficult to conjure up an impression of formal education from the period of Angkor to French colonization. Where we know that Vietnam opened its first university on or about 1045, it was not until Cambodia achieved independence in 1953 that there is evidence of strong national interest in the creation of a formal education system. Higher education was not installed for another ten years.

France imposed a protectorate over Cambodia as a result of its direct military intervention in Vietnam and in an effort to consolidate its territorial expansion into the so-called "Far East" (Thomson, 1945). The protectorate was explicitly linked to French hegemony over Vietnam (at that time formed by Tonkin, Annam and Cochinchina) and followed a series of French military attempts to conquer the fragmented empire. During 1887–1893 the French formed the Indochina Union consisting of Vietnam, Cambodia and Laos. The record of colonial history thereafter was largely concentrated on Vietnam which mounted a number of strong resistance movements and uprisings over the first half of the twentieth century (Huynh, 1971; Osborne, 1974; Marr, 1981). Cambodia remained a backwater during the colonial period with the urban development of Phnom Penh occupying French interest.

With the granting of independence in 1953, Prince Norodom Sihanouk injected a strong national interest in education. Teacher colleges were established in several provincial capitals and secondary schools increased in number. (Before 1953 there were only nine high schools in the country and rural populations had limited access to all but basic education.) From the early 1960s, there was a rapid expansion in the provision of education and an equally rapid escalation in the levels of education offered. The University of Phnom Penh opened in 1963 with a Khmer national as its first vice-rector. The number of universities grew as the major provinces identified higher education with increasing levels of development. This rapidly growing modern system remained largely confined to the urban areas of Kampot, Kompong Cham and Battambang with each of these centers being served by universities during the 1960s.

This education system contained faults that can still be found within Cambodia today. The system did not allow for the integration of Church and state. Rural Wat schools provided rudimentary schooling appropriate for an agrarian society. The urban schools were those of the state. This urban system was highly bureaucratized with mechanisms for internal efficiency largely absent. It also allowed for the dual development of education: central and provincial. Still, expenditure on education was significant. According to Chandler (1993), Sihanouk insisted on large expenditures on education "amounting in some years to over 20 percent of the national budget." This in itself created problems. Chandler (1993) claimed:

> the prince could not foresee the discontent that would affect tens of thousands of high school graduates and hundreds of university graduates in the late 1960s when they found it hard to obtain well-paid employment . . . [many] blamed Sihanouk for their plight.

According to Vickery (1985), before the 1970s, Cambodia developed an education system restricted to the major urban areas. He noted that before independence education had been neglected, but

> after independence some degree of rapid development was desirable and laudable. The attitude of the Cambodians however, seemed to be that of the maximum amount of modern education in any field at all for the maximum number of children was an absolute good in itself, without ever taking into account the absorptive capacities of the society. (Vickery, 1985)

Chandler (1993) argued that post-1953 was heavily influenced by events outside Cambodia with the country becoming "a hostage to Vietnamese events." Decisions to expand education were not helped by an economy and political structure subject to external control with a resultant history "orchestrated from the east, and from such faraway cities as Hanoi, Washington, and Beijing" (Chandler, 1993). After independence, the spread of education was far more comprehensive but at odds with the human capital requirements of the nation. The education system provided by Sihanouk was biased towards the nation's largest cities. Rural Cambodia did not benefit from the selective expansion strategies employed by the Prince and handsomely built universities did not assist rural children and their family's poverty.

During the early 1970s Cambodia was consistently drawn into the war in Vietnam. With different factions within the country enabling Vietnamese troop and supply movements, on the one hand, whilst the US-supported government troops combated communist resistance groups including the Khmer Rouge, the country suffered heavy human and capital losses. As the

USA progressively lost control of that war and whilst the Khmer Rouge became more powerful within Cambodia, the socioeconomic achievements gained during the 1950s and 1960s were soon lost. By early 1972, with the Vietnam War nearing its end, civil war and aerial bombardment throughout Cambodia resulted in serious damage to all facets of Khmer life and greatly weakened the education system. By 1974:

> the economy was in ruins, heavy deficit spending and related hyper-inflation were endemic. The value of the Riel declined by 462 percent . . . foodstuffs rose by 230 percent and non-food items by 636 percent in the year. 64 percent of the national budget was allocated to military expenditures and 36 percent to civilians. (UNICEF, 1990)

As is now well known, wide-scale discontent resulted in civil war and whether Cambodia's history was determined by Hanoi or not, it was the education system and educated that were dispensed with after April 1975. The heavy investment in education during the 1960s did not improve the economy and well-being of the Khmer and under Pol Pot this was used as an excuse to destroy the economy, the educated and the sector itself. Clearly, the investment in education during the 1960s, an investment based on consequent rapid national economic growth, was destined to fail.

THE SITUATION SINCE 1975: THE KHMER ROUGE

It is fair to say that education in Democratic Kampuchea was at a virtual standstill, and that whatever central policy may have been, most local cadres considered higher education as useless and people who had obtained it less reliable than the uneducated . . . The proper mien was to tread a very fine line between ignorance and reluctant admission of a very small amount of skill. . . . (Vickery, 1985)

The situation in Cambodia from 1975 to 1979 is now well known. Democratic Kampuchea, under the Khmer Rouge, sought to destroy much of the institutional and physical infrastructure of the country and education as an institution and body of personnel was a prime target. Teachers and higher education students were sought and "taken out." During the 1975–1979 upheaval formal education was abandoned, books and equipment destroyed and teachers and students were sought and interned. It is estimated that between 75 and 80 percent of Cambodia's teachers and higher education students fled or died (Klintworth, 1989; UNICEF, 1990; UNESCO, 1991).

A less well-known outcome was the loss of some 67 percent of primary and secondary students during the same period (UNESCO, 1991). A great many of these left the country. The United Nations Transitional Army in Cambodia (UNTAC) assessed that by 1979 "there were no more than three hundred qualified persons from all disciplines left in the country

[and] all educational books, equipment and facilities had been destroyed" (UNTAC, 1992). Importantly, all universities, except one were destroyed and the institutional infrastructure of higher education, rapidly developed during the 1960s and 1970s, disappeared. It is important to note however, that the Khmer Rouge was not the only army active in this destruction of plant. The University of Kompong Cham was levelled by the government of Cambodia in 1972 when it was discovered that Vietnamese troops were billeted there.

Under the Khmer Rouge, literacy education beyond the lowest grades was abolished and formal schooling of the Western kind was eradicated. According to Vickery (1985), the policy of the Khmer Rouge was to conduct basic schooling in "factories and cooperatives" where students could study two to three hours a day and gain experience at manual work at the same time. There is much evidence that basic primary education was not eradicated under the Khmer Rouge, and Vickery (1985) suggested that a revision of wholesale destruction of a system and people needs to be considered. However, the institutional infrastructure that housed and supported schooling was all but eradicated so that by 1979 the former public education system, in all subsectors, had effectively disappeared. The process of recovery was hampered further through the Khmer Rouge having destroyed productive capital assets.

Training institutions and buildings escaping destruction were closed. Buildings housing the bureaucracy of education were also closed. It is often not recognized that many schools were not damaged by the war and although the University of Phnom Penh was emptied and other regional universities destroyed, a significant number of French-designed school buildings and colleges were left intact. A report by United States Agency for International Development (USAID) (1994) made a reasonably accurate assessment of this period of educational loss when estimating the combined effects of twenty years of war on human and physical capital:

> Although physical infrastructure has been neglected for over thirty years and has deteriorated significantly, the physical infrastructure deficit pales in comparison to what happened on the human side . . . The purposeful killing by the Khmer Rouge of the risk takers, the educated and the skilled is probably the single most important factor constraining the private sector today. (USAID)

The effects of the Khmer Rouge regime on Cambodia are enduring and in many cases inform policy priorities of the Royal Government today, policy priorities that may be at variance with the objectives of donor-financed projects. What needs to be appreciated is that the loss of teachers and students under the Khmer Rouge resulted in an almost urgent restoration of teaching as a profession after 1979. There is a sense, when discussing education with the Khmer and also after examining current and proposed donor-financed education programs, that the restoration by means of in-service training is still incomplete.

THE EMERGENCY PERIOD: 1979-1981

The Cambodia that has survived Pol Pot is like a dismembered body that is trying to come back to life. Its economy is shattered, its communications severed. Millions of hectares of rice paddies have been temporarily abandoned. A population of refugees is returning home along pitted roads and highways or assembling in the suburbs of empty and dilapidated cities . . . In Phnom Penh itself, there are three Vietnamese advisers for every Cambodian official, ten Vietnamese soldiers for every Cambodian one. (*Agence France Press*, 1979)

The installation of a Vietnamese-backed government in Phnom Penh in 1979 did not reverse the trend of previous years. Nearly ten years of war and an impoverished occupying army did little to rejuvenate a country and society characterized by widespread social and economic dislocation. Certainly, the commune farms were disbanded and people returned to the towns and cities. Although economic recovery was slow across many sectors, attempts to rejuvenate the education sector were vigorous. Within twelve months of the liberation of Phnom Penh, the United Nations claimed:

> Enthusiastic community interest combined with the determination of national and provincial authorities has resulted in the reopening of over five thousand primary schools, with more than 60 percent of eligible children back in the classroom along with twenty-one thousand teachers. (ICORC/UNICEF Joint Mission, 1980)

There are mixed versions of developments under the Vietnamese. On the one hand, a celebrated period of education renaissance as a result of Vietnam's attempt to unify Cambodia is remembered by the Khmer and major aid agencies involved with education. Other commentators report a bleak period in Cambodia's history and refer unsympathetically to "Vietnam's Vietnam" (Morris, 1985) and a "Vietnamized Cambodia. A silent ethnocide" (Martin, 1986).

Academically, literature highly critical of the Vietnamese occupation, has not been well received and revisionist histories have been condemned (Rowley, 1995). This hardly helps to clarify educational developments during this period.

The literature suggests that 1979 saw a massive expansion in the provision of basic education through the initiation of comprehensive primary schooling (and primary school enrollments) and teacher "training"; in point of fact, the recovery was much slower. Data suggesting a rapid escalation in enrolments must be balanced against very poor teaching standards, unqualified teachers and low quality in the provision of a standardized curriculum, texts and facilities. It was during the 1979–1986 period that quality provision problems emerged, became manifest and, in some cases, remain permanent. Those quality provision concerns included large numbers of unqualified teachers, an absence of curriculum and relevant and quality teacher training programs and high wastage and drop-out rates at all levels. The primary schools received the greatest attention with some five thousand schools opened and over one million enrollments recorded during the emergency phase. A curriculum was released the same year with a strong emphasis on national identity and unity. No revisions to the curriculum or organizational structure of schooling were made until 1987.

During this "emergency" phase, teachers from the pre-1975–1979 period were located and recruited. They provided crash training to new recruits. They were farmers, artisans and menial workers who could find some status in assuming the role of teacher. Kiernan (1982) noted that:

> By late 1980 the number of children in school had risen to 1,300,000, with 30,000 teachers, and a year later the figures were 1,503,000 . . . and 37,000 respectively . . . Such expansion was largely possible because of the reopening of the Ecole Normale Superieure and the Ecole de Pedagogie in the capital, where 3,000 teachers were trained, and the creation of twenty provincial training centers which produced a total of 12,000 teachers over the 1979–81 period.

The objective of the time was "massive rehabilitation" through enrolling in "school as many as possible of the large numbers of youngsters who had missed their education" (UNICEF, 1989). Training programs varied in length and intensity from 1979 to 1985. UNESCO (1991) explained that:

> In the course of the last ten years of educational reconstruction, teachers, virtually picked up from city streets and village pathways, were provided a highly variable range of short term training (three weeks, one month or one-half month). By 1982/83 there were some thirty-two thousand teachers with an enormously wide range of competencies, or lack of them, nevertheless maintaining the education system. These thirty-two thousand teachers ranged in subject competence from primary level to university.

These courses focused "on upgrading general knowledge rather than teaching skills or pedagogical methodology" (UNICEF, 1989). Crash programs were unable to make inroads into the knowledge and skill gap left after the 1975–1979 period. Schooling was basic, often conducted under trees and aimed at little more than basic literacy.

This highly focused attention on rapidly reinstating the education system was in some ways driven by a need to institutionalize schooling after the Khmer Rouge excesses. Other, more deep-rooted psychological factors may have assisted the focus. With many people still recovering from the trauma of the 1975–1979 period, it may have been that formal schooling conducted by "traditional" teachers assisted children and adolescents to re-create the normality of everyday life lost under the Khmer Rouge. The knowledge and training gap was one thing. Cultural dislocation was another. A USAID (1994) report noted that:

> The most serious deficit in human capacity is one of the most serious constraints impacting on future and programming assistance . . . Most of the pop-

ulation aged eighteen to thirty-six lack critical education and basic skills because of genocide, starvation, and massive emigration during the reign of the Khmer Rouge, continued starvation and emigration under the subsequent Vietnamese sponsored regime. . . . (USAID)

Expansion in higher education was slow given the absence of physical and institutional infrastructure outside of Phnom Penh. Growth in secondary education was equally slow as adolescents were required to service other sectors of the economy. This was particularly evident with the loss of females. At this time some 65 percent of households were headed by women. They required adolescent daughters to assist them in essential economic and household activities. Consequently, although enrollments were high in the lower grades, the drop-out rate after Year 3 was high.

RECONSTRUCTION AND REHABILITATION POST–1981

In 1983 a concrete expansion in education occurred. Previously, the emphasis had been on getting children into primary school and recruiting adults willing to be teachers. From 1981 to 1983, thirty-two thousand teachers were trained under the crash program and, whilst all received follow-up training, it was inadequate. Indeed, in Kampot, it took from 1983 until 1994 to provide a three-month in-service training program for 50 percent of the province's two thousand five hundred teachers. Nationally, these untrained teachers were responsible for the education of tens of thousands of children. Attempts to retrain teachers were intensive; however, there is little evidence to indicate that there was any qualitative improvement in skill level under an in-service program. As one senior ministry official noted, of Cambodia's sixty-five thousand teachers, perhaps all were trained but fifty-five thousand were unqualified.

The government considered that a continued expansion in primary enrollments coupled with a rapidly expanding teaching population would rapidly address problems of low literacy and numeracy. Efforts to expand the secondary and higher education sector were not as systematic. Thus, when in 1983 the teacher training model of eight years general education plus one year teacher training (8 + 1) was considered (Blom and de Nooijer, 1992) it was not until 1989 that the fruits of that training filtered into the system. The 8 + 2 training for primary teachers and 8 + 3 training for lower secondary teachers were introduced soon afterwards, but again it was not until the early 1990s that fully schooled teachers entered the system.

In the meantime, the "chaotic situation" of wide-ranging teacher competencies prevailed (UNESCO, 1991). In all, by 1990, some fifty-three thousand teachers had been trained under widely varying pre-service training programs. Students were exposed to great variation in teacher competency. It was not unusual for children to take between seven and ten years to complete primary school. This emergency approach left another legacy: high levels of repetition and a general overcrowding of schools—particularly primary schools—owing to overenrollments based on high repeater numbers. UNESCO (1991) noted that:

> Dropout and repetition represent considerable wastage to Cambodian society in terms of frustration caused to the child and the family by not achieving the aspired goals for schooling. The causes of repetition and dropout raises questions on the adequacy of the *content, organization and structure of education*, among the internal factors and at the same time would explore some economic, social, cultural and geographical constraints operating as external factors influencing the education system or achievement at school.

Repetition was more indicative of the low skill level of teachers and corruption. Students wishing to progress from one year level to the next were required to pay a bribe. This practice had become institutionalized and by the early 1990s, failing year 1 became almost mandatory. For instance in 1993–1994, by age cohort, there should have been around 260,000 children in Year 1; there were over 500,000.

Within higher education, the picture was not much better. Through the assistance of technical expertise from Vietnam, teacher trainers and academics were taken through intensive retraining programs to update knowledge and skills. Other Khmer trainers and ministry staff were sent to Vietnam for further training in the universities. Universities and institutes of technology destroyed in the provinces were not restored so access to higher education was confined to Phnom Penh. This left higher education fragmented. If the influence from Hanoi was so great, as has been argued by Martin (1986), it must be explained why higher education, including teacher education, proliferated throughout Vietnam albeit through the creation of numerous highly specialized universities and colleges, whilst the situation in Cambodia was very much the opposite.

POLICY REVIEW: 1990–1995

The restoration of education in Cambodia came as a result of the significant national effort to restore basic education and teacher training. That national orientation remains strong. It also comes as a result of international commitments to reconstruct the system. There is no doubt that films such as *The Killing Fields* and personal accounts of life under the Khmer Rouge, for instance Teeda Butt Mam's *To Destroy You is No Loss*, did much to shape the image of modern Cambodia in Western thought. Both records dramatically detail the danger school- and university-educated citizens in Cambodia faced. This image of the eradication of a people owing to education certainly aroused international interest and pressure to restore the education system. However, images of the Pol Pot regime should not disguise the fact that there was little educational development as a result of the liberation in 1979 and the many thousands of teachers "trained" during that period remain, hindering educational development. Current indications suggest that the international investment in education at least until 2000 will be directed to the retraining of unqualified teachers and will not be disbursed in secondary schools and the teacher training colleges where the future of the country can be more directly shaped. It is this type of investment that has concerned analysts who worry that external aid has not been able to affect educational development in developing nations positively (Nash, 1984; King, 1991; Jones, 1992; Verspoor, 1993; Tilak, 1994b).

Until 1990, aid workers, primarily the UN and NGOs were confined to Phnom Penh and one or two provincial cities. This enabled government authorities to maintain surveillance of NGO activity and ensured that the capital brought into the country remained tied up in Phnom Penh. From 1990, when security throughout the provinces improved, UN and NGO activity systematically shifted out of Phnom Penh into the provinces. To the consternation of central government, provincial governments became increasingly involved with the approval of donor programs. The provinces of Battambang, Kompong Cham, Kandal, Takeo and Kompong Speu witnessed a proliferation of education and health projects.

With the arrival of the UNTAC in 1992, increasing numbers of bilateral programs were approved and monitored by the central government. The successful outcome of the May 1993 elections saw the International Monetary Fund approve programming of activities. Cambodia's arrears were cleared and bilateral programming was strengthened. Bilateral programs expanded so that by early 1993, in excess of thirty international providers, UN, bilateral and NGO, had installed around one hundred educational programs. USAID (1994) noted that:

> Besides the United States, which has provided the highest cumulative level of assistance to the Cambodian people since the mid-1980s, other major donors are the Japanese (who have focussed on specific infrastructure projects), the French (who have targeted the education sector, with emphasis on French language-based higher education) and the Australians (who have focussed on support for specific [private voluntary organizations] programs). In addition, close to thirty other bilateral donors are involved in providing assistance to Cambodia. (USAID)

But all was not well. By late 1993, the newly formed national government expressed concern over the lack of project coordination. With World Bank, Asian Development Bank and Japanese, US and French bilateral programs on the verge of a rapid phase of disbursement and expansion, a growing sense of anxiety about the purpose and impact of investment programs was evident. This concern centred on the fact that project activity was confined to one area: teacher training.

Teacher in-service training has dominated the international agenda for education. The cause of the focus can be traced to a 1990 sector analysis by UNESCO. The UNESCO (1991) *Intersectoral Basic Needs Assessment Mission to Cambodia* sought to provide a sector analysis and policy priority assessment of the key sectors of the economy. The sector study for education raised and set firmly in place a government priority that has remained in place and largely unchallenged. The study urged that "*teacher training is, and will continue to be in the future, the critical pivot in the quality improvement thrust of the Government for basic education*" (UNESCO, 1991). The needs assessment of UNESCO and others painted a bleak picture of education in the early 1990s. UNTAC (1992), the military arm of international aid observed that "the system [was] in danger of collapse. Salaries are low. Facilities are poor and classrooms crowded . . . There are high dropout and illiteracy rates." The so-called NUFFIC Report, relying on UNESCO's intersectoral study found teacher training centers to be substandard, all of which had a "negative effect on the quality of training" (Blom and de Nooijer, 1992). The generalization applied to all training facilities: health, agriculture, higher and technical education. The mission assessed the government policy of in-service training for unqualified teachers by 1995 as "unrealistic" (Blom and de Nooijer, 1992) yet the bilaterals concentrated efforts in this area. Meanwhile, conditions and facilities for learning and teaching throughout the whole sector remain in a poor state. UNICEF (1990) claimed that:

> Many buildings have leaking roofs, earthen floors and no windows and doors. They are usually ill-equipped as regards furniture and teaching aids . . . Water and sanitation are also major problems in all education facilities and many schools have no potable drinking water or latrines. . . .

Thus despite the sector being totally run-down and being characterized by high repetition rates (of primary school students), a substandard and outdated curriculum and unqualified teachers, the government pushed teacher in-service training as its major strategy. Indeed, in 1992, the pre-service training of secondary school teachers ceased altogether and, in 1994, access of women to pre-service training was greatly reduced owing to the introduction of a Year 11 examination pass to enter training (it had previously been Year 8). None of this could contribute to a quantitative or qualitative improvement in education.

It is possible that the then State of Cambodia had actually predetermined in 1990 the major inputs for intervention in education for UNESCO. In that year, the Secretary of State urged the full training of teachers and management staff to operationalize the system. He claimed:

> We have set the objectives and priority tasks as follows. Draw up an appropriate plan [of action] for *teachers* taking into account . . . the overcrowding in classrooms and the inadequacy of building available. . . . (Cross, 1990)

By stating this, he set in place a "mind set" that predicated quality improvement in education on the quality improvement of teachers in service. The UNESCO sector report effectively endorsed this policy emphasis on in-service training so that by 1994, the government had convinced external financiers of education, both current and new, that the teacher retraining remained the dominant policy priority. The Secretary of State was eventually supported by formidable arguments from the World Bank. The bank argued that in the case of Cambodia, a strengthening of the education system would reduce poverty and stimulate economic activity elsewhere through a strengthening of the nation's skill base. It stated at an international conference that:

> For the government to be able to play a more active role in education, it will have to strengthen institutions and the human resource base, focusing primarily on improving the implementation capacity in key ministries and agencies while reducing the number of civil servants. Immediate action is envisaged to restructure and strengthen ministries and agencies in the areas of government coordination, finance and education, to name a few. (World Bank, 1994b)

This argument hardly seems to endorse a heavy financing of teaching training in isolation from retraining across many sectors. But in its following sector report the bank concluded that:

> To launch a meaningful assault on poverty, the government will need to improve the quality of education so that its labor force can begin to compete with those of neighboring countries in basic skills . . . progress in this respect is constrained by the government's inability to finance the training and recruitment of enough teachers and, more important, to pay them adequate salaries which will allow them to teach full time. Alleviation of this constraint with donor support would raise the sectors' absorption capacity for investments, opening the way for more rapid and sustainable developments. (World Bank, 1994a)

The European Union and the US accepted these conclusions and proposed and mounted vigorous programs in in-service training for the 1994–1997 period. As donors responded favorably, coordination across the whole sector decreased and the crucial funding required for curriculum development for instance, was not available. Indeed, by the beginning of 1995 some thirty international organizations were providing in-service training in some shape or form.

France, Australia, the European Union, Norway and the USA were amongst the key financiers and providers. The US's bilateral agency, USAID, a new player in 1994, at first questioned this evident lack of coordination and proposed joint programs in the disbursement of its aid budget but nonetheless endorsed further activity in teacher training:

> UNICEF is already undertaking a successful program in primary education in Cambodia, but it does not have funding sufficient for massive primary teacher training. USAID/Cambodia will support strategic planning, teacher training, limited materials development, and provision of textbooks . . . with benefits accruing in a large part to Cambodia's predominantly female primary teacher corps. USAID/Cambodia will provide a grant to a consortium of NGOs to work with UNICEF to continue and geographically expand these primary education support activities. (USAID, 1994)

The sentiments seemed reasonable enough, but with the majority of international assistance being locked into teacher training programs, the premise that the quality improvement in teacher training would result in both a quality improvement in education and the strengthening of the nation's skill base was being stretched. Importantly, a key quality improvement in teacher training—the establishment of a benchmark that only allowed Year 11 graduates to enter teacher training—had greatly reduced the numbers of girls entering training from 45 percent to less than 10 percent. A strategy by USAID to overcome this was not available at the time of writing. (The World Bank [1994a] sector review expressed concern about regional disparities and lack of coordination between the government and donors. Noting that the country "is divided between fairly well-serviced areas and areas that are poorly serviced or not serviced at all" it argued that even national coverage was required if economic development in other sectors was to be realized.)

Despite these efforts, it was clear by late 1994 that things were beginning to go wrong owing to the concentration of programs and resources in one major activity. Repetition in the lower grades and high drop-out rates after Years 7 and 8 were not being addressed by any of the donors. The fact that children were often taking between seven and ten years to complete five years of primary school had not been attended to.

UN representatives noted that despite the UNICEF assessment of 1990, investments had not altered the poor situation in schools:

> The school system is inadequate both in qualitative and quantitative terms and is stressed by a dramatic growth of the school aged population which adds 400,000 children a year. (Joint Statement of UN Resident Representatives in Cambodia, 1994)

Around this time, evidence against a heavy investment in teacher in-service training was starting to emerge. In one pre-service college in Battambang three bilateral agencies were running three or four separate in-service programs concurrently, while a nearby secondary teacher training college lay empty. An Asian Development Bank funded education sector review had argued that the nation's twenty-six training colleges should be rationalized into six major provincial colleges to improve efficiencies and to strengthen teacher trainers and training. This recommendation was overlooked as more bilateral effort was put into in-service training. Indeed, bilateral programs for 1994–1997 contained insignificant provisions for the training of teacher trainers. That same report argued for a much leaner teacher training curriculum and the reduction of school subjects from fourteen to six with a lengthening of the school day and year.

Again, these were not acted upon. Yet, it would be readily acknowledged that these strategies and the overcoming of gaps and constraints therein would significantly improve the quality of education. To concentrate on in-service training alone would not seem sufficient. A heavily funded Australian four-year Bachelor of Education program at the university was certainly producing quality graduates to teach in schools, but as their training contained a compulsory major in English, the graduates (and the teaching staff) were entering the private sector on graduation where their English language capacity could be put to work for commercial purposes. In this case, teacher training was stimulating the economy but was not providing a qualitative improvement to education.

CONCLUSION

The national and international effort to rehabilitate and reconstruct the education system of Cambodia appears to be committed to at least the year 2000 and beyond. Investments from the USA, Australia, France and the Asian Development Bank have been locked into five- and ten-year plans which are assured. By the end of 1996, three-year investment programs in the in-service training of teachers by the European Union, the USA and France, will have been fulfilled. It will have to be established then if the investment in teacher training has actually increased the skill level of teachers resulting in higher levels of commitment, lower levels of student repetition and related lowering of poverty (as a result of increased skills). From the beginning of 1997, the Asian Development Bank will have in place its major program of education reform which will see a heavy investment in curriculum development and associated teacher training and a significant strengthening of the Ministry of Education through skill-building programs. Whether, as the World Bank reasons, these endeavors will improve Cambodia's competitive position with neighboring nations and economies remains to be seen. However, it would seem that the conviction is strong. Still, the strengthening of a nation's economy through a strengthening of its education system is a risky business as there has been little direct evidence to support the equation both historically and economically. During the 1960s, a heavy investment in education in Cambodia certainly saw the proliferation of universities and the establishment of many fine schools, but as has been observed by Chandler (1993) and Vickery (1985) any consequent strengthening of the workforce and economy was localized to major cities. Inevitably, extravagances in the education sector without an allied strengthening of the labor market contributed to civil war and a holocaust with a strong mandate to eradicate the sector. Thus, the current emphasis must be viewed with some caution.

Ironically, in one of Cambodia's most feared neighbors, Vietnam, something of the opposite is occurring. With a literacy rate of 92 percent, Vietnam has long presided over one of the strongest and most comprehensive education systems in the Greater Mekong Subregion. But the literacy rate has dramatically declined recently owing to increasing numbers of students departing from schools to staff the rapidly expanding private sector economy. As Vietnam undergoes its transition to the market economy, the secondary school system is being weakened as students labor in factories and small businesses and the higher education sector is being weakened as more and more highly educated (English- and French-speaking) staff take on higher paid positions in the private sector. The irony is taken further when it is recognized that the government has refused loans from the World Bank and Asian Development Bank to upgrade secondary and higher education, respectively. It would seem then, that the government of Vietnam has quickly grasped that in its case accepting large loans for education may not necessarily strengthen the nation's economy.

It is hard to predict whether World Bank and Asian Development Bank predictions that a strengthening of the nation's skill base through investments in education will reduce poverty and stimulate economic activity. Certainly, bilateral and multilateral investments which do not need to be paid back by the government will increase the volume of cash in the economy and will also increase the nation's consumption capacity. However, the assumption that better-trained and better-paid teachers will result in a qualitative improvement in the education system will have to be tried and tested. As noted earlier, the high-quality training of English language teachers at the University of Phnom Penh, has only seen increasing numbers of graduates enter the private sector to sell their skills; it is arguable that the University of Phnom Penh has undergone a transitional period resulting in higher quality staff and programs as a direct consequence of Australia's investment in education. It will therefore be necessary at the turn of the century to re-examine the education sector thoroughly and establish whether the projections of multilateral and bilateral financiers have been correct; then it will be clear whether the vigorous investments and training programs have in fact stimulated economic growth.

Evidence against an investment in teacher training resulting in a qualitative improvement in education and the economy has and will be restricted by the absence of similar strategies in key related areas. Despite the sustained long-term call by the government for modernizing and improving teacher training, the international community has not invested in pre-service training, the training of teacher educators and an overhaul of the teacher training curriculum (pre-service and in-service) in forward planning. Whilst donors provide trainers for retraining programs, there will be little opportunity for Khmer teacher trainers to achieve the necessary skill and qualification level to assume responsibility for training in the lead-up time to 2000. Whilst primary and secondary schools remain marginal to the mainstream donor-financed programs, there will be little opportunity to achieve quality improvement in student learning.

REFERENCES

Asian Development Bank. (1992). *Cambodia. Socio-economic Situation and Immediate Needs.* Asian Development Bank, International Monetary Fund, UNDP: World Bank.

Blom, H. C. J. and De Nooijer, P. G. (1992). *Focus on Higher Education and Vocational Training in Cambodia.* The Hague: NUFFIC.

Chandler, D. (1993). *A History of Cambodia*. Colorado: Allen & Unwin.

Cooperation Committee for Cambodia. (1992). *Humanitarian Assistance in Cambodia*. Phnom Penh.

Cross, S. (1990). *Extracts from a Report Presented by Mr Mom Chi Huy, Vice-Minister of Education*. Phnom Penh.

Galasso, E. (1990). *Education in Cambodia. Notes and suggestions* (Phnom Penh, Redd Barna).

Huynh K. K. (1971). "The Vietnamese August Revolution Reinterpreted." *Journal of Asian Studies*, 30, pp. 761–782.

ICORC/UNICEF. (1980). Joint Mission Report, December.

Jones, P. W. (1992). *World Bank Financing of Education: Lending, Learning and Development*. London: Routledge.

Kiernan, B. (1982). *Kampuchea 1979–81*. Singapore: Heinemann Asia.

King, K. (1991). *Aid and Education in the Developing World*. Essex: Longman.

Klintworth, G. (1989). *Vietnam's Intervention in Cambodia in International Law*. Canberra: Australian Government Printing Service.

Malhotra, M. M. (1994). *System Analysis of the Education Sector. Education Management and Resource Management: Education Sector Study*. Phnom Penh: Asian Development Bank.

Marr, D. G. (1981). *Vietnamese Tradition on Trial 1920–1945*. Berkeley: University of California Press.

Martin, M. A. (1986). "Vietnamised Cambodia. A Silent Ethnocide." Indochina Report, 7, pp. 1–31.

Ministry of Education. (1990). *Education: State of Cambodia*. Phnom Penh.

Ministry of Education. (1993). *Year-end Report on Achievements in the 1992–93 School Year and Objectives and Activities for the 1993–94 School Year*. Phnom Penh.

Morris, S. J. (1985). "Vietnam's Vietnam," *The Atlantic Monthly*, January, pp. 70–82.

Nash, M. (1985). *Unfinished Agenda: The Dynamics of Modernization in Developing Nations*. Boulder: Westfield Press.

Thu No. (1995). Higher Education in Vietnam: Key Areas Need Assistance. Paper presented to the *Fourth International Symposium on the Role of Universities in Developing Areas*, Melbourne, 11–14 July.

Osborne, M. (1974). "Continuity and Motivation in the Vietnamese Revolution: New Light from the 1930s." *Pacific Affairs*, 47, pp. 37–55.

Psacharopoulos, G. (1989). "Why Educational Reforms Fail: A Comparative Analysis." *International Review of Education*, 35, pp. 179–95.

Ratnaike, J. (1991). *Perspectives for Quality Improvement of Teacher Training*. Phnom Penh: Ministry of Education.

Rowley, K. (1995). Review of M. Martin, "Cambodia: A Shattered Society." *Asian Studies Review*, 18(3), pp. 195–198.

Sharma, M. (1992). "Teacher Education: The Quest for Quality." Paper presented at the *Colloquium on Alternatives in Initial Teacher Training*. (Colombo, Sri Lanka), 23–28 April.

Shawcross, W. (1991). *Sideshow*. New York: Simon & Schuster.

Teeda But Mam. (1989). *To Destroy You Is No Loss*. New York: Anchor Books.

Thomson, R. S. (1945). "The Establishment of the French Protectorate over Cambodia." *Far Eastern Quarterly Review*, 4, pp. 313–340.

Thu, N. (1995). "Higher Education in Vietnam: Key Areas Need Assistance." Paper presented to the *Fourth International Symposium on the Role of Universities in Developing Areas* (Melbourne), 11–14 July.

Tilak, J. B. G. (1991). "Why Educational Policies Can Fail?" *Journal of Educational Planning and Administration*, 5, pp. 317–323.

Tilak, J. B. G. (1994a). *Financing Education in Cambodia*. Phnom Penh: Asian Development Bank.

Tilak, J. B. G. (1994b). "External Financing of Education." *Journal of Educational Planning and Administration*, 8, pp. 81–86.

UNESCO. (1991). *Intersectoral Basic Needs Assessment Mission to Cambodia*. Bangkok: UNESCO.

UNESCO. (1992). *Education for All. Proceedings of the 1992 Annual Conference*. Phnom Penh.

UNESCO. (1994). *Programme of Assistance and Support to Cambodia 1994–96*. Tokyo: The Second International Committee on the Reconstruction of Cambodia.

UNESCO/UNICEF/UNDP. (1991). *National Conference on Education For All. Final Report*. Phnom Penh.

UNESCO/UNDP. (1994). *Rebuilding Quality Education and Training in Cambodia*. Phnom Penh: UNDP.

UNICEF. (1989). *Master Plan of Operations 1989–91*. Phnom Penh.

UNICEF. (1990). *Education For All: Cambodia*. Phnom Penh.

UNICEF. (1991). *Master Plan of Operations for a Programme of Services for Children and Women in Cambodia (January 1991–December 1993)*. Phnom Penh.

UNICEF. (1994). *Revised Master Plan of Operations 1992–1995*. Phnom Penh.

UNTAC. (1992). *United Nations Transitional Authority in Cambodia*. Phnom Penh.

USAID. (1994). *USAID Assistance Strategy for Cambodia*. Phnom Penh.

Verspoor, A. (1993). "More than Business-as-Usual: Reflections on the New Modalities of Education." *International Journal of Educational Development*, 13, pp. 103–112.

Vickery, M. (1985). *Cambodia: 1975–1982*. Boston: South End Press.

World Bank. (1993). *Viet Nam: Transition to the Market*. Washington, DC: World Bank, East Asia and the Pacific Region.

World Bank. (1994a). *Cambodia: From Rehabilitation to Reconstruction*. Washington, DC: World Bank, East Asia and the Pacific Region.

World Bank. (1994b). *World Bank Statement, International Committee of Reconstruction for Cambodia Conference*. (Tokyo), 10 March.

Contributor Notes

Zebun M. Ahmed received a Ph.D. in Social and Comparative Analysis in Education (under Administrative and Policy Studies) from the School of Education at the University of Pittsburgh. Before embarking on her doctoral work in education, she received a Master's Degree in Sociology from the University of Pittsburgh. Currently, she is an adjunct faculty member at both Duquesne University and Robert Morris University in their sociology departments, as well as a Research Associate in the Women's Studies Program at the University of Pittsburgh. Her area of interest is women, education, and third-world countries.

Sheila Aikman has carried out ethnographic research with the Harakmbut peoples of southeastern Peru over the past 20 years and worked closely with the indigenous organization, FENAMAD. For the past 6 years she has been a lecturer in Education and International Development at the University of London, Institute of Education and has recently taken up a post with Oxfam GB as Education Policy Adviser. Her work continues to focus on policy/practice issues of basic education, and in the areas of interculturalism, equity and diversity in curriculum and development and language policy.

Robert Aspeslagh is Senior Researcher at the Netherlands Institute of International Relations, "Clingendael." He has written a number of articles on education for peace, several of them in close cooperation and co-authorship with Robin Burns.

Robin Burns retired from the Graduate School of Education at La Trobe University in Melbourne, Australia, at the end of 1998, and now holds honorary positions at Monash University in Melbourne and the University of Technology, Sydney. She continues her research in comparative education and the sociology of science. She is the author of *'Just tell them I survived!': Women in Antarctica.*

Carmen Colazo is Paraguayan, a lawyer, and a graduate of the Information Science program at the Universidad Nacional de Córdoba in Argentina. She has been a university professor in Argentina and Paraguay and a researcher in law and communication for several NGOs. She consulted for the women's caucus of the constitutional convention of Paraguay in 1992, and she was Director of the Office of Social Development for the Ministry of Health and Welfare between 1991 and 1993. Her publications include *Los* *partidos politicos en el Paraguay* and *Desarollo de los temas educación, comunicación y mecanismos de participatión*, presented in the IV International Conference on Women in Beijing.

Robert Cowen is a Reader in Comparative Education in the Institute of Education University of London, a member of the Editorial Board of Comparative Education and a Vice-President of the Comparative Education Society in Europe. His comparative interests include quality control systems in higher education. His most recent article is "Socrates was right? Teacher education systems and the state" in *The World Yearbook of Education 2002.*

William K. Cummings is Professor of International Education and at the Graduate School of Education and Human Development of George Washington University. Dr. Cummings has a Ph.D. in sociology from Harvard University and is a past president of the Comparative and International Education Society. He has served as Policy Advisor in Education to the governments of Ethiopia, Indonesia, and Sri Lanka. He has published a number of books and articles on the academic profession, the service role of universities and colleges, and on the dynamic of reform in higher education.

Stephen J. Duggan is Director—Education, Overseas Projects Corporation of Victoria Ltd. (Australia). As an education and institutional reform specialist, he undertakes major assignments for the Asian Development Bank in Cambodia, Vietnam, Indonesia and Mindanao (the Philippines). He is currently leading the design and development of major education programs for Papua New Guinea.

Irving Epstein chairs the Department of Educational Studies at Illinois Wesleyan University. His intellectual interests include educational policy, comparative international education, and children's rights. He is Associate Editor of *Comparative Education Review* and the author of numerous publications, including the book *Chinese Education: Problems, Policies, and Prospects.*

John Knodel is Professor of Sociology and Research Scientist at the Population Studies Center, University of Michigan. He conducted extensive research in the area historical demography, social demography, aging, AIDS related behavior and the impact of the AIDS epidemic on older persons. He has extensive experience in both qualitative and quantitative research in Southeast Asia, especially Thailand and Vietnam.

Leslie Limage is a program specialist in the Educational Policy and Strategies Division of UNESCO. She has graduate degrees in comparative and international education from the University of Paris and the University of London Institute of Education. She has twenty-five years of experience in international organizations, teaching, and research, focusing on educational reform and equality of opportunity, diversity and mutual respect, language policy and practice, and literacy and basic education.

Angela Little has been Professor of Education at the Institute of Education, University of London since 1987. She was previously a Fellow of the Institute of Development Studies at the University of Sussex. She has extensive research and teaching experience in Asia, Africa and Europe, with specialized knowledge of Sri Lanka. Her current subject interests include policy and planning for Education for All; multigrade teaching in poor and remote areas; and globalization and qualifications. She is the current President of the British Association of International and Comparative Education and past President of the British Comparative and International Education Society.

H. Dean Nielsen is Senior Education Specialist in the East Asia Pacific Region of the World Bank, where he has been concerned with improving access to quality education in the region, both through schooling and less conventional means. He is co-author, with William K. Cummings, of *Quality Education for All: Community Oriented Approaches.* He has been an Associate Professor at the University of Hawaii, where he taught courses in Educational Policy Studies, Education and Society, and Education and Development. He has worked as a consultant under USAID in Indonesia and Egypt and held positions in numerous development agencies.

Rolland Paulston is Professor Emeritus at the University of Pittsburgh. He is Past President and Honorary Fellow of the Comparative and International Education Society. Today, he questions how a postmodern turn opens space to map and compare representations of educational change.

Ronald Price is Scholar Emeritus, Graduate Institute of Education, La Trobe University, Melbourne, Australia, and Research Associate, Department of Science and Mathematics Education, Faculty of Education, University of Melbourne. Well known for his pionerring work on education in China, he focussed recently on issues of social responsibility in science.

Reijo Raivola is Professor of Education and Dean at the University of Tampere, Finland. Widely published in the fields of higher education, politics of education, and comparative education, he has continued his work through the research committees of the European Union, the OECD/Ceri Governing Board, and the Association for the Development of Education in Africa.

Nobuo K. Shimahara, formerly Professor of Education and Anthropology in the Graduate School of Education at Rutgers University, is now Vice President for Academic Affairs at Tokyo Jogakkan College, Tokyo, Japan. He is the author of *Teaching in Japan: A Cultural Perspective* and *Learning to Teach in Two Cultures: Japan and the United States* (with Akira Sakai).

Rosa Maria Torres's education experience has taken her across the world on advisory, training, and evaluation missions, primarily with UNICEF and UNESCO. She currently Director of Instituto Fronesis, and has been the Program Director for Latin America and the Caribbean for the Kellogg Foundation (1996-1998), and Senior Education Advisor and Editor of "Education News" at UNICEF Headquarters (1991-96). The author of numerous articles and nearly twenty books on education, she conducted Ecuador's National Literacy Campaign "Monsignor Leonidas Praoño" (1988-90).

Frank Youngman has been Director of the Institute of Adult Education and Dean of the Faculty of Education at the University of Botswana, where he has taught since 1975. His extensive publications have covered many issues of adult education, particularly in relation to the political economy of development.

Index